A HISTO

NORTH CAROLINA

IN THE

PROPRIETARY ERA,

1629–1729

The Carolina Charter from Charles II to the Lords Proprietors, 1663.
Courtesy of State Archives of North Carolina.

A History of North Carolina

— *in the* —

Proprietary Era, 1629–1729

LINDLEY S. BUTLER

The University of North Carolina Press

Chapel Hill

Designed by April Leidig
Set in Caslon by Copperline Book Services, Inc.

Manufactured in the United States of America

The University of North Carolina Press has been
a member of the Green Press Initiative since 2003.

Cover illustrations: The seal of Albemarle County served as the seal for
proprietary North Carolina. Courtesy of State Archives of North Carolina.
Background: Courtesy of Burgerbibliothek, Bern, Switzerland.

Library of Congress Cataloging-in-Publication Data
Names: Butler, Lindley S., author.
Title: A history of North Carolina in the proprietary era, 1629–1729 / Lindley S. Butler.
Description: Chapel Hill : The University of North Carolina Press, [2021] |
Includes bibliographical references and index.
Identifiers: LCCN 2021049357 | ISBN 9781469667553 (cloth) |
ISBN 9781469667560 (paperback) | ISBN 9781469667577 (ebook)
Subjects: LCSH: North Carolina—History—Colonial period, ca. 1600–1775.
Classification: LCC F257 .B928 2021 | DDC 975.6/02—dc23/eng/20211020
LC record available at https://lccn.loc.gov/2021049357

IN MEMORY OF

Hugh T. Lefler

(1901–1981)

and

William S. Powell

(1919–2015)

It being the Lords Proprietors Intent, that the Inhabitants of
Carolina should be as free from Oppression, as any in the Universe.
—John Lawson,
A New Voyage to Carolina, 1709

There is Liberty of Conscience allowed in the whole Province, . . .
no Disputes or Controversies were ever observed to arrise
among them about their Religious Principles.
—John Brickell,
Natural History of North Carolina, 1737

Albemarle County was American, and thus possessed qualities better
understood today than in that day. . . . North Carolinians, as later they
would be known, seem largely to have gone their own way.
—Wesley Frank Craven,
Southern Colonies in the Seventeenth Century, 1949

CONTENTS

ILLUSTRATIONS

Figures

Maps

Tables

PREFACE

AT A VERY EARLY AGE I was drawn to history, increasingly to that of my native state. Once I decided to be a North Carolina historian, my path led to Chapel Hill, Hugh T. Lefler's undergraduate and graduate courses, and the riches of the North Carolina Collection and its then curator, the indefatigable and generous William S. Powell. Taking a seat in Professor Lefler's graduate seminar on colonial America in 1962, I had no inkling that a six-decade odyssey was beginning that would lead to this modern history of North Carolina's proprietary period. His suggestion of "Culpeper's Rebellion" for a seminar topic led to a master's thesis on Albemarle County, and my course was set in the enigmatic proprietary era, a remote period of such intermittent and scant documentation that few had attempted it.

"Through a glass darkly" aptly describes the prevalent view of proprietary North Carolina, the least-known and -understood period of the state's history. Why is this so? For many historians the colony's distant era has appeared to be of little consequence, and in the past it was difficult to research. A key factor, however, may be the propriety's invisibility, because there are few physical remains of public buildings, dwellings, or graves. Of the handful of period residences standing in the state, only one, the Newbold-White house in Perquimans, is open to the public. By contrast, in New England, settled from the beginning in towns, there are hundreds of structures that date partially from the early period, and a number of houses in each state are open to the public. Marked graves from the seventeenth century abound in early New England town cemeteries. In North Carolina few graves from the era survive, some of which have been moved for preservation. It is as if the genesis period, the first century in which the foundation of the future state was laid, has simply disappeared.

It is time to open the curtain on proprietary North Carolina. There we will discover a fascinating world long occupied by nations of Indigenous peoples, where doughty European pioneers were drawn to the "Roanoke Country," a watery place of wide rivers, blackwater swamps, and a broad sound tucked between the Outer Banks and the Dismal Swamp. On their own these settlers created a unique frontier society and government that served their needs but was largely ignored at the time as an aberration and nearly forgotten as the history of colonial America was written from the perspective of more accessible regions.

With gaps in the sparse written documentation, it was evident to me that some of the narrative would have to come from the ground and underwater. A secondary field of historical archaeology evolved from my participation in an excavation in Israel and study at Hebrew University, summer seminars at Flowerdew Hundred on the James River, and excavations at Charles Towne on the Cape Fear and in Barbados. As historian and diver for the *Queen Anne's Revenge* shipwreck project, I was peppered with questions about proprietary North Carolina, which by 2008 led to my launching this essential contextual study of the period. For those of us who remember North Carolina's tercentenary, which was celebrated in every county, one need look no further than the noncommemoration of the state's 350th anniversary in 2013 to understand how much this book is needed.

Decades ago, except for the published *Calendar of State Papers* of Britain and *North Carolina Colonial Records*, researching sources buried in the state archives and county records took an inordinate amount of time for little yield. Born in the state's tercentenary in 1963, the second series of the *North Carolina Colonial Records*, superbly edited with historical introductions by Mattie Erma E. Parker, William S. Price, Robert J. Cain, and Jan-Michael Poff, has made accessible the executive and judicial records and the correspondence of Church of England missionaries that touch on every phase of life in the era. The priceless legacy of the modern colonial records project is the exhaustive search of public and private repositories in the United Kingdom for documents that were copied and deposited in the state archives to feed scholars for generations to come. Another invaluable source is Powell's *Dictionary of North Carolina Biography*, containing character sketches of many of the early colonists.

CONCEIVED AS a narrative synthesis of North Carolina's proprietary period, this study probes the genesis of our state to reveal insights about the origins of American culture, society, and values. By the mid-twentieth century the standard narrative had been created by the state's premier academic historians, Robert D. W. Connor and Hugh T. Lefler. As I delved deeper into the records over the past decade, their view was generally confirmed. However, my findings about some of the specifics were surprising. For example, in that crucial first century some of the Lords Proprietors, whom many historians previously considered irrelevant, were founding fathers, laying a solid foundation by visionary and pragmatic governance documents that enabled free North and South Carolinians to enjoy significant political and religious liberty that matched or exceeded the freer of the North American colonies—Rhode Island, Maryland, New Jersey, and Pennsylvania.

The colony's numerous political upheavals have fostered the image of a confused and rebellious government. In reality, the turbulence resulted from a drive for self-determination by the early settlers. Enabled by the proprietors' benign neglect and the liberal constitutional structure that established a broad electorate, the pioneers formed a governing coterie that resisted any challenge to their position, overthrew corrupt and tyrannical governors, and controlled the colony's destiny. Thus, self-government emerged very early in North Carolina.

For generations historians thought that the dangerous outer coastline, which limited entry, and the treacherous interior sounds so isolated the colony that its development was retarded, leaving an impoverished "poor Carolina." In fact, the uncertain navigation was mastered by a combination of knowledge and experience among Indian, European, and African watermen and women who created a rich maritime heritage in Indigenous craft—the log canoe and the periauger. Local mariners built sloops, shallops, and brigs and sailed them to Bermuda, the West Indies, and mainland colonial ports. In addition, commerce carried by intrepid New England merchants and sea captains connected the colony to North Atlantic trade well enough for it to prosper as a middling economy that occupied a secondary but secure place in the North Atlantic world.

By the end of the royal period North Carolina was the fourth most populous continental British colony and had evolved into a major contributor to the wealth of the empire by exporting the products of its pine forests—lumber, staves, shingles, and the leading production of naval stores: tar, pitch, and turpentine.

THROUGHOUT, and especially in the quest for illustrations, I have been grateful for the assistance of the staff of the state archives, particularly Kim Andersen of the image collection and the search room staff, whom I besieged with uncommon requests for obscure documents and maps. Over the years the North Carolina Collection's Robert Anthony and his staff have provided vital support for my research. Others who have helped me acquire illustrations are Eric Blevins of the North Carolina Museum of History and Paul Fontenoy of the North Carolina Maritime Museum. Through participation in the *Queen Anne's Revenge* Shipwreck Project I enjoyed a direct encounter with the material culture of the early eighteenth century and benefited from the perspective of archaeologists Richard Lawrence, Mark Wilde-Ramsing, and David Moore, and Sarah Watkins-Kinney of the *Queen Anne's Revenge* Conservation Laboratory at Greenville.

I owe much to my elders and mentors in North Carolina history who encouraged and inspired me, influenced my writing, and provided opportunities—

Hugh Lefler, William Powell, H. G. Jones, Burke Davis, and David Stick. James Deetz of Flowerdew Hundred instilled a global view of historic archaeology. Special thanks to a fellow student of colonial North Carolina, William Price, for his support. My contemporaries, some of whom have been collaborators in research and have gently prodded me to complete this much-needed study, are Thomas Loftfield, Joe Schwarzer, Barbara Snowden, Alan Watson, and the late Jerry Cashion, Gerald Bray, George Stevenson, and Gerald Shinn. I am grateful to the Archie K. Davis Fellowships of the North Caroliniana Society for supporting my research in Barbados for two summers. Kara S. Stultz keyed into the computer my pre-digital-age papers. Julie A. Hampton compiled targeted research from the second series of the *North Carolina Colonial Records*. Betty Kirkpatrick helped prepare an image for publication. Throughout my career I have been privileged to be teamed with a talented editor and writer, my wife T, who has been integral to crafting all of my books, especially this one. She was once again undaunted by the challenge of deciphering, keying, and editing my longhand. Together we have refined it into this version. Any errors or omissions are mine alone.

A MISCELLANY OF

SEVENTEENTH-CENTURY USAGES

Thorn

The Anglo-Saxon thorn character stood for the "th" sound and is represented by the letter *y*—hence "ye" for "the" and "yt" for "that." "Ye" is pronounced "the."

Calendar

In the late sixteenth century Pope Gregory XIII promulgated a reform of the ancient Julian calendar by beginning the year on 1 January and adding a correction of ten days. The English did not adopt the Gregorian calendar until 1752, when eleven days were added.

In the proprietary period the Julian year began on 25 March, and March was the first month. Dates from January to March were often written as, for example, "14 January 1690/91," but sometimes the old year was used, as in "14 January 1690." Quakers replaced the pagan names for the months with numbers and wrote dates as day, month, and year. In this study the months and days are written as recorded in the Julian calendar, but the new year is begun on 1 January. No attempt has been made to reconcile the ten-day discrepancy between the two calendars.

Currency

Money was reckoned in English pounds (£), shillings (s), and pence (d), and written £1.10.6, or £1.10s.6d. There were twenty shillings in a pound and twelve pence in a shilling. Common coins were a guinea (£1.1s), a crown (5s), a half crown (2s.6d), a half penny, and a farthing (one-quarter of a penny). There was little cash in the colonies, and Spanish and other foreign coinage circulated, but most business was transacted by bartering commodities—tobacco, pork, beef, hides, deerskins, furs, naval stores, whale oil, and so on. The assembly set the cash value of commodities.

A HISTORY OF
NORTH CAROLINA
IN THE
PROPRIETARY ERA,
1629–1729

INTRODUCTION

DISTANT EONS AGO, the American continents lay open, empty of human beings, separated by oceans from the migrations out of Africa that populated the planet. Eventually some of the ancestors came by land across the ice, some by water, and spread from the northern frozen tundra to the stormy cape overlooking the southern polar sea. They coalesced from families into tribes that spoke many tongues and created cultures and civilizations.

About 12,000 years ago, from the west, north, and south, the first folk trickled into the region midway along the eastern coast of the northern continent. Across forbidding wooded slopes of the highest eastern peaks they came, down to the rolling hills of piedmont forests, prairies, and rushing streams, through the broad flat coastal plain, into the swamps and marshes of the tidewater and great sounds, finally to the ephemeral sandy barrier islands. Thousands settled as hunters, gatherers, fishers, and then farmers living close to the land, shaping it by fire and stone to yield a living. Most remain nameless, but they left their traces in implements of rock, bone, and clay; burials and earthen mounds; shell middens; and stone fish weirs in the streams.

About a thousand years ago, the land was dotted with communities joined by a network of trails and supported by agricultural fields. Extending across the Southeast from the Mississippi River valley to North Carolina's mountains and piedmont were cities of the hierarchical Mississippian culture—religious and administrative centers where central plazas were dominated by earthen temple mounds.

Then some 500 years ago a new wave of interlopers arrived from the eastern sea in vessels propelled by wind. They came from another world that had mastered iron, technology, and science to a level not seen on this continent before. Fleeting coastal contacts by the Spanish, French, and English gave the intruders little hint of the patchwork of highly organized cultures and polities that characterized the interior. The Spanish were first to penetrate the hinterland, an initial overreach with disastrous consequences for both themselves and the Native cultures. Drawn to the wondrous things brought in trade by the strangers, Indians also came in contact with enslavement, epidemic disease, and murderous warfare—a holocaust that struck down countless numbers. In the early stages the Native Americans expelled the invaders or pinned them to the coast.

The Spanish fell back to a toehold in what is now Florida, but the invasion caused a catastrophic transformation, ultimately shattering the Mississippian world that had thrived for half a millennium.[1]

Following explorers came traders and soldiers, then a wave of colonists—men, women, and families—many of whom were so poor and had so little hope that they willingly sold themselves as contract laborers, embarking on the unforgiving ocean in search of a new life on this continent reputed to have limitless resources. These immigrants made their living from fur trading, ranching, plantation agriculture, and forest products, increasing their success by expanding the labor force of indentured servants and enslaved Indians, who were gradually augmented by enslaved Africans. Over time, the Europeans became so numerous that they could not be denied: they conquered the land and claimed it as their own.

A portrait of a place in time, this book spans an era from the late sixteenth century through the early eighteenth, when, with the exception of eight years, what became the colony of North Carolina was in private hands.[2] This transitional period witnessed the shift from the Elizabethan model of privatized empire building to the early modern empire of centralized metropolitan oversight by Crown authority, a process begun by James II and accelerated by the career soldier William III. The narrative examines the colony's formative years, revealing how Indians, Europeans, and Africans were gradually shaped by interacting in that place. Under proprietary charters North Carolina was a province of heterogeneous people and faiths who enjoyed freedom of conscience—"soul-liberty."[3] Here, regardless of background and status, a free person could make a living and rise in the world, secure dignity, and worship as mind and conscience led. From this seminal legacy of freedom and toleration the future state was born, and these principles were forcefully expressed in 1776 in the new state's "Declaration of Rights" and constitution.[4]

North Carolina Genesis

In *New Voyages to Carolina* Larry E. Tise and Jeffrey J. Crow reorganize the North Carolina narrative in the context of a half century of social history, emphasizing a modern interpretation of race, gender, and social and class struggle that will reshape the state's historiography. They also deplore the apparent lack of a genesis story—a tale of origins that reflects an understanding of what North Carolina would become.[5] Other colonies on the coast of North America originated in a place, such as Jamestown, Plymouth Rock, Philadelphia, or Savannah, with a legendary founder like John Smith, William Bradford, Roger Williams, William Penn, or James Oglethorpe. While North Carolina's enduring legend, the Lost Colony of Roanoke, was set in the heroic Tudor Age of such giants as Elizabeth I, Sir Richard Grenville, and Sir Walter Raleigh, the problem is that it failed, as did two other lesser-known North Carolina lost colonies, the Spanish Fort San Juan and the Cape Fear Charles Towne.

There is a North Carolina genesis story, but it is so different from that of the other twelve original colonies that neither her people nor many historians recognize it. As historian William S. Powell commented, "North Carolina frequently puzzles the uninitiated . . . ; sometimes the state puzzles its own natives as well."[6] The most perceptive scholars of early North Carolina have understood its origin, emphasizing the uniqueness. North Carolina's genesis is not the stuff of heroes and myths. What is known is that prior to 1660 European settlement began in the Roanoke country that became Albemarle County, but there was neither specific location nor rock nor larger-than-life leader present. Rather, it was a land of promise that attracted immigrants who were self-motivated, searching for better land and opportunity and a refuge from intolerance and persecution—the ongoing American historical experience.

That North Carolina would spring from Albemarle County was pure happenstance. The colony's settlement was unintentional. Few came directly from Europe; instead, most arrived from other colonies, initially Virginia. An assortment of borderers, yeoman farmers, mariners, artisans, traders, husbandmen, planters, and merchants, they wandered in on their own and purchased land from the Indians. Given the limitations of isolation imposed by the coastline and the Dismal Swamp, they prospered slowly, creating a middling economy through diversified farming, ranching, Indian trade, forest products, and eventually naval stores. Although the colony had no towns or ports for years, undaunted New England sea captains and merchants routinely navigated the shallow inlets and ever-changing estuarine channels to provide a window to the outside world.

In 1663 the Roanoke settlement was incorporated by the Carolina Charter into the vast transcontinental grant from Charles II to eight Lords Proprietors, English knights and nobles who had defended the Crown through the civil wars, suffering property loss, imprisonment, and exile. These men accepted radical changes wrought by the revolutionary age, incorporating political and religious freedom in the charters and constitutions of their colony. Instead of a single founder, Carolina had eight founders, all of whom were committed to expanding the empire and reaping a profit from their domain. With a self-made colony underway, now renamed Albemarle County, the Lords opted for a light hand and low expectations after trying several direct initiatives that came to naught. Thereafter, their attention was focused on the potentially more prosperous Charles Town settlement on deepwater Ashley River. The result was that self-governing Albemarle became one of the freer colonies in America, nurturing values that are considered foundational to the political and religious liberty of the United States.

Albemarle pioneers were a plain people, and their descendants have proudly embraced that heritage and its difference from neighboring states. There is no better expression of this genesis legacy than the state motto, suggested by Walter Clark and legislated in 1893: *Esse Quam Videri*, "To Be Rather Than To Seem."[7] A variation on the theme is the motto of the North Caroliniana Society, "Substance, Not Show."

Historiography of Proprietary North Carolina

In the more than 350 years since the founding of the Carolina propriety, there has been only one previous history of the era, the second volume of Francis Hawks's *History of North Carolina* (1858). An Episcopal priest and scholar, Hawks compiled a topical account interspersed with documents. Many more sources are accessible today, allowing a more comprehensive study. Yet Hawks understood the essence of the proprietary legacy to North Carolina. Regarding the government established in the 1660s, he noted that the "two great principles" of the right of the people to elect their representatives and not to be taxed without their consent became "part of the political creed of our whole country." Hawks summarized the liberal proprietary policy thus: "Here was a grant of all the freedom rational men could desire, and . . . the system was alike simple and judicious, and possessed the great merit of being *adapted to their condition*."[8]

The history created earlier by the state's nineteenth-century amateur historians was significantly revised by the publication of the monumental *Colonial Records of North Carolina* (1886–90), edited by William L. Saunders, and the subsequent history by Samuel A. Ashe (1908). This legacy portrait of the state became the basis of the narrative of academic historians into the twenty-first century. According to Saunders, the state's first permanent English settlement of Virginians in the future Albemarle County was the "parent settlement of North Carolina."[9]

Although there had been professionally trained historians in the state for some time, not until 1919 did scholars produce a multiauthored comprehensive survey. The first volume was by Robert D. W. Connor. In keeping with the prevalent imperial school, Connor emphasized North Carolina's connection to the British Empire but made little effort to interpret the state's origins.[10] However, a decade later in his second survey, Connor described Albemarle County as the "Genesis of North Carolina."[11]

By the mid-twentieth century Hugh T. Lefler, the leading state historian, called Albemarle County the "Cradle of North Carolina," "unique" in comparison to other American colonies. Among the characteristics that set North Carolina apart were the lack of a town or port for four decades, settlement mostly from other colonies rather than directly from overseas, and the dangerous coastline, which retarded population and economic growth. Political isolation fostered self-government and a "spirit of independence" as well as "individualism and democracy." Finally, no other colony was shaped more by geography than North Carolina.[12]

As part of the commemoration of the national bicentennial, a series of histories of the original thirteen colonies was published. The North Carolina volume, the state's first colonial history, was written by Lefler and Powell. Few outside the state have thought that North Carolina had anything to contribute to the American colonial narrative, but Milton M. Klein and Jacob E. Cooke, editors of the series, made insightful observations. The editors noted that the "enigmatic character" of North Carolina had made it the "proverbial exception" to the other continental American colonies. The colony "from the beginning was strikingly different" from South Carolina, lacking a plantation aristocracy, large numbers of enslaved people, and centers of commerce and culture. Preoccupied with local problems and geographically and culturally isolated, the colony had "a uniquely parochial character."[13]

In a 1989 monograph on the seventeenth-century Albemarle County genesis of North Carolina, I emphasized the geographic isolation and the lack of proprietary oversight that enabled self-sufficiency, individualism, and independence of thought and action. Living in an age when society is organized around institutions, modern North Carolinians cannot imagine how the colony could have survived without such basics as towns, schools, or churches—in effect having almost no social, cultural, or economic infrastructure. Although institutions enable society, conversely they may impose limitations. The Albemarle settlers were free to create pragmatically what structure they needed. I concluded that the colony's "political unruliness" reflected an "emerging democracy" and that Albemarle County was "unlike any other English colony," having a "volatile blend of diverse population, turbulent politics, and official indifference."[14]

Twentieth-century American historians, including some historians of the state, have been baffled by proprietary North Carolina, treating it largely as local history with few implications beyond its borders. The colonial American interpretation has been compiled primarily from New England and the Chesapeake, with passing nods to the mid-Atlantic and South Carolina. For generations, "poor" North Carolina has been viewed as an isolated backwater, settled by Virginia immigrants with a leavening of religious dissenters, who subsisted in an underdeveloped economy with a reasonably equal distribution of wealth. Depicted as diffident and profit-minded, the proprietary overlords were portrayed as soon losing interest in their impoverished settlement. With little support or direction, local governance was characterized by instability and insurrection. Yet in the years of political unrest the colonists learned how to govern themselves and laid a solid foundation for a free state.

In the national story, North Carolina, an exception that simply doesn't fit, has been largely disregarded. A reader looks in vain in American history surveys to find more than a paragraph or two about early North Carolina. Nevertheless, the settlement's early years in fact may shed more light on what the country became. In the nascent colony there was an alternative, grounded in a self-governing polity and religious freedom, that was more like the future United States than were New England's Puritan theocracy or the Chesapeake's auto-cratic plantocracy, both of which suppressed religious and political freedom.

More than any other colonists, early North Carolinians were in a remote and peripheral settlement soon cut loose by their proprietors and left to them-selves. There is no better illustration among the American colonies of a free society maturing through the creative tension of practical social, economic, and political experiences. Fostered by their Anglo-Celtic cultural heritage and centuries of participatory English governance and judicial practice, the British and other European immigrants coped with a challenging frontier setting. Be-fore they and their sister colonies realized it, over time they became something new—Americans—and were ready by the late eighteenth century to cast off imperial oversight and face the future on their own terms.

Among colonial American historians who have grasped the essence of Al-bemarle County were Herbert L. Osgood, Charles M. Andrews, and Wesley F. Craven. In summing up the development of the American colonies, Osgood wrote that by the end of the seventeenth century the majority of the colonists were native born or had come as children. Through language, cultural patterns, and family stories there were grounding ties to the motherlands, but no direct memories. Their lives had been lived entirely in the New World, coping with the Atlantic frontier. Their forebears, mostly of middle- and lower-class ori-gins, had been drawn overseas by opportunity and had created a society that had greater equality and less class distinction, without the extremes of wealth, poverty, and status of the Old World. The majority were farmers and artisans, with some in trade. Isolated by the transoceanic distance, the colonists were insular and provincial, focusing on local issues, which encouraged commitment to self-government and their own nascent institutions.[15]

This description of the colonial experience in that first century particularly applies to North Carolina, which is acknowledged to be the most remote and insular of all the continental colonies. When coupled with the neglect of the

Lords Proprietors, the colonists' drive toward self-determination and local institutions marks them as the earliest examples of what comes to be considered American.[16]

To Osgood, "the foundations of American liberty were laid" in that first century. Practical institutions, both local and colonial, were fashioned through "slow and natural growth," often by trial and error, and were directed to increasing and preserving independence and self-sufficiency.[17] It is not surprising that Americans have a global reputation as pragmatic, inventive, and creative problem-solvers. Also descended from the first century is Americans' dual materialistic and spiritual nature, which reflects motives of immigrants desperate for economic opportunity and freedom of conscience. It is said in jest that the Quakers came to America to do good and did well, but their economic success resulted from practical application of their religious principles of honesty, fairness, justice, human dignity, and equality, which built trust among their neighbors, regardless of race, ethnic heritage, or creed.

Andrews conceived a sweeping context for the seventeenth century: two distinct periods of colonization separated by the 1640–60 "pause" of the English Civil War and the Interregnum. The "Heroic Age of Puritanism," centered spiritually and intellectually on the Elizabethan age, saw the colonization of the mainland Chesapeake and New England and the offshore and Caribbean islands of Bermuda, Bahamas, Leewards, and Barbados. The conquest of Jamaica in 1655 was the precursor of the Restoration colonization of the proprieties, beginning with Carolina. Characterized by a "gloss of modernity," this new era in the English Enlightenment looked to the future humanistic, secular world of commerce and science, of the Royal Society, Isaac Newton's *Principia*, and John Locke's treatises *On Government* and *On Toleration*.[18] Spiritual concerns were joined by the study of humanity and nature, aptly illustrated in Carolina by John Lawson's *New Voyages* (1709) and Mark Catesby's *Natural History* (1731). The Puritan zeal of the early colonization was replaced by the evangelical spread of Quaker missionaries across the Atlantic to every English colony on the mainland and in the islands, a movement appropriately named the "heroic age of Quakerism." Born in the English Revolution, this radical Christian sect, eschewing orthodox theology and ritual, freed its adherents to bridge the transition to the future, embracing the English Enlightenment's humanism, materialism, and science without compromising their unique core belief in the individual's "Inner Light."[19]

Wesley F. Craven voiced the most perceptive insight, observing in his definitive *The Southern Colonies in the Seventeenth Century* (1949) that Albemarle County "presented to men of the late seventeenth century a more perplexing problem of identification than any other along the Southeastern coast. . . .

Albemarle County was American, and thus possessed qualities better understood today than in that day." Although the roots of Albemarle lay in Virginia,
the American persona of this "coastal backwoods" had evolved in isolation behind the ramparts of the Dismal Swamp and the Outer Banks, providing a refuge for Quakers, other religious dissenters, and the independent-minded, who
"seem largely to have gone their own way."[20] By the late seventeenth century,
if the isolated Albemarle frontier had evolved into an American community,
as Craven has suggested, then it is the first to emerge in the colonies and offers a different insight into colonial American history than the Chesapeake or
Puritan New England.[21]

The last half century's scholarly emphasis on social history has focused on
the forgotten common people, women, and minorities and generated gender,
racial, and regional studies and conceptual interpretive frameworks based on
social change through class struggle and confrontation. In this vein, Noelleen
McIlvenna's study of Albemarle, *A Very Mutinous People: The Struggle for North
Carolina, 1660–1713* (2009), imagined an oppressed multiracial underclass that
established a "utopian community" of "a society of equals."[22] Recently McIlvenna
extended her study of the development of representative self-government in
the Chesapeake in *Early American Rebels: Pursuing Democracy from Maryland
to Carolina, 1640–1700* (2020). From her viewpoint, the series of rebellions that
successively swept across the region originated with poor white settlers who
were inspired by the English Revolution and led by connected families, some
members becoming governors of their colonies. Successive failures in Maryland
and Bacon's Rebellion in Virginia finally culminated in Culpeper's Rebellion in
Albemarle, which established a representative government that successfully ran
the colony for two years and was accepted and protected by the proprietors.[23]

Although a revolution can accelerate change, social and political transformation does not necessarily require class conflict. On the contrary, the free society
of Albemarle emerged under the aegis of the Lords Proprietors. The colony's
promise of living was achieved by continually evolving dynamic social interaction as the people together experienced common challenges and creatively
solved problems.

Another step toward understanding the era through social theory was taken
in the essay collection edited by Bradford J. Wood and Michelle LeMaster,
Creating and Contesting Carolina: Proprietary Era Histories (2013). Theoretically
grounded in social history, these articles explore aspects of the thesis that creative tension stems from confrontation, whether verbal or physical. To test this
theory, the editors chose the turbulent first decade of the eighteenth century,
when the interplay of different visions and conflicts drove the adaptation of
both people and place. This nuanced premise offers a more plausible direction
for social historians to pursue in unraveling the conundrum.

Founding Proprietary North Carolina:
The Principles and the Colonists

This book introduces the reader to a different proprietary North Carolina than previously portrayed by the state's historians, including this author. Albemarle County, the foundation of the province, was neither so poor nor so isolated as earlier thought. Although a secondary market, the colony was well connected to North Atlantic commerce by resolute local and New England sea captains who routinely carried the products of the fields, savannahs, forests, and sea through North Carolina's shallow inlets to the other English mainland colonies, Bermuda, and the West Indies, and indirectly to England, Scotland, and mainland Europe. The frustration for economic historians is that transshipped illicit commerce is hard to document, and many of North Carolina's products were shipped off the books of imperial customs, leading to the assumption that the colony was backward and poor.

However, North Carolinians were industriously engaged in making a living, and they succeeded beyond a subsistence level, creating a diversified viable economy of middling planters, ranchers, farmers, merchants, and frontier traders who assumed the political leadership of the colony. As in other colonies, indentured servants, freeholders, yeoman farmers, planters, and merchants shared the common goal of accumulating property, real and chattel. In North Carolina the gulf between rich and poor was not as great as in neighboring colonies, and there was enough upward mobility to make the emerging slave-based plantation economy an aspiration for success. The result was less class tension than existed in wealthier colonies.

From ancient times slavery had been integral in warfare, with prisoners among the spoils of war and the property of the captor. Not seen in Europe since the Middle Ages, slavery was well established in Africa and the Americas. The voyages of the Portuguese around Africa and the Spanish across the Atlantic, followed by the seafaring nations of Europe, revealed a plentiful source of labor and lucrative trade. Beginning in the sixteenth century, for nearly 400 years slavery spread throughout the European Atlantic colonies—the Spanish, Portuguese, French, Dutch, and, from the seventeenth century, all of the British colonies.

An abomination to modern Western values, slavery was fundamental to the colonial economies and the Atlantic trade. The practice was so ingrained in the background of the future United States that the nation split, fought a bloody and destructive civil war for union, freedom, and the eradication of slavery, and after a century and a half continues to struggle to resolve the reprehensible effects of racism, slavery's offspring.

The promise of social and economic mobility, political freedom, and religious liberty was reserved for the free colonists, regardless of race, and indentured servants who had completed their contract. Although class deference was the era's norm, among free colonists on the rough-and-tumble Albemarle frontier there was a free and easy camaraderie that sometimes bordered on contempt for conventions. Liberties were taken in social relations that would have been more consequential in the stratified societies of wealthier colonies; yet the courts offered an outlet for settling most altercations, and violent crime was rare. Provincial officials were judged by their actions rather than position or birth, although here, as in England, family connections did count, creating a governing elite through marriage and blood relations.

The freedom of mind and spirit offered by the proprietors attracted many dissenters and created a setting in which egalitarian Quakers flourished and became the colony's first and only organized church for some thirty years. The policy of subscription or affirmation for sworn oaths enabled Quakers to hold office and with other dissenters to wield the dominant political influence, briefly creating a Quaker-led colony.

The English colonies that offered greater political, social, and religious liberty were Rhode Island and the proprietary colonies of Maryland, the Carolinas, New Jersey, and Pennsylvania. Founded as a refuge from religious persecution, Roger Williams's Rhode Island is acknowledged as the birthplace of American religious liberty. Williams guaranteed freedom of worship, whether he agreed with a church's beliefs or not, and he was the first to advocate the separation of church and state.

Maryland's Act Concerning Religion (1649), commonly known as the first colonial act of toleration, was designed to protect the founding minority Catholics. The often-quoted few lines on the "free exercise" of religion for "professing" Christians and condemnation of "reproachfull Language" toward various denominations are buried in a morass of harsh punishment aimed at dissenters who were not orthodox Trinitarians. The controversial law gave temporary respite to Catholics but was revoked by Puritans in five years, briefly reinstated, and permanently repealed in 1692. Catholics lost freedom of worship early in the next century.[24]

The first governance documents for the Carolinas, New Jersey, and Pennsylvania are all descended from the Carolina Concessions and Agreement of January 1665, which offered subscription (affirmation) for an oath—a direct appeal to Quakers—and complete freedom of conscience. Within six months a second Carolina charter removed dissenters from ecclesiastical law. In February 1665 Sir George Carteret and Lord John Berkeley, proprietors of New Jersey, issued their Concessions and Agreements, a copy of the Carolina Concessions with minor wording changes. Berkeley sold his share in 1674 to Quaker proprietors that soon included William Penn. The Concessions and Agreements of West Jersey incorporated liberty of conscience and expanded political freedom. It was this document that became a basis for Pennsylvania's Frame of Government (1681), considered an important source for the U.S. Constitution.

However, no other colony can match the statement on religious liberty in Carolina's Fundamental Constitutions, which explicitly extended freedom of worship to Indians, Jews, heathens, other dissenters, and enslaved persons. Only atheists were excluded. With the important role of Quakers in governance, late seventeenth-century North Carolinians enjoyed complete soul-liberty. The simple rule defining a church would have allowed Jewish and Muslim worship. To grant enslaved persons freedom of worship, the proprietors recognized that religion does not change a person's civil obligations, in effect separating church and state.[25]

North and South Carolina shared the same Lords Proprietors, charters, and the Fundamental Constitutions, but the colonies became very different. Isolated Albemarle County, first settled by Virginians who purchased land from the Indians, preceded the propriety and was self-governed by the founders, who remained in power for decades. After Albemarle did not meet their economic expectations and Clarendon County (Charles Towne on the Cape Fear) failed, the proprietors turned south. By 1670 under Lord Ashley's direction they recruited Barbadian planters and invested in the colonization voyages, settled the second Charles Town on a deepwater harbor with direct connection to England, and favored a plantation economy based on enslaved labor. Nevertheless, South Carolina under the Fundamentals did attract a diverse population, including a number of dissenter Huguenots, as well as Quakers.

The source of Carolina's liberal ethos was the founding fathers, the eight Lords Proprietors, who have previously been characterized as irrelevant absentee aristocratic landlords driven solely by the pursuit of wealth. It matters not that profit was a prime motive of the Lords, for these courtiers, especially the Duke of Albemarle, Sir John Colleton, and Lord Ashley, had imbibed the principles of freedom and toleration from their experiences in the English Civil War and Commonwealth. Like most Englishmen of that troubled age, great or small, they had all experienced privation and discrimination and, in some cases, imprisonment and banishment for their beliefs. To attract colonists, their vision for Carolina included their strong commitment to protect the rights and liberties of Englishmen and to establish representative government, economic opportunity, and freedom of conscience.

The proprietors incorporated these concepts in the foundational documents of their province—the charters, the Concessions and Agreement, the Fundamental Constitutions, and the governors' instructions. These documents enabled the development of a broadly representative General Assembly elected by freeholders, as well as some elected General Court judges. Furthermore, frontier challenges fostered a pragmatic society that encouraged social mobility and an expansive status for women, who were accepted in professions and business. Despite the absence of towns, deepwater ports, schools, or the established church for four decades, this colony enjoyed some literacy, free religious worship, and sufficient commerce. It was not only a self-governing polity but also a self-made society. Through the later writings of the proprietors' secretary, John Locke, their liberal principles eventually became embedded in the Declaration of Independence, state constitutions, the U.S. Constitution, and the Bill of Rights.

From freeholders to indentured servants, those who came to North Carolina were seeking the economic and social promise of unlimited land, a fluid society, a representative government, and religious liberty. When the Lords early concluded that their northern colony was unlikely to prosper, they abandoned the Albemarle and sponsored a settlement on the deepwater Ashley River. Left to find their own way, the Albemarle settlers discovered that learning self-government can be a long and painful process, especially the manner of peacefully transferring power. The troublesome politics of Albemarle County from 1673 to 1690 yielded a nearly unbroken series of coups, countercoups, deposing of tyrants, and rebellion. These upheavals were caused neither by restrictive proprietary policies nor by class conflict, but rather by the age-old question "Who should rule at home?"[26] From this turbulent period a "governing founders" class emerged. From their experiences in English and Virginia local courts these founders brought a respect for the rule of law. With proprietary sanction they shaped the new colony by effectively meeting the challenges of a frontier wilderness on their own.[27]

While oppressive governors were occasionally removed in other colonies, none surpassed Albemarle County, where rebels overthrew a governor, elected a free assembly, held office for nearly two years, became the de jure government, and suffered no consequences. Local gentry of long-resident planters, traders, merchants, and artisans of moderate means—a middle class—emerged to fill positions on the council, the General Assembly, and the courts. By the 1690s North Carolina was stabilized by a Quaker polity and largely influenced by the egalitarian principles of the sect. The political consensus achieved by Quakers, other dissenters, and Anglicans was supported by experienced and astute deputy governors and provincial governors, one of whom was a Quaker proprietor.

By the end of the century the governing founders who had created and defended self-government were mostly deceased, as was the last of the original proprietors, William, Earl of Craven. To the new generation of proprietors, financial gain was of greater concern than the ideals born in conflicts a half

century earlier. In 1701 John, Lord Granville, an Anglican zealot, became palatine with an agenda of establishing the Church of England in both colonies.

In the early eighteenth century the local Anglicans, long resenting and
chafing under dissenter government, purged Quaker officials, overturning the
colony's stability by prohibiting subscription for an oath of office. This was
not a revolution by force of arms but a manipulation of political elections to
achieve the establishment of the state-supported Anglican Church. Juxtaposed
on the growing sectional challenge by the new Bath County (1696) against
Albemarle's dominance, this fundamental shift in power began with the 1701
vestry act and ended in 1711 in the nearly bloodless Cary Rebellion and the
triumph of a mostly Anglican oligarchy of elite planters. Having lost their
political status, Quakers continued to be a spiritual and moral force, exerting
influence by witnessing against war and eventually opposing slavery. Religious
liberty was reduced to religious tolerance. Although personal political confrontations continued, especially between the last governors, transfer of power after
1712 was under constitutional proprietary oversight. The colony was maturing
politically, but at the cost of submerging a sizable minority that had nurtured
an inclusive government that ensured freedom of conscience.

After more than a half century of social historians' focusing on the role
of the common people, especially neglected minorities and women, to some
scholars it will seem heretical to conclude that Carolina's aristocratic founding
fathers, the Lords Proprietors, are the source of Carolina's political and religious
liberty—the colony's most significant legacy. Nevertheless, in the absence of
preconceptions, that is what the documents have revealed. Key to this development was the shift in 1690 of proprietary oversight to the potentially more
lucrative colony on the Ashley River, thereby allowing the Albemarle settlers
to chart their own course in a self-governing colony. Doubtless this conclusion
in the early twenty-first century is also influenced by the era in which we live:
a time in which uncompromising adherence to ideology has created polarized
state and national governments that threaten crucial American principles of
political and religious liberty, which were evolving in all of the colonies at various stages. In North Carolina that process began with the proprietary charters
and governance documents that allowed the founding settlers to set their own
course toward self-government.

Proprietary North Carolina and the Atlantic World

Poor, backward Albemarle County, isolated by North America's most dangerous Atlantic coastline, has been relegated by most historians to a minor role,
little more than a footnote, in the Atlantic World interpretation that has set
the tone of colonial history for the past half century. Although first suggested

in the early twentieth century by a journalist advocating American intervention in the Great War in 1917, the pivotal role played by the United States did
not resonate with many scholars until after the Second World War, when the
United States was forging the creation of the Atlantic community through the
Marshall Plan, the Truman Doctrine, and the North Atlantic Treaty Organization. The solid foundation of the imperial historians, notably Osgood and
Andrews, had broadened the horizon of American colonial historians by placing the continental colonies in the context of the British Empire, particularly
the wealthy Caribbean colonies. The next step was integrating the Atlantic
world of the European maritime nation-states—Portuguese, Spanish, French,
Dutch, and English—and their overseas empires that wove together four continents—the two Americas and the Caribbean, Europe, and Africa. From the
fifteenth century onward the Atlantic Ocean became the latest "inland sea of
Western Civilization."[28] In fact, Western civilization has always been water-
centered, migrating west from its origins in the Nile and Tigris-Euphrates river
valleys five millennia ago, to the Mediterranean Sea in the third millennium,
and finally to the Atlantic Ocean over 500 years ago.

The concept of an Atlantic region is well founded by countless studies about
the interrelationships of the colonies and the European overseas empires, the
integral African slave trade to the Caribbean and the mainland colonies of the
American continents, the immigration of ethnic and religious refugees and indentured servants, the cultural origins of diverse free migrants, the institutional
and commercial networks, and geographic and environmental influences.

IF ALBEMARLE COUNTY was so isolated and poor, how was the "Cradle of
North Carolina" integrated into the Atlantic world? As will be discussed in this
study, trade connections were much greater than previously believed, linked by
coastal small vessels to New England, New York, Philadelphia, Bermuda, the
English West Indies, and Dutch Curaçao. From these ports North Carolina
products then were transshipped to the British Isles and Europe. In the last
decade of the proprietary period the gradual shift from diverse products to
exploitation of the great eastern pine forests moved the economic center to the
Cape Fear River, the colony's first deepwater outlet. This made North Carolina
a full and important participant in the North Atlantic trade network, setting
the stage for the colony's role in the royal era as the empire's leading producer of
strategic naval stores—tar, pitch, turpentine, and masts—as well as other forest
products of staves, shingles, and lumber.

The domestic maritime culture of Albemarle County also connected it to
the Atlantic world. The colony was centered on the internal broad sounds and
rivers, which required riverine and estuarine watermen—Indian, African, and

European. The region's Indians had depended on the dugout canoe for more than 3,000 years. Enslaved West Africans came from a riverine culture that had built and navigated dugouts, some much larger than the Carolina craft. Furthermore, the French, Dutch, Irish, Scots, and English all had log canoes in their deep past and were experienced fishermen and skilled coastal boatmen with skiffs and small sailing craft. The dugout canoe and its descendant, the periauger, were the common artifacts that tied together Native Americans, Africans, and Europeans. Furthermore, on the shores of the rivers and sounds, boatwrights used indentured, enslaved, and free labor to fashion plank-built vessels—flat-bottomed fishing skiffs for both oars and sails to ply the interior waters and, for the open sea, shallops, sloops, ketches, brigs, and brigantines.

———————

QUAKERS IN ALBEMARLE were part of an Atlantic network created in the mid-seventeenth century. Beginning in 1652 George Fox, founder of the Religious Society of Friends (Quakers), established an evangelical ministry that swept through England, attracting thousands to his radical concept of the "Inner Light"—that of God in every person. Within a few years Quakers spread the message to less receptive Europe, ranging as far as the Near East and especially across the Atlantic to the English colonies in the West Indies and North America. Among Quaker testimonies was their refusal to take an oath, since it implied failure to speak the truth at all times. By 1665 North Carolina's proprietors had authorized complete religious liberty, including affirmation, or subscription, in place of oaths, which would allow Friends not only to conduct business and commerce but also, more important, to serve in government positions.

Arriving as missionaries in North Carolina in 1672, Fox and William Edmundson found an unchurched people and ready converts, leading to the formation of monthly meetings in two precincts as the only organized church in the colony. Quakers grew rapidly, becoming part of the Atlantic community of Friends nurtured by further visits of missionaries, traveling or "public" Friends, and epistles, or correspondence with London Yearly Meeting and the meetings that were found in all of the English colonies. Albemarle Quaker merchants established ties to North Atlantic commerce through their Quaker counterparts in Rhode Island, New Jersey, and Philadelphia.[29]

———————

AT THE OPPOSITE END of the social spectrum, pirates of the Golden Age were an active component of North Atlantic and African commerce. Random visits of pirates to North Carolina began to occur in the late seventeenth century, usually for repair, wood, and water. With neither port nor significant trade, the

isolated colony had little wealth to attract pirates. However, the sound country
hidden behind barrier islands offered a haven for rest, recuperation, and repairs,
where there was little chance intruders would be found. For the colonists, the
foreign visitors brought news of the world and an infusion of cash and trade
that bolstered their meager economy.

Stranding in 1718 at Beaufort, *Queen Anne's Revenge* and her consorts carried some 300 to 400 men, predominantly British but also representing other
seafaring European nations—France, Spain, and Portugal—with over a fourth
from West Africa, mostly enslaved, although some were freed and had joined
the pirate crew. The artifact assemblage of the former French slaver with a
mostly British crew also reflects the North Atlantic world. Pirates, after all,
were indiscriminate in their theft. The cultural origins of the several hundred
thousand artifacts excavated so far are 36 percent English, 26 percent French,
and the remaining 38 percent divided among Swedish, German, Italian, Spanish, Dutch, Portuguese, Chinese, and African.[30] The host of pirates who came
ashore received a pardon for past crimes, and many of them settled down in
the colony and contributed to its future. North Carolina briefly harbored the
early eighteenth century's only mainland North American bases of pirates at
Ocracoke and Cape Fear, forever linking the colony to some of the most notorious pirates of the age.

FROM BETTER TRADE CONNECTIONS than previously thought, the local maritime culture that entwined four continents, the transatlantic Quaker community, and the pirates who came to its shores, North Carolina was a participant
in the North Atlantic world and therefore, to be understood, can be approached
from that overarching interpretive perspective. But North Carolina's different
course from the universally accepted view of the colonial American experience
in fact sheds light on what the United States became. A new history of colonial America awaits its scribes who look to the colonies that followed another
way—Rhode Island, Maryland, North and South Carolina, New Jersey, and
Pennsylvania. In these colonies the seeds of liberty for free people were sown
on good ground and flourished, creating a nation of immigrants that with all
of its shortcomings and missteps may still represent a beacon of hope for many
people of planet Earth.

CHAPTER ONE

Aliens in a Strange Land

Land has been found by modern man which was unknown to the
ancients, another world with respect to the one they knew.
—Verrazzano, 1524

IN THE YEAR OF OUR LORD 1524, a far-flung expedition commanded by
Giovanni da Verrazzano was dispatched from the kingdom of France to
cross the Great Western Ocean with two aims—to seek a northern route
to Asia and to establish a claim to new territory hitherto consigned by treaty to
Spain and Portugal. From the European perspective, England's right to North
America had been established by John Cabot's 1497 voyage to Newfoundland
sponsored by King Henry VII, and Juan Ponce de León had discovered Florida
for Spain in 1513. The North American coast from Florida to Newfoundland,
however, was terra incognita, "unknown land," and the position of France and
England was that new lands were secured by occupation, not discovery. When
Verrazzano sighted land north of Cape Fear on the first of March, he thought
it "a new land which had never been seen before by any man."[1]

In 1521, news of Hernan Cortés's conquest and despoiling of the fabulously
wealthy Aztec Empire in Mexico had swept through the courts of Europe. The
trickle of gold coming to Spain from the West Indies now became a glittering
torrent of silver, gold, and gems that for nearly two centuries fueled Spain's effort to dominate Europe. The next year, Juan Sebastian de Elcano returned to
Spain in *Victoria*, the only ship of Ferdinand Magellan's flotilla to survive the
first voyage around the globe. Again Europe was agog, for the discovery of an
alternative sea route to China raised the prospect of great riches. Spurred by
these events, King Francis I collaborated with the Italian expatriate community
in France to launch Verrazzano's voyage.

Francis I was a French king with a global vision who looked to Italy for leadership and counsel. Leonardo da Vinci was the most celebrated of the Italian
state ministers, merchants, bankers, and mariners who served him. His chief
navigator, the well-educated Verrazzano, may have been born in France. Italian
silk merchants and bankers, including relatives of Verrazzano, had been drawn

to Lyon, where the community they established provided funds and technical support for the voyage of exploration.[2] At thirty-nine, Verrazzano's experience included years as a mariner and navigator in the Mediterranean and at least one voyage across the Atlantic from France to Newfoundland.

Sailing from the Madeira Islands in 1524, Verrazzano commanded *La Dauphine*, the 100-tun ship provided by the Crown.[3] Except for a fierce storm that forced a course change to the north, the voyage was uneventful. On the first of March on latitude 34° north of Cape Fear, Verrazzano caught his first glimpse of a "rather low lying" coast. Approaching within a mile of the beach, the French could see bonfires onshore, evidence that there were inhabitants, although they saw no one. After a fruitless voyage south fifty leagues (about 110 nautical miles), they returned to the original landfall and anchored offshore, likely just north of the cape near present-day Kure Beach.[4]

As the French longboats rowed toward the beach, they attracted a group of curious but cautious Natives. Demonstrating "great wonderment" and "great delight at seeing us," they reached out gingerly to touch these odd-looking men from another world—their peculiar and excessive clothing and their "whiteness." To Verrazzano the inhabitants looked "not unlike the Ethiopians," with dark complexion, black hair and eyes, broad faces, and tall, "well-proportioned" physical stature. He commented that in their agility, swiftness, and "sharp cunning" they "resemble the Orientals." Most striking was their near nakedness, barely covered by loincloths of animal skins and grass belts festooned with animal tails. The surroundings—the forest of palms, laurel, bay, cedar, and cypress unknown in Europe—also suggested Asia. In the "salubrious" early spring breezes, trees exuded "a sweet fragrance over a large area."[5]

Continuing their reconnaissance, the French sailed up the coast that angled toward the east, reporting more fires, possibly beacons. In need of fresh water, *La Dauphine* anchored offshore at a place Verrazzano named Annunciata in honor of the Annunciation of the Virgin Mary. Here he observed a chain of islands less than a mile wide. Looking northwest across the island, he saw a vast body of water with no land in sight that he thought must be the "eastern sea" (Pacific Ocean), the eagerly sought way to fabled India and China. What Verrazzano saw at Annunciata was the Outer Banks. With a sea visible to the northwest, he was off either Ocracoke or Hatteras Island, where Pamlico Sound appears to be a limitless ocean.

As before, friendly Natives motioned to the French to come ashore. Finding the breakers too rough to risk a landing in their longboat, Verrazzano sent a strong swimmer with "little bells, mirrors, and other trifles" to the waiting crowd. Caught by the heavy surf and half drowned, he was rescued by the Natives, who built a fire by the dune to revive him. The terrified sailor and his

GIOVANNI DI PIER ANDREA DI · BERNARDO DA VERRAZZANO
PATRIZIO FIOR. GRAN CAPP. · COMANDANTE IN MARE PER
IL RÈ CRISTIANISSIMO · FRANCESCO PRIMO,
E DISCOPRITORE · DELLA NUOVA FRANCIA.
nato circa il MCDLXXV. · morto nel MDXXV.
Dedicato al merito sing.° dell' Ill.° e Rev.° Sig.° Lodovico da Verrazzano
Patrizio, e Canonico Fiorentino Agnato del Med.°
Preso dal Quadro Originale in tela esistente presso la sud.° Nobil Famiglia
g. Zocchi del. · F. Allegrini inc 1767.

Sailing for France in 1524, Giovanni da Verrazzano began the
first exploration of North America's eastern coast at Cape Fear.
Courtesy of North Carolina Collection, Wilson Special Collections Library, University of North Carolina at Chapel Hill.

shipmates were convinced that he was about to be roasted and eaten. To everyone's great relief, when the youth recovered, he was gently led to the sea's edge,
embraced, and watched until he had safely returned to the boat.[6]

From Annunciata, *La Dauphine* rounded the cape and sailed north along the
Outer Banks to another offshore anchorage at a land "much more beautiful and
full of great forests." This country Verrazzano called Arcadia after a hilly woodland in ancient Greece, envisioned by Virgil as an ideal landscape. A low-level

flight from North Carolina to New Jersey has identified the area around Kitty Hawk and Kill Devil Hill as the sole candidate for Arcadia.[7] Kill Devil Hill and nearby Jockey's Ridge, the highest sand dune on the East Coast, boast elevations close to 100 feet. Tucked behind Jockey's Ridge is Nags Head Woods Preserve, a mature maritime forest of tall pines and hardwoods, interspersed with freshwater ponds and rich with wildlife. Walking into this national natural landmark, one enters a haven of harmony and peace, a rare place that European explorers of five centuries ago would recognize.

Anchoring offshore, the French saw a solitary man on the beach, studying them and their ship. Verrazzano himself led a twenty-man shore party. As the French boat approached, the few other people in sight scurried into the woods, but the stoic man stood his ground and was gradually enticed closer. Verrazzano observed a handsome man, naked and olive-skinned, with his hair tied in a knot at the back of his head like a sailor's queue. The Native made a friendly overture of a "burning stick," probably a pipe of smoking tobacco, a central element of their ritual. The puzzled French, who had never seen such an object, responded by striking flint and steel to ignite gunpowder in a flash and a cloud of smoke and then fired a shot from a harquebus. The Indian was "thunderstruck" and, trembling, fell to his knees in apparent prayer, pointing to the sky, the sea, and their ship.[8]

Leaving the man shaken but unmolested, the search party spread out into the woods and open marshes. In a glade deep in the forest they stumbled upon a frightened old woman, a "very beautiful and tall woman" some eighteen or twenty years old, and six children—five girls and a boy about eight years old. Confronted with armed men in strange garb spouting gibberish, their faces bizarrely hidden by beards, the terrified little band cried out in alarm. With good intentions, the French offered food that the old woman took eagerly but the young woman dashed to the ground in disgust, perhaps fearing the men's intentions. The French, abandoning kindliness, seized the young boy and tried to capture the young woman as well, but she began screaming. Realizing that they were totally isolated from their shipmates and vulnerable to an ambush, the men hastily retreated to their boat.[9]

The contrast between these Natives' fear and the curiosity of those near Capes Fear and Hatteras may indicate that the "Arcadians" had had hostile encounters with Europeans and perhaps had witnessed kidnappings by Spanish slavers. By taking the youth, the French reinforced the wicked reputation of the strangers from the sea. The fate of the boy is unknown.

Verrazzano described these people as bareheaded, lighter in color than the Natives farther south, and dressed in clothing woven from Spanish moss and hemp thread. The French discovered a clearing where dugout canoes were fashioned from large logs by burning and scraping. Verrazzano was impressed with the country's fertility, particularly noting the abundance of wild grapevines laden with "dry fruit sweet and pleasant, not unlike our own." He thought that with cultivation the grapes could produce "excellent wines."[10]

After three days *La Dauphine* headed north along the North American seaboard as far as latitude 50° on the coast of Newfoundland. Although Verrazzano missed Chesapeake and Delaware Bays, he did enter New York's harbor and explore the shores of Long Island, Narragansett Bay, Cape Cod, and Maine. His narrative would stimulate further exploration of the southeastern coast and the ongoing search for the Northwest Passage to the Orient. The identification of Pamlico Sound as an arm of the Pacific Ocean was recorded on the 1529 map of his brother, Gerolamo da Verrazzano, who was on the voyage.[11]

Verrazzano was the first European explorer to describe the coast of North Carolina from Cape Fear to Kitty Hawk, and decades passed before other Europeans revisited the area. Beyond North Carolina, Verrazzano had found a continent "larger than our Europe, than Africa, and almost larger than Asia."[12] His discoveries fired the imaginations of Spanish, French, and English alike, and through the remainder of the sixteenth century all would stake their claims and attempt to possess the new country.[13]

––––––––––

THE SPANISH CONQUISTADOR Juan Ponce de León had been the first European to set foot in southeastern North America. The seasoned warrior accompanied Columbus on his 1493 voyage to Hispaniola and later conquered Puerto Rico. On an expedition north, on 2 April 1513 he made landfall, probably at an inlet south of Daytona Beach that still bears his name, christening the land La Florida, which delineated the entire Southeast for over seventy years. Turning south, León encountered the north-flowing Gulf Stream, the great offshore current destined to convey countless ships to Europe. Returning in 1521 to colonize the Gulf Coast, he was mortally wounded in a savage clash with Natives and withdrew to die in Puerto Rico.[14]

That same year a series of Spanish voyages explored the mainland as far north as the Carolinas, seeking land, slaves, and gold. Lucas Vázquez de Ayllón, a judge from Santo Domingo, dispatched Francisco Gordillo, who in the Bahamas met another slaver, Pedro de Quejo. Together they made landfall on 24 June at the mouth of the wide South Santee, which on a subsequent voyage was christened the Jordan River.[15] Excited by the discovery, Ayllón secured a royal patent granting exclusive rights to the land from Chicora, the Winyah

Bay region, north to Chesapeake Bay. Since Chicora corresponded to the latitude of Andalucía, one of the most productive provinces in Spain, Ayllón had
high hopes for his colony.

In 1525, Ayllón sent Quejo to La Florida to reconnoiter the mainland from
present northern Florida to Chesapeake Bay. From Chicora at the Jordan River
he sailed north, exploring Cape Fear, Cape Hatteras, and the inlets near Roanoke Island. Quejo's report of desolate marshes, sandy islands, and dangerous
shoals in the northern range of Ayllón's patent confirmed that Chicora was
the most promising site for a colony.[16] Thereafter, the area that became North
Carolina no longer figured in Ayllón's colonization plans.

The next adventurer to succumb to the allure of the region's reputed wealth
was Hernando de Soto, a middle-aged conquistador who had made a great fortune with Pizarro in Peru. Bored by a courtier's life in Spain, de Soto received
a royal appointment as governor of Cuba with the right to colonize La Florida.
From Havana in 1539 he set sail in a large fleet, carrying nearly 600 men, including priests, gentlemen, slaves and servants, and over 200 horses, the largest
and best-equipped expedition ever sent to the Southeast. Landing in May near
Tampa Bay, the Spanish plunged into the interior, trailed by hundreds of pigs
for provisions and mastiffs for hunting both men and game.

The invaders soon discovered that they were not in an uncharted wilderness
but in the homeland of the highly civilized Mississippian culture that flourished from 800 to 1700 C.E. Radiating from the great urban ceremonial center,
Cahokia, in modern East St. Louis, the culture spread along the Mississippi
valley north toward the Great Lakes and southeast to the shores of the Gulf
and the Atlantic as far north as Tennessee and North Carolina. Characterized by agrarian villages and fortified towns centered on plazas dominated by
earthen ceremonial mounds, the Mississippians were organized into regional
chiefdoms.[17]

De Soto arrived in the period when the culture was waning, having been
pushed to the brink by a smallpox epidemic, which weakened the traditional
chiefdoms. The invaders carved a bloody and tragic swath across the Southeast
as far north as North Carolina and west across the Mississippi River. In town
after town the Spaniards seized hostages, demanded ransoms, and impressed
hundreds of men and women to serve as bearers and concubines. The Natives
frequently harassed the Spanish with guerrilla tactics and occasionally met
them in open battle. When queried about gold and silver, the Indians pointed
northward, luring the intruders farther into the interior.[18]

Once they left the trackless forests of the Savannah River valley, the Spanish
entered the realm of the legendary city of Cofitachequi, where fields flanked
trails that were arteries of commerce linking villages, towns, and cities. Through

the early morning mist on the Wateree River, the exhausted Spanish saw the three high mounds of the large city. Arriving by canoe, the "Lady of Cofita-chequi," niece of the ruling queen, ceremonially greeted de Soto, bedecking him with a long string of pearls. The Spanish were invited to the city, where they found a diminished population, a food shortage, and no gold, but were permitted to loot great quantities of pearls from the temples and mortuaries of the realm. At nearby Talimeco the iron axes, knife, rosary, and trade beads they discovered surely came from the Chicora voyages.

Continuing up the Wateree-Catawba River valley, the Spanish entered North Carolina's western piedmont in late May 1540. Eight days' journey brought them to Xuala, a sizable town in the foothills of the Blue Ridge that archaeologists consider the regional center of the Mississippians. Surrounding the central plaza of Xuala were a council house, an earthen temple mound, and nearby mortuaries. The whole town was protected by a log palisade. Although settled in an earlier period, the reconstructed Town Creek Indian Mound, a North Carolina historic site in the Pee Dee River basin, conveys a sense of the sixteenth-century townscape.[19]

From Xuala de Soto followed the Catawba River west up the Blue Ridge escarpment, passing through Swannanoa Gap toward the lands beyond. After turning back in modern Arkansas, de Soto died of fever and was buried in the Mississippi River. The remnant of his army, about 300 strong, reached Mexico in September 1543, over four years after the invasion had begun.[20] Having suffered catastrophic failures in La Florida, the Spanish avoided the region for nearly twenty years.

Piratical attacks on the treasure-laden ships plying the Gulf Stream forced a change in policy. In 1561 an expedition commanded by Angel de Villafañe, the new governor of La Florida, was sent to Santa Elena to select a site for a military base to protect the treasure fleets. Villafañe sailed from Havana with four vessels: two caravels and two small *fragatas* for close inshore work. It is not clear from the voyage's meager and contradictory accounts whether Villafañe actually explored Santa Elena or another bay nearby. What he reported, a shallow and unsafe anchorage, was certainly not the broad and deep Port Royal Sound.

Moving north, Villafañe's next landfall was about 34° north at what he thought was Cape San Román but was almost certainly Cape Fear, near Verraz-zano's landing several decades earlier. Meeting no one, the dons trooped across the peninsula and discovered a major river, the Cape Fear. Reboarding, Villa-fañe sailed around the treacherous cape and entered what he thought was the Jordan River. From the middle of the wide Cape Fear River they beheld what is visible to this day—a low-lying wooded shore lined with grassy marshes and a scattering of small islands that appeared too miry and desolate for a colony.[21]

As Villafañe retraced his course around the shoals, in a storm he lost sight of his consort caravel, and it did not return. Undeterred, Villafañe sailed up the coast with his flagship and the *fragatas*. On 14 June near 35° north he sighted Cape Hatteras, its shoals extending far out to sea, which he misidentified as Cabo de Trafalgar, or Cape Lookout. That night the flotilla was caught on the lee shore by a hurricane that caused both of the *fragatas* to founder. Through howling winds and blackness the Spanish were haunted by screams and cries for God's mercy from the nearest *fragata*, which they were powerless to help. The next morning, facing an empty and turbulent sea, he set a course for Cuba, safely returning to Havana by late July. Although Villafañe had been essentially lost on his voyage of discovery, he unwittingly discovered North Carolina's preeminent river—the Cape Fear. His report to the king described the coast below 35° north as poor, uninhabited, not suitable for a colony, and not likely to be encroached upon.[22]

The Spanish conclusion that "there was no reason 'to fear that the French will set foot'" in La Florida could not have been more wrong.[23] The French were the first to attempt to found a privateering base in the region. The Huguenots, Protestants who were being persecuted at home, received permission to establish a colony as a refuge and privateer outpost on the North American mainland. They made two efforts—first in 1562 at Charles Fort on Port Royal Sound, which collapsed through poor organization and support, and two years later at Fort Caroline on the St. John's River. This second colony was so close to the treasure route that it triggered a decisive response from the illustrious Admiral Pedro Menéndez de Avilés. In 1565 Menéndez mounted a thousand-man expedition that massacred the French heretics, destroyed their settlement, and founded Saint Augustine, the first Spanish colony in La Florida, as a military outpost to secure the western flank of the sea lane. The massive coquina walls of Castillo de San Marcos rose in the next century to ensure that Florida remained Spanish for nearly 250 years.[24]

To solidify Spain's possession of the region and to protect the treasure ships, Menéndez expanded military outposts, personally seating a colony at Santa Elena in 1566 that became the first capital of La Florida. Menéndez established friendly relations with the local Indians and constructed Fort San Felipe on the ruins of Charlesfort. Reduced by mutiny and desertion, the Santa Elena colony was in jeopardy until Captain Juan Pardo stabilized it.[25]

Menéndez's vision was to settle the interior, acquire the allegiance of the Native American population, and discover an overland route from Santa Elena to the silver mines in Zacatacas, Mexico, which was much farther away than the Spanish realized. Given these orders, Pardo set forth with 125 men on 1 December 1566, marching north into largely unknown country that was heavily

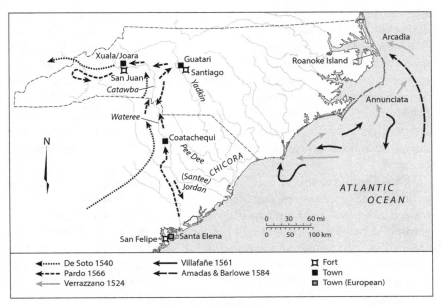

European Exploration

populated with intact Indigenous cultures.[26] In recent memory, the inhabitants had had violent encounters with de Soto's incursion and were no longer awed by these grasping and violent strangers. Except for trade possibilities, the Indians had no reason to tolerate the intruders and knew they could be easily enticed away by fanciful tales of riches lying deeper in the heartland.

Pardo intersected the route de Soto had taken a quarter of a century earlier and followed his trail up the Wateree-Catawba River into the Blue Ridge Mountains. In January 1567 the Spaniards reached the town of Joara, de Soto's Xuala. Facing snow-covered mountains to the west, for secure winter quarters they constructed Fort San Juan north of the town's central mound, equipping it with adequate powder, shot, match cord, crossbows, and tools. Ongoing archaeological excavations at the site of Joara have uncovered burned remains of five buildings, a log palisade, and sixteenth-century Spanish metal and ceramic artifacts.[27] Over the next month, Pardo visited other Native towns and built the imposing Fort Santiago at Guatari on the Yadkin River, where he left a few soldiers and a priest to found a mission.

Recalled to Santa Elena to repel an anticipated French attack, Pardo left a garrison of thirty men under Sergeant Hernando Moyano. Intended to be a permanent outpost of La Florida and supported by other fortified garrisons,

Fort San Juan thus housed the first European settlers in North Carolina, pre-dating by eighteen years the celebrated Roanoke Island settlement of Captain Ralph Lane. Fort San Juan would be occupied for eighteen months; Lane's En-glish colony lasted less than a year before being abandoned. Sergeant Moyano cannot be faulted for initiative, but his actions led directly to the failure of the Spanish outposts. Moyano imprudently involved his garrison in tribal con-flicts, supporting the Joara chief against his enemies and spearheading raids into southwestern Virginia and Tennessee. Finally, he moved a garrison west to Chiaha and constructed a fort, where he awaited reinforcements from his captain.[28]

When Pardo returned to Fort San Juan in September 1567, he was alarmed to find that the Joarans were embittered by the arrogant Spanish demands and seizures of women and supplies. After placating the Indians, he increased the garrison at San Juan; marched into the mountains to rescue Moyano's men, narrowly escaping a trap; and retreated to Joara. There Pardo, ordered back to Santa Elena, left Moyano well supplied with arms and provisions. Through their greed and lust, however, the Spanish had ensured their own doom. In the spring of 1568, the Natives throughout the region finally rose up, massa-cred most of them, and burned their forts.[29] The European presence in North Carolina's backcountry was violently erased, forgotten, and held at bay for over a century.

An unintended consequence of the Spanish expeditions was that dozens of Spanish and African deserters and captives were scattered across the South-east, lost to their country and to history, but living with the Indians, first en-slaved and then gradually by marriage or adoption incorporated into the tribes and nations. These sons of Iberia and North Africa are likely ancestors of the mixed-race people called Melungeons found throughout the Southeast, espe-cially in the mountains and backcountry.[30]

SIXTY YEARS PASSED before the Native Americans of coastal North Carolina would have significant interaction with other strangers from the sea. From Ver-razzano's 1524 first contact to the landing of Philip Amadas and Arthur Barlowe in 1584, the inhabitants of the Outer Banks infrequently saw Spanish vessels passing offshore and an occasional shipwreck. The Spanish and French incur-sions on the North American mainland had nettled the English, who believed that John Cabot's discovery gave them prior claim to the northern continent, but not until the flood tide of the Elizabethan Age would England be able to exploit that claim.

North of Santa Elena there was no European presence on the southeast-ern coast. Since the reign of Henry VIII, the English had had Gerolamo da

Verrazzano's map of the region. They were intrigued by the dream of "Andalucia" or the mythical "Arcadia," and Verrazzano's belief that he had seen an arm of the Pacific Ocean. In the 1580s his reputed discovery was incorporated into maps by the influential scientist and astrologer Dr. John Dee for Queen Elizabeth and Humphrey Gilbert and was also published by Richard Hakluyt.[31] The possibility of reaching Asia through a midcontinental passage was very much in Walter Raleigh's plans for the Roanoke voyages.

The true legacy of France's ravaged colonies in Florida, however, was the narratives of Jean Ribault and René Laudonnière, published in English translation. In Ribault's timely description, *The Whole and True Discoverye of Terra Florida* (1563), the English had their first glimpse of mysterious, exotic La Florida. Laudonnière's *L'histoire notable de la Floride*, dedicated to Sir Walter Raleigh, was published in Paris in 1586, and the next year in England. Jacques Le Moyne de Morgues, the artist of Fort Caroline, relocated to England and joined Raleigh's household. The German engraver Theodor de Bry acquired Le Moyne's paintings from his widow and published them in 1591.[32]

Under the firm hand of Elizabeth I, England was poised for economic growth, overseas expansion, and cultural flowering. The English were on the cusp of a great era, the Elizabethan Age, and when it ended in the early seventeenth century, England was a major European nation-state. In the forefront of overseas expansion were the Elizabethan "sea dogs"—sea captains, traders, privateers, and pirates—Sir Humphrey Gilbert, Sir Walter Raleigh, Sir Francis Drake, Sir John Hawkins, Sir Richard Grenville, Thomas Cavendish, and Sir Martin Frobisher.[33]

Many of these men were from Devon in southwestern England, and several were related. Gilbert and Raleigh were half-brothers, and Grenville was a cousin of both Raleigh and Drake. The sea dogs earned their knighthoods through extraordinary exploits in subduing and colonizing Ireland, raiding Spanish treasure ships and ports, defeating the Spanish Armada, circumnavigating the globe, seeking the Northwest Passage to Asia, and attempting to establish overseas colonies in Newfoundland and on Roanoke Island. They laid the foundation for England's maritime dominance of Europe (and, indeed, the world), which lasted from the sixteenth century to the mid-twentieth.

England's concept of overseas conquest and colonization was forged in the Tudor subjugation of Ireland. Although the English had long been in Ireland, by the sixteenth century rebellions and dynastic clashes threatened their tenuous hold. The Crown countered with military garrisons, new plantations of English colonists, and brutal repression. Gilbert, Raleigh, Grenville, and Ralph Lane had all been engaged in terrorizing the Irish, perfecting tactics that would be imposed on the Native Americans.[34]

The early settlements of soldiers fresh from the bloody fields of Ireland were transported by admirals, sea captains, and pilots who were more committed to chasing Spanish and French prizes than to seating a colony. The seeds of failure for England's first settlement in Virginia were sown in the harsh reaction to Native intransigence; the pursuit of piracy, privateering, and raids against the Spanish; and the inability of settlers to adapt to the New World environment.

The voyages that brought the English to North Carolina's Outer Banks were inspired by Sir Humphrey Gilbert, who was interested in the Northwest Passage to Asia and colonization in North America. In 1578 the queen gave him a six-year proprietary charter, by letters patent, to search for "remote heathen and barbarous lands," which he would own and govern. In return for his grant, Gilbert was obligated to colonize within the six-year limit and give the Crown one-fifth of the gold and silver.[35] Although the monarch at times participated as an investor, from Gilbert onward English North America was first explored, financed, colonized, and governed by individuals and corporations. Gilbert finally reached Newfoundland in 1583 at Saint Johns Harbor, but on the return voyage he disappeared in a storm.[36]

Gilbert's dream of overseas colonies did not die with him but was taken up by Walter Raleigh, who received a six-year renewal of the charter on 25 March 1584. The ambitious, mercurial Raleigh possessed wide-ranging interests and seemingly unbounded energy. This brilliant light of the English Renaissance has been embraced as the protofounder of the United States. Over a lifetime of achievement, the visionary Raleigh was a soldier, pirate, privateer, scientist, poet, and historian. Introduced at court by a relative, Raleigh quickly entered the inner circle of the queen's courtiers and made himself indispensable.[37]

In 1583 Queen Elizabeth gave him Durham House, his London residence on the Thames River. Sparing no expense, Raleigh modernized the rambling medieval structure into an elegant home befitting a powerful courtier and royal favorite. High in his aerie overlooking the river, surrounded by his books, maps, globes, and scientific instruments, he could dream and plan his overseas ventures. His widening circle of scientists, soldiers, artists, merchants, and mariners became, in modern parlance, a "brain trust" that would lay the foundations of the British Empire.

Raleigh's first long voyage, to the Cape Verde Islands as captain of *Falcon*, sparked a lifelong passion to explore and colonize the New World. His mentor at sea was the Portuguese pilot Simon Fernandez, a veteran of thirty years as merchant-seaman, privateer, and sometime pirate. Fernandez, who had crossed the Atlantic twice for Spain and explored the mainland, possibly as far north as the Outer Banks, became an integral part of the team that Raleigh assembled at Durham House.[38]

At the intellectual center of Durham House were Raleigh, Richard Hakluyt, and Thomas Hariot. Raleigh and Hakluyt met as students at Oxford University, and Hakluyt's publications had made him the foremost proponent of overseas colonization. Completing the creative hub was Thomas Hariot, a graduate of Oxford, for whom Raleigh provided a residence, study, library, laboratory, and observatory. A contemporary of Galileo, Hariot became a prominent scientist of his era who independently experimented with atomic theory, laws of motion, refraction, and the telescope. His *Briefe and True Report of the New Found Land of Virginia* (1588) was the first ethnographic and natural history of North Carolina. Hakluyt and Hariot were among the English "metropolitans," whose goal was to establish "dominion and civility" on the verges of the empire by trade, colonies, and converting the Natives to Protestant Christianity. Under Hariot's guidance, Fernandez, Thomas Cavendish, and Sir Richard Grenville taught navigation to Raleigh and the youthful Philip Amadas and Arthur Barlowe.[39]

Charter in hand and eager to launch a full-fledged overseas colonial enterprise, Raleigh dispatched two small barks under Barlowe and the nineteen-year-old Amadas, the expedition admiral, to explore north of Santa Elena. Leaving Plymouth on 27 April with Fernandez as pilot, they sighted Wococon (Ocracoke) on 4 July and sailed up the Outer Banks to a navigable inlet near Roanoke Island that they dubbed Port Ferdinando.[40]

Amadas and Barlowe led a party ashore on the north end of Hatteras Island. They were entranced by their surroundings. Grapes were so plentiful that the vines spilled down to the edge of the surf, where "the surge of the Sea, overflowed them." From the sandy beach the men trudged south toward hills later called Kenricks Mounts, which were covered with a "goodly woods" of red cedars. From the hilltops as far west as they could see there appeared to be "another great Sea."[41]

Two days passed before any inhabitants appeared. First contact was with three fishermen, one of whom was lured aboard, where he was plied with clothing, wine, and meat, "which he liked very well." The three Natives reciprocated by filling their canoe with fish for the strangers. News of the visitors spread rapidly. The next morning brought a large party led by the imposing Granganimeo, brother of King Wingina, who held a formal council with the English, conveying through speech and gestures his "joy and welcome." The English reciprocated with gifts, which were graciously received. Coming from an aristocratic society, the Europeans were impressed by the deference shown to Prince Granganimeo and his family, and they learned that King Wingina was "greatly obeyed" and "reverenced."

The council ended with trading and a bountiful feast. For sailors who had spent weeks subsisting on salt meat and ship's biscuit, the cornucopia of victuals from Indian gardens and hunts was welcome indeed. In trade, the Natives offered "Chammoys, Buffe, and Deere skinnes." The English laid out copper kettles, hatchets, axes, and knives, but refused to part with their swords.[42]

Within days Granganimeo honored the English with a family visit including his wife, his daughter, and several younger children. In return, Barlowe sailed to the Roanoke village, where he was greeted "cheerfully" by Granganimeo's wife, who treated the boat's crew to a bath, laundering of their clothes, and another feast. Amadas and Barlowe learned that they had entered a complex geopolitical world of shifting alliances. Wingina's realm was limited to the towns of Roanoke and Dasemunkepeuc on the mainland. Although urged to become Wingina's ally in regional politics and conflict, the English wisely demurred.[43]

The Natives related intriguing stories about two shipwrecks that had been tossed up on the Outer Banks over twenty years earlier. The Secotans had helped survivors from one wreck fashion a double-hulled craft from two canoes, with sails sewn from shirts, but the derelict canoes were later found on a nearby island. The other ship had no survivors. From its wreckage strewn on Croatoan the Secotans recovered nails and spikes that they shaped into crude cutting and scraping tools. Very likely these were the *fragatas* lost by Villafañe in 1561 near Cape Hatteras.[44]

After several weeks in the region, Amadas and Barlowe set separate courses for England. They had located a usable inlet, established friendly relations and trade with the Roanokes, briefly reconnoitered inland waters, experienced the bounty of the land, and located an island for a potential settlement site. Overall, it was an auspicious beginning. Reflecting their gracious welcome, Barlowe wrote, "Wee found the people most gentle, loving, and faithfull, void of all guile, and treason, and such as lived after the manner of the golden age." Two Natives, Manteo and Wanchese, joined the English for the return trip to England.[45] The English were interested in interpreters; for his part, Wingina hoped to take the measure of these men from across the sea.

Amadas and Barlowe arrived in England in mid-September. Raleigh was ecstatic. His presentation of Manteo and Wanchese at court was a sensation. Delighted with Barlowe's glowing report, Raleigh presented it to the queen with a Hakluyt essay on colonization. Elizabeth demonstrated her pleasure by knighting Raleigh on Twelfth Night, 6 January 1585, allowing the new land to be named Virginia, for the Virgin Queen, and appointing Sir Walter lord and governor. The queen's chief contribution was the royal ship *Tiger*, to be the flagship of the fleet preparing to take a colony to Roanoke Island.[46]

By April Raleigh dispatched seven well-equipped vessels, four of which he owned, under the command of his cousin, Sir Richard Grenville, who sailed with Fernandez on *Tiger*. Among those commanding the other vessels were Amadas (now admiral of Virginia), Barlowe, and Thomas Cavendish. The goal was to establish a privateering outpost that could be expanded into a permanent colony. Soldiers made up about half the complement, and Ralph Lane, a veteran officer, was appointed the outpost's governor. To document the natural and mineral resources and the Native people, Thomas Hariot led the scientific team, which included the artist John White and a Jewish metallurgist, Joachim Gans from Prague, who would establish what is known today as "America's first science center."[47]

Via the West Indies for trading and taking Spanish prizes, Fernandez brought the fleet to Ocracoke on 26 June. There *Tiger* grounded and was damaged, along with the bulk of the colony's supplies. Grenville launched a reconnaissance to map the sound, meet other Indians, and seek Verrazzano's purported passage to Asia. In July a pinnace and three boats embarked on Pamlico Sound carrying some fifty men, including Grenville, Amadas, Lane, Cavendish, Hariot, White, and Manteo. They were pleasantly welcomed at the villages of Pomeiooc near Lake Mattamuskeet and Secotan on the Pamlico River. At Pomeiooc, a palisaded town of seventeen longhouses and a circular temple, John White began his sketches of the Algonquians, drawing their daily activities and charming portraits.[48]

A colder reception awaited them at Aquascogoc on the Pungo River, where a silver cup disappeared. Amadas returned to recover the cup, but it could not be found. Angered by this perceived faithlessness, Amadas ordered the village and its crops burned, leaving the inhabitants, who had fled, to face a bleak winter and squandering forever the goodwill fostered the year before.[49] Over such a trivial matter as a silver cup, this was foolhardy and did not bode well for the handful of Englishmen surrounded by thousands of Natives.

At Port Ferdinando by 27 July, Grenville accepted Granganimeo's invitation to settle on Roanoke Island, and the colonists began work on housing and a fort. Lane was enchanted by the prospect of the colony, writing from the new fort that the country had "the goodliest soile under the cope of heaven" and noting that the climate was "so wholesome, that we have not had one sicke, since we touched land here." A month later, Grenville sailed for England, leaving Lane and his men, the first English colony in Virginia.[50]

Hariot began compiling notes about Virginia that would become his most lasting contribution. He wrote of great migratory flocks of geese and swans, spring runs of sturgeon and herring, abundant shellfish, and land and sea tortoises. He singled out maize, the versatile keystone crop of Native farming, which could be baked into bread, boiled into a "pappe" (cornmeal mush), or as corn "mault" brewed into "as good ale as was to be desired."[51] Tobacco, or "uppowoc," used in religious rituals and for health and pleasure, fascinated the scientist. Soon an inveterate smoker, Hariot was convinced that it opened "pores

"Village of Pomeiooc" in "Wunderbarliche, doch warhafftige Erklärung,
von der Gelegenheit vnd Sitten der Wilden in Virginia . . ." [*America*,
pt. 1, German] (Frankfurt: Theodore De Bry, 1590), 81. Courtesy of
North Carolina Collection, Wilson Special Collections Library,
University of North Carolina at Chapel Hill.

and passages" to purge excessive phlegm and other "gross humors" and "notably
preserved" the health of the Algonquians.[52]

Hariot's vision for the Algonquians was to civilize and convert them to the
"true religion" of the Church of England. Using his otherworldly technology
—compass, magnifying glass, guns, fireworks, and books—he demonstrated
the superior power of the "God of England." When he preached the gospel,
the Natives reverently mimicked his prayers and singing, but as more of them
sickened and died after visits from the English, they begged Hariot to heal

them. Despite eventual open warfare with the Roanokes, Hariot "sought by all meanes possible to win them by gentlenesse," hoping that they could be persuaded to embrace "the trueth, and consequently to honour, obey, feare, and love us."[53]

In the spring of 1586 Lane scouted the interior rivers, seeking a protected harbor and settlement site. Ever the soldier, among the powerful Chowanoac the arrogant Lane took their king, Menatonon, and his son, Skiko, hostages, ensuring their enmity.[54] Far up the Roanoke River, seeking rumored pearls, gold, and copper, Lane's party encountered ambushes and destroyed crops, and had to eat their mastiffs to survive. Back at Roanoke Island food was critically scarce. Probably manipulating Lane, Menatonon convinced him that Wingina, now called Pemisapan, was conspiring with other tribes to surprise and destroy the English. Urged by Skiko, Lane launched a preemptive strike at Dasemunkepeuc, slaughtering a number of the warriors, including Pemisapan, whose head was mounted on a pole at the site as a warning.[55] Such vicious assaults on the Algonquians would echo down through centuries of hostilities between Native Americans and the European invaders.

Threatened on all sides and facing starvation, the colonists were overjoyed when Sir Francis Drake's fleet arrived, fresh from looting Saint Augustine and Spanish towns in the Caribbean. Drake's offer of ships and supplies was aborted when a storm damaged and scattered his fleet. When he offered to take the colonists home, they fled so precipitously that three men were left behind. Within days a supply ship arrived at the abandoned settlement, followed a fortnight later by Grenville's entire fleet. No colonists could be found, and a captured Native informed them of Drake's rescue. Loath to lose the foothold, Grenville chose fifteen men to maintain an English presence.[56]

Undeterred by the failure of the Lane colony, Raleigh planned a permanent colony, and on 7 January 1587 a corporation was created for the "Cittie of Ralegh in Virginia." Appointed governor, John White was accompanied by his pregnant daughter Eleanor and her husband, Ananias Dare. On 26 July three vessels bearing 117 colonists, including 17 women, 9 children, and 2 Natives, Manteo and Towaye, arrived at Port Ferdinando. The plan was to pick up Grenville's men and relocate the colony to Chesapeake Bay.[57]

Simon Fernandez, arguing that the hurricane season was well underway and eager to return to the Caribbean for privateering, refused to take them north and instead set them ashore at Roanoke Island. Of Grenville's men only an ominous single skeleton remained. Nevertheless, the hopeful colonists set to work repairing the standing houses and unloading supplies. Within days they were shocked by the brutal murder of George Howe, who was crabbing alone in the shallows. Alarmed, White sent Manteo to assuage the distrust, but the effort was undone by the colonists' mistaken attack on friendly Croatoans. Trying to maintain a semblance of normality, White conducted three christenings—Manteo, a Harvie child, and his newborn granddaughter Virginia Dare. With growing apprehension the colonists insisted that White return to England to advocate for timely resupply while they moved to a more secure location.[58] White set sail for England, no doubt anxiously watching from the deck as the dark forest holding his little family and his hopes for the future receded from sight.

War with Spain and the Spanish Armada thwarted White's desperate efforts to return. When he finally reached Roanoke Island in 1590, the only traces of the colonists were cryptic carvings of "Croatoan" and "CRO" that suggested Manteo's tribal home south of Hatteras. A storm forced White to leave Virginia without finding the colony. Having done all he could, he never lost hope that his daughter's family still lived in Virginia. From his home in Ireland in 1593 White sent his friend Richard Hakluyt the report of his last voyage, ending his letter with the poignant prayer "Thus I commit the relief of my uneasy company of planters in Virginia to the merciful help of the Almighty, whom I most humbly beseech to help and comfort them, according to His most holy will and their good desire, and so take my leave."[59] Despite efforts by Raleigh himself and later from Jamestown, the English men, women, and children left on Roanoke Island were never seen again. The heartbreaking story of the Lost Colony continues to fascinate and has become America's best-known historical mystery. While numerous theories have been advanced and considerable archaeological and historical research has produced a few intriguing clues, over four centuries the colony has remained lost. Most recently, in 2012 a hidden town symbol was discovered on a John White map, perhaps indicating the intended refuge for the harried colonists, which White knew before he left. Subsequent archaeological excavations near Salmon Creek at the head of Albemarle Sound have uncovered sixteenth-century artifacts, which may finally lead to the elusive settlement.[60]

THROUGHOUT THE sixteenth century Native Americans and intruders from Spain, France, and England vied for dominance in the Southeast. The hubris of Spanish conquistadors who explored and conquered the Americas is breathtaking. Driven by unquenchable greed, hunger for power, and a fanatical faith honed by centuries of conflict with the Moors, they could not conceive of failure. But they, like the English and French, suffered one loss after another as over a thousand Europeans died or disappeared in the wilderness, and countless

Natives perished from conflict and from diseases unintentionally brought by the invaders.

With the destruction of Fort San Juan, North Carolina's first "lost colony," the Spanish tide receded to the environs of Saint Augustine's stout ramparts and a few struggling Franciscan missions. To the north, England viewed the coast and hinterland as a no-man's-land occupied by Indian tribes and chiefdoms. It was not a foregone conclusion that the region would be possessed by English-speaking colonists. Although Raleigh's two Roanoke Island colonies began with great promise, they also failed because of poor decisions, lack of support, and Native hostility caused by English arrogance and brutal retaliation, leaving the new name "Virginia" on the map and the poignancy of the English Lost Colony to tantalize future generations.

But in England, now committed to overseas colonies for trade and empire, it was no longer questionable whether she would expand beyond her immediate vicinity. The English clung to the belief that their countrymen were living somewhere in Virginia and that very soon more Englishmen would cross the Atlantic to join them. From first contact at Roanoke Island, just twenty-three years passed before the English stepped ashore on the Chesapeake Bay and planted the tiny fortified settlement at Jamestown that survived to inaugurate the British Empire and become the foundation of the United States.

CHAPTER TWO

The Carolana Propriety

We do erect and incorporate them into a Province,
and name the same CAROLANA.
—Charles I, 1629

SIR WALTER RALEIGH sent several voyages to search for his colonists between Cape Hatteras and Chesapeake Bay. Although the expeditions
returned with medicinal plants, they never found the English settlers.[1]
Nevertheless, because it could not be proven that the colonists had perished,
the belief persisted that somewhere in Virginia the colony survived, and that
was enough to maintain Raleigh's charter rights and England's claim. After
Elizabeth's death, Raleigh's 1603 arrest and conviction for treason led James I
to seize his property, including Virginia.[2] Imprisoned in the Tower of London
for most of his last years, until beheaded in 1618, Sir Walter Raleigh did live to
see the incarnation of his vision, the establishment of an English presence in
the New World.

Bridging the failures of the sixteenth century to successes in the next, the
proprietary charters of Gilbert and Raleigh provided the model for privatiz-
ing England's overseas expansion into a world empire. With the royal treasury
chronically in need of revenue, James I followed Elizabeth I's example of letting
the risk of empire building fall on courtiers, statesmen, and merchants. In 1606
the king issued a charter to the Virginia Company, which founded Jamestown.
Rather than to individual proprietors, the new Virginia grant was to a group
of investors, including gentry and merchants. Connections to the past were
represented by Richard Hakluyt and Raleigh Gilbert, a son of Sir Humphrey.[3]

When Jamestown was founded in 1607, the leaders were instructed to look
for Raleigh's colonists, presumed to be still alive. Hearing from the Indians that
whites were living to the south, in 1608 John Smith ordered two searches of the
Chowan and Roanoke Rivers, but no Englishmen were found. Although al-
luring rumors of Europeans in the region continued, Smith concluded that the
Roanoke Island settlers were "all dead."[4] Tottering Jamestown, barely surviving

through the tragic "starving time," launched no further explorations for Roanoke survivors.

Although Virginia found a lucrative export, tobacco, the colony remained tenuous—underfunded, undersupplied, plagued with an appalling death rate. On 22 March 1622, a surprise onslaught by the Powhatan confederacy struck James River farms, plantations, and towns. By sundown, over one-quarter of the colony's white population had perished, beginning many months of brutal warfare that would end in a crushing defeat of the Indians.[5] The prolonged conflict profoundly affected the development of Virginia, forcing the transition from a proprietary colony of joint public and private participation to a royal province.[6]

Shortly before the 1622 massacre, the urbane John Pory, Virginia's secretary of state, traveled some sixty miles south to the Chowan River. His observations were widely circulated in England in a sermon and pamphlet, in John Smith's *General Historie* (1624), and in a promotional tract in 1649.[7] Pory reported extensive stands of pine trees that could provide England the strategic naval stores of ships' masts, tar, and pitch. On the river he was impressed by large fields of maize that produced two harvests a year. Pory was welcomed, probably at the principal town of the Chowans, the largest in the region, where "the great king" entertained him, expressed interest in "a league" with the English, and regaled him with tales of copper farther west. Soon after Pory returned to Virginia, the Powhatan assault and war quashed any immediate interest in settling deeper in Indian country.[8]

———

WHEN THE VIRGINIA CHARTER reverted to the Crown in 1624, the decision was made to separate the territory between Virginia and Spanish Florida and offer it for private colonization. The uneasy peace that James I had maintained with Spain crumbled in 1625 with the accession of his son, Charles I, who was willing to confront England's traditional enemy. Within the year, war began with both Spain and France. As part of a broader strategy to curb Spain's dominance in the West Indies and Florida and to advance English colonization, Charles made a flurry of proprietary grants to influential advisers and courtiers—particularly in 1627 to James Hay, Earl of Carlisle, who was granted Caribbean islands; in 1629 to Sir Robert Heath, the region south of Virginia; and in 1631 to George Calvert, Lord Baltimore, land north of Virginia.[9]

Long interested in overseas colonies, Sir Robert Heath, a close adviser of the king, had been appointed attorney general in 1625 and would become chief justice. Heath's propriety granted on 30 October 1629 was by far the largest—the territory between latitudes 31° and 36° north. It included all of what is now the

Sir Robert Heath, whose Carolana propriety of 1629 from
Charles I became the basis for the future Carolina charters.
Courtesy of State Archives of North Carolina.

southern United States from the southern shore of Albemarle Sound in North
Carolina to the St. Johns River in Florida and west "so far as the Continent
there extends itself." The grant encompassed the offshore islands, extending
well below 31° to the unclaimed Bahamas. Heath and his heirs were named the
"true and absolute Lords and Proprietors" of this new province of Carolana,
named for Charles I.[10]

Conceived as a buffer to protect Virginia from Spanish incursions from
Florida, Carolana bore a striking resemblance to the English medieval palatine
counties next to Wales and Scotland. England's troubled borders, perpetually
threatened by raids and uprisings, required the quick response of a resident
administrator. On the Scottish frontier the Bishop of Durham had long been
empowered with viceregal authority to rule his autonomous palatine county as

a prince-bishop, sovereign within his borders. In effect, at its peak in the thirteenth century the palatine county was a kingdom within the kingdom. Using the Bishop of Durham's precedent, the king bestowed viceregal authority on the proprietor, which became the legal basis for governance in the province and would appear in the charters of Maryland and Carolina.[11]

Lord Proprietor Heath held his fief by knight's service and was primarily obligated to settle and protect the province. Remote "New Carolana," bordering hostile Spanish Florida and located "among so many barbarous nations" (that is, the Native Americans), was also subject to piratical incursions. As captain general, the proprietor had full authority to defend the province from all rebellions, invasions, robbers, and pirates. Laws were normally to be enacted with the "counsel, assent, and approbation of the Freeholders of the Province, or the major part of them," although in emergencies the proprietor could promulgate executive ordinances. Whether passed by an assembly or by the executive alone, laws could not be "repugnant or contrary" to the laws, customs, and rights of Englishmen. Inhabitants of Carolana would be considered natural subjects and lieges of the king and possessed of "all liberties, franchises, and privileges of this our Realm."[12]

Despite repeated efforts, no colony would be established in Carolana. Eventually the charter was revoked, but the Carolana Charter would live on in its direct descendant, the Carolina Charter of 1663. Carolana has been described as a colony in a time of "false steps, not triumphs,"[13] but in an era when colonization was largely a matter of trial and error, the failures ultimately taught colonizers how to succeed.

At the time Heath petitioned the king for a propriety, he was negotiating with leaders of the London refugee community of French Protestant Huguenots. Their rapid growth in a rigid Catholic country touched off religious persecution and massacres, and many fled to England. Conferring with Heath was M. de Belavene, representing Antoine de Ridouet, Baron de Sancé, who proposed a colony of 2,000 men supported by farming and trade. Heath informed the king that he was "about to lead thither a Colony of men, large and plentiful, professing the true religion . . . applying themselves to the culture of the said lands and to merchandising." These plans came to naught due to a lack of financing but were a catalyst for the Carolana patent.[14]

Heath drew additional supporters to his enterprise by temporarily dividing the propriety into two fiefdoms—a northern tract for George, Lord Berkeley from southern Albemarle Sound to Cape Fear, and a southern tract to Sir Richard Grenville from Cape Fear to the Satilla River at latitude 31° north. Whether the venture was on sound footing as Heath claimed, by the time the charter was granted, with winter coming on, it may have been too late to proceed.[15]

During the winter Hugh L'Amy negotiated with Berkeley and Heath as the representative of Sancé's expanded Huguenot group, which now included Samuel Vassall. L'Amy expected to lead a colony to Carolana and was commissioned receiver general of rents. Sancé requested the region between 34° and 35° from Cape Fear to Ocracoke Inlet but by March 1630 received territory between the Neuse and Pamlico Rivers. He envisioned an initial settlement of 100 to 150 men with mariners, artisans, and laborers. Detailed plans for the colony included sketches of fortification and housing, but the want of funding and settlers precluded any voyage that year. Further discouraging the Huguenots was an inopportune order by the Privy Council that required colonists to be adherents of the Church of England.[16]

As months passed and plans failed to materialize, the partners drifted to other colonial interests. By 1632 only Samuel Vassall was left to carry the Carolana project forward, and he retained his interest in the region for the rest of his life. Son of John Vassall, a Huguenot refugee merchant, Samuel was born in England and had become an ardent Puritan and a founder of the Massachusetts Bay Company. Earlier he had outfitted his shallop as a privateer. Now a London merchant and ship owner, he had extensive experience trading in the Mediterranean, Africa, and the American colonies. Known as a cloth merchant, he also dabbled in various other products, including tobacco, currants, silks, hemp, flax, and enslaved Africans. Over a long political career he served as a London alderman, a member of Parliament, a navy commissioner, and a commissioner for plantations. Often at odds with the Crown over trade policy, he has been characterized as a "restless opponent of the Caroline régime."[17]

In the summer of 1632 Vassall had an agreement with a partnership headed by Edward Kingswell, who was appointed governor of a colony in Carolana. Vassall was to transport the initial settlement of forty persons, followed by twenty more. Knowing that Carolana's northern coast was dangerous and lacked deepwater ports, Vassall dispatched Henry Taverner, who spent nine months mapping the coast from Virginia to St. Helena Sound. Based on this reconnaissance, Vassall requested the rights to the southern half of Carolana from latitudes 31° to 33° north.[18]

To navigate the shallow rivers, Vassall offered his shallop and the pinnace *Henry*, but both required extensive refitting before going to sea. Impatient at the delay, Kingswell, his family and servants, and three dozen colonists set sail for Virginia on Vassall's larger *Mayflower*, commanded by his brother-in-law Peter Andrews. In Virginia by October 1633, they were stranded for a year because they lacked supplies. Several months later Vassall sent Taverner in *Thomas of London* with twenty-eight new settlers. He was preparing *Henry* for sailing when an ill and despondent Kingswell landed in England demanding compensation for his losses and Vassall's failure to fulfill the contract. The next two years were consumed with litigation. A government commission finally settled partial restitution on Kingswell, but Vassall refused to pay and served brief prison terms instead. Kingswell died in 1636 during a later hearing, leaving Carolana available for yet another initiative.[19]

Of the nearly seventy colonists who had landed in Virginia in the Vassall-Kingswell venture, forty-six were issued land headrights and apparently remained. Some of these may have gone south to Carolana. In 1636 a party of Virginians went "adventuringe in ye Chowan country for sperrits resin." There they met a group from Bermuda, also seeking naval stores, who were discouraged by the "overplus" of men already there. Although Carolana's pine forests were well known from John Pory's report, this curious reference to overcrowding in the Chowan is puzzling, as explorers a decade later encountered no one of European descent.[20]

NEXT TO SEEK HIS FORTUNE in Carolana was Henry Frederick Howard, Lord Maltravers. Related to several of England's most powerful families, Maltravers was a court favorite and a member of Parliament and the Council of New England.[21] Using his considerable influence, Maltravers persuaded Charles I to direct Virginia's governor and council to create the County of Norfolk from the headwaters of the Nansemond River south to the Neuse River, lying mostly in Carolana. The new county was patented to Maltravers, who had seven years to settle it and had to pay an annual rent of twenty shillings.[22] Before the patent was actually issued, however, on 2 December 1637 Maltravers purchased the entire Carolana propriety from Heath and thereby became Lord Proprietor of the province.[23]

Eager to settle his new colony, Maltravers employed Captain Henry Hawley, who as governor of Barbados had brought order out of chaos. On 2 August 1638 Governor Hawley was commissioned lieutenant general of Carolana and deputy governor of the northern half of the province and promised 10,000 acres. His brother, Captain William Hawley, became deputy governor of the southern half of Carolana. There is no further mention of Henry Hawley, but by April 1640 William Hawley was in Virginia, where he secured permission to recruit up to 100 Virginia freemen for Carolana.[24]

Whether any settlement took place then is not known. Much later, seeking to establish his claim to Carolana, Daniel Coxe stated that Maltravers had "planted several parts of the said county." Moreover, Carolina proprietor Sir John Colleton had the impression that a plantation had been seated by the "steward to the Duke of Norfolk." Maltravers's interest in Carolana faded as he became absorbed by events in England, serving as a general in the 1639 Scottish war and being drawn into the ensuing Civil War as a royalist.[25]

Before 1646 only individuals or small groups of explorers had visited the Roanoke country. All that changed when Governor Sir William Berkeley authorized punitive expeditions against Indians in the region in another war with the Powhatan confederacy. Reprising the earlier massacre, Opechanconough, Powhatan's brother, ordered a massive surprise attack that began on 18 April 1644 and left some 500 colonists dead. Governor Berkeley countered with an aggressive "scorched earth" policy, destroying villages and crops and leading to Opechanconough's capture and death and finally to a treaty in the fall of 1646.[26]

Two military incursions south of the James in 1646 were described by a militiaman, Henry Plumpton of Nansemond County. One was an overland strike commanded by Major General Richard Bennett that targeted the bitter Weyanokes, who had earlier in the war been harried south from their home on the James River. A planter of Isle of Wight and Nansemond Counties, General Bennett was a council member and a Puritan leader.[27] Apparently Bennett's foray drove the Weyanokes farther south, so deep into swampy wasteland that the militia could not safely pursue them.

To complete the suppression of the Weyanokes, a second campaign was organized and led by Colonel Thomas Dew, also a Puritan and planter of Nansemond County, who was under the command of General Bennett.[28] Probably using shallops, pinnaces, and other small craft, the militia force sailed from Chesapeake Bay to Currituck Inlet, across the sounds, and some twenty-five miles up the Chowan River to Weyanoke Creek, where the tribe had resettled. Plumpton mentioned a fight there with the loss of one man. Native tribal elders years later remembered that the Weyanokes moved to the Moratock (Roanoke) River after this attack. Although contemporary maps are confusing, Weyanoke Creek was either the Meherrin River or its tributary, Potecasi Creek.[29]

For the first time these frontier military campaigns introduced a number of Virginians to a little-known land as far south as Roanoke River and its vast estuary. They found a country centered on a broad sound whose wide and deep tributaries were lined with abandoned Indian fields and extensive pine, cedar, and cypress forests. In the face of armed invaders, the Natives surely remained hidden, making the land appear virtually uninhabited. After accompanying Colonel Dew, in 1648 Henry Plumpton, Thomas Tuke (Tooke) of Isle of Wight, and others acquired from local Indians a huge tract on the west bank of the Chowan River, from the mouth of the Roanoke north some forty miles to Weyanoke Creek. This is the earliest record of a land purchase by Virginians in the region. While no settlement occurred at that time, within a decade the area would attract some of the first colonists to the Roanoke country.[30]

Fort Henry was built at the falls of the Appomattox River during the hostilities in 1645. After the war it became the primary trading post for the fur trade extending south and west into Carolana, as well as the base for exploration of the region. It was owned by Captain Abraham Wood, formerly an indentured servant who had risen to be a planter and Indian trader. A member of the House of Burgesses and later the council, Wood became militia colonel and eventually a major general responsible for defending the southwestern arc of the frontier.[31]

THE YEAR 1649 opened with the execution of King Charles I, the ensuing proclamation of the Commonwealth, and Oliver Cromwell's actions to solidify his grip on the nation through an Irish campaign and suppression of rebellions in England. The civil wars had taken an enormous toll on the country, leaving it economically depressed, deeply divided, and faced with the unimaginable uncertainty of a government without a monarch. With such a state of affairs in England, the time was ripe for literature promoting the American colonies. Five tracts appeared in London from 1649 to 1651 on Carolana and southern Virginia alone.[32] Since the authors relied on the reports of Hariot, Lane, White, and Pory, their portraits of the region were markedly similar; however, each one also incorporated personal knowledge from those who had visited the region.

Three accounts were published in 1649: William Bullock's *Virginia Impartially Examined*, the anonymously written *A Perfect Description of Virginia*, and a newspaper promotion by a "well-willer." In *Virginia Impartially Examined*, Bullock included "the rich and healthful Countries of Roanock." Drawing on experiences of acquaintances, Samuel Vassall and Peter Andrews and Andrews's father, who had resided in Virginia, Bullock included practical advice for potential colonists regarding equipment, clothing, and crops that could be grown.[33] *A Perfect Description of Virginia* reprinted Pory's 1622 report and included a narrative based on a fresh look at the region.[34]

In the spring of 1649 a letter appeared in the *Moderate Intelligencer*, a London weekly newsletter. The detailed description of Carolana by an anonymous "well-willer" encouraged "*Adventurers, Planters, and Servants*" to join an unnamed governor who was organizing a venture of "*many Gentlemen of quality and their families.*" From the "flourishing Plantation" of Virginia, a source of livestock and provisions, they would enter Carolana by the Elizabeth and Nansemond Rivers.[35]

In contrast to the low estate to "which the late War" had brought England, the "well-willer" portrayed a land that would make Adam and Eve weep with envy. In Carolana the deer and elk were bigger and tasted better; turkeys roosted in large flocks and reputedly topped the scales at forty pounds. The "stately" open pine forests were filled with a pharmacopoeia of herbs and drugs and would provide tar, rosin, and turpentine. For those who farmed, abandoned Indian fields of black mold soil two feet deep returned two corn crops a season and would increase the yield of English grains and fruits.[36] The identities of the "well-willer" and the proposed governor are unknown. The plans were apparently overshadowed by the troubled early years of the Commonwealth.

Edward Williams's 1650 *Virgo Triumphans: or, Virginia richly and truly valued; more especially the South part thereof; viz. The fertile Carolana* acknowledged his debt to John Farrer, who provided him "the whole substance of it." Farrer, a member of the Virginia Company of London and a merchant, published a map of the coast from Cape Fear to Cape Cod that is the only extant map in which the region south of Virginia is designated "Carolana."[37] Williams extolled the potential of the southern region and expected his readers to "discover the beauties of a long neglected Virgin the incomparable Roanoke, and the adjacent excellencies of Carolana," arguing for a colony as a buffer against the Spanish.[38]

The last and most important of the midcentury promotional tracts was Edward Bland's *The Discovery of New Brittaine* (1651). Bland, sent to the colony in 1646 to oversee his family's land and mercantile interests, received Governor Berkeley's permission to explore southern Virginia to assess the potential for Indian trade. Joining Bland were Captain Abraham Wood and other gentlemen, indentured servants, and Pyancha, an Appomattox guide.[39] In August 1650 they headed southwest on a nine-day journey into Indian territory. In Nottoway Town they were received ambivalently by the king and his brother, Oyeocker, who were at odds over the English. Despite the king's attempt to discourage them, Bland was committed to his Tuscarora destination. In a tense setting, the party rode out the next morning, accompanied by Oyeocker, while the Nottoway king secretly dispatched warnings to the Meherrin, Weyanoke, Chowan, and Tuscarora.[40]

In Meherrin town, the English were welcomed with feasting and dancing and received an invitation from a Tuscarora visitor. On the trail, however, Bland learned that the Weyanokes were spreading lies, unsettling the Indians with stories of English treachery.[41] At the Roanoke River Hocomawanack village, with hostile Weyanokes and Chowans possibly closing in on them, Bland finally recognized their danger and set up camp outside the town. Both Pyancha and Oyeocker suspected betrayal and urged withdrawal.[42]

Early the next morning the English left abruptly. Back at Meherrin town, which had been so friendly, they were greeted coolly, and here Bland learned that Weyanoke spies were shadowing them. The region was clearly aroused, although the unfriendly response probably had more to do with Native rivalries than with the English interlopers. Pyancha located alternate routes, and the sight of Fort Henry on September 4 brought welcome relief. Although intended to establish relations for future trade with the southern tribes, the Bland exploration had the opposite effect, temporarily dampening interest in the region. The Virginia assembly granted Bland permission to settle there, but his ardor had cooled. He departed for England in 1651 to publish his narrative, which included the John Farrer map of Virginia and Carolana, and died two years later in Virginia.[43]

In July 1653, acting on a petition of Roger Green, an Anglican clergyman then residing on the Nansemond River, the assembly granted 10,000 acres to the first 100 persons who would settle on the Roanoke River and the south side of the Chowan River.[44] For his "hazard and trouble of first discoverie, and encouragement of others for seating those southern parts of Virginia," Green received 1,000 acres "next to those persons who have had a former grant."[45] Although it was formerly believed that Green initiated settlement in North Carolina, there is no evidence to support this assertion.[46]

———————

AFTER TWO DECADES of promotion, exploration, and tantalizing clues to colonization, Carolana was still devoid of English settlers. But new initiatives were stirred by the eyewitness accounts of returning explorers and militia. Unplanned and unexpected, the first permanent settlement in North Carolina was realized through the Virginia-based fur-trading enterprise of Colonel Francis Yeardley and his lead trapper, Nathaniel Batts, the colony's unwitting founders.

A trader and planter, Colonel Francis Yeardley lived in Lower Norfolk County at Lynnhaven with his wife, the twice-widowed Sarah Thoroughgood, and four stepchildren. The Yeardley family had been in Virginia since Francis's father, Captain George Yeardley, came from Bermuda in 1610 and married Temperance Flowerdew, who brought him Flowerdew Hundred plantation. He served as governor of Virginia and was knighted. During the Commonwealth period, Francis Yeardley was in the House of Burgesses and on the Maryland council. In addition to fur trading, Colonel Yeardley raised livestock and tobacco and was a ship owner and merchant.[47]

In September 1653 a young beaver trapper, Nathaniel Batts, who was set to go to Roanoke, was accidentally left behind in Virginia when his sloop sailed. On his own, Batts secured permission and supplies from Colonel Yeardley. The customary practice was for a sloop or pinnace to serve as a mother ship for periaugers and log canoes that could transport trade goods and provisions on the shallow creeks. Batts hired a small boat and took four other men with him, including two of Yeardley's neighbors and a member of Yeardley's family, probably his teenage stepson, Adam Thoroughgood.[48]

Sailing through Currituck Inlet to Roanoke Island, Batts's party did not locate the sloop but encountered the "great emperor" of Roanoke in a hunting party on the island. The Virginians spent several days with the friendly Natives, touring the nearly seventy-year-old remains on the site of Sir Walter Raleigh's colony, where Batts recovered a souvenir for Yeardley. Fluent in the Native languages, Batts persuaded the emperor, his war captains, and the king of another province to keep the peace with the English. The other king may have been Kiscutanewh of the Yeopim, who later sold land on the Pasquotank River to Batts. The Indians agreed to go with Batts and his men to Yeardley's house in Virginia for a week's stay.[49]

Yeardley and the Roanoke emperor established an immediate rapport that blossomed into a trusting friendship. Observing the Yeardley stepdaughters reading and writing, the Roanoke asked Yeardley to teach his only son to "speak out of the book, and make writing." Yeardley enthusiastically agreed. On departing from Lynnhaven, the Roanoke expressed a desire to serve the Christian God and also wanted his son to be raised as a Christian. He promised to return in four moons with his son. The new friends parted with "expressions of love, and many presents."[50]

While Yeardley was away in Maryland, the Roanoke emperor returned to Lynnhaven and was graciously entertained by Sarah Yeardley. When she took him to worship at the parish church, some of the congregation were outraged, acted "uncivilly," and threatened to have the Indian whipped and sent home. The Roanoke was frightened and "much appalled" by such treatment, but the gritty Sarah "kept him in her hand by her side," standing firm against the mob and successfully backing them down. When Yeardley returned, to make amends with the Roanoke he sent a carpenter and five helpers to build a furnished English house for his new friend. Yeardley also sent £200 to purchase land, acquiring "three great rivers" and tributary streams. Enamored with his "ample discovery of South Virginia," Yeardley wrote that "we find a most fertile, gallant, rich soil flourishing in all the abundance of nature, especially in the rich mulberry and vine, a serene air, and temperate clime." He also mentioned the "stately timber" and wrote that the region was "rich in precious minerals."[51]

With his house under construction, the Roanoke sent ambassadors to invite the Tuscarora emperor to meet with Yeardley's men. A two-day journey led the English to a hunting camp, where they were entertained by the Tuscarora emperor and his 250-man retinue. The emperor told them of a rich Spaniard who for seven years had lived in his chief town with thirty in his household, seven of whom were Blacks. There was also a report of a Black living with the Neuse Indians.[52] The Tuscarora offered to take the English to the Spaniard and tempted them with stories of copper mines and salt from the sea. With Batts, their interpreter, ill and an Indian war ongoing, the English declined. When the Virginians left, the Tuscarora emperor sent along his son, accompanied by his tutor and other retainers. As they passed through the sounds, other Indian leaders joined the party, so that a group of forty-five Indians, including the Roanoke, the Tuscarora prince, and other important Indian chieftains, arrived at Yeardley's house in Lynnhaven on May 1. Two days later the Roanoke brought his son to the church to be baptized before the Indians and the congregation. One can imagine Sarah Yeardley's satisfaction on the occasion.[53]

Through these contacts, Yeardley had laid the groundwork for large-scale fur trading with the area's Indians. He optimistically requested that Farrar send him silkworm eggs, olive trees, fruit trees, and other plants suitable for the latitude. Yeardley planned another exploration in July, but if this expedition did occur, there is no record of it. His untimely death ended the fulfillment of his vision, but the trade contacts remained in place.[54] Yeardley contributed the vision and the financing, amounting to some £300, and Batts, who spoke the Native languages, provided the requisite experience and diplomatic skills to build the trade. Both men afforded the Natives respect and dignity, fostering harmonious and trusting relations and securing generous land purchases.

After the English house was completed for the Roanoke emperor, Yeardley instructed the carpenter, Robert Bodnam, to build a dwelling and trading post for Batts, who was to run the operation. Since Virginians considered the Chowan River the western boundary of Lord Maltravers's County of Norfolk, the former land purchases and grants were west of the Chowan or on the Roanoke River. Yeardley's purchase of "three great rivers" likely referred to the Chowan and Roanoke Rivers' confluence, which creates Albemarle Sound, then called Roanoke Sound. There could not be a more strategic location for control of the fur trade than the point at the head of the sound, which is precisely where Yeardley sent the crew for five months in 1655 to construct Batts's trading post. For his labor on the two-room twenty-foot-square house with a chimney, Bodnam was paid 1,000 pounds of tobacco.[55]

The most important source on the midcentury settlement is the colorful map drawn by Nicholas Comberford in 1657 that depicts Batts's house and has English place-names still found on modern maps. Two slightly different versions of this map of the "South Part of Virginia" exist. The copy at the National Maritime Museum, London, includes illustrations of large animals and a small boat being rowed on the sound. The New York Public Library copy has a later addition to the title that reads, "Now the North Part of Carolina."[56]

Batts's House, the earliest-known English dwelling in Carolana, was located on the point between the Roanoke and Chowan Rivers on the south bank of Salmon Creek. The important navigation notes include the warning that Currituck Inlet was "Barrd" and that the inlet at Wococock (Ocracoke) Island was the access to the Neuse and Pamlico Rivers and Roanoke Sound. Written on the sound is the sailing direction "Heare is Passage for Great Sloopes up to South Key," indicating that sloops, including the fur trade mother ships, were sailing up the Chowan and Blackwater Rivers for over fifty miles to South Key landing. From there a portage of less than twenty miles connected travelers to the headwaters of the Nansemond River that flowed north to Chesapeake Bay.

Today South Quay is a crossroads on the Blackwater River, and the backroad connection to the Nansemond is called Indian Trail. This interior route from Virginia southward up the Nansemond, then down the Blackwater to the Chowan and thence to Albemarle Sound, became the main access for traders and settlers between Roanoke and Virginia. On the east side of the Chowan River, Rockahock, derived from an Indian word, survives in Rockyhock, a community and creek in Chowan County, North Carolina. Finally, Comberford's is the only map designating Currituck Banks as Lucks Island, which would later become an important landmark for Carolina and the geographic basis for the colony's northern boundary in 1663.[57]

Batts had been in Carolana as early as the fall of 1653, and the trading post built two years later made him a seasonal resident, the first-known settler in the region.[58] Although Batts retained his residence in Lynnhaven, where his family lived, the trading post launched a lifelong permanent connection to the Roanoke country. In May 1656 Batts married the widow Mary Woodhouse and moved to her plantation, which became known as "Batts Quarters."[59] Although a skilled diplomat, he lacked business sense. The morass of his personal finances kept him in debt and embroiled him in litigation the rest of his life. In hindsight, Mary Batts would have been well advised to execute a prenuptial agreement to protect her property. A few months after the marriage, her daughter Elizabeth sued Batts for recovery of property willed to her by her father. Before a year was out, Mary herself sued her husband on her children's behalf for their inheritance, and she informed the court that her new husband was demanding that his stepchildren pay for their board.[60]

In the summer of 1657 the court granted Batts some relief from his perennial financial troubles by ordering that he have a year's protection from his creditors for the "great pains & trouble" that he endured while discovering an inlet "to the southward," possibly the inlet north of Lucks Island.[61] As the most knowledgeable resident of the area, Batts likely was also with Colonel Thomas

Dew and Captain Thomas Francis in July 1657 when they embarked on "a discoverie of the navigable rivers to the southward between Cape Hatteras and Cape Fear [present-day Cape Lookout]." The result of the survey is the sailing directions on the Comberford map that confirm the earlier trading ventures.[62] As his personal and financial problems mounted, Batts spent more time in the Roanoke country.

From Kiscutanewh, king of the Yeopim, on 24 September 1660 Batts acquired land on the west bank of the Pasquotank River from the river's mouth to New Begun Creek. The deed, which documents the earliest extant land purchase in North Carolina, is recorded in Norfolk County, Virginia. The former Hariots Isle in Albemarle Sound at the mouth of the Yeopim River became known as Batts Island and finally Batts Grave.[63]

When Quaker founder George Fox stayed with Batts in 1672, he was living on a plantation on the east side of the Chowan River. Fox described Batts as "a rude and desperate man."[64] Yet Fox called him Captain Batts, formerly governor of Roanoke, "who hath a great command over the country, especially over the Indians."[65] While Batts never held an administrative post in Carolana, as the first settler and manager of the region's lucrative fur trade, his was clearly the dominant English presence in the region.

PRIOR TO THE Carolina Charter, Carolana's Roanoke country had been the southern frontier of Virginia for a decade, and the stage was set for permanent settlement. One motive alone enticed Virginians to move south—land, the basis of wealth and status. By word of mouth, fur trappers spread news of this fertile open country, and the region's fine natural qualities were praised in promotional tracts. The area could be entered directly from the sea by small craft through shallow Currituck or Roanoke Inlets or by the back door of the Nansemond, Blackwater, and Chowan Rivers. Prime locations on Virginia's waterways had been taken for over a generation, and now at midcentury new colonists eagerly sought unclaimed land. Blocking westward migration were forbidding mountains and unfriendly Indians made hostile by the Bland exploration and the still-fresh memory of the last war. To the south, however, lay a copy of the familiar Chesapeake: an estuarine system of broad sounds fed by navigable swamp-fed rivers—the Chowan, Yeopim, Perquimans, Little, Pasquotank, North, Alligator, and Scuppernong. Looming over the waterside abandoned Indian towns, fields, savannahs, and marshes were the giant longleaf pine and cypress forests bordered by the Great Dismal Swamp on the north and vast unnamed wetlands on the south. The six rivers on the north shore sliced the land into peninsulas or necks that were no hindrance to travel or communication because this "watery world" was so easily traversed by canoes and small sailing vessels.

Fur traders had been welcomed by the dwindling local tribes, and a friendly interdependence prevailed. Yeoman farmers, some of means and most from border counties, heeded the call of productive soil and fallow Indian fields ready for their hoes, and their steady trickle southward became a stream. From all existing evidence, the period from 1658 to 1661 was when English immigrants first moved into the Roanoke country in numbers. These incoming settlers, remembering two bloody wars in Virginia that had ravaged Europeans and Indians alike, respectfully and wisely purchased their land from the Roanoke Natives, nurtured the mutual reliance in trade, and lived side by side in peace. There was more than enough room for hunting, field crops, and livestock grazing.[66]

After Nathaniel Batts, the first settlers known to have moved permanently to the Roanoke country were John Harvey and his wife Dorothy Tooke. Unlike Batts, who was at first a part-time resident, the Harveys purposefully left their Virginia home and moved their household furnishings and livestock to "the Southward." John Harvey had come to Virginia in 1640 with his parents, who located on the James River. Although the circumstances of the couple's move are not known, by 1659 John and Dorothy Harvey had settled, probably on the Chowan River. It may be that they, like Batts, purchased land from Kiscutanewh, but if so, the deed is lost. To help his daughter set up housekeeping, James Tooke gave the Harveys a feather bed and bolster, sheets, a blanket, a rug, four cows, and a heifer.[67]

In his will, written in 1660 and administered two years later, James Tooke left Dorothy additional household items, including another feather bed, linens, a copper kettle, a pewter candlestick and chamber pot, two rings, and a silver beer bowl, dram cup, and spoon.[68] In 1663 Harvey secured patents from Sir William Berkeley to 250 acres in the Chowan area and 600 acres on Symons Creek on the east bank of the Little River in the Pasquotank region. The Harveys sold the Chowan tract and moved to the larger plantation, where they raised livestock, accumulating about sixty cattle, numerous hogs, forty sheep, and four horses.[69] John Harvey would become an important and trusted political leader, serving on the council and eventually as governor.[70]

Some of the Harveys' neighbors arrived before 1663. Hugh and Elizabeth Smithwick were in Chowan by 1659;[71] Samuel and Elizabeth Davis of Isle of Wight were in Pasquotank by 1660;[72] and in 1661 Richard Sanderson had come to Currituck[73] and Robert Lawrence of Nansemond County had located west of the Chowan River.[74] By 1660 three distinct communities had emerged—west of the Pasquotank River, on the necks or peninsulas at the mouth of the Perquimans River, and west of the Chowan River.[75] Following Nathaniel Batts's example, these early settlers probably purchased land from the Native Americans. Batts's 1660 deed for land west of the Pasquotank mentioned previous owners John Mason and John Willoughby and was witnessed by George Durant and Richard Batts, Nathaniel's brother.[76] Durant's deeds for a tract on the Perquimans River adjacent to Samuel Pricklove are dated 4 August 1661 and 1 March 1662. Also from Kiscutanewh, they are the earliest conveyances recorded in North Carolina. On this land, henceforth known as Durant's Neck, George and Ann Durant established their plantation. A witness on the 1662 deed was Caleb Calloway, who with his wife Elizabeth lived on the Yeopim River.[77]

Aware that the southern population was growing rapidly, on 9 October 1662 Deputy Governor Francis Moryson and the Virginia council appointed Captain Samuel Stephens "commander of the Southern plantation" with authority to appoint a sheriff. A native-born Virginian, Stephens was well connected to the colony's merchants through his father and his maternal grandfather, Abraham Peirsey, and to government through his stepfather, Sir John Harvey, a former governor.[78] Combining judicial, administrative, and military responsibilities, commanders in Virginia had for some time served on plantations, in county government, and on the frontier. The remote Albemarle was ideally suited for such an officer. As a magistrate Stephens was responsible for maintaining law and order and protecting the region, and he would administer the colony until a proprietary governor was appointed in 1664.[79] It may be that the influential Nathaniel Batts was deputized by Stephens to keep the peace. While explorers, fur traders, and planters were flowing into Virginia's southern frontier, the region's future was destined to be determined not in Virginia but by momentous events already underway in England—events that were once again shaking the foundations of the nation.

CHAPTER THREE

Carolina

Founding a Colony

Carolina is a fair and spacious Province on the
Continent of *America*: so called in honour of His
Sacred Majesty that now is, *Charles the Second*.
—Robert Horne, 1666

O N THE MORNING OF 25 May 1660 an English fleet from Holland
bearing Charles II and his brothers, James, Duke of York, and Henry,
Duke of Gloucester, approached Dover. Everything had been done
to ensure a triumphant return. After twenty years of darkness, Charles's ex-
hilaration must have been nearly overwhelming. When civil war erupted in
his twelfth year, his privileged life as a royal prince had ended, and ascending
the throne seemed impossible as royalists were defeated, his father executed,
and the Commonwealth established under Lord Protector Oliver Cromwell.
Cared for by Sir Edward Hyde, his guardian and closest adviser, the sixteen-
year-old Prince Charles had fled England to join his mother in France, finding temporary sanctuary with Sir George Carteret on the Isle of Jersey. From
France Charles began a fourteen-year odyssey through European courts as a
penniless exile.

Cromwell's death in 1658 and the Commonwealth's rapid disintegration
brought General George Monck, military governor of Scotland, and his army
to London by February 1660. Parliament appointed him lord general of all the
armed forces on land and sea, enabling him to become the kingmaker, key to
Charles's return to England. While maintaining good relations with Parliament, in late March Monck opened secret communication with Prince Charles
and sent terms that Hyde drafted into the Declaration of Breda, promising a
general pardon for actions during the Civil War, security of property acquired
during the wars and the Interregnum, and liberty of conscience.

Monck ordered a fleet to Holland under Sir Edward Montagu to bring the king home. At the harbor in Dover a great throng of English people, from laborers to great nobles, gathered to greet him. In the early afternoon the king stepped from his barge and knelt on the pier, giving thanks to God. He rose and walked toward the kneeling Monck. Helping him rise, the king embraced and kissed him and called him "father." Monck handed Charles a sheathed sword, and the mayor of Dover presented the king with a richly bound Bible. The king, Monck, and others moved aside to a canopy and briefly chatted, beginning their acquaintance.

Charles II and his general then entered a "stately" coach and left immediately for Canterbury along a road lined with thousands gathered to see the return of their king. Buildings were festooned with tapestries, bells were ringing, flowers were strewn along the streets, and the crowd was in a holiday mood. On Sunday the royal party worshiped in the run-down Canterbury Cathedral, followed by the investiture of Monck and Montagu with the Order of the Garter, with the royal dukes handling Monck's regalia.[1]

Without Monck's support for Charles, the throne had been unreachable, and the grateful king recognized his pivotal role, writing, "I must acknowledge your extraordinary affection to me and your very discreet conduct of this great work . . . , which you have wonderfully composed."[2] A few days later, the king reached London on his thirtieth birthday and was welcomed by tens of thousands of cheering subjects celebrating a peaceful Restoration. By July Monck had been named the Duke of Albemarle.

Within three years Charles II granted to eight Lords Proprietors a princely domain in America that closely corresponded to the propriety that his father had earlier given to Sir Robert Heath. The proprietors were George, Duke of Albemarle; Edward, Earl of Clarendon; William, Lord Craven; John, Lord Berkeley; Anthony, Lord Ashley; Sir George Carteret; Sir William Berkeley; and Sir John Colleton.

The Lords Proprietors of Carolina were extraordinary men living in extraordinary times. Between 1642 and 1660 they had endured the trials and privations of a long and bitter civil war, the beheading of the king, and the persecutions of the republican Commonwealth. Throughout this era, with two exceptions, they had suffered the consequences of remaining loyal to the monarchy, losing both property and position; some had been forced into exile in Europe.

Most of the Lords Proprietors were first-generation peers, new to great wealth and position. Although some had ancient connections, others were from the country gentry—respectable families with modest estates. Living through nearly a generation of enormous political, social, and religious upheaval, these self-made men thrived on the opportunities spawned by turbulent times. Prior

General George Monck became the Duke of Albemarle in 1660.
Chairing the meetings of the proprietors, he was elected the first palatine in 1669. Courtesy of National Portrait Gallery, London.

to the Restoration, all of them had been knighted except Monck and Colleton, but none of them held a great title. Once the king was in power, a shower of offices, titles, and honors poured onto the future Lords Proprietors.

George Monck, Duke of Albemarle (1608–70), from Devonshire, the son of Sir Thomas Monck, was related to the noted Grenville family. His distinguished military career on both sides of the civil wars exhibited personal courage and initiative on the battlefield, first for king and then for Parliament. A volunteer at age eighteen, he achieved regimental command during the Scottish and Irish rebellions. Captured in a royalist defeat in 1644, he was charged with treason and held in the Tower for two years. A new Irish rebellion led to his release and a parliamentary commission as major general. From Ireland he went to Scotland, earning trust and praise from Cromwell, who named him commander and governor of Scotland.

Lord Chancellor Edward Hyde, Earl of Clarendon,
was a mentor of Charles II for years. Courtesy of
National Portrait Gallery, London.

Monck excelled in land and sea warfare. Appointed a general-at-sea, he was
credited with naval victories in both the first and second Anglo-Dutch Wars.
His control of the army in 1660 was the crucial factor in the bloodless Restoration. As captain general charged by the king with defending the nation, he
labored tirelessly during the crises of London's Great Plague and Great Fire in
1665–66.[3] Monck confounded his contemporaries and historians alike. Samuel
Pepys declared him a "blockhead," perhaps because of his taciturn nature, but
nothing could be more wrong.[4] One need only look at his record to surmise
that behind the stolid mask was a sharp and calculating mind. His diplomatic
skills were demonstrated with the difficult Irish and Scots, and his astute handling of the various political and religious factions at the time of the Restoration was masterful.

Lord Chancellor Edward Hyde, Earl of Clarendon (1609–74), held the

William Craven, Earl of Craven, was elected the fourth palatine
in 1680. Courtesy of State Archives of North Carolina.

highest political post in the government. From Wiltshire gentry, the Oxford-
educated Hyde served in Parliament and became chancellor of the exchequer
under Charles I, who knighted him in 1643. Following Prince Charles into
exile in 1646, Hyde became his surrogate father and closest adviser. Although
he personally disliked Monck, Hyde relied on him to pave the way for the
Restoration. Of all the proprietors, Hyde, selected primarily for his name and
position, demonstrated the least interest in Carolina.[5]

William, Lord Craven (1606–97), son of Sir William Craven, Lord Mayor
of London, attended Oxford but at age sixteen went to the Continent. As an
officer serving the Prince of Orange, he earned a knighthood and was made
Baron Craven in 1627. While aiding the deposed Bohemian monarchs Frederick and Elizabeth, the sister of Charles I, he became infatuated with Elizabeth
and served as her protector for the rest of her life. Although there is no evidence

John Berkeley, Baron Berkeley of Stratton, was
Carolina's second palatine and a proprietor of New
Jersey. Courtesy of State Archives of North Carolina.

of any unseemly relationship, he never married. Because of Craven's crucial financial support for Charles I, the Commonwealth government declared him an enemy of the state and confiscated much of his property. He returned to England with the Restoration, became lieutenant general, and in 1664 was created Earl of Craven. He was a stalwart aide to the Duke of Albemarle during the Great Plague and the Great Fire and an early member of the Royal Society, founded in 1660.[6]

From the ancient family of Berkeley Castle of Somersetshire, John Berkeley, Baron Berkeley of Stratton (1602–78), and his brother William both attended Oxford. For military and diplomatic service John earned a knighthood in 1639. During the civil wars, as a royalist general, he surrendered Exeter in 1646 and was exiled to the court of Queen Henrietta Marie in France, where he became the governor of James, Duke of York. Charles II named him Baron Berkeley

The only original proprietor to live in the North American
colonies, Virginia's governor, Sir William Berkeley, was given
oversight of the founding of Albemarle County.
Courtesy of State Archives of North Carolina.

of Stratton in 1658. Undoubtedly, he was responsible for the inclusion in the
proprietors of his brother, Sir William Berkeley, the longtime royal governor
of Virginia.[7]

Sir William Berkeley (1605–77) received a master of arts degree from Oxford in 1629. Through family connections he became a courtier of Charles I
and was fortunate to have Sir Edward Hyde as a mentor. Possessing a keen
mind and broad interests, he took advantage of opportunities in the arts and
sciences at court, learning agriculture, botany, horticulture, and silk production
and becoming a dramatist. He was knighted in 1639 for service in the first
Scottish rising. Appointed governor of Virginia in 1641, he was ousted in 1652

Anthony Ashley Cooper, Baron Ashley, was the catalyst
for the founding of Charles Town (1670) and principal author of the
Fundamental Constitutions. He was named Earl of Shaftesbury
in 1672. Courtesy of State Archives of North Carolina.

by a Commonwealth expedition and retired to his estate, Green Spring. After
the Restoration, in 1660 Virginia's assembly elected him governor, confirmed
by Charles II the following year.[8]

The youngest proprietor was Anthony Ashley Cooper, Lord Ashley (1621–
83), who descended from a wealthy family of Dorsetshire. Educated at Oxford
and Lincoln's Inn, Ashley served in Parliament during the Civil War and the
Interregnum. Like Monck, he switched sides from royalist to Parliament, then
back at the time of the Restoration. He was named Baron Ashley and chancellor of the exchequer in 1661. A former owner of a Barbadian plantation, he
had also invested in slave-trading voyages. Possessing a brilliant mind, Ashley

Sir George Carteret became the third palatine of
Carolina and was a proprietor of New Jersey.
Courtesy of State Archives of North Carolina.

was drawn to political intrigue. Initially somewhat diffident about Carolina, he
emerged as a key supporter of the development of Charles Town and, advised
by John Locke, was the principal author of the Fundamental Constitutions.[9]

Sir George Carteret (ca. 1610–80), from the ancient Carteret family of the
Isle of Jersey, was a royal naval officer and in 1643 became the bailiff of Jersey.
He fortified the island as a royalist stronghold and aggressively unleashed privateers on Commonwealth shipping. Parliament declared him a pirate and
excluded him from amnesty. Holding the last refuge for royalists, in 1646 Carteret hosted Prince Charles and Sir Edward Hyde and was knighted. Hyde
characterized Carteret as "truly a worthy and most excellent person." When
Cromwell's forces captured Jersey in 1651, Carteret was allowed to go into exile
in France. After the Restoration, he resumed the post of vice-chamberlain and
was appointed to the Privy Council. The Carteret family was initially very active in developing northern Carolina.[10]

Sir John Colleton (1608–66) was the son of Peter Colleton, sheriff of Exeter
in Devonshire. As commander of a regiment under General Sir John Berkeley,

Colleton was at the royalist surrender of Exeter in 1646. He chose self-exile in 1650, fleeing to Barbados, where he established a plantation and became a moderating influence in the political disorder of the Interregnum. A moderate royalist, he allied himself politically with Barbados's governor, Sir Thomas Modyford, who was, like himself, a cousin of the Duke of Albemarle. After the Restoration, he returned to England, reconnecting with the Duke and Lord Berkeley. He was knighted in 1661, and because of his colonial experience he served on the Council of Foreign Plantations and the Council of Trade. His son, James, retained the family estate on Barbados, and a grandson, John, later migrated to South Carolina.[11]

Carolina was just one of the overseas interests of the Lords Proprietors, who with London merchants and other courtiers promoted the commercial and territorial expansion of the realm. As imperialists, Lord Berkeley, Carteret, Colleton, Clarendon, and Ashley served on the Privy Council's important committees for foreign plantations and trade. In the inner circle of the king's brother, Lord High Admiral James, Duke of York, Berkeley was on the admiralty commission and Carteret was treasurer of the navy. In 1660 the Duke of York organized the enterprise that became the Royal African Company, with Berkeley, Carteret, and Colleton initially among its members, joined later by Sir Peter Colleton, Craven, and John Locke. Granted a monopoly on the slave trade to the English colonies, the company established posts in Africa and opened the continent to English commerce. The board of the Hudson's Bay Company (1670), headed by Prince Rupert, included Craven, Ashley, Carteret, Sir Peter Colleton, and Christopher, the second Duke of Albemarle. In 1664 the Duke of York bestowed the colony of New Jersey on proprietors Carteret and Lord Berkeley. Six years later the Bahamas became the propriety of Ashley, Craven, Berkeley, Carteret, Sir Peter Colleton, and Albemarle. If the Duke of York, Prince Rupert, and William Penn were added to the Carolina proprietors, it would be "a remarkably complete list of those who during the reign of Charles II held the leadership in efforts to expand English interests in the Atlantic basin."[12]

The record is silent on how these "improbable bedfellows,"[13] the Lords Proprietors, were cobbled together and who first suggested a new propriety to supplant the dormant Carolana grant. The two knowledgeable advocates of colonization who had lived overseas were Sir William Berkeley, who had been in Virginia since 1642, and Sir John Colleton, a planter of Barbados for a decade. Sir John returned to London before Sir William and quickly joined the Duke of Albemarle and Lord Berkeley and the other imperialists. Expansion of the empire was high on the Duke of York's agenda, and, as always, a propriety promised to enhance England's power and wealth without burdening the royal treasury. In committee meetings and social gatherings the future proprietors discussed how modest investment on their part could enrich themselves and the nation. Out of this ferment the group that became the Lords Proprietors began to coalesce, encompassing men united by blood or by shared experiences during the civil war.[14]

In July 1661 Sir William Berkeley, recently restored to his royal governorship of Virginia, arrived in London seeking exemptions for his colony from the new Navigation Act.[15] Sir William always put Virginia first, taking little initiative for Carolina but bringing firsthand experience to the vexing task of governing a colony. He found a rejuvenated London and a court bustling with ideas. Through his brother, Lord Berkeley, and his old friend, the Earl of Clarendon, he met the Duke of Albemarle and the Earl of Craven and quickly entered the highest levels of government. He was a natural choice for a seat on the Council on Foreign Plantations, where in August he was introduced to Ashley, Carteret, and Colleton. By the time Berkeley sailed for Virginia in September 1662, the Carolina propriety was underway.[16]

OF THE ATTEMPTED North American proprieties, Maryland had been the most successful until the Restoration, when Charles II and his brother James, Duke of York, enormously increased the area of colonies on the mainland with four proprietary grants—Carolina (1663), New York and New Jersey (1664), and Pennsylvania (1681). The Lords Proprietors of Carolina were, in modern terms, a gigantic real estate partnership, with the right and responsibility to govern their domain. By far the largest of the proprieties, Carolina was breathtakingly sweeping in extent, spanning the continent from Atlantic to Pacific.[17]

Essentially regranting the Carolana patent, on 24 March 1663 Charles II conferred on the Lords Proprietors of the Province of Carolina all of the territory from the north end of Lucks Island (Currituck Banks) "within" 36° north to the River Saint Mathias (St. Johns River) in Florida "within 31° north latitude" and "west as far as the South Seas" (Pacific Ocean). The significant change in the province's northern boundary was from Carolana's 36°, the south shore of Roanoke Sound, to "within six and Thirty Degrees," beginning at Lucks Island, the second island south of Currituck Inlet on the 1657 Comberford map. Since the inlet at the north end of Lucks Island was several miles above modern Corolla, the 1663 charter included most of the territory north of Albemarle Sound that would ultimately be in Carolina. Although the description was vague, the proprietors had moved the boundary well north of the sound and intended to include the southern Virginia settlement.[18] Although Virginians would argue in future negotiations that their colony's southern boundary had been established in 1629 at 36°, in reality the disputed territory was a sliver about six miles wide.[19] The colonial boundary, a point of contention throughout the life of the

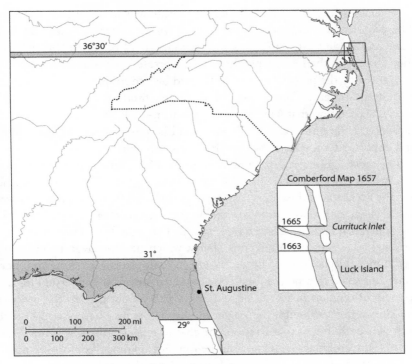

Carolina Charter Boundaries

Carolina propriety, would not be settled until the end of the era. Throughout the period it was the Virginians, knowing that their claim was specious, who always found an excuse to postpone the survey.

Like the Carolana propriety, the Carolina charter included feudal elements, such as the right to establish manorial courts presided over by the manor's steward and the granting of titles and honors that did not duplicate existing titles in the realm. In contrast to Heath, who had had his propriety by knight's service, the Carolina proprietors held their domain by free and common socage for an annual rent of twenty marks.[20]

As in previous proprietary charters, the Lords Proprietors' governing authority was patterned after the medieval viceregal Bishop of Durham. The province's laws were to be passed by an assembly of the proprietors or their representatives, "with the advice, assent, and approbation of the Freemen of the said Province or of the greater part of them, or their Delegates or Deputies." In an emergency, executive orders could be issued. In all cases the laws had to be "reasonable and not repugnant" to the laws of England, and the colonists were guaranteed all of the liberties and privileges of the king's subjects.[21]

Several sections of the Carolina Charter encouraged development and trade. The proprietors could incorporate cities, towns, and boroughs and establish ports and landings. Local duties and customs could be levied "by and with the Consent of the free people there, or the greater part of them." Land sold or granted by the proprietors was to be held by "fee simple," although subject to quitrent. Because Carolina was in the same latitude as North Africa, there was an expectation that Mediterranean products—silk, wine, currants, raisins, capers, wax, almonds, oil, and olives—could be produced there. These items and imported tools were to be duty-free for seven years.[22]

The most significant departure from the Heath Charter concerned religion. In Carolana, all colonists had had to be adherents of the Church of England, and the exclusion of dissenters may have been a factor in the propriety's failure. In Carolina, the proprietors, who were Anglicans, were charged with establishing and expanding the Church of England. The king, however, had a strong personal commitment to religious liberty, which he unequivocally expressed in the 1660 Declaration of Breda, saying, "We do declare a liberty to tender consciences and that no man shall be disquieted, or called in question for differences of opinion in matter of religion, which do not disturb the peace of the kingdom."[23] Although the Anglican proprietors may have varied in their personal commitment to toleration, the charter reflected the king's view, stating that if Carolinians could not "in their private opinions" conform to public worship by the liturgy of the Church of England, the proprietors could grant "Indulgences and Dispensations."[24]

On 23 May 1663 the proprietors began meeting at the Duke of Albemarle's lodgings in Whitehall Palace. Six attended the first meeting—Albemarle, Craven, Lord Berkeley, Ashley, Carteret, and Colleton. Having returned to Virginia, Sir William Berkeley never attended a meeting, and Clarendon appears to have done little more than lend his influence and prestige, which was enough. Albemarle was at the helm as chair of the group, and Colleton as secretary and treasurer guided the project until his death three years later. The business in this first meeting was minimal. The proprietors agreed to contribute twenty-five pounds each to an expense fund; to set aside 20,000 acres for themselves and public buildings; to appoint a surveyor; and to order maps and a "declaration drawne to invyte the planters."[25]

The Duke of Albemarle's leadership of the proprietors is clear in the various governing documents they developed for Carolina. As captain general of His Majesty's forces, Albemarle was acutely aware of military needs, and the old soldier's influence is evident in the attention to detail in this regard. Each adult male, whether master or servant, was required to have a good firelock musket, ten pounds of powder, and twenty pounds of bullets. Land policy, the essence of the propriety, was based on smaller plots that would concentrate enough armed men in the colony to defend it.[26]

Just when the proprietors were approached by potential colonists, a challenge arose from the Duke of Norfolk, whose father had acquired the Heath propriety. Planning for the Carolina grant had been so thorough that this seems a surprising oversight. In fact, prior claims under the Carolana patent had been considered, but since Heath and his successors had established no colony, it was assumed that the patent was void. Norfolk's claim threatened to compromise title to the land; however, the main concern recorded by Colleton was that "liberty of conscience" in Carolina would be nullified by the Heath patent.[27]

Faced with Norfolk's "Pretensions to Carolina," the proprietors sought relief from the king and Privy Council, and "pretendors to the former Grants" were summoned to document their claims before the council. Since neither "pretendors" nor evidence appeared to claim settlements in Carolana under the prior grants, the former letters patent were ruled null and void, and the king and council revoked all previous grants and charters. In future documents a clause would be inserted requiring settlement within a set time to avoid nullification of the grant. The proprietors were cleared to "proceed in the planting of the said Province of Carolina."[28]

There were competing settlement initiatives from New England and Barbadian groups that would stimulate the proprietors to create a governance document for future colonies. The first proposal the Lords received for a colony came from Puritans in London and Boston, the "Adventurers about Cape Fayre." They had earlier explored the region and sent ill-prepared settlers who left after six weeks.[29] The proprietors responded to the New England initiative in August with "A Declaration and Proposals to all that will Plant in Carolina." First applied in 1664 to the colony at Cape Fear, it was in effect only a year. The Declaration and Proposals reiterated many of the charter's important provisions: liberty of conscience, a representative assembly, and a seven-year immunity from selected import and export duties.[30] Departing from Virginia's customary fifty-acre headright, the proprietors created a far more complicated land allotment that was more generous to planters but niggardly to freed servants. The quitrent would be a half penny per acre. Although the New Englanders welcomed the rights they were granted, crucial land policy and governmental oversight fell short of their expectations. Because their initial settlement was abandoned in early 1663 and the proprietors refused to grant corporate status and administrative autonomy, the New Englanders lost interest in Carolina.[31]

To govern their dominion, the proprietors envisioned independent self-governing counties represented in a provincial council that would provide for the common defense and confirmation of laws. In the north, the resident

Virginians in Roanoke country had to be incorporated in the propriety. The proposed Cape Fear settlement nearly 200 miles away would be the first colony under proprietary governance. From the colonists' nominees the proprietors would select the governor and six councilors for three-year terms. Two delegates elected by freeholders from each county would comprise a unicameral provincial assembly to pass laws with the advice and consent of the governor and council. These laws would then be sent to the Lords Proprietors for ratification.[32] Although the Declaration and Proposals was never officially implemented in the northern part of the colony, its liberal governance principles would be incorporated in the successor constitution, the Concessions and Agreement.

In September 1663 the proprietors dispatched by Captain John Whittey an important packet to Governor Berkeley in Virginia. So that the "Kinge may see that wee sleepe not with his grant but are promoting his service and his subjects profitt," the documents included copies of the Carolina Charter and the Declaration and Proposals, instructions for organizing the new colony, and a commission authorizing Berkeley to appoint governors in Carolina.[33] The proprietors informed him that the Crown had voided prior claims to the region, clearing the way to proceed with land grants and government for Carolina. Berkeley was authorized to appoint a governor and six council members for the existing settlement north of the sound, now named Albemarle, and a governor and council for a colony south of the sound when needed. Newly appointed officials Monsieur Lepreyrie, surveyor, and Richard Cobthrop, secretary, were expected to embark within a month.[34]

With the colony's economic development tied to trade, the proprietors urged Berkeley to send a reconnaissance to the south to locate a rumored "boald and deepe" inlet (Ocracoke) that would give deepwater vessels access to the sound. Carlyle Island, near shallow Roanoke Inlet, was granted to Sir John Colleton and would be known thenceforth as Colleton Island. This was the first proprietary grant in the province and began the Colleton family's extensive involvement in Carolina. Berkeley was cautioned to keep the Declaration and Proposals secret, because the proprietors were not pleased about having had to concede to the New Englanders' demands. They hoped that Berkeley would find a "more fassill [facile] people, whoe by your Interest may setle upon better termes for us." Nevertheless, they would rather "grante as much as possible" than discourage potential colonists.[35]

The all-important land policy was outlined in detail. In an age of water transportation, it was a foregone conclusion that settlement would be concentrated along Carolina's sounds and rivers. For defensive capability the proprietors' ideal was 200 armed men within 1.25 square miles, which they endeavored to ensure by creating ten-acre plots in strips along the waterways.[36] Although the proprietors meant well, their plan of narrow waterfront plots separated from the interior grants bore no relationship either to the existing settlement pattern or to the topography of sandy necks interspersed with creeks, swamps, and marshes.[37]

Early Albemarle settlers had bought large tracts from the Native Americans, which the proprietors feared would "weaken the plantation" by dispersing population. Although the Lords urged Berkeley to "persuade and compell" them to give up their large plantations, he never considered overturning the Virginia grants he had already issued.[38] Even though he knew that the Carolina charter was being drafted when he left England in late 1662, the Roanoke settlement was part of Virginia, and very likely landowners were pressuring him to confirm their purchases from the Indians. He also knew that the proprietors would accept patents granted under Virginia jurisdiction. In this transition period, as a Carolina proprietor and governor of Virginia, Berkeley occasionally used the title "Governor of Virginia and Carolina."[39]

Acquiring land from the Indians, or simply squatting, engendered ample opportunities for confusion and controversy over titles. A case involving George Durant and George Catchmaid, two prominent pioneer residents, was not settled for decades. Durant had purchased a tract from the chief of the Yeopim Indians on the neck bordered on the west by the Perquimans River. Catchmaid settled on property adjacent to Durant and went to Virginia to secure his title, offering to do the same for Durant. Governor Berkeley signed the earliest of these grants on 1 April, conveying 3,333 acres to George Catchmaid of Nansemond County between the Perquimans and Little Rivers.[40] Unbeknownst to his neighbor, Catchmaid included Durant's plantation in his own patent. The two men agreed on a division, and Durant obtained signed confirmation from Catchmaid and a subsequent owner, Timothy Biggs, acknowledging his ownership of the property—but he neglected to record the title during his lifetime. After his death, Durant's sons sued in 1697 in the court of chancery, which finally cleared their title to the property.[41]

On 20 March 1663 Thomas Woodward, clerk of court for Isle of Wight County, received a Virginia commission as surveyor for the Roanoke region.[42] By the fall, Governor Berkeley issued patents for land in Carolina. These Virginia grants went to new planters and to some, like John Harvey, John Jenkins, Samuel Davis, and Robert Lawrence, who had been in the area for several years. The terms were those customary in Virginia: a fifty-acre headright for each individual entering the colony and a quitrent of one-quarter cent per acre.[43]

On 25 September Berkeley authorized twenty-eight grants in Carolina for land west of the Chowan River, on the Perquimans River, on the Pasquotank

River, and north of the Carolina River (Albemarle Sound). The individual tracts ranged from 250 to 2,500 acres and totaled nearly 30,000 acres. Among the larger grants were 5,250 acres in three tracts to the Thomas Woodward family, 2,500 acres to William West, 2,000 acres to Mary Fortsen, another 1,500 acres to George Catchmaid, 950 acres to Samuel Davis, 850 acres in two tracts to John Harvey, 750 acres to Thomas Relfe, 700 acres to John Jenkins, 625 acres to Robert Lawrence, 500 acres to William Jennings, and 450 acres to Henry Palin.[44]

———

FOLLOWING PRINCIPLES included in the Carolina Charter, the Declaration and Proposals, and their instructions to Governor Berkeley, by midsummer of 1664 the proprietors developed a constitution that incorporated their progressive governance concepts and their land policy. Issued on 7 January 1665 to address a Barbadian initiative for a Port Royal colony, the Concessions and Agreement incorporated the principle of dividing their continental domain into self-governing palatine counties: Albemarle, Clarendon, and another south of Cape Romain that became Craven. With a different agreement and minor changes in governance, the same document was issued a month later by proprietors Sir George Carteret and Lord John Berkeley for their colony, "Nova Caesarea," or New Jersey. The Concessions and Agreement was thus the founding constitution not only for North Carolina, where it was in effect for at least five years in Albemarle and about two years in Clarendon, but also for New Jersey, where it served for nearly two decades. Furthermore, it was the basis of William Penn's liberal 1677 Concessions and Agreements for the Quaker colony of West Jersey and his proprietary charter of Pennsylvania (1681) and "Frame of Government" (1682), considered precursors to the U.S. Constitution and Bill of Rights.[45]

Under the Concessions and Agreement the proprietors appointed the governor, the surveyor general, and the secretary or register of public records. With proprietary approval the governor selected the council of six to twelve colonists; then, advised by the council, the governor appointed a deputy governor and all other civil, military, and judicial officers from the freeholders of the county. The governor and council were responsible for the colony's defense, oversaw administration of the courts, issued writs of election to fill a vacancy in the assembly, issued land grants and warrants, and were authorized to "do all other . . . things that may Conduce to the safety, peace, and well Government of the said Counties." To ensure security of property from arbitrary executive action, the governor and council were expressly forbidden to levy a tax or custom without the assembly's consent; to alter or resurvey grants settled and planted for seven years; or to assess damages for trespass by stray livestock on ungranted land. All appointees of the governor served at the pleasure of the proprietors.[46]

Public officials had to "swear or subscribe [affirm]" allegiance to the king, be "faithful to the Interest" of the Lords Proprietors, and "do equal Justice to all men according to their best skill and Judgement." On taking an oath or affirmation of allegiance to the king and loyalty to the proprietors, all freemen would "enjoy the Freedoms and Immunities" of the province.[47] Allowing subscription for an oath was designed to attract Quakers and other dissenters who would not swear. The proprietors' 1665 constitutional guarantee of this right, coupled with liberty of conscience, made the province a haven for dissenters. Affirmation is recognized in North Carolina to this day.

Government commenced in a county when the governor presented his commission to a gathering of freemen who then chose twelve deputies, or representatives. The governor, council, and deputies formed a temporary legislative body to make "Laws, Ordinances, and Constitutions" for the "present good and welfare" of the county. When this assembly subdivided the county into precincts (electoral districts), the freeholders would meet annually on 1 January to select representatives to constitute with the governor and council the county's unicameral General Assembly. The assembly had authority to appoint a president or speaker if the governor and his deputy were absent.[48] The first session of the legislative body was in the spring of 1665, and over a year later it was referred to as the General Court and Committee, "being ye Legislative power . . . for ye time being." Both Maryland and Virginia accepted this designation as the colony's legislative assembly.[49]

After the provisional assembly had served the colony about two years, the county was divided into four precincts, each of which had five elected representatives, for a total of twenty. Pasquotank's existence is documented by a militia commission of October 1668 and presumably was accompanied by Chowan, Perquimans, and Currituck. According to Concessions procedure, the division may have taken place the previous year, with the first precinct election for the permanent assembly being held on 1 January 1668.[50] These four original precincts of 1668—Chowan, Currituck, Pasquotank, and Perquimans—are North Carolina's oldest counties.

The proprietors conceived the General Assembly as a powerful legislative body, in some respects more autonomous than Parliament. Unlike Parliament, which was subject to the whims of the monarch, the assembly determined their time and place of meeting, their adjournment, and their quorum, provided that it was at least one-third of the members. They enacted laws "necessary for the good prosperity and Settlement of the said Counties"; levied taxes; established courts; erected political divisions; designated ports, landings, and forts; incorporated municipalities; organized the militia; granted citizenship to immigrants; determined land allotment; and provided for the governor's maintenance. The few limits on the province's laws were that they must conform to the laws and customs of England and not be contrary to the proprietors' interests or the Concessions, especially as related to the "Article for Liberty of Conscience." Laws were to be sent to the proprietors for ratification within a year and were in effect for at least eighteen months unless disallowed. Nothing prevented the assembly from reenacting a disallowed law for subsequent eighteen-month periods.[51]

Since the propriety was essentially a real estate venture, a significant portion of the Concessions was devoted to land policy. The foundation of wealth and power in the age was land ownership, which in Britain was concentrated in the hands of squires and aristocrats. For the most part, the common folk of the British Isles were village craftspeople or small business owners or lived as tenant laborers on agricultural estates. A tenant might aspire to become a yeoman farmer with a smallholding, but few would achieve that dream. The American colonies, on the other hand, lured the downtrodden through the hope of possessing land, and not just a small plot but possibly hundreds of acres. Penniless tenants, male or female, could sign or make their mark on an indenture, or labor contract, for a period of several years, which would be sold on arrival to pay their passage to the colonies. Toiling for the term of the contract yielded the valuable payoff of a headright for the former servant and each family member, as well as freedom dues, such as clothing, seeds, and tools.

Carolina's land policy under the Concessions was the most expansive of all of the colonies, but it was so complicated that it had little chance of success. Proposed headrights for free men and women ranged from 80 acres in Albemarle to 150 acres in the future Craven, with the amounts diminishing over four years. Christian, or indentured, servants who had completed their terms were allotted from 20 to 75 acres, with similar restrictions. Speculation was discouraged through the requirement that within three years the owner must have every 100-acre tract occupied by someone, whether free, servant, or enslaved, or else it would be regranted or sold unless the General Assembly intervened.[52] The reversion policy, coupled with a doubling of the quitrent and a random casting of lots for property, alarmed potential settlers.

In the Concessions and Agreement the proprietors asserted their deep commitment to liberty of conscience, paraphrasing the king's Declaration of Breda that no freeman "shall be any ways molested, punished, disquieted, or called in question for any differences in opinion or practice in matters of religious Concernment, who do not actually disturb the Civil peace."[53] Under the 1663 charter the Lords Proprietors had been authorized to establish the Church of England and grant dispensation to dissenters if they could not conform to the state church. Now, under the Concessions and Agreement, the responsibility of establishing the state church was given to each county's General Assembly so that there would be no infringement of the "General clause of Liberty of Conscience." The assemblies could appoint and maintain "so many Ministers or Preachers" as needed and could set aside 100 acres in each parish for the minister's support. Dissenters were authorized "to keep and maintain what preachers and Ministers they please."[54]

It may have been an afterthought, but reflecting the progress made by Parliament in the Civil War and the Commonwealth, the Concessions allowed the colonists to check the abuse of executive authority. The General Assembly was given the right to address the Lords Proprietors directly "Concerning any Grievances whatsoever . . . without the Consent of the Governor and Council."[55]

ON 30 JUNE 1665, six months after the Concessions and Agreement was issued, a second Carolina Charter was signed. For years the accepted explanation has been that the inhabited area north of Albemarle Sound was not included in the 1663 grant, when, in fact, most of it was. Another reason offered has been that the 1663 charter was issued before the title was cleared from the Heath propriety claimants; however, the Privy Council dismissed those claims in August 1663 because the area had not been colonized. Lacking substance, neither of these conjectures stands.

A compelling alternative lies in the proprietors' vision of governance for their enormous province: the concept of the palatine county that was embedded in all of the Carolina charters, from Heath's 1629 Carolana to the two charters of the Lords Proprietors. As the Lords began to grasp the sheer scope of their continent-sized dominion, they received settlement proposals for Cape Fear and for areas as far south as Port Royal. Hundreds of miles separated these potential colonies from the inhabited area north of Albemarle Sound.[56] Their pragmatic solution was to subdivide their domain into separate palatine counties. Although they had covered nearly every contingency in the 1663 charter, they had no explicit authority to create independent colonies within the province, nor was there a precedent in other colonial charters. Faced with a de facto settlement on the northern border and a proposed Cape Fear colony 200 miles south, the proprietors created independent governments for the two areas.[57]

To dispel any doubts about the legality of separate counties and to quash any future questions concerning the title, the Lords requested a new charter so that for "good and happy Government" they could create "several Counties, Baronies, and Colonies" within the province. As in the first charter, the counties had representative assemblies with the right to levy taxes by the consent of the freemen.[58]

The new boundary with Virginia was sited on the northern side of Currituck Inlet and extended west to intersect the Weyanoke River "within or about" 36°30' north and thence to the continent's western coast. This roughly six-mile shift north was apparently made to anchor the border on better-known points. Furthermore, Currituck Inlet would be entirely within Carolina and not subject to regulation by Virginia. Overreaching absurdly deep into Spanish territory, the new southern Carolina boundary was expanded 2° of latitude, some fifty miles south of Saint Augustine, the capital of Spanish Florida.[59]

The 1665 charter strengthened the guarantee of liberty of conscience. Henceforth, dissenters were no longer subject to ecclesiastical law and must abide by civil law only. The charter incorporated the statement on religious liberty from the Concessions and Agreement that all may "freely and quietly have and enjoy his and their Judgements and Consciences in matters of Religion."[60]

Carolina is unique among the American colonies in having the possibility of being constitutionally divided into autonomous states to be represented in a provincial assembly or parliament. However, with only two self-governing colonies the provincial assembly did not evolve. Albemarle County was the only autonomous colony in North Carolina. When Bath County was created in 1696, it was incorporated for governance into Albemarle because the separate colonies of North and South Carolina had emerged. The governmental equivalent of the modern county was the precinct, for which South Carolina used the Barbadian term "parish."

In two senses Carolina was a "colony of colonies," both in being settled primarily by seasoned immigrants from other colonies, and now in its governing structure. If Carolina's expanse across the continent had survived into modern times, it might very well have become the United States of Carolina. More far-reaching in the areas of liberty of conscience, a free legislative assembly, and the concept of a federal structure of self-governing states, Carolina, as much as any other colony, was the precursor of basic constitutional principles of the United States.

Although the provincial assembly never materialized, the provincial governor of Carolina, residing in Charles Town, would later appoint deputy governors for North and South Carolina. Furthermore, under the Lords Proprietors, the Bahamas were organized as another palatine county until they became a royal province in the eighteenth century. Under royal government, the Province of Georgia would be carved out of the southern buffer of Carolina adjacent to Spanish Florida. Carolina's proprietary charters and constitutions had laid the foundations for future colonies—North Carolina, South Carolina, Georgia, and the offshore Bahamas—as well as for New Jersey, Pennsylvania, and, over a century later, the United States.

CHAPTER FOUR

Clarendon County

Puritans and Barbadians on the Cape Fear

Ye many Palmettos growing na[tur]ally there,
wch renders it a summer Contry.
—William Hilton, 1662

I T WAS 14 AUGUST 1662. Preparations were complete, and all supplies and provisions were aboard the ship *Adventure* anchored off Charlestown in Massachusetts Bay Colony. The crew waited expectantly as a longboat pulled away from the dock bearing the ship's captain, William Hilton. An excellent choice to command the exploration, Hilton at age forty-five had long experience on transatlantic and Caribbean voyages. He had lived most of his life in New England and nearly a decade in Charlestown, long enough to be well connected to his fellow sea captains, mariners, and merchants.[1]

When Hilton reached the deck, he gave orders to weigh anchor, and so began the long-anticipated journey to explore the southern coast of North America. Sponsored by the Committee for Cape Faire at Boston, a group of businessmen from Boston and surrounding towns, this voyage was one in a continuum of exploring and colonizing missions by New Englanders to expand their faith and opportunities for trade. The doughty Puritans had planted their theocratic refuge on Massachusetts Bay in bleak New England, whose stony fields afforded little more than subsistence. Their wealth came partly from the forests but primarily from the sea, which generated the continent's first important maritime culture of seamen, fishermen, shipwrights, and merchants engaged in the North Atlantic trade network. Trading and colonizing ventures pushed southward into warmer latitudes, from the southern Atlantic coast to the legendary riches of the Caribbean and Old Providence Island off the Spanish Main in Central America. The quest was also prompted by the needs of younger generations for land and a future. Like other Puritan towns, Newbury and Charlestown had granted all of their land by the mid-seventeenth century, leaving little economic opportunity except on the sea for the founders' children and grandchildren.[2]

About half of Hilton's crew are known from the officers who cosigned his report and from river and feature names on the accompanying map. The five signers were Major Samuel Goldsmith, a London merchant; Lieutenant Enock Greenleefe of Boston; John Greene, a Charlestown scholar; James Bate of Dorchester; and Edward Winslow, from a prominent Boston merchant family and son-in-law of Hilton. Others known from map nomenclature are Henry Douglas of Boston; Sergeant John Badger of Newbury, a nephew of Hilton; Joshua Browne, a stepbrother of Badger; William Hurry, a Charlestown mariner; and Thomas Burges of Charlestown. Most of the men were middle-aged, except Winslow, Browne, Badger, and Hurry, who were in their twenties. Hilton's men represented experienced seamen, militia officers, and the expedition's sponsors.[3]

When *Adventure* slipped downriver on the tidal current, Captain Hilton carried orders to explore Cape Fear as a potential site for a colony and to reconnoiter the "South parts of Florida," the region below Virginia claimed by Spain. *Adventure* sailed leisurely down the coast for twenty days, arriving at Cape Fear on 3 September, but contrary winds would not allow the ship to round the dangerous tentacles of sand that reach some sixteen miles out into the Atlantic. In a test of his seamanship, Hilton was forced to pick his way cautiously through the breakers several miles off the cape. On clearing the shoals, *Adventure* arrived in the "faire haven" of the road and a safe anchorage at 33°45' north. Europeans had not seen Cape Fear in more than a century, since Villafañe's discovery in 1561. The rest of that day a boat crew searched unsuccessfully for the entrance to the river.[4]

Having located the cape and with a favorable northeast wind, the next day Hilton set a course south to complete his reconnaissance of the shores that the English considered "undiscovered country." Over the next month erratic winds, storms, and currents prevented him from carrying out his mission. Twice fierce nor'easters drove *Adventure* almost 300 miles south, nearly to Saint Augustine. Finally, in fitful breezes Hilton was able to work laboriously up the coast to Cape Fear Road, anchoring there on 3 October.[5]

Luckily the channel was found quickly, and *Adventure* began a three-week exploration by sail and longboat covering about forty-five miles of the river. Hilton named his discovery the Charles River. The first week was spent in the lower river taking soundings, sampling the fish and oysters, and interacting with Native Americans in a nearby village. Embarking in the longboat, Hilton worked upstream two more weeks, taking the Northeast Cape Fear River as the main branch.

To his New England sponsors Hilton reported a "most temperate" climate without "any considerable winter." As he penetrated deeper into the interior, his detailed and sanguine observations noted an abundance of fish, shoals of oysters, extensive pine and hardwood forests, plentiful game and waterfowl, and swarms of bees. On one night, they heard the eerie howls of wolves. Observing Natives adding snake meat to their stews, Hilton opined that there were no rattlesnakes in the area.[6] Most of the land appeared fertile, with "scarce a stone to be seene," a remark that would appeal to his New England sponsors. Besides ample farm sites, there were grassy meadows, marshy wetlands, and large fields where the Natives harvested maize. Beyond any crop that could be grown in New England, Hilton speculated that oranges, limes, plantains, olives, cotton, and pineapples would flourish. Grapevines were ubiquitous, as was cane, which raised the prospect of growing sugarcane, the golden crop of the Caribbean.

During three weeks of exploration the English were surprised to find fewer than a hundred Indians, who appeared to be mostly elderly and "very poor and silly Creatures." Although the Natives were shy and courteous toward the English, Hilton reported that they were "very theevish." The majority of the Indians, especially the young men and women, apparently hid from the intruders. Their shyness may have been a strategy to entice the visitors to trade and settle there. If this was the case, it worked, for the English were sufficiently impressed with the riverside land to purchase it from the local chieftain.[7]

Having completed a survey of the Cape Fear, Hilton headed home, anchoring *Adventure* at Charles Town on 6 November. He presented his report to the Boston Committee, who engaged Nicholas Shapley of Charles Town, an experienced mariner and surveyor, to prepare a map of the discoveries. Completed within the month, the original sketch map has been lost but was copied by John Locke. The coast was charted with depth soundings, and the cape was accurately drawn, showing the two anchorages in the road.[8] Hilton's report and Shapley's map provided the earliest geographical details of the Cape Fear area, placing the hitherto unknown region on subsequent maps of Carolina.

The map's most striking feature is located on the east side of the river—a crenellated tower symbol, complete with a banner, named James's Fort. Most scholars have rejected the idea of a fortified site, observing that the explorers were not there long enough to have built such a structure. Others have suggested that the castle symbol may mark a future settlement location. However, for two of the three weeks that *Adventure* was there, Hilton and half his crew were exploring upriver. The remaining sailors stayed at the anchorage awaiting his return. Once ashore they would have erected sailcloth awnings to shelter themselves and their supplies and then protected their position. A fortified shore base could have been built in a day or so and augmented over time. Even hastily dug ditches and earthworks with crude fencing would deter wolves and discourage hostility from nearby Natives. The name "James's Fort" likely honored James, Duke of York.[9] There was a certain symmetry in naming the river for the king and the shore base for his brother.

Hilton's glowing report and Shapley's map identified a southern haven for the New England settlement. Expectations were already high among the Puritans, who were easily persuaded to join the venture, recognizing opportunities to expand their community, increase trade, and provide prospects for young families. Organized in just two months, the expedition embarked for Cape Fear in February 1663 on two vessels: the ship *Constant*, with Captain John Long, and the bark *Plyer*, with Captain Richard Price. Since Hilton would have been the obvious choice for commander, he probably was at sea.[10]

A few of the participants may be identified from local court records. From Boston came Henry Douglas, who had earlier accompanied Hilton, and his son Thomas. Staking their future on the Cape Fear, the Douglases took a sow and goods and supplies in two barrels, two chests, and a hogshead. In his will written just before leaving, Henry Douglas bequeathed his "sheare of lande at cape feare" to his infant grandson. Two other returnees from the fall voyage were John Greene and Enock Greenleefe. Daniel Pierce, a Newbury blacksmith, and Abraham Shepard of Malden were said to have gone to "Cape Faire." Considering the broad mercantile interests of the Boston Winslows, young Edward surely returned to stake claim to Point Winslow. Important investors in the project were Bostonians John Paine, who sent two agents to the colony, and merchant Thomas Clarke, both of whom were probably members of the sponsoring committee.[11]

What is most puzzling about this New England foray into the Cape Fear is the sudden mysterious collapse of the enterprise. If the colonists arrived in late February, it was only six weeks before a decision was made to leave. On 4 April a reluctant Henry Douglas and others, including Greene and Greenleefe, were on the bark *Plyer* negotiating for passage to "Roanoack" (the Albemarle settlement) or a return to New England. In the midst of the discussion, a young man came on board and took one of Paine's agents aside to *Constant*. The agent returned shortly and reported that "we have nothing to doe but to goe home."[12]

We may never know who the young man was, but it is possible that he had been sent by Sir William Berkeley, Virginia's governor. Berkeley had recently returned to Virginia from England, authorized to act for his fellow proprietors and knowing that their grant was imminent. In March, the same month the charter was issued, Berkeley wrote to the Earl of Clarendon that he had heard that 200 families from New England had "seated a little to the South of us."[13] Such a rumor would alert Berkeley about an unauthorized settlement in Carolina. If the Cape Fear colonists were already disheartened, a messenger from Berkeley warning them that they were trespassing could have been the final straw.

Whatever transpired in April, the colony was abandoned and the Puritans sailed away to New England, leaving their livestock on the barren cape. Reflecting their utter disappointment, they posted a sign on the cape to discourage future settlers.[14] At this juncture when Cape Fear, now a pariah, might have dropped out of sight for years, there was one final approach by New England interests, and in London and Barbados others arose who were willing to venture their lives and fortunes on this subtropical land.

The Carolina Charter marked a dramatic new colonial venture that stirred immediate interest, and by June Sir John Colleton noted that there were "divers people that desire to settle and plant" in Carolina.[15] A London-based group called Adventurers about Cape Fayre, which included Boston merchants, approached the proprietors with a proposal, patterned after the New England colonies, for a corporate colony to be guaranteed freedom of conscience and complete self-government, including the right to select the governor, to make their own laws, and to enjoy immunity from taxes other than those they approved.

The proprietors wanted nothing to do with a corporate colony and countered in late August with a governance document that met many of the Adventurers' requests, including liberty of conscience, a legislative assembly, and a seven-year immunity on selected trade duties. The proprietors, however, would appoint the governor and council from nominees submitted by the colonists and would review and ratify the laws.[16] Because of the failure of their initial settlement in early 1663 and the proprietors' refusal to grant corporate and administrative autonomy, most of the New Englanders lost interest in Carolina. The few who remained, some of whom had relatives in Barbados, joined the Barbadian Adventurers, and some returned with Hilton on his next voyage.

––––––––––

AS THE PURITANS looked elsewhere, interest in Cape Fear was kindled in Barbados. First settled in 1627, Barbados had in just thirty years wrested from the gentle, forested landscape a phenomenally rich plantation society unmatched in the English colonies. Typical of contemporary comments bestowed by travelers and sojourners was that it was the "fair jewell of your majesty's crown."[17]

Adaptive to the changing economic realities and constantly searching for a viable living, Barbadian planters ran the gamut of the staple crops of the day—tobacco, indigo, and cotton—before establishing the first English sugar colony and reaping enormous profits. Barbados may have become "one of the Riches spotes of ground in the wordell,"[18] but this wealth would be enjoyed by a minority of the island's sugar planters. The high investment required for sugar factories forced the buyout of small farms and plantations by wealthier neighbors, who consolidated their landholdings chiefly in the fertile soils of the south central plateau. This social dislocation was aptly described by contemporaries as being "wormed out."[19] Beginning in the 1660s over 12,000 smaller planters, yeoman farmers, former indentured servants, and younger sons made up waves of emigration, "the Barbadian Diaspora," that made the island one of "the greatest colonising countries in history."[20]

Although the Caribbean islands, primarily Jamaica, would siphon off most of the Barbadian migrants, Carolina became the first mainland venture. Hoping to capitalize on the proprietary need for settlers, some 200 Barbadian gentlemen organized the Corporation of Barbadian Adventurers to sponsor a colony. Serving as managing agents were two cousins of the Duke of Albemarle: Sir Thomas Modyford, former governor of the island, and Peter Colleton, son of proprietor Sir John Colleton.[21] That summer the corporation welcomed William Hilton's arrival in Barbados with his report of ideal conditions at Cape Fear, as they were interested in both the cape and the more southerly Port Royal Sound.

Key guidance in the future colony came from a Huguenot family, the Vassalls of London, Massachusetts Bay, and Barbados, leaders in commercial and colonial activities for three generations. The current patriarch, Samuel of London, had sponsored an unsuccessful settlement in Carolana some thirty years earlier. Samuel's brother William, who had lived in both Massachusetts Bay and Plymouth colonies, became a planter-merchant in Barbados in 1648. His son John, a Bridgetown merchant, was a Cape Fear sponsor from the outset. Samuel and his son Henry represented the family interests in London.[22]

A fellow Massachusetts man, William Hilton undoubtedly had ties with the Vassalls and other former New Englanders in Barbados. His enthusiastic description of the Cape Fear dispelled any doubts raised by disparagement from "ill willers," prompting the corporation to engage him for another reconnaissance of the region. In *Adventure*'s crew of twenty-five men were masters John Hancock and Pyam Blowers and experienced New England seamen Captain Anthony Long and Peter Fabian, who, like Hilton, were commissioners for the corporation.[23]

On 10 August 1663 *Adventure* sailed from Speightstown, on the northwestern coast of Barbados. Blessed with fair weather, in sixteen days they sighted land north of Santa Elena Sound and scouted the coastal waters for several days. Accustomed to the steep rocky shore of New England, Hilton instead found broad prairie-like marshes laced with interconnected waterways through a rich estuarine nursery. Having interacted with Europeans for over a century, the unintimidated Indians readily approached them with news of shipwrecked English sailors. Hilton dispatched the longboat to scout Port Royal, and plied the cagey Edisto king with trade goods to secure the release of four of the seamen. As hostages for the last castaway held by the Edisto, Hilton kept an Edisto "captain," Shadoo, and two other warriors, which aroused the countryside.[24]

The longboat crew returned from Port Royal, where they had found five more shipwrecked Englishmen. Anxious to retrieve them, Hilton entered the sound by the headland that thenceforth would be Hilton Head. He negotiated the release of the men from a Spanish captain who had been sent from Saint Augustine, and the parting was friendly.[25] Three Indians—Edisto warriors Shadoo and Alush, as well as Wommony from Port Royal—remained on board for the voyage to Cape Fear and Barbados and were later returned to their homelands, where they became contacts for future English explorers.[26]

Adventure sailed north in late September into a prolonged nor'easter, finally reaching the welcome shelter of Cape Fear Road on 16 October.[27] Indians, probably old acquaintances from the village at Sachems Point, brought fresh fish and told Hilton what they knew of the failed New England venture. These Natives remained friendly and from time to time traded salt and "very good" beef and pork. Led by a Native guide, the English searched unsuccessfully for cattle abandoned on the cape, but they did find the "scandalous" sign posted by the disgruntled New Englanders. Hilton dismissed the sandy and barren cape as having "little worth."[28]

Over the next six weeks, using the yawl and longboat, the English penetrated up the Cape Fear River and its tributaries until the channel was blocked by fallen trees. *Adventure* was anchored on the east shore opposite the mouth of Greens River. Hilton's description of the region mirrored his findings of the previous winter, assuring his fellow sponsors that the Cape Fear was a Garden of Eden. A new sighting was "great flocks of Parrakeetos," the Carolina parakeets that would become extinct within two centuries. Upriver on the west bank the exploring party discovered a savannah so extensive that they walked for miles and "saw no end of it." Among waist-high grasses that at times reached their shoulders were few trees, except for "here and there a very great Oak." A stately buck inspired him to name the prairie Stag Park, while a nearby rock outcrop on the river became Rocky Point.[29]

After only friendly encounters with the Natives, far up the Cape Fear a solitary warrior suddenly shot an arrow that narrowly missed one of the men. This singular hostile act was repudiated at a council with a chief and his retinue. Expressing friendship, the chief offered Hilton two "very handsom proper young *Indian* women" that Hilton thought were the "King's daughters." The offer was politely refused; the king was placated with a hatchet and beads; and additional beads were distributed to the women and the rest of the gathering. On Hilton's return, *Adventure* moved downriver to Crane Island below Town Creek. There on 1 December in a ceremonial gathering, commissioners Hilton, Long, and Fabian met King Wattcoosa and other chieftains, who brought a large quantity of fresh fish for the ship. The day concluded with the purchase of the "River and the land of *Cape-Fair*."[30]

Hilton and his fellow commissioners, having fulfilled their purposes by thoroughly exploring Port Royal and Cape Fear, concurred that both exceeded expectations for settlement sites. Hilton closed his report by declaring that the Cape Fear valley had "as good Land . . . as any we have seen in any other part of the world, sufficient to accommodate thousands of our English Nation." With a fair wind on 4 December *Adventure* weighed anchor, and Hilton set a course for Barbados.[31]

In the five months while Hilton was exploring Carolina, the proprietors and the agents of the Barbadian Adventurers exchanged a flurry of correspondence. Sir Thomas Modyford and Peter Colleton notified the Lords of Hilton's voyage from Port Royal to Cape Fear. They requested a copy of the Carolina Charter and permission to purchase from the Natives up to 1,000 square miles to organize a "County or Corporation," for, they assured the proprietors, there were "many hundreds of noble famillyes and well experienced planters that are willing and ready to remove spedily theither to begin a settlement."[32]

Meanwhile in England, in late August the proprietors announced and soon dispatched to Barbados "A Declaration and Proposals to all that will Plant in Carolina." Developed over the summer, the document stated the proprietors' land policy, established a governing procedure, and guaranteed religious liberty. Unlike the New Englanders, the Barbadians were satisfied with nominating their own governor and council, electing their assembly delegates, and enjoying liberty of conscience and immunity from certain customs duties. Given the number of smallholdings on their home island, the Barbadians were also pleased with headrights of up to 100 acres and a half-cent-per-acre quitrent.[33]

The proprietors were aware of Lieutenant Colonel Robert Sandford's testimony before the Privy Council about his experience in Surinam, where he had been tried by court-martial and banished for opposition to a high-handed elected governor.[34] Under a corporate charter, officials were chosen for life and could be removed only by their peers "whoe may be apter to wincke at the misdemeanors of there fellow Governors" than those being governed. The Lords were therefore adamant that appointing the governor and council to limited three-year terms was "better for the people in Generall."[35]

Because of the latitude, the proprietors suggested that the colony concentrate on high-profit Mediterranean imports and not crops that would compete with

Barbados. The Duke of Albemarle assured the governor of Barbados that the proposed colony would not rival his island but would instead produce provisions that Barbadians needed, such as cornmeal, flour, beef, and pork.[36]

Long attracted by the warm climate and safe anchorage at Port Royal, the proprietors were delighted that the Barbadians had borne the cost of Hilton's voyage to that very region. They warmly expressed appreciation that "soe many publick spirrits" in Barbados were interested in colonizing Carolina south of Cape Fear.[37]

When word reached Barbados that the Lords were encouraging a colony at Port Royal, a rift opened among the Adventurers, with John Vassall and Robert Sandford advocating for Cape Fear, while Modyford, Colleton, and Colonel John Yeamans, an influential planter and Barbados council member, preferred Port Royal. The division also reflected the diverging interests of those with New England connections, such as the Vassalls, and the planters with long ties to Barbados. John Vassall organized a splinter group of Barbadians under the name "Adventurers and Planters of Cape Feare" and asked his London cousin Henry Vassall to negotiate with the proprietors for acceptable concessions.[38] Just as the Lords were on the cusp of an agreement with Vassall, Major William Yeamans, representing his father, appealed to the proprietors for a colony at Port Royal. When Yeamans obtained the proprietors' endorsement, Henry alerted his cousin John that their Cape Fear colony was not sanctioned, but the momentum was too far advanced for the Adventurers to turn back.[39]

Adventure's arrival in Carlisle Bay on Epiphany, 6 January 1664, drew an outpouring of excited townspeople to the waterside. Eyes were wide as exotic Indians set foot on Barbadian soil in the company of intrepid explorers. Hilton's report to Modyford, Colleton, and the Adventurers was so gratefully received that the Corporation rewarded all in the ship's company with generous land grants in Carolina.[40] Rumors spread rapidly through the streets of Bridgetown that large plantations of fertile soil in a lush climate were waiting for those with energy and ambition. This news could not have been better timed for overcrowded and overplanted Barbados.

A copy of Hilton's report was sent to the proprietors and by June was published in London as *A Relation of A Discovery lately made on the Coast of Florida* (1664). Containing a description of the explorations and detailed navigational information, the pamphlet also included courteous letters between Hilton and a Spanish captain, Alanso Argüelles, regarding the recovery of the English castaways. If anyone had qualms about settling deep into the territory of England's traditional foe, the peaceful settlement was designed to assuage their fears. Appended to Hilton's *Relation* was a new version of the Declaration and Proposals

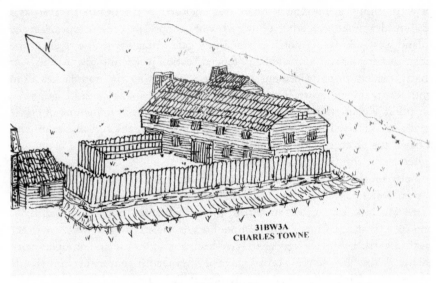

Charles Towne on the Cape Fear (1664–67). Clarendon colony, fortified center,
based on archaeological research. Original sketch by the author.

intended for Carolina "Southwards and Westwards" of Cape Romain, the Port
Royal region.[41]

Drawing on his family's long experience in business, overseas trade, and colonial affairs, John Vassall had lived in New England and Barbados and was now
ready to cast his lot with Carolina. With no approval from the proprietors, but
with full confidence that it would be forthcoming, over the next few months
Vassall organized a colony for the Cape Fear. Setting sail with a small fleet,
Vassall arrived at the cape on 29 May 1664 and located the central settlement
of Charles Towne on a low bluff on the west side of the river. On the peninsula
between deepwater Town Creek and the river there was an Indian town site,
likely with cleared fields. It is not known whether it was occupied when the
colonists arrived, but Hilton had twice purchased tracts from the Natives that
may have included this location.

Archaeological excavations revealed that the colony's central complex was
formed by an earthfast, or post-in-ground, two-story, timber-framed building,
seventy feet long, paralleling the river and fronting a square fifty feet wide. The
structure had clay-daubed chimneys, and the frame was probably covered with
sawn boards. The roof could have been either lapped planks or split cypress

or cedar shingles. The town square was enclosed by ditches that served as a shallow dry moat protecting a low earthwork capped by a plank fence. On the inland west side facing north was a sturdy gate. Adjacent to the river on the northeast corner was a moated and fenced bastion projecting toward the river that provided an emplacement for cannon, protecting the approaches from both upstream and down. The fortified compound brings to mind Ligon's description of plantation houses on Barbados that were "built in manner of Fortifications and have Lines, Bulwarks, and Bastions." The enclosure also resembles a bawn for protecting the homestead and livestock, common in Ireland and suited to the frontier setting.[42]

Between the main building and the artillery bastion was a small building, fifteen feet square, that supported the battery, probably for storing powder. Here was found a concentration of military artifacts—gun flints, lead balls, and sprue castings. Outside the compound adjacent to the gate were two other earthfast structures that appear to have been a guardhouse and an open work shelter. Across the site was a broad range of seventeenth-century ceramic shards representing Chinese porcelain, Delftware, Bellarmine jugs, salt-glazed stoneware, earthenware, and several types of Spanish ceramics, including the common olive jar. Over one-third of the ceramics were Delftware, and there was a quantity of ceramic tobacco pipe stems and bowls. The evidence supports an interpretation of the site as the fortified administrative trading center of Charles Towne.[43]

The land along the river is bordered by intermittent marshes, which forced the colonists to scatter out some sixty miles along the river's branches, seeking higher ground. Since the Indians were friendly, they felt no apprehension about living on dispersed and isolated farmsteads. According to a contemporary account, within two years the settlement comprised some 800 people from Barbados, New England, Bermuda, and Virginia.[44] So few names of the colonists are known that it is difficult to determine their origins apart from Barbados; however, the Vassalls were Puritans, and other families in Barbados had come from New England.

The Clarendon Assembly's Charles Towne residents from Barbados included planters, tradespeople, and mariners. John Knight, John Brant, Thomas Gibbs, Richard Whittney, Will Grig, John Nevinson, and Thomas Clifton were landholders, but only Knight, with 350 acres, could be considered wealthy. He had also served on the Barbados council. Vassall and Humphrey Davenport, both of whom had New England ties, were Bridgetown merchants. The militia officers Robert Sandford, George Cary, and Henry Brayne were active sea captains. After the Vassalls and Yeamanses, no other family was more important than the Gibbses of St. Andrews Parish, of whom four brothers were

Adventurers—Basill, John, Robert, and Thomas. The younger brothers, Robert and Thomas, sought their fortunes in Charles Towne.[45]

The publication of Robert Horne's promotional tract *A Brief Description of the Province of Carolina on the Coasts of Floreda* (1666) introduced Charles Towne to Londoners. Declaring that "Carolina is a fair and spacious Province on the Continent of *America*," Horne rhapsodized about the "most Temperate Clime," the wholesome air, the fecundity of the soil, the abundant natural resources, the variety of the crops, and the rapid growth of the population. Addressing the province's political and economic advantages, Horne reiterated the Lords Proprietors' offer of "Liberty of Conscience," a representative government, and generous headrights offered to free men and women and to indentured servants of both sexes when their terms expired. The tract concluded with an appeal to young gentlemen who could, with a few servants, create a "great Estate"; to indentured servants, artisans, and craftspeople "who could advance their fortunes"; and to single women who would believe that they had come to "the Golden Age when Men paid a Dowry for their Wives; for if they be but Civil, and under 50 years of Age, some honest Man or other will purchase them for their Wives."[46]

The record is silent about enslaved people and indentured servants living in Clarendon County. By the time Charles Towne was conceived, however, the plantation economy in Barbados had been established for a generation, and enslaved labor had surpassed indentured servitude as the labor force of choice. From their very first proposal to the proprietors, the Barbadian Adventurers had stated that "experienced planters" expected to have their "Negros and other servants fitt for such labor" as the new colony would need. The proprietors had included headrights for indentured servants and, probably at the instigation of the Barbadians, had incorporated allotments for enslaved laborers in the "Concessions and Agreement" (1665) and publicized these offers in the promotional tracts.[47]

The need in the Caribbean islands for provisions and livestock overrode any concern about economic competition. The Cape Fear valley had "as rich ground as any in the world," with a "blackish mold" overlying sand and clay subsoil. Most of the seeds, roots, and herbs were brought from Barbados, supplemented by some from New England, Bermuda, and Virginia. The colonists' main cash crops were potatoes, indigo, tobacco, and cotton, and they harvested two plantings of corn a season. Lime, orange, and lemon trees thrived, and apple, pear, and other fruit trees were planted. Cattle grazed on the broad marshes and savannahs, eliminating the need to plant hay, while hogs fattened on mast in the woodlands. Although sugarcane could not be grown that far north, the planters anticipated that rice, rapeseed, and linseed would thrive in the colony.[48]

The colonists seemed willing to try practically anything that could be grown in North America and the West Indies.

Supplementing the colony's agriculture, Charles Towne was a center for the Indian fur trade that attracted Natives from as far south as Kiawah and probably Port Royal.[49] Local clay was used at first to daub chimneys, but soon the colonists began making bricks, fragments of which have been found on the Town Creek site. Discarded oyster shells yielded abundant lime for mortar.[50] Forest products—lumber, staves, and shingles—were likely exports to Barbados, which had limited timber. In February 1667 *Elizabeth* under Captain Anthony Langston was dispatched to Carolina for cypress masts for the navy. Since Albemarle rarely saw vessels from England, this was likely a voyage to Charles Towne.[51]

Meanwhile, in London Henry Vassall and Robert Sandford continued to promote the Cape Fear colony's interests. On 22 August they dined with several of the proprietors to discuss an agreement about Carolina.[52] Recognizing that on their own the Barbadian Adventurers and Planters had established a flourishing colony in Carolina, in November 1664 the proprietors included Charles Towne in the new Clarendon County and appointed Robert Sandford as secretary and chief register and John Vassall as deputy governor and surveyor general. With these commissions in hand, Sandford sailed for Barbados and Charles Towne.[53]

Unfortunately, the thriving Vassall settlement was eclipsed in Barbados and London by enthusiasm for the potentially richer Port Royal Sound colony sponsored by the Barbados Adventurers, led by Colonel John Yeamans. These eighty-five Adventurers were planters, merchants, mariners, and professional men who held offices in the militia, the parish vestry, the assembly, and the council. Primarily from the rugged Scotland District parishes of St. Peter and St. Andrew, they were related by kinship ties, and several of the families had intermarried.[54]

Issued on 7 January 1665, the Concessions and Agreement began with the "agreement" between the Lords Proprietors and Major William Yeamans, representing the Corporation of Barbados Adventurers. The proprietors would provide arms for the colony and would grant 500 acres to every planter who paid 1,000 pounds of sugar and settled his plot with an armed man. The planters promised to adhere to the provisions of the Concessions and Agreement and to provide two armed transports.[55] The new constitution authorized separate governments for the province's counties, guaranteed religious freedom and a legislative assembly, and granted a larger headright for Craven County than the other counties were allowed. The differences between land allotments for Clarendon and Craven were destined to be a major point of contention that would undermine the Cape Fear colony and erode confidence in the proprietors.[56]

Noting John Yeamans's role in planning the new colony, in January the Lords persuaded the king to raise him to a knighthood and the title of baronet. On 11 January 1665 Sir John Yeamans was appointed governor of Clarendon and all of Carolina to the south and was granted 6,000 acres.[57] Bearing his father's commission and the Concessions and Agreement, Major Yeamans arrived in Bridgetown, creating a new fervor for Carolina as his father set about organizing the expedition. The Port Royal fleet under Governor Yeamans set sail from Barbados in October 1665, bound first for Charles Towne to deliver supplies and then to Port Royal to found the new colony. As his flagship, Yeamans chose a fly-boat or flute of 150 tuns, accompanied by his small frigate and a sloop purchased by the Adventurers. The first of a string of mishaps and disasters began with a "great storm" that dismasted the frigate, but the fleet reached Cape Fear Road safely in early November. There a "suddaine violent Gust" grounded the fly-boat on a shoal, and a rising wind "beat her to pieces." Miraculously, all on board made it to shore, but the ordnance and substantial food, clothing, and supplies were lost.[58]

Shaken by the loss, which was critical for Port Royal and threatened Charles Towne, the Charles Towne settlers, in dire straits, implored Sir John to send for relief. The sloop went to Virginia for food and clothing, but on the return it wrecked at Cape Lookout. The supplies were lost, but most of the crew reached the Albemarle in their small boat. Sir John then prepared to sail his damaged frigate to Barbados. Meanwhile, en route from Barbados the vexed Captain Edward Stanyarne, delayed for weeks by contrary winds, "lost his reason, and . . . leapt overboard in a frenzye." A youth somehow brought the vessel safely into the Cape Fear River.[59]

Having taken steps to relieve the colony, Governor Yeamans presented his commission and the Concessions and Agreement to the Clarendon County Assembly in Charles Towne. Dismayed by the unfavorable land policy, the assembly drafted a petition for redress of grievances. Specifically, the half-penny-per-acre quitrent, the distribution of land by drawing lots, and the requirement of maintaining one man per 100 acres were considered unreasonable for the estuarine topography.

The assembly proposed practical solutions to the problems. The colonists would pay a penny an acre on arable land if the quitrent was cancelled on the wetlands. They requested that their current grants be confirmed and not subject to division by lot. Yeamans listened sympathetically and gave his consent, declining to sign the petition but agreeing to support it in a private letter to the proprietors.[60] The matter apparently was tabled at the time, and soon thereafter Governor Yeamans returned to Barbados. Several months later in August, the petition was revived with additional advice to the proprietors that unless the land tenure questions were resolved, the province might be "utterly lost." Deputy Governor Vassall, Secretary Sandford, and twelve other assembly members signed the document, which was sent to London.[61]

Having permission from Governor Yeamans, Secretary Sandford, although not skilled in navigation, hired Stanyarne's small vessel at twenty-five pounds per month and departed on 14 June 1666 for Cape Romain and Port Royal Sound.[62] Sandford's crew of twenty included officers from the Clarendon County militia, colonists from Charles Towne, and three seamen from the earlier crew. Accompanying the rented vessel was a small shallop owned by the Lords Proprietors, commanded by Ensign Henry Brayne, an experienced mariner.[63]

On the third night of the voyage Brayne's shallop disappeared and was presumed lost. A few days later Sandford anchored near Edisto Town and welcomed the familiar Shadoo aboard. At Edisto Town, the cacique and his wife greeted Sandford's party and presented them with ceremonial gifts. They also met a visiting Kiawah who had traded in Charles Towne. Joining Sandford as his pilot, the Kiawah extolled the reception that Sandford would have in his country.[64]

On 1 July Sandford safely entered Port Royal Sound. At Parris Island he visited a settlement where Spanish influence was evident from a tall cross on the plaza. Noting excellent crops and a superior harbor, Sandford found the Port Royal region ideal, saying the discovery "exceeded all our . . . expectations." He was also overjoyed when the missing Ensign Brayne's shallop appeared. Just prior to departure, the cacique allowed his nephew to go with the English, enabling Sandford to leave Henry Woodward, a physician eager to learn more about the country and the Native languages. For his support Woodward was ceremonially honored with a maize field and the cacique's niece to cook and serve him.[65]

With Edisto, Kiawah, and Port Royal delegates aboard, Sandford observed that the "three principall Indians" of these tribes were vying for preferential friendship and trade with the English. Aware of the nuances of these relationships, Sandford was careful to treat them equally. On the return voyage, at the behest of the Kiawah, Sandford briefly entered a broad anchorage that he named the Ashley River in honor of proprietor Lord Ashley Cooper. By the evening of 12 July he arrived at Charles Towne "to the great rejoiceing of our friends." Sandford believed that Port Royal could hold "many thousands of our Nation," and a colony planted there would soon become "a perfect commonwealth."[66]

Far from being a "perfect commonwealth," the Charles Towne to which Sandford had returned was in distress. In that same summer of 1666 Carolina's first Indian war, the Cape Fear War, engulfed the colony. When and why it started may never be known, but since mutual suspicion nearly always underlay Native and European coexistence, it would not have taken much to ignite hostilities.[67]

On exploratory visits to the Cape Fear River, Hilton's friendly relations with the Indians had led to land purchases and a beneficial trade relationship. Occasional visits by trading vessels, however, were an entirely different matter from the permanent settlement of hundreds of residents from overseas. Seeking well-drained headlands among the wide marshes and jungle-like swamps, colonists took over Native fields and towns already occupying these preferred sites. The first clash may well have been over the limited arable ground, and isolated farmsteads along the river made easy targets. At Charles Towne the fortified compound was too small for more than a few dozen settlers and some livestock, although other "forts" or refuges were mentioned.

Another flashpoint may have been ownership of the cattle and hogs that New Englanders had abandoned on the cape in 1663. The Natives rapidly became proficient in husbandry, and the livestock prospered so well that they were able to supply Hilton with fresh beef and pork. The settlers from New England, some of whom could have been in the failed 1663 colony, may have tried to reclaim the animals.

Cattle were precious, but far more dear were the human inhabitants. Secretary Sandford's terse comment in July 1666 that the colonists had "killed and sent away [enslaved] many" of the Indians merely hints at the ferocity of the conflict that had begun.[68] Some forty years later John Lawson recorded that he had heard about "irregular Practices" of persuading Natives to send their children away under the pretense of educating them and teaching them Christianity. Since the children did not return, the Indians became "so disgusted" by the colonists' treachery that "tho' they had then no Guns, yet they never gave over, till they had entirely rid themselves of the *English*, by their Bows and Arrows." After slaughtering many of the colonists' animals, the Indians strategically withdrew into the forest, taking the remaining livestock with them.[69]

The Cape Fear War was on Sandford's mind as he reported his voyage to Port Royal, where, he assured the proprietors, security would not be a problem. The friendly Kiawah, Edisto, and Port Royal chiefs freely discussed the ongoing war in Clarendon, promising Sandford that such would not happen in their countries. The southern Indians had dealt with Europeans for over a century, and the economic advantages of trade outweighed the palpable risks that came with inviting Europeans into their homelands. Sandford reassuringly observed that the new region was secure from "Massacres" and could be more "cheaply defended" from "Indian Barbarisme" than could other English colonies.[70]

The favorable report Sandford brought back from Port Royal in 1666 did little to encourage the crumbling colony on the Cape Fear. Under the constant strain, internal complaints and bickering had increased, further dispiriting the planters. The Cape Fear War was more than enough to threaten the colony's existence, but other problems bedeviled the settlement: disastrous shipwrecks that lost crucial supplies, lack of support from other colonies, and uncertainty over the changing land policies. The Lords had rejected a final appeal about the headright presented by Henry Vassall, holding the colonists to the proprietary scheme of allotting land in contiguous parcels along the river. Based on Barbados, which has abundant tillable land and virtually no surface water, the proprietors could not comprehend why settlement was so scattered.

Faraway events ultimately sealed the fate of Charles Towne as an unprecedented series of disasters struck England and Barbados. With the catastrophes of the Great Plague (1665) and the Great Fire of London (1666), government was brought nearly to a standstill. During the bubonic plague, which took thousands of lives in London, the king and most of the government decamped to Oxford. The Duke of Albemarle was left in charge of the country with his compatriot, the Earl of Craven. Despite the relief measures and medical support they organized, the epidemic peaked in September with 30,000 deaths, finally winding down with the onset of cold weather. Over a five-day period the next fall a massive fire devastated the heart of London, destroying thousands of buildings. This time the king remained in London and with his brother, the Duke of York, was personally involved in fighting the conflagration. Once again, he relied primarily on the stalwart Albemarle to organize and direct the suppression and containment of the fires. At times the king, York, Albemarle, Craven, and Ashley were in the streets directing the firefighting efforts and supervising the creation of fire breaks to contain the blazes.[71]

The Second Dutch War (1665–67), which also consumed Albemarle's time, had a more direct effect on the survival of Charles Towne. A destructive naval raid by Admiral De Ruyter on Barbados in 1665 threatened English commerce. After several reverses, including a Dutch raid on the Thames shipping, the Duke and Prince Rupert took command of the fleet and fought the Dutch to a draw in the last major action of the war. In June 1667 a shallop bound for Charles Towne from Virginia, which may have been carrying supplies, was taken by a Dutch fleet that entered Chesapeake Bay. With these distractions in England, Barbados, and Virginia, there was little chance that Charles Towne would be supplied from abroad.[72] The death of Sir John Colleton in 1666 removed the proprietary driving force behind the Carolina colony and left the proprietors temporarily without leadership, as the duke was not in position to fill the gap.

As problems mounted within the colony, by the fall of 1666 Governor Vassall faced increasing unrest, reporting, "The rude Rable of our Inhabitants [are] more dayley redy to mutany against mee for keeping them there soe long." From Massachusetts Bay the desperation of the Cape Fear settlement elicited a colony-wide appeal to raise relief supplies.[73] In April 1667 the Roxbury congregation gathered support for "our Brethren & countrymen who were reduced to extrimeties at Cape-Feare."[74] If any aid was sent from New England to Charles Towne, it was not enough to stem the decline.

Gradually the colonists began to drift away overland to Virginia. Vassall finally bowed to the inevitable and at his personal expense accumulated enough ships to return the colonists to Boston, Barbados, and Virginia. The final blow was dealt when, in a cruel twist of fate, Samuel Vassall and his son Henry, who organized a relief supply ship in London and sailed for Virginia, both perished on the voyage. The supplies arrived too late to save the colony. For over thirty years Samuel Vassall had envisioned a colony in Carolina, and his attempts had ruined the fortune of his nephew John and cost him and his son their lives.[75]

In a last letter addressed to Sir John Colleton, who had actually died the year before, John Vassall wrote in October 1667 from Nansemond in Virginia that he and his "poore Company of deserted people" had not had enough clothing or supplies to continue, nor were they able to "defend ourselves from the Indians." He blamed the Concessions that favored the Port Royal initiative at the expense of Charles Towne. Having about two years' supply of corn on hand, Vassall attempted to persuade just twenty men to stay at Cape Fear, but he could not find "6 men that wold be true." Reluctantly, he yielded and took all the remaining colonists to Virginia.[76]

Despite its failure, Charles Towne deserves more recognition in North Carolina history. It was the first overseas expansion from the English Caribbean to the North American mainland. It was the first English town in the Carolina propriety and the only colonial town in North Carolina in the seventeenth century. The related voyages not only rediscovered Cape Fear but also explored, described, and mapped the southern coast down to Port Royal, opening the region to English settlement. In 1670, just three years after the colony failed, Barbadians returned to Carolina and founded the second Charles Town on the Ashley and Cooper Rivers. The Cape Fear valley remained devoid of English inhabitants for half a century. Then, during Indian wars in the Carolinas, step-grandsons of Sir John Yeamans, James and Maurice Moore, passed through the region, and subsequently Maurice and his brothers, Roger and Nathaniel, acquired land, built their homes, and settled alongside the great river, leading the pioneer influx of colonists from both of the Carolinas.

CHAPTER FIVE

Albemarle County

The Cradle of North Carolina

To thenke that any men will remove from Virginia upon harder
Conditions then they can live there will prove (I feare) a vaine
Imagination, It bein Land only that they come for.
—Thomas Woodward, 1665

I N THOMAS WOODWARD'S June 1665 letter to Sir John Colleton expressing gratitude for his appointment as the colony's surveyor general, he
strongly urged the proprietors to heed the General Assembly's petition to
base Carolina land policy on Virginia practices. In 1663 Governor Sir William
Berkeley had granted significant tracts in Carolina under customary Virginia
terms. Among these grants were those to Woodward, his wife Katherine, son
Thomas, and daughter Philarite, who together received 5,250 acres in three
tracts on both sides of the Pasquotank River and west of the Chowan River.
As the largest landholders in Carolina, the Woodward family would personally
suffer if the quitrent were doubled. His neighbors expressed their resentment,
and his Virginia contacts reported discouragement among planters considering
relocating to the region.

Thomas Woodward (1604–77) was a man of erudition, equally familiar with
Sir Francis Bacon's essays and Spanish proverbs. Former assay master of the
Royal Mint, he had been removed for his loyalty to the king in 1649 and sought
sanctuary in Virginia, settling in Isle of Wight County, where he served as clerk
of court. Appointed surveyor of the Roanoke region by the Virginia council on
20 March 1663, Woodward laid out the grants issued by Governor Berkeley. No
doubt Sir William had recommended Woodward to his fellow proprietors for
the crucial position of surveyor general, now that Roanoke was in the Carolina
propriety.[1]

The proprietors in London, focused on the Concessions and Agreement
and the Barbadian colony on the Cape Fear, sent Governor Berkeley instructions to establish a proprietary government in northern Carolina. Sir William

received authorization to appoint a governor and council for Albemarle County in September 1663, the same month he issued over two dozen Virginia land grants in the region. He felt no haste to act, since the small colony was under the jurisdiction of Virginia and he was confident that his friend Commander Samuel Stephens had matters well in hand. As the resident proprietor, Berkeley was free to exercise nominal control over the region and for a time used the title "Governor of Virginia and Carolina," but his first responsibility was Virginia. Casting about among his friends and acquaintances, in October 1664 he notified the Lords that he had chosen as governor his neighbor, William Drummond, a native Scot with some education and mercantile experience.[2]

Drummond had arrived in Virginia in 1637 as an indentured servant under an abusive master who discovered his servants' "dangerous conspiracy" to run away. The servants, including Drummond, were taken before the county court and punished by a public flogging and having their contracts extended one year. By 1648 a free Drummond began his rise by leasing from Berkeley a tract in the "Governor's Land," where he established his own plantation and married Sarah Prescott, with whom he raised a family of five children. Accumulating several thousand acres, Drummond prospered, growing tobacco and cattle and acting as an attorney and a merchant. Within nineteen years after entering Virginia under indenture, Drummond had risen to be county justice, then sheriff, and was described as a "Gentleman."[3]

Drummond's commission as governor and his instructions, as well as the commission of Thomas Woodward as surveyor general, were sent to Carolina with Peter Carteret, a cousin of proprietor Sir George Carteret. Also with Carteret were his own commissions as assistant governor, council member, and secretary and chief registrar that were signed on 3 December 1664. He landed in Albemarle on 23 February 1665. Soon afterward, the Concessions and Agreement, which the proprietors had signed on 7 January, also arrived in the colony.[4]

During the spring, Drummond set about organizing the colony's government. Peter Carteret and Thomas Woodward are the only known members of his council. The governor's instructions authorized him to call together the freemen of the colony to select twelve representatives to constitute an assembly with the governor and council. Sometime in the spring of 1665 Drummond summoned the freemen for the election, and the first session of the General Assembly was held before June, commencing over three and a half centuries of representative government in North Carolina.

In that first year Drummond had the task of instituting a government that conformed to the Concessions and Agreement. At the same time, he had to allay fears raised by the proposed land distribution policy. Since the colony had been settled under Virginia practices, the simplest solution was to convince the proprietors to acquiesce to the status quo. The proprietors' generous headrights were packaged with the disturbing quitrent increase to a half penny per acre, distribution of land by random allotment, and repossession of property if an armed manservant was not settled on every hundred acres within three years.[5]

These policies dismayed the newly installed governor and his fellow planters. The notion that they must give up their extensive waterfront plantations, which they had purchased from the Natives and secured with Virginia land grants, for ten-acre narrow waterfront strips and noncontiguous interior tracts, for which they would then have to pay twice the quitrent, was preposterous and indicative of the proprietors' ignorance of the coastal geography. Accompanying the first legislative assembly's petition for confirmation of Virginia terms, Woodward's letter warned the proprietors that their proposed land allotments and rent discouraged new settlers. He advised them to allow planters "to take up what tracts of Land they please at an easie rate."[6]

Although Drummond had established an Albemarle plantation, he maintained his family at his home near Berkeley. In September 1665 he had moved most of his indentured servants and cattle to Albemarle, but his family remained in Virginia because of the uncertain proprietary land policy. He continued his business of importing goods from England and transshipping them to Albemarle. A year later, Governor Drummond had still not moved his family to Carolina, since the Lords had given "noe assurance of land." If the servants were not maintained, a planter's land could revert to the proprietors, and there was no allowance for orphans to keep their property. Having aired these issues with the proprietors, he was ready to resign in frustration, for "they will make those that are there already leave" and "have hindered a thousand people already that weare really reminded to remove thither." He added, "I hate to bee where I can doe them any service nor my selfe noe good."[7]

Although the proprietors were well-intentioned in contriving a dense settlement model to ensure the colony's security, they failed to grasp the reality of Carolina's coastal terrain, decreeing complex and irrelevant land distribution patterns in both Clarendon and Albemarle Counties. In Clarendon, the misguided land policy contributed to the colony's failure, and in Albemarle it was folly not to continue the Virginia policies already in place. Fortunately, the well-established Albemarle colony could challenge the Lords. Proprietor Berkeley knew better than to attempt to "perswade or Compell" the Albemarle planters who had "bought great tracts of lande from the Indians" to accept "such proportions as we allot to others."[8] Surveyor General Woodward, advising that "Those that live upon a Place are best able to Judge of that Place," urged the Lords to give "serious consideration" to the "Petition of the General Assemblie."[9] But the proprietors were unmoved. In the fall of 1666, Sir John Colleton wrote to Peter

Carteret, "They shalbe obliged to keep . . . people on their land," noting that without settlers the land had little value. Furthermore, "ye way of ye Virginia Setlemt: is pnissious [pernicious] to ye planters."[10]

Beginning with the first patent granted to Sir Humphrey Gilbert in 1578, overseas colonists were granted "all the privileges of free denizens and persons native of England."[11] The Carolina Charter, emanating from the king and tested in the crucible of the civil war and the Commonwealth, was replete with such phrases as establishing the "Privileges and Jurisdictions requisite for . . . good and happy Government"; providing "establishment of Justice"; enacting laws "agreeable to the laws and Customes" of England "with the advice, assent, and approbation of the Freemen"; extending "all liberties, Franchises, and Privileges" of native-born Englishmen; and requiring customs and duties "to be reasonably Assessed . . . by and with the Consent of the free people there."[12]

The Virginians who settled Albemarle brought with them nearly fifty years of experience with self-government based on English liberties and rights that had evolved over centuries—a rich birthright of the rule of law, due process of law, trial by jury of their peers, the writ of habeas corpus, parliamentary representation, taxation by consent, and the institution of the county court. For more than a generation local administration, peacekeeping, and justice had been dispensed in Virginia by justices of the county court, few of whom had formal training in law. Customary practices in English village life and commerce had been tempered with living on the overseas verge of the emerging empire. Albemarle was a separate colony peopled by a heterogeneous mix of middle-class planters; yeoman farmers; indentured servants; Native Americans, some of whom were enslaved; and free and enslaved Africans. As in other colonies, the concept and expectation of law was that it would be simple and pragmatic, addressing the needs of the community. Law grew out of familiar traditions, with adaptations to the requirements of the frontier society.[13]

The sparse population, settled for some years in loose agrarian communities along the waterways, knew one another and required little from their new government. Although proprietary land policies might become troublesome, the charters and the Concessions granted the colonists significant voice in their government, which they surely expected to use to their advantage. The required registration of grants and deeds with the secretary provided security for land titles, so that most court actions arose from commercial transactions, personal disputes, and settlement of estates.

In addition to petitioning the Lords on land policy, the first assembly also established a county court of the governor and council, which is known from the will of Mary Fortsen, who held a 2,000-acre Pasquotank River grant. Dated 20 June 1663, this earliest extant will was recorded on 15 November 1665. The

General Court was the colony's only judicial body until the establishment of precinct courts after 1668.[14]

An early political question for Albemarle that became perennial was the location of the colony's northern boundary. In a letter of 7 January 1665 the proprietors notified Drummond that Albemarle County was to be 1,600 square miles, but wisely left it to him to recommend changes to the boundaries if necessary to encompass all of the existing plantations.[15] Since the colony was naturally defined by the sound on the south and the Chowan River on the west, no survey was undertaken, but the area west of the Chowan and the southern shore of Albemarle Sound were considered to be included.

Despite the two proprietary charters that clearly incorporated the Albemarle region, Virginia would never agree on the boundary location. Along most of the border, wilderness separated the colonies, except at the head of Currituck Sound, where there was a settlement that Virginia continued to claim. In 1665 George Durant was hindered in his attempt to survey the Currituck boundary. Thereafter, he and John Willoughby, a council member, were sent to England as agents to present the Albemarle position.[16]

The tobacco cessation negotiations with Virginia and Maryland plunged the colony, barely a year old, into a rare intercolonial agreement. In the Chesapeake the single-crop boom-and-bust tobacco economy had declined through over-production to a low price of a penny a pound. Albemarle County entered the market handicapped by low prices, a glut of harvests in Virginia, and hostilities in the current Anglo-Dutch War.[17] Furthermore, Albemarle planters, required by geography to transship to deepwater ports, were permanently saddled with higher shipping costs.

Past efforts to curtail production had failed. Long an advocate for economic diversification, Governor Berkeley had experimented with alternative products such as silk, but few had followed his example. Pressured by the excessive tobacco on hand, early in 1666 Berkeley initiated a second meeting with Maryland authorities in St. Mary's to propose a cessation of tobacco planting for the following year. The Maryland assembly responded with "An Act for Encouragement of Trade" in April that prohibited planting tobacco for a year beginning on 1 February 1667, and the Virginia assembly followed suit two months later.[18] When Governor Drummond was notified, the Albemarle legislative body appointed Drummond and Woodward as commissioners to represent the colony.

On 12 July a conference of the three colonies was convened at Jamestown to work out the details of the agreement. For Drummond, a tenant of Berkeley, it was gratifying recognition of Albemarle County and of himself to participate as an equal partner with his fellow governors on an issue so vital to the region.

The conference concluded with the cessation agreement, provided that Albe-marle County's legislature approved and sent the act to the other colonies by the end of September. Drummond and Woodward promised to deliver the act.[19]

That fall Albemarle County was disrupted by Indian hostilities. Details are sparse, but apparently Tuscarora warriors raided exposed farms and plantations west of the Chowan River and killed several colonists. Drummond called up the militia and repelled the aggressors.[20] As a result, the cessation act did not reach Maryland until 5 October, nearly derailing the pact. Trying to keep the fragile agreement on track, Virginia and Maryland commissioners met at St. Mary's on 11 December. Although a few days late, the Albemarle legislation was accepted, and the cessation was declared in effect for 1667. The three governors would issue proclamations to be enforced by county justices empowered to destroy plants and to fine or imprison offenders.[21] After all the time and effort expended, Lord Baltimore, the proprietor of Maryland, unexpectedly vetoed the act, thereby nullifying the agreement. An overwrought Berkeley wrote to the king that Baltimore's action was "like an impetuous wind" that "leaves us & his owne Province weithering & decaying in distresse and poverty."[22]

The following summer the intended goal of the aborted cessation was achieved by horrendous weather in the Chesapeake region—a spring hailstorm that stripped the plants, a long and heavy rainy season that ruined the remain-ing crop, and on 27 August a strong hurricane that leveled houses and fields and caused high tides to flood the river-bottom lands. Peter Carteret reported that a "great storme" devastated Albemarle, damaging houses, farm buildings, and the corn and tobacco crops.[23] In Virginia the natural disasters were compounded by Dutch naval raiders who invaded Chesapeake Bay, destroyed the British guard frigate, and captured or burned some eighteen vessels in a tobacco convoy.[24]

During the tobacco cessation negotiation, the personal relationship between Berkeley and Drummond deteriorated over a dispute about terms of a lease Drummond had from the governor. Unable to get satisfaction from Berkeley, Drummond twice petitioned the Virginia House of Burgesses, which replied that they lacked jurisdiction. Meanwhile, in a private letter Drummond indis-creetly criticized Berkeley, saying that "here are abundance of people that are weary of Sir Williams Government more I could say as to his obstructing all things of Carolina, but I conceive it not safe in regard I live soe neare him."[25] Berkeley soon had the note in his hands and placed it in Virginia's public record. This letter was the last straw that precipitated a rupture between the governors and may have led to Drummond's leaving office the next year.[26]

By 1667 Drummond was back in Virginia permanently and alienated from further interest in Albemarle County. He may have followed his inclination, expressed the previous fall, to resign. Whatever the reason, Drummond left the government in the care of the well-qualified Deputy Governor Peter Carteret, who had lived in the county since 1665 and had been in charge during Drummond's frequent absences.[27]

According to Berkeley's biographer, Drummond and Berkeley "came to detest each other," although Drummond continued as Berkeley's neighboring tenant. The long-term bitterness between them came to a head in 1676 with Drummond's key role in Bacon's Rebellion. When the rebels burned Jamestown, Drummond put the torch to his own house. After Nathaniel Bacon's death and the rebellion's collapse, Drummond and the remaining leaders were hunted down and brought before a contemptuous Berkeley. The next day, on 20 January 1677, the rebels were tried by a court-martial and hanged.[28]

THE PROPRIETORS ISSUED a commission to Samuel Stephens as governor of Albemarle County on 8 October 1667.[29] Presumably, they had again asked Berkeley for a recommendation. Still smarting from his ill-fated choice of Drummond, Berkeley selected his friend Stephens, who was well-known in Albemarle after two years' success as its administrator. With timely dispatch, Stephens's commission and instructions may have been received in the late fall.

A native of Virginia, the thirty-eight-year-old Stephens was from a wealthy and politically well-connected family. His father, Richard Stephens, emigrated from London in 1623 and became a Jamestown merchant, serving in the assembly and on the council. He married Elizabeth, daughter of Abraham Peirsey, the leading merchant factor in the colony and a councilman. After Richard's death, Elizabeth married Sir John Harvey, governor of Virginia, and the Harveys embarked for England in 1639, leaving ten-year-old Samuel in the care of guardians to oversee his education and his considerable property. His home plantation was the 1,350-acre Bolthorpe on the Warwick River.[30]

From such a privileged background, Stephens circulated easily among the colony's leaders, including Governor Berkeley, who later characterized him as a "mild" gentleman with "many other p[er]sonall virtues."[31] Sir Thomas Culpeper of Kent, a prominent royalist long associated with the Berkeley family, sought refuge in Virginia about 1650 and established his family on Mulberry Island on the Warwick. Stephens soon fell in love with the beautiful, vivacious, intelligent sixteen-year-old Frances Culpeper. They married in 1653 and settled into a comfortable life at Bolthorpe. In 1662, Stephens, then serving as a militia captain, began a two-year stint as commander of the Albemarle region.[32]

Stephens acquired Roanoke Island and a baronial estate of 4,000 acres, strategically located at the confluence of the Chowan and Roanoke Rivers at the head of Albemarle Sound. When the governor and his lady set out for Albemarle in early 1668, a home surely awaited them at the mouth of Salmon Creek, gracing the point that commanded a majestic view of the meeting of the great rivers and the sound.[33] By October, on receiving a report from Peter Carteret, proprietor Sir Peter Colleton observed, "I perceive ye people are well sattisfyed with Mr Stephens for theire governor."[34]

THE PROPRIETORS' INSTRUCTIONS to Governor Stephens, almost verbatim from the Concessions and Agreement, placed the obligation for the colony's defense on the governor, council, and assembly. As in all the other colonies, every home in Albemarle County had weapons for hunting and personal protection. The ever-present Native menace was reason enough, and abundant game provided a ready source of meat for the table. The forbidding swamplands and forests also harbored wolves that threatened livestock on the open range of meadows and woodlands. Not only were free men and women and manservants required to be armed with a good firelock or matchlock, powder, bullets, and match, but all adult men, free or servant, were also expected to serve in the militia.[35]

With the council's advice, the governor as commander-in-chief appointed militia officers from the county's freeholders. The Albemarle government had to supply all fortifications, supplies, weapons, and ammunition and had to raise the "trained bands and Companies." The proprietors made no commitment to protect the colony: Albemarle County was on its own. Although it probably was for the protection of Colleton Island, Sir John Colleton had consigned a barrel of powder and shot to Governor Drummond in Virginia to be sent to Peter Carteret.[36]

After Governor Drummond's successful mobilization of the colony in 1666, nothing more is known about colonial defense until 28 October 1668, when Governor Stephens issued a warrant to Peter Carteret as lieutenant colonel, effective commander of the militia, with responsibility to muster, train, and drill the entire county's armed forces. He was specifically charged with organizing the militia of Pasquotank Precinct, calling quarterly musters for training, and seeing that they had proper firearms and ammunition "soe that they may be in a redinesse att all times."[37] By 1670 the Fundamental Constitutions declared that all "Inhabitants and freemen" between the ages of eighteen and fifty-nine were obligated "to bear Arms and serve as Soldiers."[38] In the next decade military ranks such as "captain," "major," and "lieutenant colonel" are common in government documents, and there are passing references to military activities, such as a magazine to store the public powder and shot and an October "training day," or muster, in Pasquotank.[39]

FOR ALBEMARLE PLANTERS the most significant occurrence of Stephens's administration came when the proprietors accepted what would be known as the Great Deed of Grant. From Carolina's earliest days, when the settlement pattern was established by Virginia grants, land tenure had been an ongoing and critical issue. The proprietors' policies of changing land allocation rules and doubling the quitrent were so disruptive that Governor Berkeley ignored them. With strong endorsement from Governor Drummond, Secretary Carteret, and Surveyor General Woodward, the first General Assembly in 1665 petitioned the proprietors to adopt Virginia's prevailing land policy.[40] Sir John Colleton's official reply to Governor Drummond is lost, but apparently the proprietors refused their request.[41] The Albemarle assembly persisted by sending a second petition, which arrived simultaneously with a similar petition from the Clarendon assembly. The two pleas may have finally gotten the Lords' attention, although it was too late for the disintegrating Clarendon colony. On 1 May 1668, responding to yet another Albemarle petition signed by speaker George Catchmaid and endorsed by Governor Stephens, the proprietors relented, granting the Virginia terms of a fifty-acre headright, no limits on the size of the grant, and a farthing per acre quitrent. The Great Deed of Grant was recorded in the land office and in the precinct court minutes. The people of Albemarle embraced the document and considered it unalterable, standing firm despite the proprietors' later efforts to renege on the agreement and to increase the quitrent.[42]

Accompanying the Great Deed of Grant was a letter to Governor Stephens that addressed the proprietors' concerns about expanding land distribution. They urged a law to prevent engrossing, or accumulating, large tracts of land for speculation that would lie idle and disperse population. Criticized for reserving one-eleventh of the county for their own use, the proprietors promised not to infringe on current freeholders but to set aside noncontiguous parcels that would "not incomodate the people." Finally, they expected the governor, council, and assembly to enforce the colony's land distribution policy.[43]

MEANWHILE, unknown to the Albemarle settlement, another European, the first since the sixteenth-century Spanish, was exploring the Carolina backcountry. John Lederer, a native of Hamburg, Germany, had studied medicine and had a scientific interest in the Native Americans. Soon after his arrival in Virginia in 1670, he was commissioned by Governor Berkeley to seek a western route to the East India Sea (Pacific Ocean) and southward to prepare the way for trade with the Natives.

The indefatigable Lederer completed three expeditions during 1670, two of them to the Blue Ridge in Virginia. His second and longest journey, from May to July, began as an exploration to the falls of the James River. In early June Lederer and a Susquehanna Indian guide, Jackzetavon, left the main party and turned south and west, traversing the breadth of North Carolina. On his return to Virginia, Lederer claimed to have traveled hundreds of miles and to have witnessed fantastic and wonderful things, including strange Native customs, extensive savannas or prairies, a great inland sea, and a vast desert. Even in his day some scoffed at his tales, and some scholars have been uncertain about his credibility. Shortly after returning to Virginia, Lederer moved to Maryland, where his narrative was translated from Latin to English. It was published in England in 1672 and had an immediate impact on new maps of Carolina.[44]

Much of Lederer's journey can be identified through tribal locations and the rivers he mentioned. From the James he and Jackzetavon, with trade goods and a packhorse for supplies, traveled south through Saponi towns to Akentazy Island (Occoneechee) near the confluence of the Staunton and Dan Rivers, where the Roanoke is formed. From there they followed the great trading path to Oenock (Eno) village through a country of open woods, fields, and prairies. Continuing southwest, they successively visited the Shakori (Saxapahaw), the Watary (Uwharrie), the Suala (Saura), the Wisacky (Waxhaw), and the Ushery (Catawba).[45]

The Catawbas' report of a powerful nation of bearded men to the south (the Spanish) caused Lederer to turn northeast on 28 June and return through miry swamps and a barren "Sandy desert," probably the Sandhills. By mid-July he was at the headwaters of the Neuse River at the town of Katearas, seat of the "grim Majestic" Tuscarora emperor Kaskusara, who demanded Lederer's weapons and ammunition as ransom for release. The final stretch of his trek brought him to the Roanoke and then to Virginia's Appomattox River.[46]

Lederer had bypassed the Tuscarora trade monopoly in the east and gained direct access from Virginia to numerous small piedmont tribes and the major nations of the Catawba and the Cherokee. Stimulated by these discoveries, in 1673 trader Abraham Woods of Fort Henry (Petersburg) sent James Needham and Gabriel Arthur on Lederer's route across the Carolina piedmont to Tomahitan, a Cherokee town over the mountains.[47]

Within a decade the trade patterns were established. Pack trains from the James River traversed the Great Trading Path through Virginia and Carolina as far south as the Catawbas and west to the Cherokees. William Byrd II later described this heyday when caravans of up to 100 horses departed Virginia with 150–200 pounds of trade goods on each animal and returned laden with furs and skins.[48] From Charles Town, traders fanned south to the Savannah River, northwest to the Cherokees, and north to the Catawbas. From coastal

North Carolina, however, the Tuscaroras controlled access to the piedmont Indians, restricting traffic primarily to local tribes in the coastal plain, limiting trade west across the Chowan to the Roanoke, and serving as middlemen for Albemarle and Bath County markets.

In 1665 everything in Carolina appeared to be working for the proprietors. As the year began, they issued their liberal new constitution, the Concessions and Agreement; Charles Towne in Clarendon County was flourishing; and the colonization of Craven County in the southernmost Port Royal area was proceeding. The government of Albemarle County was established, and a Lords Proprietors' plantation, their first direct investment, was underway on Colleton Island.

But troubles soon arose. At home, from 1667 onward, the Duke of Albemarle heroically managed crisis after crisis, including the catastrophes of the plague and the London fire, as well as the Second Anglo-Dutch War, in which he took command of the fleet to battle the Dutch to the peace table. In Carolina the first Charles Towne failed and the Port Royal initiative proved to be stillborn. Also during this time, when the war had momentarily curtailed trade and imperial momentum, death took Sir John Colleton (1666) and Albemarle (1670), the driving forces behind the entire project. With the Earl of Clarendon exiled to Europe and Sir William Berkeley away in Virginia, there were at most six active proprietors, of whom four were original—the Earl of Craven, Lord Berkeley, Sir George Carteret, and Lord Ashley. Fortunately, the young Christopher Monck, second Duke of Albemarle, and Sir Peter Colleton shared their fathers' overseas interests. The future of the propriety, however, would rest with Ashley, who stepped up to fill the void left by Sir John and the duke.

Despite the prevalent view that Lord Ashley played a key role among the proprietors from the beginning, not until Colleton's death and Albemarle's preoccupation with England's woes was his leadership evident. As chancellor of the exchequer and on both the Council of Trade and the Council for Foreign Plantations, Ashley oversaw imperial economic development and overseas commerce.[49] The youngest proprietor by over a decade, he initially deferred to his elders: the Duke of Albemarle, a close and highly respected friend, and Colleton, who, like himself, owned a Barbados plantation.

In 1666 a fortuitous meeting at Oxford brought together Lord Ashley and a tutor, John Locke, who formed an immediate friendship based on their wide-ranging intellectual interests. The next year Locke joined Ashley's household at Exeter House in London, serving as his patron's physician and confidant and as secretary of the proprietors at twenty pounds a year. A sometime student of medicine, Locke supervised an emergency surgery on Ashley to remove a near-fatal liver cyst, extending his life by three dozen years.[50]

Enlightenment philosopher and physician John Locke (1632–1704)
was a protégé of Lord Ashley and secretary of the proprietors
1667–83. Courtesy of National Portrait Gallery, London.

For Locke the move to Exeter House was life-changing. At midlife he
seemed destined for obscurity as a minor academic tutor who dabbled in science and medicine. Over his years with Ashley, the stimulation of scintillating
conversation with a fellow inquiring mind reinforced his predilection for political theory and contributed to his becoming one of England's foremost political
philosophers. Locke's seminal "Essay concerning Toleration," written in 1667,
was surely stimulated and enhanced by his relationship with Ashley.[51]

Ashley and Locke collaborated on the Fundamental Constitutions of Carolina, also called the Grand Model or the Fundamentals, an attempt to transpose
English government and society to Carolina. The Grand Model based governance on property and a three-way balance of power among the common people, a local aristocracy, and the monarchy, represented by the proprietors. This
balance was expected to protect all parties from concentration and corruption

of power. Sir Peter Colleton later acknowledged Locke's contribution, describing the Fundamental Constitutions as "that excellent forme of Government in the composure of which you had soe great a hand."[52] Furthermore, the Fundamentals elaborated the proprietors' consistent commitment to religious toleration and representative government. They endeavored to create a government "without confusion," a state "agreeable unto the Monarchy," while avoiding "a numerous Democracy"—that is, an unstable mobocracy.[53]

The proprietors derived some of their concepts and terminology from a variety of sources, including the contemporary Republic of Venice and James Harrington's *The Commonwealth of Oceana* (1656). Harrington held that land was the basis of political participation and social rank and that political power should not be concentrated in one class over another. This was achieved by wide distribution of land and rotation of officeholding by annual ballot. With the Civil War and Interregnum fresh in their minds, Locke, Ashley, and the other proprietors followed the framework of the Restoration state, which had replaced chaos with stability through equilibrium among the monarch, the aristocracy, and the commons, thereby protecting property and basic liberties through shared power.[54]

Unique in the North American colonies, the Grand Model envisioned feudal elements in Carolina that were never implemented. About half of the provisions in the Grand Model concerned the organization and function of the Lords and were minimally related to the colony. There would be neither manors nor manorial courts. Each county was to have three nobles—a landgrave, a German title; and two caciques, an Indian word for "chief." But in Albemarle there would be too few to be a factor in the government. Strangest of all were leetmen, hereditary serfs, who had long ago disappeared in England and would never appear in Carolina.[55] For stability, the Lords had thought to transpose some of the institutions of old England, but on reflection they realized that these had little relevance to their faraway colonies.

The proprietors became the Palatine's Court, which combined administrative, legislative, and judicial functions in eight courts, each headed by a proprietor. Chairing the court was the eldest of the Lords, henceforth known as the palatine.[56] To perpetuate a landed aristocracy, the counties were to be divided into 12,000-acre tracts—two-fifths for the eight proprietors and the nobles, with the remaining three-fifths for freeholders and manors.[57] So much of Albemarle County was already settled that there was no attempt to survey these parcels. In 1681 and 1684 proprietor Seth Sothel, a man on the make, did patent three 12,000-acre plantations: one adjacent to his home at the head of Albemarle Sound and the other two on the Pamlico River, which then was deep in Tuscarora country and some fifty miles south of the sound.[58]

More important than the dormant feudal elements were the Grand Model's articles on religious freedom that strengthened the proprietary commitment stated in the charter and the Concessions. Freedom of conscience was extended to all who believed in God, including "heathens, Jews, and other dissenters," but denied to atheists. Seven persons remained the minimum to establish a "church or Profession," defined as a group that acknowledged the existence of God and conducted public worship. In consideration of Quakers and other dissenters who would not take oaths, each church decided how they would "witness a truth." Individuals were explicitly forbidden to "disturb or molest any Religious Assembly," to "use any reproachful, Reviling, or abusive language against any Church or Profession," or to "disturb, molest, or persecute another for his speculative opinions in Religion or his way of worship."[59]

While verifying that freemen "have absolute Power and Authority over" their "Negro Slaves" that was not compromised by religious beliefs or worship, the Grand Model also includes a remarkable statement on religious freedom for enslaved persons:

> Since Charity obliges us to wish well to the Souls of all Men and Religion ought to alter nothing in any Man's Civil Estate or Right, it shall be lawful for Slaves, as well as others, to Enter themselves and be of what Church or Profession any of them shall think best, and therefore be as fully Members as any Freeman. But yet, no Slave shall hereby be exempted from that Civil Dominion his Master has over him, but be in all other things in the same State and Condition he was in before.[60]

Within this grant of freedom of conscience for the enslaved is a rare colonial reference to the separation of the spiritual from the civil or material life. In Rhode Island Roger Williams had practiced separation of church and state for decades, and in this instance of protecting freedom of conscience for the enslaved, the Lords Proprietors had arrived at the same conclusion.

Copies of the Fundamental Constitutions, adopted 21 July 1669, were dispatched in August with colonists bound for Port Royal and the following January to Albemarle. In October six proprietors elected the Duke of Albemarle the first palatine. By their next meeting in January 1670, the ailing duke had died and was replaced by his son, Christopher Monck. Lord John Berkeley, now the eldest proprietor, became palatine. The Lords appointed their deputies from the existing council members—Governor Stephens for the palatine, John Jenkins, John Willoughby, Peter Carteret, Francis Godfrey, Major Richard Foster, and the recently arrived John Nixon.[61]

Accompanying the copy of the Fundamentals was a letter to Governor Stephens and the council expressing the proprietors' views toward their new government. They believed that the freemen of Albemarle would have "a Greater Share in the Gover[n]ment." Furthermore, "an equall distribution of power" among the proprietors would prevent tyranny by any one of them and protect every man's "property & liberty" and the colony's peace. Although the document was developed for the Port Royal colony, the proprietors planned to activate the Grand Model in all of their counties and promised a final draft soon.[62]

In their instructions to the governor and council, the proprietors took a pragmatic approach to implementing the Fundamental Constitutions. Realizing that Albemarle had no landgraves and caciques, nor even enough eligible freeholders to staff all the required government positions, they delayed full implementation, hoping "to Come as nigh it as we cann in the present State of affaires."[63] Governor Stephens was authorized to issue writs of election for each of the four precincts to elect five freeholders. In November these twenty representatives would meet with the five proprietors' deputies, who represented the nobles in the assembly. After organizing and electing a speaker, the assembly was to elect five of their members to join the deputies for an expanded council that had the powers of the Grand Council. By maintaining the legislative delegation and making half the seats on the council elective, the proprietors had in fact given the colonists a greater share in the government. As in the Concessions, the Lords confirmed that officeholders could subscribe or affirm rather than take an oath of office. This temporary arrangement became permanent as the years went by, supplementing the Fundamentals and the governor's instructions. The governor and five deputies comprised the Palatine's Court, which had the jurisdiction of the General Court.[64]

The new council of governor, deputies, and elected assistants was granted legislative initiative, which many historians have interpreted as weakening the assembly. The unicameral assembly, however, had always included the governor and deputies. Adding the elected assemblymen to the council increased the role of the freeholder, and the expanded council likely functioned as a legislative committee, strengthening, rather than weakening, the assembly.[65]

The compensation for use of private property for public needs, such as roads, bridges, public buildings, towns, markets, or draining swamps to improve public health, was addressed by the precinct courts. An appointed jury of twelve men, called surveyors, would assess the damage, and the council would levy a precinct or county tax to cover the claim.[66]

To this day, local courts in North Carolina are descended from the precinct courts authorized under the Fundamental Constitutions. These precinct courts established a strong tradition of local government in the colony. Composed of a steward and four justices, the court met quarterly and heard all noncapital criminal cases and civil suits for less than fifty pounds, so that the courts' business concerned almost every aspect of the colony's daily life. Constables, elected annually, were the precinct peace officers. The earliest surviving minutes are for Perquimans Precinct in 1688, although references to precinct courts exist from earlier in the 1680s and the first mention of a precinct official is Justice of the Peace Francis Tomes in 1672.[67]

Drawing on their experiences in revolutionary England and in Virginia, the founding settlers in Albemarle's isolated frontier anchored their courts on English rights, liberties, and justice as embedded in the liberal proprietary Fundamental Constitutions. Although often portrayed by historians as a disorderly colony wracked by turmoil, the general and precinct court records reveal a well-established system of courts dedicated to maintaining a stable society by securing property and protecting life and liberty. The dockets were dominated by civil suits regarding property transfer, debts, contracts, commodity values, administration of estates, and regulation of public infrastructure—roads, mills, landings, bridges, and ferries.

Less than 20 percent were criminal cases, mostly about property theft, damage, and trespass. Indicative of a relatively permissive backcountry society, the small number of cases for slander, contempt for authority, and flouting public morality far outweighed the violence of assault or the rare murder. Punishment was surprisingly lenient for the era, usually fines and forfeitures or, for those unable to pay, a whipping or the stocks. There were rare banishments and occasional executions by hanging. Often severe sentences were reduced on an appeal to the court for mercy and a bond for good behavior for a year and a day.[68]

All officials were to swear or subscribe allegiance to the king and fidelity to the proprietors and the Grand Model. Reiterating liberties provided in the charters and the Concessions and Agreement, the Fundamentals stated that any man who "For Religeon sake be not Free to Sweare" the oath of allegiance to the king and the proprietors was allowed the alternative of subscribing in a book.[69] This provision, which liberated Quakers to serve in the government, would stand for thirty-five years.

Under the Concessions, freeholders had the right to vote and hold office. Proposed property qualifications in the Fundamentals were 100 acres for constables, 200 acres for General Court jury, 300 acres for precinct register, grand jury, and judges, and 500 acres for county judges, sheriff, and assembly delegates. These requirements would have excluded all who could meet only the 50-acre requirement for voting, precinct jury, and precinct register.[70] Since the instructions wisely allowed "freeholders" to continue to serve in the assembly and other positions, the extant records indicate no significant changes in officeholders.[71]

An innovation in the Grand Model was a register of births, marriages, and deaths to be kept in each precinct. Quakers also kept such records in their meeting minutes, as did Anglicans in their vestry minutes after the church was established in the next century. Early registers for Pasquotank and Perquimans precincts survive, but North Carolina's vital statistics would not be kept by the government again until the twentieth century.[72]

Also dispatched with the Grand Model were assembly acts that addressed immigration, land policy, trade, and marriage, which were ratified by the Lords in January 1670. To conform to the Fundamentals, the laws were "enacted by the Pallatine and Lords Proprietors with the advice and consent of the Grand Assembly." To encourage immigration, there was a five-year prohibition on suing colonists for past debt, and new settlers were exempted from taxes for one year. Three laws favored settlement over land speculation: a two-year residence requirement was imposed for sale of headrights; over the next five years grants were limited to 660 acres in single parcels; and vacant improved land had to be occupied, or it could be repossessed and sold. For better regulation of trade, monopolizing commodities for resale was forbidden, and to discourage inroads by Virginia traders, Carolina residents had exclusive rights to the fur trade. Finally, marriage was recognized as a civil contract. Since there were no ministers in the colony, couples appeared before the governor or a council member with witnesses and declared their willingness to be husband and wife; a certificate would be signed and registered in the county or the precinct.[73]

Fortunately, the proprietors encouraged implementation of the articles of the Fundamental Constitutions that retained the established governance principles of the Concessions and Agreement. The few landgraves and caciques in northern Carolina bore their titles as an honorific. The "sacred and unalterable" Grand Model, revised five times over thirty years, was never officially accepted in either of the Carolinas and would, after the last bare-bones version in 1698, disappear.[74] Longer than southern Carolina, Albemarle County maintained a stable relationship with the Lords because the proprietors recognized the inappropriateness of imposing such an elaborate scheme of government on its sparsely settled frontier. Furthermore, the colonists had learned that if they persisted in advocating a practice that worked, the proprietors would eventually acquiesce.

How would the Grand Model, which had some features with so little relation to life in Albemarle County, have been received by Governor Stephens, who had so far navigated a rocky course and compiled a record of solid achievement? We will never know, since the constitution, the proprietors' instructions to the governor and council, and the acts of the General Assembly were being sent into a void. Governor Stephens had died early in 1670.

CHAPTER SIX

Unrest, Upheaval, and Rebellion

Testing the Limits of Freedom

First the occasion of . . . imprisoning the Presidt is, that thereby
the Countrey may have a free parlem[en]t & that from them
their aggreivances may be sent home to the Lords.
—John Culpeper, 1677

S IR WILLIAM BERKELEY entered his study at Green Spring plantation and
crossed wearily to his writing table by the window. It was 7 March 1670.
For twenty-one years he had borne the burden, mostly alone, of governing Virginia, His Majesty's most important North American colony, through
one of England's most turbulent eras. The sad news of the death of his ami-
able friend and protégé, Albemarle governor Samuel Stephens, had torn him
with conflicting emotions. His genuine grief at the loss was tempered by vexa-
tion, even anger, over the perpetually troublesome little colony on his southern
border—a situation for which he bore some responsibility as an inattentive
proprietor.

Sir William sharpened his quill and wrote to the Albemarle council and
assembly of his "inexpressible griefe" and his concern that "this unexpected
Losse of this worthy person" might affect the colony's growth. Berkeley valued
Stephens as "a man of approved Courage great Integrity and a lover of the Collony." Overseeing Albemarle as commander and proprietary governor, Stephens
had guided the region well, effectively balancing the proprietors' instructions
with the colony's established land and governance practices.

Having heard that "great factions fomented against" Stephens, some even
"Soe Insolent as to draw their Swords against him," Berkeley insisted that the
council not elect as governor anyone who had offered "violence and indignityes
to the late worthy Governor."[1] Sir William had no cause for concern, for the
council met on 10 March and chose Peter Carteret to be governor. A council
member since 1665 and assistant governor under both Drummond and Stephens, this cousin of proprietor Sir George Carteret managed the proprietors'

plantation on Colleton Island. As acting governor during Drummond's frequent absences, he had been vital to the success of the colony's first administration. Carteret continued to serve capably in his posts under Governor Stephens, who had also appointed him commander of the county militia.[2]

THE FINAL DRAFT of the Fundamental Constitutions and the governor's instructions, dispatched in the fall of 1670, were probably received late in the year. While increased participation in the government was welcome, many were appalled by the Fundamentals' proposed policies that threatened the Great Deed of Grant's land distribution and quitrent. Governor Carteret and the council responded respectfully to the Lords on May 16, pointing out changes that contributed to "various Comotions disorders & irregularities." Confident that the proprietors meant them to be "a free happy & florishinge people," they outlined their grievances: the mandated survey of the county into 10,000-acre tracts, which the colonists declared "Impossible"; doubling the quitrent; limiting landholding to occupants; and removing the assembly's right to initiate legislation. In hopes of redress, the assembly had delayed convening, and it was evident the government had not yet been altered.[3]

The April 1672 assembly elected Valentine Bird speaker, and James Blount, Thomas Jarvis, William Jennings, Edmund Chancy, Thomas Pearce, and Speaker Bird as assistants to join the deputies for the Grand Council. Faced with an impasse, the council chose delegates to present their concerns to the Lords "Man to Man." Governor Carteret and the respected John Harvey, as agents of the "People of Albemarle," were to request

- that quitrents be the same as in Virginia;
- that the Lords provide arms and ammunition for the colony's defense;
- that children have the same headrights as servants;
- that laws be changed that limited tracts to 660 acres, forbade suits for five years, and established monopolies; and
- that Virginia repeal their restrictions on shipping and their two-shilling-per-hogshead fee.

In an accompanying letter, the council reported that they had organized under proprietary instructions, having "extracted the best and as wee Conceive ye most usefull" elements of government.[4] That summer Carteret and Harvey embarked for England. In New York, business matters forced Harvey to return home, leaving Carteret to continue alone.

Years later, attempting to deflect blame for their rebellious province, the proprietors declared that Governor Carteret had left the county "in ill order &

worse hands."They berated him for failing to curb the New England trade and, at the behest of Indian traders, discouraging settlement south of Albemarle Sound.[5] The leaders of Albemarle, however, knew that both fur traders and New England mariners were essential to the local economy. Furthermore, at this stage settlement was too sparse to desire expansion into dangerous Indian territory. The last word on Carteret came from the council, who informed the Lords of the "goodness of our Governor by whose prudence and Integrity God hath blessed us since his receiveing yt charge wth more unity & tranquility than ever before."[6] Unity and tranquility would rarely grace the colony over the next twenty years.

With the Duke of Albemarle in failing health, Ashley emerged as de facto chair of the proprietors. After the Cape Fear colony failed, he realized that if Carolina were to succeed the Lords must be directly involved and must invest more. Although Albemarle County was on course, the proprietors were more interested in the promising new settlement proposed for Port Royal. To support this venture, in early 1669 Ashley persuaded his partners to ante up £500 each and to invest an additional £200 a year for the next four years. For the first time the proprietors were making a significant financial commitment to the province, and the result was the successful seating of a new Charles Town the next year.[7] By 1672 Lord Ashley would reach the apogee of his political power as the Earl of Shaftesbury and Lord Chancellor.[8]

The indifferent Berkeley did not join the others in supporting Carolina, which would compete with Virginia, and since he was separated from them by an ocean, they had little recourse. Frustrated, the other partners decided that the way out of Sir William's noncompliance was to acquire his proprietary share in exchange for a swath of northern Carolina. Having garnered little from Albemarle County but complaints, Shaftesbury considered this a satisfactory solution. Secret negotiations with Berkeley began, but rumors circulating in Albemarle that the officious Sir William might become sole proprietor sent shudders through the populace. Documents authorizing this agreement were secretly signed in May and November 1672, and the Lords, considering that a deal had been struck, proceeded as if Sir William were in charge. This may explain why the council deputies, who had four-year terms, were not reappointed in 1675, allowing the colony's legal government to lapse.[9]

Why was the transaction never completed? It may have been simply a matter of timing. Disposing of a proprietary share that had emanated from the Crown would have required a charter amendment, if not a new charter. In 1675 Virginia was headed toward Bacon's Rebellion and Sir William's ultimate removal, disgrace, and death. To quell mounting criticism and persistent rumors that they wished to divest themselves of Albemarle, in October 1676 the proprietors reassured the colony's council and assembly, vowing that "wee neither have nor ever will parte with the County of Albemarle to any person whatsoever" and will "mayntaine and preserve you in the English Rights and Liberties."[10]

———

FOR NEARLY A CENTURY historians have attributed the political turmoil in Albemarle County to factional strife. Although launched as a power struggle, political unrest in the 1670s became much more than that, ultimately stretching the limits of freedom. Furthermore, the long-standing view that well-defined "proprietary" and "antiproprietary" parties vied for control does not bear close scrutiny.[11] Sir William Berkeley's hearsay about "great factions" at odds with Governor Stephens apparently referred to individuals rather than cliques. The earliest settlers, most of whom preceded the propriety, consistently filled the council seats, won election to the assembly, dispensed justice on the Palatine's and precinct courts, and desired to maintain their hegemony. The issue was not pro- or antiproprietary, but merely holding on to the reins of power. These men would oppose any policy, law, or individual that threatened the colony's precarious economy or the freedom, openness, and tolerance that derived from the Lords Proprietors. For their part, the Lords would continually turn to them to restore the colony's stability. Although there would be personal challenges, too few colonists were connected to English officials to mount significant opposition to those who had led the government since 1665.

Then what was the source of the unrest? The answer to those involved was personal vendettas fueled by "ambition and envy or the private pekes [piques] and particular disgust" toward opponents.[12] In a 1670 suit, Surveyor General Thomas Eastchurch suffered distraint of property for alleged debt. Eastchurch, who considered the case frivolous and unjust, was absent from the county at the time. When he failed to appear in court, Judge John Willoughby issued an order for his appearance. Under warrant from Governor Carteret, Captain Thomas Cullen seized goods to cover the indebtedness. In December 1671 Eastchurch protested the "spoyle of my estate" and urged the governor to protect his property from "some mens madness." When Eastchurch attempted to appeal his case to the Lords, Willoughby refused, calling his court "the Court of Courts and Jury of Juries."[13] The consequences of this altercation would be profound. From that point on, Eastchurch methodically accumulated political power, plotting revenge on the entrenched leaders—especially Willoughby and Cullen.[14]

Contemporaries called the founding planter-merchants the "Popular" party, or "Populists." Their opponents, loyal to the proprietors, were known as the "Loyal" party, or "Loyalists."[15] In reality, neither faction supported the proprietors' land policies, and both welcomed the political and religious freedom granted by the Lords. Both sides firmly believed they represented the colony's best interests, but Populists, drawing on their long experience as county leaders, had the stronger case. In an age of class deference, Loyalists viewed "the people" as a "mutunous" mob and held that the future lay in accommodating the proprietors.[16] Whether factions or vendettas, until 1676 a struggle for power between the "ins" and the "outs" subsumed the colony's political life. Albemarle became the most contentious of the North American colonies, enduring coups and countercoups in which citizens publicly berated their officials, engaged in court altercations and brawls, and overthrew tyrannical officials and governors.

PRIOR TO HIS DEPARTURE for England on 16 May 1672, Governor Carteret, following Grand Model procedure, appointed council member Lieutenant Colonel John Jenkins as deputy governor to serve until Carteret returned or until the proprietors sent a new governor. Among the earliest settlers in the Albemarle, John and Joanna Jenkins had obtained a 1663 grant for 700 acres where they were already living, on Harvey's Neck. A Virginia planter of some means, Jenkins was also a master mariner and ship owner who had been engaged in trade with Bermuda. Throughout the stormy times that ensued, no new governor commissioned by the proprietors would be installed until John Harvey became president of the council in 1679.[17]

Carteret was confident that he had left the colony in capable hands. The November 1673 assembly, again led by Speaker Bird, was the first assembly under the Fundamental Constitutions, which established a biennial pattern that is followed to this day. Precinct elections were held by the freeholders in early September, and the session convened a month later.[18] No one could foresee that the colony would face trade duties that threatened its fragile economy, a two-year Indian war, and a political and constitutional crisis that would split the colony and spin out of control, leading to a coup, a countercoup, and, finally, a rebellion.

The colony's purported "unity and tranquility" masked a seething personal and political power struggle that erupted soon after Carteret embarked. Thomas Eastchurch had returned to Albemarle, still nursing resentment over the seizure of his property. Emboldened by his proprietary commission as surveyor general, Eastchurch sought the vacant governor's office through an influential relative in England. Although the proprietors considered Eastchurch "a gentleman of a very good family" and "a very discreet and worthy man," they were too absorbed with their southern colony and negotiations with Sir William Berkeley to fill the post.[19]

When his feelers to the Lords failed, in 1673 Eastchurch won election to the assembly and began to build a power base that became the Loyal party. Among his minions were the newly arrived Timothy Biggs and Irishman Thomas Miller, who became his most ardent supporter. Biggs married the widow Mary Catchmaid and lived at her plantation on Durant's Neck in Perquimans. A council member, he also served contentious terms as a customs official. Miller, an apothecary and merchant prone to overimbibe, could be vulgar and abusive, especially when in his cups. Controversy swirled about him throughout his political career. Eastchurch and Miller were truly an odd pair.[20]

Compounding the adversities of a hazardous coastline and Virginia's high freight rates, England's navigation acts were a credible threat to Albemarle's economy. The acts restricted carriers to English or colonial vessels and crews and required certain products, including tobacco, to be shipped only to England. Enterprising New Englanders, who dominated intercolonial coastal trade, circumvented the law by landing the tobacco in Massachusetts Bay or Rhode Island. Relabeled as fish, it was illegally shipped to Ireland, Scotland, the Canary Islands, and mainland Europe.[21] The navigation acts succeeded in driving away Dutch competitors, but an unintended consequence was the proliferation of smuggling by New England merchants. To curb the illicit trade, the Plantation Duty Act of 1673 required a duty of one penny per pound on tobacco shipped without a certificate of bond from the port of origin. This law struck directly at Albemarle County's planters because the outlets for their tobacco were either Virginia or New England.

The proprietors considered that New England traders, by paying low prices for commodities, "eate out & ruin'd ye place" and complained that the half dozen New England merchants who handled Albemarle's tobacco "Bostoniz'd" the trade.[22] In 1676 the Lords instructed the governor to "deverte the trade of our People under you with those of New England." To encourage direct trade with England, they requested the inlet depths, believing that the measurements had been concealed by persons who had "joyn'd with some of New England to engross that poore trade you have and Keepe you still under hatches."[23] In truth, the ever-changing inlets were shallow and restricted safe entry to smaller sloops and ketches engaged in the intercolonial trade.

Despite declining population, the Chowanokes, who resided in the Chowan River valley, were the largest Indian tribe in Albemarle County. In 1675, beginning in New England with King Philip's War, hostilities between colonists and Natives swept down the Atlantic seaboard into Virginia, prompting Nathaniel Bacon to raise an unauthorized militia force that he eventually led against the unresponsive Governor Berkeley, igniting Bacon's Rebellion. With the frontier aflame, Bacon's militia tracked the Susquehanna Indians to southern Virginia near the Carolina border. There Bacon persuaded local Occaneechi to attack the northern invaders on the nearby Meherrin River, and some Susquehanna remnants fled east to join their Meherrin kinsmen. After Bacon's men destroyed and looted the Roanoke River Occaneechi stronghold, the Meherrin-Susquehanna sought refuge with the Chowanokes. Although the Chowanokes had lived peaceably under a proprietary treaty since Albemarle's founding, the recent violence and Bacon's treachery convinced them that no Indian was safe, and they yielded to appeals from their new neighbors to join them in retaliation. Thus in the fall of 1676 began the Chowan River War, the colony's first protracted Indian conflict. Few details of the hostilities are known, but the Chowanokes and their allies reportedly committed "sundry murders and depredations" that nearly interdicted overland travel with Virginia. The Indians were not "wholy Subdued" until the militia, partly raised from fugitive Bacon rebels, engaged in a yearlong "open war" that produced losses on both sides.[24]

By the summer of 1675 colonists' apprehensions were fueled by lack of communication from the proprietors, rumors that Virginia would absorb the colony, and the questionable status of council deputies whose terms had ended the previous year. Only Deputy Governor Jenkins could claim legitimacy. There was no term limit on his commission: he was to serve until Carteret's return or his replacement by the proprietors. As Eastchurch solidified Loyalist opposition in the assembly and the council, the Populist leaders—Governor Jenkins, George Durant, Valentine Bird, and a recent arrival, John Culpeper—laid plans to protect their hold on the government. Formerly serving as an assemblyman and surveyor general in South Carolina, Culpeper arrived in 1673 with a dicey reputation. His enemies would later say that he was "forced to fly from Ashley River for his turbulent and factious carriage there."[25]

To thwart Eastchurch's growing strength, the Populists focused on Miller, whose loose tongue when under the influence was the Loyalists' weak link. In the taprooms of local ordinaries Miller often disparaged the royal family in ways that bordered on treason. Once he declared in a "Rebellious Trayterous Manner" that there would never be "good times in England" as long as there was a king. On hearing a false report that the Duke of York had died, Miller declared that "som of the rest would not bee long after him." John Culpeper reported Miller's indiscretions to John Nixon, a justice and council member, but Nixon dismissed the charges, knowing Miller's propensity to "bee always talking of such Matters."[26]

Meeting in Jenkins's home, the Populists conspired to entrap Miller by prodding him to more egregious denunciation of the king. At Harris's tavern Miller declared he would not defend the king because he "setts his people to fight in unrighteous Causes," that the Cavaliers were "Rogues," and that "there was noe

Righteous dealinge amongst the Cavaleares, for the King had his hand in a Whores placket."[27] That autumn in Francis Godfrey's tavern Miller was caught in blasphemy, saying in a "most Atheisticall and Blasphemous Manner" that the sacrament of the Lord's Supper is "a litle Hogg's wash powred in a piggs Trough."[28] Such sacrilege would have offended virtually everyone.

When commissions for customs officials arrived from the Lord Treasurer, the nominees were absent. In such a case the governor could fill local appointments. Since the Popular party opposed enforcement of the customs duties, Governor Jenkins took no action.[29] In September, however, Loyalists won a surprising majority in the assembly. Eastchurch was elected speaker and implemented well-laid plans to impeach Jenkins under charges of "severall misdemeanours." The governor was arrested and held prisoner. Eastchurch promptly reported his actions to the Lords, who, having heard only Eastchurch's side, replied that they were "very well pleased" with Jenkins's removal and the "Order and settlement" of the government.[30]

Hearing rumors from Populist councilman William Crawford and New England traders that prices would double if the duty were collected, the planters became "very mutunous and reviled & threatened" the council. Eastchurch allayed their fears by appointing former speaker Captain Valentine Bird as collector of customs. Accepted by both factions, Bird had just begun his duties when the Chowan River War began.[31]

Still smarting from the General Court's earlier injustice, Eastchurch was now in position to take revenge. When he ordered his old nemesis, Judge Willoughby, to appear before the Palatine's Court, Willoughby refused the summons and thrashed the constable. Outlawed for contempt, Willoughby was forced into exile in Virginia along with Patrick White. Another easy mark was councilman Thomas Cullen, who as a frontier trader had earlier sold weapons to Indians, some of whom were now hostile. Since selling arms to an enemy was punishable by death, warrants for Cullen's arrest were issued, but he, too, fled.[32]

In early 1676 the Popular coalition, well equipped because of the Indian threat, organized resistance against the tobacco duty. Bird, White, and George Durant led armed men who forced Speaker Eastchurch to remit three farthings of the duty, ostensibly to pay for defense.[33] Durant, "one of the ablest and most influential men in the county," was one of the colony's founders and a leader of the Popular party. Rarely holding public office, over a long career he generally wielded his influence behind the scenes.[34] His open involvement in this armed tax protest was unusual, and opponent Timothy Biggs attributed it to Durant's desire to ship a "considerable quantitie of Tobacco" to New England. While Eastchurch reeled from this confrontation, the armed "riotous persons" in a "Rebell Rout" released Jenkins and elected him "Generalissime." The rebels

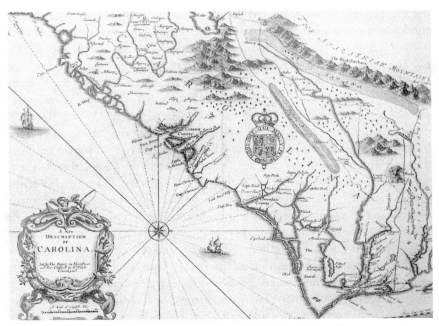

John Speed's map, *A New Description of Carolina*, was published in 1676.
Courtesy of the author.

closed the General Court and dissolved the assembly, forcing Eastchurch to
scurry to Virginia and thence to England. By late March Jenkins had resumed
his position as deputy governor, with Durant as attorney general.[35]

Miller was arrested, indicted for blasphemy and seditious and treasonable
utterances, and tried in the assembly in March. Depositions were entered and
witnesses' testimonies recorded, but Miller was not sentenced immediately because of the judges' uncertain tenure. He was held in irons until May, when
Governor Berkeley ordered him to Virginia for trial. Under armed guard,
Miller was taken to Jamestown, accompanied by John Culpeper and council
deputy Timothy Biggs. Acquitted in June by Berkeley and the council, Miller
departed for England.[36] With Eastchurch and Miller gone and the government
controlled by Populists, the Loyalists were left in disarray.

Before the proprietors that fall, Eastchurch presented a convincing version
of the past year's events. The Lords were swayed by his gentlemanly demeanor,
family connections, and apparent concern for the welfare of the colony. Proprietary commissions were issued naming Eastchurch governor and surveyor
general of Albemarle County and governor of the region south of the sound on

the Pamlico and Neuse Rivers. Miller was commissioned a council deputy and the colony's secretary, or register. The other deputies appointed were James Hill, Timothy Biggs, Richard Foster, and John Nixon. With the exception of Foster, the new council members were Loyalists, marking the most significant change in the government in a decade.[37] George Durant, an emissary for the Popular faction, had arrived too late. Hearing about Eastchurch's elevation, Durant supposedly retorted that if Eastchurch became governor, he "would turn Rebell."[38]

From Eastchurch and Miller, as well as Durant, the proprietors gained fresh knowledge of potential perils facing Albemarle County. The Indian conflicts that had spread throughout the colonies had reached Virginia and threatened to spill over into their colony. Their instructions to Governor Eastchurch warned him to practice "strict justice, friendship and amity with the neighbour Indians and not suffer them to have any just cause to complain of any oppression or Injustice." Knowing that Albemarle's prolonged political strife could very well spawn another Bacon's Rebellion, the Lords stressed that the governor "take spetiall care that Justice be duly administered" and not be "tedious, troublesome nor chargable," for "men of prudence and of estates" would not come to the colony if "liberty and property" were not secure. They advised that the assembly pass laws that protected the ancient rights of Englishmen. In accordance with the Fundamental Constitutions, the Lords specifically listed trial by a jury of freeholders, due process of law, no arbitrary arrests, a speedy trial, and assurance of a "just defense."[39]

Meanwhile, both Virginia and Maryland had faced rebellions of their own. In Virginia the entrenched Berkeley was nearly toppled by Nathaniel Bacon, who took Jamestown and temporarily ousted the governor. Bolstered by English troops and Bacon's untimely death, Berkeley subdued the rebels and executed their leaders.[40] Maryland, founded as a Catholic refuge, suffered from continual tension between Catholics and Protestants. The discontented Protestant majority launched a protest in Calvert County that was crushed by prompt action and the execution of its leaders.[41]

The flight of surviving Baconites into forests and swamps south of the James may have influenced events in neighboring Albemarle. Nansemond County was rife with Bacon's followers, while Albemarle's first governor, William Drummond, was a key adviser to Bacon and paid for it with his life. For several months in early 1676 John Culpeper was in Jamestown, where he may have conferred with Drummond or other Baconites. That September Bacon commented, "It is the mind of this Country [Virginia] and of Maryland, of Carolina alsoe to cast off theire Governors."[42] Bacon himself planned that in the event of failure Albemarle would be a refuge. Oddly, the known Bacon rebels in Albemarle became the governor's personal guard, a reversal of their roles in Virginia. Whether Carolinians were stimulated by Virginia's uprising or not, the swift and bloody vengeance exacted by Governor Berkeley was a vivid warning to proceed with caution.

In the spring of 1677 Eastchurch and Miller left England for Carolina by way of the West Indies. In Nevis, Eastchurch courted and married an heiress to "a considerable fortune."[43] Tarrying on Nevis for an extended honeymoon, Eastchurch sent Miller ahead with an appointment as president of the council and commander-in-chief. From Nevis Miller sailed to Bermuda, where he booked passage with Solomon Summers on the shallop *Success*, which reached Currituck on 15 July.[44] Shortly after landing, Miller, considered Eastchurch's pawn, was confronted at Major Richard Foster's house by the volatile Patrick White, who threatened him at knifepoint, declaring that he "would never have the Kings Customes settled there." Bearing a commission to Foster as a proprietor's deputy, Miller did not blame him for White's assault. Foster was leery of Miller and at first refused the appointment but changed his mind when he was offered command of the county's militia with the rank of lieutenant colonel.[45]

From Currituck, *Success* sailed to the Little River landing of Timothy Biggs on Durant's Neck. Miller and the crew lodged with Biggs, who joined Miller in plundering the cargo, taking it for personal use or sale. When Summers protested the theft of the cargo entrusted to him, Miller threatened him, driving Summers and the enslaved Jack across the peninsula to George Durant's inn, managed in his absence by his wife Ann.[46]

Miller summoned the assembly, presented his commissions, and had Eastchurch proclaimed governor.[47] Since Eastchurch had not followed the protocol of confirmation by the council in person, he was not officially governor, and his appointment of Miller had no legal standing, an oversight that eventually undermined Miller. Nevertheless, the assembly, packed with Eastchurch Loyalists, accepted Miller as acting governor. The Populists suspected that he would seek retribution for his prior treatment, which indeed he did. Prolonged disruption of the courts had caused a backlog of cases, and Miller and the new deputies, meeting as the Palatine's Court, concentrated on punishing Populists who had deposed Eastchurch in 1676. As election time neared, Miller issued writs for the burgesses and attempted to manipulate the election by setting new procedures and disenfranchising those convicted by the court. Running on the issue of the burdensome one penny per pound duty on tobacco, the Popular faction prevailed, but Miller refused to seat them.[48]

Although the Chowan River War was waning, Miller recruited a "pipeing guard," ostensibly to defend the colony from the Indian menace. Funded by customs revenue, the company of nearly forty soldiers was described as "Loose fellows & of Bacons Company runn out of Virginia after Bacon was dead."

A hardnosed set, this armed band made a colorful show, bedecked in brightly hued knots and flowered ribbons. Personally loyal to Miller, they served primarily as his bodyguard and enforcers to intimidate his opponents.[49] The Loyalist assembly's investigation of the conduct of the war not surprisingly found the Jenkins government guilty of neglect and subject to heavy fines.[50]

The thorniest problem continued to be customs collection. Summoning Bird, Miller demanded his resignation and appointed two new deputy collectors, Henry Hudson in Currituck and Timothy Biggs in Pasquotank. Miller used his guard to collect customs, and duties began to flow into the government's coffers. Miller proudly claimed that in five months' time his subordinates had accumulated tobacco and bonds equal to 327,068 pounds, or 817 hogsheads, and seized illegal imported goods, including the vessel *Patience*, for a total of £1,242.82.01, £700 of which Bird had previously gathered.[51]

As his power increased, Miller arrested Populist leaders and put prices on their heads, levied excessive fines, and manipulated and restricted the assembly. Hearing that George Durant was expected from overseas, Miller vowed to imprison him and "hang him as soone as he came home." When he finally realized that the colony "would not endure his Governm[en]t" any longer, Miller used his guard to disarm the inhabitants.[52] From the Loyalist viewpoint, Miller took his obligations as governor seriously, tackling issues that had plagued the colony for years. Miller himself believed that he had ended the Indian threat and unified "to the generall satisfaction of ye inhabitants" a divided colony that had been in "miserable confusion."[53] The opposition, however, seethed over Miller's arbitrary and perverse pursuit of his adversaries.

Obviously, the rebellion was well planned and organized, waiting only for the arrival of weapons on the brig *Carolina*. Miller considered it not "accidentall," but a conspiracy, or a "mature or deliberate contrivance" of "poysoning the peoples eares, unsetling and disquieting their minds" with lies, such as claiming that the quitrent was to be doubled to two pence per acre and then raised to six pence. The Loyalists labeled the Populist leaders "Infamous & Scandalous persons" who had duped "poore & ignorant Subjectes . . . through fals delusions."[54]

On 1 December 1677 *Carolina*, armed with five guns, sailed into the Pasquotank River and dropped anchor at Crawford's landing. On her maiden voyage, laden with trade goods, rum, arms, and ammunition, *Carolina* was commanded by New Englander Zachariah Gillam, with George Durant as chief mate. As first officer, Durant was left in charge of the brig when Gillam went ashore to clear customs. Questioning Gillam about tobacco he had shipped earlier, Miller demanded duties for "180 hogsheads." When Gillam produced proof of payment, Miller ignored the evidence, had Gillam and his crew arrested, and seized the ship's papers. Learning that Durant was aboard, Miller, armed with a brace of pistols, rowed out to the vessel at eleven o'clock that evening. Confronting Durant on deck, Miller, in an "insolent and Hectoring manner," drew a pistol and threatened to arrest him.[55] Replying that his duty was to protect the brig and cargo, Durant refused to yield and was backed up by Gillam's crew. When Gillam returned to the vessel at midnight, he found the two men conversing in the great cabin. Miller soon left, but Durant, distrusting Miller, remained on board.[56]

When word of the shocking incident on *Carolina* spread through Pasquotank Precinct, the insurrection erupted. The next day Lieutenant Edward Wells and William Nevill led over thirty soldiers who forcibly entered Timothy Biggs's house, frightened his family, and ransacked the public records, seizing commissions and customs receipts. The same band, now led by Wells, Bird, and Captain William Crawford and armed with pistols and cutlasses from Gillam's brig, seized Miller, Biggs, and John Nixon at Crawford's house. Biggs wrote that they were taken with "great viallenre" by the mob, who imprisoned them, "Searching . . . for writteings takeing all we had." The president and the two council deputies were held in close confinement at Crawford's plantation.[57]

The leaders of the rebellion—Culpeper, Crawford, Durant, Bird, and Gillam—gathered on *Carolina*, which was anchored offshore with "Jack Ensign Flag and Penon flying." During the afternoon of 3 December, Culpeper wrote the "Remonstrance," a call for the entire colony to revolt, declaring that President Miller had been overthrown so that a "free parlem[en]t" could appeal the county's grievances to the proprietors. Omitting "many heinous matters," Miller's major transgressions were

- denying free election of the assembly,
- cheating the county of 130,000 pounds of tobacco,
- levying an excess tax of 250 pounds,
- spending 20,000 pounds of tobacco on his "pipeing guard,"
- demanding an excessive £1,000 entry fee, and
- arbitrarily arresting Captain Gillam and attempting to arrest George Durant.

These actions, Culpeper declared, and his "many other Injuries, mischiefes and grievances," will lead to "inevitable ruein . . . (unlesse prevented) which wee are now about to doe and hope & expect that you will joyne with us." Copies were immediately dispatched to every precinct.[58] Samuel Pricklove carried a copy of the "Remonstrance" to Perquimans but was arrested by Marshal Edward Wade, a Loyalist. Three days later, Culpeper led an armed band to Chowan, seized Wade, and released Pricklove. Chowan officials were taken to Durant's house and imprisoned until a general meeting could convene. Accompanying

the "Remonstrance" to Currituck was a message to the county's militia commander, Lieutenant Colonel Foster, to muster soldiers, seize deputy collector
Henry Hudson, and bring him to Durant's plantation, now headquarters of
the rebellion.[59]

Foster called a meeting, ostensibly to elect burgesses for the coming assembly. On hearing the "Remonstrance," the surly crowd vented their frustra-
tions, shouting, "Wee will have noe Lo[r]ds noe Landgraves noe Cassiques we
renounce them all and fly to the King's protection." After half an hour, Foster
cautioned them that "that way would not doe" and regained control of the
throng, who then "cryed up" in favor of the Lords. The burgesses were elected
and instructed to insist on free trade, no duties, and freedom to send their
tobacco where they wished, and to try Miller for "odious crimes." With shouts
of "God dame ye Collector" ringing out, Hudson feared that he might be murdered on the spot. When the mob cooled down, the meeting adjourned and the
delegation departed by water for Durant's Neck, where all of the prisoners were
now guarded by more than sixty soldiers. When the Currituck flotilla passed
Carolina, a salute of three guns was fired.[60] *Carolina* thereafter weighed anchor
and sailed to Durant's landing, uniting all of the rebel forces.

On the morning of 20 December, a patrol led by Bird ransacked Miller's
farm. Buried in a tobacco hogshead was a box containing the county seal and
papers, which they took to Durant's plantation. By then a crowd had gathered,
and in the afternoon Miller was brought out in irons. According to the prisoner's later report, the rowdy throng, fortified by a generous flow of rum from
Gillam's ship, overturned the stocks and pillory and threw them into the river.
Miller claimed that Crawford boasted that "if ye Govr came among them there
or the Lords either, they would serve them ye same sauce." Scouts were sent
out to "seize, imprison, or chase out of ye county" those refusing to join them.[61]

The Currituck contingent arrived on 24 December with collector Hudson
as their prisoner, and to the sound of a drum roll the eighteen-member rebel
parliament was convened. Thomas Cullen, whom Eastchurch had outlawed,
was elected speaker. The delegates were James Blount, Anthony Slocum, John
Varnham, Henry Bonner, John Jenkins, Samuel Pricklove, William Therrill,
Caleb Calloway, Alexander Lillington, William Crawford, Valentine Bird,
William Jennings, Thomas Jarvis, Enoch Billings, Richard Sanders, Patrick
White, and William Sears, the drummer. Miller believed the government
reached a new low with the drummer's election to the assembly, which he
derided as a "confused rabble" or a drunken mob.[62] In truth, the delegates were
planters and merchants who had governed the colony from the beginning.
Most were either the colony's founders or longtime residents; about half were
militia officers; several were justices of the precinct and county courts; two had

been speakers of the assembly; nine had served on the council; many had been burgesses in the assembly; and the ranks included a former governor. These men regarded Miller, Eastchurch, and their supporters as usurpers.[63] From the General Assembly "ye supream Court" was formed. Richard Foster was elected chief justice, with associate justices Jenkins, Crawford, Blount, White, and Bird, of whom all except White had judicial experience. On fabricated charges, council members Timothy Biggs, accused of murder, and John Nixon, accused of treason, were brought out to be tried before this court.[64]

Miller was dragged out again in irons, and a grand jury was impaneled to indict him. Mordecai Bowdoin, a New England trader in arrears for customs duties, was elected foreman. According to Miller, others from the crowd, of whom "scarce 4 . . . could read or write," were selected for jury duty. Culpeper guided the inexperienced jury through the indictment. The sheriff summoned "scandalous infamous and illiterate persons" from the "confused rabble" for the petit jury, and another New England trader, Joseph Winslow, was appointed foreman. When the jurors began muttering "threats vows and bloody oathes of stabbing hanging, pistolling or poisoning," Miller was convinced his life was forfeit. Before the proceedings spiraled out of control, Durant pulled Gillam aside and asked him to intercede quietly with the court.[65]

At this moment, in "ye very nick of tyme," a proclamation of Governor East-church, now in Virginia, was read before the crowd, condemning the rebellion and ordering the rebels to give up their arms, release the prisoners, and send representatives to him to explain the causes. Distrusting Eastchurch, the as-sembly ordered militia to the border region to prevent his entrance.[66] Culpeper was elected collector of customs, and the customs receipts were sequestered, some being used to pay the troops. Miller, still in irons, and the other prisoners were returned to confinement. Their work completed, the assembly adjourned. In the mood for celebration, many crowded on board *Carolina* for a "frolick" fueled by free-flowing rum, "very joyfully fireing" the brig's guns. After confer-ring with Foster, Crawford, and Culpeper, Gillam "opened store" and began trading with the "Insurrectors."[67] The vivid descriptions of chaotic drunken behavior of the "Rabble" assembly and trial at Durant's headquarters came primarily from eyewitness accounts by Loyalists, notably Miller, who expected to be murdered, and Biggs. In that hard-drinking era alcohol flowed freely at political and public meetings, market days, and court sessions. The ever-present backdrop at the events in this case was a corps of disciplined soldiers who kept the potentially volatile situation in check, as well as the subtle backstage man-agement of Culpeper, Durant, and Gillam.

Although the Albemarle militia had successfully protected the colony in two Indian conflicts, it had had little effect on the political turmoil that preceded

Culpeper's Rebellion. To one historian the failure to defend Miller's government indicated poor organization and discipline.[68] On the contrary, it demonstrated how bitterly most of the colonists resented Miller's gross abuses of
power, persecution of the colony's traditional leadership, and the insult of his
employing a personal guard. The rebels were not an armed mob. The militia
exhibited effective organization and discipline in full support of the rebellion.
Some 80 to 100 soldiers were commanded by their highest-ranking officers,
colonels Jenkins and Foster, with six captains and a lieutenant representing all
precincts. Without unnecessary violence the soldiers responded swiftly to arrest
Miller and the Loyalist council and seized government and customs records.
There was no opposition. Miller's transgressions had cost him the people's
support, and, taken by surprise by superior numbers, his "pipeing guard" melted
away into the swamp and forests. It was a bloodless revolution.

THE REBEL COUNCIL of Foster, Crawford, Bird, Cullen, and Blount promptly
wrote to Virginia's governor, Colonel Herbert Jeffreys, on behalf of the "almost
Unanimous Inhabitants," to counter the effect of "Mislead persons" who had
gone to Virginia to "Stirr up your Honors mind against us your Neighboring
Collony." They admitted detaining Miller, who "was Illegally sent here President by Thos. Eastchurch," described as the pretended governor because "we
never saw any Commission." Miller was accused of using his armed guard to
commit such "Horrible Injustice" that the colony would have "Inevitably been
Ruined." Miller's alleged crimes included blasphemy, treason, infidelity to the
proprietors, and his effort to "Destroy This County." The council asked Jeffreys
to delay action until he had the full record of circumstances in Albemarle.[69]

Governor Jeffreys, an experienced professional soldier, had command of a
sizable contingent of Royal troops to pacify the colony in the aftermath of
Bacon's Rebellion. When he received word of "some Mutineers in Armes" in
Albemarle, he promptly sealed the border by calling up the southside militia
"lest the fire bursting there might set us A flame" and prepared to provide Eastchurch with soldiers to quell the uprising. The startling news in early February
1678 that Eastchurch had died from a fever ended his threat to the rebellion.[70]

The untimely escape of Timothy Biggs and his voyage to England created
new anxiety for the rebels. Among those convening at the home of John Jenkins
on Harvey's Neck were leaders Culpeper, Durant, Willoughby, Foster, Blount,
and Crawford, as well as Captain Gillam. The rebels took steps to consolidate
the new government. Biggs's getaway prompted them to authorize a ten-foot-
square log prison to hold Miller in solitary confinement. Measures were taken
to organize the county's defense under Lieutenant Colonel Foster. Two agents,

George Durant and John Willoughby, were appointed to represent the rebels to the proprietors. And Gillam provided bills of exchange to conduct business for the government.[71] Now with popular approval and in firm control of the county government and the customs office, the rebels would successfully govern the colony for nearly two years. Jenkins, who could claim a valid commission as deputy governor, may have resumed his office.[72]

By April 1678, Biggs was in London and went straight to the proprietors, informing them of the rebellion and urging a "speedy and effectuall suppressing" of the rebels, which could then be achieved by a "small force." He recommended a vessel armed with eight to ten guns, volunteers from Virginia, and the offer of indemnity for all but two or three leaders. Biggs further advised that if the rebellion was not swiftly subdued, "great Injury" might ensue "by servants, Slaves & Debtors flying thither" from New England, New York, Maryland, and Virginia. This disturbing news came at a particularly bad time for the Lords, for the Crown was questioning the wisdom of all proprieties, and a rebellion would be a convenient excuse to bring Carolina under royal control. The proprietors initially downplayed the incident. To placate Biggs, in September the lords secured a lucrative Crown appointment for him as comptroller and surveyor of customs.[73]

Timothy Biggs landed in Albemarle in February 1679 when the General Court was in session at Durant's house. The court summoned Biggs, ordering him to present all of his papers and records. After reading his commission aloud, Biggs imprudently nailed it to the door and prepared to assume his office. Incensed over this affront, Culpeper ripped off the notice and posted a proclamation that he was the only collector in the county.[74] Fearing reprisal, Biggs stayed close to home and slept with loaded pistols by his bed.

Culpeper was dispatched to London that summer to explain the causes of the rebellion. In a hearing before the proprietors on 17 November, Culpeper admitted rebellious acts and placed himself under a £500 bond, agreeing to return the missing customs receipts within a year.[75] This discreet arrangement satisfied the relieved proprietors, who hoped their colony's unrest was now over. Culpeper prepared to return home.

Having found it a "very difficult matter to gitt a man of worth and trust," the proprietors again searched for a reliable governor. For the first time they looked within their inner circle and persuaded one of their own, Seth Sothel, who had purchased the Clarendon share, to take the post and settle the rebellion as soon as possible. The plan went horribly awry when Governor Sothel, en route to Carolina, was captured by pirates, enslaved, and held for ransom in Algiers.[76] On receiving this distressing news in February 1679, the Lords wisely chose planter John Harvey as president of the council and therefore acting governor.

Harvey, one of Albemarle's first settlers, was respected by all and supported by the Populists. Furthermore, he had remained neutral in the rebellion. It was a conciliatory appointment for a new beginning in the colony. To settle the controversy in the customs office, the proprietors selected Robert Holden.[77]

Sailing in late spring, Holden arrived in Albemarle in July with commissions, laws, and a copy of the Grand Model. It had been years since Albemarle County had had an executive commissioned by the proprietors. For eighteen months the colony had been governed by the rebel leaders, who warmly welcomed the new governor. With no hint of retribution from the Lords, Harvey was instructed "to come as nigh" as he could to organize a government based generally on the Fundamental Constitutions and to institute land policy that had been in abeyance throughout the upheaval. The former rebels were pleased that the seat of government would remain at the centrally located Durant plantation at the mouth of the Perquimans River.

Before Harvey could initiate reform and reorganization, there was the perennially unfinished business of Thomas Miller, who had been festering in the filthy log jail. Prior to the rebellion, Miller's opponents had failed to secure a conviction for his abuses. Again in August 1679 he was brought before Attorney General George Durant in the Palatine's Court of Governor Harvey and deputies Anthony Slocum, James Hill, and Timothy Biggs and indicted for treasonable words and blasphemy. The original depositions were accompanied by new evidence from John Davis, who had heard Miller call the Lords Proprietors "fooles or sotts," which was hardly treasonable. Miller was held for trial in November, but the indictment was so blatantly political that Hill, Biggs, Henry Hudson, and others helped him escape. Although pursued with "hue & cry" into Virginia, he succeeded in boarding a ship for England.[78]

The return to de jure government began when Governor Harvey issued writs for the September assembly election. When the burgesses convened in November, the Populist majority elected George Durant speaker and William Crawford, James Blount, and John Varnham as assistants on the council to join proprietors' deputies John Jenkins, Richard Foster, John Willoughby, Anthony Slocum, and Robert Holden. The other known burgesses were Alexander Lillington and William Wilkinson. All except Holden, who was not present in 1677, had been leaders of the late rebellion. The election of 1679 marked the final triumph of the bloodless revolt, as the rebel leaders were duly elected and installed as Albemarle County's legitimate government.[79]

Under the leadership of speaker Durant, the assembly enacted a comprehensive agenda of at least fifty-eight laws. Sadly, they are nearly all lost; however, many were incorporated in the 1715 codification of sixty-six acts that reached back to the earliest laws of the colony.[80] One of the extant laws was an Act for

Precinct Courts that reauthorized the lower courts. The precincts were renamed for proprietors—Shaftesbury (Chowan), Berkeley (Perquimans), Carteret (Pasquotank), and Craven (Currituck). The court organization, jurisdiction, and administrative duties were unchanged. The commission of peace for Berkeley Precinct in 1692 empowered two justices and juries to investigate "witchcraft, enchantments, sorceries, [and] magic arts," in addition to the usual felonies, trespasses, and extortions. With the exception of an imprisoned woman accused of witchcraft in 1680, the court records are silent about the "dark arts" until 1703, when a singular occasion erupted.[81]

In the last week of July two Currituck residents, Susannah Evans and Martha Richardson, allegedly "Diabolically and malitiously" bewitched neighbors at the instigation of the devil, causing extreme pain that resulted in one death and possibly another in the same family. As in the earlier witch hysteria of Salem, in the Massachusetts Bay Colony, this disturbing incident could easily have spun out of control. According to the deposition of Thomas Bourchier, his entire household, including a servant couple, declined overnight from excellent health to grave suffering with severe pain in extremities and internal organs. His wife, Deborah, described it as a thousand nails piercing her feet that moved to her bowels, tormenting her unmercifully. In her agony she blamed Susannah Evans, "an evil woman," and urged that she be examined for witch signs. Thomas was also struck with "chronic strange and unusual pains in his stomach, belly and Prevyiparts." Other family members were afflicted, as well as the nearby Thomas Taylor family. In a less dramatic incident, Martha Richardson was accused of bewitching and tormenting William Parker and others.

Imperiled by the slander of witchcraft, John and Susannah Evans met the Bourchiers at a neutral site to attempt reconciliation. When the Evanses denied any responsibility for the illnesses, the meeting dissolved into verbal abuse and threats. After an agonizing month Deborah died, turning the conflict into a potential capital crime, and the case moved to the General Court at Little River, many miles up the sound by water. The province's high court convened in late October with the Evans and Richardson cases on the docket. Depositions concerning both were presented to the Grand Jury, which returned verdicts of Ignoramus, or lack of evidence. Thus there would be no trial, both women were exonerated, and no witchcraft accusations are recorded for the rest of the proprietary era. Thomas Bourchier died soon afterward of his afflictions.[82]

THE LAND POLICY for settlers arriving before December 1684 set headrights at sixty acres for free persons and male servants and fifty for all other servants or enslaved persons, including women, Blacks, and Indians. The governor was authorized to reissue or confirm earlier grants at either a farthing or a half penny quitrent per acre, but new grants required a penny per acre. The disparity of rents would not be solved until later governors Ludwell and Archdale approved the 1668 Great Deed of Grant that allowed acquisition on Virginia terms.[83]

Two patents issued for plantations in Shaftesbury (Chowan) precinct reflected the new land distribution policy. Under Governor Harvey, John Varnham received 250 acres in November 1679 based on his earlier Virginia grant. In March 1680 under Governor John Jenkins, Robert Winley received a 280-acre patent based on the Great Deed of Grant. In both cases the quitrent was a farthing per acre.[84]

In London, Miller presented a petition to the king and Privy Council, stating that the rebels had challenged Crown authority and seized royal customs revenue. The Crown, having no choice, issued a warrant for Culpeper's arrest on 19 December 1679. A week later Culpeper was arrested on Gillam's *Carolina,* which was awaiting departure for Albemarle. The Lords of Trade and Plantations and the Commissioners of Customs ordered a full investigation of the affair. Imprisoned about twenty days, Culpeper requested that he be brought to trial. The Crown ordered the proprietors to present a copy of their charter and a full report of the rebellion on 4 February 1680.[85] Facing the potential loss of their charter if Culpeper were convicted of treason, the Lords chose to defend him.

At the Lords of Trade and Plantations hearing, the proprietors were represented by the Earl of Shaftesbury, the Earl of Craven, and Sir Peter Colleton. Handling the defense, Shaftesbury opened by stating that Miller had had no legal authority to assume control of the government. A commissioner of customs countered that Culpeper had no authority to seize the customs receipts. At this point, Culpeper testified that he was lawfully elected by a legal assembly. After the prosecution brought in overwhelming testimony against Culpeper in the sworn statements of Miller, Hudson, and others, the hearing ended. Culpeper sought the mercy of the court and requested a trial in Albemarle, but his motion was denied. About a week later, Gillam was called before the Lords of Trade and Plantations, but no concrete evidence could be presented against him. At this hearing, Shaftesbury reported that further evidence was forthcoming from Carolina and secured a delay.[86]

The investigation dragged on nearly nine months until 20 November 1680, when Culpeper was tried for high treason before the Court of King's Bench. Lord Shaftesbury presented a masterful defense, arguing that since there was no legal government in Albemarle at the time, there could not possibly have been a revolt. He further declared that Miller "*without any legall authority* gott possession of the government" and performed many unlawful and arbitrary acts. Shaftesbury pointed out that since Governor Harvey and collector Holden had taken office, all was "quyet and his Majtyes Customes quietly paid by the People." Furthermore, Holden had returned customs receipts to the treasury and, remarkably, the people of Albemarle had "laid a Taxe upon themselves" to repay the revenues seized during the uprising. These arguments secured Culpeper's acquittal.[87] Thus ended the active rebellion, but the colony's bad reputation in Virginia remained.

Although peace had returned to Albemarle and the government was sanctioned by the proprietors, Governor Jeffreys's successor, Lord Thomas Culpeper, continued to see a menace in his southern neighbor. To justify a Virginia garrison, Culpeper reported to the Privy Council in 1681 that North Carolina had "always been dangerous to Virginia" because it was "the resort of the scum and refuse of America." Reputedly some of that "scum" was former Bacon rebels who fled Virginia fearing for their lives.[88]

———————

THE REBELLION OF 1677, eventually named Culpeper's Rebellion, was much more than a coup or factional bickering.[89] It was not a drunken mob run amok, as portrayed by deposed president Thomas Miller, who stood before the rebel court fearing for his life.[90] Nor was it, as recently described, the struggle of an underclass of runaway servants, slaves, and debtors against a ruling class of planters and merchants to establish a "Quaker-Leveller republic."[91] In "poor Carolina" there was no great gulf between wealthy colonists and the "preponderance of small to middling landowners."[92] As for supposed Quaker involvement, after restoration of legal government the "peacable people" sent a petition to the Lords denouncing the rebels' "seditious actions" and denying any participation in the rebellion. Among their "sufferings" from the rebel militia was the brief arrest of Quaker officials—councilman James Hill and two burgesses, who had been Loyalists. Furthermore, not trusting the pacifists' neutrality, the militia confiscated the firearms from their homes.[93]

Miller branded the rebellion "treasonable and tyrannicall" and reported to the Lords that the Albemarle freemen had assumed "to themselves the supreme and sovereign power, by first dissolving then erecting Courts of Judicature, convening Parliaments without Writs," and taking control of customs. Having sifted through the evidence and the hearings, the proprietors themselves summarized the case between Miller and the rebels in February 1680. They concluded that Miller had "startled and disaffected the people" by doing "many extravagant things, making strange limitations for ye choyce of ye Parliamt, . . . laying fynes, . . . sending out strange warrants to bring some of ye most considerable men of ye Country alive or dead before him" with a price on their heads. The proprietors, who had endured the trials of the English Revolution, understood that the men of Albemarle, faced with Miller's oppression, "had formed themselves into w[ha]t Mr Culpeper calls ye Governt of ye Country by their owne authority & according to their owne modell."[94] This government of the people was inspired by the English Revolution—the Civil War, the execution of Charles I, the Commonwealth, and the Restoration—that had challenged the authority of the Crown and the Anglican Church and had spawned radical political and religious ideas. Everyone understood that the execution of the king in 1649 passed sovereignty to the people of the nation, represented by Parliament. Parliament established the Commonwealth and offered the crown to Charles II. The king, the Lords Proprietors, and the Albemarle colonists had all been transformed by living through these revolutionary times.

Culpeper's Rebellion was decidedly a middle-class revolution of a planter-merchant gentry, most of them the colony's founding settlers, who had filled government posts from the outset in precinct and general courts, the assembly, the council, and even the governorship. Just as their descendants over a century later initially sought justice from the king, they looked to the Lords Proprietors for redress of their grievances, as the source of their political and religious liberty, and as the guarantors of their rights as Englishmen. In this sense, Culpeper's Rebellion was more a precursor of the American Revolution than were other rebellions or coups d'état in the colonies. Albemarle was a colony where rebels deposed a governor and successfully governed the colony for nearly two years, after which de jure government was restored to the former rebels with no retribution. Uniquely, "the North Carolinians, as later they would be known, seem largely to have gone their own way."[95]

WHILE CULPEPER'S treason trial was being played out in England, a new political drama took the stage in Albemarle—the rise and fall of a despot, Robert Holden. A Virginia merchant, Holden was drawn to Albemarle in 1671 by the Indian trade, but he kept his Virginia residence and was swept up in Bacon's Rebellion. As one of the "great offenders," he was imprisoned until he paid a fine of 5,000 pounds of tobacco. Financially ruined, he sailed to England to appeal to the Lords Proprietors, hoping to recoup his fortune in Albemarle County. In the aftermath of Culpeper's Rebellion, in 1679 Holden secured a Crown commission as customs collector. Soon he was showered with lucrative proprietary appointments as a council deputy, secretary, receiver general, escheator of estates, and surveyor of shipwrecks and other "Ejections of the Sea." As receiver general he collected quitrents, either in cash or in tobacco, and received a 10 percent commission.[96]

On his way to Albemarle, Holden stopped over in Boston in June to investigate the smuggling that was endemic in New England. Based on his subsequent actions in Albemarle, he may have learned more about customs fraud than was good for him. Holden reported that about half a dozen local traders were purchasing most of the Albemarle tobacco, which was then shipped from Boston without inspection to Ireland, Scotland, or the continent under the label of any commodity not subject to duties.[97] Holden arrived in Albemarle that summer bearing President Harvey's commission. By the end of 1679, however, Harvey died, and the council confirmed as its president the former governor John Jenkins, who served until his death in December 1681.[98]

As the only official who had both royal and proprietary commissions, the ambitious Holden recklessly overreached, assailing both the Crown customs officers and the county officials. As a proprietors' deputy, he joined the inner circle of Harvey's council, composed predominantly of Populist former rebels. Holden ingratiated himself with such long-entrenched officials as Jenkins, Foster, Crawford, and Durant and was secretary at the council's second trial of Thomas Miller. Resenting his downfall and perceived persecution, in a petition to the king Miller stated that Holden, "a Ringleader in ye late rebellion in Virginia has made it his business to close with ye rebells there [Albemarle]."[99]

The quickest way for Holden to concentrate wealth and power was to defraud customs, exploiting the confusion created by having two customs officials. Holden's rival, Timothy Biggs, Crown comptroller and surveyor of customs, was vulnerable as a Loyalist. Because Biggs had enabled Miller to escape in the fall of 1679, he was virtually ostracized by the government.

Brooking no opposition, Holden willfully arrested his opponents and held them without bail. As customs collector, he levied extortionate duties by devaluing tobacco so that the duty became two pounds of tobacco for every pound shipped. On some tobacco hogsheads assigned to customs by a broad arrow mark, Holden illegally altered the symbol and placed the tobacco in his personal account. Other infractions included theft and sale of public powder, which left the magazine supply dangerously low; altering the text of an assembly act after it had been passed and signed; browbeating a grand jury; and insolence toward officials and the governor. In the General Court, Holden contemptuously declared that there was "neither Governor nor Government" in the colony.[100]

In the fall of 1679 Biggs's Currituck deputy, Samuel Pricklove, observed Holden releasing bags of ginger that had been seized as an illegal import. When Holden cleared the New England ketch *Speedwell* with twenty-two hogsheads of his own tobacco on board, Pricklove inquired about the duties. Calling him a "Foole and Loggerhead," Holden told him it was none of his business. Subsequently, when Pricklove attempted to inspect a barque bound for New England,

Holden had him arrested and held without bail. The extent of Holden's vicious-
ness, as well as his dominance of the ruling clique, was revealed in March 1680
when Pricklove received an abhorrent sentence to stand in the pillory for three
hours, to have his right ear cut off, to be banished forever, to stay in prison in
irons without bail until he was transported in irons, and to pay court costs and
fees. On the same day, the court suspended Biggs's commission as comptroller
and surveyor general of customs, leaving Holden as the only customs official.[101]
Not only did the General Court have no authority over Crown officials, but neither Pricklove nor Biggs had committed a crime: both were fulfilling their duties of office. Since Pricklove remained in the colony and gave evidence against
Holden the next year, he was not banished, and it is doubtful whether his harsh
sentence was executed.

Throughout the remainder of 1680 Holden continued his reign of fraud,
intimidation, terror, and gross miscarriage of justice. How could men of good
sense, who had not hesitated earlier to oppose tyranny, tolerate such behavior?
Although his drive to power had begun against Biggs, one of their opponents,
they were slow to recognize that he might well turn on them. Indeed, he did
just that in midyear. Using trumped-up charges of abusive words and involvement in Miller's escape, Holden orchestrated arrests in the dark of night and
imprisonment without bail. Among those detained were Sheriff Edward Wade,
planter Edward Smithwick, and Burgess William Wilkison. Captain William
Woollard, Holden's personal armed guard, arrested Wade in Currituck. Smithwick, who was out on bail, was seized at night, trussed up, and taken by boat
to the noxious Perquimans log prison. Wilkison challenged the bogus charge
of abusive words, whereupon Holden flew into a tirade, denied him appeal,
and ordered him to be incarcerated. En route, Wilkison appealed to Governor
Jenkins, who took him into his home in Chowan. Holden was enraged by the
governor's interference. Declaring that he had made Jenkins governor and was
thereby "above the Governor and had greater power," after dark Holden arrested Wilkison at gunpoint and sent him to jail.

For three weeks that fall Smithwick and Wilkison were held along with a
woman accused of witchcraft. The prison was kept tightly closed, and Wilkison wrote that he was forced to "eat[,] Lye and voyd his Excrements . . . Soe
that we were almost poysened with the Stink." At the grand jury hearing in
November, most of the charges were dropped for lack of evidence. Grand jury
members later testified that Holden browbeat them into returning two indictments against Wilkison.[102] The grand jury's intimidation finally convinced the
ruling party to close ranks and arrest Holden in 1681.

The evidence for Holden's alleged crimes was contained in twenty depositions sworn in court with Holden present, apparently either a grand jury

hearing or a trial. He was accused of numerous crimes committed over the span of 1679–82: customs extortion and fraud, theft of public property, contempt of government and court officials, illegal arrests, denial of bail, cruel punishment, and false imprisonment. Unfortunately, the court records are missing, but he disappeared from Albemarle, either through banishment or escape, and never returned. In England he ingratiated himself with the proprietors and in 1707 applied for the governorship of the Bahamas. Asked for a character reference, proprietor John Archdale wrote that Holden was "no ways qualified for the meanest Post in the Government." Holden did not receive the appointment.[103]

GOVERNOR SETH SOTHEL arrived in Albemarle in 1682 with the proprietors' expectations that they had sent a "very sober discreet gentleman" who would "by his prudence" establish "quiet and good Government."[104] In 1675 the Earl of Shaftesbury, believing Sothel a gentleman of "considerable estate" and "my Friend," encouraged him to migrate to southern Carolina and take up a 12,000-acre manor. Soon after Sothel purchased a proprietary share, in October 1677 he was asked to become governor of the turbulent Albemarle County.[105] On the voyage over in 1678 he was captured by Turkish pirates near Gibraltar and held captive in Algiers.[106] By the following summer the Crown had offered to exchange two pirate captives, "Hadgamore (Hadji Omar), commander of the Tiger of Argier (Algiers)," and "Buffillo Ball," for Sothel's release. Word reached England that Sothel labored as a slave, carrying "Morter, Brick and stone for the Masons with a heavy Chaine . . . upon his legg besides Bolt and Shackle." Finally, the hostages were exchanged in 1681, with Sothel's ransom of 6,000 pieces of eight bonded by two Englishmen in Algiers.[107]

On Sothel's return to England, the proprietors issued a proclamation to the Carolina colonies declaring his appointment as governor. But the Sothel who arrived in Albemarle was a different man, evidently warped by his harrowing experiences among the Barbary pirates. No longer a "sober moderate" gentleman, Sothel reimbursed just half of the ransom before he sailed to Carolina. Only the threat of debtors' prison forced him to pay the remainder. Nevertheless, Quaker proprietor John Archdale, who served as Sothel's acting governor, initially thought well of him.[108] Sothel immediately began accumulating land, including the 4,000 acres once owned by Governor Stephens on Salmon Creek. Although he had other holdings on the Pasquotank and Little Rivers, he lived on the Chowan property and was engaged in agriculture and the Indian trade.[109]

Governor Sothel, like Holden, was more interested in his own wealth and power than in the welfare of the colony. During his tenure piracy appeared in Albemarle for the first time, and on 23 November 1685 the General Assembly made piracy punishable by death without benefit of clergy. Ironically, considering his experiences, Sothel was later charged with rewarding and protecting pirates.[110] He accused two Barbadian shipmasters of piracy, despite their producing papers of entry and clearing. These men were imprisoned without trial, and one of them, Richard Humphrey, died in prison. Sothel refused to have the will probated and claimed Humphrey's estate. When executor Thomas Pollock threatened to seek redress from the proprietors in England, Sothel arrested and imprisoned him. Sothel reputedly took bribes to reduce criminal charges and seized estates, including one from an orphaned boy. His alleged thefts included an enslaved Black, seven pewter dishes, a herd of cattle, and imported lace. Finally, he imprisoned George Durant for saying "reflecting words." Claiming that Durant had forfeited his bond, Sothel seized his estate.[111]

The jailing of George Durant was the final straw. In 1689 Thomas Pollock led an armed band who surprised Sothel at his plantation, arrested him, and put him in prison. At Sothel's request, he was tried by the Albemarle assembly, which banished him for twelve months and forbade him from holding office in the colony. Having learned of the assembly's verdict, in December the Lords formally suspended Sothel from the governorship of Albemarle County.[112] Ever a survivor, the next year Sothel went south to Charles Town, where he parlayed his position as a proprietor into replacing Governor James Colleton, who was weakened by warring political factions. Prideful and unreformed, Sothel soon overstepped his authority and was accused of illegal and unjust actions similar to those that had caused his downfall in Albemarle.[113]

Recognizing that settlement had spread south of Albemarle Sound, the proprietors appointed the new governor, Colonel Philip Ludwell, to administer "that part of Carolina that lyes North and East of Cape feare."[114] Ludwell's title marked the beginning of the division of the proprietors' domain into North and South Carolina.

CHAPTER SEVEN

Life in the Tidewater

Family and Society

You write me your son is Intended into this Country to se me I should
be glad to se any of my relations but the Country is sickly and the
Inlet bad and a dangerous place to corrupt Youth that I
cannot give him the least Incouragement.
—Anna Willix Sothel, 1694

WHEN ANNA SOTHEL sat down in March 1694 in her manor house on Salmon Creek to reply to her sister Hazelponi Wood in Ipswich, Massachusetts Bay Colony, she was understandably depressed, having just buried her third husband, former governor Seth Sothel. Despite her husband's controversial career, she had remained loyal and was grief-stricken, saying, "My losses are incomparable for the losse of my dear husband who am left a widdow my pen canot expres my greife and troubles."[1] Like many of her contemporaries, however, Anna Sothel rapidly recovered her zest for life and in the next year married her fourth husband, Colonel John Lear of Nansemond County, a wealthy planter and Virginia council member. Sadly, she shared only a few months with him before she died in May 1695.

In England birth determined social status, and few rose above their class. Anna Willix Sothel's life fulfilled America's promise that regardless of one's birth a person could accumulate property and ascend to the pinnacle of society, political influence, and wealth. She rose from toiling as a bound maidservant in New England to reigning as mistress of large plantations and as wife of a governor of both Carolinas during a turbulent political era. Born in New Hampshire, Anna was the daughter of Belshazzar and Anna Willix of Exeter. When his first wife was murdered, Belshazzar took his young daughters to live in Massachusetts and remarried. The Willix sisters were soon orphaned by their father's death and their stepmother's mental illness. Anna and her two sisters, Hazelponi and Susannah, became indentured servants. In 1666 Anna moved to Boston to live with Hazelponi, and there she met her first husband, Robert

Riscoe, master and part owner of the brigantine *Good Hope*, which sailed to Albemarle, Ireland, and England. The Riscoes had moved to Albemarle by 1670. Widowed by 1683, Anna married widower Captain James Blount, a planter of Chowan Precinct, longtime member of the council, and burgess in the General Assembly. The Blounts resided at his plantation, Mulberry Hill, on Albemarle Sound.[2]

After Blount's death in 1686, Anna became the wife of proprietor and governor Seth Sothel, and they moved to Sothel's manor on Salmon Creek. Sothel's term as governor began in 1683 and was marred by such gross abuse of power and corruption that he was overthrown in 1689, tried by the General Assembly, and banished for a year. The Sothels went to South Carolina, where as a Lord Proprietor he assumed the governorship for a contentious two years until suspended by action of the proprietors. On leaving South Carolina, the Sothels resided in Nansemond County, Virginia, as well as Albemarle, where he died.[3]

Sothel left most of his property to Anna, who married Colonel John Lear before the estate settlement was complete and died in 1695 before it was finalized. Lear's death a few months after Anna's demise left two estates unsettled. Thomas Pickering, a nephew, came to Albemarle from New Hampshire to represent his mother-in-law, Hazelponi Wood, and his aunt, Susannah Jones. Through litigation these sisters gained title to 12,000 acres and the Sothel homeplace on Salmon Creek, which the Pickerings subsequently purchased from them for their residence.[4]

North Carolina began as a small self-sufficient colony of Virginians, who were well established by 1663, when the Roanoke country became a propriety. The proprietors inherited a colony that owed them nothing. In the wild swamps of Pasquotank or Currituck, what mattered was not your birth or family's status in England, but whether you could ride well, shoot well, wield an axe or hoe, pole a canoe, and work through a sweltering midsummer day in the fields. Little wonder that the Albemarle farmers, planters, artisans, and traders ignored the distant proprietors. Tucked behind the treacherous Outer Banks and protected from the south and west by the water barriers of Albemarle Sound and the Chowan River and on the north by the Great Dismal Swamp, Albemarle planters followed their own course with little concern about what transpired in London or Jamestown.

The colony's free and bound population had always been somewhat diverse—mainly English, some Scots and Irish, a few other Europeans, and some free, bound, or enslaved Indians and Africans. The early land grants indicate several hundred settlers scattered along the waterways, with small concentrations west of the Chowan and on the Pasquotank and Perquimans Rivers. By 1679, in the aftermath of Culpeper's Rebellion about 1,400 tithables, or "working

TABLE 7.1. Precinct Population

Year	Precinct	Total	Anglican	Quaker	Black	Atheist
1709	Pasquotank	1,332	900	210	211	11
1710	Currituck	839	735	1	97	5–6

hands," were reported, of which one-third were "Indians, Negros and women."[5] Estimates based on these tithables indicate over 3,000 free people, including a few free Africans, and less than 500 indentured servant and enslaved laborers of the three races and both sexes.[6] Tithables, or taxable persons, were probably defined then as in Virginia—enslaved males and females twelve years or older, indentured servants of both sexes fourteen or older, and free males sixteen or older.[7] The 1715 North Carolina law defined taxables as enslaved males and females aged twelve or older and all other males aged sixteen or older, whether free or bound.[8]

Surviving documents from 1715 to 1721 list fewer than three tithables in most households, with only ten householders having ten or more. Prominent among them were two council presidents, Thomas Pollock with thirty-one and William Reed with fourteen tithables, and councilmen William Duckenfield with seventeen, Richard Sanderson with twelve, and Edward Moseley with ten. When Thomas Pollock died in 1722, in addition to his many plantations he bequeathed seventy-four enslaved persons. These exceptions notwithstanding, the phrase "a society of small farmers" aptly described the colony in 1729.[9]

In its most complex form, a plantation household could include the master and mistress and their children; indentured white, Indian, or African servants; enslaved Indians or Africans; and children of all races and conditions of servitude. Fluidity of status was largely confined to free persons and indentured servants completing their contracts, with occasional manumission of those enslaved. By the end of the century the labor force was shifting toward fewer indentured servants and more enslaved people, with Africans outnumbering Indians.

By the early eighteenth century it was noted that "the Fame of this new-discover'd Summer-Country spread thro' the neighbouring Colonies, and, in a few Years drew a considerable Number of Families."[10] In the same period an Anglican missionary, the Reverend James Adams, compiled a census in his two precincts that included adults of both sexes, but probably not children.

Perquimans and Chowan would more than double these figures, and when the precincts in Bath County were added, the population could approach 10,000. Reports sent to England after the destructive Tuscarora War recorded

1,600 whites and 500 Blacks as tithables.[11] A modern estimate projected a population by 1700 of about 10,000 whites and less than 1,000 Blacks, most of whom were enslaved.[12] Not until the eighteenth century did the colonial free and bound populations reach parity with the Indian tribes in the tidewater.

Most of the European colonists traced their origins to the British Isles and had migrated to the county from Virginia, the West Indies, New England, England, Scotland, and Ireland; however, some French and a few Dutch settled in Albemarle and Bath. Described as a French alien, Benjamin Massague settled on a 328-acre plantation south of the Scuppernong River.[13] William Gascoigne, a Pasquotank planter, also had a plantation on the south shore east of the Scuppernong River, mostly for cattle. When young mariner James Sarason was stranded by his indicted former captain, the court gave responsibility for the boy to Gascoigne, who claimed to know his Maryland family and offered to return him to his father. Gascoigne died soon thereafter, and his widow retained Sarason until the General Court had him discharged from her care in 1704.[14]

French Protestant refugees fleeing from persecution, Peter Furree and his son John and Isaac and Francis DeLaMare settled in Pasquotank. Residents for years, John Furree and Francis DeLaMare applied for and received naturalization in 1697.[15] Shortly after receiving his citizenship, DeLaMare served on a jury and soon became a precinct justice, a vestryman of his parish, and by 1706 a General Court justice, serving until his demise in 1713.[16]

Jacob Peterson, probably Dutch, who had originally been naturalized in Maryland, migrated to Albemarle in 1681. Owner of a 300-acre plantation in Perquimans, he was granted Carolina citizenship in 1698.[17] On the Trent River in Bath County by 1708 there was a settlement of French Huguenots who had migrated from the James River in Virginia and were described as "very industrious" and "good Neighbours amongst us."[18] In 1710 the German Palatines and Swiss arrived to found New Bern.

Immigrants came from a hierarchical society that had been roiled by the Civil War and Interregnum, "a world turned upside down," which had increased class fluidity both up and down. Those who braved the frightening transoceanic crossing had initiative, energy, and motivation to seek a better future in the economic and social opportunities of the Caribbean and American colonies. The era of the English Revolution profoundly affected all who experienced it, from the Lords Proprietors to the poorest yeomen and tenant farmers, many of whom voluntarily immigrated to the Chesapeake as indentured servants or freeholders. From Virginia some headed south to Roanoke country, soon to become Carolina. More common in the eighteenth century, transported prisoners and war refugees had enormous impact on the overseas colonies, especially on the Chesapeake colonies of Virginia and Maryland and the West Indian

Leeward Islands, where so many were sent that the term "Barbadosed" referred to involuntary transportation. The prisoners and many of the refugees ended up as indentured servants or plantation laborers.

Prior to 1700 there were many more indentured servants than enslaved persons in the colonies, and servants remained a significant labor factor well into the eighteenth century. A majority of white immigrants came to the colonies as bound servants. "Servant" was a generalized term that chiefly referred to white indentured servants and a few Indians and Africans, but also to apprentices bound by their families or by the courts if orphaned or illegitimate, whether white or part African or Indian.[19] In North Carolina the earliest reference to indentured servants was the proprietors' Colleton Island plantation, established in 1664. The next year saw the arrival of manager Peter Carteret and three servants, one French and two English, who subsequently completed their contracts, received clothing and freedom dues, and were then hired as free laborers.[20]

Indentured servants entered into a labor contract for several years; the time span depended on the circumstances. Farm tenants could escape grinding poverty by immigration, paying their passage by an indenture that was sold to a planter upon arrival. Servants received clothing and room and board. At the end of the contract, they were given freedom dues that might include clothing, tools, seeds, corn, provisions, livestock, or a gun. These dues, with a fifty-acre headright, enabled the former servant to become a freeholder.

Since fifty acres was too little land to support cattle, the usual entrée into farming, the newly freed person would often trade or sell the headright. If the former servant received a good reference from the master, a man could find employment as a plantation steward or overseer. A woman with a good reference could become a hired domestic and was free to marry. According to Brickell, overseers were paid by every seventh calf and foal, half of the newly born hogs, and a seventh of grain and tobacco produced on the plantation. In addition, they were free to grow their own crops. Thus in a few years a former servant could accumulate enough resources to purchase a plantation. Servants who had been indentured as artisans, such as carpenters, coopers, or blacksmiths, could find work in that craft. The less industrious and untrained could enter an apprenticeship. For those who had not received a good reference because of misbehavior or negligence, there was little choice but to be a hired unskilled laborer, working periodically for a few days and living a "loose and indolent" life.[21]

Apprenticeships were another form of bound labor, usually arranged by parents for their children to learn a trade or craft. Orphaned minors under court protection were also apprenticed. Often they could choose their master or mistress, and the term of service usually ended at twenty-one years of age or, in the case of females, upon marriage. At age ten John Hallum was apprenticed by his parents to Benjamin Massegue, with obligations to keep his master's secrets and not to frequent ale houses or contract matrimony. His service was to be for eight years, and he was to receive a mare and a heifer. The death of his master a year later resulted in a second indenture until age twenty-one to a widow, Elizabeth Bartley, who was to educate him. Young Hallum received a cow and her offspring, and his freedom dues would be a suit of clothes and two breeding sows.[22]

Indentured servitude, which was available to anyone, became the most powerful agent of social mobility in the colonial period. The majority of the servants were young and single, although some were married couples. Most servants came from the middling tenants, freehold and leasehold yeoman farmers, and free artisans and tradesmen. A few were younger sons of country gentry, while some were unskilled laborers. A study of thousands of migrants embarking from Bristol and London in the latter half of the century revealed that over a third were yeomen, nearly a quarter were artisans and tradesmen, a quarter were women, a tenth were laborers, and 1 percent were gentlemen.[23] Tens of thousands from Britain and some from Europe availed themselves of the opportunity of free passage, training, and land in exchange for several years of work. Three single women who had indentures were Elizabeth Jersey, Katherine Gardner, and Alice Gardner, who each contracted in 1684 for four years of labor to pay their passage to Albemarle.[24]

Whether for a penniless laborer, maid, or gentleman, the five-to-six-pound fare to the colonies was covered by an indenture, or contract, with the ship's master to work, usually for four to seven years. On arrival, the contract was sold to a planter or artisan. The concept of the indentured servant, sometimes called an English or Christian servant, was derived from the medieval apprenticeship that provided education and vocational training for youth and young adults while ensuring care and fostering for orphans and bastards. In addition to teaching a skill or craft, contract holders were obligated to provide room and board, just and fair treatment, and, at the expiration of the term, negotiated freedom dues. In 1695 Thomas Houghton, a tailor of Yawpin, entered his son Richard into a seven-year apprenticeship with Henry Norman, a Perquimans cooper. The freedom dues were a mare delivered after three years, and at the end two suits of clothes and a set of cooper's tools. In 1703 Richard Houghton sued Norman for a breach of covenant over the dues. The court awarded him a new suit of clothes and more cooper's tools—a handsaw and a drawing knife.[25] In 1715 the assembly set freedom dues at three barrels of corn and two suits of clothing valued at five pounds. A man could substitute a gun for one of the suits.[26]

Precinct courts or church vestries had oversight to ensure that the terms of the indenture were fulfilled and to protect both parties from abuse. An unjust master might lose the servant by the court's ordering purchase of the remainder of the contract. For simple infractions, guilty servants were usually punished by extension of their time. The precinct court was also responsible for selecting guardians for orphans to provide education and protection of an estate. All chattel and real property, or the equivalent, was to be turned over to the orphan when of age. If the child was poor, then an apprenticeship was established, although Quakers were excluded as masters or mistresses.[27]

Precinct courts also heard cases involving runaways or criminal acts by servants. For misbehavior an unruly or runaway servant was usually punished with an extension of the contract, frequently double the time lost, and sometimes corporal punishment. For example, a maidservant who had a bastard child often was sentenced to serve an extra year. Petty theft by a servant in one case brought thirty lashes, plus eighteen months added to his five-year contract to cover court costs. Returned runaway servants and enslaved persons were observed wearing a heavy neck yoke until their masters felt they could be trusted.[28]

Free Blacks resided in the colony but left little trace beyond occasional court appearances. Thomas Andover and Francis Johnson entered suits, served on jury duty, and gave testimony in courts.[29] An experienced waterman, Andover was hired in 1694 to pilot a sailing canoe from the Scuppernong River to South Quay in Virginia. Involved in the Indian fur trade, Andover had business connections with two factors: Governor Seth Sothel and council member William Duckenfield. When Andover was sued by the New Pennsylvania Company, an intercolonial fur trading firm, Duckenfield covered his three-pound debt.[30] In 1694 the recently widowed Anna Sothel agreed to settle a debt owed to Andover with three cows and four pigs. After the debt became entangled in four estates, the executors withheld payment until Andover's attorney, Captain Anthony Dawson, secured a judgment from the court in 1698.[31]

Francis Johnson, described as a "mulatto," resided south of the sound on a 191-acre farm on the Scuppernong River, which he sold in 1704.[32] Earlier he was a partner with William Steel of Currituck in wreck salvage on the Outer Banks. When Steel refused to release Johnson's share of a wreck, Steel and his cohorts William Lee and John Spelman were charged with contempt on Johnson's testimony in General Court. However, lack of proof resulted in dismissal.[33] The case took a bizarre turn when Lee and Spelman testified that Johnson had intercepted and concealed a letter from Steel to the governor. Unable to refute the accusation, Johnson was found in contempt and received thirty-nine "stripes on his bare back well laid on." Subsequently, Johnson was saddled with court orders, court costs, and a damage suit.[34]

Manumission, or voluntarily freeing an enslaved person, was a legal agreement or bequest. An example of manumission by an indenture was the agreement between Alexander Lillington and Anthony, alias Toney, his enslaved laborer. Toney was bound to serve under strict conditions just over ten years, until Christmas Day 1705, when he would be set free.[35] In his 1675 will, Francis Godfrey left a canvas pillow to a "mulatto" child called Black Will, or Dicks Will, and mandated that he would serve the Godfrey family for over thirty years, after which he would be set free and receive the value of 400 pounds of tobacco and a good suit of clothes.[36] The General Court ordered Thomas Symons, executor of the estate of Charles Jones, to pay five pounds for "Bringing up a Negro Boy," who likely was free, since an enslaved person would have been either inherited or sold in the estate settlement.[37]

The status of free Black persons in a slavery setting was precarious, fraught with the constant threat of an unscrupulous white person's illegal claim that they were enslaved and collecting rewards or even selling them. Judith Spellman, a free woman of color, narrowly escaped enslavement in the fall of 1729. She had worked for some time as a hired domestic for Pasquotank planter Joseph Stoakley. When he began to treat her like a slave, she fled to seek the protection of a magistrate. Stoakley caught and forced her to return to the plantation, where he tied her, whipped her "Naked Body" until she was bloodied all over, and put her in leg irons so tight that her feet swelled painfully. Somehow she escaped after several days and reached a precinct justice. Charged with assault and wounding, Stoakley had to post a £100 bond to ensure that Judith could attend General Court. Meanwhile, he fell seriously ill and died by January 1730, whereupon the case was dismissed. Spellman successfully defended her freedom in court against the claim of Stoakley's son and heir and later secured freedom papers for her daughter, Milly.[38]

According to his petition, Peter Vantrump, a free Black sailor, fell into such an entrapment in North Carolina in 1726. He had been at sea on several voyages out of New York and other ports. That summer he was on St. Thomas Island and wanted to go to Holland. He joined the crew of a brigantine commanded by a Captain Mackie, supposedly bound to Europe. Mackie sailed instead to Edenton, where he allegedly colluded with Edmund Porter, then a judge of the admiralty court, for Porter to entice Vantrump to stay in North Carolina. Although Vantrump insisted he was free, he apparently carried no written proof, and Porter claimed him as his slave. Vantrump's petition to Chief Justice Christopher Gale was heard in February 1727. Gale ordered Vantrump to be held by the provost marshal for trial in General Court for "his liberty and freedom." In the interim Vantrump was allowed to be employed by "Safe persons" who would guarantee his appearance. After hearing testimony from both Vantrump and Porter in its session in March, the General Court ordered the petition dismissed, leaving Vantrump enslaved to Porter.[39]

The next year Porter filed a related suit against Robert Hicks for trespass concerning his enslaved man, now a cooper known as Peter VanKamp. Porter's deposition claimed that Hicks had taken possession of VanKamp and detained him for two months, taking the profit from his work. Porter sued for fifty-nine pounds in damages. Although VanKamp apparently had been returned, both parties agreed to continue the case. It was postponed a second time until March 1729, but Porter did not appear, so Hicks was absolved, and Porter was charged court costs for "false Clamour."[40]

———————

IN THE MID-SEVENTEENTH CENTURY Virginia's bound labor force of indentured servants and enslaved Indians was on the verge of being supplanted by enslaved Africans. This was the time when the Roanoke country south of Virginia was being settled by Indian fur traders, farmers, and planters, some of whom had indentured servants. These settlers had little need for many workers on their smaller tracts in an isolated region. By the century's end, however, Roanoke, now North Carolina, had developed a diversified economy of commercial agriculture, ranching, and forest products with better connections to the North Atlantic trade network. As in Virginia, by that time enslaved Africans were the preferred laborers, although well into the eighteenth century the labor force included free and indentured whites, Blacks, and Indians side by side with enslaved Indians and Blacks.

From the beginning of settlement, fifty-acre headrights were granted to colonists, primarily entering overland from Virginia, who sponsored family, friends, acquaintances, indentured servants, and enslaved African and Indian men, women, and children. Among the 1663 Virginia land grants in the Albemarle are several hundred headrights for free men and women, but no indentured servants. Brought by Phillip Evans, Tony Negro, presumably enslaved, is the sole individual identifiable as African. After 1694, when land grants and sales resumed, numerous headrights were awarded for servants and those enslaved. Although the preponderance of headrights were granted for free whites, in the whole proprietary period there were 491 for nonwhites, of whom 56 were Indians and the rest Africans.[41]

Headrights were granted for every entry into the colony, resulting in multiple rights assigned to individuals. Rights were also gifted, traded, and purchased. In Perquimans James Minge cobbled together 1,000 acres for twenty rights, using six for himself, three for his wife Ruth, four for Robin (a Black), and seven for individual Blacks. No one else came close to John Blaney's 1,650-acre claim in

1698 for "transporting himself thirty-three times." While this could be taken as apparent fraud, Blaney, a New England sea captain, had tallied his many voyages to the colony over more than a decade.[42]

The colony's largest landholder, Thomas Pollock, submitted headright claims for six grants in 1694 and 1712. About one-third of the headrights were for enslaved or bound labor, including twenty-four Africans, five Indians, and a female servant.[43] By 1717 Pollock had accumulated about 31,000 acres, most of which was in longleaf pine and cypress, used for timber and naval stores that required an expanded labor force. He corresponded with Boston merchants for enslaved Africans at any price, particularly seeking "Sound" young men and women to work in the pine forests for tar and pitch. Reflecting the dehumanization of slavery, he also sought to acquire a young woman for a "breeder."[44]

Documented in the headright claims of planters with large landholdings is the preference for enslaved Africans over Indians and indentured servants.

Susanna Hartley of Perquimans, the widow of councilman Colonel Francis Hartley, managed an 1,100-acre plantation, where her diverse laborers included five enslaved Africans, two English boys, two Frenchmen, and a Dutchman.[45]

A list of headrights recorded in General Court in February 1694 is more representative of the small-to-middling planters and shows little preference for enslaved over servant laborers. Thirty-two men and two women claimed 192 headrights, mostly for family members. Sixteen headrights claimed for servants and enslaved persons included eight Africans, six indentured servants, an Indian boy, and a hired man. Only three of the thirty-four planters claimed ten or more headrights. The largest number was thirteen, which garnered 650 acres for Edward Mayo, a Quaker leader and longtime resident who claimed ten for family members and three for enslaved Africans. The smallest claim was by Jenken Williams for himself.[46]

To help his cousin John Arderne staff his Salmon Creek plantation, William Duckenfield sold him twenty-three enslaved Africans, Indians, and "mulattos," twelve male and eleven female. With the exception of Mustapha, Sukee, and Sambo, their names are common English designations. One man, Cheshire, is named for Duckenfield's home county. When the bill of sale was signed, Duckenfield gave Arderne an Indian boy, Natt.[47]

About the same time, Quaker planters and merchants were also acquiring bound labor and large landholdings with headrights granted partly for enslaved and indentured labor. Councilman Francis Tomes received 1,150 acres for twenty-three headrights, including allotments for three maidservants, two servant women, a manservant, eight enslaved Africans, and two Indians. Merchant Patrick Henley's 1,100-acre grant was based on twenty-two headrights, half for enslaved Africans. Sea captain John Hunt claimed 1,300 acres for twenty-six

TABLE 7.2. Headrights Granted in 1694

Grantee	Acres	Headrights	Africans	Indians	Servants
William Wilkinson	1,400	28	13	0	0
Alexander Lillington	1050	21	5	0	0
Richard Pope	650	13	6	0	1
Thomas Harvey	640	13	8	0	2
Henry Slade	600	12	5	2	0

TABLE 7.3. Importation of Enslaved Africans

Origin	Enslaved	Voyages
New York	18	10
South Carolina	16	2
Virginia	13	3
Bermuda	2	1
Maryland	1	1

headrights, including six Africans and an Indian. William and Gideon Therrill received 400 acres for eight headrights granted in part for two Africans and four Indians.[48]

Estate wills and inventories reveal such mixed labor forces as former governor Seth Sothell's 1695 listing of three Africans and three Indians; Valentine Bird's 1680 roster of eleven Africans, one Indian, and one female servant; and Mary Porter's 1717 bequest of four Africans and two Indians. None could equal Thomas Pollock's bequest of seventy-four enslaved Africans, probated in 1722.[49]

Dr. John Brickell noted that most of the enslaved persons originated in Guinea in West Africa and were usually purchased by gold and silver for sixteen to twenty-six pounds sterling, depending on age, sex, condition, and skills. Treacherous inlets and lack of a deepwater port meant that no transatlantic slave ships docked in the colony. Consequently, North Carolina was a secondary market for enslaved Africans, for whom headrights could be claimed. For the overseas trade, local customs records are few, and a duty was not levied, possibly to encourage importation of bound labor.[50] However, a partial portrait comes from sources in other continental colonial ports and Bermuda, where seventeen voyages to North Carolina can be documented between 1702 and 1730 that carried a total of fifty enslaved Africans, about half of whom entered in 1727.

Enslaved Africans were shipped to North Carolina as part of mixed cargoes in small coastal vessels that had carried the colony's goods for decades. Of the ten known vessels engaged in this trade, eight were sloops varying in size from seven to thirty tuns, mostly ten tuns or lighter. The three vessels registered in North Carolina were two ten-tun sloops, *Ann* and *Lark*, and a three-tun peri-auger, *Greyhound*. *Pheby*, a thirty-tun schooner, was based in South Carolina; four sloops were registered in New York; and the fifteen-tun *Bersheba* was from Bermuda. The majority of the enslaved traveled as individuals or groups of fewer than five. Two exceptions were eleven from Charles Town, South Carolina, and ten from Virginia's York River.[51]

The story of "Negro Boy Jack" provides insight into such commerce between Albemarle and the offshore islands. In February 1707 Chowan planter John Blount, a council member and General Court justice, commissioned his factor, Charlesworth Glover, to acquire an enslaved boy. Glover sailed for Bermuda in the sloop *Non Such*, under John Wilkins, master, where Glover purchased Jack and accompanied him on *Non Such* as an enslaved passenger for a fare of twenty-five shillings. Arriving first at a Pasquotank River landing, Glover left Jack on the sloop with Master Wilkins's assurance that *Non Such* would be at Little River soon. Using a lightering canoe, Wilkins, his mate, two sailors, a hired man, and two enslaved men were engaged in unloading cargo and stowing the outbound shipments. Jack also was hired to help. Last noted playing in the canoe, Jack fell unobserved into the water and tragically drowned. When it was discovered that he was missing, the sloop was thoroughly searched and his body was eventually found in the water. Because Wilkins had temporarily hired Jack, Blount sued him in General Court for £50 damages. The jury awarded £4.10s to cover the cost of passage and expenses, but not liability for the accidental death.[52]

In 1710 Colonel Christopher Codrington of Barbados, a benefactor of the Society for the Propagation of the Gospel (SPG), a missionary arm of the Anglican Church, had bequeathed two plantations staffed by hundreds of enslaved Africans to endow a theological and medical college. The Reverend John Urmston's desire for enslaved Africans to work his plantation led to his unusual effort to acquire them through the SPG. Beginning in 1711, Urmston twice sent requests for two Blacks who could speak English and work either as domestics or in the field, but his inquiries went unanswered.[53]

Enslaved Indians and Africans numbered from about 200 in 1680 to fewer than 1,000 in the early eighteenth century. Both Africans and Indians were typically listed in families, suggesting that they lived as family units.[54] Carteret described dormitory quarters for his servants, and barracks or duplex multifamily structures were common well into the eighteenth century. Family dwellings would consist of a small single room with a loft accessed by a ladder, similar to the home of a freeholder, usually an earthfast wood structure covered with siding and a split shingle roof with a mud-daubed wood-frame chimney. Minimal furnishings would include stools, tables, and a chest, with sleeping pallets in the loft.[55]

THE ONLY KNOWN PORTRAIT of enslaved African life in the colony is the sketchy description by Brickell, who lived in North Carolina 1729–31. Despite the restrictions of control endemic to slavery, the enslaved Africans managed to instill elements of their native cultures into a vibrant African American cultural life. Organized into tenuous families that were subject to dissolution by their owners at any time, the enslaved Africans created meaningful family relationships, sealed by a simple marriage ceremony recognized by the exchange of a token, such as a "Brass Ring or some other Toy." If after a year or so the couple had no children, always hanging over them was the threat of separation, as their owners were primarily interested in increasing their enslaved labor force. Divorce, marked by return of the token, would be followed by another marriage, perhaps repeatedly.

Enslaved children were raised by their parents or older women. When of age to work in the fields, they were allowed to plant a plot of tobacco for themselves and to earn income for personal needs by gathering and selling medicinal herbs, such as snakeroot, valued highly as an antidote for snakebite in a region rife with venomous serpents. Except for wintertime, clothing for the enslaved was minimal. Children wore "little or no" clothes, and in the summer young men and women worked in the fields "stark naked" except for a loincloth. Some enslaved Blacks were taught to read and write, and some were apprenticed to a trade or craft and became highly skilled.

Given the prevalence of runaways and the fear of rebellion, the colonists felt justified in passing punitive servant and slave laws. Compared to Blacks born in the colony, some of whom had been baptized and raised as Christians, the native Africans were thought to have "very harsh and stubborn Dispositions." Brickell agreed with this attitude after witnessing some Africans' stoic fortitude while experiencing brutal whippings that shredded their backs.[56]

Among the enslaved in Sothel's 1695 estate were three Africans and two Indians—Dina, who was "very lame" and pregnant, and a boy named Harry.[57] Sothel's enslaved family of Manuell and his wife Frank not only claimed personal property—bedding, a chest, and a gun barrel—but Manuell and the estate appraisers were at such loggerheads that neighbor Thomas Pollock intervened more than once with armed men "keeping the peace."[58] Impressed by the abilities of Manuell and Frank, Pollock acquired them and sent them across the sound to manage his distant plantation on the Scuppernong River. There their family expanded to two daughters and three sons. In addition to his farm supervision, Manuell engaged in trade with passing travelers, on one occasion providing roasting ears and tobacco. Pollock listed five enslaved families in 1709—Rowman and Judith, London and Betty, Thom and Nancy, Jackfiddle and Grace, and Scipio and Moll and their two sons, Tom and Scipio—but in his estate settlement in 1722 he divided his sixty-eight enslaved persons among his three sons without consideration of family ties.[59]

In 1680 Valentine Bird, a prosperous planter, listed thirteen bound laborers: Ann Farmer, with four years left on her indenture; an enslaved Indian named Mary; and eleven enslaved Africans: three men—Mingo, Andrew, and Thom; four women—Hanna, Betty, Betty, and Bess; and four children—boys Mustapha, Robin, and George and a girl, Jane. The planter Thomas Jarvis had two enslaved Indians—Anne and her child, Harry—and five enslaved Africans—three men, a woman, and a child. Their values ranged from £35 to £40 for adult males, £30 for adult women, and £10 to £20 for children, depending on their age.[60]

Headright claims recorded in 1694 reveal the diverse labor groups on Albemarle's farms and plantations. Thomas Harvey had eight enslaved Africans (Hector, Maria, Tom, Peter, Nick, Betty, Maria, and Nick) and two indentured servants (William and Elinor); Benjamin Laker's enslaved Africans were Mingo's family of his wife and two children (Francisco and Maria); Perquimans Quaker Timothy Clare had two indentured servants (Charles and Eliza), two enslaved Indians, and three enslaved Africans.[61]

The 2,000-square-mile Great Dismal Swamp had been occupied by Native Americans for millennia. It has been asserted that by the eighteenth century there was a Maroon community, or refuge for fugitive servants and slaves. In the previous century the labor force had been predominantly indentured servants, with enslaved Indians and Africans. Runaways then were usually sought on Currituck Banks. By the end of the seventeenth century the number of enslaved Africans was increasing rapidly as larger plantations became more common. Dr. Brickell is singular in his observation that runaways hid in the woods, sometimes for months. He asserted that Africans were fearful of Indians, who had a "natural aversion to the *Blacks*" and often shot them on sight or occasionally hunted down fugitives, torturing and killing some and forcing others to return and face the harsh punishment awaiting them.[62]

There is little documentary evidence of a fugitive community in the Great Dismal Swamp prior to the eighteenth century. In recent years archaeological excavation of hammocks scattered throughout the swamp has documented both Native American inhabitants from the Archaic to the Woodland cultures and later European and African artifacts from the eighteenth and nineteenth centuries. The few European artifacts of the seventeenth century could very well have been acquired through trade.[63]

AFTER 1700 up to a dozen remnant Native American tribes numbering several hundred persons lived peacefully in small villages scattered across the Albemarle. John Lawson recorded fifty Meherrin warriors, fifteen Chowan, ten Pasquotank, thirty Poteskeet, and just six total Yeopim. Having traversed the backcountry, Lawson estimated that the five eastern piedmont tribes totaled about 750 persons.[64] South of the Albemarle Sound, the "Greate nation" of the "very Civilised" Tuscarora and their satellite tribes reputedly numbered over 5,000 in fifteen towns, about three-fourths of the coastal Indians.[65]

Native Americans were economically integrated with the colonists not only as a source of furs but also in the agricultural economy. John Lawson observed, "The neighboring *Indians* are friendly, and in many Cases serviceable to us, in making us Wares [weirs] to catch Fish in, for a small matter. . . . Some of them hunt and fowl for us at reasonable Rates. . . . The poorer Sort of Planters often get them to plant for them, by hiring them for that Season."[66]

Regarding the mastery of the water by Native boatmen, near the end of the Tuscarora War Thomas Pollock described recalcitrant Mattamuskeet and Core warriors who used boats and canoes on the sound and streams to raid settlements on the Alligator River and Roanoke Island. Pollock wrote that these "expert watermen" could "transport themselves where they please" and fade back into impenetrable quagmires and swamps of "one of the greatest deserts in the world, where it is almost impossible for white men to follow them."[67]

Peaceful coexistence with the Native inhabitants began with the early settlers' purchase of land. The Quaker belief in treating everyone with dignity and equality certainly reinforced good relations, but the colony's policy of accommodating the Indians was already in place before Quaker missionaries arrived. Uncommonly fair treatment included extending legal protection to the Native peoples. Indians living in their villages among the settlers, especially the Yeopim and Chowan, sought and won the protection of the General Court for damages to their property by encroaching English.[68] As early as 1684 in the county court a council member, Thomas Jarvis, represented an Indian whose gun had been kept by a colonist, Richard Edge. A few years later an Indian named John King, whom colonists had stopped from hunting, sued for protection of Native hunting rights on unoccupied land and the right to pass through settled land for the purpose of hunting. The court upheld those rights as long as Indians were "behaveing themselves sivilly and doeing noe Injury."[69]

The darkest side of the Indian-English relationship was the impact on both resulting from the enslavement of Natives, which would peak in the aftermath of the Tuscarora War. Although a source of labor for farms and plantations, runaway enslaved and servant Indians were brought before courts, often in company with enslaved Blacks, for a variety of criminal offenses, primarily theft from their masters. Henry Norman, a carpenter, and his wife Anne alleged that their runaway Indian manservant, George West, stole a canoe, a gun, blankets, men and women's clothing, shoes, and an array of carpenter's and joiner's tools.[70] In a similar incident, James and Mary Cole returned home to find themselves robbed of goods and a trunk of clothing, apparently by a trio of their enslaved persons—two Black and one Indian. Despite pursuit by the constables in Pasquotank and Currituck Precincts, the runaways were never caught.[71]

Even during and after the Tuscarora War, the courts were capable of treating Indians as they would colonists. While the war was raging, John Durant, a Yeopim Indian fighting in the colony's defense, captured an enslaved Indian woman. His commander, Matthew Midget, commandeered her without compensation. Durant turned to the Court of Chancery, which ruled that the enslaved Indian was his and ordered Midget to pay him ten pounds for her. In the case of John Cope, a Christian Indian, the grand jury indicted him for breaking and entering the Belgra home of President Thomas Pollock, arguably the most prominent and powerful person in the colony. However, the trial jury believed Cope's plea of not guilty, and he was discharged.[72]

ALBEMARLE WAS a "relatively remote and poor corner of the British Atlantic World," with limited commercial staple products or ready sources of bound labor. Historians have generally agreed that the physical isolation of North Carolina by barrier islands contributed to slow socioeconomic development. Although New England skippers sailing their small ketches and sloops indirectly connected Albemarle to the North Atlantic trade network, with no deepwater port the colonists were predominantly midlevel planters, yeoman farmers, artisans, and merchants. What gentry there were lacked the wealth of those with pretensions to aristocracy in neighboring Virginia and South Carolina. North Carolina elites might aspire to create a slave-based society more like South Carolina's, but the colony remained instead a society based on diverse free and bound labor. Regardless of what Pollock and his peers did, Albemarle was destined to be largely a middling economy, one in which many farmers engaged in commercial agriculture.[73] Bertie planter Cullen Pollock, son of Thomas Pollock, one of the colony's grandees and its largest landholder, observed that "the badness of our Navigation makes our Land and Slaves of very little profit to us."[74]

Albemarle was populated primarily by middling families who lived on several hundred acres with a few indentured servants or enslaved persons, and the gap between low and high status was narrower than in the neighboring colonies. Furthermore, opportunities for social mobility proved a powerful enticement to hazard the Atlantic crossing. A survey of eighty estates in the years 1680–1719 revealed that the net average value was seventy-three pounds.[75] Whether planters or merchants, the county's leaders owned sizable estates, possessing considerable livestock and household goods but not comparable to the wealthiest Virginians and South Carolinians. Valentine Bird, a member of the council, could boast an estate worth about £583. The estate of council member Edmund Chancy was valued at £226.13, while his fellow council member, Francis Godfrey, left assets totaling nearly £131. When proprietor and former governor Seth Sothel died in 1694, the value of his estate was just over £301.[76]

In Albemarle, with no great riches to flaunt, less ostentation fostered a casual informality that baffled English critics unaccustomed to egalitarian behavior from the "poorer sort." This contributed to the colony's reputation as barbarous and uncivilized and lent credence to the claim that it was inhabited by runaways and debtors. These assessments merely reflect the prejudices of observers unaccustomed to the rustic manners of the backwater settlement. The Reverend John Urmston, who described Albemarle as "a wretched corner of the world," never adjusted to the colony's classless values, which recognized "noe difference between a Gentleman and a Labourer, all Fellows at Foot Ball." To him, the lack of class deference made his neighbors "lawless," rejecting any "power or Authority in either Church or State save what is derived from them[;] a Proprietor were he here would be look't on no better than a ballad singer."[77]

The local attitude still lingered over a century later when a Chowan planter, James Johnston, was furnishing his elegant plantation seat, Hayes. He told a New York merchant that he wanted furniture "of the plainest and neatest kind and not in the extreme of the fashion. . . . A man by appearing very different from his neighbours is more apt to excite their ridicule and perhaps envy than their esteem and respect."[78]

Freeholders, artisans, or laborers generally lived in one-room frame or sawn-log earthfast post-in-ground houses. The chimney usually was a wood-frame structure daubed with mud. The single room accommodated daily living, socializing, and cooking, with a sleeping and storage loft accessed by a ladder or enclosed staircase. William Byrd II observed in 1728 that most of the dwellings were "Log-houses, covered with Pine or Cypress Shingles 3 feet long, and one broad: They are hung upon Laths with Peggs, and their Doors too turn upon wooden Hinges, and have wooden Locks to secure them, so that the Building is finish't without Nails or other Iron-work."[79]

Along the sparsely settled border, Byrd's survey party took shelter wherever they could, sometimes in appalling accommodations. In March, in a "wretched Hovel" at the mouth of the Northwest River, they bedded down on "a very dirty Floor, that was quite alive with Fleas & Chinches." On the return trip in November at Captain Embry's on the Nottoway River, another "dirty Room" housed the visitors and the family of men, women, and children—"no less than Nine Persons, who all pigg'd loveingly together."[80]

In contrast to the propertied class, the estate of a small farmer, who might have a hundred acres or less, consisted of a few head of livestock and the minimum of household goods. George Branch, who died in 1696, left £2 of property. The £9.06.10 estate of John Butler was gutted by illness, funeral expenses, and debts, leaving only 12s.9d. A mate of New England sea captain Samuel Woodes—Ralph French, who had accidentally drowned—possessed a few pieces of old furniture, some old clothing, a watch, a gold ring, 550 pounds of pork, three bushels of peas, and old navigation instruments, including a forestaff, a gradient, and a compass. Lawrence Mearle's estate of nearly £7 included two sheep, a small amount of corn, and a few old household items. By contrast, the planter Henry Palin's estate of just over £61 was mostly in a herd of thirty-seven cattle, and his household had a bed, four chests, a table, two chairs, a fireplace and cooking equipment, and two silver spoons.[81]

Descriptions of households of tenants, servants, or enslaved persons are rare. Peter Carteret mentioned a "Quartering House" on the plantation on Powell's Point that housed three male indentured servants.[82] Like small planters, servants and those enslaved probably lived in one-room frame or sawn-log houses with handmade or cast-off stools, chairs, tables, and storage boxes. Sleeping quarters might be beds or rush or cattail pallets with worn canvas or duck sheeting and coverlets.

The frame, or occasionally brick, dwellings of more prosperous settlers were one-and-a-half-story hall or hall-and-parlor "Virginia" style, with brick end chimneys. Typically serving for entertaining visitors, dining, and sleeping, the hall was dominated by a massive fireplace used for heating and cooking. Gradually the kitchen became a separate building, as were quarters for bound laborers and various farm outbuildings.[83] The earliest-mentioned English house in the region was the dwelling and trading post built for Nathaniel Batts, described as "20 foote square with a lodging chamber and a Buttery and a chimney." Requiring the skills of a carpenter for five months, this house was more substantial than a rude cabin—probably an earthfast timber-framed structure sheathed with horizontal planks.[84]

Similar in size was the twenty-foot frame and weatherboarded dwelling house that awaited Peter Carteret on Colleton Island in 1665. Located on Little River in Perquimans, Francis Godfrey's spacious dwelling was described as a "framed house forty foot Long 20 foot wide; with a shade [shed room] on the back side; and a porch on the front, beeing all Sawed worke; and all Ready framed." It was an inn and for many years accommodated sessions of the council, courts, and assembly. A hall with a chamber above comprised the two-room house of wealthy Governor Seth Sothel and his wife, who were childless. Their two outbuildings were a dairy and a kitchen. In his enclosed two-story entrance, planter Francis Tomes of Old Neck in Perquimans furnished the "porch Chamber" with feather beds as a guest room for visiting Quaker ministers.[85]

A larger house usually had partitions on both floors that created four rooms, and a hall-and-parlor house often had a shed room attached to the rear that housed the kitchen.[86] Houses in Perquimans Precinct that survived into the twentieth century provide examples of the primary types of construction in use by the early eighteenth century: frame, brick, and frame with brick ends. Built by Thomas Peirce after 1705, the Theopilus White house, now demolished, was twenty-eight by eighteen feet and had massive brick gable-end chimneys laid in English and Flemish bond. The Newbold-White house is a well-built Flemish-bond brick hall-and-parlor house. The property was first granted to Joseph Scott in 1684, but the surviving house was built in 1730 by Quaker Abraham Sanders.[87] Based on architectural and archaeological research, it has been restored to a seventeenth-century appearance and is open to the public for interpretation of early domestic life.

Also in Perquimans are two examples of brick-end frame houses—the Sutton-Newby, built after 1713 by Joseph Sutton, and the Myers-White, built after 1721 by Thomas Long. The former boasts elaborate medieval Flemish-bond brick with glazed headers laid in a chevron pattern, while the latter has a gambrel roof and brick ends in English bond.[88] In 1715 a gentleman of Chowan Precinct, Thomas Bray, contracted with carpenter Edward Jackson to construct a dwelling at the mouth of Indian Town Creek. A prosperous planter, Bray held 1,280 acres in tracts on both sides of the Chowan River and was part owner of the ship *Albemarle*. The house was to be twenty feet long by fifteen feet wide, with an eight-foot-wide shed room.[89]

Other extant early colonial homes remain hidden in the walls of modernized structures across North Carolina's coastal plain. The number of identified houses from the proprietary period will grow as preservation-minded individuals acquire neglected buildings and discover through historical, archaeological, and scientific research, such as dendrochronology (tree-ring dating), that they have a rare survivor of our early history. Such a case was announced in 2013:

The Newbold-White house was built by Abraham Sanders in 1730. It is restored
and open for tours. Courtesy of State Archives of North Carolina.

a small apparently Victorian dwelling in Edenton is in fact a 25-by-16-foot
story-and-a-half frame weatherboarded 1718–19 building, currently the oldest
documented house in the state.[90]

Plans to replace the Chowan River Bridge just north of Salmon Creek led
in 1996 to the discovery and salvage excavation of the Eden House archaeological site. At Eden House Point was the plantation of Governor Charles
Eden (1714–22), a later resident of this oldest settled colonial area. While not so
significant as Charles Towne on the Cape Fear (1664–67), Eden House is the
region's most important early colonial site uncovered to date.[91] This desirable
property on the west bank near the mouth of the Chowan River was included
in one of the earliest land grants in North Carolina, the 600-acre Virginia patent issued in 1663 to Saint Mount Wells.[92]

The earliest structures found on the site were two earthfast frame buildings
with wooden siding that were interpreted as a house and a barn or quarters,
probably built in the 1670s or 1680s, using the type of construction common in
seventeenth-century Virginia for both rich and poor. Indicating a high quality

of life that would match a comparable Virginia planter's home, the dwelling had a single-room hall that measured sixteen by sixteen feet and a rear shed that was eight by sixteen feet. The corner hearth was clay, the base of a typical wood-framed clay-daubed chimney. Decorative tin-glazed blue-and-white ceramic tile depicting biblical scenes adorned the chimney hood, and there was evidence of leaded casement glass windows. Ceramics and glass from the site were dated from the late seventeenth to the early eighteenth century and reflected North Atlantic connections: English, Dutch, and New England decorated earthenwares, German stoneware, and Chinese porcelain. Typical kitchen and dining vessels were milk pans, porringers, cups, pipkins, leaded glass stemware, and green blown-glass wine bottles. A rich and varied diet was represented by the bones of domestic animals, wild game and fowl, and fish from the rivers and sound. Found at the barn was a diminutive but important artifact—a copper alloy cufflink button with a portrait of Charles II that linked the site directly to the early years of settlement.[93]

A second period at Eden House is represented by a ballast stone half cellar paved with brick that underlay a larger frame structure. The cellar fill contained lead strips for casement windows, fragments of slate roof tiles, plaster, and glazed brick from a massive chimney, indicative of an elite lifestyle appropriate for council deputy William Duckenfield, who had purchased the property in 1702. Here Governor Edward and Catherine Hyde and their household may have resided from 1710 to 1713 when they were living on the estate.[94]

Other features excavated on the site were a barn, a well, a privy, and extensive fencing. Because there was open-range livestock, the homes and farm buildings, gardens, and orchards were enclosed. A contemporary description of Thomas Luten's Sandy Point property in Chowan Precinct provides a portrait similar to Eden House in the 1720s. Luten's 440-acre Chowan County plantation had a manor house, a kitchen, a barn, a stable, a garden, an orchard, 30 acres of "arable plow land," 17 acres of meadow, 70 acres of pasture, and 320 acres of woodland.[95]

Although Albemarle houses were small and many contained only one to four rooms, the wealthier planters' homes were adequately furnished not only for the families in residence but for hosting public meetings of the assembly, the courts, and the council. Furnishings ranged from simple handmade benches, stools, and tables to finely crafted Jacobean-style turned chairs, stretcher tables with turned legs, and wainscot chests.

Valentine Bird (d. ca. 1679) was a speaker of the General Assembly, a council deputy, a customs collector, and a leader in Culpeper's Rebellion. His considerable estate included trunks, chests, a couch, two tables (one of black walnut), ten chairs, a hammock, five beds, a cradle, and two pewter chamber pots. The floors and tables displayed a striped carpet and numerous colored rugs. Silver plate and pewter items that bespoke status were exhibited in open cupboards. Margaret Bird could entertain large groups with two dozen pewter plates, a number of pewter porringers, and over fifty other pewter dishes. She could set her table with an ample supply of fine and everyday napkins and tablecloths, pewter and large brass candlesticks, and salt shakers. For the best company she had a silver tankard and silver spoons. Her linen closet was well stocked with fine and common sheets, numerous pillows, plenty of towels, and cupboard cloths.[96]

Another council deputy, Francis Godfrey (d. 1675), who operated an inn and was a factor for a Barbados merchant, owned a plantation of 1,400 acres and one of the larger houses in Perquimans Precinct, which was used for council and court sessions for decades. Francis and Joane Godfrey and their three children enjoyed a well-furnished home that could accommodate nearly forty guests. The Godfreys' community status was reflected in her fine wainscoted standing cupboard graced with silver spoons, sack bowls, Durham cups, and a beer bowl, as well as her pewter-laden sideboard.[97]

Practical domestic items on the farmsteads included butter tubs, stoneware jugs, churns, cheese presses and tubs, tin pudding pans, and copper kettles; linen presses, tin candlesticks, and brass candle snuffers; trundle beds, cedar chests; sewing implements, such as a silver thimble and a silver bodkin; and a variety of weapons, including fowling pieces, pistols, cutlasses, and rapiers.[98] Early Albemarle may have been a backwater settlement, but it was not backward. High-quality furniture, silver, pewter, and linens were readily available from Virginia merchants or through the intercolonial trade supplying English goods through New England, New York, and Philadelphia.

———————

LIKE FRONTIER WOMEN throughout history, Albemarle women carved out a more independent life than their sisters in England, Virginia, or even South Carolina. While engaged in locating the boundary between North Carolina and Virginia in 1711, the Virginia commissioners were entertained by a border housewife of some means, Mrs. Francis Jones, who lived near the North River. Although her husband was away, she sent a Black servant to seek help from neighbors and provided canoes for crossing the river. She was admiringly described as "a very civil woman and shews nothing of ruggedness or Immodesty in her carriage, yett she will carry a gunn in the woods and kill deer, turkeys, &c., shoot doun wild cattle, catch and tye hoggs, knock down beeves with an ax and perform the most manfull Exercises as well as most men in those parts."[99]

Although women in Albemarle enjoyed more freedom and more favorable status than their counterparts in more settled societies, their primary duty remained rearing children, whether their own, stepchildren, or adoptions. John Lawson described the native-born women as "often very fair. . . . They marry very young; some at Thirteen or Fourteen; and She that stays till Twenty, is reckon'd a stale Maid. . . . The Women are very fruitful; most Houses being full of Little Ones."[100]

In addition to parental duties, women managed household establishments, from small farms to large plantations. In Albemarle their responsibilities might include the domestic chores of the house, nursing the sick, gardening, spinning, weaving, sewing, dairying, tending barnyard livestock, preparing and preserving food, including slaughtering, cleaning, and preserving meat and fish, as well as working in the fields beside their menfolk, indentured servants, and enslaved laborers. The equality of the frontier meant that Albemarle women quite often were expected to fulfill a man's role. Lawson was impressed by the abilities of the Carolina women, observing that "the Women are very handy in Canoes, and will manage them with great Dexterity and Skill, which they become accustomed to in this watry Country. They are ready to help their Husbands in any servile Work, as Planting."[101] Albemarle women held property, managed plantations, owned and ran businesses, served as attorneys in court, dispensed medicine and health care, and exerted indirect influence as hostesses to council meetings, courts, and political gatherings, which were usually held in their homes.

Many marriages were shortened by the death of a spouse, and over the course of a lifetime, women who were married several times might accumulate significant property. Although a married woman's dowry was protected by law, prenuptial agreements that preserved a wife's property were not uncommon, especially among the wealthy, and tended to concentrate estates for women widowed multiple times. A 1705 prenuptial contract between Edward Moseley and Anne Walker, the widow of Governor Henderson Walker, ensured that Moseley would will her £500 in "Money Plate Jewells Slaves or household stuff."[102] Before Frances Culpeper, from English gentry, would marry Samuel Stephens, he had to agree to leave her his 1,350-acre Warwick River plantation in Virginia. Two months after Stephens's death, she exacted a similar settlement from Sir William Berkeley, including a lifetime interest in his English property, an annual income of £600, and his Green Spring estate on the James River.[103]

Under English law of the time, a single woman or widow enjoyed the legal status of *feme sole*, essentially the same rights as a single man. She could sue and be sued, hold land, enter a contract, will her estate, administer estates, and be guardian of minors. On marriage she became *feme covert*, with her rights "suspended or incorporated" to her husband, who was responsible for protecting her rights and property. Albemarle's remoteness ensured that *feme covert* was more a theory than a reality. A married woman held property, had power of attorney for her spouse, and jointly owned property with her husband. Like spinsters and widows, wives operated businesses, appeared in court, and represented their husband's legal and business interests.[104]

Troubled marriage property decisions were regulated by the General Assembly and the General Court. Although divorce was not an option, the court did intervene on behalf of wives who had been abused or abandoned and could grant annulment or legal separation. In a petition Saphia Vince stated that she had been for seven years a "loving and obedient Wife" to her impotent husband, Humphrey Vince, but the marriage had not been consummated, which her husband confirmed. The court declared her marriage "Null and void," releasing her to marry again. Her husband was ordered to return her dowry or its value.[105] When John Steward "squandered away" much of her "considerable estate" and left the colony, his crippled wife, Ann Steward, petitioned the court for protection of her remaining property from her husband's creditors. She also filed a request for 30s from the estate of Emannuell Albory for caring for him through his final illness at her home.[106]

Deserted by her husband, Elizabeth Atkinson petitioned the General Court for support, as she had no way to make a living. When the court was informed that Richard Atkinson, of "Evill fame," was "Scandalously" involved with Sarah King, a married woman, he was cited for contempt, arrested, and ordered not to have company with Mrs. King. The court's settlement for the deserted wife required her husband to give her two cows and calves, a bull, a horse, a barrel of corn, and all of the household goods. The couple promised to neither disturb nor molest one another, and the court confirmed a deed of gift for the property awarded to Elizabeth.[107]

When Chowan weaver John Cockrill twice failed to appear in General Court to settle a sixty-pound debt and fled the colony, goods and chattels of that value were seized to satisfy the debt. In November 1723 his wife Mary petitioned the council that she and her small children had no source of income and were reduced to "deplorable Circumstances." She requested remission of the fine and property, and the council readily complied.[108]

In the precinct and general courts of the late seventeenth century, women served as attorneys, executrices, guardians over minors, plaintiffs, and defendants in civil and criminal actions. In February 1694 the widow Susanna Hartley appeared as an attorney in place of her recently deceased husband. In addition to answering judgments on the administration of her husband's estate, she served as an executrix of the estate of Thomas Slaughter. In the same session, two women, Hannah Gosby and Tabitha Haskett, proved headrights to land for transportation of new arrivals in the colony.[109]

The freedom afforded Albemarle women opened opportunities for business, wealth, and status. Several well-known taverns were owned and operated by women, usually widows who had been business partners with their husbands and then continued, whether they remained single or remarried. One widow inherited and operated a ferry. A number of women inherited plantations and farms. Since they very likely had been involved in the management while their husbands were alive, it should be no surprise that they were usually successful on their own.[110]

At age sixteen a Quaker maiden, Sarah Mayo, became the third wife of Pasquotank planter and merchant John Culpeper, a middle-aged widower. While managing her household and raising two daughters, she helped her husband in his correspondence with New York trading partners. After his death she married another middle-aged merchant, Patrick Henley, master of the vessel *Jane and Sarah*. A stepdaughter, two more daughters, and a son completed her family. In 1698, late in her last pregnancy, she sailed to Philadelphia to nurse her seriously ill husband. Shortly after her arrival she gave birth to a daughter, and within three months she lost her second husband. Sarah remained in the city settling his debts and estate. She married her third husband, Mathew Prichard, a Pasquotank Quaker, before she left Philadelphia. Back home she took over the family business as executrix and administrator.[111]

Innkeeping was a woman's most prevalent business opportunity. Diana Harris accompanied her husband, Thomas, to Albemarle around 1665, where they settled on 600 acres in Perquimans Precinct. Thomas Harris became secretary of the colony and clerk of the council and operated a tavern at their home. After his death in 1677 Diana married William Foster, a widower and county justice. The couple continued to keep the tavern. When Foster died in 1687, Diana took over the business and operated it with her son, John Harris; she became sole owner when he died in 1693. During the joint tenure, the inn was known as the house of John Harris, although from the meager record, it is clear that Diana managed it and employed Thomas Hassold as bookkeeper. In 1694, at the age of fifty, Diana married Thomas White, who was fourteen years younger. This time Diana had chosen poorly. White sued to collect delinquent accounts and was countersued by his creditors. Soon the inn was teetering on bankruptcy and the marriage failed. Diana sued for separate maintenance, claiming that he had sold most of her furniture and left her destitute and homeless. White died in 1696, leaving a wasted estate. Diana recovered some of her household furnishings, but she did not resume tavern keeping.[112]

Although women could not participate directly in public affairs, some exerted influence by accumulating wealth and position through advantageous marriages. Like Anna Willix, Frances Culpeper achieved the pinnacle of power and wealth in the American colonies through marriage to men of talent and

ambition. She was the wife of three colonial governors and by inheritance became a Lady Proprietor of Carolina. Two months after the death of Samuel
Stephens in 1670, Frances married Sir William Berkeley. Although she was a
generation younger than the governor, Sir William doted on her, taking her
into his confidence as a political adviser. Dame Frances hosted a salon at Green
Spring, lavishly entertaining the colony's leaders, and staunchly supported her
husband during Bacon's Rebellion. When Sir William died in 1677, she gathered a coterie of planters and officials at Green Spring who virtually controlled
the colony. In 1680 Lady Frances wed Colonel Philip Ludwell, a near neighbor
who later was named governor of northern Carolina. He came to Albemarle in
1690, possibly accompanied by his wife. A vivacious woman of charm, wit, and
strong conviction, Lady Frances died in 1695 at the age of sixty-one.[113]

Ann Marwood Durant, a remarkable woman in any age, adeptly balanced
extensive domestic obligations with a business, professional, and public life.
Ann Marwood was living in Northumberland County, Virginia, when George
Durant, a mariner, arrived there from England in the summer of 1658. Six
months later the Durants were married in an Anglican service. Not long afterward, George became involved with Nathaniel Batts and the Albemarle fur
trade. In August 1661 he purchased land from the Yeopim Indians on a peninsula that became Durant's Neck.

Whenever her husband was at sea, Ann Durant managed the family's en-
terprises, including an inn, a mercantile business, and a plantation. She hosted
court and political meetings in her home, dispensed medicine and health care,
sewed clothing, arranged funerals, and even had the coffins made. She held
power of attorney for her husband and appeared in court for him, as well as
on behalf of herself and others. On her first day in court on 25 May 1673, Ann
Durant became the first female attorney in North Carolina, paving the way for
others to follow. Meanwhile, she reared nine children, including three sons and
six daughters born between 1659 and 1681. All but one son survived to adult-
hood. She also raised two granddaughters who had been orphaned in infancy.
By all accounts the thirty-five-year Durant marriage was a partnership that
weathered long periods of separation. They depended on each other but could
make their way independently. When George died in January 1694, Ann survived him by only a year.[114]

———————

FROM THE BEGINNING, explorers and colonists praised the region's rich abundance of game, waterfowl, and seafood. Hospitable Indians offered meals of
maize in various forms, venison, small game, fish and shellfish, and an array
of vegetables and fruits in season, chiefly beans, peas, squash, pumpkins, and

This portrait of Frances Culpeper (ca. 1660) is the only known
likeness of a woman related to North Carolina in the proprietary
era. In addition to successively marrying three colonial governors,
she was a Lady Proprietor of Carolina. Private collection;
photo courtesy of MESDA Object Database, File S-6958.

melons. The Natives broiled, roasted, and cured by smoking, but their standard
repast was a stew of meat, fish, and vegetables simmered in a large earthen
pot.[115] On his extensive journey through the backcountry, John Lawson recorded eating "barbacu'd Turkeys, Bear's Oil, and Venison," and later combining
venison scraps with "3 Teal and a Possum; which Medly all together made a
curious Ragoo."[116]

Maize, or Indian corn, was the cereal of the Americas, the heart of the diet of
the Native Americans and the newcomer Europeans and Africans. Writing in
the early eighteenth century, naturalist Mark Catesby observed that it was the
grain "of most general use, and is eat, not only by the Negro slaves, but by the

generality of white people." As roasting ears, green corn, bread, and pudding, corn is still the foundation grain of the southern diet, although Catesby noted that in his day boiled hominy was "more in esteem than any other preparation."[117] John Urmston described eating a common corn "hominy-Bread," but believed it "fitter for Hoggs."[118]

From their West African homelands, enslaved Blacks brought new vegetables, fruits, seasonings, and cooking techniques. Coming initially to Carolina from Barbados and other West Indian islands, Black cooks familiar with Creole cuisine contributed such ingredients as yams, peanuts, okra, black-eyed peas, and watermelons. To food preparation they added deep-fat frying and exotic sauces seasoned with ginger, thyme, parsley, basil, shallots, or hot peppers.[119] Over time the southern diet became a rich mélange of Native American, British, West African, and Caribbean ingredients and cooking methods.

Colonists brought their familiar English fare to Albemarle but complemented their heavy diet of meat, dairy products, and bread with native fruits, vegetables, and game. Settlers consumed fresh, salt, and cured pork; beef, mutton, bacon, cheese, butter, and honey; and wheat and corn breads. All households grew vegetables, as well as herbs for seasoning and medicinal use. For familiar domesticated fruit, colonists planted orchards and berry patches or reclaimed them from their Native predecessors. Wild nuts were plentiful, and favorite wild fruits and berries were persimmons, mulberries, haws, fox grapes, strawberries, blackberries, blueberries, and raspberries. A new delight was the native pawpaw, described as soft and very sweet, from which "rare Puddings" were made.[120]

Like their contemporaries throughout the empire, Albemarle planters were fond of beer, wine, and spirits, consuming quantities of flip and punch made from imported rum, brandy, and wine. Although some rum came directly from Barbados and Jamaica, most was imported through New England. William Byrd thought this rum "so bad and unwholesome, that it is not improperly call'd 'Kill-Devil.'"[121] The preferred sweetener was molasses, called "Long Sugar," which originated in the Caribbean but was also brought in from New England. Byrd described a local punch known as Bombo that was equal parts of rum and water mixed with "Long Sugar."[122] An overnight council meeting at the Perquimans house of John Pettiver in 1708 where four servants attended twenty men resulted in a bill of £17.11 to cover a barrel of "Strong Drink," seven gallons of rum, fifty pounds of sugar, and meals of beef, pork, fowl, wheat bread, and butter.[123]

Locally made cider and quince-drink were also popular. At the tavern of Thomas and Diana White one bill of £27.13.8 was paid primarily for bottles of flip, cider, quince-drink, and rum, although meals and entertainment were also included.[124] In addition to persimmon beer, John Lawson noted that "they make a Wine, or Liquor, which they call Quince-Drink, and which I approve of beyond any Drink which that Country affords, though a great deal of Cider and some Perry is there made."[125] In the earliest reference to a southern staple, corn whiskey, Thomas Ashe mentioned in 1680 that the Carolinians "have lately invented a way of making with it [corn] good sound Beer; but it's strong and heady: By Maceration, when duly fermented, a strong Spirit like Brandy may be drawn off from it, by the help of an Alembick."[126]

Albemarle's most popular recreational pastimes were hunting, fishing, and fowling, which had the useful result of providing meat for the table. For less practical entertainment, Dr. John Brickell observed that colonists were "fond" of horse racing and that "Race-Paths," usually a quarter mile long, were laid out near the towns and across country. Contests were normally match races, with two horses running at "all the speed imaginable." Furthermore, Brickell wrote that colonists were "much addicted to *Gaming*" with cards, dice, and cock fighting. The "darling Amusement," however, was dancing to the music of a fiddle, a bagpipe, or unaccompanied singing. The wheat harvest in June was a time of celebration that brought planters and laborers together from miles around for the harvest, great feasting, music, dancing, and "Revelling."[127]

WAS THE "COUNTRY SICKLEY" OR NOT? A statistical study of mortality in the colony determined that the median age of death for white males rose from thirty-five to fifty-one by the turn of the century. Although their life expectancy was less than that of New Englanders, it was greater than in Virginia, contrary to the general view that one's lifespan decreased proportionately as one moved south in the colonies.[128] Knowing that the low, swampy environment was similar to the Virginia tidewater, researchers are surprised to find better health in the Albemarle region. Two contributing factors may be that more of the Albemarle settlers were seasoned, native-born colonists and that the colony's isolation reduced exposure to communicable diseases.

Among the colony's medical practitioners were John Hecklefield, Patrick Maule, Thomas Taper, John King, John Feillett, Jerome Armor, George Alleyn, and Godfrey Spruill, who used the title "Chyrurgion." A Bertie couple, James and Ann Speir, served their community as surgeon and midwife. In England medical men were ranked as physicians or doctors educated in a university, chirurgeons (surgeons) who had learned as apprentices, and apothecaries who prescribed and dispensed drugs. Most of the practitioners in North Carolina were really chirurgeons, although some used the title "doctor of physick," and one called himself "Practiser of Physick and Surgery."[129]

An ailing patient received care from family, neighbors knowledgeable about the practice of medicine, physicians, or tavern keepers. In 1690 John Culle, a laborer in a sharecropping arrangement with Ann Durant and living in her inn, died after a two-week illness. About half of the £4.16.2 bill to his estate related to the sickness: daily attendance, rum, a gallon of cider, quince-drink, accommodations, bedding, and a burial rug.[130] Women who served as midwives often also had knowledge of herbal remedies, and many women "attended" or nursed the sick in homes or inns. Alice Wade, for example, received three pounds for treating and curing James Lundy's leg.[131] In 1725 Patience Cotton Speir died following childbirth under the care of midwife Ann Speir. Although Patience had absolved her of any blame, the distraught parents, James and Martha Cotton, accused Ann Speir of murder, and she was indicted. The protracted case went to trial the next year, resulting in a verdict of not guilty.[132]

Treatment in the period could be strenuous. Still believed to be caused by the ancient notion of imbalance in humors, or bodily fluids, disease was treated by bleeding, purging, and vomiting. "Physic" and emetics were used to induce vomiting, and "glisters," or "clysters," for evacuation of the bowels. Anodyne pills were given as painkillers and muscle relaxers. One common compound, "anodyne balsam," was a concoction of castile soap, opium, camphor, saffron, and wine.[133] In midsummer 1694 Dr. John King treated Arthur Workman for eight days, administering two physics, two emetics, several clysters, and ten anodyne pills. Medicine and treatments were expensive: anodyne pills cost five shillings each, emetics and physics were three shillings, and "glisters" were five shillings. Counting two follow-up visits, Dr. King's total bill came to £9.13. Workman survived the treatment, only to be arrested for nonpayment of his bill. By the time the case came to court, he had died. His executrix, Mary Clarke, secured a reduction of the charges and paid the remainder.[134]

In the early eighteenth century James Feillett, self-described as "Dr. Medicine," attempted to treat several incidents of "country distemper," or endemic yaws. Yaws was common in the colony, associated with poor hygiene and sanitation and eating fresh pork. Known to be related to venereal syphilis, the non-venereal yaws was treated internally with mercury and mercurial ointments. Finding an advanced infection of many years' duration in Dorothy Jennings, who had over three dozen sores and "malignous" ulcers on her atrophied right arm and leg, Feillett prescribed daily baths, physics, chemical and galenical remedies, ointments, salves, and powders. Feillett claimed to have nearly cured her, but she stopped the treatment. The total bill for extensive attendance and medicines came to £21.5. Jennings worked off £4.10 of the bill by cooking and washing for the doctor's family and providing corn, beeswax, and pasturage for the doctor's horse. When she contested the remainder, a jury reduced it to £2.10. For the same affliction William Jennings successfully contested Dr. Feillett's entire bill because the doctor allegedly stated that he "would make an absolute Cure of the distemper," which he was unable to do. Gradually, as living conditions improved, the historical record contained fewer mentions of "country disease."[135]

Irishman Dr. John Brickell, author of *The Natural History of North Carolina* (1737), arrived in the colony in 1729 and practiced medicine in Edenton until 1731, serving as personal physician to Governor Sir Richard Everard and his family. Although highly regarded, Brickell likely received his training from an apprenticeship and hospital experience. His list of common illnesses and disorders included "*Agues* or intermittent *Fevers, Cachexia, Diarrhaea, Dysenteria,* the *Clap* and *French Pox,* the *Yaws, Chollicks, Cholera-Morbus, Convulsions, Hooping-Cough,* and *Cutaneous Disorders* such as *Tetters, Ring-worms, Rashes, prickley-Heats,* and the *Itch.*"[136]

To treat cachexia, or swellings, which he attributed to eating excess fruit, dirt, and clay, Brickell recommended iron filings and rust, accompanied by purging. He used a regional treatment for yaws concocted from tree barks and berries. For rashes and itches, Brickell prescribed camphor mixed with wine or any other spirit. The serious symptoms of "cholick," convulsions and violent aspiration, were countered by strong vomits, purges, clysters, and ointments. He arrived during an epidemic of whooping cough, which he treated with bleeding, vomiting, and "Jesuits bark."[137]

The courts provided for the handicapped, as in the case of eleven-year-old orphan John Maccee, described as "lame and decrepit." The General Court placed him under the care of William Jones, who was instructed to provide him with housing, food, and clothing at public expense.[138]

A frontier agricultural and trading economy leaves little leisure for education or cultural life. Nevertheless, Albemarle society encompassed a spectrum, from men such as Thomas Woodward, who could quote Bacon's *Essays* and a Spanish proverb, to illiterate council members Thomas Pearce and William Jennings.[139] Personal libraries were few and spare, as estate inventories reveal only an occasional book or small collection of volumes, and often the only book in the home was the Bible. George Durant's Bible (London, 1599) probably was with the family when they immigrated by 1661. It remained in the family until the nineteenth century, when it went to the University of North Carolina; it is now housed in the university's North Carolina Collection. In the early years, even prominent planters had tiny libraries: Thomas Harris had a Bible and three other books, while Francis Godfrey possessed but nine books, including a Bible. Christopher Butler, who may have been Irish, had a Latin Bible, rare in the colony.[140]

By the eighteenth century there were more substantial personal libraries. Edward Salter, a Bath County merchant, had a library catalogue of various subjects: Bible commentaries, divinity, law, history, and mathematics. Those in public office and the general courts often owned large libraries. Councilman John Lovick's shelves housed law books and Clarendon's history of the civil war. The largest known collection in the colony was that of Edward Moseley, a dominant political figure for decades. He founded a public library in Edenton in 1723 with a gift of 76 books, mostly theology and church history. In his estate Moseley left 200 law volumes to his son-in-law; several volumes of biblical commentary, history, and physic to his wife; and to a daughter and sons over 150 volumes, among them dictionaries, three volumes of John Locke, and books on religion and gardening.[141]

In the late seventeenth century the scattered rural population of Albemarle County could boast neither schools nor any formal education, and some residents remained illiterate. Typical might be the 1663 will of Mary Fortsen of Pasquotank: it bears her signature, but the four witnesses, two men and two women, signed with marks. Similarly, two members of the 1672 governor's council could not write their names.[142] However, a statistical survey of document signatures and marks in Perquimans Precinct revealed a surprisingly high literacy rate, comparable to that in Puritan New England, where schools were established. From 1661 to 1695, among Perquimans adults 67 percent of free males and 30 percent of free females were literate.[143]

Education during that time took place in the home under tutelage by parents or neighbors. Alexander Lillington's will directed his executors to "carry on my Son, John, in his learnings as I have begun, and that All my Children be brought up in Learning as conveniently can bee."[144] Chowan widow Henretta Butler contracted with a Daniel Leigh, lay reader in St. Paul's parish, to teach her son Christopher reading, writing, and arithmetic, but Leigh did not follow through and was sued for the fee.[145] Planter Thomas Clarke, who signed his will with a mark, intended that if his legatees were deceased, his estate was to support a schoolmaster to teach the "poor fatherless Children" of Chowan. He died shortly thereafter, and the will was contested and settled on behalf of a minor grandson.[146]

The colony's reputation for religious freedom drew many Protestant dissenters, largely Quakers but also Baptists and Presbyterians, who depended on the Bible for guidance and therefore valued literacy. Quakers educated both sexes, and Perquimans had the largest Quaker community in the colony. Their custom was to worship in homes, but early in the next century they began building meetinghouses that quickly became educational centers. In the 1690s Quakers were influential in governing the colony, creating a period of political harmony and progress when education could flourish.

Youngsters were trained to become skilled workers through apprentice bonds, usually requested by their parents. For a girl, the apprenticeship term ended when she married or reached the age of eighteen, while boys remained apprenticed until age twenty-one or older. Apprentice masters for both Grace Plater, ten years old, and John Hallam, eleven years old, were also directed to provide "Christian Education." Hallam's first master, who had died, was French, and his apprentice bond to widow Elizabeth Bartley required that he learn "to read English." Court-appointed guardianships and apprenticeships of orphans specified education, as well as training for a trade, and widows often received foster children to their mutual benefit. The widow Susannah Hartley was granted the apprentice Jabel Alford to learn the trade of carpenter or joiner. The court ordered the guardian of Johanna Kingkate to "bring her up in Learning," and Thomas and Sarah Harvey were obligated by the court to teach William Pead to read.[147]

The colony's first schoolmaster was Charles Griffin, "Gentleman," who migrated from the West Indies to Albemarle in 1705. A "devout" Anglican, Griffin settled in Pasquotank precinct, which, like Perquimans, was heavily populated by Quakers. Griffin was engaged by the local vestry as the lay reader, and because of his diligence and "general Good Caracter and Esteem," the congregation prospered. His school, the first in North Carolina, was for boys and girls. Because of its success, attributed to his "descreet Behaviour," it attracted Quaker children, despite the Anglican instruction and daily prayers.[148] The location of his school is believed to have been at the Symons Creek Monthly Meeting, which had a meetinghouse by 1703.[149]

In 1709 an Anglican missionary, the Reverend William Gordon, recommended that Griffin be appointed lay reader and clerk of the vestry for Saint Paul's Parish, Chowan. The vestry hired him at a salary of twenty pounds per year, and he also opened a school but did not stay long. By October Adams reported that Griffin, "who had behaved himself very remarkably" as lay reader and schoolmaster, "had fallen into the Sin of Fornication" and joined "the Quakers Interest."[150] Whether Griffin "had fallen" for a Quaker lass is not known; however, he remained an Anglican and was unmarried all his life. From 1714 onward he was employed very successfully in Indian education in Virginia, capping his career as Brafferton Professor at the College of William and Mary in charge of the Indian school.[151]

The only other school in the region was established at Sarum near the border in Virginia by Edward Mashborne to serve youth from both colonies and nearby Indian towns. When peace returned, Thomas Hoyter, a Chowan king, planned to send his son to the school. The Reverend Giles Rainsford, then minister in Chowan, was "Strangely Surprized" at the proficiency of the students and their grounding in Anglican "Principles"; in 1712 he recommended that Mashborne be supported by the Society for Propagation of the Gospel (SPG). Mashborne himself wrote to the SPG in April 1716, expressing his concern over the "lamentable circumstances" in North Carolina "for want of Education." About two weeks later Governor Charles Eden solicited the SPG "please to Send us Schoolmasters," stating that the inhabitants would support most of the salaries. Neither Mashborne nor the governor received a reply.[152]

In North Carolina the prospects for resourceful men and women of ability far exceeded the social norms of England or the more institutionalized colonies characterized by class deference. The proprieties, especially the Quaker-led North Carolina, West Jersey, and Pennsylvania, attracted dissenters seeking economic opportunity, political participation, and freedom of conscience. As North Carolina came under royal control, the possibilities would narrow. However, the colony never became oligarchic, aristocratic, or so intolerant as Virginia and South Carolina. Poorer than these adjacent colonies, Albemarle developed on its own, remaining more egalitarian and less stratified. We may reply to Anna Sothel that although her "Country was sickley and the Inlet bad," she and her contemporaries struggled, survived, and often prospered in their mid-Atlantic enclave.

CHAPTER EIGHT

Making a Living

Planters, Traders, and Merchants

This Countrey would holy perrish for want of goods it being a place
soe sholy that noe Vessell can come directly from England hither.
—Henderson Walker, 1698

ACTING ON Captain John Whitty's glowing report of Carolina's healthful climate and economic potential, on 8 September 1663 Sir John Colleton secured a grant for Carlyle Island, renamed Colleton Island, marking the first grant to a proprietor in the colony. At the mouth of Albemarle Sound directly north of Roanoke Island and protected on the east side by the Outer Banks, it was strategically located for trade at the juncture of Albemarle and Currituck Sounds and near Roanoke Inlet.[1]

Shortly thereafter, Colleton, the Earl of Craven, Lord John Berkeley, and Sir George Carteret formed a partnership to operate a plantation on the island and Powell's Point across the sound.[2] The Colletons, Sir John and after his death in 1666 his son Sir Peter, managed the partnership from England. Whitty, a Devonshire sea captain who was a courier for the proprietors, was advanced £218 to set up a livestock breeding operation on the island with cattle, horses, and hogs for the Barbados market. The stock was to include 100 sows with piglets, ten boars, ten cows with calves, a bull, a horse, and a mare. Whitty hired William Crawford as overseer and ordered enough salt to preserve thirty tons of pork.[3]

The partners engaged Peter Carteret, Sir George's young cousin, to manage the plantation and serve as a public official. When Carteret arrived on Colleton Island on 23 February 1665 bearing commissions, instructions, and documents, he was dismayed to find little beyond a twenty-foot dwelling, a "10-foot hogg howse & apsell of wild hogs." When the Lords received Carteret's gloomy assessment, they called in Whitty for an explanation. He shifted the blame to the overseer, Crawford, and his London partner, Bonnefeild, both of whom allegedly "plaid the Knave" to the proprietors and Whitty, causing the enterprise to "goe to wrack."[4]

On the island Carteret endeavored to make the best of the situation. With three indentured servants from France and England, "out of the wilderness wee cleered what ground we could on powells pointe." The corn they planted grew poorly because "wee were all Sick all the Sumer that wee could nott tend it & the Servants Soe weake the fall & Spring that they could doe little work."[5] The period of illness afflicting Carteret and his servants was the "seasoning" that most new colonists experienced, to which some succumbed.[6] The next year Carteret and his men cleared and fenced more fields and built an eighty-by-twenty-foot partitioned hog house on Powell's Point. The hogs were moved to the point, but a third of them died, despite tending by a servant and corn for fodder. The plantation did produce 150 barrels of corn, which was consumed on site.[7]

Added to the difficulties of seating an overseas plantation on a distant frontier were a series of destructive storms, common on the Carolina coast. In 1667 corn and tobacco were planted, and plans were developed for a land-based whaling operation to exploit the whale pods that migrated off the Outer Banks. Disaster struck on 27 August when a hurricane "destroyed both corne & tob: blew downe the roof of the great hogg howse" and ruined two houses. That season the only success was thirty barrels of whale oil, but the shipping was so delayed by weather that much of it was lost through leakage. A three-month drought the following year "burnt up all the tob. & stented the corne," and when heavy rains finally came in August, much of the tobacco rotted, leaving only five hogsheads of tobacco to accompany eighty barrels of whale oil for the year's exports.

Another hurricane in 1669 ruined the entire tobacco crop, except for one stored hogshead. The corn was flattened and spoiled, and whale oil production dropped to fifty-two barrels. The "violent" hurricane of 6 August 1670 pounded the plantation twenty-four hours and "blewe downe howses," downing timber and leveling the corn and tobacco crops, a dwelling house, the hog house, and two storehouses that had sheltered thirty barrels of whale oil and four tons of cork. Carteret thought the storms had kept the whales offshore, as he could only show thirty-eight barrels of whale oil. He wrote that "it was Lick to bee a famine amongst us," and little relief could be expected from Virginia, which had been ravaged by the same violent tempests.[8]

The next two years, the servants' terms of indenture having been completed, they were hired to plant corn and maintain the livestock. Since Carteret did not mention any natural disasters these years, they apparently harvested the crops. Carteret's final assessment of his experience was, "It hath pleased God of his providence to Inflict Such a Generall calamitie upon the inhabitans of these countreys that for Severall yeares they have Nott Injoyed the fruitts of their

Labours which causes them Generally to growne under the burtyn of poverty
& many times famine."[9]

After eight years of arduous toil, Carteret's balance sheet showed a debt of
£605.16.10, offset by significant assets, primarily at Powell's Point. The plantation had a dwelling, a servants' quartering house, nearly seventy acres of
cleared land, and a herd of 111 cattle, for a total value of £566.11. In addition, the
shore-based whaling operation had produced 195 barrels of whale oil, valued
at £241.05.[10]

Captain Whitty's early report to the proprietors that one could "easily pass
by land and river" from Virginia to the Chowan River and "ryde but 25 myles
by land" describes the preferred overland entry to the colony. Using rivers connected by a trail in Virginia, one skirted the western edge of the Great Dismal Swamp with less risk than sailing through the sand-choked inlets.[11] The
vast swamp was a formidable barrier, although travelers could follow tortuous
trails through the dank wilds. The Quaker missionary William Edmundson
described the Great Dismal as "all wilderness, and no English inhabitants or
path-ways, but some mark'd Trees to guide People." He became "sore foyl'd
in Swamps and Rivers."[12] Journeying in November 1672 the Quaker founder
George Fox spent three days on horseback, seeing "neither house nor man
through ye woods, & swamps, & many cruell boggs & watery places."[13] As if
the natural obstacles were not enough, Indians occasionally menaced overland
travelers.

The sound and rivers provided excellent internal transportation for people
and goods by canoe or boat. The journey overland from Currituck to Chowan
was hindered by the six rivers that sliced from north to south, creating peninsulas, called necks, where settlement was concentrated. Decades after Quaker
missionaries visited the area, the Reverend John Urmston bought horses and
hired a guide to attempt east–west overland travel. Quickly realizing that the
rivers, which were formidable barriers to his progress, were conduits for water
travel, he hired a large "Boat" and a crew of "Experienced Watermen," and later
he acquired a sailing canoe.[14]

No resident would attempt the east–west trek by land, but between the rivers, sandy trails marked with blazed or notched trees provided local connections, winding through forests and fields to numerous landings on the necks.
Years later John Brickell described pleasant traveling on improved roads,
singling out the broad, level highway from Edenton to Virginia, which was
wide enough for coaches, carriages, wagons, and carts. Blazed trees marked
public paths that also could accommodate coaches and wagons; however, travelers could easily lose their way on the myriad of unmarked animal or Indian
paths wending through the woods.[15]

The precinct and general courts supervised and planned roads, with free-holders, servants, and enslaved persons who lived along a road responsible for its construction and maintenance. Daily traffic might include individuals on foot or horseback, herds of livestock, rolling hogsheads of tobacco, and high two-wheeled carts. In the coastal plain the roads drained quickly and were passable except in periods of heavy rainfall. Marshy creeks were occasionally bridged; some low places were spanned by log and earthen causeways; but fer-ries on major rivers were rare. In 1704 the Reverend John Blair, a newcomer, found a guide necessary to enable him to cross the rivers and traverse "the worst roads I ever saw." To reach the Pamlico River settlement, Blair had to canoe the five-mile-wide Albemarle Sound and then slog fifty miles through uninhabited, trackless wilds.[16]

Travel difficulties were only one obstacle that Albemarle planters had to overcome. Uncertain and oft-changing proprietary land tenure policies cre-ated anxiety, although the Albemarle settlers usually won concessions from the distant Lords. When the proprietors promptly reneged on the Great Deed of Grant's terms, which were similar to those in Virginia, the colonists insisted that the document was irrevocable.[17] After the dispute was finally resolved a quarter century later, a pent-up demand for land grants and sales was unleashed.

Plantation and farm size in early Albemarle varied from the 50-acre head-right to the 44,000 acres granted to proprietor Seth Sothel, of which he devel-oped only his two 4,000-acre plantations in Chowan and Pasquotank.[18] Not many grants exceeded 1,000 acres, and a study of land patents revealed that prior to 1680 the mean size was 833 acres, with a median size of 600 acres. From 1680 to 1704 the mean had dropped to 447 acres, with a median of 300 acres, as reflected in the table.

The main reason for this change was a 1670 act of the General Assembly to curb speculation by restricting single grants to 660 acres.[19] Of the over 3,300 North Carolina proprietary grants issued, about half were for 375 acres or less. Although the restriction was relaxed in the eighteenth century, still two-thirds were for 640 acres. Landowners could accumulate significant acreage by obtain-ing multiple grants, although they might not be contiguous. Overall, Albemarle County was most like the poorer and middling counties of Virginia.[20]

In the early eighteenth century, however, a few individuals and families amassed enormous landholdings. Between 1706 and 1729 the largest landown-ers were the Pollock family (88,152 acres), Frederick Jones (49,730 acres), the Moore family (48,172 acres), the Moseley family (47,973 acres), and John Lovick (42,137 acres). These five families owned over a quarter of a million acres, about 17 percent of the total patented land, and their concentration of land and wealth affected the colony from Albemarle to Cape Fear.[21]

TABLE 8.1. Comparative Acreage

Acres	1663–79	1680–1704
50–249	8%	38%
250–849	65%	59%
850+	26%	2%

Birds soaring above Albemarle County would have seen houses and out-buildings hugging the sound shores and riverbanks, with fenced fields for crops and open meadows for livestock nearby and the dark green of swamp and forest behind them. On closer inspection, the fenced-in manor house, surrounded by its brood of outbuildings, would resemble a small village. Around the owner's dwelling, often a four-room story-and-a-half of frame or brick, would be clustered a smokehouse, a dairy house, quarters for servants and enslaved persons, and storage sheds. Slightly apart would be set the barn, a stable, tobacco storage and curing houses, a corncrib, and a variety of sheds. Described in construction contracts were a large barn for wheat storage and specific buildings to house hogs and chickens.[22] In addition to his own considerable landholdings, in 1722 Francis Tomes was renting a nearby 327-acre plantation on the east bank of the Perquimans River that had a mansion house, kitchen, garden, orchard, 30 acres of arable plow land, 17 acres of meadow, 70 acres of pasture, and 200 acres of woodland.[23]

As plowshares were uncommon, the land was normally cultivated by hand, "breaking the Earth with Hoes."[24] In addition to the weeding, grubbing, and hilling hoes, prevalent farm tools included tobacco-cutting knives, spades, trowels, pitchforks, and steelyards for weighing tobacco. Reflecting the needs of a self-sufficient society, most plantations had some carpenter's tools—usually axes, hatchets, drawing knives, hammers, adzes, augers, chisels, various saws, and wedges. Since wooden barrels and casks were used for shipping, many planters had an array of specialized cooper's tools. Depending on the size of the plantation, there might be grindstones, millstones, hand grain mills, meal trays, caulking equipment for boats, and a wine or cider press. Those planters with dairy houses had churns, butter tubs, cheese presses, and an assortment of earthenware vessels, barrels, and casks.[25]

Soon after coming to Chowan in 1710, the Reverend John Urmston acquired a sound-side 300-acre plantation, mostly wooded, with twelve cleared acres. He, his wife, their three children, and an indentured domestic servant moved into a new home with a half-finished separate kitchen. Hired help was scarce, so he resorted to indentured and enslaved labor. Cattle and corn, the colony's main products, were his goal. With English goods he purchased livestock—a horse, three cows and calves, five sheep, and fowls, as well as fourteen bushels of wheat. He expected to have for their table butter, cheese, milk, beef, and mutton. Soon he planted peas and beans in his garden. His neighbors allocated most of their crops for the purchase of imported expensive rum, molasses, sugar, and other necessities for themselves. After several years on the plantation, Urmston's total expenses were for labor, tools, and equipment. To the purchase price of £50 was added £80 for repairs, £5 for a hand mill, a canoe and sails at £7, two carts at £4.10s, a plow and harrow at £3.15s, and a variety of farm, carpenter's, and cooper's tools.[26]

Urmston's labor expenses included £79 for three enslaved Blacks, two of whom died, and £16 for an English servant who ran away in ten days. He was never satisfied with the female indentured servants, one of whom he described as a "Sorry wretch." Another was a "Notorious Whore and theif" who had come with them from an English prison but was "preferable" to anyone who could be hired locally. After the death of his wife in October 1719, partly due to the privations they had endured, Urmston sent his younger children to England in the care of the SPG. Prior to leaving for England himself in March 1721, Urmston disowned his son for fathering a child with the domestic servant.[27]

———————

CONSIDERING THE Virginia origin of many Albemarle planters, it would be surprising if they had not brought tobacco culture with them. The type of tobacco they grew was an air-cured dark variety called Orinoco. The seeds were planted in the winter in beds located in the woods. Around May, the slips were transplanted into fields where broken ground had been hilled into low mounds four feet apart. Following Indian practice in the maize fields, legumes and melons were customarily planted alongside. On the predominant smaller farms and plantations, labor- intensive tobacco involved the whole household, from the landowner and his or her family to the servants and enslaved—all toiled in the fields side by side through the hot, humid summer days. The plants required topping when the leaves began to mature, seemingly endless hoeing to control weeds, removal of the suckers or shoots, and constant collection of hornworms. When the plants were ready for curing, stalks were cut and hung on sticks in an open barn. The final phase was "seasoning" in a cellar to increase moisture content so that the leaf was pliable.

Most planters had their own landings and packhouses where they prepared, stored, and shipped tobacco, which was packed in hogsheads. Tavern keeper Thomas Harris had five cooper's adzes and two pairs of steelyards, indicating that a packing house at his landing served neighboring plantations.[28]

Sometimes stemmed, but not always, graded tobacco leaf was packed tightly in hogsheads that were weighed by large steelyards. In the early years, a hogshead weighed 400 pounds, and over time more than doubled in weight.[29]

While tobacco was the first important crop, the economy was not dependent on it. From a small beginning, by 1677 the annual production of tobacco for Albemarle County was 2,000 hogsheads, or 800,000 pounds.[30] In Virginia and Carolina, tobacco values fluctuated widely throughout the seventeenth century, remaining depressed in the latter half of the century. In the accounts of Peter Carteret, the price of tobacco from 1666 to 1671 was about two pence per pound.[31] Even with the high freight cost charged by coastal traders, two years later Thomas Miller expected to net a profit of six pence per 100 pounds on his thirty-six hogsheads sent to Ireland or England. His hopes were dashed when the sloop carrying his shipment ran aground in the inlet. The water-soaked cargo ended up in Newport, Rhode Island, and Boston. Miller sued to recover damages but was unable to prove negligence.[32]

Begun under the Commonwealth, navigation acts had closed colonial trade to foreign shipping by imposing duties and mandating exclusive use of British or colonial vessels and crews.[33] The acts benefited the colonies by guaranteeing sales and stimulating shipbuilding and employment of mariners. The disadvantage was the elimination of free market competition that could lower prices for imports and raise prices for exports. Because all of the colonies had an unfavorable balance of trade with the mother country, smuggling became rampant, from New England to the Carolinas. Among the colonies, North Carolina had the unique burden of its dangerous coast, which relegated its trade to shallow-draft New England and local coasters who could manage the challenging navigation. This restricted direct connections to the North Atlantic and Britain, further exacerbating the trade imbalance. Notwithstanding this constriction, the colony persevered and developed a middling agrarian economy based on diverse crops and products. Although commonly viewed as backward and benighted, North Carolina possessed the same, if not better, economic and social opportunities as the other American colonies, especially with a relatively narrow gap between poverty and wealth that resulted in a shorter path to success and status. The shipping disadvantages would not be relieved until the opening of the deepwater Cape Fear River in the 1720s and the related expansion of pine plantations that rapidly vaulted the colony into the empire's leading producer of naval stores.

Attempting to stem the flood of colonial smuggling, in 1673 Parliament passed the Plantation Duty Act, which levied a tobacco duty of one penny per pound to be either deposited or bonded when the ship cleared port. Later in the century the price of tobacco dropped to a penny per pound, and by 1715 it brought just one and a quarter pence per pound.[34] The return from tobacco shipped through Virginia was further reduced by an entry and clearing fee of two shillings per hogshead.[35] Finally, in 1679 Virginia embargoed North Carolina tobacco shipped by sea and in 1726 by land.[36] With the tax consuming the profit from the crop, plus shipping charges and fees on top of that, Albemarle planters and merchants were forced to evade customs if they were to avoid economic ruin. As late as 1728 William Byrd noted that new Currituck Inlet, at ten feet in depth, was navigable for the small sloops that carried the bulk of the colony's tobacco. After encountering a New England sloop on the sound, he observed that the "Saints of New England" avoided "paying that impertinent Duty of a Penny a Pound."[37]

Easternmost Currituck Precinct was considered remote, yet the old and new Currituck inlets were the early entryways to the colony, especially to and from Virginia. The port of Currituck provided important ingress throughout the proprietary period, with deputy customs collectors stationed at Currituck and at the centrally located Little River settlement that was the de facto seat of government. Despite the tobacco embargo that Virginians were clearly ignoring, Norfolk became the entrepôt for North Carolina. By the early 1730s North Carolina governor Burrington noted an annual trade of £50,000 with Norfolk carried in shallops, periaugers, and even canoes that risked the thirty-five-mile open ocean voyage from Currituck Inlet to Cape Henry. Although some Virginians complained about the Albemarle competition, the furs, tobacco, provisions, and naval stores pouring into Norfolk from the south were the making of the Virginia port.[38]

The meager return on tobacco steered planters toward diversified agricultural products—provisions, livestock, and mixed grain crops, chiefly corn and some wheat. In the eighteenth century, forest products of lumber, shingles, staves, and naval stores—tar and pitch—expanded to become the colony's leading export. Whereas tobacco had been the primary medium of exchange, other commodities were added, including corn, wheat, whale oil, pitch, pork, beef, and dressed and raw deer skins. Bath County, established on the southern frontier in 1696, based its economy on the Indian fur trade, livestock, provisions, and fishing. French Huguenots on the Pamlico and Trent Rivers and Swiss and German Palatines on the Neuse experimented with wine and linen.[39]

Since West Indian planters were committed solely to sugarcane products, the mainland colonies became their chief source of meat, grain, provisions, and livestock. As early as 1666 Sir John Colleton urged Peter Carteret to "stocke Colleton Islande wth Cowes bulls horses & Mares to run & breede there . . . [and] yor hoggs on ye poynt. . . . You know w[ha]t a Comodity hoggs flesh is at Barbadoes & beef Likewayse."[40] By 1679 Robert Holden described a colony

TABLE 8.2. Livestock

Year	Planter	Cattle	Hogs	Sheep	Horses	Total
1680	Valentine Bird	18	48	22	0	88
1680	Edmund Chancey	60	17	0	0	77
1680	Francis Godfrey	31	0	11	5	47
1680	Thomas Harris	41	47	0	2	90
1694	Thomas Jarvis	115	24	5	5	149
1695	Seth Sothel	0	0	200	3	203

overrun with livestock: "catle allredy so plentifull that hundreds of them runnes Wild and breeds in the Forest." Horses and wild goats also ranged freely in the woods, and hogs fed on a variety of orchard windfall fruits. Sheep abounded but were kept in check by wolves.[41] In the eighteenth century, John Lawson praised Albemarle's excellent beef and pork, the thriving sheep that often bore two lambs, and "well-shap'd and swift" horses.[42] By the end of the seventeenth century, a planter's livestock s could total over 200 animals.

Stock values recorded in the 1680s were 30s for cows, 15s for sows, 5s for shoats, and 10s for sheep, all depending on the animal's age and condition.[43] In the 1680s resident proprietor John Archdale was engaged in ranching on several tracts in Pasquotank Precinct, producing cattle and beef and probably hides and tallow. One of his sales in 1686 was to rancher Daniel Axtell of southern Carolina for fifty cows at three pounds per head.[44] Although the necks between the rivers were occasionally fenced off, most Albemarle stock foraged all year on open range. Besides Colleton Island, stock grazed on Roanoke Island and Batt's Grave. Fencing prevented livestock damage to settlers' houses, yards, gardens, fields, and burial plots, and cattle pens protected calves from predators. A planter on Batts's Grave lost a damage suit over hogs destroying his cornfield because he had not enclosed it.[45] In addition to losses from wolves and panthers, periodic murrains, or plagues, caused mass deaths of cattle, sheep, and hogs. A murrain in early 1717 took most of the colony's black cattle. If mast was not plentiful, starvation could claim large numbers of hogs over the winter.[46]

The market for salt pork included New England, Bermuda, Barbados, and other West Indian islands.[47] In addition to the preparation and shipping of salt beef and pork and tanned cowhides, cattle and hogs were increasingly driven north to Virginia and sold on the hoof. Drovers herded the stock on forest trails that widened into thoroughfares over time. Toll keepers at bridges and ferries had the dual role of keeping tolls and recording livestock.[48]

Governor Hyde reported to Governor Spotswood of Virginia that Virginians were periodically rounding up Albemarle's free-range cattle, sweeping up some that belonged to North Carolinians. If challenged, the drovers would destroy the disputed cattle. Individual ear crops (patterned notches) were registered in the precinct courts so that livestock ownership could be determined. The Meherrin Indians, tributary under Virginia, also were accused of killing Carolina livestock. Spotswood apologized for his Indians but regarded the unsurveyed border as disputed territory. In 1715 the General Assembly responded with a law to regulate Virginia drovers, who were known to take unmarked livestock. Tollbooks were stationed on the Carolina road in Chowan, at the head of the Perquimans River, and at the mouth of the Northwest River for Currituck. Rangers kept the tollbooks, collecting two pence for horses and cattle and a penny for hogs.[49] The livestock trade to Virginia continued to expand. Governor George Burrington reported to the General Assembly in 1733 that when mast was plentiful, up to 50,000 fat hogs were driven to Virginia, along with most of the oxen and many horses, cattle, and calves.[50]

With cattle and hogs roaming a heavily wooded range, livestock rustling was a common crime. Altering registered ear crops on livestock was a felony. Convicted in 1697 of mismarking a cow, James Fisher had to pay 2,000 pounds of beef to the plaintiff. Fisher was back in court the next year accusing Christopher Butler of killing one of his cows, generating a countersuit "for many Molestations Vexations etc." Following years of litigation, Fisher finally was awarded a heifer.[51]

Although grain crops were important, neither wind- nor water-powered mills appeared in the colony before the eighteenth century. Hand mills were used to grind cornmeal and hominy for personal use, and a hollow log or stump with a sturdy wooden staff for a pestle was very common. Unground wheat was exported and partly returned as flour from New England mills. As the new century arrived, a horse-drawn mill in Bath and a water-powered mill in New Bern were among the first to be built. Carpenters constructed a millhouse for Pasquotank planter Joseph Commander for £4.10s. By the 1720s there were a few millwrights in the colony: Edward Jackson in Perquimans, John Salisbury in Chowan, and John Cox. In Chowan James Cole had a mill dam and pond, and presumably a mill.[52]

The earliest explorers noted the rampant overgrowth of the native muscadine grape and its cultivated variety, the scuppernong, which produced distinctive sweet table wines. Sir John Colleton encouraged wine production at the Colleton Island plantation, for which he sent seeds from a white Rhine grape that he was confident would thrive if there was sufficient dry weather for proper ripening. He urged manager Carteret to "goe boldly on with yor: Viniardes," advising him to experiment with seeds and cuttings. In Colleton's last letter to

Carteret in March 1666 he requested a small cask of wine from the native grape: "Let it bee well made & have its Naturall & full workeing." Whether Sir John received his cask of muscadine wine is unknown, for he died that year.[53]

A half century later John Lawson "well relisht" the "very strong" wine made from the native grapes and promoted Carolina as "Wine-Country." Huguenot pastor Philip de Richebourg conferred with Lawson at Bath, sharing plans to "propagate Vines" from slips. Having recently acquired seeds of a white grape from Madeira, Lawson had successfully planted them and anticipated other imports of seed.[54] Dr. John Brickell, who lived in Edenton from 1729 to 1731 and visited Bath and Beaufort, saw a vineyard in Bath town and another of the Madeira white grape on the Neuse that could have descended from Lawson's seeds. Brickell declared that the white wine of this vineyard was "exceeding good," and he believed that the colony could be "as fine a Wine and Oil Country as any in *Europe*."[55]

Hampered from the outset by geography, North Carolina at first grew slowly. The colony attracted chiefly English yeomen who carved out modest farms and plantations that relied for labor primarily on white indentured servants, and to a lesser extent on enslaved or indentured African and Native American laborers, and hired free workers of all three races. By the turn of the century, enslaved Africans outnumbered indentured servants and enslaved Indians. However, in stark contrast to South Carolina, which built a plantation society on Indian and eventually African slave labor, North Carolina's European population always outnumbered the Native American and African laborers. When Lawson arrived, North Carolina had fewer than 1,000 Africans out of about 12,000 total colonial inhabitants, which increased to 15,000 by 1710. In that same decade, South Carolina's colonial population, which was half African in origin, grew from 6,000 to 10,000.[56]

Free laborers usually worked for wages, but sharecropping agreements did exist.[57] Peter Carteret hired the three indentured servants who had worked for him in the years 1666–71 when their term of service was over. They were paid 1,000 pounds of tobacco a year, worth just over eight pounds sterling, while Carteret received twenty pounds for managing the plantation.[58] Wages were usually paid in commodities. Peter Brock, master of the vessel *Prosperous Galley*, engaged two ships' carpenters in Pasquotank to "pull to pieces" and rebuild his vessel at the rate of six shillings a day. In Chowan a brick chimney was constructed for ten pounds. With the owner providing the timber, boards, and shingles, a dwelling was to be constructed in Perquimans for five barrels of pork and sixteen barrels of tar.[59]

STRATEGICALLY CENTERED between Ocracoke Inlet, the colony's best gateway, and the Tuscarora nation, Bath County was poised to thrive on the Indian
trade and seaborne commerce. North Carolina's first port town, Bath on the
Pamlico River, was followed in a few years by New Bern on the Neuse River
and Beaufort on the Atlantic near Cape Lookout. Of necessity the colony's
trade was dominated by the shallow-draft small sloops, ketches, shallops, and
brigs mastered by New Englanders in partnership with Carolina traders and
planter-merchants. Two Pamlico River planters, Thomas Dereham and prominent Bath County official Levi Truewhitt, were heavily involved in Indian
trade as partners, sometimes copartnering with Robert Quary and the New
Pennsylvania Company, John Porter, and Richard Smith. They were supplied
by Thomas Jones, a Virginia merchant of James City.[60] Henry Lisle, a Chowan
laborer made prosperous through the Indian trade, acquired a plantation at
Rockyhock. After a poor year left him with a forty-two-pound debt to his local
factors for the New Pennsylvania Company, he was forced to sell his plantation,
livestock, and "great Conoo."[61]

Illegal trade to avoid customs duties was rampant in all the colonies, and
North Carolina's long irregular coastline made it ideally suited for smuggling.
In Bath County the sparse population and a rapidly expanding frontier-driven
economy grounded in the Indian fur trade opened numerous opportunities for
customs evasion. Although clerk of both county and precinct courts and a well-
known Pamlico River planter-merchant, Levi Truewhitt, like most of his peers,
was willing to attempt nonpayment of duties when possible. Master and owner
of the six-tun sloop *Pamlico Adventure*, Truewhitt landed her in August without
entry papers at Thomas Dereham's plantation on Dereham Creek. The cargo
was being unloaded when deputy customs collector Captain William Barrow
seized the vessel and cargo under orders of Governor Robert Daniell, who lived
directly across the river. At the admiralty court meeting in October at Little
River, Attorney General Christopher Gale presented the case and urged forfeit
of the vessel and cargo. Ruling in favor of Truewhitt, the court dismissed the
case, only requiring him to pay costs.[62]

In 1704 collector Samuel Swann caught Indian trader and planter John Pettiver unloading goods from Virginia from his two-tun shallop *Thomas and Mary*.
Not only was the shallop not registered, but Pettiver had no Virginia clearance
papers and had failed to secure an entry. Swann seized the vessel and cargo,
both of which were condemned and sold.[63]

From the colony's earliest days at the trading post of Nathaniel Batts to the
expansion south into Bath County, Indian and English trappers, hunters, and
fur traders were the vanguard of settlement, providing a mainstay of the economy. The General Assembly's attempt to regulate commerce and maintain local

control, including a fine of 10,000 pounds of tobacco to dissuade "Strangers from other parts," proved unenforceable in the remote backcountry.[64] In the fall of 1705, Charles Gee, a Virginia Indian fur trader, brought five packhorses laden with seven hatchets, eighty-eight yards of blue and red coarse cloth, forty-five pounds of powder, fifty-five pounds of shot, a gun lock, thread, and scissors. Although he had no clearance to trade, he openly bartered for cash, furs, and skins in Chowan and Pamlico, where the deputy governor, Thomas Cary, seized his remaining truck and ordered a special court for a condemnation hearing. Gee was not present, but the court ruled that any of his North Carolina property could be attached for value.[65]

With direct access to the North Atlantic, Virginians were the chief suppliers of North Carolina traders. In 1695 Captain William Randolph of Henrico County, Virginia, sponsored Dr. Godfrey Spruill of Albemarle, selling him trade goods for buckskins, doeskins, beaver, and other pelts, and encouraged him to acquire enslaved Indians. Dorothy Busskin of Nansemond County similarly backed William Duckenfield, a Chowan planter and trader. Merchant John Bates of York River provided merchandise to Bath County fur trader Christopher Gale. Gale noted, "English goods are here verry valuable," naming nails, carpenters' and farmers' tools, linens, powder, shot, hats, and stockings for a "sortable store."[66]

Native American tribes north of the sound dwindled rapidly after European settlement, but the populous Tuscarora nation to the south remained strong throughout the century, serving as middlemen with the Siouan Indians to the west.[67] The trade goods, or "truck," consisted of trinkets and glass beads; steel axes, knives, tomahawks, and tools; iron cooking vessels; colored cloth, clothing, and blankets; powder, shot, and guns; and whiskey and rum. Deerskins dominated the fur market, but pelts from beaver, wolf, otter, fox, muskrat, raccoon, wildcat, and bear were also collected. Skins and furs became the currency of the frontier economy, with the values set at two shillings for dressed buckskin, eighteen pence for dressed doeskin, four shillings for otter skins, three shillings per pound for beaver pelts, and eighteen pence for fox and wildcat skins.[68]

At the time of his death Governor Sothel, who conducted business from his Salmon Creek plantation on the Chowan River, had in his storehouse 300 gallons of rum, 18 gallons of whiskey, 90 glass bottles, 600 pounds of shot, 50 pounds of gunpowder, 8 guns, door hinges, 203 pounds of nails, and 21 bushels of salt. His furs and skins included over 250 deerskins, and bear, beaver, fox, and wildcat pelts.[69] Whiskey, rum, arms, and ammunition formed the cornerstones of the Indian trade, leading directly to the tragic destruction of the province's Native Americans and their cultures.[70]

During Queen Anne's War in the early eighteenth century, as the tobacco economy of the Chesapeake region became depressed, the long-established Indian fur trade expanded. Bath County attracted newcomers who saw the potential of immediate profit in trading with neighboring Indians. Well-known Bath County traders included John Buntin and Captain Richard Smith, who lived south of the sound in Pampticough (Pamlico) Precinct. In one trapping season Buntin sold 200 deerskins and assorted pelts from fox, wildcat, muskrat, otter, and raccoon. Furs and skins that Smith handled in 1701 included 140 buck, 194 doe, 39 fox and wildcat, 47 beaver, 29 raccoon, and a few wolf, bear, and otter.[71]

Christopher Gale exemplified the young gentleman who made his fortune in North Carolina's Indian fur trade and rose to the pinnacle of political leadership, serving as the colony's chief justice, a council member, and militia colonel. From Yorkshire, Gale first settled on Harvey's Neck in Perquimans, where in January 1702 he married the well-connected Sarah Laker Harvey, recent widow of Governor Thomas Harvey; a year later a son was born. Gale was prospering, although he missed "Books & pleasing Conversation." Raised a devout Anglican, he was concerned about the "Decay off Christian piety" in the colony, which seemed overrun with Quakers. Responding by holding worship services in his home with a lay reader, he still longed for clergy, especially because his son of seven months "to my great greeif" was unchristened. It did not help that the first minister to North Carolina, Daniel Brett, had recently left in disgrace.[72]

Gale's fur trade connections spread north to Virginia, Boston, and other New England ports and reached into the province's backcountry to the Appalachian Mountains. Within a few years the peripatetic Gale had had dealings with a dozen Indian tribes in Albemarle and Bath Counties, as well as the Tuscarora nation. To his family in England he described the Indians as living "in small Townes and barke Cabbins, pallisado'd in with 2 or 3 Rows of Stakes; every Towne or nation has its perticular King & different language." In 1703, on the eve of a projected four-month journey west, Gale wrote home, hoping to entice his brother Miles to join him as a "Carolina Coaster." A shallop Gale had dispatched two months earlier to the Cape Fear River was laden with enough English goods for an extended journey to the western mountain tribes. The Cape Fear penetrated far into Indian country, bypassing the Tuscarora and greatly shortening the overland trek to the lucrative potential of the Catawba and the Cherokee.[73]

To be nearer the center of the fur trade, in 1705 Gale relocated to Bath County, establishing Kirby Grange, a plantation near Bath, the colony's first port town.[74] A partner of Gale was none other than his neighbor, John Lawson. Gale and Lawson also dealt directly with the London firm of Micajah Perry and the New Pennsylvania Company, which traded tobacco and furs in the mid-Atlantic colonies.[75]

Although Christopher Gale (ca. 1679–1735) began his life in
North Carolina as an Indian trader, he is pictured here as chief
justice of the Bahamas. His portrait was drawn in 1719 by Henrietta Johnston in Charles Town. North Carolina Museum of History; photo courtesy of MESDA Object Database, File S-1423.

ALBEMARLE COUNTY was a smaller version of the Chesapeake Bay region,
with navigable tributary rivers feeding the great estuary of Albemarle Sound.
However, North Carolina's dynamic barrier islands made her internal estuarine
rivers and sounds as daunting as the dangerous inlets, especially the poorly
charted, sand-choked sounds, where storms frequently resculpted the channels.
The convergence of Native American, British, European, and African cultures
that created the Albemarle society was embodied in the region's dominant craft,
the maneuverable dugout canoe. Developed over millennia and virtually inde-
structible, the dugout was ideally suited to frequent grounding in the shallow
waters of the sounds. A logical modification of floating logs that early humans
used as watercraft, the dugout was indigenous around the world and was widely
used in Europe, Africa, and America for thousands of years before the English

reached America. Archaeological remains of dugouts, some remarkably preserved, have been found dating from 3,000 years ago in North Carolina, 4,000
years ago in Ireland, and 8,000 years ago in Nigeria.[76]

Massive cypress logs up to thirty-six feet in circumference were burned,
using rosin as fuel, and "scoop'd" with sharp stones and shells. The Native
American "digging" by fire and scraping was vastly improved by English metal
saws, hatchets, axes, knives, and adzes. Brickell observed that no "People in the
World" were "more handy and dexterous" at sailing, rowing, or paddling canoes
and periaugers than Indians.[77] West Africans, many from the riverine Guinea
Coast, had grown up with even larger dugouts hewn by hand from silk cotton
trees taller than the grandest cypress. Since Guinea Coast rivers flowed directly
into the ocean, African boatmen were often at home in heavy surf and open
seas.[78] As adept with paddle and pole as the Natives, these experienced mariners
soon mastered the unpredictable Carolina sounds.

The Indian method of harvesting abundant fish and shellfish with nets and
weirs was not unfamiliar to their European and African neighbors. What the
Indians could impart was specific knowledge of the estuarine currents, channels, and sites for shellfish and placement of weirs. Unexpected hazards, at least
to the English, were huge alligators drawn to the fence-like weirs by entrapped
fish. To escape, the massive reptiles thrashed until the sides were shattered.[79]

In addition to labor-saving metal tools and construction techniques, Native Americans gleaned from their European neighbors the knowledge of Old
World poled and sailing craft—scows, flats, skiffs, shallops, ketches, sloops—
and the New World periaugers, indigenous to the southern colonies. Plank-
built skiffs, shallops, and sloops were constructed from durable red cedar, also
used for house posts, sills, fences, and coffins. White cedar was preferred for
masts, booms, yards, and bowsprits.[80]

Adapted from the dugout to increase cargo capacity, the sturdy periauger,
built by sawing a dugout lengthwise and joining the halves with thick planks,
was usually about forty feet long with a beam of eight feet. Whereas the largest
canoes held up to 30 barrels of cargo, periaugers could carry 80 to 100 barrels
weighing several tons. Propelled by paddles, poles, oars, or sails on one or two
masts, periaugers were well adapted to the shallow sounds and inlets. According
to Brickell, no European vessel of the same burden could "out Sail" a periauger.[81]

Periaugers and shallops, although open or partially decked, were also sea-
worthy for coastal voyages and offshore islands—Bermuda, the Bahamas, and
the Caribbean. Lawson related the story of "a foolish Man" who decked a canoe
that held sixteen barrels, intending to sail to Barbados. The customs collector,
convinced that the man had "lost his Senses" to think he could make such a
voyage in a "hollow Tree," refused to clear him.[82] Canoes and a crew of two or

North Carolina replica periauger under sail on the Neuse River. It was built in 2004
by the North Carolina Maritime Museum and is based near Hertford.
Courtesy of Perquimans County Restoration Association.

three men could be hired for commerce at the rate of two shillings sixpence to
five shillings a day and were sailed to Virginia.[83] Seaborne exports and imports
passed through the tricky inlets in small sloops, schooners, ketches, and shallops
and the larger brigs and brigantines. In 1673 the General Assembly set an entry
and clearing fee of fifty pounds of tobacco for decked vessels but exempted
open boats.[84]

William Byrd recorded a detailed account of navigation of Currituck Sound
in March 1728. Byrd and the Virginia boundary survey commission embarked
from a landing on the Northwest River in two periaugers piloted by Captain
William Wilkins. Rowing eighteen miles downstream to Currituck Sound,
they sailed south of Knotts Island to their rendezvous with the North Carolina
delegation at old Currituck Inlet, now virtually closed and filled with tempes-
tuous breakers that presented "a very wild Prospect." Byrd described the new
inlet, opened in 1713, as five miles south and ten feet deep, adequate for small
sloops, one of which they saw in the sound. Captain Wilkins treated the two
dozen men in the group to a feast of "Savoury and well-tasted" local oysters.

When the survey began on 7 March, the larger periauger, laden with baggage, retraced the southern route to the mouth of North River. Exploring the
passage north of Knotts Island, Byrd's periauger became foiled in the shallow

water, running aground in the "perpetual Shoals." Fearing that they might become stranded in the middle of the sound, Byrd concluded that it would take
a "Skilful Pilot to steer even a Canoe safe over it." Determined to conduct the
survey, they chased down a local canoe whose occupants guided them to Back
Bay, where after wading a half mile knee-deep in muck they were relieved to
reach dry ground.[85]

What North Carolina lacked was an easily navigated deepwater inlet. The
prominence of New England traders in the Albemarle economy was directly
correlated to the dangers of North Carolina's coast. The shifting sands of the
Outer Banks dictated that the bulk of Albemarle's trade be carried by small
coastal sloops, ketches, shallops, and brigs that could safely traverse shallow inlets into Albemarle Sound. Once one was inside the sound, the wide and deep
tributary rivers—the North, Pasquotank, Little, Perquimans, Yeopim, Roanoke,
and Chowan—provided excellent protected internal sailing waters. Reporting on the hazards of navigation, the colony's first surveyor general, Thomas
Woodward, reported to the proprietors that at Roanoke Inlet, the main entry,
vessels "must always be of very small burthen . . . so uncertaine are all those In-
letts." Even when taking the inlet at high tide through a channel marked with
beacons, in early 1665 Captain Whitty "struck twice or thrice" on his passage.[86]

Robert Risco, master of the Albemarle brigantine *Good Hope*, weighed anchor on 20 March 1673 in the Pasquotank River, outward bound for New England. Reaching New Inlet two days later and finding that the channel "seemed
to be quite barred up," the experienced Risco nevertheless decided to attempt
the passage.[87] *Good Hope* ran hard aground, and Risco vividly described the
consequences. "Notwithstanding all our endeavors with ancor & Cables and all
the meanes wee could use shee cast thwart & Imediately there arose a violent
storme . . . which caused the Sea to breake sheer over her." That night the damaged *Good Hope* broke free in the high tide and cleared the inlet, but the cargo
of tobacco was ruined.[88]

Albemarle's overseas trade originated at numerous plantation landings on
the rivers north of the sound. Although handicapped by isolation and navigation difficulties, the colony participated in the North Atlantic trading network,
dealing with other mainland colonies, chiefly New England and Virginia, and
the West Indies, Bermuda, and England.[89] Resident proprietor John Archdale
noted that the products of tobacco, oil, hides, and tallow could be safely shipped
in vessels of 150 tuns that drew up to nine feet.[90] The diversity of the colony's
exports is revealed in the cargo of the sloop *Peter*, which in 1697 carried corn,
peas, beans, feathers, pork, tobacco, wine, whale oil, hides, deerskins, and furs.
By the turn of the century the products of the pine tree, tar and pitch, appeared
on manifests. Classified as "naval stores," tar and pitch were strategic materials
used in caulking ships and preserving sails, rigging, sheets, lines, and cables.

These products were essential to keeping England's growing merchant and naval fleets at sea.[91]

An observer noted in 1696 that "the Inlet of Roanoke is frequented with small vessels trading to & from the West India Islands."[92] More than a decade later, former customs official Robert Holden reported that the "barrd" inlets admitted small vessels from New England and Bermuda.[93] Albemarle's exports to the West Indies were chiefly livestock and provisions, exchanged for the island imports of rum, sugar, molasses, and salt. Typical of small vessels engaged in trade with the islands was the five-tun, sloop-rigged shallop *Success* owned by Bermuda merchant Thomas Leech. From Bermuda in 1677 Thomas Miller and two others booked passage for Albemarle on *Success*, which arrived in July. Carrying a cargo that included calico and a barrel of salt, the vessel was crewed by Master Solomon Summers; a sailor, Richard Gamble; and an enslaved sailor named Jack.[94]

The dominance of livestock, provisions, and Indian furs in the eighteenth century is illustrated by two shipments—Thomas Pollock's outbound cargo to Boston in 1704 of leather and furs, 244 barrels of pork, and 2,690 dressed deerskins and Edward Moseley's consignment to Bermuda on *New Speedwell* in 1707 of 100 bushels of Indian corn, four barrels of pork, and a barrel of lard.[95] Customs collector Holden's list of exports added to these tobacco, wheat, beef, hides, tallow, tar and pitch, and drugs—sassafras, calamus (sweet flag), aromaticus (mushroom), asarabacca (wild ginger), capillus veneris and polypodium (ferns), and quercus (oak bark).[96] Lawson's more extensive goods, many of which moved through the port of Bath, included forest products—lumber, staves, ship timbers and masts, and the naval stores of tar, pitch, turpentine, and rosin; diverse agricultural crops—hemp, flax, dairy products, dyes, silk, grains, beans, peas, and wine; and two representatives of a nascent seafaring industry— whalebone and oil.[97]

During the years 1676 to 1679 Zachariah Gillam exported 889 hogsheads of tobacco from Carolina through New England to England and Holland in five different vessels.[98] Anna Sothel used the ketch *Dove*, commanded by John Blaney, to send pork to Massachusetts.[99] In 1694 the executors of a deceased local merchant, Joseph Hallet, shipped to Boston on the sloop *Industry* ninety-six barrels of pork, five barrels of whale oil, six barrels of fat, one and a half casks of beeswax, twenty-seven cured cowhides, thirteen deerskins, a panther skin, and a cub skin. In storehouses at seven plantation landings Hallett had on account another seventy-eight barrels of pork.[100] Other vessels sailing to New England, Virginia, and Barbados were the brigantine *Elizabeth*, the ketch *Speedwell*, the sloop *Durbartus*, and the ketch *Rebecka* of Rhode Island. Ships trading directly to London were the ketch *Tryall* and the *London Merchant*.[101]

Massachusetts registrations and customs records document vessels trading with North Carolina at the turn of the eighteenth century. Clearing port in the years 1687–88 were a sloop, a bark, and a brigantine and for 1701–2 five sloops and a ketch. Each of these vessels normally had four crewmen, with Bostonian masters. Exceptions were John Tooke, from Pasquotank precinct, and Nicholas Thomas Jones, who lived on the Pamlico River. Voyages to North Carolina were frequent, sometimes habitual, as illustrated by the 1698 headright claim of Massachusetts sea captain John Blaney, who filed for 1,650 acres for transporting himself thirty-three times, as documented by his ship's papers.[102] Other Albemarle seafarers were Jeremiah Goodridge of Chowan, captain of the pink *Adventure* of London, and George Durant, who was mate on the brig *Carolina*. The estate of the mate Richard French, who died by drowning, possibly at sea, included navigation instruments: a quadrant, forestaff, and compass. Thomas Matthews hired out as a sailor on Thomas Pollock's brigantine *Martha* at the rate of thirty shillings a month.[103]

A variety of partners co-owned the vessels trading with North Carolina, mostly local merchants or planters partnering with New England shipmasters or merchants. Examples of these connections were Thomas Pollock with captains of the ketch *Dove*, brigantine *Martha*, and sloops *Speedwell* and *Return*; and William Wilkinson with captains of the sloops *Susanna* and *Reserve*. Sometimes local masters and merchants formed partnerships: Captain John Tooke and John Porter co-owned the thirty-tun sloop *Elizabeth*, and Captain Thomas Phelps and Pollock had the twenty-five-tun sloop *Greyhound*.[104] Emmanuel Lowe and William Vaughn were trading partners and co-owners of the sloop *Roanoke Merchant*, which they had purchased in 1709 for £184 from the New Pennsylvania Company.[105]

Entry and clearing data in the *Boston News-Letter* for 1704–29 document significant traffic from North Carolina, which is not surprising, since North Carolina's trade was monopolized by New England sea captains. What is surprising is the volume. From 1704 to 1715 North Carolina's annual entries and clearings totaled between 18 and 62, whereas the number doubled for 1716–29, with over 100 entries and clearings in most years. In many of those years, North Carolina's coastal traffic was two or three times that of Virginia and South Carolina. Intercolonial coastal trade carried the bulk of North Carolina's exports and imports, while her neighbors, with deepwater harbors, conducted mostly transoceanic commerce with England.[106] Since the New England sloops and ketches were small, the total tunnage of the deepwater ports was much greater than that of North Carolina. Nevertheless, the colony was well connected to North Atlantic commerce.

In the Albemarle region, a half century passed before the port that would become Edenton emerged on Queen Anne's Creek. By contrast, early in Bath

County two port towns were founded—Bath on the Pamlico and New Bern at the confluence of the Neuse and Trent Rivers. Ocracoke Inlet, long known as the colony's best connection to the sea, served these Pamlico Sound ports well. At Topsail Inlet, which offered direct access to the sea, was the fishing village of Beaufort.

Of North Carolina's proprietary-era ports, only Albemarle's Port Roanoke records survive, with woefully few before 1725. Since both Port Roanoke and Port Bath were reached through Ocracoke Inlet and the exports and imports were similar by the eighteenth century, the Roanoke data provide the best available portrait of the colony's early economic activity. Most of the forty-nine documents date from 1703 to 1704. For these two years the customhouse entries, clearings, permits, bonds, and inventories cite seventeen vessels—two brigs, two shallops, and thirteen sloops. The largest vessel listed was the forty-tun brig *Martha*, which sailed to and from Boston. Outbound from North Carolina, *Martha*'s cargo was pork, deerskins, leather, hides, and furs. Imported from Boston were rum, molasses, ship rigging, and shop goods. The other known brig was the New England–owned *Speedwell*, rated at fifteen tuns. The two shallops, rated at four and five tuns, sailed to Virginia carrying pork, lard, deerskins, leather, tallow, nails, and beeswax. Imports from Virginia, obviously transshipped, were rum, sugar, and European household goods.[107]

The thirteen sloops sailing prior to 1717 ranged from five to forty tuns and were, on average, smaller than sloops just a decade later. They sailed to other colonial ports, chiefly Boston, Philadelphia, Charles Town, Patuxent River and Annapolis in Maryland, and York, Virginia. The offshore destinations were Bermuda and Barbados. Exports varied slightly from those carried earlier on the brigs and shallops: they now included beeswax, snakeroot, and feathers. Imports consisted of rum, wine, beer, molasses, sugar, cloth, shoes, clothing, household and dry goods, nails, salt, grindstones, silverware, and rugs. In the aftermath of the Tuscarora War between July and October 1715, seven vessels entered the port with powder and firearms. The only recorded transaction involving London was a 1717 transshipment of cloth, clothing, saddles, ironware, nails, and copper kettles, handled by a Virginia merchant.[108] Quaker Caleb Bundy, a Pasquotank planter, owned the sloop *Jane and Mary*, which sailed to Jamaica in 1715, stopping along the way at the salt pans, presumably on the Turks and Caicos, and returned to Albemarle with freight for Virginia.[109]

A North Carolina sea captain regularly involved in trade to the Caribbean and New England was the colorful and restless James Wimble. Born in England, Wimble went to sea early and by 1718 had sailed his own vessel to New Providence, Bahamas. Out of Nassau he entered the West Indian trade with the mainland, frequenting Albemarle. In 1723 he acquired 640 acres on the

Scuppernong River adjacent to Albemarle Sound, eventually accumulating over 2,000 acres. The next year he married in Boston, where he established a home and opened an inn and distillery. Wimble relocated to the Cape Fear River and in 1733 became a cofounder of the town that became Wilmington. That same year he drafted a detailed sea chart of the North Carolina coast that was published in 1738. Heavy losses to storms and Spanish privateers were recouped by successful privateering in the War of Jenkins' Ear, but he disappeared in 1744, presumably at sea.[110]

The extant ship registrations began in 1725, by which time tobacco had made a comeback as Port Roanoke's major export. Schooners had appeared in the colonies and rapidly rivaled sloops as the workhorse of colonial trade. For the period 1725–26, vessels hauling tobacco included five schooners that ranged from ten to thirty tuns and five sloops with a spread of twenty to forty tuns. The two brigs rated at thirty and forty tuns. All of the vessels except the small ten-tun North Carolina schooner were New England–owned, mostly from Massachusetts.[111]

FROM EARLIEST TIMES the offshore Outer Banks had a reputation as a place of refuge from the law, a harbor for smugglers, wreckers, and pirates. Royal customs official Edward Randolph characterized North Carolina in 1700 as "a place which receives Pirates, Runaways, and Illegal Traders." Randolph was always keen to find the worst in proprietary colonies, but there was some truth to his observation.[112] The previous year, a resident of "ye sand-banks had entertained some persons suspected of being runaways."[113] Ocracoke would become the last lair of the notorious pirate Blackbeard in 1718. A generation later, the royal governor described Bankers as "very Wild and ungovernable."[114] The harsh environment of these ephemeral strips of sand shaped a sturdy race. Gradually, small clusters of squatters and freeholders with meager plots were scattered among the islands, mostly subsisting on the occasional shipwreck or beached whale and the free-range livestock still remembered in the name "Cowpenpoint" near Currituck Inlet.[115] Making a living from the sea has ever been at the core of life on the Banks. Generations of stalwart sailors, masters, fishermen, crabbers, shrimpers, whalers, and inlet pilots have been drawn there to wrest a living for their families from the unforgiving sea.

Throughout the colonial period on most of the Atlantic seaboard, shore-based whaling ventures processed whale oil and bone from beached whales and kills made from small boats. On North Carolina's outer islands, close to the Gulf Stream and the migratory routes of the great mammals, whale strandings were so frequent that harpooning them from land-based boats was seldom practiced. Under the 1663 charter the Lords Proprietors were granted the rights to all the fish and whales in the inland and coastal waters, and they controlled the whaling industry by issuing licenses. In addition, the charter allowed duty-free export and import of oil for seven years. The colony's first whale oil was produced in 1665 on the proprietors' Colleton Island plantation, launching what became the plantation's most successful venture.[116]

Albemarle's first record of offshore whaling was Governor Peter Carteret's 1667 license to three New England fishermen sailing out of Southampton, Long Island, on the sloop *Speedwell* to "make use of all whales," whether taken at sea or stranded on the islands north of Roanoke Inlet. Several years later, hearing of "many Whales" off the Carolina coast and desiring to encourage the colony, the proprietors granted the "Inhabitants of our Province free leave" for seven years "to take what Whales they can, and convert them to their owne use, excepting onely such Whales as are throwne dead upon the Coast."[117]

Producing whale oil consisted of "flensing," or stripping the blubber with knives, and boiling it in large cast-iron vats known as try-pots to render the oil. When a beached whale was discovered, the finder struck an agreement with his neighbors, probably on shares, to flense the carcass and try out the oil. The stripped skeleton was then cut up for the bone. Whale strandings were too infrequent for the industry to be a major factor in the colony, but oil and bone continued to be exported throughout the era. Whale oil, used as commodity currency, retained its value. The Colleton Island plantation oil was sold in 1668 at £1.05 a barrel, and in 1715 the price of a barrel of oil was set by law at £1.10.[118]

Disputes over ownership and work shares of a stranded whale could result in a legal action. In March 1694 a resident of the banks, Mathias Towler, who held a whaling license from the governor, learned that a beached whale was being processed by Timothy Pead and his associate, Charles Thomas. They were flensing and trying the carcass, aided by Anne Ros and her family, who provided barrels for the oil. When Towler discovered the operation, he claimed the whale under his license and sued Pead. In the settlement for labor on the whale, Pead received £2s.6d, and Thomas, who claimed ten days' labor, received 10s. When Anne Ros and her family were arrested, they had filled three barrels with oil. She sold her remaining empty barrels to Towler, receiving restitution from him of £2.11.03 for her barrels and oil and £16s.8d for testifying in court.[119]

Whales were taken off North Carolina's shore mainly by New Englanders, some of whom migrated to the colony. In 1719 four New England whalers transported over 500 barrels of oil and a quantity of bone from North Carolina to Boston. Later, New Englanders were reputed to have shipped 340 barrels of oil off Ocracoke without paying the required tenth; prudently, they did not return to this coast. Samuel Chadwick, a native New Englander, had settled

at the Straits in Carteret Precinct by 1725. The next year he secured a license
to pursue whales with three boats, paying a tenth share of oil and bone to the
governor. The Cape Lookout bight at the east end of Shackleford Island had
by this time become a harbor of refuge for New England whalers who were
harpooning whales from small boats.[120]

THE MYTHOLOGY OF the Outer Banks is rife with tales of wrecking, but no
evidence supports persistent legends that vessels were lured onshore. In fact,
nature's combination of shifting shoals, fickle winds, and frequent storms on
this most dangerous of coasts made wrecks and vessel strandings common oc-
currences. Clinging to their narrow sandy reefs, Bankers existed mostly on livestock and sea life, and abandoned vessels and cargoes that washed up on the
beach were welcome gifts from the sea that constituted legal salvage.

Word of a wreck or cargo spread rapidly among the residents, who gathered
at the site and laid claims on a first-come, first-served basis. Ship timbers and
scattered shipments of lumber were collected and parceled out for homes and
boats. As with stranded whales, the proprietors claimed wrecks, but local officials made little systematic effort to regulate salvage until vice-admiralty courts
appeared in the early eighteenth century.

Wrecking or salvage normally occurred out of sight, but the cases of two
Royal Navy guardships stationed in Virginia, the HMS *Swift Advice* (1698) and
HMS *Garland* (1709), ended up in court and required government response.
The former was the more complex and bizarre of the incidents. In January 1698
the frigate *Swift Advice* was threatened by ice in Chesapeake Bay. The panicked skeleton crew ran her ashore, hastily abandoning her with the sails set. A
westerly wind drove the derelict out of the bay, and she drifted onto Currituck
Banks. On February 2 the solitary vessel was discovered with masts and rigging
intact and the naval ensigns flying.[121]

Concluding that the frigate was abandoned, over the course of a week a
group of colonists plundered the vessel. Mostly planters and residents of Currituck Precinct, those present or later accused were an odd assortment of Bankers
and mainlanders, including a married woman. The wreckers swarmed into the
hull, hauling out weapons, hammocks, bedding, rugs, men's clothing and shoes,
and, oddly, some gowns and petticoats. Two days later, Captain Anthony Dawson, a council member from Perquimans, arrived with Tony, an enslaved African; Charles, a borrowed enslaved Indian; and Richard Sanderson Jr., the son of
a council member. They were joined at the site by David Blake, a "Dangerous
person and of Evill fame." Claiming to represent the proprietors, Dawson took
charge, lowered the ensigns, and removed the sails and rigging, the guns, and

the remaining ships' stores and victuals. Whatever Dawson's original intentions were, the court found that he "did feloniously Imbezell purloyne and convey away" the king's property. To gain better access, Tony fired a "great" gun through the hull. It was a wreckers' jubilee.[122]

Meanwhile, the frigate's captain, Nathaniel Bostock, learned of the despoiling and requested aid from Governor Thomas Harvey and the council. An order was published announcing the vessel's "plundering by some evil persons" and demanding the return of the looted goods. The provost marshal arrested twenty suspects, and sea captains John Hunt and John Blaney were sent to Currituck to survey the wreck.[123]

A grand jury returned felony indictments on ten of the suspected looters, who were tried in the General Court. The judges were aware that salvage of an abandoned wreck was legitimate, but breaking into, vandalizing, and robbing a king's ship could result in the death penalty. The jury's lenient verdicts imply that the provost marshal recovered much of the loot, as most of the accused were found not guilty. Of those declared guilty, Thomas Young and Roger Snell were convicted of a felony but pled Benefit of Clergy, which reduced the sentence to being branded on the left thumb with the letter *T.* Snell's poor health won him a suspension. Anthony Dawson received the death penalty and was to be "hanged by the neck." Dawson humbly begged for and was granted a reprieve and banishment overseas. Finally, the marshal was ordered to deliver all of the stolen property to Captain Bostock.[124]

At the May court session, others were tried for misdemeanors and were discharged or received suspended sentences. Only Tony, convicted of firing the cannon, was punished with thirty-one "stripes" on his bare back. Captain Dawson, perceived to be the ringleader, had already been banished and settled in New Jersey, never to return to North Carolina. As for the "Dangerous" David Blake, he was apprehended and tried in October 1699. Despite his notoriety, the jury found him not guilty. The survey report was presented to the governor, the council, and the House of Burgesses on June 8. The committee had found that although the hull was intact, the vessel was bound firmly by seven feet of sand, and relaunching was impossible.[125]

The looting of *Swift Advice*, a unique criminal conspiracy in the province's history, involved a full range of the colony's residents: a high government official, the son of an official, planters, freeholders, a married woman, an enslaved Indian, an enslaved African, and an alleged criminal. The trial appears to have been for show, as the few severe sentences pronounced were later set aside or reduced for all but one of those convicted. Only three punishments were ultimately meted out—the banishment of Captain Anthony Dawson, the branding of the planter Thomas Young, and the whipping of the enslaved Tony.

Considering that the crime was a felony and all found guilty could have been executed, the court's leniency appears to condone wrecking as an element in the colony's economy.

ALBEMARLE PLANTERS and merchants were directly engaged in their farming and businesses, and those with smallholdings shared the field work with their servants and enslaved workers. In a backcountry region where colonists raised sheep and flax, there were spinning wheels, looms, and weavers. The everyday garb of Albemarle settlers, whether rich or poor, free or bound, was sewn from common cloth more in keeping with the toil of the farm, storehouse, and home. John Lawson noted that the "Women are the most industrious Sex in that Place, and, by their good Housewifry, make a great deal of Cloath of their own Cotton, Wool, and Flax," providing clothes for their entire family.[126]

Local merchants stocked a wide range of imported fabrics, sewing implements, and accessories, indicating that better clothing was sewn not from homespun but from ready-made cloth. Joseph Hallet offered blue linen, osnaburg cloth, buttons, needles, silk thread, and wool cards, as well as women's shoes and men's and women's stockings and gloves. John Goddard's detailed inventory comprised blue, green, and brown linen and large quantities of brown osnaburg, along with kersey, calico, Holland, crepe, and Scotch. His sewing items consisted of over ten pounds of shoe thread, four pounds each of cotton and brown thread, 9,000 pins, a dozen knives, a dozen ivory combs, a dozen pairs of scissors, seven horn combs, and four dozen pewter buttons. In addition to blue linen and Holland, Samuel Gambel's shop had green stockings, forty-eight pairs of shoes, eight pairs of scissors, 2,500 needles, a gross of buttons, and six dozen buckles.[127]

Accessories routinely imported were shoes, hats, gloves, stockings, and lace. Genre paintings of the period depict flamboyant, colorful clothing, and those colonists who could afford the latest fashions imported them. In Sarah Mayo Culpeper's order to a New York firm were five pairs of women's hose, a child's cap and wires for her young daughter, and a variety of yard goods—serge, striped, crepe, dyed linen, brown osnaburg, and white Hamburg.[128] A governor, William Glover, purchased blue linen, skeins of silk, and "crowned" buttons. Mrs. Elizabeth Banks's imports from England included broad lace, narrow lace, black silk gloves, white kid gloves, and an evening suit lined with broad lace.[129]

IN THE SEVENTEENTH CENTURY the colony's foundational occupations were trader, merchant, planter, farmer, rancher, mariner, and tavern keeper. Court records reveal that as the colony's population grew and port towns emerged,

the abilities of basic artisans and craftspeople were augmented by the specialized skills of blacksmiths, pewterers, carpenters, sawyers, coopers, shipwrights,
tailors, weavers, cobblers, cordwainers, wheelwrights, and saddlers. By the turn
of the century additional workers included factors, butchers, bakers, barbers,
wigmakers, feltmakers, hatters, millwrights, joiners, turners, bricklayers, tanners,
silversmiths, and hosiers. By that time professions, originally restricted to physicians and apothecaries, included attorneys who had gradually acquired proficiency through repeated appearances as amateur legal counsel. Since Quakers
had no professional ministers, the clergy appeared in the colony only after the
church establishment.[130]

Carpenters Thomas and William Stephenson contracted in January 1698
with merchant and Provost Marshall Joseph Commander for extensive repairs
on his Pasquotank plantation: roofing the dwelling (£2.10s); underpinning the
house (2s); finishing the house (7s); building a millhouse (£4.10s), a henhouse
(14s), and a cart (12s.6d); mounting a grindstone and trough, 2s; making a new
table leaf, 5s; and mending a canoe, 1s). Commander partially paid the total
bill of £9.3s.6d with merchandise—a pair of shoes, four dozen buttons, rum, a
handsaw, an ogee plane and chisel, and a pair of compasses—and by covering
two debts for the Stephensons.[131]

Carpenter's tools were in evidence on most plantations, but one carpenter,
Thomas Harris, seemed particularly well equipped with his inventory of two
adzes, six augers, nine chisels, three hammers, two planes, a broadaxe, a hatchet,
a drawing knife, five files, five cooper's adzes, two handsaws, one whipsaw, a
crosscut saw, a framing saw, and four wedges. Henry Norman's runaway Indian
servant took with him a broadaxe, a gouge, a saw, a file, two chisels, an auger,
and a joiner's square, compass, and plane.[132]

Since commodities were shipped in wooden barrels or casks in that era, the
cooper was an indispensable member of the community. In addition to the cooper's tools found on plantations, which imply repair and possibly limited production, among coopers mentioned in the court records were Cornelius Terry,
John Wilson, John Spelman, and John and Richard Bentley.[133] Only coopers
could craft the 400-pound-capacity hogsheads in which tobacco was packed.
The largest container made in the period was the tun for shipping wine, which
had a capacity of four hogsheads.

Albemarle's relative isolation prompted the community to be self-sufficient,
making what would be needed to farm, to trade, and for daily life. Other known
artisans included the blacksmith William Secherverell, the weaver John Ley,
the cordwainer Charles Tailor, the bricklayer Jacob Overman, the wheelwright
Gabriel Newby, and tanners, tailors, and millwrights.[134] One smith, Nathaniel
Tomes, had acquired the skill to cast spoons.

Regardless of the challenges of geography, after difficult beginnings on

Colleton Island, Albemarle planters created a continually evolving diversified agricultural economy that resulted in prosperity. In the eighteenth century, especially in the burgeoning Lower Cape Fear valley, naval stores (tar, pitch, and turpentine) and wood products—lumber, shingles, staves, barrelheads, and hoops—became North Carolina's major exports and further ensured the colony's secure niche in the commerce of the North Atlantic.

CHAPTER NINE

A Dissenter's Colony

Quakers and Baptists

I find Quakers and Baptist[s] Flourish amongst the North Carolinians.
—Governor Sir Richard Everard, 1729

A ROOT CAUSE OF the English Civil War was the intolerance and persecution that the Church of England, or Anglican Church, practiced against dissenters. Like the Catholics they supplanted, Anglicans were certain that their particular theological beliefs comprised the "one true faith" and that all non-Anglicans were heretics. As the Protestant Reformation spawned numerous dissenting Christian sects across Europe, Anglicans were alarmed by the rampant religious diversity, which flirted with chaos. Supported by the absolutist Stuart monarchs James I and Charles I, they launched such severe oppression of dissenters that many emigrated from England, removing to the more tolerant Holland or to the American colonies to establish their own refuges.

Forged in the fires of the English Civil War, the regicide of Charles I, and the Commonwealth, which involved both parliamentary failure and the military rule of Oliver Cromwell, most of the Lords Proprietors shared with many of their countrymen a desire for greater toleration in the British Isles. Fortunately, prior to his restoration to the throne, the exiled Charles II, having personally experienced these upheavals, readily agreed to the conditions sought by the Lord General George Monck. The promises of a general pardon, the confirmation of land ownership, and religious liberty, subject to Parliament's approval, were incorporated into the Declaration of Breda of 4 April 1660. Charles stated, "We do declare a liberty to tender consciences, and that no man shall be disquieted, or called in question for differences of opinion in matters of religion, which do not disturb the peace of the kingdom."[1] The king's view on toleration was stated in the 1665 Carolina Charter and became the basis for the proprietary policy on freedom of conscience in Carolina, the most liberal of any English colony.[2]

Charles's commitment to tolerance, however, was nearly undone by the

overwhelmingly Anglican and royalist Cavalier Parliament, which began re-
pealing Puritan restrictions on social behavior and returning the Church of
England to dominance. A series of noxious laws were passed, unfairly labeled
the Clarendon Code for the Lord Chancellor, the Earl of Clarendon. While
Clarendon favored returning to the Anglican establishment, he advocated a
moderate compromise and could not support vindictive acts. The new laws
were designed to continue suppression of Catholics, to root out Puritans and
Presbyterians from church and state, and to persecute radical dissenting sects,
such as Baptists and Quakers. The king attempted to counter these measures
by periodic Declarations of Indulgence that temporarily removed restrictions
and emptied the prisons of dissenters. In the face of this poisonous atmosphere,
the Anglican proprietors demonstrated a far deeper commitment to religious
liberty than was necessary to attract colonists.[3]

In contrast to the Carolana charter, which mandated all colonists to be com-
municants of the state church, Carolina welcomed dissenters. The charter authorized the proprietors to grant "Dispensations" for those who could not publicly worship following the "Liturgy, forms, and Ceremonies" of the national
church. In return, the dissenter was to be loyal and obedient to the monarchy
and the laws of the province.[4] The result of this provision was that Carolina
would share with Rhode Island, New Jersey, and Pennsylvania the reputation as
the most tolerant of American colonies for religious nonconformists and would
attract numbers of these dissenters as settlers. When the Carolina Charter was
unsuccessfully challenged by claimants under the Heath patent, proprietor Sir
John Colleton's primary concern was that the offer of religious liberty might
be nullified by the earlier charter's Anglicans-only policy. Colleton observed
that those preparing to immigrate to Carolina "expect liberty of conscience and
without that will not goe."[5]

In the 1665 Concessions and Agreement, the Lords strictly adhered to their
deep commitment to liberty of conscience by paraphrasing the Declaration of
Breda that no freeman of the province "shall be any ways molested, punished,
disquieted, or called in question for any differences in opinion or practice in
matters of religious Concernment," and they may "freely and fully have and
enjoy his and their Judgements and Consciences in matters of religion."[6]

The proprietors declared that they would not infringe on the "General clause
of Liberty of Conscience," and the General Assembly was expressly forbidden
to pass laws against it. Regarding the Church of England, they authorized the
assembly of each county to appoint and support ministers by creating parish
glebe farms of 100 acres. A provision to accommodate dissenters allowed them
to maintain preachers and ministers as needed.[7] The 1665 charter broadened the
guarantee of liberty of conscience by deleting the requirement that dissenters

be "subject and obedient" to ecclesiastical as well as civil law. Religious tolerance now shifted to freedom of conscience, and the statement on religious liberty from the Concessions and Agreement issued six months earlier became a charter right.[8]

Among the original proprietors, the three most influential were also the most deeply committed to liberty of conscience for the colonists. During his pre-Restoration negotiations with Charles II the future Duke of Albemarle, who became the proprietors' first palatine, or chairman, had secured that guarantee from the king.[9] After the duke's demise, Lord Ashley, later the Earl of Shaftesbury (1672), was the mentor of the political philosopher John Locke and became the dominant proprietor until his fall from power in 1682. The enduring Earl of Craven became palatine in 1680 and with key support from the Quaker proprietor John Archdale maintained religious tolerance until his death in 1697 at the age of ninety-one.

Ashley and Locke drafted the Fundamental Constitutions, or Grand Model, in 1669 to be the permanent frame of government for Carolina. Much in the document harked back to the medieval past, but the startlingly liberal provisions guaranteeing freedom of conscience were a harbinger of complete religious liberty and eventual separation of church and state. Fifteen articles in the document were devoted to religion. To be a freeman, or to live in the province with legal protection, one had to acknowledge and publicly worship "a God." Unique for the time was the explicit inclusion of Native Americans, "whose Idolatry, Ignorance, or Mistake gives us no right to expel or use them ill." Others specifically mentioned were new colonists who might have "different Opinions concerning Matters of Religion," and "heathens, Jews, and other dissenters." Only atheists were excluded.[10]

In the context of separating religious and civil authority, an article recognized enslaved persons as human beings and granted them "soul-liberty," stating, "It shall be lawful for Slaves, as well as others, to Enter themselves and be of what Church or Profession any of them shall think best, and thereof be as fully Members as any Freeman." Lest this freedom should extend too far, the Grand Model confirmed that religious beliefs or worship could not compromise a master's "absolute Power and Authority" over his enslaved persons.[11]

A church could be organized by seven or more persons and was officially recognized by filing the names with the colony's register. Three simple rules defined a legitimate church: to acknowledge the existence of God, to publicly worship that God, and to state how the church would bear witness to truth. Any religious assembly not observing these rules would be declared unlawful.[12]

Liberty of conscience was protected by powerful constitutional guarantees unmatched in England or any other colony:

- "No Person of any other Church or Profession shall disturb or molest any religious Assembly."
- "No Person whatsoever shall speak any thing in their religious Assembly irreverently or seditiously of the Government or Governors or State Matters."
- "No Man shall use any reproachful, reviling, or abusive Language against the Religion of any Church or Profession." . . .
- "No Person whatsoever shall disturb, molest, or persecute another for his speculative Opinions in Religion or his Way of Worship."[13]

Consequently, in the seventeenth century, North Carolina enjoyed absolute freedom of conscience. This soul-liberty was reinforced and protected by the only organized church in the colony, the Religious Society of Friends, or Quakers, who had also achieved political prominence.[14]

Although religious freedom would be compromised by church establishment in the early eighteenth century, religious toleration remained a fundamental tenet throughout the proprietary era and beyond. John Lawson was not exaggerating when he observed that Carolinians "enjoy at this Day an entire Liberty of their Worship; the Constitution of this Government, allowing all Parties of well-meaning Christians to enjoy a free Toleration . . . it being the Lords Proprietors Intent, that the Inhabitants of *Carolina* should be as free from Oppression as any in the Universe."[15] Two decades later, Dr. John Brickell noted that in North Carolina "no Disputes or Controversies are ever observed to arise among them about their Religious Principles." According to Brickell, the dissenters in numerical order were the Albemarle Quakers, Presbyterians mostly on the Neuse, Roman Catholics chiefly around Bath, and Baptists living primarily in Albemarle. Anglican missionary Thomas Newman, who served Chowan, Bertie, and Bath, reported about a dozen Catholics in the colony in 1723.[16]

The political and religious ferment of the English Revolution era had literally upended the world of the mind. Freedom of thought now enjoyed by the common people bred radical political, social, economic, and religious ideas. From the spectrum of new religious groups and sects, including Anabaptists, Quakers, and Baptists, came such beliefs as God present in everyone, the equality of all before God, absolute freedom of conscience, free will and grace, separation of church and state, and rejection of ecclesiastical and biblical authority, as well as such testimonies and practices as rejection of infant baptism and other sacraments. Both the Quakers and the Baptists would exert important influences on the religious life of North Carolina in the late seventeenth century.[17]

Through the evangelical ministry of the itinerant George Fox and others, by midcentury the Religious Society of Friends, popularly called Quakers, had spread throughout England, drawing chiefly from laborers and artisans. Quaker founders emphasized the biblically based vision of the Inner Light, or the Light of Christ within each individual. Related to this revelation were beliefs in the sacredness of human life and sacramental living. From these insights stemmed their radical testimonies of equality of all, regardless of birth, race, or sex; a dedication to truth that disallowed oaths; pacifism; and a rejection of ecclesiastical authority that rendered church hierarchy, clergy, rituals, and creeds unnecessary. Their testimonies of simplicity and equality were expressed in plain dress and speech. Quaker organization was based on the local congregation, known as a meeting for worship, which conducted business in monthly, quarterly, and yearly sessions. Quakers did not observe religious holidays because of the pagan origins. For the same reason, they adopted a plain calendar, numbering the days and months; hence, Sunday was First Day, and March was First Month.[18]

Particularly heretical to the Anglican Church were Quaker practices of open worship, marriage and burial without officiating clergy, and rejection of the physical observance of the sacraments of baptism and communion. Orthodox Christians viewed with suspicion Friends' mystical worship in silence to wait for direct leadings of the Holy Spirit that might be expressed by any man or woman present. Quakers' recognition of women as ministers and missionaries was abhorrent to church, state, and society. Unrecognized by the Church of England, Quaker marriages were held in a meeting for worship in which the couple promised before God and witnesses to be loving and faithful to each other. Placing the emphasis on the personal experience of the Inner Light, Fox considered the rituals of outward communion and water baptism unnecessary. He had taken to their logical extreme the foundational Protestant beliefs: priesthood of believers and justification by faith.

On fire with Fox's breathtakingly simple and direct vision, Quaker traveling ministers, both men and women, dispersed across England, Ireland, and the Atlantic colonies, appealing to seekers estranged from Anglican formalism and unfulfilled by the bleakness of Puritan authoritarianism. Quakers' unorthodox theology, heretical practices, and radical social and political witness made them targets of prolonged and harsh persecution and punishment by the Anglican Church and the state, in both England and Virginia, and by the Puritans in Massachusetts Bay. Especially galling to the orthodox were Friends' conventicles, or secret religious gatherings; their lack of class deference; and their unconventional actions: refusing military service, protesting parish tithes, failing to accord due respect toward public officials, and refusing to take oaths. For these transgressions they were subjected to fines, imprisonment, public whippings, banishment, and, in Massachusetts Bay, execution.[19] To attract Quakers, a section of the Fundamental Constitutions allowed all civil officials to "subscribe and not swear" allegiance to the monarch and loyalty to the proprietors.[20]

In neighboring Virginia, religious liberty for Protestant dissenters was a foreign concept. From the founding of the colony, strict conformity to the Church of England had been imposed by acts of the assembly and enforced by the courts. The most insignificant departure from orthodoxy was considered "public scandal," and individuals were hauled before the courts for fines, imprisonment, corporal punishment, and banishment. By 1660 a major contention was the absence of infant baptism among Puritans and Baptists, and, even worse, the Quakers' rejection of water baptism at any age. Because of their heretical doctrine and practices, Quakers, who had been in Virginia for only four years, were viewed as social and political threats. That year the assembly passed "An Act for Suppressing Quakers," which characterized Friends as "an unreasonable and turbulent sort of people" and authorized their imprisonment and deportation.[21]

Ignoring the king's 1662 instructions that dissenters were not to be "molested or disquieted" for their religious beliefs, Governor William Berkeley, an Anglican zealot, was persistent in imposing the "true faith" and persecuting the "pestelent Sect" to prevent the growth of "the abominated seede of the Quakers."[22] The secluded Albemarle region might have been considered a haven for the oppressed, but Albemarle then was part of Virginia. Even after it was in the Carolina propriety, Governor Berkeley, their chief tormentor, was a Lord Proprietor with potential oversight of the colony.

Knowing that Virginia strictly enforced conformity to the Church of England and persecuted Quakers in particular, historians initially surmised that the Albemarle settlement was a sanctuary for religious refugees. Three of the earliest known land grants in 1663 were west of the Chowan River to Quakers Robert Lawrence Jr. (625 acres), his brother John Lawrence (625 acres), and John Murdah (420 acres), all from Chuckatuck Monthly Meeting in Nansemond County.[23] The evidence, however, reveals that most settlers came to the Albemarle to raise tobacco and livestock, rather than churches. By the time Quaker missionaries arrived in the colony to plant their faith, these first Quaker settlers had moved away.

The Society of Friends began in Carolina in 1672 with the missionary visits of Quaker evangelists William Edmundson and George Fox. Edmundson found only one Quaker family, Henry and Hannah Phelps, on the Perquimans River. For their faith the Phelps family had suffered severe persecution in Salem, Massachusetts Bay Colony, including imprisonment, whipping, and banishment. They had fled to Albemarle in 1665 but had not seen other Friends in the colony in the seven years since.[24] Two other oppressed Quaker couples from Massachusetts Bay who later migrated to Albemarle were Christopher and Hannah Nicholson from Marblehead and Isaac and Demaris Page of Salem.[25] From tolerant Rhode Island came William Bundy (who later served on the council), Thomas Kent, and Henry Stanton. New Englanders would play an important role in developing commerce and the crafts, especially furniture, in the eighteenth century.[26]

Edmundson and Fox arrived in Albemarle just two years after the Fundamental Constitutions made Carolina one of the most tolerant of American colonies. Destined to lay the religious foundation of North Carolina, Edmundson, an English carpenter and joiner and a soldier for Cromwell, married after the war and moved to Ireland. During his spiritual journey he became intrigued with Quakers. On a business trip to England he was convinced (converted) by James Nayler and thereafter met George Fox and began his ministry in Ireland in 1655.[27]

Fox had long planned a mission to colonies in the West Indies and North America and was considering establishing a Quaker colony as a refuge from persecution. Accompanied by twelve ministers, both women and men, Fox sailed in March 1671, landing first in Barbados, where there was a thriving Quaker community, and then continuing on from Jamaica to the mainland. Entering Chesapeake Bay, their ketch anchored in the Patuxent River in Maryland. From there the missionaries spread out in the colonies, with Fox and his companions heading to New England and Edmundson's party turning south.[28]

After attending meetings in Virginia, Edmundson wrote that, the leading of the Holy Spirit "being upon me, I travelled to *Carolina*." Apparently unaware of the well-worn overland and river route, in late April the forty-five-year-old Edmundson and two companions plunged into the aptly named Dismal Swamp. After spending a rainy two days and nights "sorely foiled in Swamps and Rivers," they discovered a path that led them to the Perquimans River and the house of Henry and Hannah Phelps. Seeing other Friends after seven long years, the Phelpses "wept for Joy."

Since it was First Day (Sunday) morning, Edmundson, although wet and exhausted from his difficult trek, took only a few hours' rest before conducting the first Christian worship in North Carolina since the Roanoke Island colonies. Settlers gathered and "sat down in the Meeting smoking their Pipes," causing Edmundson to observe that they had "little or no Religion." But he found these people receptive, for in "a little Time the Lord's Testimony arose in the Authority of his Power, and their Hearts being reached with it, several of them were tendered and received the Testimony." Among the converts at this first religious service were precinct justice Francis Tomes and his wife Priscilla, who "received the Truth with Gladness." At Tomes's urging Edmundson crossed the river the next day and held a "blessed Meeting" in Tomes's home that garnered more new Friends. Edmundson spent that night with the Tomes family and departed for Virginia the next morning.[29]

On his return to Virginia, Edmundson offered encouragement and spiritual comfort to the beleaguered Friends meetings. Following another Quaker precept, "speaking truth to power," Edmundson visited Governor Sir William Berkeley at his Green Spring plantation. Using "soft Arguments," he beseeched the governor to be "*kind to our Friends*," in the same way that his brother, Lord Berkeley, was in Ireland. The vindictive Sir William, however, was "very peevish and brittle." At a subsequent Friends meeting, the newly convinced Major General Richard Bennett, a former Puritan, asked Edmundson if the governor had called him "*Dog, Rogue*, etc." When the evangelist answered that he had not, Bennett commented, "*You took him in his best Humour . . . for he is an Enemy to every Appearance of Good.*"[30]

That fall, George Fox, who had returned to Virginia, headed to Albemarle County. On 20 November Fox and three companions left Somerton in Nansemond County on horseback and, although traveling the well-known back route, still became entangled in the "woods, & swamps & many cruell boggs and watery places," passing a very uncomfortable night in the wild. By the next evening the weary Quakers had reached a house on Bennett's Creek in Carolina, where they spent the night.

Despite its inauspicious beginning, Fox's missionary journey became a brilliant success. From Bennett's Creek his party canoed down the Chowan River to the house of Hugh Smithwick in Chowan Precinct, where a crowd gathered to meet them. Among the settlers was the influential Captain Nathaniel Batts, who offered the hospitality of his nearby house. Although Fox described Batts as "a Rude desperate man," the two men became well acquainted, for Fox remained with Batts for three days and held his first meeting for worship there. Batts enhanced Fox's reputation by spreading the story of a Friend who, directed by Fox, had healed the sick by the laying on of hands. When Batts questioned Fox about the incident, he simply answered that "many things had beene done by ye power of Christ."[31]

Exchanging their canoe for a boat, on 25 November Fox's band paddled along the north shore of Albemarle Sound to the Harvey's Neck home of Governor John Jenkins and his wife Joanna, who "Received us Loveingly." At the governor's house, Fox engaged in a theological discourse with a "doctor" that "was of great service . . . of openinge much to the people Concerneinge ye Light & the spiritt." As they debated the nature of the human conscience, Fox queried an Indian, who confirmed that if "hee did lie and doe yt to another" there was "somethinge in him, that did tell him of it, that hee should not doe soe."[32]

Sir Peter Lely's portrait of George Fox is at Swarth-
more College. Frontispiece from Norman Penny,
Journal of George Fox.

The next morning Governor Jenkins sent Fox's boat thirty miles around the
point while the men walked two miles through the woods to the Perquimans
River home of Joseph Scott, a burgess in the assembly. There Fox held a meeting that "was tender, & a sound pretious [precious] meettinge." A subsequent
meeting at the house of Henry Phelps included the colony's acting secretary,
Thomas Harris, who had been convinced by Edmundson. The following day,
29 November, Fox "went amonge" and preached to a large gathering of Native Americans and "their younge Kinge," who subsequently brought his wives,
some elders, and his son to worship with Fox.[33]

Two days later, while en route to Harris's home, some ten miles down the
Perquimans River through "much raine" in a "Rotten boate," Fox and his crew
ran aground in the offshore shallows. Emerging from the mist was the "bare-
footed and barelegged" innkeeper Diana Harris, the secretary's wife, who took
them into her canoe and paddled them to shore, where they spent the night
at the Harrises' inn.[34] After raising and repairing the sunken boat the next day,
Fox's party endured a long and harrowing voyage on the sound through rough

seas and high winds, persuading him that "the great power of God was seen in carrieinge us in that boate."[35]

Holding his last meeting in the Perquimans region on 3 December, Fox recorded that it was "glorious & pretious." Five days later he was back at Hugh Smithwick's house. There his final meeting in the county was attended by a Native shaman and an "Indian captain," who became a convinced Friend. Following this service, Fox and his companions left for Virginia, satisfied that their busy three-week mission to Albemarle's European settlers and Indians had nurtured the meetings that William Edmundson had planted a few months earlier.[36]

Returning to Virginia four years later, in 1676, Edmundson found the colony "in great Trouble, . . . the *Indians* being at War with the *Christians*, and the Governor, Sir *William Berkeley* and Col. *Bacon* at fierce War one against another." Undaunted by the peril, Edmundson was again "moved of the Lord to go to *Carolina*." To the rigors of the swamp were added the risks of the Chowan River War, which had erupted during Bacon's Rebellion. In the border wilderness he would traverse, "the *Indians* were not yet subdued but did Mischief and murdered several." Virginia Friends attempted to dissuade him from going, but Edmundson followed his leading, accompanied by one elderly Friend who dared attempt the hazardous journey.

Suffering no mishaps, in two days the pair reached the Henry Phelps house, where Edmundson learned that his friend had died but that his widow, Hannah, had married James Hill, another Quaker whom Edmundson had known in Ireland. Edmundson held a meeting for worship at the home of Francis Tomes on First Day and several other "precious Meetings" in the area. When he left, Edmundson reported that the "People were tender and loving, there was no Room for the Priests . . . for Friends were finely settled."[37]

As the only organized church available to meet the colonists' spiritual needs, the Society of Friends grew rapidly. Albemarle's unchurched dissenters readily accepted the preaching of the missionaries Fox and Edmundson. Doubtless, the egalitarian nature and directness of Quakers appealed to Albemarle's individualistic and self-sufficient settlers. By 1677 several groups of Friends had emerged in the center of the colony that developed into the Perquimans and Pasquotank monthly meetings. Worship gatherings in private homes were designated preparative meetings, which together constituted a monthly meeting. The monthly meeting business sessions, held separately for men and women, were the core of Quaker organization.

Within four years George Fox suggested a single yearly meeting for the two Carolina settlements, but the distance between Charles Town and Albemarle was too great to make this practicable.[38] From the first monthly meeting at the home of Francis Tomes, others developed at the home of Jonathan Phelps in Perquimans and in Pasquotank on Little River. The minutes of Perquimans Monthly Meeting record four meetings for worship on the Perquimans, Pasquotank, Yeopim, and Little Rivers.[39]

Quaker monthly meeting minutes contain references to their social practices and discipline. Leaders in a Friends meeting were called overseers or elders, and to be "eldered" meant to be counseled by a committee of elders for disciplinary purposes. Robert Harman was visited by a committee in the Perquimans Monthly Meeting for drunkenness and dancing, and John Lawrence was cautioned for being "Carless of Coming to Meeting." In a later period concern was expressed for "much Wildness at friends maridges," and the meeting designated two members "to be thear to Keep A Good decorum."[40]

Quakers continued to meet in homes for worship and business through the 1690s, but Pasquotank and Perquimans meetings approved five meetinghouses in the early eighteenth century.[41] In its June 1703 minutes, Pasquotank Meeting proposed that a meetinghouse be constructed with "as much speed as can be." Within a year a meetinghouse had been built in Perquimans on an acre fronting the river. By 1706 another stood on an acre that Francis Tomes donated to Thomas Peirce, Gabriel Newby, and others on behalf of "a Society of Protestant Desenters Vulgarly called Quakers." This building was twenty-five feet long, covered with clapboard, with a chimney at one end.[42]

The Quaker adherence to honesty and truth, signified by their refusal to swear an oath of any kind, was widely known. In the 1665 Carolina Charter the proprietors had provided that indulgences and dispensations would be given to those who could not "for Conscience sake . . . take and Subscribe the Oaths and Articles" of the Church of England. For civil oaths of allegiance and loyalty the alternative was subscription, which the proprietors granted in the Concessions and Agreement. As stated in their 1670 instructions to Governor Samuel Stephens, "In Case any man For Religeon sake be not Free to Sweare then Shall he Subscribe the same in a Book . . . provided which Shall be deemed the same with Swearing."[43]

For nearly forty years the practice of subscription or affirmation allowed Quakers to participate fully in the colony's political life in any office— governor, council, assembly, and the courts, from precinct to county. The council and court records contain numerous examples of subscription. As late as April 1708 when Gabriel Newby, one of the last Quakers to serve on the council, was installed as the deputy of proprietor John Archdale, he declared that he would "subscribe after the manner of his profession being a Quaker."[44] His father-in-law, Francis Tomes, had made a similar declaration several years earlier when he began another term on the council.[45] The subscription of Quaker Thomas

Symons for serving as foreman of a grand jury stated, "I Do in the Presence of God and under the Penallty of perjury promise to Declare the truth the whole truth and Nothing but the truth acording to the best of my Judgment in the Case."[46]

Not until the early eighteenth century, after the Anglican Church was established, was oath-taking used to purge Quakers from government. Although Quakers were excluded from holding all public offices, the courts accepted subscription, or affirmation, for testimony in civil and criminal cases, including probate, testimony, jury duty, petitions, depositions, and business transactions.[47] However, having lost their voice in government and no longer being protected by the original proprietors' broadminded policies on religious liberty, Quakers faced the possibility of losing the right of affirmation under an all-Anglican judiciary. Rejection of affirmation would mean being held in contempt of court, resulting in fines or imprisonment and seizure of property "to the Ruin of themselves & familyes."[48]

In 1715 the General Assembly, now also dominated by Anglicans, finally addressed this uncertainty in a law defining "Liberty of Conscience." The religious freedom granted by the proprietors, which for decades had protected all Christian and non-Christian faiths, was narrowed to allow only "all Protestant Dissenters" to practice public worship "without Molestation," as long as British parliamentary laws and restrictions were satisfied. The new law specified that Quaker "Solemn Affirmation" would be accepted for an oath; however, Quakers were excluded not only from serving in public office but also from giving evidence in a criminal case and from serving on a jury, thereby limiting Quakers to civil suits and business and property matters.[49] Gone was the all-inclusive proprietary freedom of conscience, although in fact Quakers would be protected from judicial and economic persecution for the remainder of the colonial period.

The testimony that has been a recurring source of persecution to Quakers throughout their existence has been the peace witness. Many of the early convinced Friends had been veterans of the English Revolution, fighting under Cromwell; but George Fox had refused military service because of his belief in the value of human life and in the principle that a follower of Christ should not take another's life.[50] To non-Quakers, anyone refusing militia service, especially in times of war, constituted a threat to the survival of the state. In England, imprisonment and fines were levied, but Friends eventually won the right to conscientious objection as a witness of their faith.

In the unruly politics of Albemarle there were several instances of Quakers' publicly witnessing for peace. Neutrality is often interpreted by those in conflict as either covert opposition or support for their side, and Albemarle proved no exception. During Culpeper's Rebellion, even though they attempted to avoid involvement, several Friends leaders were seized by the rebels. The most prominent—burgesses Francis Jones and Christopher Nicholson, and James Hill, the deputy of the Duke of Albemarle—were briefly imprisoned. To counter rebel accusations, in 1679 Friends submitted a petition to the Lords Proprietors, signed by twenty-one Quakers, which stated that Friends "in Scorne called Quakers . . . have stood single from all the seditious actions." They denied the rebels' charges that Friends were "plotters and contrivers of Treason and Wagers of War and *vile* persons and disquiaters of the peace and scandalous base Intelligencies," and affirmed that they had always adhered to their testimonies against "such wicked practices."[51]

Other protests were lodged in 1680 and 1683 in response to a law passed by the General Assembly that would sentence "all that would not bear arms in ye Musterfield" to six months in prison and a fine according to their estate. In the first instance, nine Friends from Perquimans Monthly Meeting suffered imprisonment rather than serve in the militia. Among them was William Bundy, then a precinct justice, who would become a council member by 1684.[52] In 1704 Pasquotank Monthly Meeting approved a paper on the "Friends Principle concerning fighting wars, & Sheading of blood," which was posted at the courthouse during court sessions.[53] In the 1715 militia law there was no provision for pacifist Quakers, who would be liable for a five-shilling fine levied for absence at quarterly musters and a fifty-shilling fine for refusal to serve in time of war.[54]

The devastating assault on Bath County that began the Tuscarora War did not immediately heal the long-standing political divisions in the colony. Largely residing in "safe" Albemarle County, Quakers maintained their peace witness and would neither serve in the militia nor provide supplies for defense. One exception in the first weeks of the hostilities was Ephraim Overman, who was eldered by Pasquotank Friends Meeting for taking arms with the militia "contrary to our known principles." Overman admitted his error and promised to "take better care and walk more circumspectly."[55]

Quakers tended to live in communities centered on their monthly meetings, but they maintained ties with the broader Atlantic Quaker society of the other continental and West Indian colonies and the British Isles, anchored by London Yearly Meeting. The Albemarle Quakers, virtually all convinced Friends, brought into the faith their diverse religious backgrounds and experiences. Ties were solidified by the traveling ministers, letters, epistles, and tracts sent between the colonists and the homeland.

The first known traveling Friend from the Albemarle was elder Gabriel Newby, who went north in 1701 to New Jersey and Pennsylvania, and again in 1715, this time accompanied by Matthew Prichard. English native Joseph

Glaister, convinced in 1692 at age nineteen, commenced preaching two years
later. After evangelizing as a traveling minster in the British Isles and the
American colonies, he settled in 1709 on New Begun Creek in Pasquotank,
where he married Mary Palin and lived until his death in 1719.[56]

A Quaker leader, Henry White Jr., wrote the earliest known North Carolina
literary pieces, a prose epistle and a 302-line religious poem, which he copied
into the minute book of Symons Creek Monthly Meeting in 1698.[57] White
had migrated to Albemarle from Virginia and settled on a 700-acre plantation
on Little River purchased in 1663. An early member of Pasquotank Monthly
Meeting, he hosted meetings for worship in his home until 1707, when a meetinghouse was built adjacent to his plantation. White later was a justice on the
precinct court and the General Court.[58]

Recounting man's fall from Eden and redemption through Christ, White's
poem reflects an orthodox theology but has passages that illustrate Quaker
beliefs in the inward Light—the God within:

> and com to Crist whom thou hast sent
> into the world a blesed light . . .
> this is a day he may be founde
> waite enwardly to here his sound
> for what is to be known of God is manifest
> in Man: that is our chefest test
> and rule of life for to walke by[59]

Couched in expressions of peace and love, the epistle that accompanied the
poem takes a more overtly Quaker perspective. Filled with "love in his harte
to all mankind," White captured his belief in the light of Christ within in such
lines as "We are the children of god because ye presious love of god abounds
in our harts towards one another," and "Let our souls be ever hongering for
. . . devine elumination of the lord to drope down as the small raine . . . that
our souls may therby be refreshed . . . and like a well watered garden floresh."[60]

Throughout his life White demonstrated his commitment to the Quaker
testimonies of equality and peace. After Culpeper's Rebellion, he was among
the signers of the Quaker petition to the proprietors that both explained their
pacifist stance and answered the slanders heaped upon them by their critics.
An itinerant Quaker minister, Thomas Story, described the worship of White's
enslaved persons in a meeting and reports that they had become Quakers. In a
memorial after White's death, the yearly meeting cited his "Christian conduct
and loving behavior" to the Indians, which was reciprocated by "great love and
tenderness" toward the colonists.[61]

Since the Church of England was not established in North Carolina until the early eighteenth century, an act authorizing civil marriage was passed by the assembly in October 1669 and ratified by the Lords Proprietors on 20 January 1670. Titled "An Act concerning Marriage," it stated that a couple desiring marriage should go to the governor or a council member with "three or fower of their Neighbors" as witnesses and declare that they accept "one and the other for man and wife." The official then issued a certificate, which was recorded by the colony's secretary or by the precinct registrar.[62] Since Quakers served on the council and the general and precinct courts, appropriate officials were always available to witness weddings.

The early Albemarle monthly meeting minutes contain records of many marriages, the earliest being that of Christopher Nicholson and Ann Atwood on 21 April 1680 at a worship meeting in the Tomes home.[63] When a couple were ready to marry, they announced their intent in a monthly or quarterly meeting. The meeting then appointed a committee to ensure there were no other attachments before granting clearance to proceed. On the appointed day during the meeting for worship, the couple recited simple vows, which were witnessed by all in attendance. In April and May monthly meetings in 1689 Gabriel Newby and Mary Tomes, the daughter of Francis and the late Priscilla Tomes, announced their intention to marry and were found to be "clear from any Engagement." At the quarterly meeting on 1 June "they took one another to be man and wife promising to live together in good order as becomes Truth in the presents of God." The marriage certificate was signed by the couple and the thirty witnesses who were present. Among the signers were precinct and county court justices and two council members, Tomes and William Bundy.[64]

The Quaker monthly meeting, which had oversight over marriage and behavior, disciplined members for straying from accepted practices. Although Robert White had a living wife who had left him for another man seven years earlier, he and Rebecca Overman ignored the advice of the meeting and married. Hasty remarriage was discouraged, with widows and widowers being counseled to wait at least a year. Edward Mayo, an elder and clerk, courted a non-Quaker widow and was required in meeting to publicly condemn his "unseemly actions" of attempting to marry too soon after the loss of both spouses. When Henry Keaton and Elizabeth Scott, a widow, expressed their intention to marry, Keaton had to assure the meeting that Scott's "fatherless" children would have the inheritance due them.[65]

The precinct register of births, marriages, and deaths was established by the Fundamental Constitutions in 1669, and a marriage was not considered legal, regardless of the "Contract or Ceremonies," until it was recorded with the parents' names.[66] The only extant register of vital statistics is one for Perquimans Precinct that began on 5 December 1679 with the retroactive listing of the marriage of George and Anne Durant that had occurred in 1658 in Northumberland County, Virginia.[67] Recorded are a variety of marriage practices, including Quakers in quarterly and monthly meetings; by ministers of the Gospel in several Virginia counties; and a number by local officials, among them Governor John Jenkins and several council members. Benjamin Laker, General Baptist founder and minister, married a couple in 1696 when he was serving on the council.[68] Around the turn of the century, 1699–1701, recorded marriages included those by the Church of England in Virginia, and in North Carolina some Quaker, some officiated by Deputy Governor Thomas Harvey, others performed by precinct justices or council members, and still others solemnized by the Anglican lay reader Richard French or by Daniel Brett, the first Anglican missionary.[69]

When a Quaker died, the deceased was simply memorialized in a meeting for worship. Describing Quaker funeral customs, William Penn wrote that "burials are performed with . . . simplicity . . . the corpse being in a plain coffin, without any covering of furniture upon it." At the grave site there was a "silent pause," but "no set rites or ceremonies."[70] In keeping with Friends' testimonies of simplicity and equality, graves were marked with ballast or fieldstones.

With few physicians in the colony, the terminally ill who lacked family members to tend them would be taken in by neighbors or, occasionally, innkeepers. If the person died, the funeral expenses were usually paid through the estate settlement. Funeral elements included the coffin, preparing and cleaning the body, food and drink at the wake, the registration fee, and any costs relating to the grave, such as fencing or a tombstone, the latter being a rarity. When the estate was small, the claim might be partially reimbursed by the court. In one case the debt was satisfied by a partial payment of cash, plus the hat and clothing of the deceased.[71]

The scant information available on the funeral customs of non-Quakers in the Albemarle is contained in the court records. At times there were significant expenses related to final illnesses and funerals. The total estate of John Butler, £9.06.10, was charged £3 for health care and funeral expenses. Ann Durant, who kept an inn, recorded expenses relating to the death of Robert Cannon that totaled £10, including £1.06 for the coffin; £2.03.06 for the Holland shirt, Holland shroud, handkerchief, and cap in which Cannon was dressed; and 2s.6d for two quarts of rum. In 1690 Durant billed the estate of John Culle for rum, cider, quince punch, accommodations and bedding, and a rug in which he was buried. Another innkeeper, Diana White, received £3 for food, attendance, and funeral costs for Richard Bentley. Other outlays for funerals were for cider, for public registration of the death, and in one instance for paling, or fencing, around a grave.[72]

Wherever they have lived, Quakers have been involved in social and political reforms based on spiritual insights. When possible, they often held political office, as did Albemarle Quakers, who served in the government until the Anglican establishment in the early eighteenth century required them to take an oath of office. Quaker members of the council were men of property and, like many Friends of the era, owned enslaved persons. By the late seventeenth century North Carolina had become a Quaker-led colony, with a majority of Quakers and dissenters in the assembly and a plurality on the council.

Francis Tomes (1633–1712), a resident of Old Neck, where he had a plantation of 1,000 acres on the Perquimans River, successfully served in dual roles as an eminent Quaker leader and an important government official. Both the Perquimans Monthly Meeting and in 1698 the North Carolina Yearly Meeting were organized in his home, where Quaker gatherings were frequently held. Tomes and his wife hosted all of the prominent Quaker leaders who visited Albemarle, including Edmundson, Fox, and Thomas Story.

Tomes's public career spanned over thirty years with positions in the precinct court by 1672, the county court in 1684, and over twenty years on the council as a proprietor's deputy. At other times he also was deputy customs collector, collector of quitrents, and clerk of the precinct court. High position, however, did not protect him when the Anglicans began their drive for power. Tomes was forced off the council in 1705 when he refused to swear an oath of office, and two years later he suffered seizure of some property for refusing to pay a tithe to the established church.[73]

Another important Quaker official was Daniel Akehurst (1653–99), who had been convinced in England and was a lifelong minister. Retaining a home in Virginia, Akehurst came to Albemarle, settling in Pasquotank Precinct by 1684, when he was the attorney for proprietor John Archdale. Akehurst served on the council and the General Court, as secretary of the Albemarle colony beginning in 1693, and as deputy customs collector in 1695. Active in Friends meetings in Virginia and Albemarle, the "devout" Akehurst was cited at his death by Albemarle Friends for the influence of his ministry among them.[74]

Other Quakers who held high office during their ascendency were William Bundy, John Hunt, Gabriel Newby, and Thomas Symons. William Bundy (d. 1692), a freeholder of 170 acres in Perquimans, served as a precinct justice and on the council. He was imprisoned in 1680 for refusing to bear arms. Sea captain John Hunt had a 1,300-acre plantation on the Little River in Pasquotank, where he was on the precinct court. In the 1680s he served on the council and later on the General Court. Gabriel Newby (1659–1735) was a burgess in the assembly in 1703 and later on the council of Governor William Glover. A supporter of Thomas Cary, Newby served on his council, 1708–11. A son-in-law of

Francis Tomes, Newby accumulated 900 acres in Perquimans Precinct. Thomas
Symons (1649–1706), a resident of Pasquotank who held a 400-acre plantation
on Little River, served as a precinct court justice, a council member in the 1690s,
an assembly burgess, and a justice of the General Court for nine years.[75]

The apex of Quaker political influence was reached under the leadership
of John Archdale (1642–1710), who was a Lord Proprietor, acting governor of
Albemarle, and governor of Carolina 1694–96, residing some five years in the
colony. Archdale shares with Seth Sothel the distinction of being the only resident proprietors in North Carolina. From Buckinghamshire gentry, Archdale
became a Quaker sometime after meeting George Fox in 1674. Four years later
he purchased a proprietor's share in Carolina for his young son Thomas. In 1683
Archdale, now collector of quitrents, sailed for Albemarle with his two daughters and soon acquired a plantation. Residing there for three years, he served as
acting governor in the absence of Governor Sothel.

Unrest in southern Carolina led to Archdale's appointment in 1694 as governor of the entire province, with deputy governors under his administration in
each colony. He moderated the dissension in Charles Town, passing a number
of laws, including one that exempted conscientious objectors from military
service. Archdale successfully negotiated peace with Native Americans, as he
had done in Albemarle, and also with the Spanish in Florida. In 1695 and 1697
he was in North Carolina visiting his family and serving as governor.[76]

───────────

DESCENDED FROM the turmoil generated by the Protestant Reformation, the
individualistic Anabaptists were organized in autonomous, democratically governed congregations. Recognizing no authority except the Bible, their most
notable witness was that in lieu of infant baptism they required adult baptism
by full immersion as an outward sign of an experience of grace. The earliest
English Baptists, known as General Baptists, were grounded in the Arminian
theology of Christ's atonement for all, stressing free will. The Particular Baptists that emerged in the eighteenth century were Calvinists who emphasized a
covenant and believed that salvation was predestined and the Holy Spirit must
be experienced before baptism.[77]

Like the Quakers, early Baptists had been persecuted in Virginia and New
England. The laws against nonconformity in Virginia were so strict that fifty
years passed before the first Baptists appeared in the colony. Oppressed particularly by Governor Sir William Berkeley, dissenters found some relief under his
successor, Governor Thomas Culpeper. However, the 1689 English Act of Toleration was not incorporated into Virginia law until a decade after its passage.[78]

In New England, beginning with the banishment of Roger Williams in 1636,

Baptists experienced the same cruel torments as Quakers. So severe was the treatment in Massachusetts that English Puritans expressed "shame," and the king rebuked the colony for imposing fines, whippings, and imprisonment on dissenters. Like other nonconformists, Baptists found freedom from oppression in Rhode Island, Pennsylvania, and New Jersey, as well as in Carolina, where the colony's first Baptist church was organized in Charles Town in 1684.[79]

Predominant among Baptists in North Carolina were the General (or Free Will) Baptists, whose earliest congregation appeared in 1729 in Pasquotank Precinct, now Camden County. Recognized as founder of the denomination in North Carolina, preacher Paul Palmer arrived in Albemarle in 1719, leaving Virginia one step ahead of his creditors. At the time a Quaker, he became a member of Perquimans Monthly Meeting and married his second wife, Joanna Taylor Peterson, wealthy and twice widowed. She was the stepdaughter of Benjamin Laker, a General Baptist minister. Influenced by his wife and indirectly through the library of the long-deceased Laker, by 1722 Palmer left the Quakers and embarked on a Baptist ministry that would take him throughout the southern colonies and into New England. Early successes in Albemarle came among dissenters on Indian Town Creek in Chowan and in Pasquotank.[80]

From earlier Baptist worshippers in Chowan and Perquimans, Palmer organized congregations in all Albemarle County precincts and spread the church into Bath County as far south as the Cape Fear. Governor Sir Richard Everard reported that when he arrived in the colony in 1725 there were few dissenters other than Quakers, but within four years Palmer, "the Baptist Teacher," had converted "hundreds." From his base in North Carolina, Palmer began itinerant evangelism that led him to the Baptists in Rhode Island and across New England and New York, followed by an extensive ministry into South Carolina, other southern colonies, and the middle colonies.[81]

The origin of Baptists in North Carolina, however, lies not with Palmer but with the life's work of Benjamin Laker. Originally from the County of Surrey, England, Laker was converted during the Interregnum by the Baptist leader Matthew Caffin, who in 1660, along with others, presented "A Brief Confession or Declaration of Faith" to Charles II, stating the beliefs of the General Baptists and affirming their acceptance of the civil authority of the monarch. Laker signed a reaffirmation of this document in 1663. The king was willing to issue dispensations and indulgences, but Parliament's Conventicle Act of 1664–66 and 1671, followed by a Test Act of 1673, suspended religious dissent.[82]

To encourage migration to Carolina, the Lords Proprietors had from the outset publicized the charter principle of religious toleration. With discrimination unlikely to wane in England, the Laker family immigrated to Albemarle County, settling in Perquimans Precinct on a 400-acre plantation with an indentured servant and a few enslaved persons. Serving as a justice on the precinct court, by 1690 Laker was appointed to the council as a proprietor's deputy and also served on the Palatine's and General Courts. Laker was well connected through his daughter, Sarah, who first married Thomas Harvey, a future governor and a scion of one of the oldest planter families in the colony.

Although Laker did not formally organize congregations, there are several links to his significant impact on the colony's General Baptists. In his library were important tracts on General Baptist doctrine that he left to his daughters. At the time of his death in April 1701 the Albemarle Baptists sent a request to the London General Baptist Assembly for books and a minister. The next year the London Baptists sent books to "our Brethren of the Baptist perswation and of the General Faith."[83]

A witness of Laker's will, Richard French, an Oxford-ordained Anglican, became Laker's neighbor in Perquimans Precinct and apparently fell under his influence. Within a few years, without church sanction, French was performing marriages as a "minister of the Gospel." By 1705, matching what was transpiring in England, the establishment of the Anglican Church had initiated both religious and political discrimination against dissenters in Carolina. The council forbade French to officiate at weddings, but he continued to baptize and celebrate marriages over protests by Anglican clergy.[84]

To biased Anglican missionaries of the early eighteenth century, Baptists and Quakers were tantamount to heathen. In 1704 the Reverend John Blair observed "idle fellows" who preached and baptized "through the Country without any manner of orders, from any sect, or pretended Church." Blair called Albemarle "the most Barbarous place in the Continent." Six years later the Reverend James Adams reported, "I have struggled these two Years with a Lawless and Barbarous People, in general, and endured more, I believe, than any of the Society's Missionaries ever has done before me."[85]

In North Carolina, religious liberty reached its apogee under the provincial gubernatorial administrations of Governor Archdale and Deputy Governor Thomas Harvey (1694–99). Although it is not certain that Harvey was a Quaker, his second wife, Sarah, was the daughter of Benjamin Laker, the prominent Baptist leader and council member.[86] Whether influenced by his personal faith, his acquaintance with Archdale, or his wife, Harvey protected freedom of conscience and dissenters' participation in the government. With Governor Harvey's death in 1699 and the election of a staunch Anglican, Henderson Walker, as president of the council, the new century would usher in a concerted drive to oust dissenters from government and establish the Church of England.

CHAPTER TEN

From North and East of Cape Fear to North Carolina

Phillip Ludwel is a Rascal, imposter, & Usurpr
all which shall be justified in England.
—John Gibbs, 1690

ALBEMARLE'S FIFTEEN YEARS of political unrest and rebellion appeared to have ended with Governor Sothel's banishment and the appointment of the experienced Philip Ludwell, but one last power struggle briefly erupted before a decade of harmony and growth closed the century. Captain John Gibbs of Norwich, England, a cousin of Christopher Monck, the second Duke of Albemarle, was appointed a cacique in October 1682, which entitled him to a council seat. Although given land grants of several thousand acres in South Carolina, he instead sailed for Virginia. Arriving there the next year, he acquired a plantation that straddled the unsurveyed border on a peninsula extending from Virginia into Currituck Precinct. In November 1689, about a month after Governor Sothel was deposed, Gibbs purchased a plantation on the Pasquotank River, establishing residence in Albemarle.[1]

When the council met to appoint an acting governor to replace the deposed Sothel, Gibbs cited the Fundamental Constitutions, which allowed a resident proprietor, his heir apparent, or a noble of the colony to be the palatine's deputy, and thereby the governor and head of the council.[2] Not only was Gibbs the only noble in the colony, but as a relative of Monck, who had died childless the previous year, he might inherit the duke's proprietorship.[3] With no doubt that Gibbs had the right to serve as interim governor, subject to confirmation by the proprietors, the council agreed. He was described in a deed of 16 November 1689 as "Governor of North Carolina," an indication that he had been elected by the council immediately after Sothel's banishment.[4]

Gibbs served as governor about nine months, presiding over a colony recovering from the abuses of power and political persecution of the Sothel regime. Directed toward "unity and tranquility," an act of the assembly while he was governor prohibited "opprobrious language" against anyone involved in recent disturbances surrounding Sothel. Among the eleven signatories of the act were councilmen Thomas Jarvis and William Wilkison, Speaker of the Assembly John Nixon, and the burgesses Thomas Pollock, Henderson Walker, and John Philpott—all planters with commercial interests as merchants, ship owners, and mariners. These were seasoned men of substance who had distinguished themselves through long public service in their precincts and the county. Three of them—Jarvis, Walker, and Pollock—left their mark as acting governors, serving as either deputy governor or council president.[5]

At the same time that Gibbs became governor, Colonel Philip Ludwell of Virginia was in London conferring with the proprietors, and on 5 December he was commissioned "Governour of that part of our Province of Carolina that lyes north and east of Cape feare."[6] With little forewarning, in the spring of 1690 the arrival of Philip Ludwell carrying a proprietary governor's commission was potentially destabilizing. Although Ludwell did not meet all of the qualifications required by the Fundamental Constitutions, any uncertainty was erased by his proprietary commission. Gibbs readily relinquished his office, but soon began to have second thoughts and gathered supporters. Thomas Jarvis remained deputy governor under Ludwell.

On 2 June Gibbs issued a proclamation declaring that Ludwell had usurped his position by an "illegal Irregular proceeding." Gibbs vowed to take his challenge to the Lords Proprietors and threatened Ludwell and his backers with single combat by swords, saying that he would "fight him in this Cause, as long as my Eyelidds shall wagg." Gibbs ordered "all Persons to keep the Kings peace, to consult ye fundamentals, and to render me due obedience." Those who accepted commissions or offices from Ludwell would do so "att their utmost peril." To prevent conflict he was willing to meet with the new council, and he assured the colony that he would not "wrong ye Lords Proprietors, or Country."[7]

Ludwell and Jarvis failed to heed his "Declaration," so on 6 July Gibbs and fifteen armed men surprised and closed the Pasquotank Precinct Court because it was meeting under Ludwell's authority. Gibbs took two hostages, councilman and secretary Francis Hartley and Captain Edward Wells, a county justice and former council member, detaining them under guard, first in Pasquotank and then at Gibbs's Virginia residence. Deputy Governor Jarvis raised the county militia and pursued Gibbs to the apparent border, which he would not cross without Virginia's permission. Jarvis sent a message to Ludwell in Virginia urging him to return to Albemarle "with all the speed Imag[in]able" to bring "peace and quietness," and to persuade Virginia governor Frances Nicholson to allow Albemarle militia to arrest Gibbs. Hearing that Gibbs had some eighty supporters, Ludwell wrote to Nicholson, requesting his intervention to defuse the "very dangerous" confrontation.[8]

Having experienced rebellion in New York, Nicholson promptly negotiated the release of the hostages, and Ludwell and Gibbs agreed to arbitration by the Lords Proprietors. Nicholson reported to London that the "stirrs I have quietted for ye present." His larger concern, however, was that in addition to disorder among Albemarle's "very mutinous people," there was also a rebellion in Maryland. He believed that disturbances in the neighboring colonies might induce unrest among the "great many idle & poor people" in Virginia.[9] Ludwell and Gibbs departed for England, and the rebellion died when the Lords Proprietors decided in favor of Ludwell. Accepting the ruling, Gibbs returned to his Virginia border plantation and turned over his Albemarle affairs to an attorney.[10] Much to the relief of Albemarle County, the Gibbs Rebellion was the last instance of the unrelenting generation of upheavals, protests, coups, and factional struggles for power.

Events in Albemarle played out against the backdrop of broad changes wrought by England's Glorious Revolution (1688–89), when the Catholic monarch James II was deposed by his daughter Mary and her Dutch husband, Prince William of Orange. James had been tolerated primarily because his successors were his Protestant daughters, Mary and Anne, by his first marriage. In June 1688, however, a Catholic son was born who preempted his half-sisters. At the invitation of Protestant leaders and the acquiescence of England's key general, John Churchill, Prince William invaded in November, and James fled into exile in France. In early 1689 Parliament proclaimed the throne vacant, and William and Mary accepted the crown jointly, proclaiming the Declaration of Rights that guaranteed such basic liberties as an independent Parliament, free elections, jury trial, and keeping arms. Parliament subsequently passed a Toleration Act and the Bill of Rights that also confirmed a Protestant succession.[11]

William and Mary were popular in the predominantly Protestant American colonies, where the overthrow of the Catholic king was greeted with relief and joy. While the issue in England was the Protestant succession, in the colonies the simmering resentment of the suspect James II and his arbitrary Dominion of New England boiled over when William and Mary took the throne. The hesitation of some colonial governors to declare for the new monarchs engendered protests and rebellions that swept away governors in New England, New York, and Maryland. Although contemporary with the tumult in England and the other colonies, the overthrow of Governor Seth Sothel in each of the Carolina colonies and the removal of Governor John Gibbs in Albemarle were not caused but, rather, encouraged by these events.[12]

A few years passed, but even in remote Albemarle the momentous events in England had not gone unnoticed. In mid-September 1694, at a neighborhood gathering at Major Alexander Lillington's home where some were drinking excessively, John Philpott of Pasquotank, one of the colony's few Roman Catholics, offered a toast to the former King James. Out of the nervous silence John Twegger countered, "I will drink to King William['s] health." Philpott retorted, "God dam King William I'le drink King James Health for he is the right King." Twegger then rebuked Philpott, who damned the king a second time. The next morning as Philpott rehashed the incident with Timothy Pead, the tiff became so heated that Philpott threatened a duel. Only Lillington's refusal to supply weapons averted violence.[13]

Although Philpott was a respectable merchant and public official, within a fortnight he was summoned before the deputy governor and council to answer for his "very dangerous words against his present Majesty." Philpott aggressively questioned whether it was a crime to drink to the health of King James. The reply was that to do so and say that James was the "rightfull King" was of "Dangerous Concequence." Philpott's pugnacious attempt to debate the council about the king's rights was declined as being "to hye [high]" an issue. Philpott was so argumentative that the marshal was ordered to remove him. He then had to post a £500 bond for a court appearance in late November. Uncertain of the law regarding treason, the council sought advice from Governor Ludwell in Virginia.[14]

On 26 November the General Court of the deputy governor, council, and assistants convened. A grand jury reviewed depositions and returned an indictment for treasonable words. In his jury trial on 28 November Philpott entered a plea of not guilty. Attorney General John Porter called witnesses to verify that Philpott had "maliciously and devilishly" cursed the king, but John Twegger could not remember which king they were toasting. Another witness, Mary Peterson, testified that when she asked Philpott if he thought he would hang, he blustered that he would have a hundred armed men with him.[15]

Found guilty as charged, Philpott was sentenced to forfeit all his "goods and chattels" to the Lords Proprietors and to be imprisoned for a year and a day without bail. The now chastened Philpott appealed to the mercy of the court, citing his "weaknes and age." The court graciously distrained only court costs, and he was released. He died within a few months. Considering Philpott's belligerent behavior, the colony's leadership was remarkably lenient at this time.[16]

The last decade of the seventeenth century was a tranquil time of harmony, increasing prosperity, responsive government, expanding territory, and growing population. The political leaders of this era were, without exception, capable men of means who had served on the precinct and county courts, in the assembly, and on the council. Mostly longtime resident planters and merchants, they were committed to the colony's well-being and development and had earned the backing of both settlers and proprietors. The Lords Proprietors'

This previously unpublished ca. 1660 portrait of the young
Philip Ludwell was painted in England prior to his migration
to Virginia. Private collection; photo courtesy of the MESDA
Object Database, file S-3906.

appointment of Colonel Ludwell to govern Carolina north and east of Cape
Fear officially recognized that by 1689 the two widely separated colonies were
well on their way to becoming North and South Carolina.[17]

The most experienced proprietary governor that Carolina would have, Philip
Ludwell had been at the center of power in Virginia for thirty years, navigating
the stormy politics of the Crown's most important North American colony.
Cousins of Governor Sir William Berkeley, Ludwell and his brother Thomas,
from a family in Somersetshire, Bruton Parish, were among the governor's
inner circle of friends and advisers. Ludwell became a planter and by 1675 was

a militia colonel and on the council as deputy secretary. Loyal to the governor, he was effective in suppressing the rebels in Bacon's Rebellion; however, Bacon's revolt led to Berkeley's recall to England in 1677, where he died within weeks of his arrival.

Ludwell gravitated to the political salon of Virginia leaders gathered by the widowed Lady Frances Culpeper Berkeley. Known as the "irreconcilables," they consistently opposed the policies of the imperialist Governor Herbert Jeffreys, who had been sent by the Crown to pacify the rebellious colony. Putting the welfare of Virginia first, Ludwell and his colleagues recognized the dual threats to their position as the ruling plantocracy and to Virginia's political independence. Finding Ludwell obstinate, Jeffreys labeled him "rash and fiery" and removed him from the council in 1679.[18]

The next year Ludwell, who for five years had been a widower with two young children, married his longtime friend and political ally, Lady Frances. He moved to her home, Green Spring plantation, and became the "arch irreconcilable," their leading strategist. By 1681 his wife's cousin, Governor Thomas Lord Culpeper, restored him to the council. At the time, Lady Frances, who had inherited her former husband's share, was a proprietor of Carolina, but in 1683 she sold her share to four other proprietors who conveyed it in trust to Thomas Amy.[19]

Ludwell continued to oppose the expansion of royal authority in Virginia and was again suspended from office in 1687 by Governor Francis Effington for "rudely and boldly" disputing with him. Arriving in London the next year as an agent of the assembly, Ludwell presented a petition to King James protesting Effingham's abuses of power, but within two months the king was overthrown. Distant Virginia was eclipsed by the extraordinary events of the Glorious Revolution. Ludwell and Effingham, however, were granted a hearing before the Privy Council the following spring, and the council backed the royal governor over the irascible Virginian.[20]

During the remainder of the year, Ludwell conferred with the Carolina proprietors about their continuing problems in Albemarle County, chiefly the corruption of Governor Seth Sothel. Ludwell has been characterized as "a man of large abilities matched with equally great ambitions," who possessed the "restless spirit of a freebooter." These qualities, coupled with his depth of experience and grasp of colonial affairs, impressed the Lords, who believed they had found the right man to calm their unruly colony. Ludwell was commissioned to replace Sothel as governor of northern Carolina and to pacify the county.[21]

Not knowing that a confrontation with Governor Gibbs awaited Ludwell, the proprietors instructed him to appoint a court of three of the "honestest and ablest" men to investigate the complaints and determine "the true reasons" for the coup against Sothel. The court was to decide whether Sothel had oppressed the colonists or had himself become a victim of injustice.[22] After he arrived in the late spring of 1690, Ludwell's first months were absorbed by the fracas with Gibbs, which ended with the Lords' confirming Ludwell as governor.

Deputy Governor Thomas Jarvis had settled in Albemarle before 1663 on Harvey's Neck in Perquimans, later acquiring a plantation in Currituck on Whites Island. There with the toil of seven enslaved laborers—Indian, Black, and "mulatto"—he raised livestock and engaged in whaling. Except for the interlude of Culpeper's Rebellion, when he was in the rebel parliament, Jarvis served on the council from 1672 until his demise. As acting governor in 1690, his leadership of the militia had been decisive in stopping Gibbs's seizure of the government. Jarvis's reorganization of the government and the courts was ended by a long illness that culminated in his death in 1694.[23]

While Ludwell was in London to confer with the proprietors, Sothel had landed in Charles Town in the midst of intense political strife. Taking advantage of the volatility, the predatory Sothel claimed the governorship as a proprietor and soon became embroiled in as much controversy as he had created in Albemarle. With complaints flowing to London regarding Sothel's arbitrary rule, the proprietors recognized that both the Gibbs crisis and this new Sothel imbroglio stemmed from provisions in the Fundamental Constitutions that gave both Gibbs and Sothel legitimate claims to the governorship. Thereupon, the Lords attempted to consolidate the two colonies under one administration. Since Ludwell was with them in London, on 2 November 1691 they commissioned him Governor of the Province of Carolina.[24]

In contrast to northern Carolina, where governance was based on a few provisions of the Grand Model, a body of temporary laws, and the successive instructions to the governors, at Charles Town a small dynastic nobility had emerged, and more elements of the Fundamental Constitutions were in effect.[25] Ludwell arrived in Charles Town in April 1692 with detailed instructions that superseded both the temporary laws and all previous governors' instructions. He was authorized to remove Sothel and reorganize the government, beginning by setting aside the Fundamental Constitutions. Having lost most of his support, Sothel reluctantly stepped down but contested his removal for several months. The proprietors' suspension of the Grand Model was publicly proclaimed on 11 May 1693.[26]

In South Carolina Ludwell failed to mediate the political rivalry that had wracked the colony for years. Unable to build a moderate coalition among the factions and losing the proprietors' confidence, a frustrated Ludwell appointed as deputy governor the widely respected landgrave Thomas Smith. In May 1693 Ludwell left Charles Town, never to return, and sailed north to Lady Frances and his Virginia plantation, Green Spring. The Lords issued a commission to Smith in November. Over the following year Governor Smith, facing declining health and wearied by the demands of the colony's intransigent factions, advised the proprietors to send one of their own as governor.[27]

Back in Virginia, Ludwell resumed contact with North Carolina, where he would serve as governor until the summer of 1695. The most important governance effect wrought by repeal of the Fundamental Constitutions related to the General Assembly. The North Carolina assembly now became bicameral, with elected representatives of the precincts comprising the lower house, known as the House of Burgesses, which regained the right to initiate legislation and to amend bills. The upper house was reduced to the governor, the council, and the nobles, losing the elected assistants. These significant changes separated appointed and elected officials, made the Carolina assemblies more like Britain's Parliament and the other colonial legislatures, and set the stage for the power struggle between the lower house and the executive in the next century.[28]

In addition to government reorganization, Ludwell untangled North Carolina's confused land policy, which had long hampered land grants and sales. After careful study, on 28 November 1693 he proclaimed that the 1668 Great Deed of Grant was "irrevocable." With this stroke, North Carolina's land policy would henceforth match Virginia practices approved by the proprietors twenty-five years earlier but subsequently shelved. Accordingly, the floodgates opened on new grants, and old deeds and land grants that had lain unrecorded over the past two decades were now registered.[29]

Throughout the next year, Ludwell presided over the council in court sessions beginning in March 1694 and remained in communication with the colony through emissaries and correspondence at his Virginia home.[30] After the midyear death of Deputy Governor Jarvis, Ludwell filled the vacancy with Thomas Harvey, who had long served on the council. When proprietor John Archdale assumed the office of provincial governor in 1695, Ludwell retired. Any expectation of domestic felicity was dashed by the death of Lady Frances that summer. Reentering the political arena, he became speaker of the Virginia House of Burgesses later that year, serving in the house for three years. In 1700, turning Green Spring over to his son, Philip, he left Virginia for England and remained there until his death in 1723.[31]

––––––––––––

THE STABILITY initiated by Governor Ludwell came to fruition under the leadership of John Archdale, who had had experience in solving problems in a troubled colony. Less worldly than Ludwell, more spiritual in his nature, the convinced Quaker brought the qualities of his chosen faith to the office of governor—patience, moderation, honesty, and practicality. Archdale excelled as a peacemaker. Of all the attributes of his Quaker faith, that of pacifier was most sorely needed in South Carolina.

As a former resident of Albemarle and acting governor, Archdale was the proprietors' key adviser on the colony's affairs and a logical choice to fulfill the appeal from Governor Smith. Nurtured in a country gentry family of Chipping Wycombe, Buckinghamshire, Archdale (1642–1717) was introduced to the colonies in 1664, representing his brother-in-law, Ferdinando Gorges, in reasserting his family's proprietorship of Maine. Engaged in a bewildering contest with Massachusetts Bay and royal commissioners, Archdale retained a semblance of proprietary governance and organized the militia in Maine, but he ultimately deferred to the Crown. Back home, Archdale assumed his role as village squire. His second wife, whom he married in 1673, was the widow Anne Dobson Cary, whose son Thomas Cary would become a proprietary official in the Carolinas.

By 1678, having met George Fox, Archdale and his two elder daughters became Quakers, while the rest of his family remained Anglican. At a time when Friends were being persecuted, Quaker leaders, most notably Archdale's neighbor, William Penn, began seeking a haven in the overseas colonies. Surely influenced by Carolina's policy on religious freedom, in 1678 Archdale purchased a proprietary share in trust for his minor son Thomas. Archdale became an active proprietor, promoting the development of the colony, encouraging the new Quaker community, and defending religious toleration.[32]

After Archdale was appointed collector of quitrents, in 1683 he and his Quaker daughters, Mary and Anne, began a three-year sojourn in Albemarle County. As a proprietor, Archdale served as acting governor during the periodic absences of Governor Seth Sothel, presiding over councils and courts.[33] He had an extensive cattle ranching operation on several plantations and owned 1,000 acres on New Begun Creek that he rented to the Akehurst family for a decade.[34] Archdale's daughter Anne married Emanuel Lowe, a London fishmonger, in 1688, and they moved to North Carolina three years later. Lowe served as Archdale's attorney in the eighteenth century, filing suits to recover rent and property damages. In 1691, Mary married John Danson, a draper, in London. The Dansons later assumed the second Archdale proprietary share.[35]

Toward the end of his stay in Albemarle, on the first day of the year, 25 March 1686, Archdale wrote a letter to George Fox describing the colony, stating that his goal was to "have the country at peace with all the Indians and one another." He was optimistic about the colony's potential, saying that it could provide "plentifully all things necessary for the life of men, with as little labor as any I have known." At the time acting as governor for the absent Sothel, Archdale referred to "my brother Sothell," indicating that Sothel's darker nature was not yet evident. Archdale had been successful in brokering peace among the Native Americans. Most recently he had intervened with the "very wise . . . great fat king" of the Tuscarora, averting conflicts with the Chowanokes and the Matchepungo. He optimistically described the Indians as "so civilized as to come into English habits, and have cattle of their own" and regarded them as an untapped potential mission field.[36]

In late summer 1694 Archdale was appointed governor of North and South Carolina, and his commission was issued on 28 November. To enhance his prestige, he was ennobled as a landgrave. Beyond his extensive instructions to end the confrontation in South Carolina, in North Carolina he was to settle land policy, to encourage development by erecting counties as needed, and to confirm the existence of the Great Deed of Grant that Ludwell had implemented without prior approval by the proprietors.[37]

Archdale and his son Thomas sailed for the colonies from Bristol in January 1695. Landing first in Maine, they traveled overland through the colonies, arriving in North Carolina in June to a warm reunion with the Lowes and Archdale's grandchildren, Nevil, Elizabeth, and Anne. The governor's main task in North Carolina was to get acquainted with the capable Deputy Governor Harvey, whose tenure he readily reaffirmed. After a pleasant six weeks, the Archdales set out for Charles Town, arriving in August.[38]

At a joint meeting of the council and assembly on 17 August, Archdale officially took office by affirmation. In his first speech to the assembly he declared that he would "endeavor to heale all ye differences amongst you, to reconcile all persons."[39] Shortly he confirmed his nephew Joseph Blake as deputy governor of South Carolina, and his stepson, Thomas Cary, was named secretary of the council. With the backing of the assembly, Archdale addressed the divisive colony in a comprehensive series of acts that became known as "Archdale's Laws," which touched on the broad spectrum of tensions, including regulation of the Indian trade and liquor traffic, quitrents, land policy, a more humane Indian policy, a slave code, and welfare. His enlightened diplomacy improved relations with the Spanish in Florida and the various frontier Native tribes. The assembly passed an unprecedented address of appreciation to the governor, praising his "wisdom, patience, and labor." After a year Archdale left the government to Blake and sailed to North Carolina. Before leaving, Thomas Archdale, who had come of age, sold his proprietary share to his cousin Blake, ending his father's long commitment to the colony. After eighteen years Archdale could no longer act as a proprietor, but he was still the provincial governor. Several months after Archdale left, the South Carolina assembly passed two laws that were dear to him—an act granting Quakers exemption from military service and an act granting religious liberty to all except Catholics.[40]

Returning to North Carolina by October, Archdale served as governor of the colony for about five months, until the following spring. In December he presided over the Palatine's Court (council) that established Bath County between Albemarle Sound and the Neuse River, organizing a territory much larger than Albemarle County. Following the South Carolina model of several counties within a colony, Bath would not be self-governing but would have precinct representation in the General Assembly. During the next months Archdale made appointments, presided in the Court of Chancery and the General Court, and efficiently conducted the colony's business.

One of Governor Archdale's most important actions was to authenticate the Great Deed of Grant of 1668. At the request of the House of Burgesses, and with corroboration from Deputy Governor Harvey and councilman Francis Tomes, on 2 February 1697 Archdale certified that the document was the original.[41] With its verification by two provincial governors, one a recent proprietor, as well as the colony's current deputy governor and a trusted proprietor's deputy, any reservation the proprietors had had about the document's validity was laid to rest. After nearly thirty years of controversy raised by their doubts, there would never again be any question about quitrent and land distribution. As in South Carolina, the North Carolina General Assembly sent an unprecedented resolution of thanks to the proprietors, commending Archdale: "It was his greatest care to make peace and plenty flow amongst us." Archdale's last public action was to accompany the Quaker missionary James Dickinson on a tour to visit the colony's Friends meetings.[42]

Bidding his family farewell, Archdale returned to England in early 1697 with the satisfaction of a job well done in both of the Carolina colonies. The following year he was elected to Parliament from Chipping Wycombe, but he was denied his seat for refusing to swear an oath of office. Although retired, Archdale never lost his interest in Carolina. In 1705 he was needed by his coreligionists during the church establishment and exclusion crisis that disrupted both colonies; that year he purchased another proprietary share, which he held until 1708, when he gave it to his daughter Mary and her husband, John Danson, of London. Archdale also published a tract, *A New Description of That Fertile and Pleasant Province of Carolina* (1707), primarily an account of South Carolina that forcefully expressed his opposition to church establishment in the colony and the attendant discrimination against dissenters.[43]

Archdale's last years were spent at the family manor, and he was buried by his Anglican widow in the High Wycombe Church. An earlier biographer, Stephen B. Weeks, who characterized Archdale as "sagacious, prudent, and moderate," wrote that "no other man exerted as much influence for good on the development and growth" of the Carolina colonies.[44] In both North and South Carolina,

Archdale's peaceful interlude ushered in a decade of stable government that enabled the settlements to weather renewed turmoil in the eighteenth century.

Deputy Governor Thomas Harvey was North Carolina's executive until the end of the century. He had been a planter in Albemarle since 1670, and after his marriage to Joanna, the widow of former governor John Jenkins, he moved to her plantation on Harvey's Neck and accumulated over 1,000 acres. By 1684 Harvey was on the council, where he served for the rest of his life.

An able advocate for the proprietors, Governor Harvey bore the brunt of implementing the governmental reorganization and change in land policy. Throughout his tenure of office, Virginia's royal governors threatened to encroach on North Carolina's territory and jurisdiction. Supported by the proprietors and employing passive resistance and obfuscation, Harvey staved off initiatives by both Virginia and the Crown to subvert North Carolina, successfully thwarting the hostile royal official Edward Randolph and ignoring periodic demands issued from Williamsburg.

Thomas Harvey was well connected to the colony's power structure by family relations and marriages. His cousin John had been acting governor in 1679. Harvey's second wife, whom he married in 1688, was Sarah, the daughter of Benjamin Laker, the colony's leading Baptist and a council member. Although Harvey's religious affiliation is not known with certainty, the respect he had in the Quaker community and the Laker connection are indications that he was a dissenter.[45]

In the placid 1690s under Governors Ludwell, Jarvis, Archdale, and Harvey, the colony was governed primarily by Quakers and dissenters. Dominant in Perquimans and Pasquotank, the Quakers and other dissenters, mostly Baptists, held a majority in the House of Burgesses. Comprising the council of proprietors' deputies were Harvey, Laker, Quakers Daniel Akehurst and Francis Tomes, and Anglicans Colonel Thomas Pollock, Major Samuel Swann, Captain Henderson Walker, Richard Sanderson, and William Wilkison. When meeting as the General Court, the governor and council were supplemented by assistants who were mostly Anglican.[46] In November 1697 the General Court justices appointed by the governor and council were Anglicans Swann, Walker, Thomas Blount, and John Durant; Captain John Hunt, a Quaker; and Quaker sympathizer John Porter. As chief judges, either Swann or Walker was required to be at any session.[47]

Under William and Mary a recurring issue for all proprieties was the expansion of royal administration of the colonies. In May 1689, citing conditions in Maryland, Pennsylvania, and Carolina, the Privy Council recommended to Parliament that in the "present circumstances" consideration should be given to "bringing those Proprieties and Dominions under a nearer dependence on the Crown."[48] As a result, proprietary colonies were besieged by royal officials seeking evidence of governmental misrule and inefficiency, especially any lax enforcement of the navigation acts. Ultimately, the goal was to nullify proprietary charters through the legal proceeding of *quo warranto*. Unsurprisingly, the consummate soldier William III drew his colonial governors from the ranks of the military, expecting them to be more effective administrators.[49]

Bolstered by their well-established commercial network, New England merchants and sea captains initially ignored the navigation acts and continued to trade with the Dutch and seek other direct markets in Europe. Customs officials overlooked the violations for a while, but Edmund Randolph reported their involvement in illegal trade and their blatant refusal to put up bonds for enumerated products. The result was increased efforts at enforcement.[50]

Violations of the navigation acts were heard by the provincial vice-admiralty court, the Palatine's Court, and the General Court. Despite Randolph's contempt for the colonial courts, cases appear to have been decided on the evidence. To increase the use of British and colonial ships in the transatlantic trade, registration was mandated after 25 March 1698. When the brigantine *Indevour* and its master, Edward Ashley, arrived in Albemarle from Boston in April, the customs collector, Samuel Swann, seized the vessel for nonregistration. Ashley petitioned the court for release because there were no registration offices open in Boston when he cleared nor in Albemarle when he arrived. Since he was quite willing to register, he argued that he should not be penalized. Regardless of the potential effect on the colony's trade, however, the jury strictly followed the law and condemned the vessel.[51] That same month another case involved the sloop *Dubartus*, co-owned by influential Henderson Walker and ship's captain Andrew Belcher, a Boston merchant. *Dubartus* was seized for importing European goods originating in London and passing through Boston, which could be an invitation to smuggle. The owner avoided condemnation by proving that the cargo was not opened en route and that the law allowed layovers on a voyage.[52]

Formerly an officer of Massachusetts Bay Colony and secretary of the Dominion of New England, Edward Randolph was the Crown's point man in the 1690s to investigate presumed mismanagement and customs fraud in corporate and proprietary colonies. His ouster in the overthrow of the Dominion of New England had so prejudiced him against private colonies that he relentlessly advocated expanding royal authority. Historians have viewed Randolph as too narrow and bigoted to be fit for office, but at the same time so skillful that he was key to shaping England's colonial and commercial policies of the time.[53]

Appointed Surveyor General of Customs in North America in 1691, Randolph traveled assiduously through the colonies searching for corruption in the customs system and documenting illegal trade from the colonies to Europe through Scotland and Dutch Curaçao. A direct result of his reports was the Navigation Act of 1696, which authorized vice-admiralty courts, appointed naval officers, and required proprietary governors to take an oath and post bond for enforcement of trade regulations.[54] In Carolina, he recorded unsubstantiated allegations that governors had consorted with pirates and smugglers, taken bribes for ignoring customs violations, and charged exorbitant fees for unregistered vessels.[55]

Based more on hearsay than evidence, Randolph's dim view of Albemarle took shape in his oft-quoted characterization of the colony: "Tis a place which receives Pirates, Runaways, and Illegal Traders."[56] Randolph alleged that proprietary governors refused to take oaths of office, approved laws "prejudicial" to trade, tolerated illegal court proceedings, and protected pirates and smugglers to the point that some of the colonies were in a state of "Anarchy and Confusion." As a solution, Randolph recommended to the Crown that proprietary colonies should become royal through annexation or consolidation. His solution for Carolina was that northern Carolina should be annexed by Virginia, and southern Carolina should be combined with the Bahamas into a new royal colony.[57]

Thanks to Randolph's findings, a bill was introduced in Parliament in 1701 for "reuniting" the proprieties to the king, but the bill failed, partly because of lobbying by the Lords Proprietors and the influential William Penn. The Lords of Trade then called on Virginia's governor general, Francis Nicholson, to make recommendations regarding Carolina and the Bahamas. Nicholson had characterized Albemarle's citizens as "a very mutinous people . . . never yet well settled." Not surprisingly, his prophetic solution was that the king should purchase the bothersome colony of Carolina for £2,000, but it was not to be at that time.[58]

A tempest was stirred up in Albemarle by Edward Randolph's challenge of the deputy customs collectors Henderson Walker and Richard Plater. Both Walker, a council member and future governor, and Plater, a future attorney general, were well-connected planters. When Randolph attempted to replace them, Walker and Plater appealed to the council, contesting the authority of Randolph, who had not presented his commission in the colony. The council sidestepped the issue, passing it on to Governor Ludwell to forward it to the proprietors.[59]

The unsettled customs issue was addressed the next year when the General Court recognized the commission of Peter Jacob Guerard as collector for the province. Governor Archdale had endorsed Guerard's commission of 30 October 1694 and then appointed Quaker Francis Tomes as deputy collector for North Carolina. Tomes, in turn, appointed as his deputy Quaker Daniel Akehurst for Pasquotank and Little River District.[60]

The proprietors countered the Crown infringement on their charter rights with passive resistance, delaying action or ignoring requests. Deputy governors in North Carolina avoided taking the required oaths and posting bond. Virginia's attempt to extend vice-admiralty jurisdiction to North Carolina, although authorized by the customs office, was resisted well into the next century. In 1694 Governor Archdale had been commissioned admiral of the colony with authority to appoint vice-admirals. When Virginia governor Sir Edmund Andros informed Deputy Governor Harvey in 1698 that an admiralty court of Virginians had been appointed for North Carolina, Harvey replied that there was no vacancy, as he had already appointed Henderson Walker the vice-admiralty judge for the colony.[61]

For some years the proprietors had urged settlers to move south of Albemarle Sound into the vast coastal plain, stating as early as 1676 that the Neuse and Pamlico Rivers "should have bin before this welplanted."[62] Not evident to the Lords were the substantial obstacles to expansion. The Pamlico and Neuse Rivers were deep in Indian country on the verge of the Tuscarora nation, and stretching from Albemarle Sound to the Pamlico River was "above fifty miles of desart [sic] to pass through without any human Creature Inhabiting it."[63]

Governor Archdale described the accelerated settlement in this isolated country, mentioning a sickness, or "consumption," that had caused "a great mortality" among the Pamlico Indians that left large areas unpopulated.[64] Hearing of abandoned Indian fields, colonists bypassed the forbidding wilderness by sailing their periaugers and canoes down Pamlico Sound to the rivers. By 1696 it was noted that "several Persons are seated" on the Pamlico River, enough to propose a new county and precinct. At a council on 9 December, with Governor Archdale presiding, writs of election were issued for two burgesses in the next assembly in January. The council authorized the creation of the county and honored the governor's request that it be named Bath County for Proprietor John Grenville, Earl of Bath.[65] From its beginnings, Bath County attracted new and more diverse inhabitants. By 1708 French Huguenots from Virginia settled on the Neuse and Trent Rivers, where they were soon joined by German Palatines and Swiss.[66]

A perennial controversy from the earliest days of the colony had been the location of the northern boundary, stemming from the Carolina charters that had included the Virginia settlement north of Albemarle Sound. Resenting the loss of territory and population, Virginia periodically brought up the boundary issue, but there was no Crown support for their position. Having the most to lose, they would back away from an actual survey and refuse to negotiate. Consequently, the North Carolina–Virginia boundary region became a no-man's-land, which suited the borderers, many of whom were squatters who could thereby evade the nuisances of law enforcement, quitrents, and taxes.

In the 1680s Virginia had authorized the sheriff of Lower Norfolk County to collect tax levies in Currituck and on the Blackwater River. The Albemarle council appealed to the proprietors, who petitioned the Committee on Plantations in December 1681 that by their charter, the boundary extended from Currituck Inlet west to Weyanoke Creek "within" 36°30' north. By 1688 Albemarle authorities were seizing household goods from inhabitants of Currituck who had refused to pay taxes.[67] Governor Nicholson of Virginia observed in 1690 that "ye Bounds betwixt us & them [are] very often in dispute." The next year Virginia sent a surveyor, Thomas Milner, who determined the latitude of the east and west anchors at Currituck Inlet and the mouth of Weyanoke Creek to be less than, but near, 36°30'.[68]

The matter simmered until 1696, when Undersheriff William Fitzgerald of Princess Anne County attempted to attach goods stored on Crow Island in North Carolina for a debt owed by a fugitive from Virginia. Before the goods could be removed, Deputy Marshall William Bray of Currituck arrived on the scene with an armed posse, "rescued" the property, and arrested Fitzgerald. This incident triggered a strong protest from Governor Edmond Andros, to which Deputy Governor Harvey replied that he would investigate the dispute. Harvey summoned Bray for an explanation, but Governor Andros meanwhile cautioned Virginia sheriffs to "be Carefull" in collecting quitrents and taxes in the disputed area.[69]

Near the end of the century, when the Crown was moving to eliminate proprieties, Virginia was emboldened to press for a survey on their terms. Anticipating a boundary dispute, Harvey requested a copy of the Carolina Charter, which the proprietors sent in December 1697 with the expectation that it would "assert our Bounds" with Virginia. In February 1699 Harvey notified the Virginia council that the proprietors had ordered him to survey the boundary. The North Carolina council appointed Daniel Akehurst and Henderson Walker to go to Virginia to represent North Carolina's interests in negotiations.[70]

On their arrival, the two men were forced to wait outside the chamber while the Virginia council discussed the legality of their credentials. When the North Carolina delegates were called into the room, Governor Nicholson laid his royal commission on the table and demanded that they display their authorizations. Contemptuous of North Carolina, Nicholson capped the insults by rejecting their commissions, declaring that without royal sanction, neither their commissions nor Harvey's appointment as deputy governor was legitimate. Although the Virginia council refused to meet with the North Carolinians, the Carolina Charter and accompanying documents were copied into their records. Nicholson wrote to Harvey, pronouncing the latter unqualified because he had neither taken an oath nor posted bond. Nicholson also reiterated Virginia's specious claim of jurisdiction over North Carolina on customs matters. By the time the letter reached North Carolina, Harvey had died and had been replaced by Henderson Walker as president of the council. After his shabby treatment in Virginia, Walker was diplomatic but firm in asserting his colony's position.[71]

By the end of the seventeenth century most of the men who had first settled in the colony and led it politically were deceased. They had constituted a governing class of founders, serving as acting governors, council deputies, assembly burgesses, general and precinct court justices, administrative officials, peace officers, and militia officers. Their dominance was essentially ignored by the distant proprietors, who were focused on more lucrative South Carolina and were quite willing to leave North Carolina in the hands of those who had, on their own initiative, created the colony that anchored their northern realm. These local leaders were challenged occasionally from within by newcomers who sought recognition and status for themselves and resented those who kept the reins of power firmly in hand. If necessary, the old guard fomented rebellion to overthrow would-be claimants to the governorship, as well as legitimate proprietary appointees who overstepped their bounds.

Concurrently, with the death of William, Earl of Craven, in 1697, the last of the founding proprietors had passed. The leaders among the original eight lords had had the vision and commitment to create a colony grounded on political and religious liberty expressed in the charters and constitutions. The proprietary shares had changed hands, in some cases several times, by inheritance or sale, primarily to individuals interested in financial return rather than in a new society shaped by the chaotic age of the English Revolution. This tumultuous era set the evolution of English constitutional government on a new trajectory that culminated a century later—in America with a revolution and constitutional republic that, within fifty years, saw the beginning of popular democracy, and in Britain with the parliamentary reforms of the nineteenth century.

THE LAST YEARS OF the seventeenth century were internally so quiet that a modern observer would conclude that North Carolina finally had begun to mature politically and culturally. Deputy Governors Thomas Jarvis (1689–94) and Thomas Harvey (1694–99) died in office, and Henderson Walker was elected president of the council in July 1699 by Quakers Akehurst and Tomes and Anglican Sanderson. Laker's retirement from the council in 1697 and Akehurst's death in December 1699 left Tomes as the sole dissenter on the council by 1700, whereupon the council permanently shifted to predominantly Anglican, setting the stage for the establishment of the Church of England in the new century.[72]

Two provincial governors of Carolina, Philip Ludwell and John Archdale, personally interested in Albemarle because of their past connections or residence, directly governed the colony. The government was free of irregularities, the economy was growing, and the society was fluid and stable. Political factional strife had disappeared under the guidance of capable leaders who resided there, understood the problems, and worked to solve them. The culture reflected the egalitarian values and positive outlook of Quakers, who thrived under the Lords Proprietors' firm adherence to religious liberty. The new century would usher in new conflicts, but in the twilight of the seventeenth century, North Carolina enjoyed a welcome respite from discord.

CHAPTER ELEVEN

A New Century

John Lawson's North Carolina

The Fame of this new-discover'd Summer-Country spread thro'
the neighbouring Colonies, and, in a few Years drew
a considerable Number of Families, thereto.
—John Lawson, 1709

There is freedom in North Carolina.
—Anna Eva Zant, 1711

I N 1701 the twenty-five-year-old John Lawson entered North Carolina toward the end of a 550-mile wilderness odyssey that began in Charles Town
and wound across western Carolina. The son of a Yorkshire physician, John
Lawson, gentleman, had been reared in London. Nearby Gresham College,
which emphasized natural sciences and mathematics and hosted meetings of
the prestigious Royal Society, nurtured Lawson's lifelong passion for learning. That passion impelled him to travel, explore, and write with keen and
sympathetic observation. In 1700, while preparing for a trip to Europe and the
"Grand Jubilee at *Rome*," he unexpectedly met a gentleman from the "*Indies*"
who convinced Lawson to change his plans, assuring him that "*Carolina* was
the best Country I could go to."[1]

Lawson's new mentor was South Carolina planter and fur trader James
Moore, who was in London conferring with the proprietors and would in September assume the governorship as president of the council. Moore provided
passage to the colony for his young friend and sponsored him during the five
months he was in Charles Town. Arriving in August, Lawson was favorably
impressed with Carolina's prosperous chief port, noting the well-built housing
and fortifications and the thriving commerce. He was especially struck by the
diversity of churches, which signaled religious tolerance in the colony. Ever
restless, Lawson listened eagerly to Governor Moore's tales of frontier Indian
trade and conflicts and readily secured from his patron an appointment to explore Carolina's Indian country.[2]

In late December, accompanied by English traders and Indians, Lawson set out for the Santee River in a large canoe, commencing an epic 500-mile journey through the virtually unknown backcountry of proprietary Carolina. Nearly two months later, on February 24 the party emerged from the forest on the Pamlico River at the plantation of Captain Richard Smith, an important fur trader and planter of Bath County.[3] There Lawson met Smith's daughter, Hannah, who may have inspired his portrait of Carolina women as being "very fair, and generally as well featur'd, as you shall see any where, and have very brisk charming Eyes."[4] Whether Hannah had "very brisk charming Eyes," she wouldn't have found it difficult to charm this intrepid explorer, who, after all, had spent two months in the wilderness. After a brief stay in the Pamlico settlement Lawson purchased property at the forks of the Neuse and Trent Rivers and built a house a half mile from the Native American town of Chattoka. The adjacent creek is known to this day as Lawson Creek. There he lived with a "young Indian Fellow and a Bull-Dog"[5] and began work as a private surveyor, often on the Pamlico, where he could visit Hannah Smith.

On the banks of the Pamlico in February 1701, Lawson confided in his journal, "The most noble and Sweetest Part of this Country, is not inhabited by any but the Savages; and a great deal of the richest Part, thereof, has no Inhabitants but the Beasts of the Wilderness."[6] The first explorer to describe piedmont Indian life in detail, Lawson approached the Natives with open curiosity and sensitivity, nonjudgmentally observing their way of living and recording their beliefs. Before his exploration, the region was known only to Virginia and South Carolina fur traders who visited the Indian towns and villages. From Lawson's colorful journal emerges a vibrant portrait of Native American customs, social intercourse, illness and medical practices, lifeways, burial and funeral customs, dances and festivals, religion and spirituality, commerce, diplomacy, and war. With an eye to the commercial future, he vividly described his natural surroundings—rivers, trees, medicinal plants, wildlife, and stone. In addition to forests, Lawson was fascinated by the large open landscapes—savannahs or prairies—and the fields and farms near Indian towns.

In upland South Carolina's Waxhaw and Catawba foothills, the Indian settlement pattern was denser. Here Lawson intersected the "Great Trading Road" that connected Virginia to the Catawba and Cherokee nations. Regularly traversed by pack trains of fur traders, the trail was a busy highway connecting flourishing towns and villages. Arriving at the Catawbas' principal town, Lawson was surprised to meet a Scot, John Stewart, a trader based in Virginia. Stewart was ready to return to Virginia with his seven packhorses, but a wandering war party of the feared Seneca had forced him to tarry until Lawson appeared.[7]

As they traveled, Lawson enriched his journal with vignettes of the Native Americans they encountered along the trail. The Waxhaws celebrated the corn harvest with hours of feasting, drinking, and dancing, culminating with the young singles selecting "Bed-fellows" and disappearing into the night. In every village it was the custom of the chief to extend hospitality to visitors, including the companionship for the night of young single women, or "trading girls." A price was negotiated between the couple, and to refuse would be a slight. On one occasion a young trader was upset to discover that he had been robbed by his overnight "bride," even losing his new moccasins. After the Indians "laugh'd their Sides sore" at the plight of "Mr. Bridegroom," a set of moccasins was provided, and the parties went on their way.[8]

Skirting the foothills, Lawson, Stewart, and their companions traveled north on the trading road in "delicate" weather for February, crossing ice-crusted streams and pleasant high and dry savannas toward Sapona Town on the Yadkin River. There the Saponas feted them, along with visiting Tutelos from the mountains, who reported plentiful buffalo, elk, bear, and deer in their region.[9] In the ancient Uwharrie Mountains, Lawson passed through Uwharrie and Keyauwee towns. With the Keyauwee king, Jack, he enjoyed discussing religious beliefs, King David, and writing. He was quite taken with the queen's daughter by a former marriage, describing her as the "beautifullest *Indian* I ever saw, and had an Air of Majesty with her."[10]

Leaving Keyauwee Town, the companions split up. Stewart and his party took the direct path toward Virginia, while Lawson and a guide stayed on the trading road toward Occaneechee Town. They crossed the broad Haw Fields, considered the richest land in the backcountry, which inspired Lawson to write that the Indians had "the Flower of *Carolina*, the *English* enjoying only the Fag-end of that fine Country." He met a pack train of thirty horses from Virginia led by a trader named Massey, who urged Lawson to engage "*Enoe-Will*," chief of a consolidated tribe of Shakori, Eno, and Adshusheer, as his guide to the coast. At Occaneechee Town Lawson met and instantly warmed to Eno-Will, whom he described as "of the best and most agreeable Temper that I ever met in an *Indian*." The next morning Lawson set out toward Adshusheer in the company of Eno-Will and his men. The remainder of the trip wound through the flat, boggy land of Tuscarora country, where he had a cordial encounter with a Tuscarora hunting party of nearly 500. Although he was treated courteously, Lawson surmised that the Tuscarora were leery of direct contact between the backcountry tribes and the English. Several more days of travel through the swamplands brought Lawson's party to the English plantations on the Pamlico on 23 February.[11]

At the dawn of the eighteenth century, John Lawson's North Carolina had no Anglican Church establishment, no towns or ports, and no schools. The colony nevertheless enjoyed political stability, with capable governors and councils and an effective assembly and court system. Lawson perceived that North Carolina, only recently doubled in size, was poised for growth, which offered opportunity for him to thrive economically, socially, and politically. Because Bath and Albemarle Counties were separated by nearly fifty miles of dense, swampy wilderness—one of the least populated areas in the state to this day—the settlements communicated by water, using the sounds and rivers. Bath's growing economy, based on the fur trade with the Tuscarora and other tribes, was enabled by better sea communication through Ocracoke and Hatteras Inlets, but the shallow waters of Pamlico Sound remained a hindrance.[12]

Quick to grasp the potential of the emergent frontier, Lawson cast his lot with Bath County, establishing his home and family and living there the rest of his life. There on the edge of Indian country, he prospered as a fur trader and surveyor while pursuing his scientific and literary interests and producing North Carolina's major contribution to colonial literature. He threw himself into the county's development, serving as a local official, holding provincial appointments from the proprietors, and cofounding the colony's first towns—Bath on the Pamlico River and New Bern on the Neuse—both in Bath County. Lawson would represent the province's interests to the Lords Proprietors and would be a confidant and adviser to governors.[13] The opening decade of the eighteenth century was Lawson's time, and he made the most of it.

From the earliest days the London-dwelling Lords Proprietors had envisioned port towns that would spur trade and population growth. They believed the colony would never be in a "happy & safe posture" or be "flowrishing" until there were "Townes amongst you." To encourage commerce, defense, and public safety, the proprietary charters and governance documents authorized establishment of fairs and markets and the chartering of cities and port towns. The Fundamental Constitutions further facilitated commerce through oversight of highways, bridges, and river navigation. The proprietors addressed public health by mandating regulation of drains, sewers, wetlands, and "anything that may corrupt, deprave, or Infect the common Air or water." Incorporated municipalities would be governed by a mayor and twelve aldermen appointed by the proprietors from a common council elected by the householders. As early as 1670, the Lords suggested that the governor and council select a site in each precinct for a port town with a "publick storehouse." At one of them, designated by the council and assembly, the proprietors would provide funds from quitrents and fines to build a "State house," a prison, and a church that would form the nucleus of a capital.[14] Despite proprietary encouragement, the only town in seventeenth-century North Carolina had been Charles Towne on the Cape Fear River, founded in 1664 and abandoned three years later.

The Lords continued to prod Albemarle County, urging expansion south of the sound in towns that would provide security from the Indians. By 1676 they had selected Roanoke Island as the site for the colony's metropolis and instructed Governor Thomas Eastchurch to establish a capital there. Another port town was to be on the western side of the mouth of Little River, where planters were concentrated and where courts and assemblies met frequently. In effect, the Little River and Durant's Neck settlement near the center of Albemarle County had been the de facto capital for years. A third port was suggested at the strategic head of the sound on Salmon Creek at the mouths of the Chowan and Roanoke Rivers, the oldest settled area of the colony. The Lords were adamant that without ports and towns the colony would "not longe continue civilized or ever bee considerable or secure."[15]

The outbreak that next year of Culpeper's Rebellion, the death of Governor Eastchurch, and the general political unrest postponed any effective port development on the rivers. The Albemarle populace seemed content with their plantation landings, which worked well enough for the shallow-draft vessels that carried the colony's trade. Forty years would pass before the Town of Bath would be laid out on the Pamlico River in Bath County—not Albemarle. There would be three new towns in Bath before Albemarle's first town, the future Edenton, began to emerge on Queen Anne's Creek.

With new arrivals from overseas and from the Albemarle region, Lawson readily found work as a private surveyor in Bath County. By 1704 Governor Robert Daniell appointed him the county's deputy surveyor. In that same year alone Lawson completed thirty-nine surveys but failed to pay the governor his share of the fees, for which he was sued. Other lapses, due perhaps to the avalanche of work, included Lawson's failure to register a survey, an inaccurate survey of a large tract, and multiple surveys of blank patents—an illegal but not uncommon practice.[16]

Despite these few incidents, Lawson retained the confidence of the Lords Proprietors, who appointed him surveyor general of North Carolina in 1708. That same year they chose Lawson and Edward Moseley, the former surveyor general, as commissioners to represent North Carolina in a joint survey of the long-disputed boundary with Virginia. Although ordered by the Crown and urged by Governors Spotswood and Hyde, the survey was delayed for over a year. Virginia commissioners Nathaniel Harrison and Philip Ludwell, son of the former Carolina governor, finally met Lawson and Moseley in Williamsburg, Virginia, but the two sides could not agree on evidence provided by affidavits from landholders in the disputed region, nor which of the different surveyors' readings were correct. The Virginia council accused Moseley and Lawson of obstructing the survey for personal gain, but the truth was that Virginia stood to lose their spurious claim to a portion of North Carolina. As for the Virginians' objections regarding the accuracy of Lawson's survey, in 1729 William Byrd II confirmed that the difference between the two surveys was a half minute, "a very inconsiderable variance."[17]

Lawson's map of North and South Carolina was published in the first installment of his natural history of North Carolina in June 1709 and was then bound into subsequent editions. Like most maps of the period, it was derived from an earlier map, but new details—the town of Bath and soundings and sandbars in Pamlico Sound—could have come only from Lawson himself. While in London arranging the publication of the book, Lawson provided a manuscript draft and descriptions for the map to an engraver. In August the proprietors paid Lawson twenty pounds for copies of the new map.[18]

Reflecting the growing settlement pattern in Bath County, in 1705 three precincts were established: Pamptecough on the Pamptecough River (Pamlico); Wickham, south of Albemarle Sound; and Archdale on the Neuse River. Seven years later the names were changed to Beaufort, Hyde, and Craven, respectively. Each of these precincts could elect two representatives to the General Assembly, giving the county a total of six. From the concentration of planters in the vicinity of Old Town Creek (Bath), which provided a deepwater anchorage, came the initiative to establish a port town.[19]

In Pamptecough Precinct early in the eighteenth century, partners John Lawson, Joel Martin, and Simon Alderson purchased sixty acres from David Perkins overlooking the confluence of Old Town Creek with the Pamlico River. In 1705 Lawson laid out a linear town of seventy-one lots, just over one acre each, with several streets parallel to the creek. The General Assembly incorporated Bath on 8 March 1706, naming Lawson, Martin, and Nicholas Daw as commissioners or trustees. By the end of October, Perkins and the trustees were joined by merchants Nathaniel Wyersdale, Thomas Sparrow, Thomas Peterson, and James Beard; a physician, Dr. Maurice Leullyn; a cooper, John Jordan; and the public figures Christopher Gale, Colonel Thomas Cary, John Porter, and Lyonell Reading. Named the seat of Bath County and Pamptecough Precinct, Bath hosted the first quarterly session of the county court in October. Lawson was named the clerk of court and public register of the precinct, serving from January 1707 until he left for England in August 1708. Describing the limited public accommodations during court sessions, one traveler wrote that "ye ordinary keepers have not beads [beds] to Lodge us," which forced them to stay in private homes or to camp around the village.[20]

Perched on a low bluff, Bath was the administrative and commercial center for a vast untamed area stretching south from Albemarle Sound to the Neuse River. Through Ocracoke and Hatteras Inlets, Bath was connected to the ports of the Chesapeake, as well as Charles Town, Boston, New York, Philadelphia,

Bermuda, and the Caribbean. When merchant sloops, brigantines, or brigs were in harbor and court was in session, the few streets bustled with mariners, Indians bearing furs, and settlers from many miles away who brought their goods by dugout canoe and the small sailing craft of the sounds—periaugers, skiffs, and shallops.

Merchants operated shops and traded from their homes, and the cooperage was busy turning out barrels, casks, and hogsheads. Lawson, Gale, and Dr. Leullyn formed a partnership in 1707 to build and operate a horse-powered gristmill.[21] The earliest description of the new village, by the Reverend William Gordon in 1709, notes that about a dozen houses had been built along the river, probably sheltering some fifty to sixty souls. Gordon predicted that with the "Better Inlet" and "most Pleasant Savenna's" for pasturing cattle, Bath would be "the Center of trade." The Reverend John Urmston, as usual, had nothing good to say, noting that Bath was "the most obscure Inconsiderable place in the Country."[22]

As surveyor and a founder of Bath, Lawson acquired two choice lots totaling more than an acre on Town Point at the corner of Front and Water Streets. In his rambles as a fur trader, naturalist, and private surveyor, he was a frequent visitor to the Pamlico River home of Hannah Smith. It is not known when they began cohabiting, but by the end of 1705 Lawson had built a house in Bath overlooking Old Town Creek. Because they were living together unmarried, a common practice in the era, John leased the house to Hannah for seven years, with lifetime domicile rights in the event of his death. For their daughter Isabella, born in April 1707 and named for her grandmother Lawson, John purchased cattle and a 320-acre tract. In 1708 he signed over to Hannah his share in the town's gristmill. In Lawson's will of 12 August 1708 he left to "my Dearly beloved Hannah Smith," who was again pregnant, the house and lot and one-third of his personal property. The remainder of the estate was left to Isabella, and Hannah was named executrix.[23]

The voyages of overseas exploration had made the seventeenth century an age of scientific discovery. Having found what they considered a "New World," Europeans quickly developed a keen appetite for knowledge about their exotic new colonies. Around the turn of the eighteenth century, amateur naturalists engaged collectors who fanned out across the Caribbean islands and North America, gathering specimens and searching for a new order to the natural world. These men and a few women were protoscientists seeking knowledge for its own sake, as well as finding practical answers as to how Europeans could thrive in the new surroundings. The cohort included such luminaries as John Ray (d. 1705), considered the father of English natural history; James Petiver, a London apothecary who became a respected entomologist; and Sir Hans

Sloane, a distinguished physician who was the preeminent British collector of the era. They garnered empirical knowledge by observing, classifying, and compiling descriptions of what they studied. By midcentury, generations of international collecting led to the modern binomial classification system developed by the Swedish Carolus Linnaeus, which imposed order on the teeming chaos of nature.

John Lawson was one of those fearless explorers, plunging into the Carolina wilderness with a curious mind. As a correspondent of James Petiver, Lawson sent reports and specimens to enlarge Petiver's important collection of flora and fauna, which was subsequently acquired by Sir Hans Sloane. Sloane had traveled to Jamaica in 1687 and over fifteen months had identified some 800 new species of plants. The first volume of his *A Voyage to the Islands of Madera, Barbados, Nieves, S. Christophers and Jamaica* . . . (1707) was surely read by Lawson when he was in London in 1709. It is plausible that Sloane's book was the model for the title, contents, and format of *A New Voyage to Carolina*.[24]

From the Pamlico River on 12 April 1701, about six weeks after entering the colony, Lawson gladly replied to Petiver's advertisement for collectors, saying he would welcome that occupation and the "Reward to have the Conversation of so great a Vertuosi." At the time Lawson was preparing to go to the "Sea Board" for shells, and he also offered to send a journal of his discoveries.[25]

Of all Lawson's accomplishments none is greater than his natural history of North Carolina published in 1709, titled *A New Voyage to Carolina; Containing the Exact Description and Natural History of That Country*. In his dedication to the Lords Proprietors, Lawson wrote, "I here present *Your Lordships* with a Description of your own Country, for the most part, in her Natural Dress."[26] North Carolina's first resident Renaissance man, Lawson had a deep curiosity about many fields of knowledge. The late seventeenth century had seen a resurgence of travel narratives and natural histories, and Lawson's *New Voyage to Carolina*, the only book written about proprietary North Carolina, became a classic of early American literature. The book is many things: a journal of his backcountry exploration, a natural history, a compilation of flora and fauna, a description of the colony, observations of the Native Americans and their customs, and a brief lexicon of Native languages. It is the first extensive account of the piedmont heartland, a region some 300 miles wide between the tidewater and the mountains. While the book was generally well received by Lawson's contemporaries, the Reverend John Urmston, the Anglican cleric who was an inveterate critic of North Carolina, commented that the Lords Proprietors should be "ashamed of their famous countrey" rather than having Lawson "write whole volumes in praise of such a worthless place."[27]

While Bath was developing, fur traders and planters were moving into new lands in the Neuse River valley on the southern frontier of Bath County. Among the earliest known settlers along this margin of Indian country were Thomas and Ann Lepper and William Powell. A prosperous planter and Quaker, Lepper had first settled on the Yeopim River in Perquimans Precinct by 1679. Rising rapidly in the colony's government, he served on the precinct and county courts, as the county marshal, and on the council. In 1697 he sold most of his land and moved south to the newly organized Bath County, where by 1701 he was on the county court. William Powell, often cited as the earliest known settler in the Neuse River valley, purchased a tract in 1702 from Thomas Lepper.[28]

Farnifold and Hannah Green moved from Virginia to Perquimans Precinct in 1697. Ten years later he received a proprietary grant of 1,700 acres along several miles of the Neuse River, which he divided into plantations from Upper Broad Creek to Greens Neck near modern Oriental to Lower Broad Creek and Piney Point. The year before, Green had petitioned the council to put cattle on Ocracoke Island. As a captain of the county militia, he played an important role in defending the region during the Tuscarora War.[29]

A resourceful French Huguenot colony relocated by 1708 from Virginia to the Trent River, where they grew hemp and flax and established a vineyard. Their spinning and weaving operations produced linen thread and cloth, which they traded first with their English neighbors and later with the Swiss and German settlement centered at New Bern.[30] The next year, Neuse River inhabitants petitioned the government for a precinct court because of the "teadgous," expensive journey that required crossing the Pamlico River to sparsely settled Bath, which lacked accommodations for court attendees.[31]

The German migration to American colonies had roots in the sixteenth-century Reformation, which triggered years of religious wars. Frederick V, the Elector of the Protestant Rhenish Lower Palatinate, married English Princess Elizabeth, daughter of James I. Briefly rulers of Bohemia, the royal couple had to flee from an overwhelming Catholic invasion. Ever after known as "the Winter Queen," Elizabeth became a progenitor of the Hanoverians.[32]

In the destructive Thirty Years' War (1618–48), the Palatinate suffered utter devastation that extended into the eighteenth century in the wars of Louis XIV, whose armies repeatedly invaded the Rhineland. William III had forged the Protestant coalition to curb the voracious ambition of the French king. During the War of Spanish Succession and the reign of Queen Anne, the English offered to naturalize foreign Protestants from the war-ravaged Palatinate. Attracted by English broadsides and driven by deprivation exacerbated by hard winters, thousands of desperate Germans and some Swiss refugees flooded England. By 1709 as many as 15,000 Germans crowded camps around London, huddling in tents and emergency shelters. Sympathetic toward her fellow

Protestants, Queen Anne allocated some £135,000 to pay for their passage from Holland, basic subsistence, and further passage to Ireland and the colonies. That year the colonies began to absorb the bulk of the refugees; most went to Pennsylvania, but many were recruited to Carolina.[33]

The seeds of North Carolina's second town, New Bern, were sown in England, the Palatinate, and Switzerland through collaboration among the Lords Proprietors, German Protestant refugees, and the Swiss colonization corporation, Georg Ritter and Company. The latter was represented by two Swiss natives of Bern, Franz Ludwig Michel and Christoph Baron von Graffenried. New Bern's founders were three of the most remarkable men ever to live in North Carolina—Michel, de Graffenried, and John Lawson.[34]

A former officer of the French army, Michel became an agent of the Ritter Company, organized to colonize and prospect for silver in the American colonies. Sent to Virginia, Pennsylvania, and Maryland, in 1703 Michel spent an "agreeable sojourn" in South Carolina.[35] He also represented the Canton of Bern, which was seeking to deport "undesirable" poor squatters and Anabaptists to the colonies, a convenient dumping ground. The Anabaptist sect was an offshoot of the evangelical Ulrich Zwingli, whose radical practices made them unwelcome even in tolerant Bern. Their alarming beliefs, which included rejection of infant baptism, separation of church and state, refusal to take oaths, freedom of worship, voluntary communal living, pacifism, refusal to pay taxes for religious or military purposes, and rejection of capital punishment, led to their oppression, imprisonment, and deportation.[36]

De Graffenried, who attended universities at Heidelberg and Leyden, learned of North Carolina through two proprietors in London, the second Duke of Albemarle and the second Sir John Colleton, whom he described as "my special friend." Chronically living beyond his means, the debt-ridden de Graffenried returned to Switzerland and married. At Bern, Michel convinced him that he could restore his fortune through colonization and silver prospecting.[37] Leaving his financial woes and his family in his father's care, de Graffenried returned to London, where the Lords Proprietors introduced him to North Carolinians Lawson and Christopher Gale. The convergence of de Graffenried, Michel, and Lawson in London in 1709 led to the Ritter Company's purchase of 10,000 acres on the Neuse and Trent Rivers. Michel received a grant of 2,500 acres, and de Graffenried purchased 5,000 acres, for which he received the titles of a Carolina landgrave and Baron of Bernburg. A twelve-year option was secured on 100,000 acres, and a thirty-year lease on mineral rights and mining.[38]

On behalf of the Ritter Company, de Graffenried and Michel contracted to resettle 150 Bernese paupers and Anabaptists and 650 Palatines from ninety-two families. In the contract with the Crown commissioners for resettlement of

Christoph Baron von Graffenried was the founder of the
Swiss and Palatine settlement at New Bern (1710).
Courtesy of State Archives of North Carolina.

the Palatines, about half the transportation cost was borne by the Crown, and each Palatine was to receive clothing valued at one pound. The company's land would be divided into 250-acre plantations that were rent-free for five years and distributed to the Palatine families by lot. In addition, they would receive free tools and household utensils, as well as a year's provisions and livestock, which would eventually be repaid.[39]

In January 1710 Lawson embarked from England with some 650 Palatines. Although the baron had selected young, healthy men and women of various crafts and trades, his careful planning was derailed by a disease that struck before they left, taking the lives of about forty of the young children. During the prolonged, harrowing voyage through winter storms on overcrowded vessels, the malignant "spotted fever . . . fluxes & the Dropsy" ran their course, taking about half of the remaining Palatines. As a final insult, when they were in sight of the Virginia coast their supply vessel was plundered by a French privateer.

Lawson and the poorly provisioned survivors journeyed overland into North
Carolina, reaching the Chowan River plantation of Colonel Thomas Pollock, a
wealthy planter and council member. On credit, Pollock provided limited supplies and small boats to convey the colonists to their destination on the Neuse
River, where they arrived on 27 April 1710.[40]

In the meantime, Michel conveyed 150 Bernese paupers and religious refugees down the Rhine to Rotterdam, where nearly all of the Anabaptists and
Mennonites chose to remain in tolerant Holland. From Newcastle, England,
de Graffenried and Michel and about 100 Swiss, mostly paupers, embarked in
July, arriving in Virginia in September after an uneventful voyage. In contrast to
the horrific Palatine experience in which about half died, very few of the Swiss
were lost. Following the route taken by Lawson and the Palatines, the Swiss
stopped at Pollock's plantation, securing supplies and boats. At the council,
which was in session there, de Graffenried was urged to enter the political
power struggle, but he begged off, citing the need to see his colonists safely to
their destination.[41]

When de Graffenried's contingent reached the Neuse in September, they
found the ill and starving Palatines in a state of "disease, poverty, and despair,"
on the brink of collapse. Many had traded their clothing for food. Lawson
considered the Palatines a "most Sloathful people," but he bore the responsibility for them. With North Carolina on the eve of rebellion and its government
dysfunctional, neither Receiver General Gale nor the assembly had delivered
the supplies promised by the proprietors.[42]

At the planned town site where the Neuse and Trent Rivers meet, the baron
found another surprise: the local Indians at the village of Chattoka were still in
residence. De Graffenried wisely decided to purchase the site again. In council with King Taylor and his elders, who came in their ceremonial finery, de
Graffenried, garbed in his best suit, was seated with dramatic flair in a throne-
like chair. The extended oratory ended in a bargain sealed with rum, which
exchanged a generous amount of gunpowder and shot for the site. The council
went well until de Graffenried was humiliated by his drunken partner Michel,
who rudely interrupted and assaulted Chief Taylor, only to repeat the insult
that night in the nearby camp. De Graffenried attempted to smooth over the
incident by paying a friendly visit to nearby Core Town on the Neuse, about
ten miles away. The reception was courteous but reserved, and de Graffenried
could not negotiate an agreement. Little did he know that his amicable over-
tures would soon save his life.[43]

De Graffenried and surveyor Lawson laid out New Bern on the point between the rivers, with two broad streets crossing in the middle and generous
three-acre lots to accommodate residents' homes, barns, gardens, and livestock.

Soon about twenty houses were under construction. A proprietor's house was built as a warehouse for the town, as well as a water-powered gristmill and a sawmill.[44] The baron's home, which also was the town's storehouse, was erected near the point, while a church was planned at the intersection of the two main streets. Earthen redoubts and a block house were built on the western side at Mill Creek and Trent River to deter hostile Indians. To transport supplies and provisions and to export the colony's products, de Graffenried purchased a barque for the sounds and rivers and an oceangoing sloop, which was dispatched to Bermuda to trade Indian corn for a cargo of salt. Later Michel acquired a brigantine that was sent on voyages to the West Indies.[45]

De Graffenried brought all the artisans and craftspeople needed to establish the metropolis the proprietors had envisioned. There were carpenters, joiners, millwrights, a mason, a blacksmith, cobblers, a tailor, a miller, a butcher, a weaver, a saddler, a glazier, a potter and tile maker, an armorer, a physician, a surgeon, and a schoolmaster. Traders received their town lots rent-free for ten years. At New Bern's monthly market and annual fair the village was lively with craftspeople hawking their wares—shoes, ironwork, cloth, leatherwork, and ceramics. Within a year the town became the seat of the precinct court, with Captain Johann Jacob Bötschi serving as clerk.[46] Much concerned for the spiritual welfare of his community, de Graffenried requested that his settlers be accepted into the Church of England. Serving as a lay reader, he conducted worship services and occasionally persuaded SPG missionaries to serve communion. The Bishop of London granted the baron permission to marry and baptize.[47]

With the energetic and steadying hands of de Graffenried and Michel at the helm, the Swiss settled in with the Palatines. By New Year's in 1711 the promised 250-acre plantations with a free four-year lease had been surveyed and allotted. Livestock, tools, utensils, furniture, and provisions were distributed, allowing families to move onto their land, where they cleared fields and erected houses. By April the colony's firm footing was confirmed in letters from the Bernese that were filled with confidence and hope for the future. Somewhat confused about his whereabouts, Hans Ruegsegger, writing from "India or America, in the Island of North Carolina on the river Neuse," was pleased with his plantation on Mill Creek, a "very good and fat land," where he anticipated having a hundred horses, cattle, and swine within a year's time. He exclaimed that thanks to Carolina's "freedom of conscience" alone he would not return to Switzerland for the best land that country could offer.[48]

Others wrote of broad pastures on the savannahs and rich sandy black soil that produced abundant crops of grain and Indian corn. The colonists portrayed their exotic Native American neighbors as "half naked, yet clever and sociable, unbelievers unsuited for work." They found that the "so-called wild" Indians were in fact "not wild" and often came to trade game, leather, beans, and corn for clothes, as well as to guide the newcomers and teach "some new ways." Many of them spoke English and went at least partially dressed in shirts and coats; however, they were not the least interested in the "true God." Evidence of the mutually beneficial trade relationship was found in the most-requested items to be sent from Bern, besides clothing, cloth, and spices: trade goods desired by the Natives, such as knives, tobacco pipes, ironware, copper kettles, and brassware.[49]

Writing home to have her savings sent to New Bern, the widow Anna Eva Zant, who had lost her daughter at sea, revealed that she was "making a beginning of housekeeping again," although it was "hard without means." After just seven months in the colony, she faced the future with optimism. She did note shortcomings: not enough colonists, a lack of good liquor, no good mills, and, most important in the predominantly male colony, "women folk are very rare."[50] After eighteen months de Graffenried was pleased to record that his colonists had "managed to build homes and make themselves so comfortable, that they made more progress in that length of time, than the English inhabitants in several years."[51]

New Bern was North Carolina's first settlement planned from its beginnings as a refuge for dispossessed paupers and sufferers for their faith. Although Huguenots and Quakers had been attracted by Carolina's religious freedom, they had come of their own volition. Never before had such a large group of refugees come to North Carolina as a sponsored colony transported directly from mainland Europe and England.

The arrival in the Neuse River valley of some 400 Germans and Swiss, who joined an earlier settlement of French Huguenots, created overnight the most ethnically diverse community in the colony. The sheer numbers were perceived as a threat by the Tuscarora and other Native tribes in the region, accustomed as they were to more gradual encroachment. Coming at a time when North Carolina was bitterly divided in a political power struggle that would culminate in armed rebellion, this sizable colony could change the balance of power. De Graffenried, courted by the contending factions and even offered the governorship, sensibly refrained from taking sides. The potential role that New Bern might have assumed as a metropolis of the colony was delayed for decades by the bloody attacks of the Tuscarora War, which would ravage Bath County and would fall heaviest in the Neuse and Pamlico valleys.

———————

AT THE PORT OF BEAUFORT, southeast of New Bern, the sea is visible through the only inlet on the North Carolina coast with direct access from the mainland to the ocean. From Beaufort it is less than two miles to the eighteenth-century Topsail Inlet, now Beaufort Inlet, which has been open and in place for centuries, although the channel has shifted repeatedly. Possessing a spacious and deep harbor on the ocean, Beaufort unfortunately lacked a good connection to the hinterland, and that was enough to prevent its developing into a significant seaport. Two short rivers—the Newport and the North—form the peninsula where the town is located, and Core Sound, the northern connector to the vast interior waters of Pamlico and Albemarle Sounds, is shallow, exposed, and treacherous. Only shallow-draft vessels—canoes, periaugers, shallops, and an occasional sloop, such as the *Core Sound Merchant* mentioned in 1712— could safely navigate the sound.[52]

Very early Core Sound was discovered to be rich in marine life. De Graffenried wrote that Englishmen from Core Sound brought oysters, crabs, clams, and a variety of fish to his settlement, and John Lawson described a fishery at Drum Inlet where red drum were salted and packed in barrels for export.[53] Other maritime occupations were shipbuilding, mentioned as early as 1713, shore-based whaling at Cape Lookout and adjacent Shackleford Banks, and offshore whaling by New Englanders at Cape Lookout.[54] Open-range cattle, sheep, and hogs grazed in tidal marshes along the rivers and Core Sound, as well as on Shackleford Banks and Cape Lookout.[55]

The enterprising Farnifold Green, while maintaining his residence on the Neuse River, acquired the future site of Beaufort, then known as Newport Town Point, in December 1707. Neighbors were John Nelson on Core Sound and Francis and John Shackleford on the North River. By 1713 Green had sold the site to Robert Turner, a merchant who obtained permission from the Lords Proprietors to establish the town. Shackleford Banks, Nelson Bay, and Turner Creek are reminders of these founders. Turner hired Deputy Surveyor Richard Graves to lay out the town in October, with lots set aside for a market and a church. The hamlet was named Beaufort for the proprietary palatine Henry Somerset, Duke of Beaufort.[56] In the emerging fishing village, the daily routine began before dawn when periaugers and skiffs laden with nets and coiled hand lines headed out on the local sounds and the sea. Throughout the day those at home cleaned, salted, and packed the plentiful catch and repaired spare nets drying on crude racks. For the regional market, barrels of oysters, clams, and crabs were packed live in seaweed or brine.

———————

WRITING ON 30 DECEMBER 1710 from his Neuse River house, Lawson described his procedures as a scientific collector and his vision for a comprehensive natural history of the colony, "if God prolongs my dayes." For every specimen, Lawson expected to record when and where it was collected, details on its reproduction and habitat, comparison with similar European examples, and its uses by both Native Americans and English. He was exchanging seeds and testing growth in a new environment. Lawson's ornithology study would comprehend specimens of all land and water birds, from the "Eagle to the wren," and describe the characteristics of nests, eggs, incubation, flight, songs, food, "beauty & colour," and migration patterns. He envisioned a comprehensive geological collection of soils, rocks, minerals, fossils, shells, and earths used for paint and medical purposes. Ever the practical observer, he was cataloguing soil types and climate related to all aspects of agriculture.[57]

Although engaged in overseeing the new settlement of Palatine refugees and Swiss at New Bern, Lawson had embarked on active collecting after his return to the Neuse in March. Since the previous summer, he had kept a diary of weather and other natural phenomena. The previous July he had dispatched through Virginia a box of specimens containing vials of insects, plants wrapped in paper, bird and snake skins, and a few fossils. The question uppermost in Lawson's mind was, How can these natural discoveries be used to provide sustenance and to "Inrich the country"? He expected Petiver and other members of the Royal Society to critique his work as he progressed toward the goal of a "Compleat History of these parts." *A New Voyage to Carolina* was intended as the first step toward that "Compleat History."

About six weeks before leaving on his ill-fated journey up the Neuse, Lawson wrote Petiver on 24 July 1711 what would be his last letter about the status of his collecting. He had recently sent an assortment of plants and four vials of insects. The governor's wife, Catherine Hyde, on a return trip to England conveyed a "book of plants" for Lawson, who had even more varieties at his Neuse River home that he had not had time to pack for the journey. Tragically, time had run out for him, and no more specimens would be forthcoming.[58]

CHAPTER TWELVE

The Church Establishment
and the Cary Rebellion

I got into No. Carolina . . . where I found the
People all in Confusion and disorder.
—Reverend Benjamin Dennis, 1711

IN CHARLES TOWN in early 1705 Sir Nathaniel Johnson, provincial governor
of Carolina, was in a quandary. His friend and adviser, Landgrave Robert
Daniell, deputy governor of North Carolina, had to be removed for, of all
things, a morals charge—living in adultery with a mistress with whom he had
a second family. For the age this was neither especially unusual nor shocking
if kept discreet, but Daniell's political opponents had used it effectively to oust
him. Much was at stake in Carolina over this incident. In the era it was customary to have a state-sanctioned and publicly supported established church,
paid for by a tithe on all taxpayers. Sir Nathaniel was succeeding with the task
given him by the proprietary palatine John, Earl of Granville, to establish the
Anglican Church in the provinces. In both of the Carolinas the project was
underway, and Sir Nathaniel was determined to keep the momentum going in
North Carolina.

From the founding of Carolina the king and proprietors had intended that
the Anglican Church, or Church of England, would be established. The first
charter allowed dissenters freedom of worship by dispensation, which became
in the second charter "Liberty of conscience." The 1670 Fundamental Constitutions reiterated "the only true and Orthodox, and the National Religion of all
the King's Dominions, is so also of Carolina," but the constitutions also stated
the strongest guarantee of religious liberty of any colony, well beyond toleration.[1] The reality was that over thirty years passed before there would be an Anglican establishment in the colony. As a result, North Carolina enjoyed absolute
soul-liberty, leaving religious life in the hands of Quakers and other dissenters.

The Church of England was established in the early eighteenth century
in the Carolinas for both religious and political reasons. Anglicans would receive spiritual succor but would also achieve political dominance by excluding

dissenters from the government. The first house of worship in the colony, begun about 1682 in southern Carolina, had been an independent Anglican church, St. Philips in Charles Town, but significant numbers of dissenters resided in both of the province's colonies. In North Carolina, Quakers and other dissenters, combined with those who professed no religion, were an influential political presence, although nominal Anglicans constituted the majority. Actively supporting South Carolina, the proprietors sponsored promotional tracts targeting Ireland, Scotland, and also Holland, where there were Huguenot refugees from France. The result was migrations of Scottish Presbyterians, Baptists, Quakers, Huguenots, and Jews, so that by the turn of the century dissenters comprised about half of the free population.

By 1700 there were more than 100 Anglican parishes on the North American mainland, but only Virginia and New York had established the church. In the next decade the Carolinas and Maryland sanctioned the church, and parishes continued to proliferate. The American church was under the oversight of the Bishop of London, who appointed commissaries to administer various colonies. Based in Charles Town, a commissary appointed in 1707 for the Carolinas and the Bahamas gave virtually no attention to North Carolina.[2]

For decades North Carolina's Anglicans, lacking a church to meet their worship needs and to provide structure for the celebration of birth, marriage, and death, repeatedly appealed to England for ministers and literature. In response to colonial requests, the Reverend Doctor Thomas Bray, the ecclesiastical commissary to Maryland, traveled throughout the colonies reporting on the condition of the church. Although Bray apparently did not visit North Carolina, he recommended that two missionaries be sent to the colony. Bray was instrumental in founding the two important missionary arms of the church—in 1699 the Society for the Promotion of Christian Knowledge (SPCK) to support religious instruction, and two years later the Society for the Propagation of the Gospel in Foreign Parts (SPG) to sponsor missionaries.[3]

Bray's initial outreach to the colonies through the SPCK supplied several dozen parochial libraries, one of which was dispatched to St. Thomas Parish in frontier Bath County. It arrived in early 1701 along with the SPG's first missionary to North Carolina, the Reverend Daniel Brett. Although the library suffered many vicissitudes, enough of it survived to receive funding and oversight from the General Assembly in 1715, making it the colony's first public library.[4]

The parish library of more than 1,000 volumes was recorded in two catalogues—a parochial library of 153 titles, and a lay library of 36 titles. The lay library included multiple copies of tracts and pamphlets intended for distribution, such as 100 copies each of *Cautions against Prophane Swearing*, *Serious Invitations of the Quakers to Return to Christianity*, *Christians Daily Devotion*, and five copies of the Bible, as well as a title on parallels between Quakers and primitive heretics.[5] The parochial titles included religious and theological works and diverse secular titles on business and commerce, English and ancient history, the classics (Virgil and Horace), foreign languages, heraldry, weights and measures, mathematics, science, and government. As in the lay collection, there were several titles exposing the heresies of Quakers.[6]

Brett, who remained in the colony about eighteen months, served both Albemarle and Bath Counties, spending considerable time in the Pamlico region. President Henderson Walker noted that during his first six months he "behaved himself in a modest manner," but thereafter acted in "a most horrid manner." Successor missionaries, transit priests, and government officials universally condemned Brett for scandalizing the colony. Christopher Gale, a devout Anglican, characterized Brett as "ye Monster of ye Age." Others complained that he caused "great trouble and grief to us who have a great veneration for the Church" and that he was a "Scandalous fellow." In 1708 President William Glover reported to the Bishop of London that the controversial clause in the Vestry Act allowing lay members to supervise the clergy was a direct result of Brett's "disorderly behavior."[7] Whatever Brett did may never be known, but in the minds of both Anglicans and dissenters his wrongdoings had a long-term effect on the local attitude toward priests. Nonetheless, the movement for establishment had such momentum now that Brett's transgressions could not hold back the tide.

Strife between Anglicans and dissenters erupted simultaneously in the two Carolinas. Until the ascendancy of John, Lord Granville, in 1701, the palatine had been a proprietor who favored toleration or was occupied with other interests. Having served in Parliament and on the Privy Council, Granville was well connected and experienced in politics. Described by a contemporary as an "inflexible bigot for the High-church," he is considered "largely responsible" for the religious conflict that vexed the Carolina colonies for a decade.[8]

Since high Anglicans believed that dissenters were unfit to hold public office, the establishment of the Church of England was coupled with an assault on dissenters in the assembly and government. In South Carolina the upheaval came in 1700 when a dissenter, Landgrave Joseph Morton, newly elected as council president, was ousted by Anglican James Moore, who was backed by the firebrand Colonel Robert Daniell and the high church Goose Creek faction. Although establishment of the Church of England topped the Goose Creek agenda, it was sidetracked by the onset of Queen Anne's War in 1702 as Daniell and Governor Moore became absorbed with provincial defense.[9]

In North Carolina the way was cleared to achieve church establishment with the July 1699 death of Deputy Governor Harvey, whose successor as president of the council was the "ardent Anglican" Henderson Walker. A resident of the colony since 1682, Walker first settled in Perquimans and by the 1690s had a sound-side plantation in Chowan Precinct. He accumulated his fortune and high status as an attorney, a planter, a merchant, and co-owner of the sloop *Dubartus*. Through his second marriage, to Anne Lillington in 1694, he was connected to the colonial elite.

Actively engaged in governance from the time he arrived, Walker served at every level in the colony's courts as either clerk or justice. He also became attorney general, secretary, a burgess, and by 1694 a council member. Described as an "adroit politician," Walker, "with a great deale of Care and management," secured a majority in the assembly of 1701, which passed the colony's first vestry act by "one or two votes." Walker's success in obtaining a sympathetic legislature may be attributed to his long residence and undisputed loyalty to Carolina and his many years of mutually respectful work with dissenters in the government. Significantly, he was elected president by a balanced council of two Quakers, a Baptist, and Anglicans. After 1700, however, the sole Quaker councilman was Francis Tomes, who had been at the locus of political power for nearly thirty years. Walker privately considered Quaker beliefs "wicked" and "pernicious," but he did not descend to political oppression of dissenters as his successors in office did. Walker's tombstone, one of the few surviving from the era, refers to the "tranquility" of the province during his administration.[10]

In a report to the Bishop of London in 1703, Governor Walker wrote that Albemarle had languished for fifty years "without Priest or Altar." Furthermore, some years earlier George Fox "by Strange Infatuations did infuse the Quaker principles" into a small group that had grown "very numerous." He credited the Reverend Dr. Bray's gift of libraries with slowing the growth of the Quaker community. Despite the nefarious Reverend Daniel Brett, Walker secured the 1701 vestry act that provided for five parishes and vestries—one in each of the four Albemarle precincts and another in Bath County.[11] The vestries were authorized to levy a poll tithe of up to five shillings for construction of churches and chapels, the purchase of glebes, and thirty-pound salaries for ministers.[12]

In accordance with the charters, the Fundamental Constitutions had always mandated that the official religion of Carolina was the Church of England and that the assembly was responsible for the construction of churches and the maintenance of the ministers. The version of August 1682, however, added that only those who conformed to the state church would be subject to the poll tax, or tithe, and that other churches, except Roman Catholic, could levy an annual tithe on their members. The limit was set at no more than a penny per acre, or twelve pence per head. Furthermore, ministers of any church were prohibited from serving in the assembly or holding any public office.[13]

On 15 December 1701 in the heavily Anglican precinct of Chowan, the vestry assembled to organize St. Paul's parish. Among the vestrymen were a who's who of Anglicans and county leadership—Governor Walker, Colonel Pollock, Colonel Wilkison, William Duckenfield, Edward Smithwick, John Blount, Nathaniel Chevin, Captain Thomas Blount, and Captain Thomas Luten. Chevin was named clerk. Their first action was to approve building a church on an acre given by Smithwick near the growing settlement on Queen Anne's Creek. Wilkison and Luten were appointed church wardens to supervise construction of St. Paul's Church. A chapel of ease was to be built across the Chowan River under the care of Pollock and Duckenfield. Lay readers were to be recruited to hold services at both locations. The church wardens were empowered to levy a poll tithe of twelve pence if voluntary contributions were not sufficient.[14]

At a subsequent vestry meeting in June a list of 283 tithables was compiled for the precinct, and a five-shilling tithe was levied for expenses related to church construction, the lay readers' salaries, and the clerk, with eight pounds set aside for the poor. John Porter contracted to build the chapel, which was finished by December. Designated by assembly law as the keeper of standards, the vestry ordered a set of weights and measures, a large Book of Common Prayer, and a volume of homilies. The brass and pewter weights and measures arrived from Boston the next spring.[15]

By 1703 two more churches were under construction, funded partly by Virginia governor Francis Nicholson's contribution of ten pounds toward each one.[16] The vestry act had been sent to the Lords Proprietors for ratification, but in late fall Governor Walker had still heard nothing from England. He was uneasy, for the Quakers had won a majority in the assembly. Knowing that their goal was to repeal church establishment in the November assembly session, less than two weeks away, Walker feared that they would succeed and the native-born children would become "heathens."[17] Notwithstanding Walker's concern, it is apparent that church establishment was not disallowed. If it had been, how can the continuous minutes of St. Paul's parish, the church tax levies, and the references to other vestries be explained? The disallowed law mentioned by the Reverend Blair appears to relate specifically to the minister's paltry salary of thirty pounds, which the Quaker-dissenter assembly did not reenact.[18]

The vigor of the church stemmed from the vestries—the parish administrative committees that were composed of appointed or elected laymen, mainly experienced government officials, planters, merchants, and militia officers. Vestries were responsible for hiring and managing ministers and lay readers, constructing and maintaining church buildings, collecting the tithe or poll tax, providing religious education, and acquiring a set of weights and measures. Although the precinct courts had had oversight and enforcement of laws on poor relief, morality, and care of orphans, bastards, and the elderly, the vestries increasingly took on those social concerns, sometimes at the behest of the courts. In addition, vestries sponsored medical care of the indigent and paupers' funerals and burials.[19]

The assembly passed a comprehensive law in 1715 declaring three legal holidays and setting rules for observing the Sabbath and suppressing immorality. The Sabbath was kept by prohibiting all normal work by freemen, servants, or the enslaved; business and trade by boats; and sales in ordinaries and taverns of liquor, wine, and beer, except for lodgers. Exception was made for necessary and charity work. The three holidays (holy days) were January 30, the anniversary of the execution of the "Royall martyr" Charles I; September 22, the anniversary of the Indian "massacre"; and May 29, celebrating the birthday and "happy Restoration" of Charles II. These days were observed with humiliation, fasting, and prayer, although there was no limitation on the sale of alcohol on Restoration Day.

The precinct courts regulated morals by levying fines or ordering corporal punishment in the stocks or by public whipping in lieu of fines. Infractions included profane swearing and cursing (with public officials subject to a double fine), public drunkenness, fornication, and adultery. Immigrant couples were allowed a year to produce a marriage certificate. If discovered to have a living spouse, one was expelled as a vagabond. If a pregnant single woman identified the father, he was required to post bond for maintenance of the child. If the woman refused to name the father or if the alleged father denied paternity, then she or he was subject to corporal punishment. The fines for sexual impropriety were designated to the parish vestry to cover the cost of caring for bastard children.[20]

Precinct courts and the Anglican parish vestries had public responsibility for the poor. Occasionally there were supplementary charitable bequests, such as those by Governors Thomas Harvey and Henderson Walker. Harvey left £100 in his estate for the benefit of the poor and poor children in Perquimans who were not under the care of the parish. Walker set aside ten barrels of corn to be distributed to ten poor people, £5 toward building a church, and £5 for the minister who preached his funeral sermon.[21]

Following the debacle of Brett, over the next three decades the SPG sent a dozen priests to minister to the colony's nascent parishes. Some were experienced clergymen and educators, while others were on their first appointments. Faced with the difficulties of travel, the indifference of the assembly and of ostensible Anglicans, and opposition from predominantly Quaker dissenters, it is not surprising that some lasted only a few months, others a year or so. Several left with their health broken, and three perished in the colony. A few, like Brett, left with their reputations ruined. Although none of them thrived under the daunting adversities they faced, the dedicated managed to carry out and expand the church's work, and one of them labored in North Carolina for over a decade.

In January 1704 Anglican missionary the Reverend John Blair found three small church buildings and glebes in North Carolina. In the largest precincts—Chowan, Perquimans, and Pasquotank—lay readers held Sunday morning and evening prayers and preached sermons. Blair himself preached twice on Sundays and during the week at vestry meetings. He baptized a hundred children but did not perform marriages, because magistrates customarily officiated at weddings. His major challenge was geographic: the population was scattered along the many rivers, and to reach the Pamlico settlement in Bath, he had to cross the sound and fifty miles of wilderness.

Although prejudiced against non-Anglicans, Blair revealed the extent of Carolina's religious diversity forty years after the charter date. He described four distinct groups, with Quakers the "most powerfull Enemies to Church Goverment, but a people very poorly ignorant of what they profess." Another group who had "noe religion" might join them if Quakers did not require their adherents "to lead a more moral life." A third body of "sort of" Presbyterians or Calvinists were led by "idle fellows" who preached and baptized without authority from any "pretended Church." Finally, Blair considered his fellow Anglicans "fewest in number but the better sort of people." Discouraged by the Quaker-dominated assembly's unwillingness to pay his meager thirty-pound allowance and burdened with poor health and travel hardships, Blair concluded that North Carolina was the "most Barbarous place in the Continent." Within a few months he returned to England.[22]

Blair's sudden departure left the colony without a pastor until the Reverend Henry Gerrard was accepted by the Chowan vestry in September 1705. Although recommended by the deputy governor, within five months Gerrard was called before the vestry to answer accusations of "Several Debauched practices." The vestry temporarily retained him until May, allowing time for him to clear his name, and no more is heard of him until he surfaced in South Carolina.[23]

The next year the Reverend Richard Marsden, who was en route to South Carolina, had a brief stopover in Pasquotank Precinct, where he conducted services, baptized infants and adults, and, for the first time in the parish, celebrated the sacrament of the Lord's Supper. Marsden's sojourn inspired the parish vestry to petition the Bishop of London for a pastor, citing the youth who lacked guidance in the faith, rampant immorality and profaneness, and the growth of Quaker numbers.[24]

The bishop responded by naming two SPG missionaries—the Reverend James Adams to Chowan and Perquimans, and the Reverend William Gordon to Pasquotank and Currituck. Traveling together, they arrived in April 1708 at the onset of the Cary Rebellion. Gordon optimistically embarked on a busy agenda of frequent worship services, baptizing, and ministering to his parishioners. As the upheavals of the political rebellion escalated, however, his health declined, and within five months, without permission from the SPG, he returned to England.[25]

Adams, too, was worn down physically and mentally by the "Lawless and Barbarous People" of Albemarle. Although feeling that he was in "a World of misery and trouble in Body and Mind," he served his parishes well, preaching twice a week, celebrating the sacraments, and making plans to work with the nearly eighty Indians in his parish who spoke English and seemed receptive to his mission. The vestries in both parishes, as well as Governor William Glover, sent testimonials to the SPG with high praise for Adams. Sadly, the careworn Adams passed away in 1710, just a month prior to his scheduled return to England.[26]

Of all the missionaries sent to the colony in the proprietary period, none was more experienced or better prepared for a backwater posting than the Reverend John Urmston (ca. 1662–1731). Better educated than most, he had been a schoolmaster, textbook author, navy chaplain, curate, and chaplain to the English merchant company in Moscow and Archangel, Russia. His references were impeccable.[27]

Urmston arrived in the colony in 1710 with his wife, three young children, and two indentured servants. Although assigned to Chowan and Perquimans parishes, when his fellow missionaries left he took over Pasquotank and Currituck and made extended trips to the Bath County parishes. On his arrival he found a weak church, barely functioning, with ruinous buildings. The colony was still in turmoil from the Cary Rebellion, and in little more than a year the horrific Tuscarora War broke out, raining violence and famine on the entire colony.

Urmston's lengthy correspondence, spiced with acerbic insights and satirical exaggerations, has become the eminently quotable chronicle of this crucial period. His visceral disdain for his archenemies—the Quakers—stemmed from his deeply orthodox religious convictions. Urmston's incessant complaints about the colony led to Governor Hyde's observation that his attitude arose from his "Unfortunate Temper which no ways suits the Humours of the Naturall born People of America."[28] Despite his invective and vitriol, there is no better source for living conditions in the colony than Urmston's correspondence with the SPG.

Few of the Anglican missionaries ever received their full stipends, however meager. Urmston, while complaining bitterly to the vestry and his English superiors, had the initiative and resources to purchase a 300-acre plantation on the sound in Chowan. Although his letters were often gloomy, he weathered the tribulations of some of the darkest, most perilous years in the proprietary era, outlasting all of his fellow missionaries and compiling an enviable record of service. Considering the unsettled conditions, adversities of travel, and lack of support from the vestries, Urmston's successful ministry demonstrated commitment well beyond that of his compatriots. His extant reports, which cover about a third of his time in the colony, compile a record of 660 baptisms, preaching on Sundays and midweek (sometimes twice a day), serving as chaplain to the assembly, influencing stronger vestry acts, and celebrating the sacraments. Because he was paid a pittance toward his annual salary, to support his family he directly managed and worked his plantation.[29]

After a dozen years of service Urmston's final word on North Carolina was his complaint that he had toiled "Among an inGratefull people . . . in Such an Obscure Corner of the world inhabitted by the dreggs and Gleanings of all other Inglish Colonies and a very unhealthy Countrey." Lesser men had been driven out, sometimes within a few months, or were broken in health, or had even died there, but Urmston had persevered and left a record unmatched by the other missionaries to the colony.[30]

The Reverend Giles Rainsford from Dublin spent about eighteen months in the colony and neighboring Virginia, beginning in May 1712. Initially he was to share duties with Urmston in Chowan and adjacent parishes, but their personalities clashed. The peripatetic Rainsford began moving from parish to parish and even crossed into Nansemond in Virginia, where he claimed to have held large meetings, turning many from Quakerism and besting in debate Joseph Glaister, the Quaker "Great Apostle." He reported baptizing forty Blacks in the two colonies. Rainsford spent five months in Chowan Indian Town, learning the language, hoping to become the missionary to the Indian nations being relocated on the border in Virginia. Another milestone he noted was converting Irish planter Patrick Lawler, a "virulent Papist."[31]

The Anglican missionaries sought converts among enslaved Africans but were ultimately thwarted by slaveholders' erroneous belief that conversion was a step toward freedom. Several missionaries reported preaching to and baptizing Blacks, but no one attempted more than the Reverend Ebenezer Taylor, who served several parishes in North Carolina over two years, beginning in Chowan in November 1717. On the western shore of the Chowan River he resided at the plantation of William Duckenfield, a devout Anglican and one of the colony's larger holders of enslaved persons. Reverend Taylor held parish worship services in Duckenfield's house and also reached out to the plantation's enslaved Africans. His annual report of April 1719 included baptizing a young white woman, thirty white children, and an enslaved young family of a Black man, a "mustee" woman, and three "mustee" children. Taylor described his further success at teaching the catechism to the couple, who had memorized it—with understanding—and recited it "perfectly" before large congregations on Sundays. He was gratified that "all that heard them admired their Saying it so well."

Taylor continued his proselytizing, preparing four more enslaved persons for baptism until stopped by Squire Duckenfield, who had been influenced by fearful neighboring slaveholders. Soon thereafter Taylor moved to Perquimans and then to St. Thomas in Bath Town. It is not known why he failed to find a satisfactory post, although one reason may be the notoriety of his ministry to the enslaved. Taylor maintained his belief that enslaved Africans, without expectation of freedom, generally were "Sensible and Civil" and "Inclined to Christianity and things that are Good." Discouraged, he finally embarked for the sparsely settled southern frontier on Core Sound. In February 1720 Taylor apparently died from exposure to bitter cold on the voyage and was buried on uninhabited Harbor Island.[32]

THE PROPRIETARY POLICY of religious liberty had been upheld particularly by the Quaker proprietor John Archdale and the early palatines, who encouraged the province's growth by recruiting dissenters. On attaining his majority, Archdale's son sold his father's share in 1696. The next year marked the death of the last of the original proprietors, the tolerant palatine, William, Earl of Craven. By 1701 John Grenville, Baron Granville, a zealous Anglican, became palatine and embarked on a mission to establish the Church of England in Carolina.[33]

At the time there were usually four active proprietors, three of whom were represented by Lord Granville. Appalled by the overbearing Granville, John Archdale, who had been absent for nine years, in 1705 purchased another proprietary share. For the next three years he was an influential advocate for the colony's Quakers and other dissenters and a protector of religious freedom. In 1708 he gave his share to his Quaker daughter and son-in-law, Mary and John Danson, who shared his beliefs.[34]

Embracing Queen Anne's "High Church" Tory policy, in 1703 Granville appointed a dedicated Anglican, Sir Nathaniel Johnson, as governor of Carolina. A former governor of the Leeward Islands, Johnson had settled in South Carolina in 1689, where he served in the assembly and aligned himself with the controversial pro-Anglican Goose Creek faction and Colonel Robert Daniell. With proprietary support assured, in 1704 Sir Nathaniel maneuvered through the assembly acts that sanctioned the Church of England and further required that anyone in public office be an Anglican communicant and swear an oath of loyalty to the Crown.

With the proprietors dominated by Lord Granville, dissenters in South Carolina petitioned the House of Lords for relief. The peers persuaded Queen Anne in 1706 that the law was repugnant to English liberties and should be disallowed, an opinion confirmed by the Crown attorney general. The queen acted in June, declaring the act null and void and instructing the proprietors to disallow the laws that violated long-standing proprietary policy. While Granville dithered, Sir Nathaniel secured passage of an establishment act that organized South Carolina into parishes and mandated a test oath, ensuring that all public officials would be Anglicans.[35]

Meanwhile, to secure church establishment in North Carolina, in 1703 Sir Nathaniel named Landgrave Robert Daniell deputy governor of the colony.[36] Although the garrulous Daniell sought and thrived on controversy throughout his life, he managed to leave an enviable legacy as assemblyman, council member, accomplished soldier, and deputy governor of both Carolina colonies. Notable contradictions marked his political life. Some governors found him a reliable confidante, while he actively opposed others. A trusted adviser to the Lords Proprietors on the final version of the Fundamental Constitutions, he then spent many years resisting their policies.

Daniell migrated to South Carolina from Barbados in the late 1670s, acquiring land warrants to 1,500 acres. By 1679 he and his wife Dorothy were settled in the new Charles Town on Oyster Point.[37] Recruited to the powerful Goose Creek faction of fellow Barbadians, he became their point man in opposing the proprietors. For his unrelenting hostility to Governor Philip Ludwell he was excluded from a general pardon in 1692. A decade later, Colonel Daniell's long militia service led his close friend Governor James Moore to appoint him as his second-in-command for a punitive expedition to Spanish Florida early in Queen Anne's War. St. Augustine was looted and burned, but the siege of the Castillo failed when Spanish reinforcements arrived. Moore shouldered blame for the failure, while Daniell's military reputation was enhanced by his actions in the campaign.[38]

In June Deputy Governor Daniell was well received in North Carolina, whose Anglicans feared that a dissenter assembly might disestablish the Church of England. Daniell reassured them that a vestry act was being developed in South Carolina, and a similar act for North Carolina was a top priority for Palatine Granville, Governor Johnson, and himself. Anglican Christopher Gale, distraught that his six-month-old son was unchristened for lack of clergy, was favorably impressed, observing that Daniell "promises very faire"

Robert Daniell was deputy governor of North
Carolina from 1703 to 1705. This pastel portrait was
drawn ca. 1715 by Henrietta Johnston in Charles
Town. Courtesy of State Archives
of North Carolina.

and "Religion & learning . . . may flourish."[39] On Daniell's arrival, however, a
threatened Indian uprising demanded his immediate attention.

Around the turn of the century, when the northern Iroquois resumed raiding
their traditional enemies—the Catawba and tribes farther south—they sought
support from their relatives in Virginia and North Carolina. These tribes, the
Tuscarora, Meherrin, and Core, were already under stress from frontier expansion and competition from the colonial fur traders. The combined pressure
spawned disturbances and violent incidents west of the Chowan and in the
Pamlico and Neuse valleys of Bath County. Despite the peace treaty with the
Tuscarora that had held for decades, rumors of war spread.[40]

Drawing on his frontier experience, Governor Daniell defused a series of
confrontations between the colonists and several Native American tribes on
the Chowan River and south of Albemarle Sound. He dampened the Keyauwee and Core threat on the Chowan by calling up the militia in a show of
force.[41] In Bath County's Pamlico-Neuse region, by contrast, isolated hostile
acts proliferated over the next year. Settlers on the Pamlico, Neuse, and Pungo

Rivers believed the source of the troubles to be the powerful Tuscarora urging the smaller tribes—Machapungo, Neuse, and Bear—into belligerence. On the Neuse a hog was killed and 250 skins stolen. Colonists were threatened and assaulted and stock was killed on the Pungo. At Drum Inlet on Core Banks, Indians robbed three fishermen, taking nets, tackle, a blanket, an axe, clothing, and provisions. William Powell was attacked by King Louther and sixteen armed warriors when he attempted to stop the theft of his ammunition. When Louther struck Powell with his bow, Powell threatened to report the chief to the governor and General Court. Louther replied that the governor could "kiss his arse." Powell took the governor a letter from John Lawson urging action against the Natives, whereupon the Indians cornered Powell on Cedar Island, berated him as a "Sonn of a bitch," and vowed to burn his house and take his corn at the next full moon.[42] Whether provoked or not, these bellicose events could easily have escalated into outright war. Governor Daniell convened a council with the Indian chieftains that summer and negotiated a treaty that brought what he called a "firm Peace"—actually, a fragile cessation of hostilities.[43]

By 1704 the previously approved Anglican parishes were organized. In the election for the next assembly, however, the Quakers, who promised to repeal the poll tax for support of the church, attracted enough dissenters to win a slim majority. The stage was set for rejection of a new vestry act. At that point Governor Daniell received a copy of the oath of allegiance to Queen Anne, and he had his solution. When the council, assembly, and courts were presented with the oath, Daniell refused to allow the long-established practice of affirmation, causing the Quakers to vacate their offices rather than violate their beliefs. In Pasquotank Precinct alone, four out of five burgesses relinquished their seats, and a new writ of election was issued. With the Anglicans now holding an overwhelming majority, the Vestry Act of 1704 was easily passed and subsequently received the proprietors' approval.[44]

Although North Carolina's 1704 act is missing, it was very likely similar to the extant South Carolina law. North Carolina's earliest surviving vestry act, from 1715, which is considered a restatement of earlier law, organized ten parishes, double the number in 1701. The section most repugnant to dissenters required a poll tithe of up to five shillings of all taxables, with a penalty of distraint of property for nonpayment. The likely model in South Carolina contained another objectionable provision for exclusion from public office for either refusal to swear oaths or noncompliance to the Church of England.[45]

In any case, exclusion was achieved by a separate law concerning liberty of conscience and recognition of Quaker affirmation. Protestant dissenters were allowed freedom to worship "without Molestation." Because Quakers had been subject to imprisonment or distraint of property for refusing to take an oath in court, this law recognized affirmation as equal to an oath, except for giving evidence in criminal cases, serving on a jury, or holding any government office.[46] Blatantly discriminatory, this act, while recognizing the right of affirmation, explicitly confirmed the earlier purge of Quakers from public office in North Carolina. The act governing assembly membership specified the same oath of allegiance required for Parliament. The 1715 governor and council were Anglicans. Of the twenty-six burgesses, twenty-one were militia officers, including nine colonels, and twenty were Anglican vestry members.[47] There were no known Quakers in the assembly, and there would be no Quakers in public office in North Carolina again until after the American Revolution.

After Governor Daniell's purge of Quakers from the government, their recourse began with a protest sent to the provincial governor, Sir Nathaniel Johnson. For three centuries historians have accepted the cryptic statements of contemporaries Pollock, de Graffenried, and others that the Quakers' complaints led to the ouster of Daniell, although considering Governor Johnson's commitment to the Church of England and the establishment in South Carolina, this explanation is suspect. In 1997 a Quaker scholar discovered the missing piece of the puzzle, which finally explains Governor Daniell's downfall, in the records of London Yearly Meeting. From time to time overseas Quaker meetings sent epistles or reports to London about their development and spiritual condition. An epistle from Perquimans Quarterly Meeting dated 31 March 1706 and signed by former council and assembly members addressed their recent political persecution: "Evill men Rose up against us and were bitter agst us because some of us that were in Commission [holding office] Reproved the Debity Governour for Cohabiting with a Woman that was not his Wife and for leaving his Wife in Ashley River."[48]

Historians have long known that Landgrave Daniell had families in both of the Carolinas, but the assumption was that his South Carolina wife Dorothy had died before he began his relationship with Martha Wainwright of Bath County, with whom he subsequently had children. The Quaker epistle leaves no doubt that Daniell was living with his northern paramour while he was still married to Dorothy. Sir Nathaniel could ignore a Quaker protest, but not Daniell's personal scandal. The silence in the colonial records suggests a cover-up by the ruling party, who were protecting their own.

From the Quakers' point of view, their expulsion from the government originated from the Anglican "Envy agst. ye Truth of God" and resentment for the exposure of Daniell's transgression. The oath requirement that excluded Quakers nearly backfired when in elections to fill the resulting vacancies, Quakers were "Chosen again and again many Times over, all ye Good men of our Province Stood by us with ye Common people." When Daniell's replacement, Thomas Cary, "proved no better," the Quakers dispatched John Porter to the yearly meeting in England, to appeal to the Lords Proprietors and the queen if necessary. North Carolina Quakers wanted nothing more than the right to affirmation that they had "Injoyed ever Since ye First Settlemt. of the colony."[49] The only other known reference to Daniell's immorality was from the Reverend John Urmston, who wrote in 1711 that Daniell was "a Monster of Wickedness."[50] Given Urmston's customary hyperbole, historians have ignored his opinion without corroboration from another source. The Quaker epistle sets the record straight.

As for the personal scandal that caused the governor's dismissal in North Carolina, Daniell remained married to his first wife, Dorothy. By early 1703 he had met nineteen-year-old Martha Wainwright (1684–1743), a native of South Carolina, who was some thirty-eight years his junior. Martha bore him four children out of wedlock—Sarah (1703), Martha (1704), John (1707), and Ann (1710)—while living in North Carolina, presumably on his Pamlico River plantation. She married him in 1711 following Dorothy's death in Charles Town.[51] Although previous biographers and genealogists have believed that Daniell's first wife had either died or been divorced before he began living with his mistress, the Quaker epistle, Urmston's castigation, and Governor Johnson's removal of Daniell support the above narrative. Dorothy, the long-suffering aggrieved party, sought no divorce, as such extremely rare action required an act of the assembly and would jeopardize her social status and her property. The only consequence to Daniell was that as a paragon of the Church of England, "defender of the faith," his hypocrisy enabled those he persecuted to oust him.[52]

Daniell maintained residences in both colonies for a time, finally moving to South Carolina after 1709. After a brief term on the North Carolina council, he served in the South Carolina assembly, commanded a contingent in the Yamassee War, and in 1715 was appointed deputy governor of South Carolina, serving for one tumultuous year. Portraits of Robert and Martha Daniell were drawn by Charles Town artist Henrietta Johnston about 1715.[53] Daniell's North Carolina property was left primarily to support his son John, who moved to the Cape Fear area as an adult. John's sister Martha (1704–79) married George Logan Jr. and became a noted South Carolina horticulturalist.[54] Originally on his Daniell's Island plantation, Daniell's grave was moved to St. Philips churchyard, where his tombstone reveals that he valued his military accomplishments above all others. Landgrave Daniell's fall from power, if not from grace, removed a decisive and experienced soldier and administrator who had the confidence of both the Lords Proprietors and Governor Johnson. After fifteen years of rare stable government, the colony fell into a chaotic power struggle of several years' duration that contributed directly to the most destructive Indian war in its history.

The Quakers had demonstrated their political acumen and were ready to take on the next governor. Under the proprietors' liberal policies, Quakers had heavily influenced North Carolina's government for more than a decade, serving in every level of administration. A state church threatened their political survival, which could lead to religious discrimination and persecution, neither of which had ever existed in Carolina. In fact, the Anglican establishment and the requirement of a sworn oath of office deliberately purged Quakers from the assembly and county and precinct offices, contrary to proprietary constitutional practice from the colony's beginning. Historian Stephen Weeks characterized the coming rebellion as an "uprising of a free people against the attempt . . . to saddle on them a church establishment with which they had no sympathy."[55]

At the same time, long-simmering tension between young, burgeoning Bath County and politically dominant Albemarle County reached the boiling point. Bath County Indian traders and planters openly challenged the hegemony of Albemarle County's "old guard" of Anglican planter-merchants. In the assembly of twenty-six burgesses, six came from Bath County, two seats per precinct, with the remaining twenty from Albemarle County, five per precinct. The proprietors had injudiciously acquiesced to this gross inequity in representation maintained by the Albemarle-dominated assembly, which had ignored a petition requesting equal representation from Bath County residents on the Pamlico and Neuse.[56] The purposeful underrepresentation of Bath County combined with the controversy over church establishment to unite opposition from the two counties into a single bloc. Those opposing Albemarle's control comprised a "loose coalition of Quakers, disenchanted northern politicians, and southern inhabitants seeking a greater voice in the government."[57]

The regional realignment would evolve into two factions of the colony's political leaders. Their power struggle culminated in the Cary Rebellion and lasted through the end of the propriety. The Albemarle party represented the next generation of the "old guard" of founding settlers, who had controlled the province from the beginning and resisted any challenge, internal or external. The Albemarle colonists, whether Anglican or Quaker, were planters and merchants engaging in commercial agriculture—livestock, grains, provisions, tobacco, and, increasingly, naval stores—and concerned with their export-import connection to the Atlantic world.

In the Albemarle, Anglicans dominated Chowan and Currituck. Although now a minority, Quakers were concentrated in Perquimans and Pasquotank and with other dissenters could elect half of the Albemarle burgesses. Bath's six burgesses constituted the balance of power. An Albemarle Quaker alliance with Bath County men could politically control the province, protecting Quaker political and religious rights and furthering the economic aims of the Indian traders. Thus the stage was set for a regional political pattern for the first time in the colony's history—a pattern that would become more pronounced and continue through the colonial period.[58]

Bath County's economy was driven by the Indian fur trade centered on deerskins and also including naval forest products, agriculture, and livestock. There were few Quakers in the county, and the Anglican influence was minimal; the most active parish was St. Thomas in Bath. North Carolina's best inlet at Ocracoke offered egress to the new port towns of Bath and New Bern and the isolated port of Beaufort at Old Topsail Inlet. Under normal economic growth the new county was set to eclipse Albemarle, but the cataclysmic Indian war would change everything. Bath County's ambitious fur traders, allied with Albemarle Quakers now threatened by church establishment, presented a formidable political challenge to the older settlement.

Forced to sack Daniell, from whom he had expected so much, Sir Nathaniel turned to Colonel Thomas Cary, another confidante and wealthy merchant of Charles Town. Although a stepson of John Archdale, and therefore potentially more acceptable to North Carolina's Quakers and dissenters, Cary was a staunch Anglican, following his mother's faith. A decade earlier he had accompanied his stepfather to South Carolina when Archdale assumed the post of governor of Carolina. Cary's first government position, secretary of the council, was bestowed by Archdale. Cary subsequently received appointment as provincial treasurer and became wealthy as a merchant and ship owner. His position and association with Governors Johnson and Archdale made him a logical candidate to fill the vacancy left by Daniell's removal. Because of Cary's relationship to the esteemed Archdale, who was once again a proprietor, North Carolina's Quakers may have supposed that he would not enforce the test oath.[59]

After an uneventful voyage from Charles Town, Colonel Cary anticipated a warm reception as his sloop anchored off the Little River settlement, the de facto capital of the colony. Cary landed on 21 March 1705 and presented his commission as deputy governor to the council, which was entirely Anglican except for the venerable Quaker leader, Francis Tomes, who had occupied his seat for over twenty years. Taking his time to assess the situation, Cary did not immediately make changes in the government. When the eminent Quaker minister Thomas Story from Pennsylvania visited the colony, he conferred with Cary about "matters of government" and had the impression that Cary would give Quakers due consideration.[60]

Cary concluded that the Anglicans already held the majority of the governmental posts and would not be denied. Tomes and the Quaker burgesses in the assembly, who had expected Cary to support Quaker affirmation, were shocked by his announcement that he would require the test oath for all public officials. Tomes refused, and his forced resignation left an all-Anglican council, the first in decades. The most influential deputies were William Glover, Thomas Pollock, and Edward Moseley. When the assembly convened in November, Quakers were completely absent from the government. The Anglican majority passed laws that discriminated against dissenters, similar to those in South Carolina, which required officials to take the oath of allegiance to the queen and adhere to the Church of England. Additionally, Cary secured a law that imposed a five-pound fine on any assembly candidate who ran for office without first swearing the oath of allegiance. Believing that the government was securely in his hands, Cary settled down on the Pamlico River, purchasing a plantation just upstream from Bath near former governor Daniell.[61]

Always vigilant regarding their religious and political liberty, the Quakers and dissenters, stunned by Cary's unexpected stance for the Church of England, took the most promising course open to them—an appeal to the Quaker proprietor John Archdale. As their agent the Quakers chose the persuasive dissenter John Porter, whom they sent to England in 1706 to confer with the Lords. Porter, a planter and merchant from a Virginia Quaker family, had settled in Chowan Precinct by 1691. He had been attorney general and speaker of the assembly and had served on the General Court.[62] With the influential Archdale's support, at their March 1707 meeting the proprietors gave Porter everything he requested on behalf of the beleaguered Quakers. It had been over forty years since the original Lords Proprietors had granted the broadest religious liberty in America to the colony, and their successor proprietors had never intended that establishing the Church of England should compromise foundational principles and rights.

His extensive property and business interests recalled Cary to South Carolina in June 1706. While there he was elected to the assembly and became speaker.[63] In Cary's absence, William Glover, a devout Anglican, was named president of the council. He was described by the Reverend John Urmston as "sober, discreet, and the only man of parts in the Country."[64] Emigrating from Virginia in 1690, Glover was an attorney and planter of the Little River settlement who had accumulated extensive landholdings throughout the colony. He had been clerk of several courts, a judge of the General Court, and a member of the council since 1700.[65] The Reverend James Adams wrote that under Glover's "pious care" the church was "in a much better Condition." Glover's devotion is evident in his letters to the Bishop of London.[66]

Glover's major challenge was the recurring boundary dispute, complicated by Indian trouble. For a quarter century a tributary tribe of Virginia, the Meherrin, had lived in the ill-defined border area on a tract north of the Meherrin River with a buffer on the south side, used mainly for hunting and grazing. English encroachment on the apparently vacant buffer led to confrontations, and the English trespassers complained that the Meherrin were burning timber, killing stock, and damaging houses. North Carolina officials held that a hundred families were threatened by loss of property by "a few vagrant and Insolent Indians."[67]

By 1707 Edward Moseley was collecting depositions to support North Carolina's position in the border negotiations with Virginia. Fed up with repeated Meherrin incursions, in August Colonel Thomas Pollock led a sixty-man raid on the Meherrin town. For two days three dozen captured Indians were imprisoned in a fort where, denied food and water in extreme heat, they nearly died. Meanwhile, Pollock's vandals pulled down cabins, threatened to burn the cornfields and kill livestock, and forced the Meherrin to flee north of the river closer to Virginia's protection. After much discussion the boundary issue remained unsettled.[68]

Having satisfied his sponsors' wishes, Porter returned to North Carolina in October 1707 and presented the proprietary orders to the council. All commissions issued to Governor Johnson were voided, including Cary's as deputy governor. Porter had been entrusted with blank commissions for new council deputies, which he issued to himself and two Quaker leaders—John Hawkins and Gabriel Newby. Retaining their seats on the council were President Glover and Francis Foster, both Anglicans. Glover, considered a man of substance and moderation, seemed acceptable to the majority and was reelected president. Hearing the bad news from North Carolina, a chastened Cary immediately sailed back from Charles Town and was accepted on the council by early November.[69]

No longer a temporary president standing in for Cary, Glover was free to reveal his true colors. Like his Anglican predecessors, he required the new councilmen to take the oath of office, which the Quakers refused to do. Porter remained on the council but was now in a minority. Taking this opportunity to return to power, Cary formed an alliance with Porter and the Quakers, promising to allow affirmation. Since Porter still had more commissions, he reappointed the Quaker councilmen, and Cary was elected president.

For a time there were two presidents and two councils—Cary's and Glover's. With Cary, who was said to be "sett up by the Roguish Quakers," were Porter, the Quakers Newby and Hawkins, Francis Foster, Edward Moseley, and Landgrave Daniell when he was in the colony. The key members of Glover's all-Anglican council were Thomas Pollock and Samuel Swann. Through the spring and summer there were two armed factions facing off, just short of violence. The Reverend William Gordon reported that there were "Great confusions in . . . that poor Distracted Collony."[70]

Since neither party considered the other legal, there was a stalemate that led to "no Law, no Justice, Assembly or Courts," moaned Reverend Urmston, who called it "Olivers days come again." To a conservative Anglican, nothing could be worse than the chaos of the English Revolution and the Commonwealth of Oliver Cromwell. Urmston's low opinion was confirmed when he attended a vestry meeting in an ordinary "where Rum was the Chief of their buisness [*sic*]."[71]

Finally, an agreement was negotiated to allow an election for the assembly to settle the issue. Writs for the assembly election were issued by both presidents, Glover and Cary. In Chowan Precinct two slates were offered for the five seats. The Glover candidates received the most votes, but Edward Moseley and his followers were not satisfied. In a setting of strife and confusion, according to Thomas Pollock, Moseley maneuvered to have both slates declared elected.

On 11 October 1708 the assembly met at Little River, with nine from Chowan seeking the five available seats. Among them was Moseley. A pro-Cary majority dominated the assembly—a political faction of Quakers, dissenters, and Bath County burgesses. Moseley manipulated the election of the Cary delegates from Chowan, and when the assembly was organized, Moseley was elected speaker, to the chagrin of his opponent, Pollock. In Urmston's opinion, the assembly was "a Strange mixture of men of various opinions, and Inclinations," including Anglicans, Presbyterians, and Independents, but mostly "Anythingarians."[72]

John Porter then presented the commission from the Lords Proprietors that suspended two laws—the one passed in Cary's first administration that levied fines on candidates who refused to take the oath, and the law under Governor Daniell that required swearing an oath. In a quick vote the assembly approved the proprietary declaration.

The assembly's next task was to determine the legitimate executive of North Carolina. The two contenders and their councils were shown to separate rooms to await the outcome. Glover, facing the reality of defeat, lodged a strong protest in the "pretended assembly," denouncing the actions just taken. Not unexpectedly, the assembly rejected Glover's protest, stating that "they would not concern themselves" in the matter. The council and burgesses then qualified some members by oath and the Quakers by affirmation.[73] The result was a resounding triumph for Cary, who added Edward Moseley to his council in appreciation for his role in securing the victory.

In 1709 a cousin of Queen Anne, Edward Hyde, obtained the queen's support for a proprietary appointment as deputy governor of North Carolina. Of the Hydes of Norbury Manor in Cheshire, Edward attended Oxford but was plagued throughout his adult life by financial difficulties stemming from debt inherited from his grandfather. The proprietors hoped that with his royal connections, Hyde would be the answer to their perennially troublesome and rebellious colony of North Carolina. Hyde's commission would originate from provincial governor Sir Edward Tynte in Charles Town.

Chief executive during the Cary Rebellion and the
Tuscarora War, Edward Hyde held the post of council president and in 1712 became the first commissioned governor
of an independent North Carolina. Courtesy of
State Archives of North Carolina.

Receiving travel funds from the queen and permission to sail on a naval
vessel, the Hyde party of fifteen, including his wife Catherine, four children,
and nine servants, were warmly welcomed to Williamsburg, Virginia, by Governor Alexander Spotswood in August 1710. There Hyde was dismayed to learn
that Governor Tynte had recently died, and his commission would have to
wait for action from the proprietors. Although he could document the proprietors' intent, without an official commission Hyde had no legal standing.
North Carolina's recent political turmoil and Colonel Cary's election as acting
governor further weakened Hyde's position. In Virginia William Glover, the
exiled former governor, hastened to tell his side of the story and blacken Cary's
name. Hyde initially decided to remain in Virginia and await a commission
from the proprietors.[74]

In September Baron de Graffenried and his contingent of Swiss bound for

New Bern arrived in Virginia, where they were welcomed by Hyde, whom he had last seen in London. Hyde hoped that the baron, known to the queen and the proprietors, might heal the breach between Albemarle and Bath Counties, which after years of religious and political strife teetered on the brink of civil war. As landgrave and overlord of some 400 German Palatine and Swiss colonists, de Graffenried was perceived to hold the balance of power and would be courted by the contending factions.[75]

At the border town of Somerton, Virginia, a delegation of pacifist Quakers met the landgrave and urged him to accept the presidency and use his influence to bring peace to the colony. He graciously declined and pledged his support to Governor Hyde, stating that he himself had witnessed Hyde's appointment to his post by the Lords Proprietors and his confirmation by the queen. De Graffenried stated that uncertainty arising from Governor Tynte's death would soon be removed by the Lords. Recognizing the Neuse River colony as his first responsibility, he agreed to negotiate between the parties and would not provide military support for Hyde.[76]

As he traveled down the Chowan River, de Graffenried stopped at Pollock's plantation, where the council was in session. Eager to involve the landgrave, the council urged him to contact Cary. At their meeting in New Bern, Cary offered to supply provisions, cattle, and grain that the Lords Proprietors had promised for the Swiss settlement. In return Cary would accept Governor Hyde. Using his firsthand knowledge of the proprietors' action, de Graffenried persuaded Cary to recognize Hyde as acting governor immediately, and not to wait for the arrival of the proprietary commission. With this guarantee, Hyde, with his family and retinue, entered North Carolina from South Quay down the Chowan River. The Hydes selected a house on the plantation of William Duckenfield in Chowan Precinct near Salmon Creek, not far from Thomas Pollock.

De Graffenried put little faith in Cary's promise when he learned that Cary threatened retaliation against some of the planters in the county if they did not support him. Calling Cary "treacherous" and the "author of all our misfortunes," de Graffenried described him as acting from "temerity, faithlessness, avarice and lack of charity." The self-serving baron typically blamed someone else for his own shortcomings.[77]

Soon de Graffenried received a commission from Hyde as Colonel of Bath County, which could put him in conflict with Cary's rebels. Consistently placing the security of his own colonists first, the baron declined, replying that his neutrality was the best the governor could expect. The next message from Hyde was a summons to the assembly at Pollock's plantation. As a landgrave and councilman, de Graffenried felt obligated to risk the journey to the Chowan River to attend. There he found the beleaguered council had organized an armed guard to protect the government.[78]

On 22 January 1711 Hyde was elected president of the council, and Cary retired to his Pamlico River plantation near Bath. If Hyde had left Cary alone in a spirit of reconciliation, all might have been well; but it was not to be. Unfortunately, years of contention had deepened distrust and a desire for revenge. Returning from exile, Glover's supporters and the Anglicans beseeched Hyde to arrest Cary and his followers. On the day Hyde took office, the council was purged of his opponents by administration of the oath of allegiance, which forced out the two Quakers, Gabriel Newby and John Hawkins, and the pro-Quaker dissenter John Porter. Also ousted was Pollock's prominent rival, Edward Moseley, the former speaker of the assembly who had maneuvered Cary's return to office in 1708. The new council was entirely Anglican and loyal to Hyde—Pollock, Glover, Thomas Boyd, Nathaniel Chevin, Richard Sanderson, and de Graffenried.[79]

Now controlling the entire government, the steadfast Anglican Hyde and his council reorganized the courts and held elections for an assembly in March. Convening in March, the new Anglican-dominated assembly voided the acts of Cary's administration, passed a stronger vestry act, and had Cary and Porter arrested and impeached for high crimes and misdemeanors. While awaiting trial, the two men escaped, Porter to England and Cary to Bath County. Up to this point the "rebellion" had been a political power struggle over the questionable legality of the governor. Now, as colonel of the Bath County militia, Cary gathered an armed force of about forty soldiers, initiating the military phase of Cary's Rebellion. Joining him were trader and sloop owner and master Levi Truewhitt and three militia captains: Collingwood Ward, William Barrow, and Emmanuel Clare. From Albemarle came Edmund Porter, former provincial secretaries George Lumley and Nevil Lowe, and Quakers Emanuel Lowe and Gabriel Newby.[80]

To meet the challenge, in late May 1711 Governor Hyde mustered the militia and led 150 troops into the "disturbed Country" to arrest Colonel Cary and his rebels. Foolishly leaving his two cannon on the Roanoke River, Hyde marched overnight through the wilds to Cary's Pamlico River plantation, Hampton. Cary narrowly escaped downstream to Daniell's plantation near Bath, defending the house with cannon and forty men. When Hyde chose not to try the fortifications, his half-hearted foray ended in ignominious retreat. A young relative of the governor was accidentally killed—the rebellion's first casualty.[81]

Emboldened by his nearly bloodless victory, Cary declared the governor and the assembly illegal and began recruiting in earnest. De Graffenried scoffed at Cary's rebels, labeling them a rabble of "tramps and rioters" enticed by "plenty of good liquor, brandy and rum." Perhaps because of this enticement, Cary raised 300 troops. He received a boost from Richard Roach, a London merchant, who arrived with trade goods, cannon, small arms, powder, and shot, and

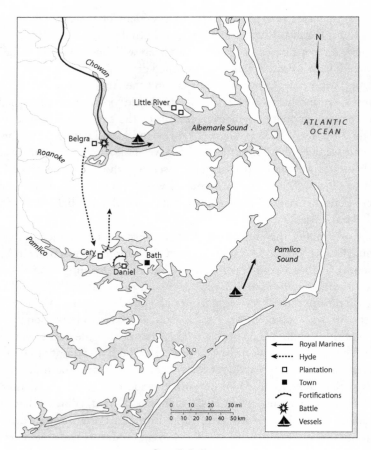

Cary Rebellion

chose to support the rebels. Ever biased, de Graffenried thought Roach "riotous and Turbulent" and a source of slander against Governor Hyde. Accompanied by his key officers, Roach and Colonel Emanuel Lowe, Cary armed Lowe's brigantine with six cannon and sixty to eighty men.[82]

Some Quakers had supported Cary, who pledged to preserve affirmation, in the political phase of the confrontation but left him when he resorted to military action. Although some recent scholars have accepted the prejudices of Anglican missionaries, Governor Spotswood, and the Hyde government, most Quakers did not violate their pacifist principles in either the Cary Rebellion or the Tuscarora War. The only verified exception was Lowe, Archdale's son-in-law, whom the yearly meeting tried and removed from their executive committee for his military participation in the rebellion, "contrary to our ways and principles." Urmston had earlier castigated Quakers, "my Irreconcileable Enemys," and after reconsideration he concluded, "I think several Quakers bore arms and . . . threaten to bring in the Indians upon us." The Anglican slander of Quakers stemmed from frustration over their neutrality and refusal to support the government in these conflicts.[83]

Fearing that events south of the border could spill over into Virginia, Governor Spotswood appointed John Clayton, an experienced attorney, for the delicate mission of mediating the growing confrontation. Clayton, known for "moderation and evenness of Temper," bore letters for both antagonists urging reconciliation.[84] At the council meeting on 26 June at Pollock's plantation, Belgra, Hyde received the mediation and truce offer with relief. The next day Clayton intercepted Cary's naval force, already in Albemarle Sound. Both parties initially agreed to meet, but the miscarriage of a message in bad weather, coupled with deep-seated suspicion, caused the breakdown of negotiations over a safe meeting place. The rebel fleet sailed to within five miles of Pollock's house, which Hyde perceived to be a blockade. Hyde was also alarmed by rumors that he would suffer the fate of Governor Daniel Parke on Antigua, who had been murdered the year before by a riotous mob.[85] Clayton now handed Spotswood's ultimatum to Cary. Spotswood sternly admonished the rebel to cease his "wild commotions" and declared that he would not allow Cary to imprison the legal governor by a "Plebeian" rout.[86]

Rejecting Spotswood's threat, on 29 June Cary weighed anchor and sailed toward Pollock's plantation. With Cary's fleet bearing down on him, Hyde dashed off a last plea for help to Spotswood, offering to pay, maintain, and transport any troops Spotswood could send. Now desperate, Hyde requested marines, who would "strike greater Terrour in the people." He promised sloops and canoes at South Quay to transport them down the Chowan River.[87]

Meanwhile, at first light on 30 June the Battle of Belgra opened with brief ineffective cannon fire from the brigantine, which was answered by a shore battery. The sixty-three loyal militia concealed themselves in the brush along the water's edge. As the rebels rowed toward the shore, they spotted de Graffenried's servant clothed in yellow livery. Believing themselves opposed by yellow-uniformed Swiss militia, long renowned for military prowess, the rebels lost heart. At that very moment of uncertainty, a lucky cannon shot from shore struck the mast of the brigantine, whereupon the rebels abandoned all notion of fighting, fled back to the vessel, and hastily sailed away. Pursued by the governor's force, the panicked rebels ran the brigantine near the shore and escaped into the swamp. Their vessel, the most powerful afloat in the colony, was easily boarded and captured, with all its armament.[88]

Prudently, the victorious Hyde declared amnesty for all the rebels except the leaders, including Cary, Roach, Lowe, and Porter, some of whom had fled to Virginia. Still possessing ample weapons, Roach retired to an island stronghold on the Pamlico River and called for other rebels to join him. Hyde sent an armed reconnaissance, which withdrew without attempting an assault. With rebellion renewing and expanding, de Graffenried and three others were dispatched to meet Governor Spotswood at the Virginia border.[89]

Although concerned about the situation in North Carolina, Spotswood told de Graffenried that since Hyde's claim to the governorship was not yet official, the Virginians were not ready to fight "against their brothers and neighbors." De Graffenried then asked if Spotswood, as "rear-admiral of the Virginia coast," could send a warship with royal troops, and Spotswood readily complied. The arrival of Captain Smith of the guardship HMS *Enterprize* with a sloop and contingent of royal marines ended the rebellion. Their commander declared before a session of the council and assembly that if all those in revolt against the government did not cease, they would face severe consequences. Shortly afterward, a letter arrived from the Lords Proprietors announcing the appointment of Hyde as governor of North Carolina, henceforth formally separating Carolina into two independent provinces and making Edward Hyde North Carolina's first governor. Cary, Truewhitt, Ward, Lumley, and Edmund Porter were arrested in Virginia and sent to London to face the Lords Proprietors. After desultory hearings dragged on for a year, the rebels were finally released on bail to return to North Carolina. By 1713 the colony was well past the rebellion and absorbed in the first stages of the devastating Tuscarora War.[90]

Over the course of 1711, Governor Hyde ended the rebellion raised by Thomas Cary, concluding several years of political strife brought on by the church establishment, unprecedented political oppression of dissenters, and the new Bath County that threatened the supremacy of Albemarle's entrenched power structure. The residue of mistrust lingered, exacerbated by two additional setbacks—a drought that decreased crop yields and a yellow fever epidemic that struck in 1711 and returned the following summer.

The Cary Rebellion was more than a confrontation about religion, although without the church establishment issue and the disenfranchisement of Quakers the growing political tension between the two counties would not have erupted into violence at that time. Beyond the church establishment controversy, the realigning of political conflicts from interest groups to a regional basis would have the greatest impact on the rest of the colonial period.

The upheaval within the white community was clearly visible to North Carolina's Native American inhabitants, who had long suffered abuses from their European neighbors and seized the opportunity to rid themselves of these interlopers. In September, not two months after Cary's defeat, a catastrophic Indian attack left the weakened and exhausted colonists reeling. Hyde valiantly endeavored to unite a bitterly divided populace unprepared for war, a war that left North Carolina's very existence in doubt. Rebellion, famine, plague, and a war for survival—any one of these would severely test a leader, and Hyde had to deal with them simultaneously.

CHAPTER THIRTEEN

The Tuscarora War

This hellish tragedy . . . [was] the grossest piece of villainy
that perhaps was ever heard of in English America.
—Christopher Gale, 1711

I N THE EARLY MORNING HOURS of 22 September 1711, 500 well-armed
Indian warriors in small "platoons," daubed with red, black, and white war
paint, fanned out across the North Carolina coastal plain along the Pamlico and Neuse Rivers and Core Sound. They came from many towns and
villages—Tuscarora, Core, Neuse, Bear River, Mattamuskeet, Wetock, and
Pamlico.[1] Their hearts burned with vengeance, kindled by years of insults, assaults, kidnappings, murders, and displacement from their ancient fields, villages, and hunting grounds. As dawn broke, the fiercely painted and feathered
men burst from the forest edges, screaming war cries, brandishing weapons,
and racing toward the houses, barns, and outbuildings of totally unsuspect-
ing settlers. Torched houses became funeral pyres for murdered families. Some
women and children were dragged away as hostages or slaves, but more often all
perished. Cattle, sheep, and oxen were slaughtered where they stood. Chickens
and geese were killed, to become the warriors' next meal. Their bloodlust slaked
for the moment, triumphant war parties filed off down the sandy tracks laden
with looted coins, weapons, axes, rum, clothing, and pots and pans as smoke
roiled up from flaming buildings and the stench of burning flesh blanketed the
farmsteads. So began North Carolina's great catastrophe, the Tuscarora War.

Only two years earlier John Lawson had written, "It is remarkable, That no
Place on the Continent of *America*, has seated an *English* colony as free from
Blood-shed, as *Carolina*."[2] While Lawson's *New Voyage to Carolina* is partly a
promotional tract, it was true that North Carolina had seen far less violence
between Native Americans and English than had many other colonies, notably
Virginia and New England. The Cape Fear and Chowan River Wars had occurred decades earlier, and recent troubles with small tidewater tribes had been
settled quickly and amicably. The irony of Lawson's observation is that he did

not foresee the coming holocaust, nor was he aware that his own actions as surveyor general would be a factor in arousing the Indians.

The roots of the Tuscarora War reach back into the first settlement of Bath County. The early years of frontier traders repeated the beginnings of Albemarle County, with fur buyers operating from small watercraft that plied Pamlico and Core Sounds and their tributaries. By the turn of the century, pioneers had acquired land on the Pamlico River and then moved south to the Neuse River and Core Sound. Storehouses were built, and plantations developed for raising cattle, hogs, sheep, and horses. Bath, the colony's first town, provided a port and commercial center just off the Pamlico River by 1705. Several hundred Palatines and Swiss led by Baron Christoph de Graffenried arrived five years later to found a town on the threshold of the Tuscarora Nation. Adapted to individual English traders and planters who provided needed and desired merchandise and weapons, the Natives viewed with apprehension this numerous tribe of Europeans who spoke strange tongues and seated their fortified settlement and outlying farms on their very doorstep.

The Tuscarora and their neighbors adopted English ways, learning to speak the language, often donning the clothing, keeping livestock, and establishing a mutually beneficial economic relationship that provided labor, game, deerskins, and furs to the colonists. At the outset relations were apparently as friendly as they had been in Albemarle for generations. A difference was that Albemarle was populated by dwindling small tribes, whereas Bath County had more viable tribes totaling several thousand people—Bay River, Mattamuskeet, Neuse, Pungo, Core, Pamlico, and the Tuscarora Confederacy, a loose alliance inhabiting the coastal plain from north of the Roanoke to south of the Neuse and westward. Dominant for more than two centuries in war, peace, diplomacy, and commerce, the Tuscarora brought goods from as far west as the Mississippi and north to the Great Lakes from their cousins, the powerful five-nation Iroquois Confederacy.

Native Americans had for generations warred among themselves, and the European colonists' insatiable appetite for furs, skins, and enslaved Indians generated more intertribal warfare. In the Indian conflicts, prisoners were part of the plunder: the victor could free, keep, trade, or sell them as he chose. Often, captive women and children had been incorporated into the victorious tribe by adoption or marriage. But a drastic change came in seventeenth-century Virginia and New England, where the major wars between Europeans and Indians were followed by wholesale exportation of enslaved Natives to other colonies. Indian towns across the southern frontier, even into Spanish Florida, were ravaged as warring tribes burned villages, killed the men, and took the women and children to the Charles Town slave markets, where they were deported to the West Indies and New England, never to be seen again.[3]

The Native peoples complained that the English kidnapped women and children, encroached on their territory, restricted hunting near plantations, confiscated game and arms from Native hunters, and failed to punish murderers of Indians.[4] John Lawson leveled harsh criticism on his fellow colonists who had led the Indians to the "Vice of Drunkenness" so as to "daily cheat them in every thing we sell." History supports his observation that practically every conflict had started over the "unjust Dealings of the Christians toward them." Lawson recognized that the "Indians are very revengeful, and never forget an Injury done, till they have received Satisfaction." Native Americans customarily followed a pattern of limited fighting, followed by parley, to negotiate "Satisfaction" for injury or insult.[5] Lawson noted the Europeans' contemptuous attitude toward the Natives, saying, "They are really better to us, than we are to them; they always give us Victuals at their Quarters, and take care we are arm'd against Hunger and Thirst: We . . . let them walk by our Doors Hungry, and do not often relieve them. We look upon them with Scorn and Disdain, and think them little better than Beasts."[6]

The weaknesses and unpreparedness of North Carolinians enabled such a crushing assault that the only result acceptable to the colonists was total war, leading to the Indians' near extermination. De Graffenried observed in hindsight that the English were negligent and careless about the potential Indian threat. The colonists had no forts, no magazines, and no plans for a coordinated defense, which seemed unnecessary in secure Albemarle.[7] Bath County, however, shared a frontier with a Native American nation that until recently had outnumbered Europeans in the colony.

Neither the North Carolinians nor the Tuscarora could speak with one voice; however, unable to bear their grievances any longer, King Hancock, the charismatic chief of Catechna, urged his people to war and forged a coalition with six southern tribes. The timing of the attack took advantage of the colony's bitter political rift that had culminated in Cary's Rebellion.[8] By 1713, acting governor Thomas Pollock concluded that "our own divisions . . . hath been the cause of all our troubles. For the Indians . . . seeing our own differences rise to such a height that we . . . were in armes each against the other, encouraged them to fall upon the county of Bath."[9] To the astute King Hancock, the English structure of a divided polity resembled his own. After five years of contention the two rival English counties, Albemarle and Bath, had finally resorted to open conflict. The Tuscarora society was equally split between the Upper Towns, owing allegiance to King Tom Blunt, and the Lower Towns, under King Hancock, but the Tuscarora had managed to keep the peace among themselves.

Having spent many months in the interior, on a fine day in mid-September 1711 Lawson invited his friend de Graffenried on a "pleasure trip" up the Neuse River. The dry summer meant extra-sweet muscadine grapes "for refreshing ourselves." Lawson hoped to locate a more direct route to Virginia, and he had long been eager to see the mountains. De Graffenried at first was apprehensive because the river traversed the heart of Tuscarora country, but he had paid well for the site of Chattoka Town, where his prospering New Bern now stood, and he was at peace with the tribe. As a precaution, the men hired two neighboring Indian guides, one of whom could speak English. Two of de Graffenried's enslaved Africans rowed the boat up the low and sluggish stream.[10] Good fortune had favored Lawson from the time he came to North Carolina, but it was about to desert him.

On the second day one of their guides happened upon the town of Catechna, the seat of King Hancock, which hosted a gathering of coastal tribes. The river party was promptly surrounded by warriors and taken to Catechna. Because the haughty de Graffenried was believed to be the colonial governor, the men were treated courteously. That evening the captives and interpreters were allowed into the council of elders, who were debating how to unify the tribes for the coming conflict and how to treat their prisoners. Lawson and de Graffenried truthfully answered that they were there to relax, gather grapes, and encourage trade and commerce. The debate took a dark turn for a time, focusing on English abuses, but the council finally decided to release them.[11]

In the morning Lawson began arguing with Core Tom, chief of the Core tribe, and the mood changed drastically. De Graffenried and Lawson were seized, their baggage was plundered, and in the council that followed they were condemned to death. On learning that their condemnation was over Lawson's quarrel with Core Tom, de Graffenried distanced himself from his companion. The elders escorted them to the "execution-ground," where the two men and one of the Africans were undressed, bound, and seated before a bonfire. The shaman began an ominous ritual, drawing white powder circles around them in the presence of an executioner, who grotesquely brandished a knife and an axe, while "a great mob . . . danced with frightful contortions." At a dramatic pause, four guns were fired, and drummers began to beat a small drum and sing a dirge.[12]

The Natives seemed "a set of Devils" to the terrified de Graffenried, who prayed for God's deliverance. Near sunset the council reconvened, and the baron made his last plea, threatening the vengeance of the "great and powerful Queen of England." The brother of King Taylor of Chattoka spoke on his behalf, and a messenger was sent for the opinion of the respected King Tom Blunt. Before daylight de Graffenried was led away to what he thought was

The Tuscarora trial of John Lawson, Baron von Graffenried, and an enslaved African as drawn by Graffenried. Courtesy of Burgerbibliothek, Bern, Switzerland.

certain death, Lawson's farewell ringing in his ears. To his surprise, the guide whispered that he was reprieved, but Lawson would die. The African was released and vanished into the darkness. Since de Graffenried did not witness Lawson's execution, he speculated that his throat was cut with his own razor. Christopher Gale took his cue from a fate Lawson himself had described—that of a prisoner being stuck with splinters of pine lightwood and set on fire, then forced to dance as a human torch until he perished.[13]

Revealing details of the massacre that he censored from his official report, Gale's personal letter of 2 November to his brother gave a searing account of the "butcheries," particularly the Indian predilection for bizarre mockery of Christian rituals. The father of the Nevil family was laid out on the floor on a clean pillow, his wife's headcloth on his head, his stockings turned over his shoes, and his body covered with new linen. His wife was propped against a chair in the chimney corner on her knees, with arms extended as if in prayer and her coats pulled over her head. Their son was laid out in the yard on a pillow with rosemary at his nose. Their enslaved African was found dead, with his right hand cut off. At the next house the husband's body was placed on his wife's grave. Women were stretched on floors with wooden stakes run up through their bodies. Pregnant women were found dead, their unborn infants ripped out and hung on trees. Gale concluded, "The blow was so hotly followed by the hellish crew, that we could not bury our dead; so that they were left for prey to dogs, and wolves, and vultures."[14]

The ghastly surprise attack temporarily paralyzed Bath County, totally overwhelming the county militia. Coordinated defense disintegrated to saving one's own family and farm. Those who survived the first attacks fled to fortified plantations, where armed men could fend off the raiding parties. More than a dozen strongpoints were hastily established along the rivers. Captain Farnifold Green wrote from the lower Neuse River in October, "We are forc'd to Keep garisons and watch and Gard, day and night."[15] From this beginning a minimal organized defense began to develop. Governor Hyde appointed one of the colony's most capable Indian fighters, Thomas Pollock, as major general of the militia. By mid-October Pollock had sent about 150 men to Bath, where they garrisoned the fort but refused to take the field.[16]

For six harrowing weeks de Graffenried remained a prisoner, constantly in fear for his life. To secure his release, he offered a ransom of clothing, powder, shot, and rum, as well as a personal treaty acceding to many of the tribes' demands, including neutrality in the war, no more taking of land, unrestricted Indian hunting, fair trade, and a fifteen-day truce for brokering a peace treaty. In the midst of this negotiation, a message came from Governor Spotswood of Virginia, demanding de Graffenried's release in the name of Queen Anne. Although the northern Tuscarora preferred compliance, the decision was deferred to King Hancock's council, and the baron remained a prisoner.[17]

Meanwhile, Captain William Brice, who commanded a garrison at his house near New Bern, led a militia reconnaissance of about sixty men, including some Palatines from New Bern, toward Catechna. Ambushed by a party of nearly 300 Indians, Brice's militia skirmished for three days before being forced to retreat. Fifteen Indians were killed and two captured, one of whom was later executed. The militia suffered one killed and several wounded. Having tasted this small victory, the Tuscarora released de Graffenried to make his way home alone. While Brice's troops were away from his fort, another war party seized the opportunity to assault his smaller garrison. Inside were nearly fifty Indian prisoners, among them nine warriors who rose against their guards but were overwhelmed and were "cut to pieces." The survivors, thirty-nine women and children, were enslaved.[18]

The gaunt, barely recognizable de Graffenried staggered home to find his town in dire straits, with little food or ammunition. Half of the settlers had left, and fifteen Palatine captives were being held for ransom. The community was appalled to learn that the terms of his treaty dictated neutrality. Sequestered among the Indians for a month, he was slow to grasp the depth of hatred aroused by the massacre. Neighboring English denounced him and attempted to kill the Native emissary under de Graffenried's protection. Nevertheless, although the treaty was signed under duress, he chose to honor it to protect his colony and effect the hostages' release. With considerable difficulty, the baron managed to convince the enemy that he had remained neutral.[19]

Captain Brice, considering de Graffenried a traitor, attempted to arrest him for trial by Governor Hyde. Informed of the plan, the baron waited at the New Bern stockade with the garrison on alert. Brice alone was allowed in to parley. De Graffenried accused him of sedition and enticing Palatine deserters. As landgrave and commander of the district, he threatened to arrest Brice if he caused further trouble and summarily sent him on his way. "So much incensed" against the Indians, Brice guaranteed the collapse of de Graffenried's truce by capturing some Bay River Indians and roasting their chief alive. After such perfidy there was no chance of an accord or obtaining the release of the Palatines. At a public sale the next spring the Bay River hostages were sold as slaves for ten pounds each and exported.[20]

Securing the northern flank was crucial to the colony's survival. Its future depended on the neutrality of highly respected King Tom Blunt of the northern Tuscarora, who had so far shown no desire to go to war. If Blunt had supported Hancock and struck the Albemarle with similar ferocity, the entire colony might have been abandoned or subject for years to Tuscarora control. Fortunately for the colonists, Blunt occupied a key position in the Tuscarora trade with Virginia and the Albemarle, and his influence with tributary tribes along the border was too lucrative to lose. Perhaps the crucial factor was that on Blunt's northern border lay Virginia, a powerful royal colony governed by Alexander Spotswood, a decisive soldier and master of frontier diplomacy who had ample force and would not hesitate to use it. Knowing that a Tuscarora attack on the Albemarle would sever his valuable trade ties and could swiftly bring down Virginia's wrath, Blunt wisely cast his lot with nonalignment.

Spotswood and the Virginia assembly did not rush aid to North Carolina, believing that the colony's desperation stemmed chiefly from their own incompetence. Virginia began by declaring an embargo on trade with the neighboring Tuscarora and other tribes. To keep the tributary Meherrin and Nottoway in line, Spotswood offered a parley with Upper Tuscarora chiefs at Nottoway Town on 22 October. At the summit the Virginia militia, 1,600 strong, was an overawing presence. The Tuscarora were given three options: become allies with Carolinians in the conflict, wage war alone against their brethren, or remain neutral. If they fought King Hancock, they would be rewarded for slain enemies and could dispose of captives as slaves. If neutrality was chosen, the colonists demanded two children of each town's headman as hostages. The

Tuscarora envoys left to confer with all towns, promising to meet the governor again on 20 November. Spotswood was encouraged that King Blunt had facilitated de Graffenried's release and relieved to hear that a South Carolina force was coming to rescue their fellow colony. But Virginia's negotiations remained unresolved. By February 1712, after South Carolina's several victories and with Blunt still on the sidelines, Hyde and his council declared that there would be no treaty with the Upper Towns until the hostile Tuscarora among them were turned over to the government. Hancock's Lower Towns were promised only annihilation.[21]

Following the September surprise attack, Major Christopher Gale of Bath County had been dispatched as Governor Hyde's special envoy to South Carolina to make a desperate plea for military support. Although politically controversial, as a fur trader Gale knew the backcountry, and the brunt of the assault had fallen on Gale's home precinct of Beaufort. Arriving in Charles Town on 21 October, he presented North Carolina's written memorial to Governor Robert Gibbes and the assembly. The formal report recounted the "calamities and miseries of so fine a country laid waste and desolate by the most barbarous enemies"—the Core and Tuscaroras. Between the Pamlico and Neuse Rivers 130 colonists had been killed in the first hours, horribly butchered, and many corpses desecrated. Homes were plundered and burned and crops destroyed, sometimes by Indians who "were esteemed as members of the several families."

Having a frontier exposed to powerful Indian neighbors, as well as the Spanish to the south, of necessity South Carolina had a better-organized militia, which customarily relied on Indian allies for the majority of their forces to battle an enemy.[22] Gale confirmed that North Carolina was unable to defend itself because the neighboring Indians could not be trusted but were "rather feared." He "implored" South Carolina to send as many of their tributary Indians as possible to wage war against 200 to 300 warriors, dangling the prize of 1,000 women and children as potential slaves. Further urgency emanated from the word that Senecas were en route to North Carolina to join the Tuscarora in the coming winter.[23]

Without hesitation the South Carolina assembly authorized £4,000 to send an expeditionary relief force of English and Indians to their beleaguered neighbors. A veteran Indian fighter, Colonel John Barnwell, was appointed to command the South Carolina contingent of mostly Native Americans.[24] Unfortunately, throughout the campaign Barnwell, described by a biographer as "a fiery-tempered Irishman," was volatile and irascible with his subordinates and casual about planning and logistics.[25]

Before Gale left Charles Town, he and Barnwell planned a joint punitive expedition into the heart of Tuscarora country. The South Carolinians and

Gale's militia would rendezvous that winter on the Neuse River and strike the Tuscarora from the rear. Bearing the news that relief was coming, Gale's sloop sailed north and simply vanished. He was waylaid by a French privateer, and months passed before he was released. North Carolina found his disappearance puzzling, as only rumors of South Carolina's decision reached them. Meanwhile, with the promise of bountiful plunder and numerous captives, Barnwell had raised an army of nearly a thousand Indians and several dozen English officers. In January 1712 he marched his army into the forest and was aghast when nearly half of his Indians deserted, perhaps discouraged by the winter campaign. He arrived on the Neuse in late January with 33 Englishmen and some 500 Indians, the most reliable being his own Yamassee company of about 150. The remainder of the Native forces represented tribes who had scores to settle with the Tuscarora—Catawba, Saura, Wateree, Winyaw, and Cape Fear.[26] At the Neuse River rendezvous Barnwell was stunned to find no one—neither Gale nor any North Carolina troops.

Still reeling from the shock of the massacre, the North Carolina assembly had approved little beyond an issue of £4,000 in bills of credit. The colony remained bitterly divided by the recent rebellion and political differences between Bath and Albemarle Counties. At this point only Bath County had suffered, while the more populous Albemarle was protected by the natural moats of Albemarle Sound and the Chowan River. Furthermore, the strong influence of Albemarle's pacifist Quakers discouraged any defense appropriations. Gale's capture had sidelined the one leader who might have rallied the assembly to action. In Virginia, Governor Spotswood was incredulous that the still-fractured colony seemed unable to "unite for common safety."[27]

Against overwhelming odds, Hyde's government managed to raise militia, gather field supplies, and keep communications open to Bath County. In February 500 bushels of corn were sent by water, the only safe supply route to Bath and New Bern. A small merchant fleet of impressed vessels operated at public expense, including a Virginia shallop and three sloops: *Core Sound Merchant* and de Graffenried's *Return* and *Dolphin*. To secure the supply line that summer, twenty men were deployed in two large canoes to patrol Pamlico and Core Sounds.[28]

Undaunted by the North Carolinians' failure to appear, Barnwell struck the western fringe of Tuscarora territory near the town of Torhunta in a thickly settled area of small villages. His approach had been scouted by the Natives, who had retired within nine hastily built forts. Barnwell threw a prolonged direct assault at Fort Narhantes, where his warriors and English officers broke through the outer walls but then faced two sturdy blockhouses. Over a half hour of desperate fighting, the Tuscarora defenders included not only men but also female archers. At the end, most of the men were "put to the sword," and the surviving remnant fled. Barnwell reported fifty-two Tuscarora dead, thirty prisoners, and considerable plunder, much of it goods stolen from the colonists. Although many of his Indians absconded with loot and prisoners, Barnwell, prone to hyperbole and braggadocio, reported to Governor Robert Gibbes that this opening battle enhanced the "honr & glory of virtuous South Carolina."[29]

Occupying a "fine Country full of provisions," Barnwell next targeted the notorious instigator of the war, King Hancock, who was reported to be in reach on Catechna Creek. A counterraid by Tuscarora from Kenta was quashed with the loss of nine enemy and the capture of two prisoners who were "burned alive" as a warning. Thwarted by the continuing desertion of his Native troops, reduced to fewer than 200, and burdened with 25 wounded, Barnwell turned east to collect reinforcements and supplies. After burning five nearby deserted villages, Barnwell withdrew his dwindling army toward Bath, which he reached on 9 February. The desperate town, cut off for over four months, was packed with nearly 300 refugees, mostly women and children, and short of food, clothing, and housing.[30] The refugees were overjoyed at their relief and reported that the Albemarle militia had descended on them in October, stayed briefly, and done little more than eat up provisions. Barnwell touted himself as "savior of Bath Town," claiming that his campaign would add "to the immortal Glory of South Carolina."[31]

Barnwell's success actually owed more to the loose political organization of the Tuscarora, their fragile and limited alliance to wage war, and the very nature of Indian warfare. His invasion route was largely through Tuscarora neutral country. Under questioning, the Torhunta captives revealed that they were unsure about the war's aims or even who their enemies were and may have been neutral. Muddling the scene even more were reports of treaty negotiations with Virginia. Blunt's northern Tuscarora belittled the campaign, saying that those killed at Torhunta were mostly old men and women, and the prisoners were children. In fact, Barnwell's unusual admission that ten women were killed indicates that not many warriors were present. His "immortal triumph," which earned him the sobriquet "Tuscarora Jack," had been a victory over largely Tuscarora noncombatants who were outnumbered ten to one.[32]

The war was five months old, and the plundered English goods may have come to Narhantes by trade. In fairness to Barnwell, Gale had indicted the entire Tuscarora nation, and not until he reached Bath did Barnwell learn that the Tuscarora were in fact divided, with many following the lead of Tom Blunt. Tragically, Barnwell's campaign had within a few weeks changed "a conflict of intermittent skirmishes and peace initiatives into a desperate war of survival."[33]

As a result of his "victory," during his remaining four months in North

Carolina Barnwell received more cooperation from local authorities. First, Governor Hyde's "catatonically inactive" government awoke and began to organize the colony's defenses. Some 200 militia were raised, provisions were sent to Bath, and magazines for powder and shot were authorized for the Neuse and Pamlico Rivers. Supplies and ammunition were distributed, although limited to seven rounds per man.[34]

After two weeks' recuperation in Bath, Barnwell marched toward Catechna in late February leading 242 men, including 70 new recruits from North Carolina. At the deserted town on Catechna Creek, they found a cache of corn and learned that Hancock had withdrawn to a strong fort upstream. Arriving at the fort on 5 March, Barnwell was dismayed to see a recently constructed formidable split-log palisade protected by a high earthen embankment with four circular bastions for enfilade fire. Obstructing the approaches were entanglements of tree branches and upright sharpened reeds and canes. Incorporating both European and Indian concepts of fortification, the fortress had been designed and constructed under the supervision of Harry, a runaway enslaved African from South Carolina. Exuding self-confidence, Barnwell directed a frontal assault. Shielded by bundles of sticks called fascines, the militia approached the walls. Under heavy musket fire and a rain of arrows, the North Carolinians were the first to break and run, some sustaining wounds "in their arses." Barnwell railed at their "base, cowardly" behavior.[35]

Cut off from reinforcement, Barnwell determined to take the fort, no matter the cost. The attack resumed but was abruptly halted by the screams of a tortured eight-year-old girl and threats to kill all the captives. The North Carolinians, unable to bear the agonies of their tormented neighbors and relatives, beseeched Barnwell to negotiate a ceasefire. Having only limited provisions and ammunition, he relented. The agreement stipulated the immediate release of twelve prisoners. Twelve days after Barnwell's withdrawal, another forty-six hostages would be released, twenty-four of them Africans. The expectation was that a formal peace treaty would be negotiated at that time.[36]

Barnwell's humiliated army retreated to New Bern, but the truce collapsed through noncompliance on both sides. When Barnwell fell ill, he sent the Swiss officer Colonel Franz Michel as his representative to the rendezvous, but no Tuscarora appeared.[37] Considering the ceasefire expired, Barnwell permitted a Yamassee raid on Core Town. Bolstered by de Graffenried's artillery, Barnwell returned to Fort Hancock, which had been strengthened during the truce with new walls and a dry moat. Establishing a base about seven miles from the Tuscarora stronghold, Barnwell had a triangular fortification, Fort Barnwell, built to protect his encampment and supplies. There he was relieved to welcome a reinforcement of seventy North Carolina militia and some Chowanoke Indians

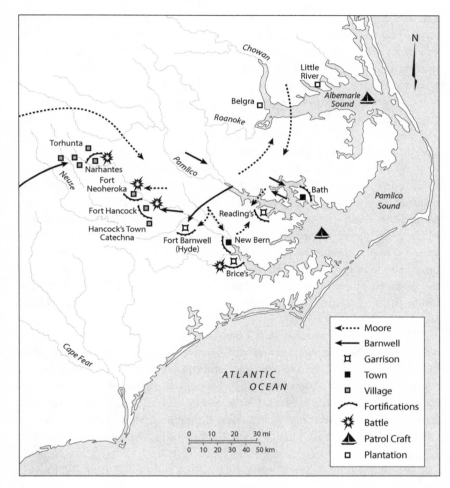

Tuscarora War

led by Colonel Thomas Boyd. Now with an army of 153 Europeans and 128 Yamassee and his artillery battery strengthened with two light three-pounder cannon from Governor Hyde, Barnwell was ready to resume the campaign.[38]

At Fort Hancock on 7 April, Barnwell deployed his troops and began a formal siege of the fort. Colonel Michel sited the battery, trenches were dug, and a diagonal was started toward the moat. Since his small cannon were unable to damage the palisade, Barnwell resorted to fire, having his troops pack combustible materials between the moat and wall, but the fort's green logs failed to ignite. Over the next ten days a series of sallies or raids from the fort were countered, with heavy casualties on both sides. As provisions dwindled, the army bordered on "extreme famine" and exhaustion. Although Barnwell had no way of knowing, the besieged Tuscarora were also near the breaking point. On hearing that Virginia traders had resupplied the Tuscarora with ammunition, Barnwell relented and called for a parley and ceasefire.[39]

The truce that Barnwell negotiated required the Tuscarora to free their European and African hostages and give up provisions and looted goods, horses, and deerskins. The Tuscarora agreed to hand over King Hancock, who had already escaped, as well as other leaders. As surety for the truce, three hostages were offered—two brothers of King Hancock and the brother of the Core chief. The fort was to be demolished and no others built. The Tuscarora were confined to the Neuse River valley and Contentnea Creek, giving up claims to territory south of the Neuse. In twenty days a conference with Governor Hyde would be convened to sign a general peace. All the Tuscarora got in return was that the remaining 160 Indians in the fort were allowed to depart unmolested, a promise that Barnwell kept. Among the captives returned was the enslaved Harry, whose brilliant defenses had thwarted Barnwell, costing him a victory. Incensed, Barnwell exacted revenge by summarily having Harry "cut to pieces."[40]

Whether anyone expected such a one-sided agreement to hold is unknown, but it did not. No one was satisfied with Barnwell's "sham" truce. The Tuscarora in Fort Hancock had been in extremity, and the unequal truce got them out of a jam. North Carolina's government had specifically directed Barnwell not to come to terms with the Indians, for the war's goal had become extermination. Barnwell's Indians were angry to discover little plunder left in the fort and the enemy prisoners set free. Having come on the promise of loot and slaves, they felt betrayed.[41]

The tenuous cooperation between the colonies evaporated. Barnwell himself was miffed by North Carolina's lack of appreciation for his service. He had lost respect for the colony's governor and other officials in February during their drunken revels at Bath celebrating Barnwell's first "victory." Governor Hyde had delayed army provisions, sequestered the site of Fort Barnwell, and not reimbursed Barnwell's campaign expenses. Before leaving in early June, Barnwell invited the Tuscarora and their allies to Fort Barnwell to receive a distribution of goods to seal the truce. Many came, and during the festivities the South Carolinians turned on their guests. In the melee some 50 visiting warriors were murdered and about 200 women and children were seized and shipped to Charles Town. Barnwell considered his action justified by the poor treatment he and his army had received after saving North Carolina. To de Graffenried, this black deed "blotted out" all the praiseworthy things Barnwell had done. Governor Spotswood branded the incident "Barnwells Treachery." While leading his army back to South Carolina in late June, Barnwell was accidentally wounded. Taken aboard a sloop at the Cape Fear River, he returned to a hero's welcome in Charles Town.[42]

In North Carolina at a council in May 1712 Hyde's proprietary commission as governor, dated 24 January, was proclaimed, and strong measures were taken to bolster the colony's defense. To entice the Upper Towns into the war, an agreement was confirmed to provide them six blankets for each head (scalp) of an enemy Indian, and the market price for women and children. Garrisons were established for two key posts: ten men for Lyonell Reading's house south of the Pamlico to protect the crossing, and an officer and thirty men for Fort Barnwell on the Neuse, temporarily renamed Fort Hyde.[43]

As expected, Barnwell's egregious betrayal of the truce brought retaliation from the Tuscarora and their allies, who raided Neuse and Pamlico settlements, killing settlers and enslaved Africans. The colony was again at war. In early June Governor Hyde sent agent James Foster to South Carolina to request a thousand Indians, "a good Commander of known courage" to replace Barnwell, and powder, shot, and flints. Within two months the South Carolina assembly once more agreed to aid their northern brethren, using unexpended funds from the original appropriation. The assembly also thanked Colonel Barnwell for his "great services" for the relief of North Carolina and awarded him sixty pounds.[44]

After nearly a year of war, through strenuous effort Hyde rallied his colony. In the called assembly of July a conscription act was passed subjecting all males aged sixteen to sixty to service and levying a five-pound fine on all who refused. Some readily accepted the fine or hired a substitute, but others, still embittered by the recent rebellion, left for Virginia. Both Quakers and non-Quakers refused to serve or to pay the fine.[45] Early in the war, in November 1711 Pasquotank Quaker Ephram Overman was disciplined by his meeting for joining the militia. Acknowledging his mistake, he apparently resigned from the militia.[46] At least two groups of draft resisters suffered legal consequences: in August 1713 the council ordered the precinct marshal to distrain property of eight men to cover fines for refusing militia service. Another group of eight, including some Quakers, were arrested after they mutinied when pressed to join a military expedition against the Indians.[47]

That summer Hyde sent Colonel Michel and a detachment of 150 militia to Fort Hyde, the exposed base that was also reinforced by South Carolinians Colonel Mackey and twenty Yamassee who had remained in Bath County. That same month Colonel Boyd led an attack against a large band of Indians, who dealt him a head wound and forced the colonists to retreat.[48] A frustrated Hyde vowed to take personal command at Bath to "end the war with honor or make such a peace as shall not reflect upon British glory."[49] But it was not to be. North Carolina had been beset for months by a yellow fever epidemic that struck down English and Natives alike. Days after his promise, the exhausted Hyde fell ill with the dreaded fever and succumbed on 8 September at his home on the Chowan River.[50]

Four days later Major General Thomas Pollock, commander of the province's militia, was elected president of the council and acting governor.[51] Pollock's first task was to reinforce and resupply the Fort Hyde garrison, which had lost nearly fifty men from desertion. By early October he had dispatched two sloops with over thirty men, provisions, guns, and ammunition. To ensure adequate rations for the army, by executive order no grain would be exported by land or sea. In Bath County the respected Farnifold Green was appointed as commissary general with authority to impress provisions and supplies.[52]

A native of Glasgow, Scotland, Pollock had settled in Chowan Precinct by 1683 and established himself as a merchant. He began a lifelong accumulation of property that by the eighteenth century made him the wealthiest landowner in the colony, as well as the largest holder of enslaved persons. After some false starts Pollock had succeeded with the full gamut of diversified exports—tobacco, beef, pork, furs, provisions, naval stores, and timber products. A ship owner, he regularly traded with Bermuda, Barbados, and other colonial ports. After 1689 Pollock married Martha Cullen West. The Pollocks had plantations in Chowan on both sides of the river, eventually establishing their main residence, Belgra, west of the river near Black Rock. Pollock strove to create at Belgra an element in the "early modern Atlantic plantation system," becoming more like the elites in other colonies where slavery was rapidly expanding.[53]

Pollock's public life began in the 1680s on the General Court, followed by a term in the assembly. He joined the opposition to the corrupt Governor Sothel, whom he arrested and jailed until trial. By 1693 Pollock was on the council, and with the exception of a few years during Cary's Rebellion, he served there for the rest of his life.[54] As an Anglican, Pollock was determined to strengthen the church establishment, although the war was his first priority. The Reverend Urmston described him as "a prudent, wise Gent. [who] hath labour'd heartily to preserve the Church and State."[55] Governor Pollock would be more effective than Hyde in organization, in negotiations with the Indians and Virginia, and in supporting the war effort.

In the fall Pollock sent an urgent plea to Governor Spotswood for men and supplies to meet the renewed Indian hostilities, but Virginians continued to view Carolinians as the author of their own woes. Nevertheless, Spotswood persuaded the assembly to allocate £1,000 for provisions and a similar amount for "duffle" for clothing. Spotswood apologized to Pollock for sending so little aid, but simultaneously he wrote to the Lords of Trade that "stupidity and Dissension" reigned in North Carolina.[56]

Pollock's effort to secure Virginia troops failed when he revealed that North Carolina could neither pay nor supply them. By the time Spotswood had arranged a face-to-face conference with Pollock near the border at South Quay, the South Carolinians were on the way. Choosing not to attend, Pollock sent two minor officials. Spotswood, miffed by such disrespect, declared that Pollock should mortgage Albemarle County to pay Virginia soldiers. By December Colonel James Moore and his expeditionary force had arrived from South Carolina, and the relieved Pollock ceased courting Virginia.[57]

Recognizing that North Carolina's survival depended on keeping the Upper Tuscarora out of the fray, Pollock negotiated with King Tom Blunt. So far Blunt had kept his towns uncommitted, resisting pressure from King Hancock to join him. Spotswood was equally concerned, for a war in the Albemarle could easily spill over the border. At the very least, it would unsettle Blunt's tributary Meherrin and Nottoway tribes, who were related to the Tuscarora. Complicating already delicate diplomacy were emissaries from the Iroquoian Five Nations in New York who were visiting their southern cousins in both colonies. Furthermore, northern Seneca warriors lurking on Virginia's western frontier waylaid a pack train, hijacking £1,000 worth of goods, powder, and shot that were then sold to King Hancock. With Pollock's encouragement, Spotswood reminded Blunt of his dependence on the Virginia trade and posted militia on the frontier to keep his tributary tribes in line and secure the border.[58]

The combination of Spotswood's actions and Pollock's diplomacy, along with the northern Iroquois' decision not to support Hancock, brought Blunt to a crossroads. With Moore's army on the way, Pollock saw a chance for victory if he could bring Blunt's followers into the war. In return for fighting the Lower Towns and capturing Hancock alive, Pollock offered a permanent peace treaty. For Blunt this opened a path to a secure future for his people. During a late fall joint hunt, Hancock was betrayed and turned over to Pollock, who had him summarily executed.

A preliminary treaty with North Carolina was signed by Pollock and by Blunt and other Tuscarora chiefs on 25 November 1712. Honoring the terms of the treaty, Blunt tipped the balance by joining the war on behalf of the colonists, attacking one Lower Town and turning in thirty scalps and prisoners. The province recognized Blunt as king of the Upper Tuscarora, eventually establishing a reservation for them, and the peace lasted a quarter century. Although Spotswood complained that he had been bypassed at the end, he welcomed the outcome.[59]

Barnwell's past heavy-handedness still galled North Carolinians, and their second appeal to South Carolina requested a different leader. The experienced Colonel James Moore, son of an earlier governor, was chosen to command the expedition. The Moores were prominent among the "Goose Creek Men" who dominated the colony's politics for decades. A native-born South Carolinian and future governor himself, James Moore built a notable reputation as a soldier in both Carolinas, fighting Indians on the Savannah River and in the Tuscarora and Yamassee Wars and rising to the rank of lieutenant general. In the latter conflict his adroit diplomacy secured Cherokee support that was critical to victory.[60]

Colonel Moore's contingent of about three dozen militia and nearly 900 Indians, mostly Cherokee and Catawba, arrived in early December. The ravaged Bath County's scant provisions forced Pollock and the council to grant them permission to cross the sound into untouched Albemarle County. There the relief force rapidly consumed all the stockpiled corn and meat, whereupon the horde of hungry Indians spread across the county, killing livestock and taking corn. Many of those plundered were Quakers, political opponents of Pollock.[61] Within a month the looting had so angered Albemarle citizens that they were ready to attack the South Carolinians instead of the Tuscarora. Desertion to avoid military service was rampant, with some fleeing to Virginia and others hiding under the "Masque of Quakerism." Pollock was exasperated but could not find a hundred men willing to campaign against the Tuscarora.[62]

Despite meager reinforcements, Colonel Moore concluded that he had enough men to take the Tuscarora fort, which would give them the plunder and captives his Native forces craved. On 17 January 1713, after weeks in Albemarle, Moore led his army south, crossing the sound and marching through the wilderness in deteriorating weather. The snow became so deep that he halted the march below the Pamlico River at Reading's Fort on Blount's Bay, resuming on 4 February.[63] From New Bern they proceeded up the Neuse to Fort Barnwell, the staging base for the attack. There Moore awaited additional supplies and ammunition from South Carolina.

Governor Pollock, recognizing the necessity of keeping the army well supplied, put the full force of government behind the effort. He and the council took the emergency step of authorizing a tax levy of five pounds, six bushels of corn, and a quarter of each tithable's wheat. For the first time, enough provisions began to accumulate to sustain a campaign.[64] A shipment of 2,200 bushels of corn was sent to the fort, and trade was embargoed until another 2,000 bushels of corn and 100 barrels of pork were stockpiled. By the end of March Pollock garnered another 800 bushels of corn and 32 barrels of meat, and Virginia sent the promised coarse woolen and heavy duffle cloth. In contrast to the previous campaign, now ammunition was plentiful. From South Carolina,

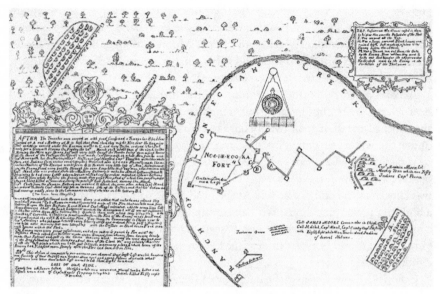

Colonel James Moore's successful seizure of the Tuscarora Fort Neoheroka is
documented by this contemporary map. Courtesy of State Archives of North
Carolina. Original in South Carolina Historical Society, Charleston.

Governor Charles Craven promised 500 pounds of powder to augment the 900
pounds already on hand.[65]

In late February Moore was ready to advance on Fort Neoheroka. The troops
marched on a well-worn forest trail with advance and rear guards and flankers
out to prevent ambush. Scouts confirmed that the Indians awaited them inside
the fort, which had been enlarged and strengthened since Barnwell's assault a
year earlier. Halting at the edge of the woods, the raw recruits apprehensively
faced an irregular hexagonal fort constructed of pine logs enclosing an acre
and a half, with high bastions anchoring each corner. The fort was situated in a
bend of Catechna (Contentnea) Creek, which protected three sides, requiring
a frontal attack from the east across a large open field. At the rear creek side,
the corner bastions were cleverly designed with blockhouses high enough to
fire across the front wall.[66]

Moore deployed his forces to surround the imposing fort. Closing the back
door on the west were the Cherokee camp and battery of 310 Indians and 10
English. On the east at the edge of the cleared field was Colonel Moore's headquarters with 88 whites and 400 Indians of "several nations." Officers included
South Carolinians Captain John Cantey and Captain Theophilus Hastings

and North Carolinians Colonel Michel, in charge of artillery, and Captain William Maule. North of headquarters was the entrenched Yamassee Battery, commanded by Colonel Mackey and James Moore's younger brother, Captain Maurice Moore, with ten militia and fifty Indian warriors. Facing the southeast corner was the protected Mulberry Battery.[67]

Accompanied by periodic cannon fire, the formal European siege opened on 1 March by beginning a zigzag trench from the Yamassee battery toward the short east wall. It took twenty days to excavate the trench and place a mine under the wall. The defenders fired muskets when in range and started their own flanking trench from the gate that they used to sally forth and attack the parallel as it approached the wall. The battered bastion closest to the parallel was chosen as the point of attack. At the head of the parallel Moore's force built a high triangular blockhouse with an elevated battery from which plunging fire could be directed over the wall. The Tuscarora had countered this threat by digging underground bunkers interconnected by tunnels to protect their women, children, and supplies.

Colonel Moore directed the battle from the advance battery on the parallel. He ordered a general storm for Friday morning, 20 March. The signal was to have been the explosion of the mine, but the damp powder produced little effect. Next, a trumpet sounded, and Captain Stone, leading the forlorn hope of a dozen English, ran the short distance to the ruined bastion. Following them came several captains, including young Moore, at the head of an English and Indian force. Within three hours the Carolinians were on the walls and in three bastions, facing "brisk" fire from the defenders. The fighting was so close that attackers and defenders were firing through the same loopholes.

At this point Colonel Moore released Captain Maule to attack the southeastern wall from Mulberry Battery. Misunderstanding his orders, Maule instead rushed the undamaged south wall, and his men were caught in a severe crossfire that inflicted heavy casualties. When the assault stalled, Moore committed Captain Cantey's unit, but it too was pinned down. Moore then concentrated artillery and musket covering fire on the bastions, allowing Maule and Cantey's men to retreat. The small lodgment near the gate was enlarged with spades so that more troops could be protected. Then a blockhouse next to the battery was set afire, and flames spread rapidly to the walls and other blockhouses. A recent study attributes the success of fire here, in contrast to Barnwell's earlier failure, to the age of the weathered fort. The Indian warriors inside the burning blockhouses refused to retire to the underground bunkers but kept firing until they perished.[68]

The provincial troops had breached the fort, and about half the walls and blockhouses were aflame or destroyed. The next two hellish days were spent clearing the tunnels and underground bunkers of their resolute defenders. Many of the crawling wounded Indians were slain as they struck at any enemy within reach. By mid–Sunday morning the last defenders were slaughtered in the covered trench that led to the creek, and the battle at last was over. Colonel Moore's terse message to President Pollock announced the victory and listed the cost in human lives.[69]

The Carolinians suffered terrible losses: 22 English killed and 35 wounded, and 35 Indians killed and 58 wounded. Maule's company sustained the most, with 12 killed and 15 wounded, or about 38 percent. Tuscarora losses were horrific: of the nearly 1,000 souls in the fort, almost all were killed, wounded, or captured. Nearly 400 perished in the fort: 200 were burned to death, and 192 scalps were taken. Another 166 were massacred outside the fort, perhaps as some attempted to escape. The 392 prisoners, mostly women and children, were taken to South Carolina, sold into slavery, and exported.[70]

Moore's ability and character won North Carolina's highest accolades. Governor Pollock could not praise him enough, especially to his fellow governors Spotswood and Craven. He wrote that Moore had behaved "nobly and gallantly" in the battle and was a "valiant, wise, and prudent commander." The commander had demonstrated "his indefatigableness in enduring the greatest fatigues, his conduct and courage at the siege and attacks were extraordinary, all which good qualities are set of[f] with so much modesty that makes them more resplendent, and renders him an extraordinary man."[71] The North Carolina troops under Captain Maule, having suffered the heaviest fire, were said to have performed "extraordinary well" and recovered the respect that their predecessors had lost the year before. There would not be another battle of this scale and intensity on North Carolina soil until Guilford Court House during the American Revolution and the late battles of the Civil War. Colonel Moore told Pollock, quite accurately, that it was "as hard a battle as was ever fought against Indians."[72]

Any doubts that King Blunt and the northern Tuscarora had about supporting the colony in the war would have been swept away by the shattering Tuscarora defeat at Fort Neoheroka. Within weeks negotiations were underway, and a peace treaty was signed in mid-May. Blunt's authority as king was extended to all of the Tuscarora south of the Pamlico River, where Indian land was to be carved out at the conclusion of hostilities. When the Yamassee War exposed the southern Tuscarora to potential attack, Blunt requested and North Carolina granted land north of the Roanoke River for resettlement. There the town of Resootska became his principal seat.[73]

Both the Indian and colonial settlements of Bath County, having suffered severely in the Tuscarora War, were left in shambles. Fortuitously, the new proprietary governor, the estimable Charles Eden, took the helm and brought stability, serving eight years, longer than any other governor of the period. Commissioned by the Lords Proprietors in July 1713, he arrived in Albemarle and qualified at a council meeting on 28 May 1714 at Little River.[74] Granted 1,000 acres by the proprietors, he first resided in Chowan on a plantation near Sandy Point and then purchased a plantation adjacent to Bath. Soon after entering the colony, he married the recently widowed Penelope Galland, who had two children, Penelope and John Galland. As a devout Anglican, he joined the vestries of St. Paul's (Chowan) and St. Thomas (Bath).[75]

Governor Eden and the council had to counter sporadic raids by renegade Indians and restore war-ravaged Bath County. Over several months, the council received petitions for maintenance of garrisons and patrols, direct relief for colonists, and resurveys necessitated after records had been burned during the conflict. In September 1714 the missionary John Urmston wrote, "The loss of Bath County if not the whol Government is threatned, to prevent which our honest Gouvernor was wholly bent. . . . We daily hear of families cutt of[f] and destroy'd."[76] The colony's treasury was depleted and the economy depressed. Following two successive bad harvests, by the winter of 1711 Urmston reported that famine stalked the colony, which had scarce pork and less than half the grain required for subsistence. His hope was that sloops from New York and Boston would soon bring desperately needed flour and provisions, even at inflated prices.[77]

Although New Bern and Bath had survived and were beginning to grow again, at war's end Bath still had only a dozen houses. To boost development on the Neuse, the destitute Palatines were allowed 400-acre plantations at one pound per 100 acres, with two years to pay.[78] The council and assembly continued to meet in Albemarle, but by choosing to live in Bath, Eden personally cast his lot where he was most needed.

IMPOVERISHED FRIENDLY INDIANS, who had sustained considerable losses, sought public restitution. To sustain them on their journey home, Hatteras escapees from "Enemy Indians" were given 16 bushels of corn, and Tom Blunt's Upper Tuscarora were granted 100 bushels. With such demands depleting the public corn reserve, the council ordered another temporary embargo on export of the grain. The Poteskeet later petitioned for protection of their hunting rights on Currituck Banks. Chowan king John Hoyter, reminding the council that his tribe had been in eight "expeditions" during the war, petitioned for resurvey of their reservation on Bennets Creek and Meherrin Neck and requested relief for losses of seventy-five hogs, a mare and colt, trampled corn, burned fences, and ravaged orchards. To facilitate a peace settlement with the still-hostile Core and Machapunga, the council sent Captain William Vaughn across Pamlico Sound with twenty bushels of corn to meet with Core leader John Pagett. When their peace talks were complete, in February 1715 the Indian tribes were permitted to settle on a reservation at Mattamuskeet.[79]

Notwithstanding the peace agreement, various truces, and the fatal blow that had been dealt to the Tuscarora, violence between the colonists and Indians did not end. Core Indians promptly violated their treaty, and renegade bands from other tribes in the Native alliance attacked isolated farmsteads and threatened settlements. To quell the raids, a group of rangers and Indians was mustered to patrol Bath County between the Pamlico and Neuse Rivers. Garrisons continued to be maintained at the homes of Brice, Reading, and James McCoy.[80]

Abruptly, on 15 April 1715 a Yamassee alliance of most of the Indian nations in the Southeast launched a murderous assault that plunged South Carolina into its own war for survival. Governor Charles Craven's plea for help brought an immediate response from North Carolina. Within a month Governor Eden raised three companies of militia from his own regiment to send south under Colonel Theophilus Hastings. In a move indicative of the fluidity of Indian alliances, a unit of militia and Tuscarora and Core Indians marched overland with Colonel Maurice Moore, who had settled in Perquimans. Moore's 1716 military and diplomatic expedition that brought the Cherokees into the war against hostile Creeks was acknowledged to have saved South Carolina.[81]

The fall session of the General Assembly at Little River addressed government reorganization with a comprehensive codification of the colony's laws. Under the practiced leadership of Speaker Edward Moseley "the ancient standing laws" were revised and ratified, beginning with six passed in 1670. The laws covered, among other things, government organization relating to the assembly, courts, militia, and public fees; church establishment, public morals, and liberty of conscience; and the economic matters of land patents, commodity fees, transportation, towns, and currency.[82]

The militia law was essentially a reenactment, but, faced with the major Yamassee War in South Carolina, the statute was enhanced to address the sometimes dysfunctional experiences in the recent Tuscarora War, the severest military test the colony ever experienced. Beyond the organization established in 1668 there were provisions regarding those exempt from service, benefits for soldiers maimed or killed in the line of duty, court-martial procedure and punishment for disobedience or mutiny, and ranks and pay, from private to colonel. All freemen between sixteen and sixty were obligated to serve, with exceptions in peacetime of Anglican ministers, physicians, and current and past appointed public officials and elected assemblymen. Fines for unexcused absences from muster were five shillings, and 2s.6d for lack of arms and equipment. In war-time, absentees were fined fifty shillings. Exemptions were suspended in war-time, with a ten-pound fine for absences. Soldiers suffering wounds or maiming were cured at public expense and given an enslaved African. If the soldier was killed, the wife and family received the African. Punishment for disobedience and mutiny were administered by the captain and varied from running the gauntlet to being tied neck and heels to riding the wooden horse. Desertion rated a court-martial by five officers who determined the punishment, excluding the death penalty.[83]

As late as 1718, Bath County was repeatedly raided by a remnant band of eight Tuscaroras supported by other Indians. Urmston reported in September that planters were deserting the county, and "Bath Town is unpeopled there is but two families the Governour and an ordinary." Four ranger units, each of ten whites and Indians, were formed to hunt down the renegades and patrol on the Neuse and Trent Rivers and Core Sound.[84]

By 4 November the council, meeting at Pollock's manor, were alarmed by a report from Secretary Knight in Bath that more Indians were menacing the town and had seized children, a servant, and an enslaved Indian of planter Thomas Worsely. The rangers launched a desperate hunt and recovered the boy, John Worsely. Unsatisfied after questioning the ranger messenger, the council asked that the boy be brought to testify before them.

Reconvening a week later at the courthouse on Mattacomack Creek, the council heard depositions and reports from militia captain John Worley that proved the "whole Affair a Villainous confedercy" of the Worsely children, servants, and the enslaved Pompey to deflect punishment for the latter's "for-mer Roguerys." The father and his daughter, Mary, were ordered to attend the council under £500 bond. The provost marshal was ordered to punish the son, John, with thirty-nine lashes. Servant Nathanel Ming received twenty-nine lashes, since he had revealed the conspiracy, and the hunt intensified for Pompey, "Dead or alive," who would be executed if found. The colony's interpreter, William Charlton, was dispatched to Tom Blunt's Tuscarora Town on the Roanoke River to report the conspiracy and offer Indians a reward for finding and apprehending Pompey. To calm the Pamlico residents, the rangers were kept in the field.[85]

Struggling to maintain themselves on the land their ancestors had inhabited for millennia, the Native Americans of North Carolina resisted, defeated, and sometimes destroyed the invaders that came by sea and land. They eradicated the Spanish outpost on the Catawba River and the English toehold on Roanoke Island—the two lost colonies—and drove away the Clarendon colony on the Cape Fear. For half a century the Indians confined English settlement to the northeastern corner, behind the Chowan River and Albemarle Sound. As the Indian population was depleted by disease, Europeans nearly reached parity with them by the early eighteenth century. Then the brutal war between the colonists and the Tuscarora alliance inflicted untold death and destruction on both sides and set the colony's growth back by several years. But the price exacted from the Lower Tuscaroras and their allies was near obliteration. Many migrated north to their Iroquois cousins, while those who remained retreated into the wilds of eastern North Carolina, where they eked out a marginal existence and faded from history until reemerging in modern times.

Did the Upper Towns fare any better under Tom Blunt's policy of neutrality and accommodation? Not really. In the short term, they did escape the fate of the Lower Towns, and they received a reservation on the Roanoke River. But their lands were gradually nibbled away by the adjacent English until they, too, chose migration to New York to join their relatives, leaving behind a few to join those in the forest who had preceded them. These became the ancestors of North Carolina's modern Tuscarora.

While the Indian conflicts' immediate effect on North Carolinians of European, African, and Native origins was horrific in the extreme, the course of the future state was set. A great region of North Carolina was now open to settlement, from the Cape Fear on the south to the Blue Ridge Mountains on the west. The smaller Siouan piedmont tribes, already decimated by disease, could not sustain themselves, leaving the country practically uninhabited, with the Catawba astride the border of the Carolinas and the Cherokee inhabiting the western mountains. By the mid-eighteenth century a wave of migration from northern colonies flowed into the backcountry, primarily along the Indian trading path that became known as the Great Wagon Road, and the future North Carolina began to take shape.

CHAPTER FOURTEEN

A Pirate Haven

The Bahamas and the Carolina Coast

North Carolina . . . has only been a Receptacle for
Pyrates Thieves and Vagabonds of all sorts.
—Thomas Lowndes, 1729

GOVERNOR CHARLES EDEN had inherited an economically distressed and politically divided colony that, while fragile, was well on its way to recovery. In March 1718 he gathered the council at the Chowan River plantation of General Thomas Pollock, who as acting governor had led the colony to victory in the Tuscarora War. Times had changed from the early days, when middling planters, Quakers, and other dissenters dominated the council. The men who sailed their periaugers to Pollock's landing were wealthy planters, some in trade, all Anglicans, and from as far away as Bath and Currituck. Pollock was the only resident of Chowan, but, drawn by the developing metropolis on Queen Anne's Creek, Governor Eden was anticipating a move to a plantation beside Pollock on the west side of the river.

This council of Governor Eden, Pollock, future governor William Reed, Chief Justice Tobias Knight, and Justice Richard Sanderson could hold their own with the Virginia and South Carolina elites.[1] The council business was routine, mostly deed registrations, lapsed grants, and new land grants. The after-dinner conversation over Madeira took a serious turn: continuing political tension, sporadic Indian raids, the perennial boundary spat with Virginia, and rumors of pirate sightings on the coast. Little did these men suspect that they were on the verge of a wave of pirate immigration.

Bearing northeast, the *Queen Anne's Revenge* ran before a freshening breeze. The notorious pirate Blackbeard leaned over his cabin table, surveying again the pile of gold and silver coins and bags of gold dust. With complete satisfaction, he relived his latest exploit: a weeklong blockade of Charles Town, South Carolina, that yielded nine prizes, over £1,500 in cash, and three dozen hostages who were ransomed for a valuable chest of medicines. He had followed his usual course of blustering intimidation, resolving the crisis without bloodshed.

Having left the Spanish Main in March 1718, Blackbeard had been at sea for months and needed to careen his ships for repairs and refitting. As he studied the chart of the North American coast, he knew the reputation of North Carolina's hazardous capes, sandbanks, and extensive shoals that jutted out to ensnare unwary vessels sailing too close to shore. He had formerly bypassed these dangers, as the colony offered little to attract his interest. The ports were few and small, and the trade carried by small craft was chiefly provisions, naval stores, furs, and tobacco. But now he sought a protected anchorage to ready his fleet for raids on the rich shipping lanes of the continent's Eastern Seaboard.

The Cape Fear River, the lair of his companion Captain Stede Bonnet, was an obvious choice that could accommodate sloops, but the poorly charted waters were dangerously shallow for his deep-draft flagship. His eyes were drawn to the hook of Cape Lookout and nearby Topsail Inlet, entrance to the harbor at Beaufort, an isolated fishing village. The sloops could safely navigate the inlet, and he trusted his seamanship to take the *Queen Anne's Revenge* through. Since both Carolinas had recently endured rebellions and devastating Indian wars, his commodities and cash would be welcome, especially in North Carolina, where demand and prices for goods were always high. Local officials could be casual about duties and trade regulations. What military force the governor had was facing the interior, where recalcitrant Indians still launched raids out of the tidewater swamps.

Secretly the wily captain pondered the sheer size of his flotilla—three sloops and the light frigate that altogether mounted nearly sixty guns, the most powerful fleet in the colonies that summer. With nearly 400 pirates and enslaved Africans aboard, there were too many hungry mouths and too many hands to claim their customary equal share of loot. If he could shed most of his crew, he could abscond with the bulk of the Charles Town treasure.

And so on a clear day in early June with a following wind and gentle swells, the pirate flotilla approached the south-facing inlet single file. The sloops passed the bar, entered the choppy inlet, and hove to in the road, awaiting the flagship. *Queen Anne's Revenge* neared the outer bar, the leadsman constantly sounding the depth. Suddenly there was a tremor, a slowing, and finally a shuddering halt that left some of the crew sprawled on the deck, sails backed, and yards swinging aimlessly. She was hard aground in the sand. Recovering quickly from the shock, Blackbeard ordered the sails clewed up, cannon shifted aft to take the weight off the bow, and a boat launched to drop a kedge anchor out behind the stern to prepare for warping the ship off the bar. He signaled *Adventure* to come out to help, but before she reached the *Queen* she too ran aground.

As the day waned, kedging efforts proved fruitless, both vessels were now hard fast, and strengthening wind brought heavier swells. Men and supplies were crowded into the small boats and ferried to the beach. There was not time over the next few days to remove the great guns, but smaller swivel or rail guns were taken ashore. Before the two derelicts broke apart, pirates and then impoverished villagers scoured the wrecks to recover anything useful. Battered over the course of the hurricane season, *Adventure* sank below the breakers. The *Queen* rolled onto her port side and capsized, also disappearing beneath the waves. Lashings parted, and the heavy cannon rolled across the tilting deck, shattered the bulwark, and came to rest on the sandy bottom. Over time the hull disintegrated, leaving a heap of ballast stones, anchors, and cannon among thousands of scattered artifacts.[2]

COVERED BY SHIFTING SANDS, the remains lay undisturbed for nearly three centuries. Meanwhile, the pirate tales grew into legends of Blackbeard, Stede Bonnet, and their cohorts until Blackbeard became a global icon of piracy ensconced in Carolina folklore. Modern fictional pirates became trivialized objects for children's entertainment, caricatures of the sociopathic outlaws of a distant age. As pirates were romanticized by novels, plays, and film, fact became so entangled with fiction that their stories would be unrecognizable to them, although they would certainly enjoy the fantastic embellishments.

Today scholars have peeled away the romantic veneer to expose the reality of pirate communities. The freebooters' democratic alternative was shocking to a society ruled by aristocrats. Pirates valued merit over birth, race, ethnicity, or religion.[3] While much evidence supports this view, we should never forget that the victims of piracy in the seventeenth and eighteenth centuries felt the same dread and terror that contemporary pirates elicit today. Far from consciously challenging the existing social and economic structure, pirates were desperate outcasts simply fending for themselves.

In the Middle Ages, burgeoning piracy provoked the custom of authorizing individuals to compensate the theft of a ship by taking as a prize a vessel from the perpetrator. Thus was born privateering. In wartime, privateers bearing licenses, letters of "marque and reprisal," preyed on enemy merchant vessels. At war's end, however, the privateer often chose piracy, prompting the observation by publisher Nathaniel Mist, using the pseudonym "Captain Charles Johnson," that *"Privateers in Time of War are a Nursery for Pyrates against a Peace."*[4] Monarchs largely turned a blind eye to the piratical activities of their erstwhile privateers as long as victims continued to be their former or likely future enemies.

Portugal was the first European country to venture out onto the Atlantic. Hugging the African coast en route to India, fifteenth-century Portuguese mariners traded for the riches of Africa, which included enslaved captives.

Spanish monarchs, envious of their neighbor's growing wealth and power, followed suit, sponsoring the voyages of Columbus west across the Atlantic toward the Orient. The unexpected discovery of the Caribbean islands and the American continents led within a generation to the conquest of two Native American empires, the Aztecs and the Incas, and an unimagined hoard of precious metals.

In 1494, through a papal settlement between Spain and Portugal, the entire Western Hemisphere, except Brazil, was declared the domain of Spain. The Spanish secured their claim to the region west of the treaty line by elaborate fortifications and a policy of "no peace beyond the line."[5] Galleons assembled in the storied ports of the Spanish Main were laden with gold, silver, gems, and commodities produced by enslaved Indians. The ships then rendezvoused in Havana for the voyage across the Atlantic to Seville. Funneled north by the Gulf Stream through the Florida Straits, convoys turned east near Bermuda and followed prevailing winds and currents across the Atlantic to the Azores and thence to Spain. From the Caribbean nearly to the Spanish coast, treasure *flotas* ran a gauntlet of attacks by English, French, and Dutch privateers and pirates.[6]

In the seventeenth century a new wave of sea wolves descended on Spanish commerce. Groups of dispossessed Europeans, chiefly French, and runaway enslaved Africans coalesced on islands throughout the Caribbean. Subsisting on pork and beef slow-cured on Arawak wooden *boucans*, these outcasts became known as buccaneers. A hard-bitten, hard-drinking lot surviving on the fringe of civilization, they supplemented their trade in cured meat and hides with small boat raids at sea.

The buccaneers' egalitarianism, an affront to their hierarchical age, resonates today. Those who freely chose to go on sea raids had an equal voice in decisions. They drew up and signed articles or rules of conduct that provided compensation for injury and the equal division of spoils. Captains were elected and could be deposed. Their rules forbade theft, assault, or murder within the group. Penalties for violations of the articles ranged from death to exile or marooning. The articles established a self-governing community based on the consent of the governed—a thoroughly modern idea, radical for their age. By the 1640s, describing themselves as "Brethren of the Coast," they had established a fortified base on Tortuga.[7]

Backwater Spanish Jamaica was captured by the English in 1655. Port Royal's commodious harbor was an ideal base for privateering and rapidly became the flamboyant and infamous buccaneer capital. A young Welshman, Henry Morgan, whose notoriety would rival that of Sir Francis Drake, was elected buccaneer commodore. His raids on the Spanish Main fueled Jamaica's economy for years as the spoils were squandered in the taverns, brothels, and gambling dens of Port Royal. Although deported to England for raiding during a truce, he returned in triumph with a knighthood and a commission as lieutenant governor to curb the lawlessness. By the time Morgan died in 1688, the Age of Buccaneers was nearly over.[8]

Spanish prayers for the destruction of the Sodom and Gomorrah of the Americas were answered on 7 June 1692 by a catastrophic earthquake that swallowed about one-third of the notorious city. The surviving buccaneers scattered throughout the islands, eventually finding a rendezvous in the Bahamas on New Providence Island.

Usually dated from the 1680s to 1725, the Golden Age of Piracy could more accurately be called the Golden Age of Privateering and Piracy. The culture of piracy in these years was far different from the buccaneers' lurid times, when Spain's transatlantic treasure fleets fostered violence overlain with international and religious factors. England and her allies fought major European wars to thwart the burning ambition of France's Louis XIV to dominate the continent. These conflicts—King William's War (1688–97), Queen Anne's War (1702–13), and the War of the Quadruple Alliance (1718–20)—spilled over to North American and Caribbean colonies.[9] Hostilities at sea among key maritime states—England, Holland, France, and Spain—were fought in the North Atlantic primarily by their privateers, many of whom became pirates during the brief interludes. Regardless of their country of origin, the sailors of these times had known war for most of their lives. During Queen Anne's War the Bahamian customs collector wrote, "War is no sooner ended but the West Indies always swarm with pirates."[10]

The Golden Age peaked in the decade following Queen Anne's War, when tens of thousands of sailors were released or furloughed and hundreds of privateer vessels were suddenly idled. Having experienced the hunt, chase, and seizure of prizes and the chance for instant wealth, few sea rovers willingly returned to the dreary life of low-paid merchantmen. All too easily they slipped into piracy, knowing that if they preyed on the shipping of former enemies there would be few if any consequences, although most succumbed to taking British prizes as well. To *great Numbers of Seamen turn'd adrift at the Conclusion of a War,* the allure of quick wealth outweighed even the risk of dying on the gallows.[11] Furthermore, guarding the entire Caribbean and North American coast in 1717 were a paltry nine frigates and two sloops stationed at Port Royal, Barbados, the Leeward Islands, Virginia, New York, and New England.[12] The odds were that few pirates would be caught.

In this era, privateers and pirates preyed on lumbering merchant ships in lightly armed, nimble sloops and brigs that could outrun better-armed naval vessels. Since their interests were served by seizure rather than destruction of a prize, no seaborne predator sought combat in which cannon fire could damage both the hunter and the hunted. Instead, the privateer and his alter ego, the pirate, usually captured prizes by firing a shot across the bow and by boarding and hand-to-hand combat if necessary, using their cannon chiefly to threaten or cripple their prey. A privateer sailed his prize to a port with an admiralty court, where the vessel and cargo were condemned and sold. The owners and crew then divided the profits. London was the seat of the admiralty, but after 1662 vice-admiralty courts were authorized overseas. The first colonial court was in Jamaica, the privateering center of the Caribbean. During Queen Anne's War in 1708 Parliament abolished the government's share, making privateering even more profitable.[13]

Called "desperate Rogues," most of the several thousand pirates active in the Atlantic were from Britain, the West Indies, and the mainland colonies, with a smattering of Dutch, Spanish, and Portuguese. Nearly all were single men with few family ties, either former privateers, volunteers from captured merchant vessels, or discharged sailors from the navy. There were a number of Africans, many doing hard and menial tasks as enslaved laborers, but others as full-fledged pirates. The conditions of life aboard ship were better than on merchant or naval vessels: access to rum and wine was limitless; they were free of harsh discipline and the detested flogging; and the chances were good that they would share booty.[14]

Following in the wake of the buccaneers, the pirates' "little Commonwealth"[15] has been described as "a rough, improvised, but effective egalitarianism that placed authority in the collective hands of the crew."[16] A majority elected the officers and decided the direction of a cruise or whether to attack a prize. Pirate captains were chosen for seamanship and command presence, and unsuccessful ones could be removed by a vote of no confidence. It was unimaginable to a naval or merchant captain that a ship could be controlled by democratic process, but pirates proved it possible. "Captain Johnson" noted that "All good Governments had . . . the supream Power lodged with the Community."[17]

Settled in the mid-seventeenth century by Bermudans, the Bahamas had always been an out-of-the-way archipelago that attracted runaways and the lawless. As early as 1667 Lord Ashley expressed interest in the Bahamas, and three years later leaders of the New Providence settlement asked the proprietors to acquire the islands. On 1 November 1670 six of the eight Lords Proprietors of Carolina received a charter to the Bahama Islands. The Bahamian proprietors were the instigator Lord Ashley, soon to become the Earl of Shaftesbury; Christopher, the second Duke of Albemarle; the Earl of Craven; Lord John Berkeley; Sir George Carteret; and Sir Peter Colleton.[18] John Wentworth, an experienced sea captain and privateer, became the first serving governor. A 1671 census listed a total of 1,097 inhabitants, living mostly on New Providence with a small settlement on Eleuthera. Enslaved persons made up 40 percent of the population.[19]

Located off main trade routes only a few days' sail from Cuba, the sparsely settled Bahama Islands lived under constant threat of raids and invasion by their Spanish archenemies. The maritime economy was based on trade with Carolina and Bermuda, fishing, and wreck salvage, supplemented by subsistence agriculture. On discovering that these were largely uninhabitable islands with thin soil and little water, the proprietors ceased investing their time or money. The result was weak government and political unrest. When England was at war with France and Spain, New Providence was sacked in 1684, then twice more during Queen Anne's War.[20]

The nearly 700 Bahama cays and islands made an ideal pirate habitat, with countless hidden coves where vessels could be careened and repaired. Commerce, including the Spanish treasure *flotas*, passed close by through the Florida Straits. An energetic proprietary governor, Sir Nicholas Trott, arrived in 1694 and rebuilt the settlement on New Providence, naming it Nassau.[21] Within two years Nassau had become a common retreat for pirates and smugglers, and Trott was described as "the greatest pirate-broker that ever was in America."[22] Ironically, his nephew and namesake would be instrumental in eradicating piracy from South Carolina twenty years later.

When Queen Anne's War ended in 1713, many unemployed privateers and former navy men gravitated to Nassau.[23] Spanish privateers operating out of Cuba ignored the war's end, eliciting retaliation from their British counterparts in Jamaica and Nassau. With the nations officially at peace, all were committing piracy. Merchants of all nationalities lodged complaints with their governments, but with limited naval forces, the colonial governors could do little to stem the lawlessness.[24]

In July 1715 the annual Spanish *flota* bearing millions in gold and silver pieces-of-eight foundered in a massive hurricane that drowned a thousand men and drove ten of eleven ships onto the Florida sands south of Saint Augustine. News of the bonanza raced throughout the Caribbean, north to the mainland colonies, and across the Atlantic, attracting soldiers, divers, and fortune-hunters, all attempting to recover the treasure. After removing much of the gold, the Spanish left 300,000 silver pieces-of-eight under guard. Soon five ships and sloops bearing some 300 men under Captain Henry Jennings swept down on the site, scattering the outnumbered Spanish detachment, which left the silver to Jennings. His triumphant return to Port Royal spurred a long debauch with rum, whores, and gambling, reminiscent of the buccaneer era, until Spanish diplomatic protests forced the thieves to relocate hastily to Nassau.[25]

Over 2,000 pirates, mostly British but including Spanish, French, and Dutch brigands, ranged from British North America to the Spanish Main and the Leeward Islands. About half were based at Nassau, organized by Captains Jennings and Benjamin Hornigold. Several pirate "commodores" amassed flotillas around frigates with lightly armed consort sloops. It was said that the pirates took more prizes in a few years than had all the European navies in the decade-long Queen Anne's War.[26] Joining the pirate rendezvous were logwood cutters ousted by the Spanish from the bays of Campeche and Honduras. Described as a "rude, drunken crew," many of the cutters were former sailors, privateers, and sometime pirates.[27]

The Crown viewed the chaotic conditions in Nassau as a dire threat to commerce that the proprietors appeared unable to address. Meanwhile, a famed privateer and mariner who had circumnavigated the globe, Captain Woodes Rogers, had formed a company of merchants to develop the Bahamas. Rogers approached both the British government and the Lords Proprietors. Under official pressure, the proprietors surrendered their governance rights and leased to Rogers's company the rents and royalties to the islands. Commissioned the first royal governor of the Bahamas in 1718, Rogers arrived in late July with troops and naval vessels. He was accompanied by Chief Justice Christopher Gale, who had held the same post in North Carolina.[28] Rogers brought a royal pardon for crimes committed before 5 January 1718—the Act of Grace—for those who would surrender by 5 September 1718, with generous rewards offered for the capture of pirates who did not. Preceding Rogers in February, Captain Vincent Pearse from Boston granted pardon to 209 pirates, some of whom reneged. Rogers reported that 300 surrendered in July. Well over 400 Nassau pirates took the pardon, including Hornigold and Jennings, who agreed to become pirate hunters.[29] To fulfill the purpose of the pardon, which was to retire the pirates, Rogers apparently ignored the deadline for absolution of past crimes.

Blackbeard and Stede Bonnet were already at sea, and the infamous Charles Vane sailed into the night before Rogers landed. Still-active pirates ranged along the Eastern Seaboard from the Carolinas to New England, preying on the shipping of Charles Town, Chesapeake Bay, Philadelphia, New York, and Boston. A who's who of pirates skirted North Carolina's coast. Most prominent were Blackbeard, Bonnet, Vane, Samuel Bellamy, Christopher Moody, Richard Worley, Calico Jack Rackham, Mary Read, and Anne Bonney.

For years freebooters had been drawn to North and South Carolina, which lay on the northwest flank of the Spanish treasure route. The Carolinas offered all the characteristics a pirate could wish—countless hiding places, war-torn societies, and weak and compliant governments divided by recent rebellions. Such a setting attracted both privateers and pirates for recreation, rest, and refitting. As early as 1684 Carolina's unsavory reputation for "harbouring and encouraging of Pirates" led the Privy Council to instruct the provincial assembly to pass an act suppressing piracy. A 1707 act to encourage settlement in North Carolina described the colony's desolate coast as a place where "Pyrates in time of Peace have hitherto made use of the Harbours therein to careen and fitt their vessels and also to Wood and Water to the great annoyance of her Majties Subjects trading along the Coast."[30]

"Consorting with pirates" was a common reproach levied against governors and officials in both colonies, but particularly South Carolina, where Charles Town was easily accessible to the Bahamas. Local merchants, chandlers, and innkeepers asked no questions but welcomed the ready cash that mariners wantonly spent for creature comforts, entertainment, and ships' provisions—cordage, sails, and fittings. Pirates brought necessities and luxuries at affordable prices, and privateers could take their prizes to the vice-admiralty courts.[31] North Carolina's obscure and treacherous inlets and remote offshore islands could easily conceal a pirate base between the busy commercial ports of Chesapeake Bay and Charles Town. When customs surveyor general Edward Randolph reported that Carolina was a refuge for "Pirates, Runaways, and Illegal Traders," the Board of Trade admonished the Lords Proprietors in 1701 that their colony was "too ordinary a Receptacle of Pyrats."[32]

In early 1718, displaced Caribbean pirates resorted to North Carolina's shores, where they found small settlements adjacent to colonial trade routes but not easily accessed from the sea. Tucked away behind barrier islands were fledgling ports where customs officials might well accommodate local merchants' and planters' needs for new trade opportunities. Governor Charles Eden was dealing with the aftermath of a double catastrophe—a rebellion that had reshaped society, eclipsed by the most destructive Indian war in the colony's history. Since the colony's military resources, the militia rangers, were protecting frontier farms and families, a band of pirates might be welcomed for even more than ready cash and cheap trade goods. As experienced men-at-arms, pirates—if they reformed and settled down in the community—could be invaluable defenders. The open question of whether they truly had retired was a source of tension, but only time would reveal the course they had laid.

North Carolina in 1718 was two colonies. The long-settled Albemarle had well-established political, judicial, religious, and economic institutions barely touched by rebellion and Indian war. South of the sound, Bath County's poor precincts struggled to recover from war and political fracture. Here pirates found acceptance, especially from war widows and orphans, and many settled down to become residents. For the unrepentant pirate, it would be easy enough to return to commerce raiding.

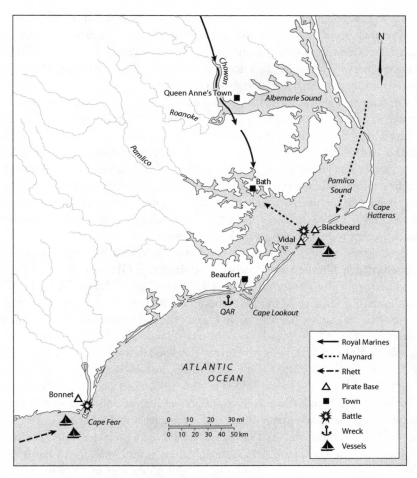

Pirates in North Carolina

Nevertheless, the pirates had to exercise restraint. There was little to fear from local authorities, although it was prudent not to antagonize their new neighbors, but taking too many prizes off the Virginia capes or Charles Town would bring retribution. Royal naval vessels were stationed in the Chesapeake, and Virginia's governor, Alexander Spotswood, was a career military man. South Carolina, like its northern sister, had recently suffered its own political conflict and devastating Indian war. In Charles Town, protected from swash-bucklers and from French and Spanish privateers by earthen and masonry walls mounting over eighty guns, pirates were no longer welcome.[33] But North Carolina, particularly Bath County, did not have the luxury of spurning a band of casual, free-spending, armed men who pumped some life into the moribund economy and might very well, if needed, defend the colony if terror once again arose from surrounding forests and swamps.

Of the many pirate captains who sailed by North Carolina, only two are known to have engaged in piracy from the colony—Stede Bonnet and Edward Thache, alias Blackbeard. Although commonly known today as Edward Teach, on the North Carolina coast in 1718 he was Edward Thache, usually spelled Thatch. He was literate, an experienced mariner, and a charismatic leader, but his origins remained a mystery for nearly three centuries. Tantalizing hints suggested that he may have been from Bristol, and a Jamaican correspondent mentioned that Thache came from "very creditable Parents," and his mother and a brother were living there in the early eighteenth century.[34]

Recent research in Jamaican public and parish records has established that the respectable Thache family probably originated in Gloustershire near Bristol. The son of the Reverend Thomas Thache, Captain Edward Thache Sr., immigrated to Jamaica in the 1690s, became a planter, and settled in Spanish Town with his family. After his wife Elizabeth died in 1699, he soon married Lucretia Axtell of Jamaica, who bore him two sons and a daughter. His son by Elizabeth, Edward Thache Jr., the future Blackbeard, went to sea on merchant vessels. In April 1706, along with four others, he was impressed near Isle of Wight into HMS *Windsor* and rated an able-bodied seaman. That December *Windsor* was at Jamaica, where Edward settled his recently deceased father's estate. After nearly seventeen months of service he was discharged in August 1707.[35] During Queen Anne's War he was said to be a privateer noted for "uncommon Boldness and personal Courage," sailing from Jamaica with Benjamin Hornigold. The earliest record of Thache the pirate was in December 1716, when Hornigold and Thache, then commanding an eight-gun sloop, plundered the brigantine *Lamb* off Hispaniola sometime after they both turned pirate and moved to Nassau.[36] Together they raided the North American coast in the spring of 1717, looting vessels from the Carolinas to Delaware Bay.

Without doubt, Major Stede Bonnet was the strangest pirate of them all. Unlike his peers from the underclass of unemployed mariners and former privateers, he was a third-generation Barbadian planter and a militia officer— "a Gentleman of good Reputation." He had never been to sea. He hired his crew and purchased his sloop instead of stealing it. Why would he abandon his high-status and growing family? Was he suffering a midlife crisis, an unhappy marriage, "a Disorder of the Mind"?[37] No one knows. Whatever the cause, he

The pirate Stede Bonnet of Barbados used the Cape Fear
River as a refuge for refitting in 1718. Courtesy of State
Archives of North Carolina (Library of Congress).

sailed from Bridgetown in his rakish ten-gun sloop *Revenge*, forsaking his
young family and his native island forever.

On his first cruise in 1717 Bonnet took eight prizes off Chesapeake Bay, New
York, and Charles Town, looting them for supplies, enslaved captives, rum, and
sugar. After months at sea, Bonnet headed for the secluded Cape Fear River to
careen and overhaul *Revenge*. In September he set a course to Nassau but was
waylaid by a Spanish man-of-war. Narrowly escaping, Bonnet was wounded,
Revenge was damaged, and the crew suffered heavy casualties. While in Nassau,
the recovering Bonnet was drawn to Thache, who had a similar background
but had the sea experience that Bonnet lacked. As owner of *Revenge*, Bonnet selected Thache to command his sloop, now armed with a dozen guns.
On another mainland foray as far north as Delaware Bay, they reaped eleven
prizes. In October a Captain Codd reported being stopped by a "Pirate Sloop

called the Revenge" with 150 crew commanded by Thache. On board, the still-recuperating Major Bonnet walked "about in his Morning Gown and then to his Books."[38]

From North America the pirate duo stopped over in Nassau to pick up Thache's eight-gun sloop, and Bonnet resumed command of *Revenge*. Cruising near Martinique in late November, they encountered a French slaver, *La Concorde*, carrying cocoa, copper, some 500 enslaved Africans, and over twenty pounds of gold dust. Although the Frenchman was well armed, scurvy and "the bloody flux" had ravaged most of the crew and many of the enslaved, taking seventy-one lives and rendering the crew barely able to work the vessel. Thache took command and sailed the prize to Bequia in the Grenadines, where they plundered the cargo, took 125 Africans, and put the remainder ashore with the French crew, with whom they left a sloop and provisions. Among the crew forced to join the pirates were three surgeons, a cook, and a Black trumpeter. Thache christened his prize *Queen Anne's Revenge* and increased its armament to forty carriage and rail guns, making it one of the most powerful armed ships in the hemisphere.[39]

Over the next year, Thache, assuming the persona of Blackbeard, cruised the Caribbean and the North American coast, establishing his reputation as "the fiercest pirate of them all." A tall and charismatic presence with his uncommon full beard, according to Johnson he created a fearsome image of "the Devil incarnate" by boarding his prey embellished with multiple weapons and trailing smoke from burning fuses in his beard and hair.[40] With Bonnet's *Revenge* as consort, the pirates cut a swath across the Caribbean that launched them toward lasting fame. The naval commander in Barbados reported the collusion of Blackbeard and Bonnet by identifying two craft sailing in the area as "a Pyrate Ship of 36 Guns and 250 men, and a Sloop of 10 Guns and a 100 men."[41]

After a winter layover in Nassau, the two sailed separately toward the Spanish Main. Hampered by his poor seamanship and lack of discipline, Bonnet was defeated by the well-armed merchant vessel *Protestant Caesar* of Boston in an intense three-hour nighttime battle. The tattered *Revenge* disappeared into the night, its captain and crew infuriated by their fiasco.[42] Quite by chance Blackbeard and Bonnet reunited in March 1718 in the Bay of Honduras. Persuaded to join Blackbeard on the *Queen Anne's Revenge*, Bonnet relinquished command of *Revenge* to one Richards, an experienced lieutenant of Blackbeard. Richards took a prize Jamaican sloop, *Adventure*, which was added to the pirate flotilla. Blackbeard now commanded the most powerful naval force in the hemisphere, mounting nearly sixty guns and crewed by up to 400 pirates and enslaved men. Relegated to being Blackbeard's companion, Bonnet became depressed and talked of seeking refuge in Spain.[43]

Establishing a base at Ocracoke in 1718, Edward Thache
(Blackbeard) brought hundreds of pirates to the colony.
Courtesy of State Archives of North Carolina.

After defeating and plundering *Protestant Caesar* and several sloops, the pirates sailed north, acquiring a Spanish sloop off Cuba and spending a brief interlude on the Florida coast diving for treasure on Spanish wrecks. Blackbeard now turned toward a far richer destination—Charles Town, South Carolina. Arriving in late May, Blackbeard and Bonnet raised the stakes dramatically with a brazen blockade that "struck a great Terror to the whole Province of *Carolina*." Over the course of a week Charles Town was humiliated: nine prizes were taken and plundered of goods and about £1,500 in specie; trade came to a standstill; and a number of hostages were seized, including a council member, Samuel Wragg. Blackbeard's demand for lifting the blockade and releasing the hostages was a chest of medicine, which the pirates sorely needed. When

Governor Robert Johnson refused to negotiate for the hostages' ransom, Blackbeard threatened to burn the prizes, shell the port, and send the heads of the
hostages to the governor. Medicine worth £400 was promptly dispatched, and
the hostages were released unharmed.[44]

With his vessels needing careening and refitting, Blackbeard set a course for
the little-known fishing village of Beaufort at Topsail Inlet. Losing the flagship
and the sloop *Adventure* in the shallow inlet, the host of pirates descended on
the hamlet. Boarding a longboat, Bonnet sailed up Core Sound to Bath, the
colony's port of entry and residence of Governor Eden. The governor granted
Bonnet and his men a pardon under the Act of Grace and permission to sail to
the Virgin Islands to seek a letter of marque as a privateer for Denmark. Either
news of the Charles Town blockade had not yet reached Bath, or the governor simply ignored the 5 January 1718 cutoff for forgiveness. In Bonnet's absence, Blackbeard commandeered the Spanish sloop, renamed it *Adventure*, and
armed it with eight guns. Abandoning all but twenty of his most trusted crew,
including five Africans, and taking the loot and forty enslaved Africans, he
marooned those who opposed him on a desolate barrier island. To avoid Bonnet, Blackbeard sailed to Bath by the outer passage through Ocracoke Inlet.[45]

On returning to Beaufort, Bonnet, incensed that he was cheated of his plunder, rescued the maroons and set out in pursuit, narrowly missing Blackbeard at
Ocracoke. Still angry, Bonnet forsook all thought of retirement and struck out
on a solo cruise up the coast to Delaware Bay. Since he had taken the pardon, he
changed the name of *Revenge* to *Royal James* and used several aliases, including
Richards, Edwards, and Thomas. In the month of July he stopped and plundered thirteen prizes, sometimes robbing, sometimes trading advantageously,
never destroying the prizes, rarely injuring anyone, and usually allowing them
to continue on their way. All vessels were stopped without a fight by either a
"shot across the bow" or boarding anchored vessels from small boats or canoes.
Seamen voluntarily joined the pirates from several of the prizes, although later,
when on trial for their lives, some testified that they had been forced.

Thievery on the high seas in these years garnered the mundane staples of
the Americas—sugar, tobacco, rum, molasses, provisions, leather, lumber, and
enslaved West Africans. Bonnet's prizes reflected the transatlantic traffic from
Chesapeake Bay and Philadelphia. The pirates acquired food, tobacco, sails and
fittings, personal items, rum, and some cash. The last two seizures in Delaware
Bay were a Barbados-bound sloop laden with provisions and a sloop inbound
from Antigua carrying valuable rum, molasses, and sugar. Bonnet kept these
two prizes as store ships and sailed to his Cape Fear hideaway.[46]

After receiving his own pardon, Edward Thatch settled down in Bath. In
no hurry to resume "pyrating," he saw an opportunity in Bath County. He had

arrived at a critical juncture in North Carolina politics: on the rebound from the Cary Rebellion and Tuscarora War, the colony had begun to experience an economic recovery. With ready cash and abundant inexpensive trade goods, the "reformed pirate" elicited few questions from the hard-pressed merchants and innkeepers. He further disarmed his critics by marrying the daughter of a local planter and entering the domestic life of the colony.

As his cash and goods dwindled, however, Thatch created an outpost at Ocracoke Inlet, the colony's main gateway to the sea. In August he sailed *Adventure* out to sea. South of Bermuda he intercepted two French merchantmen, *Rose Emelye* and *Toscin d'Or* (*Golden Fleece*), heavily laden with a cargo of sugar and cocoa. *Rose Emelye* was seized, and the French crews were sent home on *Toscin d'Or*. Back at Ocracoke while the prize was being stripped, Thatch sailed across the sound in a longboat to the Pamlico River for a midnight rendezvous with his friend Tobias Knight, the colony's chief justice and customs collector. He carried gifts of chocolate, sweetmeats, loaf sugar, and several sealed chests. At the admiralty court hearing in Bath before Governor Eden, Thatch claimed that the captured vessel was an abandoned derelict and was granted salvage rights. Both the governor and Justice Knight received substantial quantities of sugar, molasses, and cocoa, either as court fees or as gifts.[47]

Over the next four months Thatch was based in North Carolina, alternating between Bath and Ocracoke, and sometimes at sea. In October Charles Vane entered the inlet, boldly saluting his compatriot with a broadside, which was returned. The pirate companies went ashore and held a prolonged revel for days, finally ending their carousing when Vane sailed south. Thatch amused himself in the local society, probably traded, and may occasionally have pilfered.[48]

Although by some accounts no traveler on the colony's sounds was safe from the "reformed pirates," only one incident was recorded—a theft and assault on the Pamlico River that occurred the night of Thatch's mysterious voyage up the river. William Bell, a Currituck justice and merchant, testified that his anchored periauger was boarded by unknown assailants. When the intruders demanded rum and money, Bell refused. The leader declared he was "from Hell" and launched into Bell. In the struggle, Bell was struck by a sword, and the thieves seized cash, brandy, crepe, and a silver cup. The crime was initially attributed to petty thieves, and a full ten days passed before Bell implicated Thatch in the affair. By the time of a hearing before the council that blamed the incident on Thatch, he had been dead six months.[49]

While Bonnet was raiding shipping north of Carolina, Charles Vane had returned and briefly skulked off Charles Town. This was the last straw for Governor Nathaniel Johnson, who still smarted from Blackbeard's mortifying blockade. To apprehend Vane, two eight-gun sloops, *Henry* and *Sea Nymph*, were furnished with 130 men under Colonel William Rhett, who was named vice admiral. A proven soldier and sea captain, Rhett had defeated a French privateer fleet off Charles Town in 1706. Vane tricked the South Carolinians into believing he had gone south, and Rhett set off in pursuit in mid-September.

Soon realizing he had been duped, Rhett turned north to check on rumors that a pirate was careened on the Cape Fear River. Entering the treacherous river mouth on the evening of 26 September, Rhett sighted suspicious vessels upstream—Stede Bonnet's *Royal James* and its consorts. Early the next morning, Bonnet sought to escape by running past the South Carolinians. Cannon blazing, *Royal James* raced toward the adversaries. Suddenly, all vessels were aground, with *Royal James* and Rhett's *Henry* in small arms range. Tide and current tilted the adversaries so that their cannon could not bear. Over the next five hours both sloops were swept by galling musketry and pistol fire, with pirates shouting curses and oaths and the South Carolinians replying with "chearful Huzzas." The stalemate ended when the incoming tide freed *Henry*, and Rhett maneuvered to rake the pirates from bow to stern. Disregarding Bonnet's exhortation to fight on, his exhausted men ran up the white flag. About a third of *Henry*'s crew were killed or wounded; Rhett lost a total of eighteen. The pirates suffered nine dead and three wounded. Three dozen pirates, including Stede Bonnet, were captured. In early October Rhett sailed triumphantly into Charles Town harbor with his prisoners to "the great Joy of the whole Province."[50]

North Carolina's years of political conflict had bitterly divided the colony's leaders. The reins of government were held by Governor Eden, Chief Justice Tobias Knight, and council president Thomas Pollock. The opposition was headed by Edward Moseley, one of the colony's leading officials, and Colonel Maurice Moore, its most renowned soldier. Pollock and Moseley had been implacable opponents since the Cary Rebellion, and the pirate imbroglio reignited their enmity.[51] Merchants and "some of the best of the Planters" urged action against the brigands, but Governor Eden refused to divert his meager forces from defense against Indian raids. Sensing that Blackbeard was the governor's Achilles heel, Moore and Moseley secretly appealed to that dogged nemesis of piracy, Governor Spotswood, who claimed admiralty oversight of North Carolina. Spotswood welcomed news on the whereabouts of the archvillain, whose rendezvous at Ocracoke Inlet was rumored to have attracted the notorious Vane. Pirates based at Ocracoke Inlet could not only control all of North Carolina's trade but would also be poised to attack Virginia and South Carolina.

Anxious "to extirpate this nest of pyrates," Spotswood hastily planned a secret land and sea incursion into North Carolina to trap the villains. An invasion force was recruited from marines and sailors of royal naval vessels on station. Captain Ellis Brand commanded the combined operation and led the land contingent. Lieutenant Robert Maynard, first officer of the Virginia guardship *Pearl*, was given command of hired sloops *Jane* and *Ranger*, which were manned by naval volunteers. He selected *Jane* as his flagship. Guided by Moore, Moseley, and Jeremiah Vail, on 23 November Captain Brand's troops occupied Bath, where Brand confiscated a large quantity of sugar and some cotton from Governor Eden and Justice Knight. The governor was forthcoming about the sugar, identifying it as admiralty fees, but Knight had hidden his share in his barn.[52]

Meanwhile, on 20 November Maynard's flotilla entered Roanoke Inlet and sailed down the sound toward Blackbeard's *Adventure*, arriving early on 22 November. Having no carriage guns but heavily outnumbering the pirates, Maynard planned to close with Blackbeard and board, concealing most of his crew below deck. The approaching British grounded in the treacherous waters, and as Blackbeard drew near to engage them, he briefly ran aground as well. Maynard and Blackbeard shouted insults at each other, and the pirate raised his glass in a toast, declaring, "Damnation seize my Soul if I give you Quarters, or take any from you." *Adventure* came about toward the intruders, and fired a devastating broadside at close range, killing and wounding many on deck. Seizing the advantage, Blackbeard and his men clambered aboard *Jane*. Just then Maynard and his remaining crew emerged from below deck. Bloody hand-to-hand fighting lasted but a few minutes. As they dueled face-to-face, Blackbeard wounded Maynard's hand and closed to finish him off. A shot in the chest and near decapitation by a blow from behind sent the great body sprawling on the deck, riddled by five pistol wounds and many cutlass gashes. The gory business ended when Maynard severed Blackbeard's head and rigged it on the bowsprit as a grisly trophy. It had been a bloody melee. Every pirate was killed or wounded, and about half of Maynard's force suffered casualties. Maynard's men ransacked the pirate camp, uncovering a cache of cocoa, indigo, and cotton. Maynard sailed across Pamlico Sound for Bath, where more plunder was loaded onto their vessels for the return to Virginia.[53] Held in the Williamsburg jail, the surviving pirates, five of whom were African, were tried the following March, and about half were executed.[54]

While Spotswood's preemptive invasion of North Carolina was being plotted, Bonnet and his sailing master, David Herriot, escaped their guards, creating a furor in Charles Town. Search parties were organized, and the governor offered a £700 reward for their recapture. Having been forced by a storm to land their small boat on nearby Sullivan's Island, Bonnet, Herriot, an Indian, and a Black were hiding virtually under the town's nose. Acting on a tip, Colonel Rhett trapped Bonnet's party at night, killing Herriot and taking the others.

In Bonnet's absence his crew had been tried before the vice-admiralty court of Rhett's brother-in-law, Nicholas Trott. Considering pirates "Enemies of Mankind," Trott showed no mercy. Pirates quickly got the message that Charles Town was no longer an easy mark and that Trott was "a hanging judge." It was Trott who said that pirates are "Brutes and Beasts of Prey" and that "it is lawful for anyone that takes them . . . to put them to Death." Of the thirty-three pirates, only four won acquittal by satisfying the court that they were coerced against their will. On November 8, just three days later, twenty-two pirates were hanged.[55]

The recaptured Bonnet was returned to Charles Town the day after his crew's trial ended. He, too, was found guilty of piracy and condemned to die. His abject plea for mercy to the governor went unanswered. On 10 December Bonnet rode to the gallows in a cart as a drummer sounded his death knell. Nearly fainting at the scaffold, he was held up while the noose was tightened, and then the cart was driven out from under him.[56]

AS A CONSEQUENCE OF Virginia's preemptive invasion targeting Blackbeard, the government in North Carolina was temporarily torn asunder. Governor Eden and Secretary Tobias Knight were tarnished by their alleged collusion with the pirate; nevertheless, Charles Eden continued as proprietary governor until his death in 1722. Although Johnson's history initially described Eden as a partner of Blackbeard, the claim was retracted with the statement that the governor did not have "any private or criminal Correspondence with this Pyrate" and that he "bore the Character of a good Governor and an honest Man."[57] Since Blackbeard had used the colony's vice-admiralty court to have his Spanish sloop condemned as a prize and a French ship declared a salvageable derelict, legally he had not committed a piracy under the pardon. If he had lived to stand trial, however, there was enough evidence that might have condemned him for piracy at sea and robbery in North Carolina.[58]

Tobias Knight was the only official to be tried for collusion with Blackbeard. At the March 1719 pirate trial in Williamsburg, Virginia, several depositions alleged that Knight was linked to Blackbeard. The evidence was sent to Governor Eden, who brought it to the council in April. Having been given copies of all the evidence, in May Knight was tried before the council and governor as an accessory to piracy. Although suffering from a long-term illness, he ably defended himself, rejecting testimony given by a pirate on trial for his life and an enslaved Black who could not legally testify against a white person. He denied that he had failed to be forthcoming about the sugar he was storing for Thache. A witness who was staying at Knight's house when Blackbeard allegedly visited the secretary swore that no such visit had occurred. Knight was acquitted by the council. Having cleared his name, he died about two weeks later.[59]

Indicative of the political infighting in the colony was the puzzling step taken by Edward Moseley and Maurice Moore to compromise Governor Eden by capitalizing on the governor's reputation in the pirate affair. With assistance from Thomas Luten Jr., Henry Clayton, and a laborer named Joseph Moore, on 26 December Moseley and Moore broke into the home of Deputy Secretary John Lovick, nailed the door shut, and spent most of a day ransacking the provincial records, searching futilely for evidence linking the governor to Blackbeard. The provost marshal arrested them the next morning and put Moseley in irons. Moseley became so irate that he publicly defamed the governor and was perceived as stirring up sedition to subvert the government. The grand jury indicted the men, and they were tried and convicted by the General Court in July 1719. Since they had stolen nothing, the breaking and entering charge was punished by minor fines, ranging from five shillings to five pounds. Moseley, who had publicly impugned the governor, was convicted of "Scandalous words," for which he received a £100 fine and was forbidden to hold office for three years.[60]

In the midst of the investigations and hearings concerning Tobias Knight and the Moseley and Moore break-in, Governor Eden received startling news from South Carolina that he took to the council on 22 February. South Carolina was rebelling against the Lords Proprietors, having taken the government "into their owne hands" and replaced the governor and other officials. Learning that Colonel Christopher Gale had just returned from Charles Town, Eden requested his presence and asked him to submit a written report. The shocked council directed Secretary John Lovick to prepare a letter to the Lords Proprietors declaring that North Carolina "utterly detests the Proceedings" of their neighboring colony. Furthermore, the province was "intirely easy and Satisfied under their Lordships Government and will always use their utmost endeavours to maintain it."[61]

MYSTERY SHROUDS THE FATE of many of the pirates who vanished from the record after they landed at Topsail Inlet. The crews in Blackbeard's flotilla may have totaled nearly 400 pirates and Africans. Blackbeard and Bonnet sailed away with about 50 pirates and up to 100 Africans, some of whom became pirates, although most were probably sold as enslaved. Although influxes of former pirates were reported in Virginia, New York, and Philadelphia, the advantages of remaining in North Carolina were more attractive than the risks of moving to other colonies that were executing pirates. Ostensibly pardoned, perhaps up to 200 may have ended up in the North Carolina tidewater, escaping their past and becoming law-abiding settlers. With money and resourcefulness, they could contribute to the recovery of the ravaged Bath County, and reformed armed pirates would strengthen the colony's militia.[62]

Three centuries later, many individuals with deep family roots in coastal North Carolina may claim with pride that they are descended from Blackbeard. Considering the few months he spent in North Carolina, that is improbable, but these Carolinians may have an unknown pirate ancestor. Arriving in the wake of war and rebellion that had left many widows, orphans, and vacant farms, a pirate would have had numerous opportunities to lose his former identity, marry and acquire a family, and take up a respectable life. Over time these farmers, traders, craftsmen, innkeepers, fishermen, or mariners helped build a colony that flourished despite its tenuous beginnings in the proprietary era.[63]

Although there is no roster of the crews of the pirate flotilla that ended up in Beaufort, delving into precinct deeds and court records has turned up a few who fit the profile of a former privateer or pirate.[64] Likely candidates are mariners who were not in the colony before 1718 and were able to acquire property and rise quickly. As men-at-arms, some would be drawn to law enforcement or the militia. Having lived free, beholden to none, these men of action were prideful and inclined to respond violently to a personal slight. There is no evidence that Roger Kenyon had any connection to Edward Thatch, but he fits the pattern. A known privateer, he was quartermaster of *Movil Trader* from Moville, a port on the north coast of Ireland. Kenyon settled in Bath by 1720, purchasing waterfront lots, opening a tavern, and later acquiring a plantation on the north side of town. He became a precinct justice of the peace, a militia captain and major, county provost marshal by 1722, and a representative of Bath Town in the General Assembly in the 1730s. Considered a "gentleman," he defended his honor when insulted, having altercations with the volatile George Burrington and Matthew Rowan.[65]

A few pirates who can be connected to *Queen Anne's Revenge* have surfaced from local records, and more await discovery. In September 1718 the mariners James Robbins and Stephen Elsey traded three enslaved Africans for 400 acres adjacent to Bath Town. Robbins became an ordinary keeper in the town and by 1723 was provost marshal of Bath County. In 1725 a guest at Robbins's tavern, the trader John MacQueen, was robbed and held Robbins responsible. Among the items stolen were a buccaneer gun valued at eight pounds, a case of two pistols worth eight pounds, and a Cherokee basket. MacQueen claimed fifty pounds in damages, but he was not compensated, because Robbins died the next year.[66]

The most successful of the pirates known to have served with Thache was Edward Salter, a cooper, who was forced to join the pirates when Henry Bostock's *Margaret* was captured. A forced pirate who did not take up arms would be acquitted, and that saved Salter's life. Between 1721 and 1728 he acquired lots in Bath Town and over 4,400 acres in three tracts along the Pamlico River. At the time of his death in 1735, his considerable estate included a brigantine, a periauger, and enslaved Africans.[67]

William Briggs, "Chyrurgeon" on *Queen Anne's Revenge*, took the Act of Grace and raised funds by selling his damaged medicines and salves, receiving five pounds in one sale. He then embarked for England, but at Ocracoke Inlet his vessel and others were boarded and plundered by another "gang" of pirates. Briggs was forced to join these brigands, which could have jeopardized his life if he were caught again.[68]

The deaths of Blackbeard, Bonnet, and other pirate captains in late 1718 signaled the beginning of the end of the Golden Age on the Carolina coast. The brief War of the Quadruple Alliance (1718–20) spawned a flurry of privateers, and the seas remained unsafe as pirates and Spanish privateers were still lured by the commerce of the Chesapeake and Charles Town. William Byrd II noted in 1720 that "rogues swarm in this part of the world, and we are told of 70 sail at least that haunt the several parts of America." In an undeclared quasi-war throughout the decade, Spanish privateers sailed from St. Augustine, which Byrd considered "a proper nest of pyrates."[69]

Three years later, in May 1721 the impact of the specter of *Queen Anne's Revenge* was manifest when the Reverend John Urmston's voyage home from Virginia was delayed. On board a vessel in the James River, he learned of piratical activity off the Capes. For safety a convoy of five or six vessels had formed, hoping to leave within a week or so but apprehensive of the gauntlet of pirates awaiting them. A newly arrived ship that had been "ill Used" by two pirates spread a rumor that the Virginia pirate executions would be revenged by a forty-gun ship crewed by 400 men who would "not Spare man woman or Child." It could be none other than the resurrected mythologized *Queen Anne's Revenge*, the only such ship and crew ever so described. Urmston wrote, "We dare not put out to Sea," but the threat soon passed, and the missionary was safely in London by July.[70]

The last gasp of the Golden Age of Piracy in North Carolina occurred in the summer of 1727. The colony's only homegrown pirate leader, John Vidal, a merchant of Bath Town originally from Dublin, led a small "Gang of Pyrates" in an escapade at Ocracoke Inlet. Although he was described as "a man of Desperate fortune," Vidal's ineffectual efforts bordered on the comical, except that two of his men paid with their lives on the scaffold. A repentant Vidal later blamed his fall into criminality on debts and the theft of his vessel in Maryland, which brought "despair and melancholy" and "almost bereaved me of my senses."[71]

On a "business" trip by periauger to Cape Fear, Vidal and his companions,

Edward Coleman and Thomas Allen, were joined by Michael Griffing and the
Thomas Farley family. At Ocracoke Inlet on 16 June they spied an anchored
schooner and conceived the wild notion that they could make their fortune
by turning pirate, seizing the schooner, and sailing it to the Caribbean. Vidal,
Coleman, Allen, Thomas Farley, and a reluctant Griffing embarked on this
reckless course, which in less than a week saw the plundering of the schooner,
two shallops, and a wrecked sloop, in addition to numerous assaults. Although
Vidal lacked navigation skills, he did not lack self-confidence, making his cap-
tures with bluster and a pistol, first threatening the schooner's master, Jonathan
Howard, and crew with death. Roger Kenyon, a former privateer and acquaintance of Vidal, arrived in a shallop and was forced onto the schooner to join in
the effort to attempt the inlet. Strong adverse winds embayed the vessel, and it
may be that the mariners masked half-hearted efforts. Frustrated, Vidal's men
seized and looted not only Kenyon's shallop, which was transporting cattle to
Ocracoke, but also the shallop of Andrew Frazier.[72]

On sighting a wrecked sloop from Barbados on Core Banks, Vidal's band
discovered worthy plunder—rum, sugar, liquor, and a buried trove of gold coins,
a silver-trimmed sword, a watch, and gold rings. Not surprisingly, the flow of
rum and liquor fueled a drunken brawl, followed the next night by a party,
complete with a fiddler, on Ocracoke. Frazier and Howard, the former armed
with the periauger's stout tiller, subdued and bound the drunken Vidal.[73]

Deprived of their leader, Griffing, Coleman, Allen, and Farley and his wife
Martha loaded the periauger with loot and headed toward the Neuse River. At
a rest stop Griffing managed to notify a bystander about the pirates. A hue and
cry was raised on the river, resulting in the capture of all but Thomas Farley,
who absconded. Meanwhile, Vidal escaped the sheriff's custody, but Kenyon,
on commission by Governor Sir Richard Everard, hunted him down and returned him to the Edenton jail, where his companions were being held.[74]

Since North Carolina was under the admiralty jurisdiction of Virginia, the
miscreants were sent to Williamsburg for trial as pirates. The three-day trial in
August 1727 resulted in convictions and death sentences for Vidal, Coleman,
and Allen. The forced Griffing testified against the others and was released,
and Martha Farley, who could justly say she was simply following her husband,
was acquitted and provided funds for her return home. Ironically, Coleman
and Allen were hanged, but Vidal, the muddled mastermind, gained a reprieve.
Thanks to influence from associates in Virginia and North Carolina, his abject
plea for mercy secured a pardon and the expenditure of public funds for the
cost of his incarceration.[75]

ONLY A FEW MORE ALARMS were raised in the 1720s as the age of piracy in North America wound down. Over 200 brigands were captured, tried, and executed within months, making piracy suddenly very risky. Crown intervention eliminated their base at Nassau, while the threat of a pirate stronghold in North Carolina was snuffed out by prompt action from the neighboring colonies. Those remaining under the black flag scattered, some to the Indian Ocean and others to Africa, while still others quietly retired. The failure of the Lords Proprietors to act against the pirate threat of 1718 was the last in a long list of grievances that within a year brought rebellion and the end of proprietary rule in South Carolina, but proprietary North Carolina would last another decade, until the colony was purchased by the Crown.

CHAPTER FIFTEEN

The End of an Era

The Inhabitants of said Province are exceeding poor and
distressed ariseing from the calamitys of the well known
wars with the Indians of the said country.
—George Burrington, 1730

A s the lords proprietors' ownership of North Carolina came to a close, George Burrington, the newly appointed royal governor of the colony, sent a brief profile of the province to the Board of Trade in London. Having previously served as proprietary governor (1724–25) and then resided and extensively traveled in the colony for several years, Burrington ostensibly knew it well. But the past of this quarrelsome man was checkered, and the proprietors had dismissed him for reprehensible behavior. His current appointment by George II was due not only to his high-placed patrons but also to the record of his successor, Sir Richard Everard, which was nearly as bad as his own. One could take his word with more than a few grains of salt.

Burrington claimed that he reversed the population loss resulting from the Tuscarora War by encouraging immigration, "whereby the . . . miseries are greatly restored and repaired." He attributed the colonists' economic disadvantage to the "illconvenience of the Sand Banks" that hindered commerce everywhere except the Cape Fear River, generating higher costs for imports and lower prices for exports—a problem unmitigated throughout the era.[1]

Political development in the remaining proprietary decades in the two Carolinas followed divergent courses after both colonies were wracked by destructive Indian wars and pirate incursions. The second-generation proprietors, more interested in profit than in governance, let their northern colonists take control of their own affairs. The more lucrative South Carolina, however, held the Lords' attention, resulting in sporadic intervention, chiefly in the realm of land and trade policies. In addition, South Carolina was threatened by invasion from the Spanish and French and a near famine, exacerbated by proprietary vetoes of assembly efforts to relieve basic economic and political problems. The colony's long-standing frustration with inconsistent proprietary policies of neglect and interference led to a radical step, known as the Revolution of 1719. Launched as a bloodless coup grounded in English revolutionary theory and practice, it replaced proprietary governance with royal authority. In December, the Commons house of the assembly declared themselves a Convention of the People; ousted Governor Robert Johnson; elected the colony's foremost soldier, James Moore Jr., as governor; and petitioned the Crown to send a royal official. The provisional government thwarted countercoups and administered the colony for eighteen months until royal governor Francis Nicholson arrived. While North Carolinians were aware of the momentous events in their southern neighbor, they were accustomed to fending for themselves and preferred the status quo. Thus, proprietary governance was overthrown in South Carolina a decade before the Crown purchased the Carolina propriety.[2]

In the last decade of proprietary North Carolina, the colony began to lose its uniqueness and resemble its neighbors. Although most farms and plantations were small to moderate-sized, the decade saw increases in the labor force of enslaved Africans, the size of tracts, and the expansion of forest products. These items—lumber, shingles, staves, masts and yards, and the naval stores of tar, pitch, turpentine, and rosin—were produced primarily in the rapidly developing Cape Fear region, although an Albemarle plantocracy arose, exemplified by the Pollock family.

Acknowledging the province's spreading settlement, the council and assembly created new precincts: Bertie west of the Chowan River and Carteret on Core Sound from Craven. Precinct justices were now required to purchase an acre and erect a courthouse funded by a poll tax. Typical of these buildings was the Currituck courthouse contracted in April 1723 for £140. The frame structure covered by plank siding was to be thirty feet long and eighteen feet wide, supported on cedar blocks, with sash windows and a cypress shingle roof. The interior walls were to be ceiled and a second floor, connected by stairs, finished with planking. Interior treatment included the judge's bench, the clerk's table, benches, and the bar or railing. The last proprietary precincts authorized were Tyrell and Hyde south of Albemarle Sound and New Hanover in the Cape Fear valley, all in 1729.[3]

DR. JOHN BRICKELL, a resident physician in Edenton 1729–31, traveled widely, recording thumbnail impressions of proprietary towns. The largest was Edenton, the capital for several years, which had about sixty houses. Bath Town was second in size and, closer to Ocracoke Inlet, had the "most considerable and commodious" trade except for the Cape Fear. New Bern, with "few Houses or Inhabitants," had yet to recover from the Tuscarora War's surrounding devastation. Hampered by its isolation, Beaufort remained "small, and thinly inhabited." Brickell's praise was reserved for the new town of Brunswick on the Cape Fear, which he anticipated would be "very considerable in a short time, by it's great Trade, the Number of Merchants, and rich Planters that are settled upon it's Banks."[4]

To put Dr. Brickell's observations in perspective, in 1730 Charles Town, South Carolina's metropolis and the largest town in British North America south of Philadelphia, boasted 3,000 inhabitants, of whom one-third were Black, most of them enslaved. By contrast, Edenton had a few hundred residents at best, and the aggregate population of North Carolina's towns was scarcely 1,000. The sister colonies each had about 30,000 inhabitants. The striking difference between them was that in South Carolina, two out of three persons were of African origin, whereas in North Carolina there were four whites to every Black.[5]

Bath County's towns had suffered severe setbacks during the Cary Rebellion and the Tuscarora War. Communication and trade were interdicted throughout the region as Native raiding parties roamed up to the outskirts of Bath Town. With the war officially over in 1715, the village of a dozen houses began recovery with help from the proprietors and the assembly. As a stimulus to trade, the governor was authorized to appoint pilots at Roanoke and Ocracoke Inlets to mark the channels into the sound. Thereafter, the proprietors designated Bath as a port of entry, and by 1722 a courthouse was approved for the village, which became the precinct seat of government for Beaufort and Hyde.[6] Recognizing the new port's potential, in 1716 Governor Charles Eden moved from Chowan to a 400-acre plantation on Bath Creek adjacent to Secretary Tobias Knight. Another new resident was former privateer Roger Kenyon, a merchant and tavern keeper, who soon became a precinct justice, town commissioner, militia captain, and provost marshal of Bath County. The governor, Chief Justice Christopher Gale, and Secretary Knight served on the vestry of St. Thomas Parish. Services were conducted by a lay reader in private homes and the courthouse until 1734, when a simple brick house of worship—North Carolina's oldest church building—was erected.[7]

In the vortex of the war zone, New Bern's residents had been secure behind the gates but witnessed heavy loss of life and property all around them. In 1713, two years after his imprisonment by the Tuscarora, New Bern's founder, Baron de Graffenried, abandoned his colony and returned to Switzerland. Into the leadership vacuum stepped William Brice, the baron's former adversary. The most prominent remaining Palatine was Johan Martin Franck, a schoolmaster and planter who later served in the assembly and was a precinct justice.[8] The war derailed promised assistance to de Graffenried, who suffered considerable financial losses. To recoup his investment, he mortgaged his land to Thomas

Pollock, who thereby became owner of the settlement. Pollock did not press the destitute colonists for rents, but after his death in 1722 his heir, Cullen, threatened to dispossess them. Some years later, in midwinter, he carried out his threat. The "Poore pallatines" had petitioned as early as 1714 for title to their property, and the Crown eventually provided each family 250 acres rent-free for ten years.[9] Cullen Pollock did attempt to rejuvenate New Bern in 1723 by securing the town's incorporation as the seat of Craven precinct, with a courthouse, church, market, and half-acre lots,[10] but in 1731 Governor Burrington observed that the village "hath made but little Progress."[11]

Following the invasion of pirates in 1718 and their dispersion throughout the colony, Beaufort resumed its normal rhythm as a sleepy fishing village. But its notoriety as a pirate town convinced Beaufort's founder, Robert Turner, to sell out to Richard Rustull in 1720. Rustull's prospects brightened two years later when the town was incorporated as the seat of Carteret Precinct and received designation as a port. Joining Rustull on the town commission was Christopher Gale, the first collector of customs.[12] St. John's parish was organized in 1724, and worship was begun in the courthouse. By 1728 Nathaniel Taylor donated a plot where Tuscarora War victims were buried. This village burying ground is today one of North Carolina's most picturesque cemeteries.[13] Beaufort's port was ideally situated close to the open sea and had a fine deepwater harbor, but it suffered from poor riverine connections to the interior. Although a new road was cut to New Bern that improved the overland link to the rest of the colony, Burrington stated that Beaufort had "little success & scarce any inhabitants."[14]

The birth of three towns in Bath County in less than a decade had been a rude awakening for Albemarle. In accord with the proprietors' vision, Bath County's rapid growth in population, trade, and ports could overwhelm complacent Albemarle's dominance. Since the end of the seventeenth century the Little River area in Perquimans Precinct, conveniently located near the center of Albemarle County, had hosted courts, assemblies, and a customhouse. There the colony's first "Gran Court House" was used by the general and precinct courts in 1700–1701 before abruptly disappearing from the records.[15]

Stimulated by Bath County's initiative, in 1712 Chowan Precinct's assembly burgesses secured authority for the Town on Queen Anne's Creek, formerly Mattacomack Creek. Unlike Bath, New Bern, and Beaufort, which had been developed by private initiative, Queen Anne's Town was to be North Carolina's long-anticipated metropolis, the colony's capital. One hundred acres were purchased, to be subdivided into half-acre lots, each to have a small house within a year. Two acres were set aside for a courthouse for the assembly, a prison, and a church. The pressures of the Tuscarora War slowed the pace, but by 1715 the first lot had been sold.[16] Within a decade merchants' warehouses rose around the snug harbor, and artisans' shops, inns, and residences began to line the village streets.

As the capital slowly grew, the colony's government gradually relocated to public buildings on the town common. First built was a frame courthouse with interior plaster finish, financed by public and private funds, where the General Court convened in July 1716, with Chief Justice Gale presiding. In November 1718 the council also moved to the General Court House, afterward rarely meeting in the homes of governors or their deputies. After the pirate scandal, Governor Eden moved to the west bank of the Chowan in 1719 and established a plantation at Eden House, a more secure site just across the river from the capital. The August 1720 assembly first met in the courthouse, and four years later a separate council chamber had been erected. Thereafter, when the General Assembly convened, the council gathered in their chamber, and the House of Burgesses met in the courthouse. After 1722 a prison was constructed on the north side of King Street, facing the courthouse, completing the governmental complex at the head of the town common.[17] Today, standing on the steps of the fine 1767 Georgian courthouse, the view down the gentle slope of Edenton green to the bay, flanked by residences from three centuries, evokes the colony's earliest days.

On 26 March 1722 Governor Charles Eden died at his home just prior to a council meeting. He was buried next to his wife on the plantation under a tombstone that proclaimed that he had governed the province for eight years for "Ye Ease & Happynes of ye People" and that he had "Brought ye Country into a Flourishing Condition & died much lamented." Meeting at the governor's house as planned, the council elected Thomas Pollock as president before adjourning. Councilmen must have discussed how to memorialize the governor, for when they reconvened at the courthouse on 4 April, the Town on Queen Anne's Creek had been renamed Edenton.[18]

In August the assembly reorganized and incorporated Edenton, added 270 acres, and declared it the colony's "Metropolis." Town commissioners were John Lovick, Edward Mosely, Nicholas Crisp, and Gale, who was also the treasurer. Eight acres were set aside for a governor's residence, and a burying ground and market were added to the town's public land uses. A church building would be funded by the sale of lots. To solidify the government, by the next spring provincial officials were required to open their offices in Edenton, and the General Court House became the repository for the colony's records. Finally, Edenton and Bath were each granted a borough representative in the assembly.[19] With an unassailable majority in the General Assembly and now the colony's permanent capital, Albemarle's preeminence was assured for many years. Edenton, North Carolina's first capital, would remain so until 1746, when the more centrally located New Bern was selected for the future capital.

Rarely complimentary of anything in North Carolina, William Byrd II was true to form during his 1728 visit to Edenton, finding the town of forty to fifty modest houses plagued with mosquitoes and its frame courthouse having the "Air of a common Tobacco House." He declared Edenton the only "Metropolis in the Christian or Mahometan World, where there was neither Church, Chappel, Mosque, Synagogue, or any other Place of Publick Worship of any Sect or Religion whatsoever."[20] In fact, there were two Anglican chapels, one east of Edenton and another across the sound. The first parish vestry in North Carolina was St. Paul's, organized in 1701, with a simple chapel erected within a year. Plans were drawn in 1708 for an elaborate church building, but it was never built. Again in 1724 steps were taken to begin a church structure worthy of the new capital, but construction did not begin until 1736, and decades would pass before its completion.[21]

AFTER THE FAILURE OF Charles Towne in 1667, the Cape Fear valley reverted to the Native Americans, whom traders visited periodically. This lasted until the Tuscarora War, when the local Indians were forced to flee as the region was crisscrossed by South Carolina armies of militia and Indians dispatched to aid their neighbors. A few South Carolinians settled west of the river before 1725. The earliest land grant was in May 1713 to Landgrave Thomas Smith for Smith (Bald Head) Island, which remained undeveloped at the time. Among Welsh patentees in 1714 were Thomas James, John Hughes, and Enoch Morgan. The settlement was so sparse that for a few years this remote region was a lawless frontier. The Thomas Jones family had a short and tragic sojourn, cut off by raiding Indians who murdered them and plundered their plantation. Maurice Moore reported this incident, gathered evidence on the perpetrators, and retaliated by attacking and capturing Cape Fear Indians, initiating their exodus into South Carolina.[22] Another murder and robbery victim, the Cape Fear trader Peter "Pedro" in 1724, was probably Peter Perdreau, a Huguenot from Santee River. The suspected offenders, Jacob Johnson and his sister-in-law Ann Johnson, were brought before the General Court in Edenton but were eventually released for lack of evidence.[23]

Shortly after qualifying as governor, George Burrington heard promising tales of the Cape Fear country. In the winter of 1724–25 he explored the region and returned excited about what he had seen—a deep river penetrating the heart of the backcountry, its banks lined with endless longleaf pine forests, miles of open savannas, and fertile black, sandy loam. Thenceforth he never wavered from the dream that the colony's future lay on this great waterway. He lifted the Lords' ban on grants and began approving land warrants, initiating the process for patents issued by the provincial secretary.

South Carolinian Maurice Moore, who had seen the valley during the war, acquired a plantation in Perquimans Precinct and married Elizabeth Lillington Swann, daughter of Alexander Lillington, scion of one of the colony's oldest and most important families. As colonel of the North Carolina militia sent to aid South Carolina during the Yamassee War, Moore crossed the lower Cape Fear near former Charles Towne, whose governor had been his step-grandfather, Sir John Yeamans.

Although Moore rose to prominence in Albemarle, serving as parish vestry-man, councilman, and speaker of the lower house, he had not forgotten the rich land and pine forests of the Cape Fear River. In an audacious move for a middle-aged, well-established planter, Moore sold out and headed south to the untamed frontier.[24] Beginning in 1725 he acquired patents from Governor Burrington to over 7,000 acres on the west bank of the river. His enthusiasm soon attracted his brothers, Nathaniel and Roger, from South Carolina, as well as friends and in-laws from Albemarle. In less than a decade, Maurice Moore acquired about 25,000 acres.[25]

Near Old Town Creek a 1969 archaeological survey discovered the remains of a house that may be Moore's initial residence on a 1,000-acre plantation. Subsequent excavations revealed a stone foundation surrounding a massive central brick chimney with four fireplaces, an uncommon design in the South. Described as a transitional early Georgian style, the four-room house with cor-ner fireplaces measured thirty-two by twenty-seven feet, imposing for the time. Artifacts that date the house to the second quarter of the eighteenth century include a 1723 half penny and clay pipe stems.[26] Another Moore home is hidden behind the nineteenth-century classical facade of Roger Moore's Orton, the state's preeminent plantation house. Having acquired a 640-acre tract from his brother in 1726, Roger added 500 more acres for the core of his holdings. His first house was destroyed by Indians, but by 1735 he erected a story-and-a-half brick house that a century later was expanded into the Orton of today.[27]

Up the coast on Topsail Bay is Sloop Point house, dated 1726, the oldest known standing residence in the Cape Fear region. The story-and-a-half three-room home with two end chimneys and a West Indian–style porch is on a tract then owned by John Baptista Ashe. About 1718 Ashe moved from South Carolina to Albemarle and then to Beaufort Precinct. He married Elizabeth Swann, daughter of Samuel Swann, thereby becoming related to the Lilling-tons, Edward Moseley, and Maurice Moore. Ashe was in the assembly and served as speaker while he was making plans to resettle on the Cape Fear.[28]

Thanks to Governor Burrington's land policy, unlimited grants in the Cape Fear valley enabled some wealthy landowners to accumulate nearly 100,000 acres. Early on, the best river land had been snapped up by planters from

Sloop Point on Topsail Bay was built by John Baptista Ashe in 1725. It is the oldest known house in the Cape Fear region. Courtesy of State Archives of North Carolina.

Albemarle and South Carolina, mostly related by kinship or marriage, and known as "the Family." Fueled by their great plantations, large holdings of en-slaved Africans, and a few labor-intensive products and crops, the Lillington, Moore, Swann, Ashe, Porter, Moseley, Allen, and Vail families provided genera-tions of high-level military and political leadership to the colony and state of North Carolina, as well as to the early United States.

Sailing up the lower river, vessels successively passed Burrington's Walden (Governors) Creek plantation, Nathaniel Moore's York, Maurice Moore's Brunswick Town and Old Town, Roger Moore's Kendal and Orton, Eleazar Allen's Lilliput, and John Baptista Ashe's Grovely. Neighboring plantations along the Northeast Cape Fear were owned by John Porter, Samuel Swann, Edward Moseley, the Moores, Allen, and Burrington, with his 10,000-acre Stag Park. Upstream on the Cape Fear were the Moores, Swann, Ashe, and Corne-lius Harnett.[29]

Although described then as "this Remote Part of the World" and more re-cently as "one of the most marginal places in the English-speaking world,"

by the end of the colonial period the Cape Fear was the province's wealthiest region, with the highest rate of enslaved labor.[30] Describing the Family's
dominance, Governor Burrington singled out the three Moore brothers—
Maurice, Roger, and Nathaniel—from the South Carolina "Goose Creek Faction," which had been "always very troublesome in that Government and will
without doubt be so in this."[31]

Albemarle Sound planters had intermarried as elites are wont to do, but
the Family most mimicked the English aristocracy, whose great estates were
connected by a web of intermarriages. When the Family's patriarch, Maurice
Moore, married Elizabeth Lillington Swann, he acquired three stepchildren
—John, Elizabeth, and Samuel Jr.—and two brothers-in-law—Edward Moseley, husband of Anne Lillington Walker, and John Porter, husband of Sarah Lillington. Another sister-in-law, the widowed Mary Lillington, married Jeremiah
Vail, and Moore's stepdaughter Elizabeth married John Baptista Ashe. From
South Carolina, the Rhett sisters—Catherine, wife of Roger Moore, and Sarah,
wife of Eleazar Allen—were daughters of William Rhett, the scourge of pirates
and captor of Stede Bonnet.[32]

In June 1725 on a low bluff a dozen miles up the Cape Fear River from the
sea, Maurice Moore cut out 360 of his acres and named it the Town of Brunswick. The town was laid out in twenty-four squares of fourteen half-acre lots,
along with a town common and plots for a courthouse, jail, church, market,
and cemetery. An enterprising Irish merchant, Cornelius Harnett Sr., bought
the first two lots and soon opened a tavern and river ferry. By 1729 New Hanover precinct and St. James parish were established, with Brunswick as the
seat of government. Both town and precinct were named for King George I,
whose German titles were Duke of Brunswick and Elector of Hanover. The
parish vestry petitioned the Bishop of London the next year for support of
the Reverend John La Pierre, a former Huguenot pastor in South Carolina.[33]
Brunswick languished for years, described in 1731 as "a poor, hungry, unprovided
Place consisting of not above 10 or 12 scattering mean Houses, hardly worth
the name of a Village."[34]

The Cape Fear economy was built on the products of its vast tracts of native
pine trees—lumber, shingles, barrel staves, and naval stores of tar, pitch, turpentine, rosin, and masts and yards—eventually supplemented by rice. As a great
maritime trading power in the age of wooden sailing ships, Britain had a voracious appetite for naval stores, which were vital to keep her navy and merchant
fleet at sea. Tar and pitch were used to waterproof and seal ships' hulls and as a
preservative to extend the life of ropes and sails, while turpentine was an essential ingredient of paint. Heretofore, Denmark and Sweden had been the chief

suppliers, but North Carolina rapidly became the leading source, eventually exporting more than all the other American colonies combined.

Albemarle had exported forest products for years, but not in great quantity. The opening of the Cape Fear shifted the colony's economy to naval stores and timber products, which could be shipped directly to England from the deepwater port of Brunswick. Brunswick became a port of entry in March 1731 and was touted by Governor Burrington in his address to the assembly as the "Place of the greatest Trade in the whole Province." Within a decade, traffic from the Cape Fear surpassed that of Edenton's Port Roanoke, relegating the provincial capital's port to second place.[35] North Carolina had found strategic products that fit directly into the trade pattern of the British Empire. On the Cape Fear a wealthy society had emerged that was comparable to neighboring Virginia and South Carolina.

North Carolina's mature longleaf pine forests reached noble proportions, and pine heartwood ranked with cypress and cedar for durability. Harvesting and processing were done primarily by enslaved Africans, driving the rapid growth of slavery in the Cape Fear. When petitioning for more land along the river, Edward Moseley noted that he had "a considerable number of Slaves, and no Lightwood land for his Slaves to make Tar."[36] From thousands of barefoot enslaved workers engaged in producing tar and pitch came the colony's richest region, as well as the future nickname of the state's inhabitants—Tar Heel.

The working conditions were horrendous. The stifling heat and humidity of the tidewater climate rose to extremes in the pine savannahs and dank swamps that bred hordes of mosquitoes and biting flies. The men kept a wary eye out for monstrous alligators up to sixteen feet or more, six- to seven-foot rattle-snakes, and thick cottonmouth moccasins that could swallow a piglet or a small dog whole.

In a process called boxing, a long wide gash was cut into the living tree, which released clear resin that was collected in barrels and solidified into rosin. The tree died in about three years and eventually fell, becoming "lightwood." On a low rise in a large cleared circle an enslaved team dug a shallow depression with a drainage trench. Sawyers and axe men hand-cut and split the massive dead pine trunks, some a hundred feet high, to three-foot lightwood logs that were piled haystack-style as tall as a one-story house and over thirty feet in di-ameter. Earth or sod was packed over the stack to form a kiln, which was fired from the top, with vents opened successively down the slope. As the lightwood slowly smoldered over three to five days or more, tar ran to the center and drained down the trench, where workers ladled it into barrels. A second firing of tar produced pitch, and rosin was the residue from distilling turpentine. The work was hard and dangerous, with the hazards of fire and hot tar exacerbated during dry weather, when kilns were known to explode and injure or kill the workers.[37]

In addition to naval stores, the pitch pine furnished construction timbers, floorboards, and siding for houses. Cape Fear men touted Carolina pine as superior in appearance and durability to New England white pine and European pine and fir. Cornelius Harnett and Hugh Blaning petitioned the council in 1732 for additional pine land to expand sawmills on the Cape Fear. Harnett singled out the West Indian market for boards and timber. Blaning, a sea captain and merchant, was impressed by the river's navigable depth some eighty miles upstream. On his voyages to the Mediterranean and North Africa, Blaning noticed flat-roofed local dwellings built of European pine and fir and covered with clay. In addition to the Carolina pine's superior qualities, the colony's milder climate allowed harvesting and shipment year-round, in contrast to northern Europe's seasonal limits. He also calculated that Carolina timber could compete in price with Dutch supplies. Blaning foresaw the development of "Great Trade to many parts."[38]

DURING THIS PERIOD a notable contribution to knowledge of the American colonies was Mark Catesby's two-volume masterpiece, *The Natural History of Carolina, Florida, and the Bahamas . . .* (1731). While not specifically about North Carolina, Catesby's work stemmed from his time living in Virginia, South Carolina, and the Bahamas, and for sources he relied on John White's drawings, accessed through Sir Hans Sloane, and John Lawson's natural history, which he acknowledged.

Growing up in a family with property and status, Catesby exhibited a lifelong interest in nature. In 1712 he sailed to Virginia for a prolonged visit with his sister Elizabeth, wife of provincial secretary Dr. William Cocke. There Catesby formed a lasting friendship with William Byrd II and traveled to the Appalachians and to Jamaica. After a chance meeting with South Carolina governor Francis Nicholson, Catesby was invited to explore that colony. During his 1722–25 sojourn in South Carolina, Catesby made extensive treks into the backcountry collecting specimens, compiling a report, and drawing the flora and fauna. A year in the Bahamas with Governor George Phenney led to his paper at the Royal Society on Bahamian bobolinks, a seminal work on bird migration.[39]

Catesby devoted seventeen years to his natural history. His stunning monumental two-volume folio work described the region's rivers, climate, soils, agricultural products, and Native peoples. His narrative was enlivened by 220 color illustrations of birds, plants, amphibians, reptiles, fish, insects, and mammals found in the Carolinas, Virginia, Florida, and the Bahamas. Of particular interest today are his firsthand accounts of the waning buffalo and its habitat, the savannas or prairies. With Indian guides he hunted buffalo in upcountry South Carolina "towards the Mountains." There he found "spacious Tracts of Meadow-Land . . . burdened with Grass six Feet high" and observed that the buffalo "range in Droves, feeding in open *Savannas* Morning and Evening, and in the sultry Time of the Day they retire to shady Rivulets and Streams of clear Water, gliding thro' Thickets of tall Canes."[40]

The first extensively illustrated natural history of the North American colonies, Catesby's magnum opus earned him election to the Royal Society in 1733 and set a standard that influenced naturalists and scientists thereafter. Catesby's "lively portrayals" of 109 birds established him as the father of American ornithology. His illustrations remained unsurpassed until the nineteenth-century works of Alexander Wilson and John J. Audubon.[41]

PERSONAL VENDETTAS largely put aside during the Tuscarora War reemerged thereafter to plague North Carolina politics for the remainder of the era. Factions that coalesced around individuals were manifest in storms swirling around the governors and members of the council and assembly. The colony's unity ruptured over a quarrel between Governor Eden and Chief Justice Gale about court reform but soon involved Speaker Edward Moseley and the assembly over unresolved issues from the recent war.

The ambitious Gale, longtime chief justice and council member, attempted to make the judiciary independent by proposing a chief justice who could hold court alone or with two assistants. Since the reform enhanced his power at the expense of the executive, Eden ignored it but confirmed him as chief justice and appointed eight associate justices. The proprietors approved Gale's proposal and sent him a commission, which the council accepted in January 1716 over the governor's objection. Although a constitutional issue, the personal dispute led Gale to storm out of a council meeting in August and go to England to appeal to the Lords. Assembly resolves presented at that same meeting criticized the previous government's handling of the late war, pitting Speaker Mosely against the governor, who thereby was faced with another powerful adversary. In defense of the council, Eden promptly dissolved the assembly.[42]

Meanwhile, in London Gale met the charismatic Woodes Rogers, the new royal governor of the Bahamas. Nassau seemed an excellent opportunity for Gale, whom Rogers appointed chief justice and council member. Although Gale planned to move his family to Nassau, within a year the reality of the seedy former pirate base sobered him, and he departed for the mainland. By 1720 he had returned to North Carolina, relocating in Queen Anne's Town. The proprietors recommissioned him chief justice in 1721, but because of Eden's opposition, he did not take office immediately.[43]

At Eden House during the 1721 Christmas holidays, Secretary John Lovick prepared the will of the ailing Governor Eden. Other guests included Gale's son-in-law Henry Clayton and Gale's former court clerk, William Badham. Lovick was named chief beneficiary of Eden's will, with small bequests to a niece in England and a few friends. Eden's wife Penelope had died in January 1717. Most surprising was that his stepchildren, Penelope and John Galland, were not mentioned. At the time Penelope was married to Colonel William Maule, the colony's surveyor general, with whom Eden was in a dispute over fees. Widowed in 1726, she married John Lovick, becoming mistress of Eden House and its owner at Lovick's passing in 1733.[44] The day after the governor's death Gale claimed the chief justiceship, and three days later he took his council seat. Over the next eighteen months, innuendo circulated regarding the suspicious settlement of Eden's estate, as well as Gale's hasty return to power.[45]

Succeeding the late Governor Eden, Thomas Pollock was again elected president of the council but succumbed within five months. William Reed, a planter of Currituck and Pasquotank, who had been on the council ten years, was the next ranking member. Reed became president in September, and he served until the arrival of the new governor in January 1724. Reed was embroiled in the political disturbances of the propriety's latter years, becoming an opponent of Governors Burrington and Everard.[46]

From a prominent Devonshire family, George Burrington was fortunate to have the patronage of the Duke of Newcastle-upon-Tyne, a leading Whig politician. To fill the vacancy left by Governor Eden's demise, Newcastle recommended his protégé to his friend and proprietor, John, Lord Carteret. Burrington was commissioned in February 1723. The following year Newcastle was elevated to secretary of state, Southern Department, with administrative oversight of the American colonies.

When the forty-two-year-old Burrington disembarked in Edenton in January 1724, he was greeted warmly by a council and assembly who were pleased to have attracted a governor so well connected in Britain. Burrington devoted his considerable energy and organizational skills to the colony's economic development, which had been hampered by the proprietary ban on land sales and grants. Upon request of the House of Burgesses, Burrington and the council approved sales and warrants for lapsed and vacant land, a very popular move in the colony. The governor was allowed a twenty-five-shilling fee for signing patents.[47] Burrington directed the improvement of navigation, located new roads, and personally encouraged settlement of the Cape Fear valley, all of which further increased trade and immigration.

Unfortunately, the dark side of this talented man surfaced almost immediately. He was imperious and thin-skinned and possessed an uncontrollable temper and a tendency to violence. Burrington soon lost the council's support, but he successfully curried the assembly's favor. A vivid instance of his vindictiveness involved a poor laborer, Joseph Castleton, for whom Burrington had paid passage to the colony. According to Castleton, when he appealed for more time to repay the debt, Burrington beat him and forced him to kneel and beg for his life. Castleton made the mistake of publicly proclaiming that there was "not a Worse Rogue and Villain in the World" than the governor and vowing to write to the proprietors. When Burrington sued him for defamation and sedition, the indigent Castleton pled guilty and sought the court's mercy. For his conviction of "Seditious and Scandalous" words, he was sentenced to stand two hours in the pillory, beg the governor's pardon, and enter a fifty-pound bond to keep the peace.[48]

Like Burrington, former governor Reed, the senior council member, was strong-willed and prickly, and he became so disaffected with the governor that he quit attending council meetings and would not return until Burrington was removed the next year. At a November council hearing it was alleged that Reed had circulated the slanderous rumor that Burrington had been imprisoned in England for abusing an "old Woman." Reed expressed contempt for a summons to appear before the council, not only refusing to open it but declaring that he "would wipe his Arse with it."[49]

From late 1724 through mid-1725 Governor Burrington reconnoitered the "Southern parts" of the province for the proprietors on three trips that launched the Cape Fear region's future. The long-established practice was for the president of the council to act for an absent governor. Rejecting Reed, Burrington nominated and the council elected Edward Moseley to be president "to transact the publick business of the Government," and Moseley took the qualifying oath on two occasions, 31 October 1724 and 3 April 1725.[50] Moseley occupied nearly every important public office and is acknowledged to be "the single most important political figure" in the early eighteenth century, but he has not been recognized for his several months' service as acting governor.[51]

Initially Christopher Gale was favorably impressed by Governor Burrington, who qualified in January 1724 and shortly appointed Gale's sons-in-law, Henry Clayton and William Little, provost marshal and attorney general, respectively, and his brother, Edmund, and Adam Cockburne to the General Court. Within two months, however, Gale reported that the governor was abusing him, threatening to "slitt his nose, crop his ears and lay him in irons" like a common felon.[52]

It is not clear what prompted the rift between Gale and Burrington. For Gale it originated when the receiver general, Arthur Goffe, a friend of the governor, prevented customs officials John Dunston and Adam Cockburne from fulfilling their duty. Dunston was arrested and subsequently sued Goffe, but the case was dismissed on a technicality. The governor had also overstepped by personally seizing and holding a vessel without consulting the customs officials.[53]

For his part, Burrington believed their animosity sprang from the settlement of Eden's estate, which Eden's English heirs challenged as unlawful. The proprietors sent the heirs' petition to Burrington, who presented it to the council in July when Gale and Lovick were present. Lovick responded to the petition, but the hearing was delayed until October. Since the General Court was meeting concurrently, the governor and council ordered the petition to be recorded and heard in General Court. When Gale defied them by refusing to have the petition recorded, Burrington became enraged, railing at Gale, Lovick, and the court clerk, William Badham, threatening to imprison them all. He stormed into court and called Gale "a Rogue & a Villain" to his face, precipitating an early adjournment.[54]

At dawn on Sunday, 23 August, the Gale family and their Edenton neighbors were awakened by pounding on the front door, loud shouting, and swearing. It was Governor Burrington, threatening to murder Gale. When the stout door held, Burrington shattered the windows, vowing to take Gale by the throat and burn or blow up his house. Gale's wife Sarah and teenage daughter Penelope were terrorized. After securing his family's safety, Gale left the province with a letter to the Lords signed by seven of the ten councilmen testifying to Burrington's outrageous behavior and "illegal proceedings." In January 1725 he presented his sworn testimony to the customs commissioners in London, describing the sensational events in Edenton. With their long experience and confidence in Gale, the Lords were appalled and hastened to remove Burrington. Conveniently, at the same meeting Sir Richard Everard, baronet, was approved as governor.[55]

Meanwhile, at the October council session, Burrington vacated Gale's public offices and made a clean sweep of Gale's allies, removing Clayton, Edmund Gale, and Badham. Lovick replied to the Eden heirs' petition in court, asserting their claims to be false, but Burrington, ruling that his riposte was imperfect and evasive, delayed any decision until the next court session.[56] By the time the next court was held, Burrington was gone. When the Eden heirs' petition was presented to Sir Richard and the court of chancery in July 1726, it was dismissed.[57]

Sir Richard Everard (ca. 1683–1733), from an ancient Essex family of the village of Much Waltham, served as a captain in Queen Anne's War and succeeded his father as baronet in January 1706. In the previous month he had married Susannah Kidder, the daughter of the Bishop of Bath and Wells. Accompanying the Everards to North Carolina were their four children: Richard, Hugh, Susannah, and Anne.[58]

On 17 April 1725 Sir Richard, the only baronet to be a North Carolina governor, received his commission and a 2,000-acre grant and soon embarked for Edenton with Christopher Gale.[59] At the July council meeting in Edenton, Everard took the oath administered by council president Moseley. Sir Richard reinstated Gale's family and friends in their offices, enabling the council to take up routine precinct and provincial matters—appointments, land grants, and estate settlements. The council also addressed a backlog of grievances from tributary Indian tribes that had threatened the colony's fragile peace. Colonel Robert West, who was later the provincial Indian commissioner, was dispatched to defuse a looming crisis on the Roanoke River caused by incursions from northern Indians. Finally, following customary practice, the assembly was dissolved and new elections were authorized.[60]

Burrington's first inkling that he was being replaced came from the July council meeting while he was at Cape Fear. Enraged by his precipitate and unexpected suspension, the paranoid Burrington decided to remain in the province, where he plotted revenge and created an impossible situation for Everard. Unfortunately, Everard's stubborn refusal to brook opposition matched Burrington's. The poisonous mix was explosive.

Burrington was furious that Gale, his inveterate enemy, had orchestrated his removal behind his back. Superficially he accepted his fate, and the council awarded him a lapsed grant of 5,000 acres on the Cape Fear, hoping that would keep him occupied. With the council and courts controlled by Sir Richard's cabal of Gale, Lovick, and Little, Burrington built his power base in the assembly, enlisting influential supporters—Maurice Moore, John Baptista Ashe, Goffe, William Maule, Cullen Pollock, and Edmund Porter. Burrington's plan was to secure enough assembly seats "to resque the administration out of the hands of these rogues." With Bertie and Chowan securely in his camp, he spent a fortnight successfully canvassing the "Lower precincts" to counter the influence of "the Knight" and "the Gentry."[61]

With Burrington and his men controlling the assembly, Everard prorogued it to April; however, the burgesses defied the governor and met for two days in November. After electing Maurice Moore speaker, they sent delegates to the governor, claiming that "Pretended Prorogation" was illegal as an "Infringement of their Liberty & breach of the Priviledges of the People." Everard stood by the postponement and refused to see the speaker. The next day the assembly approved Edmund Porter's address to the proprietors extolling the "great happines" the province had enjoyed under Governor Burrington, who had been falsely and maliciously accused of fomenting a South Carolina revolution. The house approved sending Goffe, Porter, and Nathaniel Duckenfield as agents to the proprietors.[62]

With government at an impasse, Burrington escalated a campaign of intimidation and violence against the executive. According to allegations in grand jury depositions, in November he publicly ranted that Sir Richard was "no more fitt to be Governor than a Hogg in the Woods and that he . . . is a Noodle and an Ape." Spotting an Everard man, Burgess Thomas Parris, Burrington damned him as a fool. About two weeks later on the night of 2 December at the head of a "riotous ruffianly" gang, Burrington pounded on Sir Richard's door and yelled that he was "no more fit to be Governor . . . than Sancha pancha." Calling Sir Richard a "Calves head," he demanded "Satisfaction," threatening to "Scalp Your damn'd thick Skull." Sir Richard retorted that if Burrington did not leave, he would have him punished in court. Denied entrance, Burrington's thugs smashed the windows.[63]

From there, Burrington, his henchman Cornelius Harnett, and an armed mob broke into the home of Constable Joseph Young, whom they thrashed and knifed. His pregnant wife, Mary, was routed out of bed and so frightened that she miscarried. Hearing the tumult, their neighbor, James Pottar, rushed to their aid. Harnett seized him by the throat, and Burrington swore to run him through with his sword, but in the fray Pottar escaped their clutches.

The hoodlums next forced their way into Thomas Parris's ordinary, where Harnett beat the proprietor, whose wife, Susannah, fled into the night seeking help. On 4 January Burrington returned to the Parrisses' home, attempted to break in, and threatened to murder Parris and his lodger, Adam Cockburne, the port collector. Frustrated, Burrington shattered the windows. Throughout, Burrington taunted the governor, claiming that "not an Officer dare Speak to me or look me in the face."[64]

Suffering no consequences, Burrington took his reign of terror to Bath Town, where he assaulted tavern keeper and merchant Roger Kenyon in March 1726, smashing windows, doors, and locks and threatening to burn the house. Armed with pistols and a sword, Burrington attacked Kenyon. Kenyon, a former privateer, defended himself but was outnumbered and wounded. In court he sued Burrington for £500 damages. When Burrington failed to appear, his property was attached to ensure his appearance at the next court session.[65]

With Burrington's rampage threatening the province's stability, at the March session of the General Court the grand jury returned indictments against Cornelius Harnett for riot and against Burrington for trespass, assaults, misdemeanors, and riot. James Castellaw and John Nairne were indicted for verbal

misdemeanors in the September election and in February for "Seditious intent
to Subvert the Government" and obstruction of receiver general William Little.
Burrington attended court, represented by his attorney John Baptista Ashe,
whose request to answer the indictments in the July court was granted.[66]

Meanwhile, Burrington's political fortunes soared. In April the assembly reconvened for a week in Edenton, with Burrington as a Chowan burgess and
Ashe elected speaker. Sir Richard sent a message of reconciliation for the welfare of the colony, and the lower house replied in like manner, calling for immediate cessation of "Oppression" and "Perversion of Justice." If the assembly
resolutions could be believed, the courts were being suborned to protect the
"Evil minded" cabal of Gale, Lovick, and Little. The chief justice was accused
of having assembly members illegally indicted for petitioning for grievances
and being arrested and held without cause. Attorney General Little allegedly
took bribes to forestall arbitrary arrest.

The burgesses complained that these actions were a "great Infringement of
our Libertys as we are Freemen" and violations of the Magna Carta and the writ
of habeas corpus. Although the governor was "dangerously ill," the assembly
denounced the prorogation as "arbitrary & illegal," and rescinded the governor's
twenty-five-shilling fee for signing land grants. Once again Burrington was
thanked for his "mild administration" and his service to the province. To the
Lords Proprietors the house denounced Everard's "very Corrupt administration" and urged Burrington's restoration as governor.[67]

If Sir Richard had not resorted to persecuting his opponents, he would be
kindly remembered. Despite Burrington's assertions that he brought "infinite
Confusion on the Country" and had the "meanest Capacity, and worst Principles of any Gentleman I ever knew," Everard worked diligently for the economic and religious welfare of the colony. For years Virginia had subjected
North Carolina's tobacco to duties, fees, and sometimes exclusion. Sir Richard proposed a duty-free port on the Nansemond River for North Carolina
products that would benefit both colonies, but Virginia would not have it.[68]
After initially following the proprietors' unpopular instructions to close the
land office, Everard reopened it and distributed over 100,000 acres using controversial blank patents, a relief especially in the Cape Fear. He also benefited,
as had his predecessor. In addition to the 5,000 acres that he and his wife had
been granted, he patented 10,000 acres of the rich backcountry Hawfields.[69] By
1729, however, he ordered Secretary Lovick to desist in issuing grants, blaming
Lovick, Surveyor General Moseley, and Attorney General Little for the excessive number of grants and dubbing them "flagrant Villains," comparable to
criminals condemned to "Execution at Tyburn."[70] His most popular action was
approving an assembly issue of £30,000 of currency, for which they granted him

a gift of £500. The discounted colonial currencies were a poor substitute for the pound sterling, but the unfavorable balance of trade with Britain left too little specie circulating in the colonies to transact business.[71]

Sir Richard believed North Carolina "a most Heathenish Part of America," and he conscientiously supported the church.[72] In contrast to Burrington, who exhibited little interest in religion as proprietary governor, Sir Richard brought with him the Reverend John Blacknall, who became the resident minister in Edenton. At the time, the courthouse was used for religious services. As vestryman and church warden, Everard learned that about £600 was available to build the long-delayed Edenton church. He and Edward Moseley attempted to start the project, but they were thwarted by Secretary Lovick, who Everard said "makes a Jest of all Religion," having "no Religion" himself.[73]

Governor Everard thought highly of the Reverend Blacknall, praising him to the Bishop of London as "a very good Preacher a Gent. perfectly Sober beloved by all but Mr. Burrington's Party." Blacknall's obligation to Everard made him a pariah to Burrington, which may have compromised his ministry. In 1726 his illegal marriage in Edenton of a Currituck couple, Thomas Spencer and Martha Paul, a "mulatto," offered a way out. Blacknall informed on himself and by law was to be fined fifty pounds. He was indicted in General Court in July 1726 but was never tried or fined. Thereafter he moved to Virginia, where he enjoyed a long and successful career as a parish minister.[74]

The ne'er-do-well Reverend Thomas Baylye had previously served successive parishes in Philadelphia, Maryland, and Virginia until asked to leave for drunkenness, swearing, and fighting. He showed up in North Carolina in 1724, living in Bertie and preaching in Pasquotank and Perquimans but unreformed and cozy with Burrington. In November 1725 he was arrested for defying Governor Everard by preaching without permission. According to Everard, Baylye had been on a two-day binge in Edenton and was unfit to hold services. When the governor refused him the courthouse key, Baylye forced the door open. In a last failed effort to secure a living in North Carolina, Baylye unscrupulously forged a petition to the SPG requesting his service in Bath's St. Thomas parish. Finding that no one would have him in the colonies, he ended his days in England.[75]

Burrington's political triumph was short-lived. Facing indictments for his violent rampage in the July court, he fled to England and was never tried for his alleged crimes.[76] His absence left Sir Richard's cabal in control of North Carolina. To perpetuate their ascendancy, the government began prosecuting their opponents for libel or slander, accumulating evidence from informers in the taverns and ordinaries, and stooping to an "Inquisition" of servants. In little more than a year, Burrington's hooliganism had been replaced by the excesses of Everard's courts.[77]

Everard's simmering anger reached a boil in April 1727 when he publicly quarreled with Dr. George Allen, who had come to Edenton from Williamsburg, leaving a record of drunkenness and fighting. In the heat of the moment, the governor allegedly struck Allen with his cane. Allen took revenge in late June. Armed with a brace of concealed pistols and a sword, he accosted the governor in the street. Sir Richard seized one of the pistols, admonishing Allen to be gone and behave himself. Shouting "God damn You," Allen aimed the other pistol at him, threatened to kill him, and stormed off. On trial in the October General Court, a sullen and unrepentant Dr. Allen pled not guilty. Brazenly turning his back to the bench, he addressed the "Common people," claiming that no one could receive justice from this court. In the face of such bald-faced sedition, Gale ordered the provost marshal to arrest Allen, who fled to his home, barred the door, and threatened to kill anyone who tried to apprehend him. Shortly afterward he returned to Williamsburg to escape the pending charges.[78]

By 1728, the imminent sale of North Carolina to the Crown created uncertainty about governmental authority, prompting a breakdown of law and order. Indictments for contempt, slander, sedition, and riot multiplied, some directed at the governor and his family, others against Lovick, Gale, and the General Court. The low point came in June when Joseph Jenoure, an Edenton gentleman, led a crowd of laborers who ran amok, assaulting a man in the street with clubs and staves. Lovick and Sir Richard had an altercation, and admiralty judge Edmund Porter was embroiled in an extended fracas with the General Court. For once, George Burrington was right when he declared the province in chaos and the court unable to function.[79]

For some years the current proprietors had exhibited little interest in their overseas domain that produced more headaches than revenue. Shares had changed hands through sale or inheritance, with some tied up in litigation between heirs. The Crown had for decades campaigned to recover the proprieties through persuasion, quo warranto judicial proceedings to challenge the charters, or, as a last resort, purchase. Ironically, considering the Crown's efforts to nullify the charter, it was the Lords themselves who requested it. In January 1728 the proprietors petitioned the Crown to purchase all of Carolina. In the course of negotiations, every proprietor except the Earl of Granville agreed to sell. The Crown paid each of the others £2,500, for a total of £17,500, with an additional £5,000 divided equally to cover arrears in quitrents. Governing authority returned to the king, as did the ownership of ungranted land, with the exception of Granville's one-eighth share, which eventually became the Granville District in the northern half of North Carolina.[80]

To locate the northern boundary, the Crown ordered a joint survey by

Virginia and North Carolina. After the survey was completed, the sale was consummated on 25 July 1729, bringing North Carolina under royal authority. Governor Everard was retained in office temporarily until the appointment and arrival of the new royal governor. In 1731, to the amazement of many, former proprietary governor George Burrington became North Carolina's first royal governor.[81]

———————

THE STORY OF the boundary survey is known through the clever pen of that quintessential Virginia gentleman, William Byrd II of Westover (1674–1744). Having spent nearly half his life in England, he was a Renaissance man of great energy and enthusiasm, equally at home in a London drawing room, on the street soliciting a lady of the evening, in a meeting of the Royal Society, or in a fashionable coffeehouse discussing politics, business, love, or state affairs. Nevertheless, he slipped easily into the bucolic life of provincial Virginia, involving himself in the day-to-day management of his vast plantations, slaking his voracious thirst for land, and serving in the House of Burgesses and on the provincial council. Self-possessed and ambitious, as head of the Virginia commission to conduct the joint survey of the boundary with North Carolina he kept lively journals that brought him lasting fame. From the pages of these narratives it seems unlikely that he could ever feel more fulfilled than as the faithful "Steddy," riding forth into the wilderness with his troop of "knight-errant" companions. To Virginians, North Carolina was "the sinke of America" as profiled by a sprightly, worldly Virginian whose ironic wit reflected all the biases of his aristocratic peers.

The survey began with an order to the governors of Virginia and North Carolina to appoint commissioners and surveyors. From the Virginia council came Byrd (Steddy), Richard Fitz-William (Firebrand), William Dandridge (Meanwell), and two surveyors: William Mayo (Astrolabe) and Alexander Irvine (Orion). Because they would be entering "an ungodly Country where they shou'd find neither Church nor Minister," the party included a chaplain, the Reverend Peter Fontaine (Dr. Humdrum).[82]

Byrd wittily described the North Carolina commissioners—"the Flower & Cream of the Council of that Province"—in his "secret history." If Christopher Gale (Jumble) had not "formerly been a Pyrate himself, he seem'd intimately acquainted with many of them." John Lovick (Shoebrush) was simply a "merry good humor'd man." The distinguished Edward Moseley (Plausible), the most important political figure of his day, was portrayed as smooth tongued, possessing qualities of a Jesuit. William Little (Puzzle Cause) was dismissed as "a very wicked, but awkward, Rake." The Carolina surveyor, assisted by Moseley, was the young Samuel Swann (Bo-otes).[83]

Byrd characteristically faced the adventure in style, with adequate retainers, a tent, a marquee or dining fly, and enough wine and rum "to drink every Night to the Success of the following Day." Byrd brought two servants and fifteen experienced woodsmen, mostly former Indian traders. At Norfolk, the commission had engaged two periaugers and loaded two kegs of wine, two kegs of rum, and a quantity of bread. Betraying a curious blind spot regarding his own stores, Byrd believed the North Carolinians were "better provided for the Belly than the Business." The joint commission rendezvoused at Currituck Inlet on 5 March 1728 to commence the survey. That night, while Byrd lay in the woods sheltered from the stiff breeze by a bower of cedar branches, his mind turned from the uncharted wilderness he was facing. He "cast a longing Eye towards England, and sighed."[84]

The next day at noon the latitude was determined to be 36°31'. The afternoon was consumed by a heated debate about where to start the survey, and the next morning the expedition began when a stake was driven into the sand on the north shore of the inlet.[85] Setting sail across the shallow sound, grounding frequently, the band of explorers landed on the swampy mainland to become enmeshed for two days in a "quagmire and pocosins," finally camping at a plantation, where "All the People in the Neighbourhood flock't . . . to behold such Rarities as they fancied us to be. The Men left their belov'd Chimney Corners, the good Women their Spining Wheels, and some . . . rose out of their sick Beds to come and stare at us. They look't upon us as a Troop of Knight Errants, who were running this great Risque of our Lives." Grimly urging the surveyors to make their wills, the local people told them they were "the first of Human Race" to attempt crossing the Dismal Swamp from east to west and "dare say will be the last."[86]

Throughout the survey Byrd catalogued the primitive North Carolina borderers' peccadilloes. He described them as "Indolent Wretches" who grew no fodder for their swine and cattle but turned the animals out to forage in the woods, sometimes cutting down trees to provide Spanish moss for feed. Byrd made no allowance for the open-range husbandry practiced for generations along the frontier in all the southern colonies. Tongue in cheek, he commented that Carolinians "devour so much Swine's flesh, that it fills them full of gross Humours . . . [and] makes them likewise extremely hoggish in their Temper, & many of them seem to Grunt rather than Speak in their ordinary conversation."[87]

One evening found Byrd and Lovick at the home of "a Family of Mulattos" where "a Dark Angel surpriz'd us with her Charms." Since Byrd believed that "many Slaves shelter themselves in this obscure Part of the World," he suspected that his hosts were runaways.

Noting that the "worthy Borderers" protected not only runaways but also "Debtors and Criminals," he speculated, perhaps with irony, that from such "small" beginnings North Carolina might become "the Seat of some other great Empire."[88] Virginia's strict church establishment forced religious dissenters, little better than infidels to Byrd, to seek refuge along the border. Although Byrd knew that North Carolina had attracted few priests, he expressed dismay that civil officials could marry couples but no one was empowered to christen children, who were left to be reared as "Arrant Pagans." He surmised that the Carolinians were glad not to be "Priest ridden" and must not be "troubled with any Religious Fumes, and have the least Superstition of any People living."[89]

While the intrepid surveyors took two weeks to slog some fifteen miles through the forbidding Dismal Swamp, the commissioners circled around and made camp. Uneasy visitors came daily to the camp to inquire about the relation of their land to the new border. As Byrd saw it, if they became Virginians, they would be subject "to some sort of Order and Government; whereas, in N. Carolina every one does what seems best in his own Eyes."[90]

With relish, Byrd drew a satirical portrait of his southern neighbor: "Surely there is no place in the World where the Inhabitants live with less Labour, than in N. Carolina. It approaches nearer to the Description of Lubberland than any other, by the great felicity of the Climate, the easiness of raising Provisions, and the Slothfulness of the People." An imaginary land of luxury and laziness, Lubberland was well-known in popular literature. To Byrd, it was "Aversion to Labour that makes People file off to N. Carolina where Plenty and a warm Sun confirm them in their Disposition to Laziness for their whole Lives."[91] For generations, North Carolinians failed to grasp Byrd's playful wit, viewing him as a haughty Virginian peering down his nose at his lowly neighbors.

After the surveyors and commissioners reunited, the line was carried forward until 4 April, when rattlesnakes began to reappear in the warmer weather, forcing the end of the survey for that season. After drawing "an Elegant Plat" of the seventy-three miles of the line that had been finished, the company agreed to reconvene in September to complete the task. The various members of the party started for home the next day.[92]

With Byrd now officially in command of the Virginia delegation, the second half of the boundary survey began on 20 September. The goal was to reach the mountains before winter. The commissioners would venture into uncharted territory beyond the settlements, crossing the great warpath used by northern Indians to attack the Catawba. The night before they left "civilization," the survey party's drunken rowdiness forced their landlady to defend her honor by barricading herself in her bedroom armed with a full chamber pot. Although embarrassed by the incident, Byrd seemed more concerned the next day with the loss of a bottle of cherry brandy, broken by the jolting of the North Carolinians' rickety cart.[93]

The Virginia expedition of twenty retainers, the surveyors, and the commission expected to subsist on 1,000 pounds of bread supplemented with ten days' provisions and wild game. The three North Carolina commissioners brought 500 pounds of bacon and dried beef and 500 pounds of biscuit. Over the course of the trip the hunters, including Saponi Indian Ned Bearskin, provided dozens of turkeys, deer, and bear, augmented with a wildcat, a bison, a mountain partridge, a raccoon, a squirrel, and a skunk. The party heard panthers and wolves, found elk horns, and sighted flocks of geese, cranes, and wild pigeons. Although they saw signs of bison several times, the kill made toward the end of the trip was a rare occurrence.[94] A refreshing interlude ensued when the iconic frontiersman Epaphroditus Bainton guided them to a plantation. Byrd was awed that the sixty-year-old Bainton kept a concubine, ranged in the woods up to twenty-five miles a day, and claimed to bag about a hundred deer a year.[95]

Fifteen days out on the trail, some 170 miles from the coast and about 50 miles beyond the last settlement, the North Carolina commissioners surprised Byrd by abandoning the survey at the Hyco River. Byrd and the Virginia commissioners, except Fitz-William, chose to follow their orders to take the line to the mountains. The hot-tempered Fitz-William's strenuous argument almost escalated into a brawl, but the collapse of a table broke the tension. A joint plat was negotiated and drawn by surveyor Mayo, and the two commissions departed amicably.[96]

Relieved of the Carolinians and the irascible Fitz-William, Byrd relaxed and truly enjoyed his adventure, becoming more and more the woodsman and each day reveling in the surrounding beauty, natural phenomena, new medicinal plants, and "Company of so many Brave Fellows." Near the confluence of the Dan and Staunton Rivers, the company formed a mock order and began wearing turkey beards in their hats as cockades. As they crossed the clear waters of the Dan, which Byrd named, sunlight struck abundant mica in the sand so that it sparkled as if it were gold. Byrd considered it the most beautiful stream he had ever seen. The next day, on 11 October, the party first sighted distant western mountains that appeared "like Ranges of Blue Clouds rising one above another." Byrd named two of the major tributaries of the Dan for his surveyors— the Irvine (now Smith) and Mayo Rivers, both of which join the Dan south of the border.[97]

As the hilly terrain became rougher, on 26 October the jaded horses, which had not had proper feed for some time, forced a halt. The line had been run 72 miles farther, for a total of 241.5 miles from the coast. That afternoon the whole party climbed a hill north of the camp and beheld an "Amphitheatre of Mountains" extending some thirty miles west, with four distinct ledges to the north and one broken ledge to the south. Byrd observed, "One of the Southern Mountains was so vastly high, it seem'd to hide its head in the Clouds, and the West End of it terminated in a horrible Precipice." The mountain just to the east "heav'd itself up in the form of a vast Stack of Chimneys."[98]

Delayed for four days by heavy rain, the return to civilization began on 30 October. Although hampered by increasingly bad weather and swollen streams, the journey was uneventful, the party reaching a settler's home by 15 November. Byrd was back at Westover a week later. Of all the remarkable sights on the three-month trek, Byrd was most entranced by the upper Dan River, where he found rich soil and forests of cane. As the survey party crossed the clear river, Byrd noted that the "high Land" was "very good" and the "low Grounds promis'd the greatest Fertility of any I had ever seen." The abandoned Saura Indian fields were covered with "a sweet kind of Grass, almost knee-high, which was excellent Forage for the Horses."[99]

Having learned that North Carolina commissioners would be paid with land, Byrd may already have arranged his Dan valley purchase. His witty jibes notwithstanding, Byrd really believed that North Carolina was "a very happy country" where people "may live both in health and plenty." By 9 December he had patented 20,000 acres that he named "the Land of Eden," for which he paid Moseley and his companions £200. Although not yet connected to "a market or to navigation," he firmly believed that these "estates will be valuable."[100]

WHEN GEORGE BURRINGTON returned as the new royal governor on 25 February 1731, he "found the Province in the greatest Confusion the Government sunk so low that neither Peace or Order subsisted, the General Court suppressed, the Council set aside a year and a half, some of the Precinct Courts fallen, the admiralty Court having no restraint." Burrington blamed his erstwhile ally, vice-admiralty judge Edmund Porter, as well as Governor Everard, whom he viewed as a "very weak man."[101]

After the Crown purchased Carolina, the council appealed for relief, informing the king of the "State of this unhappy Province" caused by Governor Everard's "great Incapacity and weakness" and "Oppression and Arbitrary Power." Counted in the litany of abuses were contempt of the council, flouting the law, charging excessive fees, and frequent offenses by his "Pack of Rude children."[102] Adopting Burrington's penchant for personally attacking opponents, Sir Richard threatened to suspend Chief Justice Gale and Secretary Lovick from office and imprison them for lack of zeal in prosecuting his enemies. Everard was livid about the council's "Secret and Clandestine" letter to the king, and he blamed his troubles on bad advice from his former allies—Gale, Lovick, and Little.[103]

There was more than enough personal responsibility for the chaos; however, twenty months had elapsed between the sale of the propriety and Burrington's arrival, creating uncertainty about the legality of the government. Bearing a royal commission, Porter kept the vice-admiralty court open and "began to draw all manner of Business," which incidentally increased his revenue. A more capable and decisive governor might have been able to lead in such a void, but not Sir Richard.

Taking charge and imposing Crown policies was Governor Burrington's task. Considering his vindictiveness and removal five years earlier, what were they thinking in London? Within six months the choleric Burrington had alienated friends, verbally abused and physically assaulted officials, and aroused former adversaries. Nevertheless, nearly four years elapsed before he was suspended. Although he contributed to the colony's expansion and commercial growth, in North Carolina's long and checkered political history Burrington has a dubious distinction as the sole governor to be recalled twice—first by the proprietors and then by the Crown.[104]

Toward a New State

IN THE MID-SEVENTEENTH CENTURY, following Virginia's second devastating Indian war, migrants trickled across the southern frontier into Roanoke country, finding a lonely but safe region, thinly populated by dwindling remnants of Algonquian tribes. On their own, settlers occupied fertile abandoned Indian fields accessible from numerous tributaries of the largest sound-estuarine system of the continent—a watery world that, except for lacking a stable, deep outlet to the sea, bore an uncanny resemblance to the Chesapeake. Hampered by the absence of institutions—no towns, no ports, no churches, no schools, no infrastructure—and a government that was at times chaotic, the self-reliant pioneers of the Albemarle forged a viable economy of diversified farming, ranching, and exploitation of the abundant pine, cypress, and hardwood forests. When the Lords Proprietors shifted their focus to their more promising southern colony, the Albemarle settlers became an afterthought, left to chart their own course within the proprietary framework of representative self-government, a judicial system that guaranteed English political liberty, and freedom of conscience attractive to dissenters.

Although not wealthy, North Carolina had a middling economy with a narrower gulf between rich and poor than her neighbors. The "poor" in the proprietary colony's epithet can be attributed to the small number of port records that survive, and the shipping of most of its trade through secondary seaports—Boston, Providence, Salem, Philadelphia, Norfolk, and Charles Town—where the origin of the products was lost. Near the end of the era, Brunswick on the Cape Fear River became the colony's first port regularly trading directly with England. The resulting expansion of North Carolina's most important export, naval stores, augmented by timber and later by rice, fostered great plantations along the Cape Fear and created the colony's wealthiest region in the royal period.

In the early eighteenth century North Carolina began losing its uniqueness and more closely resembling its neighbors as the Anglican Church was established and Quakers were purged from the government. Although an elite-driven plantation economy evolved that relied on more enslaved African labor, the majority of the colonists continued to live on small farms and ranches, their lives regulated by the precinct and general courts and the elected assembly in conjunction with the governor and council. For free citizens of the colony, proprietary North Carolina was the epitome of freedom—political, religious, social, and economic.

As the proprietary era ended, North Carolina was poised for continued population growth and economic development. Over seven decades the colonists' numbers had increased from a few hundred to over 36,000. These included 30,000 northern Europeans, primarily English, and nearly 6,000 Africans, mostly enslaved, although some free Blacks had lived in the colony from the beginning. The Indian population of the coastal plain had dwindled from more than 10,000 to under 1,000, predominantly Tuscarora in the Indian Woods reservation, Meherrin on the upper Chowan, and scattered remnants of other tribes.[1] By rapid expansion in the royal era, North Carolina grew into the fourth most populous of the thirteen American colonies.

Although the Anglican Church had been established since 1701 and parish vestries were organized in every precinct, the colony had few priests or missionaries. Some chapels had been built, but worship was usually held in homes or public buildings with lay readers. In spite of political persecution, Quakers flourished in their traditional seats of Pasquotank and Perquimans. Calvinists—Presbyterians, Huguenots, and German Reformed—were increasing, and the General Baptists were multiplying rapidly. In place of complete religious freedom, North Carolina now offered religious tolerance.

Political confrontation in the royal period changed. No longer did personal and factional feuds spawn coups d'état and rebellions; instead, sectional hostilities arose between the North and South over the imbalance in assembly representation that imposed an Albemarle stranglehold over the rest of the colony. By the mid-eighteenth century, sectional conflict, exacerbated by economic, class, and religious differences, had shifted to an east–west orientation, culminating in the War of the Regulation (1765–71), the most significant rebellion in any colony prior to the American Revolution. A chiefly Anglican eastern governing class—merchants, officials, and large planters with enslaved laborers— quelled the Regulation challenge of western small farmers and planters, who were typically dissenters. The Revolutionary War saw the same triumphant eastern elite defeat the Crown.

For North Carolina, Culpeper's Rebellion, the Regulation, and the Revolution were milestones in the long continuum of political struggle that began with Magna Carta and eventually elevated commoners to power. In North Carolina in the 1770s, just as in the 1670s, the question was "Who should rule at home?" Who would shape the destiny of North Carolina—the proprietors or colonists, the Crown or Commons, the planters and merchants or the yeoman farmers, the Anglicans or Quakers, or the various factions? Imperial oversight, whether private or royal, was essentially irrelevant.

The hard-won independence of the united colonies, proclaiming political and social ideals in the Declaration of Independence that were grounded in the English Revolution of 1640–60 and the Glorious Revolution of 1688–89, unleashed a continuing struggle toward those ideals. Although it took a bloody civil war, the nation eradicated the evil of slavery and continues to strive, albeit unevenly and painfully slowly, toward racial justice, gender equality, social and economic fairness, and equal opportunity for all citizens. Regrettably, the United States and North Carolina still fall far short of these ideals, but as long as the nation and the state continue to confirm these principles as our goals, we are on the right course.

NOTES

Abbreviations

ANB   John A. Garrity and Mark C. Carnes, eds., *American National Biography*, 24 vols. (New York: Oxford University Press, 1999).

CRNC   William L. Saunders, ed., *The Colonial Records of North Carolina*, 10 vols. (Raleigh: State of North Carolina, 1886–90).

CRNC2   Mattie Erma E. Parker (vols. 1–3), William S. Price (vols. 4–5), Robert J. Cain (vols. 6–11), and Jan-Michael Poff (vol. 11), eds., *The Colonial Records of North Carolina, Second Series*, 11 vols. (Raleigh: Office of Archives and History, 1963–2007).

DNB   Leslie Stephens and Sidney Lee, *Dictionary of National Biography*, 22 vols. (London: Oxford University Press, 1921–22).

DNCB   William S. Powell, ed., *Dictionary of North Carolina Biography*, 6 vols. (Chapel Hill: University of North Carolina Press, 1979–96).

ENC   William S. Powell, ed., *Encyclopedia of North Carolina* (Chapel Hill: University of North Carolina Press, 2006).

NCHGR   James R. B. Hathaway, ed., *The North Carolina Historical and Genealogical Register*, 3 vols. (Edenton, NC, 1901–3).

NCHR   *North Carolina Historical Review*.

SCE   Walter Edgar, ed., *The South Carolina Encyclopedia* (Columbia: University of South Carolina Press, 2006).

SF   *Southern Friend: Journal of the North Carolina Friends Historical Society*.

SRNC   Walter M. Clark, ed., *The State Records of North Carolina*, 16 vols. (Winston: State of North Carolina, 1895–1906).

SSCWI   Secretary of State Council Minutes, Wills, and Inventories, 1677–1701, State Archives of North Carolina, Raleigh.

VMHB   *Virginia Magazine of History and Biography*.

Introduction

1. Ethridge, *From Chicaza to Chickasaw*, 1–5; Hudson, *Juan Pardo Expeditions*, 54, 56, 58, 59, 72, 73.

2. The Crown asserted its ownership twice: in 1603–6, when Raleigh's estate was seized on his arrest for treason, and 1624–29, after the failure of the Virginia Company.

3. The Fundamental Constitutions protected this freedom, even for enslaved Indians and Africans. *CRNC2*, 1:181, 183.

4. *SRNC*, 23:978, 983; Lefler, *North Carolina History Told by Contemporaries*, 105–7.

5. Tise and Crow, *New Voyages*, 356–57.

6. Powell, *North Carolina: A History*, xi.

7. Walter M. Clark (1846–1924) was a Civil War veteran, attorney, historical editor, chief justice of the state supreme court, and lifelong crusader for social justice. *DNCB*, 1:378–79.

8. Hawks, *History of North Carolina*, 2:457–58.

9. *CRNC*, 1:x.

10. Connor, *History*, 1:iii.

11. Connor, *North Carolina*, 1:91.

12. Lefler, *History of North Carolina*, 1:xvii.

13. Lefler and Powell, *Colonial North Carolina*, xiii–xiv.

14. Butler, *North Carolina Genesis*, 2–3, 72.

15. Osgood, *American Colonies*, 2:435–37.

16. Osgood, *American Colonies*, 2:439.

17. Osgood, *American Colonies*, 2:441–42.

18. C. M. Andrews, *Colonial Period*, 3:ix–xii.

19. Tolles, *Quakers*, 56.

20. Craven, *Southern Colonies*, 408–10.

21. Butler, *North Carolina Genesis*, 2–3.

22. McIlvenna, *Very Mutinous People*, 1. For a review, see Wood, "Struggling," 602.

23. McIlvenna, *Early American Rebels*, 42–51, 79–87, 91–96.

24. Death and property confiscation were mandated for blaspheming God and denying Christ's divinity or the Trinity. Fines, whipping, prison, or banishment awaited those guilty of criticizing the Virgin Mary, the Apostles, or the Trinity. "Maryland Toleration Act"; C. M. Andrews, *Colonial Period*, 2:310–14, 311n; Osgood, *American Colonies*, 2:319–22.

25. *CRNC2*, 1:181–83. See chapters 5 and 9 for a more extensive discussion of the origin of religious liberty in North Carolina.

26. Becker, *History of Political Parties*, 5, 22.

27. Bailyn, "Politics," 114–15.

28. Quoted in Bailyn, *Atlantic History*, 12; Meinig, *Shaping of America*, 64–65.

29. Tolles, *Quakers*, 12, 13–14.

30. Wilde-Ramsing and Carnes-McNaughton, *Blackbeard's Sunken Prize*, 157.

Chapter One

1. Wroth, *Voyages of Giovanni de Verrazzano*, 133.

2. Wroth, *Voyages of Giovanni de Verrazzano*, 7–8; Morison, *European Discovery of America: Northern Voyages*, 279–83.

3. The rating of ships' capacity in tuns refers to the 252-gallon tun wine container, which weighed about 2,000 pounds.

4. Wroth, *Voyages of Giovanni de Verrazzano*, 74–75, 133, 141, 143. For years Wroth's location of Verrazzano's landfall well south of Cape Fear convinced scholars except historian and sailor Samuel E. Morison. Verrazzano was an excellent navigator, and his first sighting at 34° north, about ten miles north of Cape Fear, was confirmed on land. He missed the entrance to the Cape Fear River because Frying Pan Shoals forced him to sail fifteen miles offshore. Verrazzano's repeated estimates of "fifty leagues" cannot be taken literally.

5. Wroth, *Voyages of Giovanni de Verrazzano*, 134–35.

6. Wroth, *Voyages of Giovanni de Verrazzano*, 135–36; Morison, *European Discovery of*

America: Northern Voyages, 290–95. By mislocating Verrazzano's first landfall south of Cape Fear, Wroth, *Voyages of Giovanni de Verrazzano*, 78, and subsequently Cumming, *Mapping the North Carolina Coast*, 6, and Hoffman, *New Andalucia*, 110, identify Annunciata near Cape Lookout. No visible body of water there could be confused with the Pacific Ocean. Morison correctly places Annunciata south of Cape Hatteras, where the mainland cannot be seen.

7. Wroth, *Voyages of Giovanni de Verrazzano*, 136–37; Morison, *European Discovery of America: Northern Voyages*, 295–97. Samuel Morison's low-altitude flight is convincing: there is no other coastal hilly area that evokes Arcadia. Arcadia has been located by other scholars on the Delmarva Peninsula. See Wroth, *Voyages of Giovanni de Verrazzano*, 78; Quinn, *North America*, 154–55; Hoffman, *New Andalucia*, 110.

8. Wroth, *Voyages of Giovanni de Verrazzano*, 137; Morison, *European Discovery of America: Northern Voyages*, 298. A harquebus was a lightweight matchlock fired by a burning match or fuse, hence the later name "fuzee" or "fusil."

9. Wroth, *Voyages of Giovanni de Verrazzano*, 136; Morison, *European Discovery of America: Northern Voyages*, 296, 298.

10. Wroth, *Voyages of Giovanni de Verrazzano*, 136–37.

11. Wroth, *Voyages of Giovanni de Verrazzano*, 141. See Cumming, *Southeast in Early Maps*, 107, plate 3, and 115, plate 8; Morison, *European Discovery of America: Northern Voyages*, 319–20n, 321 map.

12. Wroth, *Voyages of Giovanni de Verrazzano*, 142.

13. Verrazzano commanded two more transatlantic voyages to Brazil and the West Indies. In 1528 on one of the Leeward Islands, Verrazzano waded ashore alone into a gathering of fierce Caribs, who promptly killed and ate him at the surf's edge, while his horrified brother could do nothing to save him. Morison, *European Discovery of America: Northern Voyages*, 314–15.

14. Morison, *European Discovery of America: Southern Voyages*, 502–3, 506–7, 510–11, 515.

15. Hoffman, *New Andalucia*, 3–6, 8, 10, 315–28. Villafañe's misidentification of the Cape Fear River as the Jordan River has long confounded explorers and historians. There is no body of water northeast of Cape Fear to correspond with Winyah Bay, which the Spanish located just north of the Jordan River. See Cumming, *Mapping the North Carolina Coast*, 86–87, 95, 99, 10.

16. Hoffman, *New Andalucia*, 11–13, 21, 34–36, 51–58, 328. See Cumming, *Southeast in Early Maps*, Vespucci 1526 map, plate 2; Ribero 1529 map, plate 4. In 1526 Ayllón launched an ill-fated colony intended for Chicora but relocated farther south as San Miguel de Gualdape. Somewhere between northern South Carolina and Sapelo Sound in Georgia, the site of this first European colony in the Southeast has eluded archaeologists.

17. Ward and Davis, *Time before History*, 119–34, 157–93; Ethridge, *From Chicaza to Chickasaw*, 11–18; Pauketat, *Cahokia*, 1–35.

18. Hudson, "Hernando de Soto Expeditions," 74–82; Morison, *European Discovery of America: Southern Voyages*, 526–27; Quinn, *North America*, 206–10.

19. Clayton, Knight, and Moore, *De Soto Chronicles*, 1:229–30, 273–76, 2:272–76, 281, 284–89, 307–9, 312–13; Hudson, *Knight of Spain*, 168–72, 174–78, 185–87; Ward and Davis, *Time before History*, 123–33, 260–61. See Coe, *Town Creek*, 82–83, 93, 98. John Swanton's 1939 study had de Soto barely skirting southwestern North Carolina in Macon, Clay, and Cherokee Counties. Although Rights, *American Indian*, 7–8, dissented, it took new documents and

archaeological excavations to establish the accurate route up the Wateree-Catawba valley. By placing Cofitachequi near Augusta on the Savannah River rather than near Camden, South Carolina, Swanton misplaced de Soto's route by a hundred miles. De Pratter, "Chiefdom of Cofitachequi," 206–7.

20. Hudson, "Hernando de Soto Expeditions," 84, 91, 94, 99; Quinn, *North America*, 212–22.

21. Hoffman, *New Andalucia*, 175–78. Cape San Román (South Island), just north of the South Santee River, is about 100 statute miles south of Cape Fear.

22. Hoffman, *New Andalucia*, 178–81; Cumming, *Mapping the North Carolina Coast*, 18. He was at Cape Hatteras (35°13'N) and not Cape Lookout (34°35'N). See below for the shipwrecks off Ocracoke and Hatteras Islands described to the English in 1584 that suggest Cape Hatteras rather than Cape Lookout as the location of the hurricane.

23. Hoffman, *New Andalucia*, 180.

24. Hoffman, *New Andalucia*, 206–7, 209–12, 217–23, 229–30; Quinn, *North America*, 241–61; Cumming, *Mapping the North Carolina Coast*, 25; Lorant, *New World*, 30–31. Among the few French who escaped were Laudonnière and Le Moyne. See Lorant, *New World*, for the French narratives and the De Bry engravings of Le Moyne's watercolors.

25. Quinn, *North America*, 264–70; Hudson, *Juan Pardo Expeditions*, 18, 23; Lyon, *Enterprise*, 166; South, *Archaeology at Santa Elena*, 3–4. Also in 1566, Captain Pedro de Coronas landed at the northern inlet to Currituck Sound, where he reported an empty land of no interest. Hoffman, *New Andalucia*, 244–45; Vigneras, "Spanish Discovery," 405–6, 412, 414.

26. Hudson, *Juan Pardo Expeditions*, 23, 258; Blackburn, "Spain's Appalachian Outpost," 39–40; *ENC*, 867.

27. Hudson, *Juan Pardo Expeditions*, 146–52; Blackburn, "Spain's Appalachian Outpost," 38–42; Moore, Beck, and Rodning, "Joara and Fort San Juan"; Moore, Beck, and Rodning, "Warren Wilson." Since 1986 archaeologists at the Berry site (Joara) near Morganton are rewriting the prehistory and history of western North Carolina. "Archaeology at Warren Wilson College."

28. Hudson, *Juan Pardo Expeditions*, 24–29, 259, 263–64.

29. Hudson, *Juan Pardo Expeditions*, 32, 35–36, 40–41, 173–77; *ENC*, 867.

30. See Winkler, *Walking*, chap. 2.

31. Cumming, *Mapping the North Carolina Coast*, 9–10, 123, 125, 127; Morison, *European Discovery of America: Northern Voyages*, 319–20n, 321, 483–84.

32. Mancall, *Hakluyt's Promise*, 92–101, 163–64, 170–73, 175, 183–94, 211, 228–29; Morison, *European Discovery of America: Northern Voyages*, 555–60; Lorant, *New World*, 10, 30–31, 118, 280; Hulton, "Images of the New World," 200–202; Hulton, *America 1585*, 8–9, 17.

33. Bradley, *British Maritime Enterprise*, 53–130; K. R. Andrews, "Elizabethan Privateering," 3–10. See K. R. Andrews, *Elizabethan Privateering*; and Ronald, *Pirate Queen*.

34. K. R. Andrews, *Trade*, 184–86; Mancall, *Hakluyt's Promise*, 62–63; Horning, *Ireland in the Virginian Sea*, 17–100; Canny, *Elizabethan Conquest*.

35. *CRNC2*, 1:5–9; Morison, *European Discovery of America: Northern Voyages*, 563–67; Miller, *Captains from Devon*, 55–59; Ronald, *Pirate Queen*, 249–55; K. R. Andrews, *Trade*, 183–86. Letters patent is a public document issued by the monarch granting an office, title, or right. The proprietary charters convey both land ownership and governance rights.

36. Quinn, *North America*, 326–64; Morison, *European Discovery of America: Northern Voyages*, 573–77; Miller, *Captains from Devon*, 59–63.

37. *CRNC2*, 1:13–18; Adamson and Folland, *Shepherd*, 26–27, 29–31, 45–47, 55–57, 64–67, 85–86; Miller, *Captains from Devon*, 151–54.

38. Isil, "Simon Fernandez," 66–81; Quinn, *Raleigh and the British Empire*, 246–63; *DNCB*, 2:190–91.

39. Humber, *Backgrounds*, 4–8, 11–13, 15–16; *DNCB*, 1:30, 45–47, 97, 3:45–47, 4:14–15, 6:176–80; Shirley, *Sir Walter Ralegh*, 20–21, 24; Oberg, *Dominion and Civility*, 2, 8, 10, 12, 27.

40. Quinn and Quinn, *First Colonists*, 1–2, 132n; Quinn, *Roanoke Voyages, 1584–1590*, 1:78, 93; Richard Butler deposition, quoted in Quinn, *Raleigh and the British Empire*, 255–56.

41. Quinn and Quinn, *First Colonists*, 2–4, 11; Morison, *European Discovery of America: Northern Voyages*, 574. Because the inlets and shoreline of the Outer Banks are constantly changing, the modern beach is about a mile farther west than when Amadas and Barlowe arrived. Cape Kenrick, the most prominent feature on White's 1585 maps, had disappeared before 1700. See Cumming, *Southeast in Early Maps*, 117–21, 123–25, plates 10–12, 14; Quinn, *Set Fair for Roanoke*, 100, 102, 134.

42. Quinn and Quinn, *First Colonists*, 2–4; Quinn, *Set Fair for Roanoke*, 35; Quinn, *Roanoke Voyages 1584–1590*, 1:99, 116–17, 2:508. In the grant of arms to the City of Raleigh on 7 January 1587 the new land was identified as "Ossomocomuck, alias Wyngandacoia."

43. Quinn and Quinn, *First Colonists*, 4–7; Quinn, *Set Fair for Roanoke*, 35–36. "Chammoys" (chamois) was probably brain-tanned deerskin, and "buffe" may have been tanned buffalo hide. Interior savannas or prairies provided habitat for bison, whose legacy remains as the "Buffalo" in the names of creeks, mountains, and towns throughout the Southeast.

44. Quinn and Quinn, *First Colonists*, 7–10.

45. Quinn and Quinn, *First Colonists*, 8; Quinn, *Raleigh and the British Empire*, 8, 12; Oberg, "Manteo and Wanchese."

46. Stick, *Roanoke Island*, 55–59; Quinn, *Set Fair for Roanoke*, 40–41; Quinn, *North America*, 327–28; Shirley, *Sir Walter Ralegh*, 26–27, 30.

47. Hume, *Virginia Adventure*, 71–84. At "Fort Raleigh" in the 1990s archaeologists uncovered Gans's laboratory beneath the earthwork.

48. Quinn and Quinn, *First Colonists*, 17–18; Sloan, *New World*, 41.

49. Quinn and Quinn, *First Colonists*, 18.

50. Quinn and Quinn, *First Colonists*, 18, 22; Hariot, *Brief and True Report*, 31–32. Excavations have established that the fort, presumed to have been built in 1585, was constructed later, possibly as a refuge. Approaching its low grassy slopes today in a clearing among tall pines evokes the fragile origin of English America and the poignant mystery of the Lost Colony. Hume, *Virginia Adventure*, 84–90.

51. Hariot, *Brief and True Report*, 13–15, 17–21.

52. Hariot, *Brief and True Report*, 16. Hariot became a lifelong smoker and in 1621 died of cancer of the nose.

53. Hariot, *Brief and True Report*, 25–30.

54. The Chowanoac (Chowanoke, Chowan) Indians, the largest Algonquian tribe living in the Albemarle region, remained influential into the eighteenth century. *ENC*, 218.

55. Quinn and Quinn, *First Colonists*, 25–33, 35–42; Hariot, *Brief and True Report*, 24–25; Oberg, *Head in Edward Nugent's Hand*, 81–104; Stick, *Roanoke Island*, 122–26, 137–40.

56. Quinn and Quinn, *First Colonists*, 42–45, 80–81, 85–86, 97; Stick, *Roanoke Island*, 142–51; Quinn, *Set Fair for Roanoke*, 133–38, 140–41, 150–53.

57. Quinn and Quinn, *First Colonists*, xxiii, 93, 107–9; Stick, *Roanoke Island*, 152–53, 159–60; Quinn, *Set Fair for Roanoke*, 254–55, 258–61.

58. Quinn and Quinn, *First Colonists*, 97–104; Stick, *Roanoke Island*, 160–61, 164–65, 168–73, 175–76; Quinn, *Set Fair for Roanoke*, 284–85, 276–85.

59. Quinn and Quinn, *First Colonists*, 122–28; Lorant, *New World*, 168.

60. Emery, "Map's Hidden Marks"; First Colony Foundation, "Hidden Images"; First Colony Foundation, "Testing Continues."

Chapter Two

1. Quinn, *Lost Colonists*, 30–33; Quinn, *Set Fair for Roanoke*, 355–57, 360.

2. Adamson and Folland, *Shepherd*, 330–32, 437–49; Quinn, *Raleigh and the British Empire*, 173–76, 203–4; C. Lee, *1603*, 267–93. When James I succeeded Elizabeth in 1603, Raleigh's enemies falsely accused him of plotting against the new king. Raleigh's estate was confiscated, and he was imprisoned.

3. Osgood, *American Colonies*, 1:24, 27–29.

4. Tyler, *Narratives*, 162–63, 188; Quinn, *Set Fair for Roanoke*, 370–75; Quinn, *Lost Colonists*, 45–47.

5. Tyler, *Narratives*, 359, 362n, 368–69. See Hume, *Martin's Hundred*, 185–298.

6. C. M. Andrews, *Colonial Period*, 1:172–78.

7. Quoted in Powell, *John Pory*, 100–101. See Tyler, *Narratives*, 355.

8. Powell, *John Pory*, 101–2, 105–6.

9. Kopperman, "Profile of Failure," 2; Kopperman, *Sir Robert Heath*, 190–92; C. M. Andrews, *Colonial Period*, 1:308–10, 2:246, 279, 282; H. R. Paschal, "Proprietary North Carolina," 10–14.

10. *CRNC2*, 1:64–66; Kopperman, *Sir Robert Heath*, 78–105, 184, 191–92, 224–25, 231–32, 285–91; *DNCB*, 3:90–91. Heath was Chief Justice of Common Pleas and later of King's Bench.

11. Lapsley, *County Palatine*, 1–2, 31–38, 68–74, 114–15, 156–64, 196–97. The Palatine County of Durham was abolished in 1836. The Bishop of Durham clause was in the Avalon charter in Newfoundland (1623) to George Calvert, Lord Baltimore. C. M. Andrews, *Colonial Period*, 2:277, 282, 283n.

12. *CRNC2*, 1:65–66, 68–69.

13. Kopperman, "Profile of Failure," 1.

14. *CRNC2*, 1:64, 70; Kopperman, "Profile of Failure," 3, 6–7; Powell, "Carolana and the Incomparable Roanoke," 5.

15. Kopperman, "Profile of Failure," 7–9.

16. Kopperman, "Profile of Failure," 9–12, 16; Powell, "Carolana and the Incomparable Roanoke," 6–7; H. R. Paschal, "Proprietary North Carolina," 23–24.

17. *DNB*, 2:156–58; K. R. Andrews, *Trade, Plunder, and Settlement*, 59–60; Bridenbaugh, *Vexed and Troubled Englishmen*, 425–26; C. M. Andrews, *Colonial Period*, 3:189–91; Kopperman, "Profile of Failure," 14.

18. Kopperman, "Profile of Failure," 14; C. M. Andrews, *Colonial Period*, 3:190–91; *CRNC*, 1:35.

19. Kopperman, "Profile of Failure," 14–16; C. M. Andrews, *Colonial Period*, 3:190–91; H. R. Paschal, "Proprietary North Carolina," 32n; Powell, "Carolana and the Incomparable Roanoke," 7–8n. *Mayflower* was a fairly common ship's name in the era.

20. Withington, "Virginia Gleanings"; Nugent, *Cavaliers and Pioneers*, 1:171–72; Powell, "Carolana and the Incomparable Roanoke," 8n. The Virginians were Thomas Osman, his father-in-law William Purrier, and his brother-in-law James Reeve. The party from Bermuda included William Salmon, Thomas Reeve, Thomas Terrill, Thomas Benedict, and Henery Whiteney. In this period Bermuda was referred to as the Somers Islands or Summer Islands. C. M. Andrews, *Colonial Period*, 1:214–15; Jarvis, *In the Eye of All Trade*, 11–49.

21. *DNCB*, 3:214–15; C. M. Andrews, *Colonial Period*, 2:222–23. In 1646 Maltravers inherited the title Earl of Arundel and Surrey and the office of Earl Marshal.

22. *CRNC*, 1:14–16; Kopperman, "Profile of Failure," 17–18.

23. There has been confusion about the date of Heath's transfer to Maltravers since Charles Andrews concluded that the documents should be dated 1632 rather than 1637/1638. See C. M. Andrews, *Colonial Period*, 3:189n; and Kopperman, "Profile of Failure," 17–18. Herbert Paschal argued effectively that the transfer took place on the later date. See H. R. Paschal, "Proprietary North Carolina," 36n; and Paschal's sketch of Maltravers in *DNCB*, 3:214–15. Paschal relies on the Daniel Coxe claim that the transaction took place on 2 December 13 Charles I. The regnal year indicates the later date. Coxe, *Description*, 116. Also see "Virginia," 48.

24. H. R. Paschal, "Proprietary North Carolina," 36–37; Kopperman, "Profile of Failure," 18–19; Powell, "Carolana and the Incomparable Roanoke," 9–10; *DNCB*, 3:215; C. M. Andrews, *Colonial Period*, 3:188. There are contradictory interpretations of the Hawley involvement in Carolana. Paschal more clearly navigated the sources. Kopperman had the advantage of Scottish documents that had not previously been used but qualified his conclusions. Kopperman, "Profile of Failure," 18n. Henry Hawley was governor of Barbados 1630–40 and authorized the first legislative colonial assembly there in 1639. This was the third representative assembly in the colonies—Virginia, 1619; Bermuda, 1620; and Barbados, 1639. See Beckles, *History of Barbados*, 9–11, 13, 23; P. F. Campbell, *Some Early Barbados History*, 63–64, 66, 69–70; C. M. Andrews, *Colonial Period*, 2:249–51.

25. Coxe, *Description*, 87; Powell, "Carolana and the Incomparable Roanoke," 10; Kopperman, "Profile of Failure," 19. Colleton is referring here to Thomas Howard, Lord Maltravers, to whom Charles II restored the title Duke of Norfolk in 1680.

26. Beverley, *History*, 60–61.

27. General Richard Bennett suffered persecution and fled to England. When he returned with Commonwealth troops he ousted Governor William Berkeley and served as governor 1652–55. In 1672 he was converted by the Quaker George Fox in Nansemond. Boddie, *Seventeenth Century Isle of Wight County*, 52, 55, 60–61, 64, 74–76, 116; Billings, *Sir William Berkeley*, 65–67, 82–83, 88, 109–11, 114–17, 121, 125, 207; Penney, *Journal of George Fox*, 2:442–43.

28. Colonel Dew, a Puritan, became speaker of the assembly and council member during the Commonwealth period in Virginia, 1652–60. Like Bennett, he was converted to Quakerism by George Fox. Billings, *Sir William Berkeley*, 117, 125; Penney, *Journal of George Fox*, 2:233, 442.

29. *CRNC*, 1:676; Briceland, *Westward*, 50–51; Powell, *North Carolina Gazetteer*, 319, 395. See the Comberford Map (1657) and compare it to the John Ogilby–James Moxon map (1672) and Joel Gascoyne map (1682). Cumming, *Southeast in Early Maps*, plates 32, 37, 39. Plumpton explicitly denied that Weyanoke Creek could be identified with the Blackwater, Nottaway, or Meherrin Rivers. His deposition, however, was taken by a Virginia commission attempting to locate the boundary as far south as possible. See *CRNC*, 1:xxii–xxiii, 676; *CRNC2*, 1:90.

30. *CRNC*, 1:676. The Tooke family were early settlers of Isle of Wight County.

31. Briceland, *Westward*, 15, 23–27.

32. Powell, "Carolina in the Seventeenth Century," 78–82; Lefler, "Promotional Literature," 15.

33. Powell, "Carolina in the Seventeenth Century," 78–79; Powell, "Carolana and the Incomparable Roanoke," 12–13.

34. Powell, "Carolina in the Seventeenth Century," 80–81; Powell, "Carolana and the Incomparable Roanoke," 11–12. Herbert Paschal attributed the authorship of this tract to John Farrer. H. R. Paschal, "Proprietary North Carolina," 45–46.

35. Lefler, "Description of 'Carolana,'" 102–4.

36. Lefler, "Description of 'Carolana,'" 103–4; Powell, "Carolana and the Incomparable Roanoke," 10–11.

37. Cumming, *Southeast in Early Maps*, 148–51, plate 29; Powell, "Carolana and the Incomparable Roanoke," 14.

38. Powell, "Carolana and the Incomparable Roanoke," 13–14; H. R. Paschal, "Proprietary North Carolina," 40–44.

39. Briceland, *Westward*, 14–22, 24–25, 27, 69–71; Salley, *Narratives*, 5; *DNCB*, 1:176.

40. Salley, *Narratives*, 8–10; Briceland, *Westward*, 70–75. Some studies locate Hocomawanack near Clarksville, Virginia. Based on rivers, terrain features, and Bland's descriptions, Briceland's conclusions that Roanoke Rapids was the destination is the most accurate. There is no evidence that Bland went as far east as the Chowan. Briceland, *Westward*, 29–35.

41. Salley, *Narratives*, 10–12; Briceland, *Westward*, 77–81.

42. Briceland, *Westward*, 82–87; Salley, *Narratives*, 14–17.

43. Salley, *Narratives*, 17–19; Briceland, *Westward*, 61–63, 88–91; *DNCB*, 1:176; Powell, "Carolana and the Incomparable Roanoke," 15; Cumming, *Southeast in Early Maps*, 148–51, plate 29. The symbols on one edition of the map are not English settlement sites. Rather, they are Indian town symbols drawn from Hariot and White. Powell, "Carolana and the Incomparable Roanoke," 14.

44. *CRNC*, 1:17; Hening, *Statutes at Large*, 1:380–81.

45. *CRNC*, 1:17. This is very likely a reference to the 1648 purchase of Henry Plumpton and Thomas Tooke.

46. Powell, "Carolana and the Incomparable Roanoke," 15; Powell, *Ye Countie of Albemarle*, xxi–xxii; H. R. Paschal, "Proprietary North Carolina," 59.

47. Parramore, Stewart, and Bogger, *Norfolk*, 29–31, 35–41; Salley, *Narratives*, 23. Yeardley's 1642 commission as militia captain is in Billings, *Papers*, 51.

48. Salley, *Narratives*, 25; Parramore, Stewart, and Bogger, *Norfolk*, 39; McPherson, "Nathaniel Batts," 72–73.

49. Salley, *Narratives*, 25–27; Powell, "Carolana and the Incomparable Roanoke," 16. Parramore, Stewart, and Bogger, *Norfolk*, 38, suggests that the emperor was Kiscutanewh, king of the Yeopim. Yeardley always refers to him as "the Roanoke."

50. Salley, *Narratives*, 26–28; Butler, "Early Settlement," 23–24.

51. Salley, *Narratives*, 25–28. The mineral assessment was based on some copper ornaments and two gold beads. In Yeardley's original letter he used "Carolana," not "Carolina." Cumming, "Naming Carolina," 37.

52. Salley, *Narratives*, 27; Powell, "Carolana and the Incomparable Roanoke," 16.

53. Salley, *Narratives*, 27–29.

54. Salley, *Narratives*, 28–29; Powell, "Carolana and the Incomparable Roanoke," 17.

55. Norfolk County Deeds, Book C, 180, Norfolk, Virginia; Butler, "Early Settlement," 24–25; McPherson, "Nathaniel Batts," 73. For the extent of the settlement at Batts's house, see Cumming, "Earliest Permanent Settlement"; and H. R. Paschal, "State in Search of a Birthday."

56. For the New York Public Library copy, see Cumming, *Southeast in Early Maps*, 152–54, plate 32. The National Maritime Museum copy is printed in *ENC*, 103; *DNCB*, 1:411–12.

57. Cumming, *Southeast in Early Maps*, plate 32, 153.

58. Powell, "Carolana and the Incomparable Roanoke," 18.

59. McPherson, "Nathaniel Batts," 73–74, 76.

60. McPherson, "Nathaniel Batts," 73–74; *DNCB*, 1:119.

61. Hening, *Statutes at Large*, 1:422; Robinson, "Notes," 165; McPherson, "Nathaniel Batts," 74–75, 78–79.

62. Powell, "Carolana and the Incomparable Roanoke," 17–18. For a time Cape Lookout was mislabeled "Cape Fear."

63. McPherson, "Nathaniel Batts," 75, 80; Powell, *North Carolina Gazetteer*, 26. Eroded over time, this island finally disappeared after a hurricane in the mid-twentieth century. "New Begin" is now Newbegun Creek.

64. Penney, *Journal of George Fox*, 2:234.

65. Penney, *Journal of George Fox*, 2:234; *CRNC2*, 2:72.

66. Butler, "Early Settlement," 25–26, 28.

67. James Tooke Will, 1 February 1660, Will and Deed Book 1:590, Isle of Wight County, Virginia. James Tooke Collection. Southern Historical Collection. University Library, Chapel Hill. James Tooke had settled in Isle of Wight County by 1653. Nugent, *Cavaliers and Pioneers*, 1:280. Tooke's will establishes when the Harveys moved to the Roanoke country.

68. James Tooke Will; Butler, "Early Settlement," 26.

69. Nugent, *Cavaliers and Pioneers*, 1:427; *CRNC2*, 3:479. The Harveys would have entered the Albemarle by the river route to South Quay and down the Blackwater to the Chowan. Settlements were emerging on both banks of the Chowan River.

70. *DNCB*, 3:63.

71. *CRNC2*, 1:71; *DNCB*, 5:392.

72. *NCHGR*, 3:146; Grimes, *Abstract*, 94.

73. "Indians of Southern Virginia," 347–49.

74. *CRNC*, 1:677.

75. Nugent, *Cavaliers and Pioneers*, 1:249, 425–29, 473, 501; *CRNC*, 1:59–67; Johnson and Bidlack, "North Carolina Land Grants," 43–48, 77–78; Butler, "Early Settlement," 27.

76. McPherson, "Nathaniel Batts," 80.

77. *CRNC*, 1:19; *DNCB*, 2:122–23. Kiscutanewh's name is rendered "Cisketando," "Kilocanen," and "Kistotanen."

78. McIlwaine, *Minutes*, 507; Robinson, "Notes," 168; Powell, *Ye Countie of Albemarle*, xxiii; Billings, *Papers*, 181, 185; Nugent, *Cavaliers and Pioneers*, 1:48, 113, 543; *DNCB*, 5:440; Billings, *Sir William Berkeley*, 169–70.

79. Morgan, *American Slavery*, 134; Craven, *Southern Colonies*, 166–71; Billings, "Transfer," 222. A governor was the commander in chief of a colony's military forces.

Chapter Three

1. This account of Charles II's return was based on Wheatley, *Diary of Samuel Pepys*, 1:63–64, 122–23, 156–57; Davies, *Restoration*, 293, 340–41, 350–51; Ashley, *General Monck*, 209–10. See Kishlansky, *Monarchy Transformed*, 134–213; Ashley, *England*, 81–128; Lockyer, *Tudor and Stuart Britain*, 268–304; and Braddick, *God's Fury*, 241–581, for the Civil Wars and Commonwealth. The Declaration of Breda is in Bryant, *Letters*, 84–85. Dated 4 April, it was read in Parliament on 1 May.

2. Bryant, *Letters*, 90.

3. Ashley, *General Monck*, 100–108, 221–23, 230–39; Powell, *Proprietors of Carolina*, 16–25; Fagg, "Carolina," 9–10.

4. Wheatley, *Diary of Samuel Pepys*, 2:435. In the same entry Pepys also characterized Monck as "stout and honest to his country."

5. Powell, *Proprietors of Carolina*, 12–16; Fagg, "Carolina," 7–8. Hyde's daughter Anne married James, Duke of York, and was mother of two future queens of England, Mary and Anne. During his exile Hyde began his monumental *History of the Rebellion and the Civil Wars in England*.

6. Powell, *Proprietors of Carolina*, 25–29; Fagg, "Carolina," 10–12; *DNB*, 5:45–49. While campaigning on the Rhine, Craven and the queen's son, Prince Rupert, were captured and held for two years.

7. Powell, *Proprietors of Carolina*, 29–33; Fagg, "Carolina," 12–14; *DNB*, 2:361–64.

8. Fagg, "Carolina," 18–20; Billings, *Sir William Berkeley*, 6–9, 11–34, 108–12, 121–34. William Berkeley's only extant play, *The Lost Lady: A Tragi-Comedy*, was performed in 1638 at court and in theaters.

9. C. M. Andrews, *Colonial Period*, 3:185; Powell, *Proprietors of Carolina*, 33–38; Fagg, "Carolina," 15–16. See K. H. D. Haley, *First Earl of Shaftesbury*, 227–31. In 1672 Ashley became Earl of Shaftesbury.

10. Powell, *Proprietors of Carolina*, 38–43; Fagg, "Carolina," 16–18; *DNB*, 3:117–19.

11. Powell, *Proprietors of Carolina*, 47–49; Fagg, "Carolina," 20–23, 25–27; H. A. M. Smith, "Colleton Family," 323–27. Sir John's plantation and family presence on Barbados has lasted to the present day.

12. Craven, *Southern Colonies*, 322–23; Craven, *Colonies in Transition*, 56–57; C. M. Andrews, *Colonial Period*, 3:52, 138–39, 226–27; Pettigrew, *Freedom's Debt*, 25.

13. Billings, *Sir William Berkeley*, 156.

14. C. M. Andrews, *Colonial Period*, 3:52, 183–84, 226, 4:56–58; Craven, *Southern Colonies*, 321, 322n, 323; Lefler and Powell, *Colonial North Carolina*, 36–37; and H. R. Paschal, "Proprietary North Carolina," 70–71. Craven later reconsidered Berkeley's role, realizing that Berkeley came to the project late, with minimal involvement and no investment in Carolina. Craven, *Colonies in Transition*, 42, 55–56; Fagg, "Carolina," 19–21, 33–34. Colleton receives credit for the propriety in Powell, *Carolina Charter of 1663*, 74. For Modyford's influence on Colleton, see Fagg, "Carolina," 73; Fagg, "Sleeping Not with the King's Grant," 175, 177; C. M. Andrews, *Colonial Period*, 3:183–84, 187, 192, 193, 195, 198.

15. Billings, *Sir William Berkeley*, 141–43; C. M. Andrews, *Colonial Period*, 4:60–90; Osgood, *American Colonies*, 3:207–11.

16. Billings, *Sir William Berkeley*, 135–58; Billings, *Papers*, 139–42; C. M. Andrews, *Colonial*

Period, 3:182–87; Craven, *Southern Colonies*, 310–24; Billings, "Sir William Berkeley and the Carolina Proprietary," 330–34.

17. One degree of latitude in Carolina is approximately 60 nautical miles, or 69 statute miles (110 kilometers); one minute is one nautical mile, about 1.15 statute miles; and one second is about 0.02 statute miles (100 feet).

18. *CRNC2*, 1:76–77. The 1657 Comberford map was readily available to the proprietors. The Lucks Island inlet corresponds to New Inlet on Moseley's 1733 map.

19. In 1970 Daniel W. Fagg Jr. identified this long-standing boundary oversight that has been misunderstood by historians for generations. Fagg, "Sleeping Not with the King's Grant," 173–74.

20. *CRNC2*, 1:xvii, 78, 85–86. The Convention Parliament of 1660 had confirmed the abolition of feudal tenures under the Interregnum. See Davies, *Restoration*, 347. A mark was an archaic English coin equal to thirteen shillings and four pence, or more than a half pound. The rent was symbolic.

21. *CRNC2*, 1:77–81. The precedent for a representative assembly had been established in Virginia in 1619.

22. *CRNC2*, 1:82, 83–84, 86. The feudal term "quitrent" meant that the annual rent paid to the proprietors was in lieu of any obligation of service.

23. *CRNC2*, 1:77; Bryant, *Letters*, 85. To restore the Church of England to preeminence, in 1661 Parliament passed the Clarendon Code, denying public office to Protestant dissenters and Catholics and purging the clergy of nonconformists. Ashley, *England*, 125–27; Kishlansky, *Monarchy Transformed*, 232–35.

24. *CRNC2*, 1:88.

25. *CRNC*, 1:33–34. Lepreyrie (Lempriere, M. de la Prairie), who was from Jersey, was recommended by Sir George Carteret. The proprietors' accounts indicate he was paid only two months, June and July. Billings, *Papers*, 208n; Fagg, "Carolina," 68n.

26. *CRNC*, 1:45, 51; *CRNC2*, 1:110–11.

27. *CRNC*, 1:34–35. In an eighteenth-century claim after the sale of Carolina, Daniel Coxe stated that Maltravers had "planted several parts" of the country. The Crown granted Coxe 100,000 acres in upper New York in 1770 as compensation. See Powell, "Carolana and the Incomparable Roanoke," 10; C. M. Andrews, *Colonial Period*, 3:186; Coxe, *Description*, 87.

28. *CRNC*, 1:34–36, 42–43; Billings, *Papers*, 201–2. The procedures against the previous charters were by common law *quo warranto*, literally by "what right," that ordered the defendant to produce the charter and justify that the requirements were being fulfilled. The council included several proprietors or their relatives, but conflict of interest was not frowned on in that period.

29. *CRNC*, 1:36–37, 39; E. L. Lee, *Lower Cape Fear*, 31, 33.

30. *CRNC*, 1:34, 43–46.

31. *CRNC*, 1:44–46. Proposed headrights were 100 acres for freeholders, 10 for male servants, and 6 for females.

32. *CRNC*, 1:44–45; Fagg, "Carolina," 73; Webb, *Governors-General*, 479.

33. *CRNC*, 1:53, 55. Whittey, a Devonshire sea captain, was trading with Virginia by 1653. He was familiar with Carolina and carried documents for the proprietors. By 1663 he had land in Albemarle on the Pasquotank River. Billings, *Papers*, 208n; Nugent, *Cavaliers and Pioneers*, 1:409.

34. *CRNC*, 1:53. There is no evidence that Lepreyrie went to the colony. Richard Cobthrop or Cobthrib was recommended by Lord John Berkeley. Billings, *Papers*, 207–8n. He may have been the Colonel Colthrope known to have seated a plantation in Albemarle on Durant's Neck by 1662 adjacent to George Durant and George Catchmaid. Declared vacant in 1697, this plantation was described as being on the Little River in Perquimans Precinct. *CRNC2*, 3:88, 503.

35. *CRNC*, 1:54–55. The grant of Colleton Island, 8 September 1663, documents the naming of Albemarle Sound. Now known as Colington Island, it was originally named for Christopher Carleill, who accompanied Sir Francis Drake on the voyage to Florida and Roanoke Island in 1586. Billings, *Papers*, 208n.

36. *CRNC*, 1:51.

37. *CRNC*, 1:51; Billings, *Papers*, 203–4. Lots on the sound and rivers were to be 1 chain (66 feet) wide and 100 chains (6,600 feet) long, with a second row of strips separating the waterfront parcels from the remainder of the grants located in the interior.

38. *CRNC*, 1:53–54.

39. *CRNC2*, 1:xviii; McIlwaine, *Minutes*, 507.

40. Nugent, *Cavaliers and Pioneers*, 1:501.

41. *CRNC2*, 3:499–506; *DNCB*, 1:345, 2:124; Nugent, *Cavaliers and Pioneers*, 1:501.

42. Billings, *Papers*, 185. *DNCB*, 6:265–66.

43. *CRNC*, 1:61–64; Nugent, *Cavaliers and Pioneers*, 1:426–27.

44. Nugent, *Cavaliers and Pioneers*, 1:425–29; *CRNC*, 1:59, 61–67; Billings, *Papers*, 209.

45. *CRNC2*, 1:107, 112, 125; E. L. Lee, *Lower Cape Fear*, 44–45. See C. M. Andrews, *Colonial Period*, 3:140, 143, 167–68, 273–75, 286–89, for the influence of the Concessions on West Jersey and Pennsylvania. The importance of Carolina's Concessions and Agreement to the U.S. Constitution has been lost to history.

46. *CRNC2*, 1:112–13, 117–20; *CRNC*, 1:52.

47. *CRNC2*, 1:112–14.

48. *CRNC2*, 1:115.

49. *CRNC*, 1:141. In Billings, *Papers*, 287. The governor and council constituted the colony's General Court.

50. Powell, *Ye Countie of Albemarle*, 32–33; Butler, "Governors," 286.

51. *CRNC2*, 1:115–18.

52. *CRNC2*, 1:120–24.

53. *CRNC2*, 1:114.

54. *CRNC2*, 1:114, 127.

55. *CRNC2*, 1:127.

56. By sea, the Albemarle settlement was about 135 nautical miles from Cape Fear and 240 nautical miles from Port Royal.

57. *CRNC*, 1:45, 49; Fagg, "Carolina," 67.

58. *CRNC2*, 1:93–95.

59. *CRNC2*, 1:91–92; Cumming, *Southeast in Early Maps*, plate 28, 142, 147–48. The nearly two centuries of misinterpreting the boundary must have originated from the untenable Virginia position. The Albemarle settlers had spread north across the region, and only the territory within a few miles of the proposed border was disputed.

60. *CRNC2*, 1:88, 104.

Chapter Four

1. *ANB*, 10:831–32; *DNCB*, 3:145–46; Hassam, *Genealogies*, 11–13; L. Hall, "New Englanders," 90–91.

2. L. Hall, "New Englanders," 88–89, 104; C. M. Andrews, *Colonial Period*, 1:496–500, 510–15, 519; E. L. Lee, *Lower Cape Fear*, 28–30.

3. Hilton mentions that he took half his crew upriver in the longboat. L. Hall, "New Englanders," 90–94, 105.

4. L. Hall, "New Englanders," 104. Hilton's latitude calculation and description of the shoals and the road west of the cape confirm that he was at Cape Fear. A road is the sheltered threshold to a harbor, river, or bay where a ship may ride in a protected anchorage. On the Moseley map (1733) a swash about five miles off the cape has a depth twice that of the shoals.

5. L. Hall, "New Englanders," 105; Butler, "Cape Fear Voyages," 23.

6. L. Hall, "New Englanders," 105–6. Indigenous to the Cape Fear are four poisonous snakes: rattlesnake, copperhead, cottonmouth (water moccasin), and coral snake.

7. L. Hall, "New Englanders," 105–6.

8. *Proceedings*; Ford, "Early Maps," 264–65; C. M. D. Thomas, *James Forte*; Butler, "Cape Fear Voyages," 20; Cumming, *Southeast in Early Maps*, 167–70; *DNB*, 5:206. The Thames school of cartographers produced Shapley's map for William Blathwayt, an official of the Board of Trade and Plantations. See Black, *Blathwayt Atlas*.

9. Butler, "Cape Fear Voyages," 23. Previously unnoticed, the name is "James's" rather than "James." The possessive is used in most of the river names and place-names. Conflicting interpretations are in E. L. Lee, *Lower Cape Fear*, 32–33; L. Hall, "New Englanders," 94; C. M. D. Thomas, *James Forte*, 1–7.

10. *DNCB*, 3:145.

11. L. Hall, "New Englanders," 92, 93, 95, 97; Bailyn, *New England Merchants*, 70–71, 107–8.

12. L. Hall, "New Englanders," 98, 107; E. L. Lee, *Lower Cape Fear*, 33–34.

13. Billings, *Papers*, 190.

14. E. L. Lee, *Lower Cape Fear*, 34; *CRNC*, 1:38–39; Lawson, *New Voyage*, 78–79.

15. *CRNC*, 1:34.

16. *CRNC*, 1:34, 36–37, 39, 43–46; E. L. Lee, *Lower Cape Fear*, 31, 33.

17. Sainsbury et al., *Calendar of State Papers*, 5:382–83; Dunn, *Sugar and Slaves*, 83; Beckles, *History of Barbados*, xiii, 21.

18. Whistler, "journall," quoted in Handler and Lange, *Plantation Slavery*, 17.

19. Ligon, *True and Exact History*, 40–41, 44, 47, 86; Williams, *Capitalism and Slavery*, 23–25; Beckles, *History of Barbados*, 12–15, 20–24; Beckles, *White Servitude*, 23–30.

20. Williams, *From Columbus to Castro*, 111–15; Beckles, *History of Barbados*, 27–28; Beckles, *White Servitude*, 8, 10, 20–30; Bridenbaugh and Bridenbaugh, *No Peace*, 206–9; Dunn, *Sugar and Slaves*, 59–83.

21. *CRNC*, 1:40, 46–47, 58; E. L. Lee, *Lower Cape Fear*, 36. At this time Peter Colleton was managing the family plantation. After his father's death in 1666 he became a proprietor and was knighted. Powell, *Ye Countie of Albemarle*, 14n; Powell, *Proprietors of Carolina*, 58. Planter Sir Thomas Modyford was acting governor in 1660–61 under the Commonwealth. Webb, *Governors-General*, 225–49, 479.

22. *CRNC*, 1:39–40, 42, 46–47; *DNCB*, 6:95–96; *ANB*, 22:282–83; Bridenbaugh, *Vexed and Troubled Englishmen*, 425–26; C. M. Andrews, *Colonial Period*, 3:189n.

23. Hilton, *Relation of a Discovery*, 1, 29–30; *CRNC*, 1:46. The title "master" refers to merchant sea captains and also sailing masters who were in charge of navigation. Pyam Blowers was a Boston merchant. Blowers Isle appears on the Robert Horne (1666) map. L. Hall, "New Englanders," 104n.

24. Hilton, *Relation of a Discovery*, 1, 2–4, 9; Cheves, *Shaftesbury Papers*, 64–65. Hilton sailed as far south as 31° north near modern Jekyll Island, Georgia. The sound was Santa Elena to the Spanish and Port Royal to the French. Hilton's *Relation of a Discovery* (1664) is in Salley, *Narratives*, 33–61. A facsimile is in C. M. D. Thomas, *James Forte*, 10–46.

25. Hilton, *Relation of a Discovery*, 6–8, 23–28.

26. Cheves, *Shaftesbury Papers*, 20n, 21n, 64–65, 75, 170.

27. For promotional purposes Hilton tried unsuccessfully to change "Cape Fear" to "Cape Fair." The Gulf Stream was the "strong current" that pushed them nearly to Cape Hatteras.

28. Hilton, *Relation of a Discovery*, 11, 21–22. The Indians had hidden the livestock very well.

29. Hilton, *Relation of a Discovery*, 12–15. Hilton's description corresponds with a journey of some sixty miles. He used the Northeast Cape Fear as the main channel. Hiltons River is the Brunswick River.

30. Hilton, *Relation of a Discovery*, 12, 16–20.

31. Hilton, *Relation of a Discovery*, 22.

32. *CRNC*, 1:39–41.

33. *CRNC*, 1:44–46.

34. Salley, *Narratives*, 80–81. After Surinam, Sandford moved to Barbados, where he was employed by Sir James Drax and served in the assembly. There Sandford again opposed an imperious governor, was banished, and sought redress in England. Sainsbury et al., *Calendar of State Papers*, 5:64–66, 104–8, 584; C. M. Andrews, *Colonial Period*, 3:197.

35. *CRNC*, 1:58.

36. *CRNC*, 1:47–48.

37. *CRNC*, 1:40, 57.

38. *CRNC*, 1:46–47, 145; E. L. Lee, *Lower Cape Fear*, 39.

39. *CRNC*, 1:144–45, 148; E. L. Lee, *Lower Cape Fear*, 40–41.

40. Hilton, *Relation of a Discovery*, 29–30. The grants ranged from 500 to 1,000 acres for officers and 100 acres for each sailor.

41. Hilton, *Relation of a Discovery*, 22–28, 30–33.

42. Ligon, *True and Exact History*, 29; E. L. Lee, *Lower Cape Fear*, 41–42; Loftfield, "Lost Charles Towne," 34, 36–37; Stone, *Old Town Plantation*, 3, 5; Hume, *Martin's Hundred*, 237–39. Modern archaeology at Old Town began with Gerald H. Shinn's 1969 field survey, followed by periodic testing and surveys. From 1987 to 1992 archaeologist Thomas C. Loftfield opened 15,500 square feet of the site, revealing Native American artifacts and the fortified center of Charles Towne. This is the only known bawn in North Carolina, although several have been found in Virginia.

43. Loftfield, "Lost Charles Towne," 36–37, 39–42, 46.

44. Horne, *Brief Description*, 1–2.

45. *CRNC*, 1:146, 149; Brandow, *Omitted Chapters*, 47, 215; Hotten, *Original Lists of Persons of Quality*, 469–70. The author used his notes from deeds, wills, and parish records from

Barbados Archives, Black Rock, St. Michael. The two Gibbs brothers would return to the second Charles Town in South Carolina and become planters. Robert had a long career in public office, culminating as provincial governor. *SCE*, 372.

46. Horne, *Brief Description*, 1, 3–10; E. L. Lee, *Lower Cape Fear*, 42–43. Horne's promotional pamphlet is also in Salley, *Narratives*, 65–73.

47. *CRNC*, 1:41, 45; *CRNC2*, 1:121–23; Hilton, *Relation of a Discovery*, 30, 32; Horne, *Brief Description*, 71. An intriguing tradition in a local African American community near Town Creek is that they are descended from enslaved Africans abandoned when the colony collapsed.

48. Horne, *Brief Description*, 3–5.

49. Horne, *Brief Description*, 93–94; E. L. Lee, *Lower Cape Fear*, 42.

50. Horne, *Brief Description*, 3.

51. Grant and Munro, *Acts of the Privy Council*, 1:440.

52. Sainsbury et al., *Calendar of State Papers*, 5:379; Salley, *Narratives*, 81.

53. *CRNC*, 1:72–73, 160. Vassall's commission as deputy governor is not extant, but there is a notation about it in the proprietors' accounts. Carolina Proprietors Accounts, 22 November 1664; Fagg, "Carolina," 76n.

54. *CRNC*, 1:75–77, 93, 144–45. The individual information has been gleaned from deeds, wills, and parish records, Barbados Archives, Black Rock, St. Michael.

55. *CRNC2*, 1:109–12, 117; E. L. Lee, *Lower Cape Fear*, 38.

56. *CRNC2*, 1:111–20, 122–23.

57. *CRNC*, 1:93–98. Controversy followed John Yeamans most of his life. In 1661 he married the recently widowed Margaret Foster Berringer under suspicion that he had poisoned her husband Benjamin, his neighbor and friend. The council exonerated Yeamans. He would also be governor of the second Charles Town in South Carolina, where he finally lost the proprietors' favor, dying before he could be replaced. *DNCB*, 6:288–89. Lady Margaret remarried and returned to Barbados, leaving her Carolina property to her youngest daughter, Margaret, who married Colonel James Moore, founding a dynasty that settled the Cape Fear and was prominent in both Carolinas.

58. The fly-boat or flute was a beamy Dutch design that allowed greater cargo space for its size. On board were twelve guns for Port Royal. Salley, *Records*, 7–10; Salley, *Narratives*, 83–84.

59. Salley, *Narratives*, 84–85; E. L. Lee, *Lower Cape Fear*, 46–47.

60. *CRNC*, 1:145–47.

61. *CRNC*, 1:146–49.

62. Salley, *Narratives*, 85, 100.

63. Salley, *Narratives*, 85, 86n. Henry Brayne would have an important role in the second Charles Town venture.

64. Salley, *Narratives*, 93–94.

65. Salley, *Narratives*, 95–98, 100–102, 104–5; *SCE*, 1045. Woodward's experiences bordered on the fantastic. He lived among the Native Americans for years, establishing diplomatic and trade contacts that would contribute greatly to the success of the second Charles Town.

66. Salley, *Narratives*, 106–8.

67. I have chosen "Cape Fear War" over "Clarendon County War." Since the name of the Natives in the region is not known, historians have long referred to them as the Cape Fear Indians. E. L. Lee, *Indian Wars*, 15.

68. Salley, *Narratives*, 106.

69. Lawson, *New Voyage*, 79–80. In Lawson's day the kidnapping and enslavement of Indian youth was a cause of the Tuscarora War. See *CRNC*, 1:160.

70. Salley, *Narratives*, 106–8.

71. Ashley, *General Monck*, 221–22, 235–36; Lockyer, *Tudor and Stuart Britain*, 335–36; Kishlansky, *Monarchy Transformed*, 213–15.

72. Billings, *Papers*, 318–20; Ashley, *General Monck*, 221–40; Harlow, *History of Barbados*, 155–56.

73. *CRNC*, 1:161.

74. Quoted in Powell, *Ye Countie of Albemarle*, xxvii.

75. *CRNC*, 1:159, 161.

76. *CRNC*, 1:159–60. John Vassall rebounded, acquiring 1,000 acres in Virginia and becoming a militia colonel. He married Anna Lewis and had seven children. In 1672 he immigrated to Jamaica, where he lived out his life as a merchant and militia officer. His sons settled in Boston, where his descendants lived until the American Revolution. *ANB*, 22:282–83.

Chapter Five

1. *CRNC*, 1:99–101; Nugent, *Cavaliers and Pioneers*, 1:426–28; Billings, *Papers*, 185; *DNCB*, 6:265–66.

2. *DNCB*, 2:108.

3. *DNCB*, 2:107–8; Billings, *Sir William Berkeley*, 165; McIlvenna, *Early American Rebels*, 56–57. The marriage of their daughter Sarah Drummond to Samuel Swann of a prominent Virginia family and their move to the Albemarle in the 1690s began an important dynasty. *DNCB*, 5:587–88.

4. Powell, *Ye Countie of Albemarle*, 3–5, 62; *CRNC*, 1:93. The commissions of Drummond and Woodward are lost, but all of the commissions were likely signed on the same day.

5. *CRNC2*, 1:117–18, 124, 126. The council was to be constituted of from six to twelve men. The first known full council, under Governor Stephens in 1670, had six members, including the deputy governor.

6. *CRNC*, 1:100. The proprietors' unacceptable land distribution proposals for Albemarle and Clarendon were based on their unawareness of the tidewater marshes and swamps. A longtime resident of Virginia, Berkeley could have enlightened them, but he had left England before the charter was issued and took little interest in Carolina. Colleton had a plantation in Barbados, as did Ashley, but the island has no marshes and little surface water of any kind.

7. Billings, *Papers*, 293–94.

8. Billings, *Papers*, 207; *CRNC*, 1:53–54.

9. *CRNC*, 1:101.

10. Powell, *Ye Countie of Albemarle*, 7–8.

11. *CRNC2*, 1:7; Chafee, "Colonial Courts," 56–57.

12. *CRNC2*, 1:76, 78–81, 84.

13. Billings, "Transfer," 215, 219–23; Chafee, "Colonial Courts," 76–77; Morgan, *American Slavery*, 149–50.

14. Will of Mary Fortsen, Secretary of State Wills, 1712–1722; Grimes, *North Carolina Wills*, 196; *DNCB*, 2:225–28, 3:55–56.

15. *CRNC*, 1:93.

16. "Indians of Southern Virginia," 346–47; *CRNC2*, 7:xxxiv; Butler, "Governors," 284.

17. The Dutch attack on the Chesapeake is in Billings, *Papers*, 318–20; Morgan, *American Slavery*, 240–41.

18. *CRNC*, 1:117–18, 139–40; Billings, *Papers*, 231–32, 281–82, 285–86, 315–17; Billings, *Sir William Berkeley*, 192. In 1664 Maryland had turned down Berkeley's request for a reduction in tobacco.

19. *CRNC*, 1:141; Billings, *Papers*, 287–89; Billings, *Sir William Berkeley*, 193–94.

20. Billings, *Papers*, 316; *CRNC*, 1:152–53; "Indians of Southern Virginia," 345–46, 348; H. R. Paschal, "Proprietary North Carolina," 442; Hening, *Statutes at Large*, 2:230.

21. *CRNC*, 1:152–53; Billings, *Papers*, 297, 303–6, 316. The Virginia Proclamation was dated 28 December 1666.

22. *CRNC*, 1:161; Billings, *Papers*, 316–17; Billings, *Sir William Berkeley*, 194–95.

23. Billings, *Papers*, 318–22; Powell, *Ye Countie of Albemarle*, 62; Billings, *Sir William Berkeley*, 195, 207–8; Morgan, *American Slavery*, 242.

24. Shea, *Virginia Militia*, 89–92; Shomette, *Pirates on the Chesapeake*, 43–45; Billings, *Papers*, 318–20.

25. Billings, *Papers*, 284, 289, 293–94; Billings, *Sir William Berkeley*, 193–94.

26. Billings, *Sir William Berkeley*, 168, 295n.

27. *CRNC2*, 2:xxxiv–xxxv; McIlvenna, *Early American Rebels*, 67.

28. Billings, *Sir William Berkeley*, 165, 168–69; *DNCB*, 2:108; Webb, *1676*, 26–27, 64–65.

29. Powell, *Ye Countie of Albemarle*, 13–16.

30. *DNCB*, 5:440; Billings, *Sir William Berkeley*, 169–70; *DNB*, 1:450–51; Nugent, *Cavaliers and Pioneers*, 1:48, 113; Deetz, *Flowerdew Hundred*, 24. The Peirseys lived at Flowerdew Hundred, which Elizabeth inherited after long litigation.

31. Powell, *Ye Countie of Albemarle*, 38.

32. *DNCB*, 5:440; Billings, *Papers*, 453–54; Billings, *Sir William Berkeley*, 170, 213.

33. Haun, *Old Albemarle County Miscellaneous Records*, 7, 8, 23, 104; Haun, *Old Albemarle County Land Warrants*, 201.

34. Powell, *Ye Countie of Albemarle*, 30.

35. *CRNC2*, 1:120, 122–23. Match was fuse for the matchlock musket. The predecessor "Declarations and Proposals" of 1663 had a similar provision. *CRNC*, 1:45; Morgan, *American Slavery*, 239–40.

36. *CRNC2*, 1:116–19; Powell, *Ye Countie of Albemarle*, 9, 11. See *CRNC2*, 1:110–11, for the proprietors' supply of cannon and accoutrements, 200 muskets, 20 barrels of powder, shot, and 200 bandoliers for the defense of the Port Royal colony.

37. Powell, *Ye Countie of Albemarle*, 32–33.

38. *CRNC2*, 1:151, 184. The inclusive term "Inhabitants" encompassed indentured manservants. "Freemen" included free blacks, some of whom were freeholders.

39. *CRNC2*, 2:209, 221–22, 417.

40. *CRNC*, 1:100–101.

41. Powell, *Ye Countie of Albemarle*, 7–8, 12.

42. *CRNC*, 1:175–76; Powell, *Ye Countie of Albemarle*, 29. The Great Deed of Grant was thenceforth referenced in deeds throughout the proprietary period.

43. Powell, *Ye Countie of Albemarle*, 29.

44. Lederer returned to Germany in 1675. *DNCB*, 4:42; Briceland, *Westward*, 96, 101–2.

Lederer's savannas, desert, inland sea, and nomenclature influenced cartographers for some years, including John Oglilby-James Moxon (1672) and John Speed (1676). Cumming, *Southeast in Early Maps*, plates 36, 37, color plate 4. Joel Gascoyne (1682) corrected some of Lederer's misconceptions. Cumming, *Southeast in Early Maps*, 174–75. The puzzling "great lake" on maps since the sixteenth century was probably a vestige of Verrazzano's presumed arm of the Pacific. See the Mercator-Hondius map of Virginia and Florida (1606) in Cumming, *Southeast in Early Maps*, plate 20. Did Lederer actually see a flooded Catawba River backed up by a natural dam? Perhaps. A scientist, he reported what he observed or was told, much of it verified by historical records and geographical analysis. See Briceland, *Westward*, chap. 8, for various interpretations of Lederer's route. Briceland's geographical analysis challenges but does not supersede the route established by Cumming and Rights from historical and geographical sources. Cumming, *Discoveries of John Lederer*, 111–26; Rights, *American Indian*, 112–23.

45. Cumming, *Discoveries of John Lederer*, 24–29, 116–23; Ethridge, *From Chicaza to Chickasaw*, 105–6; Briceland, *Westward*, 114–19; Rights, *American Indian*, 62–65.

46. Cumming, *Discoveries of John Lederer*, 30–33, 123–26; Briceland, *Westward*, 119–23; Wright, *Prose Works of William Byrd*, 309.

47. Briceland, *Westward*, 148–50, 157–61.

48. Briceland, *Westward*, 99–100, 148–50, 152–60; Wright, *Prose Works of William Byrd*, 307–8, 400.

49. Craven, *Southern Colonies*, 322; K. H. D. Haley, *First Earl of Shaftesbury*, 193.

50. K. H. D. Haley, *First Earl of Shaftesbury*, 202–5; Cranston, *John Locke*, 119; Cheves, *Shaftesbury Papers*, 392.

51. The 1667 draft is in the Huntington Library, San Marino, California. Because of censorship, Locke's views on religious toleration remained unpublished until the expanded *A Letter concerning Toleration* was published in 1689 during the Glorious Revolution. See Wootton, *John Locke Political Writings*, 186–210, 390–436, for the "Essay" and *Letter*.

52. Fagg, "Carolina," 127; K. H. D. Haley, *First Earl of Shaftesbury*, 242.

53. *CRNC2*, 1:132. The "numerous Democracy" refers to the ancient concept of a chaotic "mob-ocracy," not the modern meaning of the word.

54. H. F. R. Smith, *Harrington and His Oceana*, chap. 8; C. M. Andrews, *Colonial Period*, 3:213–14; Craven, *Southern Colonies*, 338–39.

55. The Carolina nobility could not duplicate English titles. *CRNC2*, 1:133–37; *ENC*, 874–75; *SCE*, 533–34. "Cacique" is the spelling used in all versions of the Fundamental Constitutions, although "cassique" is acceptable.

56. *CRNC2*, 1:132, 139, 143. The seven other proprietary courts were not organized in Albemarle County.

57. *CRNC2*, 1:133, 136.

58. Haun, *Old Albemarle County Land Warrants*, 272, 274, 276.

59. *CRNC2*, 1:148–50, 164. There is no stronger commitment to religious freedom in either England or the other colonies.

60. *CRNC2*, 1:183.

61. *CRNC*, 1:179–80; *CRNC2*, 7:334; Powell, *Ye Countie of Albemarle*, 39n–40n; *DNCB*, 4:373.

62. Powell, *Ye Countie of Albemarle*, 34, 51. See *CRNC2*, 1:165–85, for the version of 1 March

1670 that has minor changes, nine additional articles, and rules of precedence. Since the county had a draft, there was no urgency in sending the permanent copy.

63. *CRNC2*, 7:335; *CRNC*, 1:181. Indicating low expectations for Albemarle County, the Lords continued the "nigh it as we cann" phrase in the instructions to President John Harvey in 1679 when the postrebellion government was reorganized. *CRNC2*, 7:350.

64. *CRNC2*, 7:335–36; *CRNC*, 1:181–82.

65. *CRNC2*, 1:142, 160, 174. English constitutional theory then considered shared power a better protection of basic rights than the modern concept of separation of powers.

66. *CRNC2*, 1:141, 149, 173.

67. *CRNC2*, 1:144–45; Haun, *Perquimans Precinct Court Minutes*; Edmundson, *Journal*, 68, 115; Ver Steeg, *Origins of a Southern Mosaic*, 66–67; Hawks, *History of North Carolina*, 2:139; H. R. Paschal, "Proprietary North Carolina," 336–37; McCain, *County Court*, v, 6–7, 9.

68. Greene, "Courts and Society," 101–2.

69. *CRNC2*, 7:335.

70. *CRNC2*, 1:143–45, 147–48.

71. *CRNC2*, 7:335.

72. *CRNC2*, 1:147–48.

73. *CRNC*, 1:183–87.

74. *CRNC2*, 1:130–31.

Chapter Six

1. Powell, *Ye Countie of Albemarle*, 37–38.

2. *CRNC2*, 7:337–38; *DNCB*, 1:335; Powell, *Ye Countie of Albemarle*, 3–5, 32–33.

3. *CRNC2*, 7:335–36, 340; Powell, *Ye Countie of Albemarle*, 51–52.

4. Powell, *Ye Countie of Albemarle*, 44–50. Jennings and Jarvis were pioneer settlers. Jennings and Pearce (Peirce) signed with marks.

5. *CRNC*, 1:286.

6. Powell, *Ye Countie of Albemarle*, 50.

7. Cheves, *Shaftesbury Papers*, 91–93; Billings, *Sir William Berkeley*, 172–73; K. H. D. Haley, *First Earl of Shaftesbury*, 241–42.

8. K. H. D. Haley, *First Earl of Shaftesbury*, 232–34, 300, 304.

9. Powell, *Ye Countie of Albemarle*, 64–65; Parker, "Legal Aspects," 113–17; Fagg, "Carolina," 239–45; Billings, *Sir William Berkeley*, 172–73.

10. *CRNC*, 1:228.

11. Connor, *North Carolina*, 1:110; Lefler, *History of North Carolina*, 1:50–51, 53; Powell, *Carolina Charter of 1663*, 64–65; Butler, "Governors," 288; Rankin, *Upheaval*, 13–14, 23; *CRNC2*, 2:xlii.

12. *CRNC*, 1:256.

13. Powell, *Ye Countie of Albemarle*, 43–44; *CRNC2*, 2:4–5; *CRNC*, 1:258; Parker, "Legal Aspects," 118.

14. *CRNC*, 1:258–59.

15. In Albemarle the Loyalists backed Eastchurch's faction, which had proprietary sanction, while the Popular party of pioneer planters and merchants represented the "people." Biggs, "Narrative," 2. In Bacon's Rebellion the Loyal Party backed Governor Berkeley and

the planter oligarchy against the "people." Stephen Webb sees these Virginia parties as parallel with the nascent country and court parties in England that became Whigs and Tories. Shaftesbury was a Whig founder. Webb, *1676*, 170–71, 176–77, 413.

16. *CRNC*, 1:292; Biggs, "Narrative," 2. In 1676 Thomas Eastchurch received a proprietary commission, but he was never installed.

17. Powell, *Ye Countie of Albemarle*, 50, 53–54; *DNCB*, 3:277–78. John Jenkins, Thomas Jarvis, and William Crawford were all early residents of Albemarle, having been involved in the Ingle's and Fendall's Rebellions in Maryland in midcentury and in Bacon's Rebellion in Virginia in 1676. Ever seeking to establish representative government, they became key players in Culpeper's Rebellion in Albemarle, which finally was successful, with Jenkins returned to his deputy governor's post and Jarvis and Crawford elected to the rebel council and assembly. Josias Fendall and his family also found refuge in Albemarle, where he lived quietly in Perquimans Precinct until his death in 1692. McIlvenna, *Early American Rebels*, 42–51, 79–96, 91–96; Haun, *Perquimans Precinct, Births, Marriages, Deaths*, 30, 31; *DNCB*, 1:458–59, 3:272.

18. *CRNC2*, 1:178.

19. Powell, *Ye Countie of Albemarle*, 43–44, 50; *CRNC*, 1:229, 287; *DNCB*, 2:129–30.

20. *DNCB*, 1:153–54, 4:274–75.

21. *CRNC*, 1:245; MacDonald, *Select Charters*, 114; C. M. Andrews, *Colonial Period*, 4:61–65, 86–89, 138–41; Harper, *English Navigation Laws*, 50–51, 57–59.

22. MacDonald, *Select Charters*, 170; *CRNC*, 1:244–45, 287; C. M. Andrews, *Colonial Period*, 4:118–24; Butler, "Culpeper's Rebellion," 56–57; Craven, *Colonies in Transition*, 129, 147, 157. Other New England traders were John Liscomb and Joseph Winslow of Boston, Joshua and Caleb Lamb of Roxbury, and Mordecai Bowden from Rhode Island. C. M. Andrews, *Colonial Period*, 3:252.

23. *CRNC*, 1:232.

24. *CRNC2*, 7:168, 413; *CRNC*, 1:278; Adams, "'Sundry Murders and Depredations,'" 149–50, 156–59, 162–64, 166–68; Dawdy, "Meherrin's Secret History," 393–94; Edmundson, *Journal*, 112–13. See Webb, *1676*; and C. M. Andrews, *Narratives*, for Bacon's Rebellion.

25. *CRNC*, 1:259. John Culpeper of Barbados migrated to southern Carolina in 1671 with his wife Judith and acquired a plantation and a town house. In June 1673 he and some partners were forced to flee the colony, most likely over a debt. Leaving the colony without permission was a capital offense. The confusion between the two contemporary John Culpepers, one of the Carolinas and another of Virginia, is addressed in the sketch cited here. *ANB*, 5:844–45.

26. *CRNC2*, 7:354.

27. *CRNC2*, 7:355–56; *CRNC*, 1:290. A placket was the laced opening in the front of the bodice. Considering the king's reputation, this comment was hardly libelous.

28. *CRNC2*, 7:356–57.

29. Shaw, *Calendar of Treasury Books*, 4:280–81, 498; H. R. Paschal, "Proprietary North Carolina," 488–89.

30. *CRNC*, 1:228, 259.

31. *CRNC*, 1:257, 291–92; H. R. Paschal, "Proprietary North Carolina," 489–90.

32. *CRNC*, 1:258–59; *DNCB*, 2:129, 6:222.

33. *CRNC*, 1:292; Biggs, "Narrative," 2; H. R. Paschal, "Proprietary North Carolina," 490.

34. *DNCB*, 2:123–25.

35. *CRNC*, 1:259, 292; Cheney, *North Carolina Government*, 83n.

36. *CRNC*, 7:355–57; *CRNC*, 1:269, 289–90. One witness saw John Culpeper among Virginia magistrates conferring with Miller prior to his leaving Virginia. This was the John Culpeper of the Albemarle rebellion and not his contemporary, the recently deceased brother of Berkeley's wife, Dame Frances Culpeper. The two John Culpepers were not related. *CRNC*, 1:235; *ANB*, 5:844.

37. *CRNC*, 1:228–29, 231–33; *CRNC2*, 2:xliv–xlvi.

38. *CRNC*, 1:258.

39. *CRNC*, 1:230–31.

40. Webb, *1676*, 3–165; Billings, *Sir William Berkeley*, 232–66; Craven, *Southern Colonies*, 360–93; Morgan, *American Slavery*, 250–70.

41. Webb, *1676*, 70–75; C. M. Andrews, *Colonial Period*, 2:343–45; Craven, *Southern Colonies*, 410–12.

42. Quoted in Webb, *1676*, 69.

43. *CRNC*, 1:287.

44. *CRNC*, 1:296; W. S. Smith, "Culpeper's Rebellion," 59–61, 63–65, 88–90; Biggs, "Narrative," 1.

45. *CRNC*, 1:297.

46. W. S. Smith, "Culpeper's Rebellion," 60, 64–65. Timothy Biggs, in Albemarle since March 1674, married Mary, the widow of George Catchmaid, who owned the neighboring plantation on the Little River side of Durant's Neck. *DNCB*, 1:153–55.

47. Biggs, "Narrative," 1.

48. Biggs, "Narrative," 1–2; Parker, "Legal Aspects," 121.

49. W. S. Smith, "Culpeper's Rebellion," 59–60, 65, 68, 73–74, 88–89; *CRNC*, 1:248, 278; Adams, "'Sundry Murders and Depredations,'" 166–67.

50. Biggs, "Narrative," 3; Parker, "Legal Aspects," 123.

51. *CRNC*, 1:265–67, 278–79, 285; Butler, "Culpeper's Rebellion," 56–57. The standard hogshead weighed 400 pounds. Miller reported that the annual crop was 2,000 hogsheads, or 800,000 pounds.

52. W. S. Smith, "Culpeper's Rebellion," 60, 65.

53. *CRNC*, 1:278.

54. *CRNC*, 1:256, 305.

55. *CRNC*, 1:249, 279, 294, 301. A master mariner and merchant, Zachariah Gillam played a pivotal role in Culpeper's Rebellion. In 1668 he explored Hudson's Bay and was involved in the Arctic fur trade. On a voyage for the Hudson's Bay Company in 1682–83 he was drowned when his ship was lost in the ice. C. M. Andrews, *Colonial Period*, 3:226–27n.

56. W. S. Smith, "Culpeper's Rebellion," 60, 68, 74.

57. Biggs, "Narrative," 4; *CRNC*, 1:279, 301, 310.

58. *CRNC*, 1:248–49; McIlvenna, *Early American Rebels*, 92–93.

59. *CRNC*, 1:279–80.

60. *CRNC*, 1:272–73, 280, 299. A partial quote of the Currituck freeholders' declaration, "Wee will have noe Lords noe Landgraves noe Cassiques we renounce them all," has been cited to support the concept that the Albemarle settlers were a community of political independents, misfits, social outcasts, religious dissidents, and runaway servants and slaves who created an egalitarian society that precipitated the several rebellions in the seventeenth and

early eighteenth centuries. McIlvenna, *Very Mutinous People*, 1–3. To the contrary, the full quotation indicates that the freemen looked to the Crown for justice, and at the suggestion of Colonel Foster they turned to the proprietors. Since there were neither caciques nor landgraves in the colony at the time, why did the freeholders denounce a nobility that did not exist? They apparently were expressing uncertainty about some aspects of the Fundamental Constitutions that, if implemented, might change the polity and society of the colony their leaders had created.

61. *CRNC*, 1:281. A pillory and stocks had been constructed at Durant's house, evidence that his house had been used for some time as a courthouse. See court minutes, *CRNC2*, 2:7.

62. *CRNC*, 1:273, 281.

63. *DNCB*, 1:161–62, 178–79, 457–58, 468–69, 3:272–73, 276–78, 4:65–66, 5:362–63, 6:94–95. The militia drummer Sears, a Pasquotank planter, was a son-in-law of council member William Jennings. *DNCB*, 3:276–77.

64. *CRNC*, 1:273.

65. *CRNC*, 1:273–74, 281–82; W. S. Smith, "Culpeper's Rebellion," 69.

66. Parker, "Legal Aspects," 125. The location of the unsurveyed border was generally understood in both colonies.

67. *CRNC*, 1:282. It was illegal to break bulk or unload a cargo without the permission of the customs collector.

68. H. R. Paschal, "Proprietary North Carolina," 443–44.

69. *CRNC2*, 7:349.

70. Webb, *Governors-General*, 370, 509–10.

71. *CRNC*, 1:274, 282–83, 298. This log prison, the first public building erected in the colony, would serve for over a decade.

72. *CRNC*, 1:273, 298, 300. Regarding Jenkins, concurring opinions are in H. R. Paschal, "Proprietary North Carolina," 178n; Rankin, *Upheaval*, 41; and Butler, "Governors," 294. According to his 1672 commission, Jenkins legally could be superseded only by Carteret or a new governor commissioned by the proprietors, but Eastchurch died before he qualified.

73. *CRNC*, 1:247–48, 277.

74. *CRNC*, 1:242, 277.

75. *CRNC*, 1:262.

76. *CRNC*, 1:276, 283, 288, 339; *DNCB*, 5:399–401.

77. *CRNC*, 1:235, 239–41, 316, 327; Hawks, *History of North Carolina*, 2:136.

78. *CRNC*, 1:313; *CRNC2*, 7:353–57; *DNCB*, 4:275.

79. Cheney, *North Carolina Government*, 11, 27; *CRNC2*, 7:350–52.

80. *SRNC*, 23:1–96.

81. *CRNC2*, 2:xxv, lxvi–lxix, 420. The proprietary precinct names appear fleetingly on a handful of grants and a commission, including a 1681 reference to Berkeley in the Perquimans County deeds. Mattie Erma Parker concluded that the proprietary names were created in 1679 when de jure government was reestablished. See Fagg, "Carolina," 170n; *NCHGR*, 3, 304–10; McCain, *County Court*, 10. The familiar Indian names soon returned. The assembly designated the precincts as counties in 1739. *SRNC*, 23:126.

82. *CRNC2*, 4:64–65, 71–72, 174–76; Spruill, *Women's Life and Work*, 327–30; Spindel, *Crime and Society*, 54.

83. *CRNC2*, 7:351–52.

84. *CRNC*, 1:253–54, 302–3; Hofmann, *Province of North Carolina*, 38, 389.

85. *CRNC*, 1:255, 263, 270.

86. *CRNC*, 1:275, 284–85, 294.

87. *CRNC*, 1:326–27; Butler, "Governors," 295.

88. Webb, *Governors-General*, 399–400.

89. Because Culpeper was the only person tried for treason, English officials always associated him with the rebellion. Locally it was simply the most successful of the "Rebellious Routs" of the times. Culpeper was cast as the leading rebel in early North Carolina histories, and since 1886 the incident has been known as Culpeper's Rebellion. *CRNC*, 1:xxi.

90. *CRNC*, 1:280–82.

91. McIlvenna, *Very Mutinous People*, 1–6, 28, 158.

92. Ekirch, *"Poor Carolina,"* xviii, 20.

93. *CRNC*, 1:250–53.

94. *CRNC*, 1:287–88.

95. Craven, *Southern Colonies*, 410.

96. *CRNC*, 1:239–41; *DNCB*, 3:168–69.

97. *CRNC*, 1:244–45.

98. *CRNC*, 1:271, 327; Haun, *Perquimans Precinct, Births, Marriages, Deaths*, 34. The proprietors continued to seek a governor from England. They commissioned Captain Henry Wilkinson, who had a military background, as governor in August 1680, hoping that he would "doe equall justice to all parties" by appointing an impartial court to investigate the rebellion. For over a year the cash-poor Wilkinson attempted to find passage to Albemarle but was finally imprisoned for debt. *CRNC*, 1:328, 333–38; C. M. Andrews, "Captain Henry Wilkinson."

99. *CRNC2*, 2:9–10, 7:354–57; *CRNC*, 1:254, 304, 313–17.

100. *CRNC2*, 2:413–18.

101. *CRNC2*, 2:9, 418–19.

102. *CRNC2*, 2:419–23.

103. *DNCB*, 3:169.

104. *CRNC*, 1:283, 288, 339.

105. Cheves, *Shaftesbury Papers*, 468–69.

106. *CRNC*, 1:276, 283.

107. Grant and Munro, *Acts of the Privy Council*, 1:838, 2:3, 4; *ANB*, 20:381–82; Riddell, "Half Told Story," 247–53.

108. *CRNC*, 1:339, 346, 350–51; Grimes, *Abstract*, 155, 411; Marley, "Minutes," 50; *ANB*, 1:574–75; Hood, *Public Career of John Archdale*, 3–4.

109. *CRNC2*, 2:315–18, 400–401.

110. *CRNC*, 1:383; *SRNC*, 25:139. By demonstrating literacy, an accused could invoke benefit of clergy and avoid the death penalty. The medieval practice stemmed from a time when few besides priests could read and write.

111. *CRNC*, 1:368–69.

112. *CRNC*, 1:359–60, 362, 369, 371; Butler, "Governors," 296–98.

113. Sirmans, *Colonial South Carolina*, 48–52; Weir, *Colonial South Carolina*, 67–68. Sothel later returned to Albemarle, where he died in 1694. Grimes, *North Carolina Wills*, 421–22.

114. *CRNC*, 1:362–63.

Chapter Seven

1. *CRNC2*, 2:215–16.

2. *DNCB*, 1:178–79, 5:398–99. In Culpeper's Rebellion, Blount was on the rebel council.

3. *DNCB*, 5:399–401.

4. *DNCB*, 5:398–99; *CRNC2*, 2:176–77, 186–87.

5. *CRNC*, 1:260. Tithables, or taxables, included all categories except children and free women. Two-thirds of the "working hands" were free men or white indentured males. "Indians and Negros" were enslaved or indentured servants of either sex. "Women" meant white female indentured servants.

6. Morgan, *American Slavery*, 404. For Virginia in this period, Morgan's multipliers are 2.25–2.39, giving a population range of 3,150–3,346.

7. Hening, *Statutes at Large*, 2:170, 480; Bruce, *Economic History*, 2:40, 100–101.

8. *CRNC*, 2:889–90; *SRNC*, 23:72. A 1694 listing of fewer tithables appears to be incomplete. *CRNC2*, 2:91.

9. Wolf, "Patents and Tithables," 273; Grimes, *North Carolina Wills*, 342–45; *DNCB*, 5:117.

10. Lawson, *New Voyage*, 70.

11. *CRNC*, 2:296, 396, 419. In 1717 Thomas Pollock estimated 2,000 tithables.

12. Clowse, *Measuring Charleston's Overseas Commerce*, 30. See also *CRNC2*, 3:xii–xiii; Sunderland, *Historical Statistics*, 756; Craven, *Colonies in Transition*, 288.

13. *CRNC2*, 3:97, 127, 154, 243, 524.

14. Hofmann, *Province of North Carolina*, 1714; *CRNC2*, 2:80–81, 207, 213–14, 231, 3:97, 113, 4:107. Gascoigne also appears as "Gascoine" and "Gaskins." In one court appearance Gascoigne was described as "turbulent and brauling." *CRNC2*, 3:243.

15. Hofmann, *Province of North Carolina*, 110, 186; Whitley and Trimble, *North Carolina Headrights*, 120, 121, 151; *CRNC2*, 3:104, 176, 220, 243–44. Sometimes Fourre is "Furre."

16. *CRNC2*, 4:230, 414–15, 5:4, 38n, 6:4, 177, 396, 10:45, 109, 251. DeLaMare's wife Ann was his executrix. *CRNC2*, 5:55.

17. Haun, *Perquimans County Deed Abstracts*, 240; *CRNC2*, 3:80, 127, 177.

18. Lawson, *New Voyage*, 90, 120.

19. Watson, "Consideration," 381, 384–86, 392.

20. Powell, *Ye Countie of Albemarle*, 6n, 56–58, 61–64.

21. Brickell, *Natural History*, 268–69.

22. *CRNC2*, 2:2, 11, 344, 337–38, 3:243, 527–28; Watson, "Consideration," 385–86.

23. M. Campbell, "Social Origins," 63–66, 68–69; Craven, *White, Red, and Black*, 5–8.

24. Smith and Wilson, *North Carolina Women*, 21–22.

25. *CRNC2*, 4:58–59, 60–61.

26. *SRNC*, 23:63.

27. *SRNC*, 23:70–71.

28. *CRNC2*, 5:345, 375–76, 396; Brickell, *Natural History*, 270; Watson, "Consideration," 396–97.

29. *CRNC2*, 3:xii–xiiin, 10, 12, 66, 73, 116.

30. *CRNC2*, 4:232, 251; *DNCB*, 2:112–13.

31. *CRNC2*, 2:265, 3:99–100, 114–15, 127, 183–84. Both Sothel and Andover signed the note with marks.

32. Hofmann, *Province of North Carolina*, 350; *CRNC2*, 4:113. Johnson signed his name.

33. *CRNC2*, 3:10, 523.

34. *CRNC2*, 3:12, 73, 97, 116. Just two months later the nefarious Lee and Spelman were convicted in one of the most lurid crimes of the period, involving abduction, adultery, and theft.

35. Haun, *Perquimans County Deed Abstracts*, 98. There is evidence, albeit inconclusive, that after Lillington's death in 1697 Toney was conveyed from the family but soon was returned by legal seizure. *CRNC2*, 4:150.

36. SSCWI, 15–17. This odd bequest and contract suggest that he may have been related to the Godfreys.

37. *CRNC2*, 4:49; Franklin, *Free Negro*, 9.

38. K. Fischer, *Suspect Relations*, 159–60; *CRNC2*, 6:617, 635; Grimes, *Abstract*, 363.

39. *CRNC2*, 6:381–82; *DNCB*, 5:125.

40. *CRNC2*, 6:491, 547.

41. Whitley and Trimble, *North Carolina Headrights*, 5, passim; Wood, "Thomas Pollock," 231n.

42. Whitley and Trimble, *North Carolina Headrights*, 46; *CRNC2*, 2:215–16.

43. Whitley and Trimble, *North Carolina Headrights*, 60, 95–96. One of the men was "Ashline the more [Moor]."

44. Minchinton, "Seaborne Slave Trade," 23; Wood, "Thomas Pollock," 218.

45. *DNCB*, 3:62; Whitley and Trimble, *North Carolina Headrights*, 97. Hartley married William Duckenfield in November 1694. *DNCB*, 2:112.

46. *CRNC2*, 2:404–6.

47. *CRNC2*, 4:204–5. This is one of the largest internal transactions in the period. Both men were vestrymen and council and assembly members. Arderne predeceased his cousin and willed all of his property, real and chattel, to Duckenfield. Grimes, *North Carolina Wills*, 13–14; *DNCB*, 1:39, 2:111–12.

48. Whitley and Trimble, *North Carolina Headrights*, 28–29, 112, 139, 161, 169.

49. Grimes, *North Carolina Wills*, 342–47, 357–59, 471, 560.

50. Brickell, *Natural History*, 272; Minchinton, "Seaborne Slave Trade," 4n, 12.

51. Minchinton, "Seaborne Slave Trade," 26–27.

52. *CRNC2*, 4:359, 363–66. Charlesworth Glover (b. 1688) was son of William Glover, who was council president in 1707. *DNCB*, 2:302–8. Trial depositions were from Thomas Danforth, the sloop's owner, and Glover. Blount was one of four justices on the court; Christopher Gale was chief justice. *CRNC2*, 4:351.

53. *CRNC2*, 10:121–22, 244. Codrington (1668–1710), former governor general of the Leeward Islands, owned two plantations, which were operated by the SPG until emancipation in 1833. Codrington College in St. John Parish, founded in 1745, is now an Anglican theological seminary, a component of the University of the West Indies. Hutt, *Exploring Historic Barbados*, 33–35; *DNB*, 11:203–4.

54. Brickell, *Natural History*, 272.

55. Carson and Lounsbury, *Chesapeake Houses*, 89–90.

56. Brickell, *Natural History*, 270, 272–76.

57. Grimes, *North Carolina Wills*, 560–61.

58. *CRNC2*, 3:63, 490.

59. *CRNC2*, 3:126–27; Grimes, *North Carolina Wills*, 344; Smith and Wilson, *North Carolina Women*, 24; Brinn, "Blacks," 68, 94; Wood, "Thomas Pollock," 219–20.

60. Grimes, *North Carolina Wills*, 472–74; SSCWI, 52–53.

61. Whitley and Trimble, *North Carolina Headrights*, 113, 114, 143.

62. Brickell, *Natural History*, 203, 273.

63. Sayers, *Desolate Place*, 87–89.

64. Lawson, *New Voyage*, 242.

65. *CRNC2*, 10:29. In 1703 an SPG missionary, the Reverend John Blair, reported a rumor of 100,000 Tuscarora. Most historians have settled on some 5,000 Native Americans in the coastal plain, with several hundred north of Albemarle Sound.

66. Lawson, *New Voyage*, 92. In South Carolina native hunters were hired for twenty shillings a year to provide game for the table. Salley, *Narratives*, 170.

67. *CRNC*, 2:45.

68. *CRNC2*, 2:95, 326, 404, 3:27, 38, 40, 62, 80, 92, 102, 180, 219, 240, 271, 351–52; LeMaster, "In the 'Scolding Houses,'" 222.

69. *CRNC2*, 2:178, 207; LeMaster, "In the 'Scolding Houses,'" 216.

70. *CRNC2*, 2:326–27. There is no record of West's arrest.

71. *CRNC2*, 3:528; Watson, "Consideration," 385.

72. *CRNC2*, 5:319–21, 481.

73. Wood, "Thomas Pollock," 212; Lowry, "Class," 131.

74. Quoted in Ekirch, *"Poor Carolina,"* 15.

75. Lounsbury, "Development of Domestic Architecture," 21n.

76. Grimes, *North Carolina Wills*, 474, 561; SSCWI, 15, 19, 23.

77. *CRNC2*, 10:120, 237.

78. Quoted in Bishir et al., *Architects*, 57–58.

79. Berland, *Dividing Line Histories*, 107.

80. Berland, *Dividing Line Histories*, 80, 214, 359, 430, 459n. Embry was in the Surry County militia.

81. *CRNC2*, 2:431, 3:373, 399; SSCWI, 30, 108; Secretary of State Deeds, 12.

82. Powell, *Ye Countie of Albemarle*, 57.

83. Lounsbury, "Development of Domestic Architecture," 18–19.

84. Norfolk County Deeds, C:180.

85. Powell, *Ye Countie of Albemarle*, 62; SSCWI, 15, 17, 19; Grimes, *North Carolina Wills*, 560–61; Secretary of State Wills, 1712–1722, 2:55–56; *DNCB*, 2:309, 3:94.

86. Lounsbury, "Development of Domestic Architecture," 22–25, 31.

87. Haley and Winslow, *Historic Architecture*, 9–12, 113; Bishir and Southern, *Guide*, 113.

88. Haley and Winslow, *Historic Architecture*, 111, 198; Bishir and Southern, *Guide*, 113–14, 116.

89. *CRNC2*, 5:106, 7:495–96. The carpenter was sued for twenty pounds for not completing the contract.

90. Hampton, "Rental Property."

91. Eden House was excavated by Loretta Lautzenheiser of Coastal Carolina Research.

92. *CRNC2*, 2:335; Lautzenheiser et al., *"I Was Moved of the Lord,"* 23–24, 28, 43.

93. Lautzenheiser et al., *"I Was Moved of the Lord,"* 80, 84–85, 88–89, 92, 96, 100.

94. Lautzenheiser et al., *"I Was Moved of the Lord,"* 101, 109–10, 112, 131–32; *DNCB*, 3:247–49.

95. *CRNC2*, 5:340; quoted in Lautzenheiser et al., *"I Was Moved of the Lord,"* 114, 118, 124, 126, 145.

96. Grimes, *North Carolina Wills*, 472–74; Spruill, *Women's Life and Work*, 28–29.

97. SSCWI, 15, 17, 19. A pottle bottle contained a half gallon.

98. SSCWI, 11–13, 23.

99. Ludwell, "Journall," 9–10. Philip Ludwell, son of a former Carolina governor, and Nathaniel Harrison were the commissioners.

100. Lawson, *New Voyage*, 90–91.

101. Lawson, *New Voyage*, 91.

102. Watson, "Women," 9.

103. Billings, *Sir William Berkeley*, 171.

104. Spruill, *Women's Life and Work*, 340–41, 359, 364; Brown, *Good Wives*, 287–91.

105. *CRNC2*, 3:188.

106. *CRNC2*, 2:384, 430. In 1694 she applied for six headrights for four Africans, an English servant, and Argill Simons. *CRNC2*, 2:39, 82.

107. *CRNC2*, 3:283, 322, 329–31.

108. *CRNC2*, 5:439, 465; Hofmann, *Province of North Carolina*, 2511.

109. *CRNC*, 1:394–95, 397.

110. Watson, "Women," 19.

111. *DNCB*, 1:471–72; *CRNC2*, 2:22, 50, 138–39, 150–54, 173–74, 244–45, 256–57, 289–90, 298–99, 3:4, 15, 474, 4:17–18, 274–75, 288–89. The dates of her marriages were to Culpeper, 1688–93, and to Henley, 1693–98. Culpeper was forty-four when they married. She died in 1729 and was survived by her third husband, Quaker Matthew Pritchard.

112. *DNCB*, 2:227–28; *CRNC2*, 2:20. At age sixty in 1705, Diana Harris married her fourth and last husband, Thomas Mercer, who died in 1706. The date of her death is unknown.

113. Billings, *Sir William Berkeley*, 170–73, 213–14, 265–66, 269–70; *DNCB*, 1:470.

114. *DNCB*, 2:122–25.

115. Crump, "Foodways," 2, 5.

116. Lawson, *New Voyage*, 31. A ragout is a thick stew.

117. Quoted in Crump, "Foodways," 9.

118. *CRNC2*, 10:116.

119. Quoted in Crump, "Foodways," 5–6.

120. Lawson, *New Voyage*, 104–7, 108–12, 113–16.

121. Boyd, *William Byrd's Histories*, 92.

122. Boyd, *William Byrd's Histories*, 92.

123. *CRNC2*, 7:65, 428.

124. *CRNC2*, 2:228–31. A flip was made from folding beaten eggs into sweetened or spiced wine or rum.

125. Lawson, *New Voyage*, 115.

126. Salley, *Narratives*, 146. An alembick was used in distilling. Carolinians have been making corn liquor for over three centuries.

127. Brickell, *Natural History*, 39–40.

128. J. M. Gallman, "Mortality," 303–4, 306–7. There are no corresponding data for the Black and Native populations.

129. *CRNC2*, 3:462, 6:210, 214, 263, 345, 414, 557; Watson, *Society*, 68.

130. *CRNC2*, 2:16; *DNCB*, 1:221.

131. *CRNC2*, 2:152, 3:84, 97, 105, 113, 147, 169.

132. *CRNC2*, 6:274–75, 309–10, 345.

133. Medical information came from *Encyclopaedia Britannica*, 1st ed. (Edinburgh, 1771).

134. *CRNC2*, 3:25, 55–56. Workman lived in Pasquotank Precinct on 375 acres acquired from Clarke. Haun, *Old Albemarle County Land Warrants*, 353.

135. *CRNC2*, 4:226, 228, 241–45; Lawson, *New Voyage*, 25; Brickell, *Natural History*, 48; Parramore, "'Country Distemper,'" 44–51.

136. *DNCB*, 1:221–22; Brickell, *Natural History*, 46.

137. Brickell, *Natural History*, 47–49. Jesuits bark, introduced to Jesuit missionaries in Peru, is from cinchona, the source of quinine.

138. *CRNC2*, 3:97–98, 109, 113.

139. *CRNC*, 1:100–101; Powell, *Ye Countie of Albemarle*, 45.

140. Grimes, *North Carolina Wills*, 473; *CRNC2*, 3:540; SSCWI, 11, 13, 15, 17, 19; *ENC*, 361.

141. Grimes, *North Carolina Wills*, 234, 287, 289, 292, 317, 388, 427; *DNCB*, 4:333.

142. Grimes, *North Carolina Wills*, 196; Powell, *Ye Countie of Albemarle*, 45, 50.

143. R. E. Gallman, "Changes," 567–68, 574, 576, 580.

144. Grimes, *North Carolina Wills*, 286.

145. *CRNC2*, 4:77, 10:437. Leigh was hired by the parish on 9 March 1703, serving as sexton and, when the minister was absent, reading the service and preaching.

146. *CRNC2*, 5:445–47.

147. *CRNC2*, 2:134, 372, 392–93, 3:243, 262, 527–28.

148. *CRNC2*, 4:407, 10:85–86; *DNCB*, 2:370–71; Boyd, *William Byrd's Histories*, 118.

149. Seth B. Hinshaw, *Carolina Quaker Experience*, 71–72.

150. The word "fornication" need not be taken literally. It was often used metaphorically by ministers to mean "being seduced or converted to another faith." Among Anglicans' epithets for Quakers were "powerfull Enemies," "wicked," "notorious Blasphemers," and "Roguish." *CRNC2*, 10:22, 28, 72, 119.

151. *CRNC2*, 10:85–86, 97, 443–44; *DNCB*, 2:370–71.

152. *CRNC2*, 10:143, 149, 222–24, 6:xxxiii; LeMaster, "In the 'Scolding Houses,'" 225.

Chapter Eight

1. *CRNC*, 1:54–55; Billings, *Papers*, 207–8, 208n; Powell, *Ye Countie of Albemarle*, 6n, 7, 8. The island was originally named in 1586 for Christopher Carleill, a companion of Sir Francis Drake, and is now Colington Island.

2. Powell, *Ye Countie of Albemarle*, 6–7; Fagg, "Carolina," 104–7.

3. Powell, *Ye Countie of Albemarle*, 6, 8, 11, 12, 58; *DNCB*, 1:457–58.

4. Powell, *Ye Countie of Albemarle*, 6, 10. Whoever played the knave, Crawford became an important resident, serving on the council and as a leader in Culpeper's Rebellion.

5. Powell, *Ye Countie of Albemarle*, 62.

6. The debilitating illness affecting many new colonists during their "seasoning" period was probably malaria. Mann, *1493*, 34, 76–99.

7. Powell, *Ye Countie of Albemarle*, 62.

8. Powell, *Ye Countie of Albemarle*, 62–63.

9. Powell, *Ye Countie of Albemarle*, 64.

10. Powell, *Ye Countie of Albemarle*, 56–59.

11. *CRNC*, 1:55.

12. Edmundson, *Journal*, 50–51.

13. Penney, *Journal of George Fox*, 2:233–34.

14. *CRNC2*, 10:210, 215.

15. Brickell, *Natural History*, 262; Wertenbaker and Schlegel, *Norfolk*, 33–34.

16. *CRNC2*, 10:27, 29; Watson, *Society*, 100–103, 106.

17. *CRNC*, 1:175–76; Powell, *Ye Countie of Albemarle*, 29.

18. Haun, *Old Albemarle County Land Warrants*, 201, 202, 272, 274, 276.

19. *CRNC*, 1:186.

20. Wolf, "Patents and Tithables," 268, 274–75. See Kelly, "In Dispers'd Country Plantations.'"

21. *CRNC*, 1:120–21; Wolf, "Patents and Tithables," 267–68.

22. *CRNC2*, 3:144–45, 301, 464; Powell, *Ye Countie of Albemarle*, 62; Grimes, *North Carolina Wills*, 561.

23. *CRNC2*, 5:344–45, 362.

24. Lawson, *New Voyage*, 80–81.

25. SSCWI, 11–13, 17–19, 23, 52–54; Grimes, *North Carolina Wills*, 472–74, 560–61.

26. *CRNC2*, 10:115–16, 120; *DNCB*, 6:77.

27. *CRNC2*, 10:210–11, 264, 271.

28. SSCWI, 11–13, 17–19, 23; Grimes, *North Carolina Wills*, 472–74, 560–61.

29. Bruce, *Economic History*, 1:438–43. A steelyard was a balance beam scale for weighing objects. Steelyards ranged from small brass instruments to those large enough to weigh half-ton hogsheads.

30. *CRNC*, 1:266–67.

31. Powell, *Ye Countie of Albemarle*, 56–57.

32. Miller v. Risco, 7, 14.

33. C. M. Andrews, *Colonial Period*, 4:61–65, 86–89.

34. SSCWI, 17–19; Grimes, *North Carolina Wills*, 560; *SRNC*, 23:54.

35. Powell, *Ye Countie of Albemarle*, 45.

36. Middleton, *Tobacco Coast*, 127–28. The Crown disallowed the Virginia act in 1731.

37. Berland, *Dividing Line Histories*, 80–81.

38. *CRNC*, 3:621; Wertenbaker and Schlegel, *Norfolk*, 30–31, 35.

39. *CRNC2*, 2:37, 49, 336, 345, 419, 442, 445, 450–51; Lawson, *New Voyage*, 21, 90; *SRNC*, 23:54.

40. Powell, *Ye Countie of Albemarle*, 12.

41. Cain, "'Early Albemarle," 138.

42. Lawson, *New Voyage*, 87–88.

43. Grimes, *North Carolina Wills*, 474.

44. *CRNC2*, 4:120–21, 3:xvin. Axtell, a Quaker, was Archdale's deputy in southern Carolina, and his daughter Elizabeth married Joseph Blake, nephew of Archdale and deputy governor of South Carolina. Hood, *Public Career of John Archdale*, 42n.

45. *CRNC2*, 2:xx, 13, 39, 51, 53, 63, 152, 208, 211, 322.

46. *CRNC2*, 10:244, 246.

47. Salley, *Narratives*, 172.

48. *CRNC2*, 3:xix; Clonts, "Travel," 22–24, 28–29.

49. *CRNC*, 1:751–52; *SRNC*, 23:60–61.

50. *CRNC*, 3:621.

51. *CRNC2*, 3:95–96, 169–70, 286–88, 308–9, 322, 336–37, 358, 365, 369, 443, 446, 452.

52. *CRNC2*, 3:301, 5:144, 522, 6:271, 356, 7:399–400; Brickell, *Natural History*, 263; *CRNC*, 1:xii.

53. Powell, *Ye Countie of Albemarle*, 7, 8, 9, 11–12.

54. Lawson, *New Voyage*, 117–19. Lawson reported that provincial Governor Sir Nathaniel Johnson in Charles Town had given up on imported vines and was making all of his wine from the native grape by grafting it onto "its own stock."

55. Brickell, *Natural History*, 92.

56. Clowse, *Measuring Charleston's Overseas Commerce*, 30.

57. *CRNC2*, 2:16.

58. Powell, *Ye Countie of Albemarle*, 56.

59. *CRNC2*, 5:333–34, 435–36, 448.

60. *CRNC2*, 4:262–63, 311, 427, 467–68; Whitley and Trimble, *North Carolina Headrights*, 42; Hofmann, *Province of North Carolina*, 746, 747, 750; *DNCB*, 2:307–8, 5:25–26.

61. *CRNC2*, 4:14–15, 157–58, 161–62.

62. *CRNC2*, 4:427–28. Two of the court's justices, William Glover and John Porter, and the attorney general were planter-merchants engaged in the fur trade. *DNCB*, 2:260–61, 307–8, 6:126.

63. *CRNC2*, 4:106.

64. *CRNC*, 1:187.

65. *CRNC2*, 4:470–72. There was no follow-up trial; apparently Gee had absconded to Virginia.

66. *CRNC2*, 3:350–51, 395, 461–62; *SRNC*, 22:732, 734.

67. Lawson, *New Voyage*, 64, 232.

68. *CRNC2*, 2:447, 3:247–48, 538–39, 4:xx, 245–46, 260–61, 420, 5:10; Grimes, *North Carolina Wills*, 560–61.

69. Grimes, *North Carolina Wills*, 500–561; *CRNC2*, 3:38–39.

70. Lawson, *New Voyage*, 211–12; H. R. Paschal, "Tragedy," 10–12.

71. *CRNC2*, 3:48, 248, 535, 543.

72. *SRNC*, 22:733; *DNCB*, 2:260, 264, 4:4; Watson, *Bath*, 14, 82, 94. Gale would be appointed to the vestry of St. Thomas Parish in 1715.

73. *SRNC*, 22:732–35.

74. *DNCB*, 2:260–64, 4:3–5.

75. *CRNC2*, 4:xx–xxi, 245–46, 393–94.

76. Well-documented dugouts include cypress canoes up to forty feet long found in Lake Phelps; the Lurgan oak canoe, over fifty feet long, exhibited in the Irish National Archaeological Museum, Dublin; and the Dufana canoe of Nigeria, over twenty-six feet long and 8,500 years old. By 3,000 years ago West Africans from the Guinea coast, home of most of North Carolina's enslaved Africans, were using iron tools to dig canoes, from which they fished and traded on the rivers and the Atlantic. Their skills in boat construction, handling, and navigation proved invaluable in the Carolina tidewater.

77. Lawson, *New Voyage*, 103; Brickell, *Natural History*, 261.

78. Bolster, *Black Jacks*, 45–50.

79. Lawson, *New Voyage*, 132.

80. Lawson, *New Voyage*, 102–3.

81. Lawson, *New Voyage*, 261.

82. Lawson, *New Voyage*, 103.

83. *CRNC2*, 2:61, 126, 417, 434, 479; SSCWI, 17–19; Clonts, "Travel," 18–19; Lawson, *New Voyage*, 103; Brickell, *Natural History*, 260–61.

84. *CRNC*, 1:219.

85. Berland, *Dividing Line Histories*, 80–81, 85, 86, 358, 362. The explorers found that Knot's Island is actually a peninsula.

86. *CRNC*, 1:99.

87. New Inlet was just south of Currituck Inlet. Inlets used by the Albemarle colony were Currituck, which was suitable for small craft, and Roanoke, which was the main entrance but was shoaling. Stick, *Outer Banks*, 25–26, 274.

88. Miller v. Risco, 11–12.

89. *CRNC*, 1:232; Bailyn, *New England Merchants*, 148.

90. Hawks, *History of North Carolina*, 2:378–79.

91. *CRNC2*, 3:xix; Lawson, *New Voyage*, 70, 88. Tar and pitch were the only available preservatives for sails and rigging. England's pine trees had long been cut down, making the nation dependent on Scandinavia for naval stores for many years.

92. *CRNC*, 1:467.

93. *CRNC*, 1:663.

94. *CRNC*, 1:296; W. S. Smith, "Culpeper's Rebellion," 63–64, 88.

95. *CRNC2*, 4:127–28, 454–55.

96. *CRNC*, 1:663.

97. Lawson, *New Voyage*, 166–67.

98. *CRNC*, 1:265, 274, 297, 310, 322–23.

99. *CRNC2*, 2:215.

100. Haun, *Old Albemarle County Miscellaneous Records*, 27; *CRNC2*, 2:18, 3:352–53.

101. *CRNC2*, 2:215–16, 279, 325, 417, 418, 434, 3:16, 65, 352, 380, 517; *CRNC*, 2:279.

102. Moody, "Massachusetts Trade," 46–47; Whitley and Trimble, *North Carolina Headrights*, 30, 76–77, 202; *CRNC2*, 3:517–19, 4:48, 224–25.

103. *CRNC*, 1:279; *CRNC2*, 2:431, 3:395, 4:72.

104. Moody, "Massachusetts Trade," 47–51.

105. *CRNC2*, 5:48–49.

106. Styrna, "Winds of War," 107–8; Devine, "Forging Alliances," 334.

107. Port Roanoke Customs House Papers, 1703–17.

108. Port Roanoke Customs House Papers; *CRNC2*, 3:350, 395; *SRNC*, 22:732, 734.

109. *CRNC2*, 3:224, 5:93–94; Grimes, *Abstract*, 55.

110. *CRNC2*, 7:125; Cumming, "Turbulent Life," 1–6, 9–10; *DNCB*, 6:238.

111. Port Roanoke Book of Registers; Goldenberg, *Shipbuilding*, 78.

112. *CRNC*, 1:527.

113. Quoted in Stick, *Outer Banks*, 23.

114. *CRNC*, 4:1306.

115. Stick, *Outer Banks*, 23.

116. *CRNC2*, 1:77, 82; Lawson, *New Voyage*, 156–57; Powell, *Ye Countie of Albemarle*, 31–32, 57, 62–63; Simpson and Simpson, "Pursuit of Leviathan," 1–2, 4.

117. *CRNC2*, 1:151, 7:359–60; Simpson and Simpson, "Pursuit of Leviathan," 6. Ten years later the whaling concession was extended for another twenty years. *CRNC2*, 6:xxi.

118. Powell, *Ye Countie of Albemarle*, 57; *SRNC*, 23:54.

119. *CRNC2*, 2:18–19, 43–44, 45–46, 74.

120. *CRNC2*, 6:xxii; Brickell, *Natural History*, 220; Simpson and Simpson, "Pursuit of Leviathan," 3, 11; Stick, *Outer Banks*, 185.

121. Margolin, "'Contrary to All Law and Justice,'" 2, 5n, 12–13; *CRNC2*, 3:191–92, 216–17.

122. *CRNC2*, 3:191–98, 217, 226. Dawson, a militia captain and carpenter of Perquimans Precinct, was elected to the council by the assembly in 1694. There is a reference to him as attorney general. *DNCB*, 2:42–43; *CRNC2*, 7:368.

123. *CRNC2*, 3:lvi, 7:375–77; Margolin, "'Contrary to All Law and Justice,'" 5, 7, 8. The Quaker John Hunt of Pasquotank was on the council and a justice of the General Court. *DNCB*, 3:231–32. John Blaney, captain of the ketch *Dove*, had sailed to and from Boston and claimed headrights for 1,650 acres in 1698 for transporting himself thirty-three times. *CRNC2*, 2:143–44, 215, 3:186, 352.

124. *CRNC2*, 3:191–98, 319, 339. The archaic benefit of clergy plea was unusual. Branding and execution were very rare in North Carolina in this period, but whipping was a common punishment for both men and women.

125. *CRNC2*, 3:216–17, 226, 243, 319, 339, 7:375–77; *DNCB*, 2:43.

126. Lawson, *New Voyage*, 91.

127. Haun, *Old Albemarle County Miscellaneous Records*, 27; SSCWI, 49–50, 70–71.

128. Osnaburg was a coarse type of plain fabric.

129. *CRNC2*, 2:245, 307, 448.

130. *CRNC2*, 2:2–6, passim; Greene, "Courts and Society," 103–4.

131. *CRNC2*, 3:11, 301–2, 316–17; Hofmann, *Province of North Carolina*, 13, 96, 97; Whitley and Trimble, *North Carolina Headrights*, 110–11, 157. The value of the merchandise was £1.5s for the shoes, 2s for the buttons, 3s for the saw, 3s for the plane and chisel, and 1s.8d for the compasses.

132. SSCWI, 11–13; *CRNC2*, 2:326–27.

133. *CRNC2*, 2:21, 23, 179, 370, 3:62, 434.

134. *CRNC2*, 2:16–18, 3:248, 353, 507, 538; Haun, *Perquimans County Deed Abstracts*, 3, 13, 19, 27. A cordwainer worked with leather, usually making shoes.

Chapter Nine

1. Bryant, *Letters*, 85; Ashley, *England*, 107.

2. *CRNC2*, 1:104.

3. R. A. Moore, *Light in Their Consciences*, 182–83; Ashley, *England*, 125–27; Lockyer, *Tudor and Stuart Britain*, 330–32; Kishlansky, *Monarchy Transformed*, 232–35. Violating the Conventicle Act, which also existed in Massachusetts Bay, was punishable by imprisonment, then deportation, and finally death. Baptists and other dissenters were subject to these sentences. G. W. Paschal, *History of North Carolina Baptists*, 1:51.

4. *CRNC2*, 1:77, 88.

5. *CRNC*, 1:34–35.

6. *CRNC2*, 1:114.

7. *CRNC2*, 1:114–15, 127.

8. *CRNC2*, 1:88, 104.

9. As general of the Commonwealth's forces in Scotland, the Duke of Albemarle had blocked Quakers from proselytizing the army, not for religious principles but, rather, to maintain military discipline. This quintessential soldier had no sympathy for pacifism. Ashley, *General Monck*, 139–40, 144, 149.

10. *CRNC2*, 1:181.

11. *CRNC2*, 1:183.

12. *CRNC2*, 1:181–82, 238–40.

13. *CRNC2*, 1:148–50, 164.

14. "Soul-liberty" was first expounded by Providence's Roger Williams, who had been banished from Massachusetts Bay and championed tolerance. R. Jones, *Quakers*, 21n.

15. Lawson, *New Voyage*, 9.

16. Brickell, *Natural History*, 35–36. Brickell traveled extensively in the colony for three years. The surprise is his observation of more Roman Catholics than Baptists. *CRNC2*, 10:283, 285, 501.

17. See C. Hill, *World Turned Upside Down*, 149–53, chaps. 10–11.

18. R. A. Moore, *Light in Their Consciences*, 115–36.

19. R. Jones, *Quakers*, 70–73, 79–88, 91–92.

20. *CRNC2*, 1:113–14.

21. Hening, *Statutes at Large*, 2:166; R. Jones, *Quakers*, 270–75; Bruce, *Social Life*, 215–16, 218, 220–22, 228, 230.

22. Billings, *Papers*, 127, 199; Bruce, *Social Life*, 231, 234.

23. Lautzenheiser et al., *"I Was Moved of the Lord,"* 23, 28; Nugent, *Cavaliers and Pioneers*, 3:426; Parramore, "Tuscarora Ascendancy," 310n; W. W. Hinshaw, *Encyclopedia*, 6:31–32.

24. Edmundson, *Journal*, 51; Weeks, *Southern Quakers*, 34–35; R. Jones, *Quakers*, 284.

25. Bjorkman, "Hannah (Baskel) Phelps Phelps Hill," 10–17. See R. Jones, *Quakers*, chaps. 4–5, for the brutal punishment of Quakers by the Puritans of Massachusetts Bay, which ran the gamut of fines, imprisonment, branding, ear cropping, tongue boring, whipping, banishment, and death. The execution of four Quakers—three men and Mary Dyer—in 1659 and 1660 provoked a reprimand from the king, who ordered the release of prisoners and their return to England.

26. Hobbs, "Complex Networks," 20–21. Stanton settled on Core Sound. Others followed these pioneers.

27. Edmundson, *Journal*, 1–8, 18–19.

28. Edmundson, *Journal*, 59–61, 64–66; Penney, *Journal of George Fox*, 2:176–77, 186, 209, 212–13.

29. Edmundson, *Journal*, 66–68. Apparently Edmundson was unaware that some of the English religious groups similar to Quakers met in taverns and ale houses and frequently smoked. C. Hill, *World Turned Upside Down*, 159–62.

30. Edmundson, *Journal*, 69–72; Billings, *Papers*, 28n.

31. Penney, *Journal of George Fox*, 2:234. Hugh Smithwick had come to Albemarle in 1659 and had a 400-acre plantation in Chowan Precinct. *DNCB*, 5:392.

32. Penney, *Journal of George Fox*, 2:234–35.

33. Penney, *Journal of George Fox*, 2:235–36. The secretary was Peter Carteret, who had left the colony the previous spring. Serving in his absence was Thomas Harris, clerk of the council and public register. *DNCB*, 3:55.

34. Nickalls, *Journal of George Fox*, 644.

35. Penney, *Journal of George Fox*, 2:236.

36. Penney, *Journal of George Fox*, 2:236–37.

37. Edmundson, *Journal*, 112–15.

38. R. Jones, *Quakers*, 299.

39. Perquimans Monthly Meeting Minutes, 1:3–10; Symons Creek Monthly Meeting Minutes, 1:32–34, 36, 175–76.

40. Perquimans Monthly Meeting Minutes, 1:8, 48; Haley and Winslow, *Historic Architecture*, 9.

41. Seth B. Hinshaw, *Carolina Quaker Experience*, 7–8; *CRNC*, 1:596, 656.

42. Haun, *Perquimans County Deed Abstracts*, 236, 260; Perquimans Monthly Meeting Minutes, 1:19.

43. *CRNC2*, 1:88, 113–14, 7:335.

44. *CRNC2*, 7:428.

45. *CRNC2*, 7:382–83.

46. *CRNC2*, 3:398.

47. *CRNC2*, 7:335, 350, 1:100, 143–44, 190, 205, 3:10, 277, 315, 398, 402, 511.

48. *SRNC*, 23:11.

49. *SRNC*, 23:11.

50. R. A. Moore, *Light in Their Consciences*, 12, 122–23, 180–81.

51. *CRNC*, 1:250–53.

52. Perquimans Monthly Meeting Minutes, 1:1; *DNCB*, 1:269.

53. *CRNC*, 1:596.

54. *SRNC*, 23:29, 30.

55. *CRNC*, 1:813; La Vere, *Tuscarora War*, 93–94.

56. Weeks, *Southern Quakers*, 133–34; Whitley and Trimble, *North Carolina Headrights*, 66; Hofmann, *Province of North Carolina*, 2763, 2764; Grimes, *Abstract*, 135.

57. Terrell, "'Some Holsom Exhortations,'" 3; Terrell, "Origins," 5.

58. *DNCB*, 6:175.

59. Terrell, "'Some Holsom Exhortations,'" 3, 9, 15; Terrell, "Origins," 8–9.

60. Terrell, "Origins," 5, 8–9, 12.

61. *CRNC*, 1:252; Terrell, "Origins," 9, 11.

62. *CRNC*, 1:184.

63. Perquimans Monthly Meeting Minutes, 1:45.

64. Perquimans Monthly Meeting Minutes, 1:8. Quaker marriages in a meeting for worship qualified under provincial law because Quaker council members and magistrates were present as witnesses.

65. Hawks, *History of North Carolina*, 2:318–19, 322. In 1702 Robert White had married Tabitha Alford in meeting.

66. *CRNC2*, 1:147.

67. Haun, *Perquimans Precinct, Births, Marriages, Deaths*, 1.

68. Haun, *Perquimans Precinct, Births, Marriages, Deaths*, 63.

69. Haun, *Perquimans Precinct, Births, Marriages, Deaths*, 65–66.

70. Penn, *Brief Account*, 32.

71. *CRNC2*, 3:25, 112. A tombstone ordered from England for the grave of Governor Seth Sothel went astray in Virginia.

72. *CRNC2*, 2:16, 152, 449–50, 3:84, 373.

73. Tomes was married three times: to Priscilla, who bore him seven children; to Abigail Lacy in 1683; and to Mary Nicholson after 1688. *DNCB*, 6:39–40.

74. *DNCB*, 1:9–10.

75. *DNCB*, 1:269, 3:231–32, 4:363, 5:494.

76. *DNCB*, 1:38–39; *ANB*, 1:574–75; Carroll, "John Archdale's Quakerism," 51, 53–55. See Hood, *Public Career of John Archdale*. Ann Archdale married Emanuel Lowe, and they immigrated to Albemarle County after 1691, when her sister Mary married John Danson of London, who became a proprietor in 1708. Carroll, "John Archdale's Quakerism," 55–56, 60.

77. G. W. Paschal, *History of North Carolina Baptists*, chap. 2; *ENC*, 88–89.

78. Huggins, *History of North Carolina Baptists*, 24.

79. G. W. Paschal, *History of North Carolina Baptists*, 38–40, 44–45.

80. *DNCB*, 5:10–13. Palmer's missionary work accelerated after 1730, expanding the General Baptists into Bath County, New Bern, and Edenton.

81. *CRNC2*, 10:321; *DNCB*, 5:10–13.

82. *DNCB*, 4:4–5. Laker's story came to light via the diligent research of George Stevenson.

83. *DNCB*, 4:4.

84. *DNCB*, 4:4.

85. *CRNC2*, 10:28, 31, 104.

86. *DNCB*, 3:65–66.

Chapter Ten

1. *DNCB*, 2:294; *CRNC2*, 2:452–53. In Currituck there is a Gibbs Point on the North River.

2. *CRNC2*, 1:143, 218–19. Although the Fundamental Constitutions had been only partly implemented, for twenty years various revisions had been sent to the colony, and terminology, practices, and titles were in use.

3. The question of who would be Monck's heir was decided in England. The proprietorship was inherited by another cousin, John Granville, Earl of Bath, in 1694. Powell, *Proprietors of Carolina*, 61–62, 66.

4. *CRNC2*, 2:452–53. This is one of the earliest uses of the term "North Carolina," which became common over the next several years. The Virginia council had used it the previous year. Lefler, *History of North Carolina*, 1:56.

5. See *DNCB* for sketches of Jarvis, 3:272; Nixon, 4:373; Pollock, 5:116–17; Walker, 6:111–12; and Wilkison, 6:200–201.

6. *CRNC*, 1:360.

7. *CRNC*, 1:363–64.

8. *CRNC*, 1:364–65; *CRNC2*, 7:366. Although the border was not surveyed until 1728, it is clear that both colonies had a general awareness of the location. The disputed area was at most a few miles wide.

9. *CRNC*, 1:366. Francis Nicholson (1655–1728) had good cause to fear what he called "the mob." After being overthrown in New York by Leisler's Rebellion and fleeing to England, in 1690 he had begun the Virginia appointment. He would serve two terms as governor of Virginia and also terms in Maryland, Nova Scotia, and South Carolina. Nicholson was one of several career army officers who became royal governors in Virginia. Reflecting the long prejudice of Virginians toward their southern neighbor, these governors were inveterate and caustic critics of what they interpreted as chaotic conditions. Webb, "Strange Career"; Webb, *Governors-General*, 475, 488–89, 491, 502, 504, 509–11.

10. *CRNC*, 1:366; *DNCB*, 2:295, 4:106.

11. Ashley, *Glorious Revolution*, 160–92; Harris, *Revolution*, 350–52. The Toleration Act allowed dissenters to worship without penalty, and Quakers were permitted to subscribe, rather than swear, to the required oath of allegiance to the Crown.

12. Craven, *Colonies in Transition*, 213–34, 236–42; Craven, *Southern Colonies*, 412–14; Webb, *Lord Churchill's Coup*, 171–218.

13. *CRNC2*, 2:93–94, 109.

14. *CRNC2*, 2:94n, 108–9, 111–12, 7:370. John Philpott had been in the assembly, was register and clerk of the county court, and was a factor for Bermuda merchants. *CRNC2*, 2:100–101, 104, 446–47, 453; Cheney, *North Carolina Government*, 27.

15. *CRNC2*, 2:86–87, 90, 93–94, 109–11.

16. *CRNC2*, 2:94, 446n. Representing the period's diversity, the General Court consisted of Deputy Governor Thomas Harvey, Quakers Daniel Akehurst and Francis Tomes, Baptist Benjamin Laker, and Anglicans William Duckenfield, Thomas Pollock, Samuel Swann, and Robert Wallis.

17. *CRNC*, 1:360–61.

18. *ANB*, 14:107; *DNCB*, 4:106; Billings, *Sir William Berkeley*, 131–32, 213, 261, 270; Billings, *Virginia's Viceroy*, 26–28, 71–72.

19. *ANB*, 14:107; *DNCB*, 1:470, 4:106; Powell, *Proprietors of Carolina*, 10, 50, 53.

20. *ANB*, 14:107; *DNCB*, 4:106; Billings, *Virginia's Viceroy*, 71–72, 91–96.

21. *ANB*, 14:107; Billings, *Virginia's Viceroy*, 71–72; *CRNC*, 1:360–61.

22. *CRNC*, 1:362–63; *CRNC2*, 2:lixlxi.

23. *CRNC2*, 2:lx–lxiv, 12, 13, 15, 49; *DNCB*, 3:272, 4:106–7; M. Hill, *Governors of North Carolina*, 83.

24. *CRNC*, 1:373. For Sothel in South Carolina see Craven, *Colonies in Transition*, 233; Sirmans, *Colonial South Carolina*, 48–52; *SCE*, 889–90.

25. *CRNC*, 1:181–83, 380, 555; Cheves, *Shaftesbury Papers*, 324–25, 367, 403–5.

26. *CRNC2*, 2:lx–lxin.

27. Sirmans, *Colonial South Carolina*, 51–53; *SCE*, 884–85; *ANB*, 14:108; *DNCB*, 4:106. Landgrave Smith died in office in November 1694, several months after the appointment of Proprietor John Archdale as provincial governor. The council's election of Landgrave Joseph Blake to be deputy governor was confirmed by the proprietors. *SCE*, 77; Sirmans, *Colonial South Carolina*, 52.

28. *CRNC*, 1:373–84; *CRNC2*, 2:lxin. Although nobles were invited to serve on the council in North Carolina, there were so few as to be insignificant.

29. *CRNC2*, 3:xxii–xxiii; Haun, *Old Albemarle County Land Warrants*, 93; Haun, *Perquimans County Deed Abstracts*, 66. The Great Deed was recorded in the land records of

Albemarle County and Perquimans Precinct. The Virginia terms were a fifty-acre headright, larger tracts, and a low quitrent.

30. *CRNC2*, 2:19, 92, 93–94, 326. Historian Mattie E. Parker speculated that what brought Ludwell to North Carolina was a protracted illness of Deputy Governor Jarvis. *DNCB*, 4:106–7.

31. *ANB*, 14:108; *DNCB*, 4:107; *SCE*, 574; Billings, *Papers*, 642.

32. Carroll, "John Archdale's Quakerism," 51–53. Archdale first married Elizabeth Booth in 1659, and they had two daughters, Mary and Anne, and a son, Thomas, who died young. Anne Cary had son Thomas and two daughters, Annabella and Alicia Marie. John and Anne Archdale had two children, Thomas and Elizabeth. Since Quakers were frequently subjected to discrimination, Archdale likely put the proprietary share in his minor son's name as legal protection.

33. *ANB*, 1:574; Hood, *Public Career of John Archdale*, vii, 1–4; Carroll, "John Archdale's Quakerism," 53–54. Archdale's service as acting governor is well documented. *CRNC2*, 2:lxxn, lxxix, lxxxi–lxxxiii, 341, 349, 351, 357, 364, 366.

34. Haun, *Old Albemarle County Land Warrants*, 14; Whitley and Trimble, *North Carolina Headrights*, 92–93; Hofmann, *Province of North Carolina*, abstracts #235, #364, #366; *CRNC2*, 2:159–61, 4:183–84, 276, 278, 322, 346–47. Archdale claimed fourteen headrights, including Mary and Anne. Akehurst, a Quaker, was Archdale's attorney. After Akehurst's demise, his daughter Filiachrista and her husband Joseph Jordan rented the property. None of the Akehursts paid the annual rent of 300 pounds of fresh pork, which resulted in legal action.

35. *ANB*, 11:574–75; *CRNC2*, 4:105, 120–21, 7:483; Hofmann, *Province of North Carolina*, abstract #235; Carroll, "John Archdale's Quakerism," 55–56. The Archdale sisters received a certificate of clearness for marriage from the quarterly meeting in Pasquotank in 1688. Lowe later became Governor Cary's secretary and was involved in Cary's Rebellion. *CRNC2*, 5:xxiiin, 7:20, 22. Archdale's power of attorney was signed in England in 1703 and witnessed by Mary Danson, Elizabeth Lowe, and Joshua Kent. The following July, Elizabeth Lowe proved the document by subscribing in General Court in North Carolina. The Dansons owned 3,600 acres on Arenuse Creek east of the Pasquotank River. *CRNC2*, 4:105, 230–32.

36. Hawks, *History of North Carolina*, 2:378–79.

37. *CRNC*, 1:389–92; R. Jones, *Quakers*, 343. Titles meant little to Quakers. Archdale did not use the title, nor did he claim the 48,000 acres that went with it.

38. *ANB*, 1:574; Hood, *Public Career of John Archdale*, 8; Weeks, *Southern Quakers*, 57–58; R. Jones, *Quakers*, 344; *CRNC2*, 4:105.

39. Quoted in R. Jones, *Quakers*, 346.

40. R. Jones, *Quakers*, 346–49; Hood, *Public Career of John Archdale*, 11, 13–17, 19–20, 23–26; *ANB*, 1:574. Most historians believe that Blake was a relative; he is usually thought to have been Archdale's nephew. Weeks, *Southern Quakers*, 60; Ashe, *Biographical History*, 1:64.

41. *CRNC2*, 3:xxii–xxiii; Haun, *Perquimans County Deed Abstracts*, 66, 113, 114.

42. Carroll, "John Archdale's Quakerism," 57; R. Jones, *Quakers*, 350.

43. Carroll, "John Archdale's Quakerism," 58; Hood, *Public Career of John Archdale*. 27.

44. Ashe, *Biographical History*, 1:62, 63. In 1704 Archdale was rebaptized by an Anglican. He wrote that he still believed in the "doctrine declared by Fr[ien]ds" and that this baptism was not into the Church of England. Many Friends did not understand his action, which appeared to refute their witness against ritual and "outward signs." The Quaker records are largely silent on this strange episode. Carroll, "John Archdale's Quakerism," 59–61.

45. *DNCB*, 3:63, 65–66, 278, 4:4. The Harveys had a son, Thomas, who became a member of the council and the assembly, and a daughter, Mary. After her husband's death, Sarah Harvey married the prominent Christopher Gale in 1702.

46. *CRNC2*, 2:29, 204, 259–60, 298, 3:483, 486.

47. *CRNC2*, 3:7, 199, 274.

48. *CRNC*, 1:359.

49. Craven, *Colonies in Transition*, 235, 236–37, 255; C. M. Andrews, *Colonial Period*, 4:272–317; *CRNC2*, 3:xxiv. Harper, *English Navigation Laws*, has not been superseded. See Webb, *Governors-General*, 510–11, and *Lord Churchill's Coup* for "garrison government." During the reign of William and Mary, Virginia's royal governors were the professional soldiers Francis Nicholson and Sir Edmund Andros. By contrast, proprietary North Carolina's civilian deputy governors were long-established local planters experienced in the colony's administration.

50. C. M. Andrews, *Colonial Period*, 4:140–42.

51. *CRNC2*, 3:519–21; C. M. Andrews, *Colonial Period*, 4:160–61.

52. *CRNC2*, 3:lviii, 517–19. Walker had been a customs official and judge of the vice-admiralty court.

53. Osgood, *American Colonies*, 3:380; C. M. Andrews, *Colonial Period*, 4:158. See M. G. Hall, *Edward Randolph*.

54. C. M. Andrews, *Colonial Period*, 4:159–74; M. G. Hall, *Edward Randolph*, 154–78; Sirmans, *Colonial South Carolina*, 73; *CRNC2*, 3:xxiv–xxv.

55. *CRNC*, 1:439–40, 461, 467–69, 545–47.

56. *CRNC*, 1:527.

57. *CRNC*, 1:441, 540–41, 548; M. G. Hall, *Edward Randolph*, 158.

58. *CRNC*, 1:366, 538–42, 25:149–50; M. G. Hall, *Edward Randolph*, 203–7, 213.

59. *CRNC2*, 2:102, 7:370; *DNCB*, 5:103–4, 6:111–12.

60. *CRNC2*, 2:205, 216–18, 240, 328.

61. *CRNC2*, 3:xxiv–xxvi; *CRNC*, 1:389, 491, 511–14. An example of a vice-admiralty case is *CRNC2*, 3:517–21; *NCHGR*, 3:36–37.

62. *CRNC*, 1:x–xi, 228.

63. *CRNC2*, 10:29. The term "desert" meant "an uninhabited, desolate place."

64. Salley, *Narratives*, 286.

65. *CRNC2*, 2:272, 275, 7:373; *CRNC*, 1:472.

66. Lawson, *New Voyage*, 90, 119; Watson, *Bath*, 8.

67. *CRNC*, 1:324, 339, 343, 356, 358–59.

68. *CRNC*, 1:366–67, 385–86.

69. *CRNC*, 1:459–60, 511–12.

70. *CRNC*, 1:478, 505–6, 507–8.

71. *CRNC*, 1:506–10, 511–12.

72. *CRNC2*, 3:313, 317, 328, 7:3, 5; *DNCB*, 1:9, 3:65, 4:4.

Chapter Eleven

1. Lawson, *New Voyage*, 7; *DNCB*, 4:34. The American colonies were commonly called "the Indies."

2. Lawson, *New Voyage*, xi, 8–11; *DNCB*, 4:34. Although Christopher Gale has been mentioned as a candidate for Lawson's "gentleman," he was too young and had yet to seek his

fortune in the New World. The worldly, middle-aged Moore was a leader of the dominant "Goose Creek" faction. *DNCB*, 2:260; *SCE*, 643; P. F. Campbell, *Some Early Barbados History*, 151; Roberts and Beamish, "Venturing Out," 60; Sirmans, *Colonial South Carolina*, 76, 81–82.

3. Lawson, *New Voyage*, 13, 66–67; *DNCB*, 4:34. At the time of Lawson's visit Smith was living on 2,000 acres north of the Pamlico River. Later he moved to the Neuse River. In 1697 Smith represented Bath County in the assembly. *CRNC2*, 5:500–502, 7:627.

4. Lawson, *New Voyage*, 90–91.

5. Lawson, *New Voyage*, xvii–xviii; *DNCB*, 4:34, 36. Later his nephew, William Kirk, lived in this house and inherited it. The name "Chattoka" went with the Tuscarora exodus to New York and survives as "Chautauqua." Powell, *North Carolina Gazetteer*, 100.

6. Lawson, *New Voyage*, 89.

7. Lawson, *New Voyage*, 46, 49–50.

8. Lawson, *New Voyage*, 35–36, 40–47.

9. Lawson, *New Voyage*, 52.

10. Lawson, *New Voyage*, 57–59.

11. Lawson, *New Voyage*, xiv, 60–62, 64–67. Occaneechee Town was near present-day Hillsborough.

12. Lawson, *New Voyage*, 71. The older inlets of Currituck and Roanoke were shoaling, while at Hatteras and Ocracoke there was twelve feet at the bar at low tide.

13. *DNCB*, 4:34–35.

14. *CRNC2*, 1:85, 86, 116–17, 140–41, 148, 173, 194; Powell, *Ye Countie of Albemarle*, 35. See T. D. Wilson, *Ashley Cooper Plan*, chaps. 1–3, for the influence of the Fundamental Constitutions of Lord Ashley and John Locke on city and regional planning in South Carolina.

15. *CRNC*, 1:229.

16. *CRNC2*, 4:442, 444–46, 7:6, 55–56, 423–24.

17. *CRNC2*, 1:716, 735–39, 744–45, 752; Wright, *Prose Works of William Byrd*, 213; Lawson, *New Voyage*, xix–xxii; *DNCB*, 4:35, 332.

18. Cumming, *Southeast in Early Maps*, 86–89, 201–2; Lawson, *New Voyage*, xxxviii; Watson, *Bath*, 11; Shields, "*New Voyage to Carolina*," 304–6. Shields attributes the Lawson map to the engraver, John Senex. Following common practice, it was based on the John Thornton, Robert Morden, Philip Lea map of Carolina (1685). To credit Senex with the map is equivalent to crediting the publisher of a book with authorship. The Thornton, Morden, Lea map is reproduced in Cumming, *Southeast in Early Maps*, color plate 6.

19. Watson, *Bath*, 5–6; H. R. Paschal, *History of Colonial Bath*, 5.

20. H. R. Paschal, *History of Colonial Bath*, 4–5, 7–10; Watson, *Bath*, 5–10, 12–13; *SRNC*, 23:73–74; Latham and Samford, "Naturalist, Explorer," 254–55. Perkins later sold the remainder of his tract to Thomas Cary. Some town lots were soon resold, suggesting speculation rather than residence.

21. Latham and Samford, "Naturalist, Explorer," 256. A gristmill powered by animals was unusual in North Carolina. Windmills were more common on the coast, and streams that could be easily dammed provided water power.

22. *CRNC2*, 10:86, 121.

23. Latham and Samford, "Naturalist, Explorer," 256–57, 259, 260; Lawson, *New Voyage*, 274–75; Grimes, *North Carolina Wills*, 280–81; *CRNC2*, 7:27.

24. Parrish, *American Curiosity*, 54, 58, 110–11, 190–94, 250–54. Sloane's collections, housed at the British Museum, include Lawson's extant specimens. Sloane introduced hot chocolate

milk to London, where it soon rivaled tea and coffee in the coffeehouses. Knighted in 1716, Sloane was president of the Royal Society and the Royal College of Physicians. See De Beer, *Sir Hans Sloane*.

25. Lawson, *New Voyage*, 267.

26. Lawson, *New Voyage*, 3.

27. *CRNC2*, 10:200–201. Urmston also wrote that his invective had reached the proprietors, who were "highly incensed against" him.

28. *DNCB*, 4:54; Grimes, *Abstract*, 214; Watson, *History of New Bern*, 4; Dill, "Eighteenth Century New Bern [Part I]," 7–8.

29. *DNCB*, 2:354; *CRNC2*, 7:8, 410, 9:21, 134; Grimes, *North Carolina Wills*, 210–12.

30. Lawson, *New Voyage*, 90, 120; Dill, "Eighteenth Century New Bern," pt. 1, *North Carolina Historical Review* 22 (January 1945): 18–21.

31. *CRNC2*, 7:424; Haun, *Old Albemarle County Miscellaneous Records*, 456.

32. Elizabeth bore thirteen children. Her son, Prince Rupert, fought for Charles I in the English Civil Wars and supported Charles II after the Restoration. Elizabeth's daughter Sophia married the Elector of Hanover and was the mother of George I of Great Britain. After Frederick's death in 1632, Elizabeth lived as a widow for thirty years, much of the time under the protection of Lord Proprietor William, Earl of Craven. Cousins of the Stuarts, the Hanoverians succeeded them to the throne of Great Britain, and their descendants rule to this day. Powell, *Proprietors of Carolina*, 26–27.

33. Todd and Goebel, *Christoph von Graffenried's Account*, 9–11, 13–18, 21–22; Dill, "Eighteenth Century New Bern [Part II]," 157–58.

34. *DNCB*, 2:327–28, 4:263–64. In North Carolina Michel's name was anglicized to "Lewis Mitchell." De Graffenried's son Christoph migrated to Charles Town and founded the American branch of the family.

35. *DNCB*, 4:263; Schütz, "Additions," 133; Dill, "Eighteenth Century New Bern [Part II]," 153.

36. Allred and Dill, "Founding of New Bern," 362–63; G. W. Paschal, *History of North Carolina Baptists*, 1:13–15.

37. *DNCB*, 2:328; Todd and Goebel, *Christoph von Graffenried's Account*, 33, 252; Dill, "Eighteenth Century New Bern [Part II]," 154–56; Watson, *History of New Bern*, 7–8; La Vere, *Tuscarora War*, 19.

38. *CRNC*, 1:707, 718, 723; *CRNC2*, 7:11–12, 434–35; Dill, "Eighteenth Century New Bern [Part II]," 162–64.

39. *CRNC*, 1:986–89; *CRNC2*, 7:13–15.

40. Lawson, *New Voyage*, 268–70; *CRNC*, 1:909–11; Todd and Goebel, *Christoph von Graffenried's Account*, 225–27; Watson, *History of New Bern*, 8–9; La Vere, *Tuscarora War*, 24.

41. *CRNC*, 1:914–15; Todd and Goebel, *Christoph von Graffenried's Account*, 46–47, 49, 228–29, 369–70; Dill, "Eighteenth Century New Bern [Part II]," 164–65.

42. Lawson, *New Voyage*, 269; *CRNC2*, 7:435–36; *CRNC*, 1:910–11; Watson, *History of New Bern*, 9; Dill, "Eighteenth Century New Bern [Part II]," 165–66.

43. Todd and Goebel, *Christoph von Graffenried's Account*, 373–74, 376–77; Dill, "Eighteenth Century New Bern [Part II]," 167; Feeley, "Before Long to Be Good Friends,'" 143.

44. De Graffenried reported "one wretched water mill" in the colony in addition to the one the Swiss built. Grain was ground in wooden mortars or hollow oak tree stumps, in hand

mills by those who could afford them, and by the enterprising Swiss with water-powered pestles. Baskets were used for sifting the flour and meal. *CRNC*, 1:913; Todd and Goebel, *Christoph von Graffenried's Account*, 315; Watson, *History of New Bern*, 9, 11.

45. Todd and Goebel, *Christoph von Graffenried's Account*, 287–88, 377, 379; *CRNC*, 1:913; Dill, "Eighteenth Century New Bern [Part II]," 168–70; La Vere, *Tuscarora War*, 26–27.

46. Todd and Goebel, *Christoph von Graffenried's Account*, 312, 377–78; Watson, *History of New Bern*, 11.

47. Todd and Goebel, *Christoph von Graffenried's Account*, 377–78; *CRNC2*, 10:112–13, 135.

48. Todd and Goebel, *Christoph von Graffenried's Account*, 306–7.

49. Todd and Goebel, *Christoph von Graffenried's Account*, 307–8, 309–10, 313, 314–15, 317, 319.

50. Todd and Goebel, *Christoph von Graffenried's Account*, 310, 311, 315, 318–19.

51. *CRNC*, 1:913.

52. Paul, "Colonial Beaufort," 143; Paul, "Factors in the Economy," 116–17; Dill, *Governor Tryon*, 32, has Graffenried's map translated.

53. Lawson, *New Voyage*, 159.

54. Paul, "Factors in the Economy," 117–18, 120, 125; *CRNC*, 2:397; *CRNC2*, 7:53.

55. Paul, "Factors in the Economy," 126.

56. Paul, "Colonial Beaufort," 143–45. The Beaufort proprietary share originally belonged to the Duke of Albemarle and had descended through John Grenville, the Earl of Bath. The Duke of Beaufort inherited it from his mother, Rebecca Somerset Grenville. Powell, *Proprietors of Carolina*, 10, 61–63, 66–67.

57. Lawson, *New Voyage*, 267, 270–72.

58. Lawson, *New Voyage*, 269–70, 273. Catherine Hyde arrived in the colony in late 1710 and resided on Salmon Creek. She returned to England in 1713 and later lived with her daughter in New York, where she died in 1738. *DNCB*, 3:249.

Chapter Twelve

1. *CRNC2*, 1:181.

2. *CRNC2*, 10:xliv.

3. *CRNC2*, 10:3; Lefler, "Anglican Church," 3–4; Hawks, *History of North Carolina*, 2:338–39. The proprietors sent a letter introducing Bray to Governor Harvey in December 1699. *CRNC2*, 10:3.

4. Lefler, "Anglican Church," 4; H. R. Paschal, *History of Colonial Bath*, 12; Watson, *Bath*, 95; *SRNC*, 23:73–79.

5. *CRNC2*, 10:9–10.

6. *CRNC2*, 10:5–9.

7. *CRNC2*, 10:15, 20, 22, 74, 498; *SRNC*, 22:733.

8. Quoted in Sirmans, *Colonial South Carolina*, 77. The last of the original proprietors, the tolerant palatine William, Earl of Craven, had died in 1697. Powell, *Proprietors of Carolina*, 67; *CRNC2*, 5:xxiv.

9. Sirmans, *Colonial South Carolina*, 76–77, 82, 85; *SCE*, 643.

10. *DNCB*, 6:111–12; Lefler, "Anglican Church," 5; *CRNC2*, 10:22, 82. After Walker's death in 1704, he was initially buried on his Chowan plantation. The widowed Anne married

neighbor Edward Moseley in 1705. Years later, remains of both Henderson and Anne Walker were moved to St. Paul's Churchyard, Edenton.

11. *CRNC2*, 10:22. The vestry was the governing committee of an Anglican parish. In some colonies, notably in Barbados and South Carolina, the parish vestry constituted the local government.

12. *CRNC2*, 10:22; Lefler, "Anglican Church," 5; Lemmon, "Genesis," 427.

13. *CRNC2*, 1:227–28. The earlier version of the Fundamentals, which excluded dissenters from the public tithe, may have been key to the passage of the vestry act. The last version, in 1698, removed the revisions concerning dissenting churches, but by that time the document was considered irrelevant in both North and South Carolina.

14. *CRNC2*, 10:431–33. Described as twenty-five feet long, St. Paul's Church was of wooden post-in-ground construction.

15. *CRNC2*, 10:433, 435. By October the tithe was reduced to four shillings.

16. Nicholson's building contribution was significant; for example, ten pounds represented 40 percent of the cost to construct the chapel of ease. He left the bulk of his estate to the SPG. *CRNC2*, 10:12n, 433.

17. *CRNC2*, 10:22–23.

18. *CRNC2*, 10:28, 44–45, 433, 438–40. Beginning with Francis Hawks and Stephen Weeks, the confusion among historians about the vestry acts stems largely from the absence of extant copies of these early acts. I concur with Robert J. Cain, editor of the Church of England documents, that the 1701 act was not disallowed and that the presumed 1704 vestry act was actually that of South Carolina. *CRNC2*, 10:xxiii–xxvi.

19. *CRNC2*, 10:431–70. *SRNC*, 23:3–6, 6–10.

20. *SRNC*, 23:36. Fines for Sabbath breaking were five to ten shillings. Punishments for sexual offenses were fines of fifty shillings for fornication and five pounds for adultery. Corporal punishment for those unwilling or unable to pay fines was three hours in the stocks or twenty-one lashes.

21. Grimes, *North Carolina Wills*, 231, 436.

22. *CRNC2*, 10:28–29, 31; Weeks, *Religious Development*, 42–43; Lefler, "Anglican Church," 6–8.

23. *CRNC2*, 10:438, 440, 499. There is a gap of two years in the parish minutes.

24. *CRNC2*, 10:44–45, 66, 73.

25. *CRNC2*, 10:497, 499.

26. *CRNC2*, 10:104, 105, 107, 108–10, 112.

27. *DNCB*, 6:77–79.

28. *CRNC2*, 10:139.

29. *CRNC2*, 10:115, 116.

30. *CRNC2*, 10:275–76. Urmston continued to serve the church with appointments that were at times controversial in Pennsylvania and finally Maryland, where he died in 1731.

31. *CRNC2*, 10:192–98, 501–2. Rainsford did not receive the Indian appointment. Urmston questioned whether Rainsford's claims of Indian and Black conversions were exaggerated; however, the men were adversaries. *CRNC2*, 10:256.

32. *CRNC2*, 10:258, 260–61, 269; *DNCB*, 2:111–12. "Mustee" was a term designating a person with one Black grandparent, or one-quarter Black. Although Taylor probably died a natural death, his property was looted and money stolen by the boat crew and drovers on the island. *CRNC2*, 10:270n, 502, 5:228, 245.

33. Powell, *Proprietors of Carolina*, 7–8, 61–62, 67; *CRNC2*, 5:xxiv, quoted in Sirmans, *Colonial South Carolina*, 77.

34. Powell, *Proprietors of Carolina*, 10, 51–52, 60–61.

35. Sirmans, *Colonial South Carolina*, 36–37, 76–77, 87–89; Roper, *Conceiving Carolina*, 128–30; Weir, *Colonial South Carolina*, 76–80; *SCE*, 174, 504–5; *CRNC*, 1:634–40, 643. The Loyalty Oath to Queen Anne, the Exclusion Act (1704), and the Church Act (1704) are in *CRNC*, 2:858–62, 863–67, 867–82. Daniel Defoe's *Party Tyranny* is in *CRNC*, 2:891–923; Salley, *Narratives*, 219–64.

36. *DNCB*, 2:9.

37. Baldwin, *First Settlers*, n.p.; *DNCB*, 2:9.

38. *DNCB*, 2:9; P. F. Campbell, *Some Early Barbados History*, 151; Roberts and Beamish, "Venturing Out," 60; Sirmans, *Colonial South Carolina*, 84–86; Craven, *Southern Colonies*, 75–76. Governor Moore and Colonel Daniell's force included some 800 colonists and Indians. See Arnade, *Siege*.

39. *SRNC*, 22:733.

40. Parramore, "Tuscarora Ascendency," 317–18.

41. Parramore, "Tuscarora Ascendency," 318.

42. Haun, *Old Albemarle County Miscellaneous Records*, 101, 106, 482; *CRNC2*, 7:396–98, 401–2; McIlvenna, *Very Mutinous People*, 116–18.

43. Lawson, *New Voyage*, 211–12; Parramore, "Tuscarora Ascendency," 314, 318. Although the undated document pictured in Parramore has been considered to be earlier, it may be a draft of Daniell's treaty. George Stevenson concluded that it was more likely early eighteenth century. Feeley, "'Before Long to Be Good Friends,'" 143, 156–57n. Text is in H. R. Paschal, "Tuscarora Indians," 160–62.

44. *CRNC2*, 7:404, 10:28, 81–82.

45. *CRNC*, 2:858–62, 863–67, 867–82; Weeks, *Religious Development*, 43–49; *CRNC2*, 10:22–23, 28; Seth Beeson Hinshaw, "Two Epistles," 70–71; Lefler, "Anglican Church," 5, 8. The Quaker Epistle, the Reverend John Blair, and President Walker concur that dissenters had enough votes in the 1704 assembly to defeat the vestry act prior to Daniell's exclusion of the Quakers.

46. *SRNC*, 23:11; Devine, "Forging Alliances," 331.

47. *SRNC*, 23:6–8, 12–15, 25:159; Cheney, *North Carolina Government*, 31; Devine, "Forging Alliances," 332. An affirmation allowed Quakers to enter civil suits, administer estates, give civil depositions, and transact business.

48. Seth Beeson Hinshaw, "Two Epistles," 70.

49. Seth Beeson Hinshaw, "Two Epistles," 70–71. The eight Quakers who signed the epistle included Francis Tomes and Thomas Pierce, former council members; Gabriel Newby, previously in the assembly and a future member of the council; and former assemblymen Samuel Nicholson, William Moore, Francis Wells, William Newby, and Isaac Wilson.

50. *CRNC2*, 10:118.

51. Dahlman and Dahlman, *Daniel Island*, 31–32, 34.

52. In this era of frequent common law cohabitation, it was not unusual to maintain a stable family without benefit of marriage, regardless of social level. Landgrave Daniell recognized his natural children from birth, and he married their mother as soon as he legally could. Chamberlaine has been suggested as Dorothy's maiden name.

53. F. Alexander, *Henrietta Johnston*, 71.

54. *DNCB*, 2:9–10; *SCE*, 563.

55. Weeks, *Southern Quakers*, 163.

56. *NCHGR*, 3:74–75; *CRNC2*, 5:xxi, xxiv.

57. Styrna, "Winds of War," 57; Devine, "Forging Alliances," 333.

58. Lowry, "Class," 160–63.

59. *ANB*, 4:524; *DNCB*, 1:338.

60. Weeks, *Southern Quakers*, 75.

61. *DNCB*, 1:338.

62. *DNCB*, 5:126; Weeks, *Southern Quakers*, 162.

63. *ANB*, 4:524; *DNCB*, 2:308.

64. *CRNC2*, 10:119.

65. *DNCB*, 2:307–8.

66. *CRNC2*, 10:65, 73–74.

67. *CRNC*, 1:570, 658–59; Lefler and Powell, *Colonial North Carolina*, 67; Dawdy, "Meherrin's Secret History," 402–3, 406.

68. *CRNC*, 1:660–62, 667–68, 2:642–44; Dawdy, "Meherrin's Secret History," 402–3, 406; Adams, "'Sundry Murders and Depredations,'" 171.

69. *CRNC2*, 7:421.

70. *CRNC2*, 10:82–83.

71. *CRNC2*, 10:119.

72. *CRNC2*, 10:119.

73. *CRNC*, 1:696–99.

74. *DNCB*, 3:246–47; *ANB*, 11:610.

75. *CRNC*, 1:914. The military reputation of the Swiss, renowned as mercenaries throughout Europe for centuries, raised expectations that they would provide a frontier protective force. However, de Graffenried's effort at neutrality was aborted by his subsequent capture by and treaty with the Tuscarora.

76. *CRNC*, 1:914.

77. *CRNC*, 1:911–15; *DNCB*, 3:247–48.

78. *CRNC*, 1:916–17; La Vere, *Tuscarora War*, 28–29.

79. *ANB*, 11:610–11; *DNCB*, 3:246–49; Cheney, *North Carolina Government*, 15, 31.

80. *CRNC2*, 7:440; Lowry, "Class," 188–90. Cary's known leaders were planters, traders, militia officers, and former officials.

81. *CRNC2*, 10:128–29; Lowry, "Class," 191.

82. *CRNC*, 1:912, 915, 917. There is no evidence that Roach was a Quaker.

83. *CRNC2*, 10:123; La Vere, *Tuscarora War*, 13–14; McIlvenna, *Very Mutinous People*, 140–41, 144–46. Stephen Weeks concluded that if there had been other Quakers involved, they also would have been tried. He contends, "They continued steadfast in their testimony against war" in both the rebellion and the coming Indian war. Weeks, *Southern Quakers*, 166; Styrna, "Winds of War," 186–87. The council named former Quaker councilman Gabriel Newby and "many other" Quakers as rebels. Newby was involved in the political phase, but Quaker records do not support the "many other" claim. *CRNC2*, 7:440. To Lowry the idea of Cary supporters' urging an Indian attack "defies plausibility." Lowry, "Class," 202n. It would have been unthinkable for any colonist to arouse the Indians to war, especially those whose livelihoods depended on the Indian trade.

84. *CRNC*, 1:758–59. Governor Spotswood appointed John Clayton (ca. 1666–1737) attorney general of Virginia in 1714. His son John became a notable botanist of Virginia. *DNB*, 3:288–90.

85. Daniel Parke, a Virginia planter, had been the aide-de-camp of the Duke of Marlborough in the War of Spanish Succession. At the time he was governor of the Leeward Islands. Miller, *Colonel Parke*, 179–204. Parke's murder had more to do with his incessant philandering than with his politics.

86. *CRNC*, 1:758–59; Lowry, "Class," 191–92.

87. *CRNC*, 1:760–61; *CRNC2*, 7:438–39.

88. *CRNC*, 1:917–18.

89. *CRNC2*, 7:440–41.

90. *CRNC*, 1:762–63, 919–20; *CRNC2*, 7:440, 10:122; Lowry, "Class," 192.

Chapter Thirteen

1. *CRNC*, 1:933–34; La Vere, *Tuscarora War*, 70. Since the Tuscarora were split and only the Lower Towns and their allies engaged the colony, arguably more Natives fought alongside the English than against them.

2. Lawson, *New Voyage*, 92–93.

3. Gallay, *Indian Slave Trade*, 288–314; La Vere, *Tuscarora War*, 52.

4. Lefler, *History of North Carolina*, 1:70–71; Lefler and Powell, *Colonial North Carolina*, 65–68; Watson, *History of New Bern*, 13–14; Todd and Goebel, *Christoph von Graffenried's Account*, 234; Styrna, "Winds of War," 134–43; La Vere, *Tuscarora War*, 15–17.

5. Feeley, "'Before Long to Be Good Friends,'" 140, 144.

6. Lawson, *New Voyage*, xxx, 243, 244.

7. *CRNC*, 1:921–22, 948; Lefler and Powell, *Colonial North Carolina*, 65–66.

8. Feeley, "'Before Long to Be Good Friends,'" 141.

9. *CRNC*, 2:39–40. Regardless of the slander the government heaped on Quakers, who were pacifists, and the Cary rebels, there is no evidence that they conspired with the Indians. Although Native American neighbors were generally treated with contempt, frontiersmen knew they lived with a "sleeping tiger." *CRNC*, 1:802; Lowry, "Class," 202n.

10. *CRNC*, 1:825, 925–26; La Vere, *Tuscarora War*, 36–37.

11. *CRNC*, 1:926–28; La Vere, *Tuscarora War*, 37–38, 61–62.

12. *CRNC*, 1:930–32; La Vere, *Tuscarora War*, 63, 65–66.

13. *CRNC*, 1:826, 931–33; Lawson, *New Voyage*, 53, 207; La Vere, *Tuscarora War*, 67–68. Execution by cutting his throat is more plausible, but the legend of the human torch became widely accepted. Feeley, "'Before Long to Be Good Friends,'" 145–46, compares the ritual drama of Lawson to what John Smith endured from the Powhatans.

14. *CRNC*, 1:825–27; La Vere, *Tuscarora War*, 70–71.

15. *CRNC*, 1:815.

16. *CRNC*, 1:949; H. R. Paschal, "Proprietary North Carolina," 449–50.

17. *CRNC*, 1:933–38; La Vere, *Tuscarora War*, 79–80.

18. *CRNC*, 1:826, 939–40, 4:955; La Vere, *Tuscarora War*, 79, 88–89.

19. *CRNC*, 1:941–42; La Vere, *Tuscarora War*, 81.

20. *CRNC*, 1:943–46; *CRNC2*, 7:8; La Vere, *Tuscarora War*, 90–92.

21. *CRNC*, 1:808–12, 815, 816–17; *CRNC2*, 7:9; Styrna, "Winds of War," 146–50; La Vere, *Tuscarora War*, 94–95, 145–47; Hawks, *History of North Carolina*, 2:393; Feeley, "'Before Long to Be Good Friends,'" 149–50, 152–53. For diplomacy, treaties, and tributary tribes see LeMaster, "In the 'Scolding Houses,'" 196–98, 201–2, 210–13.

22. LeMaster, "War, Masculinity," 171–74, characterizes the Native Americans and English as "military societies," which is appropriate for South Carolina.

23. *CRNC*, 1:827–29; LeMaster, "War, Masculinity," 168–69, 171. Gale had been attorney general and chief justice of the General Court but was currently out of office because of his support of Cary. *DNCB*, 2:260.

24. John Barnwell, "Journal," pt. 1, 391–94; Parramore, "With Tuscarora Jack," 117.

25. La Vere, *Tuscarora War*, 103.

26. John Barnwell, "Journal," pt. 1, 393–94; Styrna, "Winds of War," 155–56; La Vere, *Tuscarora War*, 104–5.

27. Quoted in H. R. Paschal, "Proprietary North Carolina," 450; Brock, *Official Letters of Alexander Spotswood*, 2:116.

28. Hawks, *History of North Carolina*, 2:394–95; *CRNC2*, 7:9–11, 20, 24, 25.

29. John Barnwell, "Journal," pt. 1, 394–97; Styrna, "Winds of War," 155–64; Parramore, "With Tuscarora Jack," 118, 120; La Vere, *Tuscarora War*, 105–8.

30. Watson, *Bath*, 19–20.

31. John Barnwell, "Journal," pt. 1, 396–97, 399–402; Parramore, "With Tuscarora Jack," 120–22; La Vere, *Tuscarora War*, 108–9, 111–12.

32. Parramore, "With Tuscarora Jack," 122–24.

33. Parramore, "With Tuscarora Jack," 128; Parramore, "Tuscarora Ascendency," 323.

34. Parramore, "With Tuscarora Jack," 129; Todd and Goebel, *Christoph von Graffenried's Account*, 243; John Barnwell, "Journal," pt. 2, 48–49.

35. John Barnwell, "Journal," pt. 2, 43–45; Parramore, "With Tuscarora Jack," 129–30; La Vere, *Tuscarora War*, 119–24; La Vere, "Of Fortifications and Fire," 363, 372.

36. John Barnwell, "Journal," pt. 2, 47–48; La Vere, *Tuscarora War*, 125–26.

37. Todd and Goebel, *Christoph von Graffenried's Account*, 281; La Vere, *Tuscarora War*, 128. Franz Ludwig Michel (Francis Louis Michel), apparently experienced with artillery, had served as an officer in the French army of Louis XIV. In the Fort Neoheroka siege in 1712, he was "much praised" for his skills as an engineer. *DNCB*, 4:263.

38. John Barnwell, "Journal," pt. 2, 48, 50–51; Todd and Goebel, *Christoph von Graffenried's Account*, 231, 243–44; La Vere, *Tuscarora War*, 128–29.

39. John Barnwell, "Journal," pt. 2, 51–52; Parramore, "With Tuscarora Jack," 131–32; La Vere, *Tuscarora War*, 130–31; La Vere, "Of Fortifications and Fire," 380–83.

40. La Vere, *Tuscarora War*, 131–32.

41. *CRNC*, 1:861–62; John Barnwell, "Journal," pt. 2, 52–55; Parramore, "With Tuscarora Jack," 132–33; La Vere, *Tuscarora War*, 131–32; Feeley, "'Before Long to Be Good Friends,'" 147–48.

42. *CRNC*, 1:900, 956; Todd and Goebel, *Christoph von Graffenried's Account*, 245; John Barnwell, "Journal," pt. 2, 48; Parramore, "With Tuscarora Jack," 134–35; La Vere, *Tuscarora War*, 132–34. There has been some disagreement about this incident. See Lefler and Powell, *Colonial North Carolina*, 78; but Parramore argues effectively that this massacre occurred before Barnwell left for South Carolina in early June. To La Vere, Barnwell was the "perfect

scapegoat." La Vere, *Tuscarora War*, 133; Parramore, "With Tuscarora Jack," 135n; Todd and Goebel, *Christoph von Graffenried's Account*, 245; *CRNC*, 1:851, 862–63, 898–901.

43. *CRNC*, 1:839–41, 843; *CRNC2*, 7:18–20, 28.

44. *CRNC*, 1:851, 863, 899–902, 956.

45. *CRNC*, 1:813, 2:113; Hawks, *History of North Carolina*, 2:324, 326; Dill, "Eighteenth Century New Bern [Part III]," 311n. Because of numerous Quakers, conscientious objection was recognized but sometimes penalized.

46. *CRNC*, 1:813; La Vere, *Tuscarora War*, 93–94.

47. *CRNC2*, 7:40, 41.

48. *CRNC*, 1:860, 2:45; *DNCB*, 1:202; H. R. Paschal, "Proprietary North Carolina," 454.

49. *NCHGR*, 1:438.

50. *CRNC2*, 10:148.

51. *CRNC2*, 7:19, 21, 25–26, 28.

52. *CRNC*, 1:878–79. Green was later killed in a surprise attack on his plantation, along with a son, a white servant, and two enslaved Africans. Another son was wounded but escaped. His wife Hannah and eldest son were away. *DNCB*, 2:354.

53. Wood, "Thomas Pollock," 212–14, 216; Whitley and Trimble, *North Carolina Headrights*, 215.

54. *DNCB*, 5:116–17; La Vere, *Tuscarora War*, 113–16; Wolf, "Patents and Tithables," 267–68, 273; McIlvenna, *Very Mutinous People*, 81–82; Grimes, *North Carolina Wills*, 342–47. Pollock had four children, a daughter and three sons, by his first wife. There were no children by his second wife, Esther Wilkinson.

55. *CRNC2*, 10:144.

56. *CRNC*, 1:888–89, 2:13; Styrna, "Winds of War," 168–69.

57. *CRNC*, 1:890–91, 2:6, 25–26; Styrna, "Winds of War," 169–71.

58. *CRNC*, 2:49.

59. *DNCB*, 1:185–86. See Parramore, "With Tuscarora Jack," 136–37, for partial reproduction of the treaty. *CRNC2*, 7:39; La Vere, *Tuscarora War*, 146–47.

60. *SCE*, 643; Baldwin, *First Settlers*; Sirmans, *Colonial South Carolina*, 52, 70–71, 81–82; La Vere, *Tuscarora War*, 154–55.

61. *CRNC*, 1:892, 2:4, 7; La Vere, *Tuscarora War*, 156, 158.

62. *CRNC*, 2:13, 15; La Vere, *Tuscarora War*, 158–60.

63. During the "Little Ice Age," snow deep enough to stop an army was fairly common in eastern North Carolina. NASA defines this period as the sixteenth to nineteenth centuries.

64. *CRNC2*, 10:158.

65. *CRNC2*, 2:19–20, 30; *CRNC*, 1:892–93.

66. Fort Noo-hee-roo-ka Map, ca. 1713. South Carolina Historical Society, Charleston. Copy in North Carolina Collection, University Library, Chapel Hill. Joseph Barnwell, "Second Tuscarora Expedition," 36, 39; H. G. Jones, *North Carolina Illustrated*, 44. Other variations are "Neoheroka" and "Nohoroco."

67. H. G. Jones, *North Carolina Illustrated*, 44; La Vere, *Tuscarora War*, 165–66.

68. Joseph Barnwell, "Second Tuscarora Expedition," 38; *CRNC*, 1:956–57; La Vere, *Tuscarora War*, 166–68; La Vere, "Of Fortifications and Fire," 386–89.

69. H. G. Jones, *North Carolina Illustrated*, 44; *CRNC*, 1:957; Ward and Davis, *Time before History*, 275; La Vere, *Tuscarora War*, 169.

70. *CRNC*, 2:27; La Vere, *Tuscarora War*, 169.

71. *CRNC*, 2:39, 60, 62.

72. *CRNC*, 2:29.

73. *CRNC*, 2:36–38, 45, 49, 283, 288–89; Styrna, "Winds of War," 173–75; La Vere, *Tuscarora War*, 171–73.

74. *CRNC2*, 7:46, 48–49, 463–64.

75. *CRNC2*, 7:427, 10:188–90; Haun, *Old Albemarle County Miscellaneous Records*, 378; *DNCB*, 2:134, 262.

76. *CRNC2*, 10:185.

77. *CRNC2*, 10:237, 244, 245–46.

78. *CRNC2*, 7:50.

79. *CRNC2*, 7:46–47, 48, 49, 51–52, 53; La Vere, *Tuscarora War*, 148, 176, 196; LeMaster, "In the 'Scolding Houses,'" 225.

80. *CRNC2*, 7:51, 57–58.

81. *CRNC2*, 7:54–55; *CRNC*, 2:180, 255–56; Crane, *Southern Frontier*, 161–86; Sirmans, *Colonial South Carolina*, 111–18; Edgar, *South Carolina*, 102–7; *DNCB*, 4:303. South Carolina armed and organized enslaved Africans for defense, indicating the province's precarious state.

82. *SRNC*, 23:1–96.

83. *SRNC*, 23:29–31. "Riding the wooden horse" meant straddling a fence rail or pole with weights tied to one's legs. Wheeler, "Development and Organization," 308–9n.

84. *CRNC2*, 7:74, 10:255, 257.

85. *CRNC2*, 7:76–77. The Worsely daughter, Mary, was fined ten pounds by the General Court. *CRNC2*, 5:198.

Chapter Fourteen

1. *DNCB*, 2:134, 3:380, 5:116–17, 187, 282–83.

2. The description of the grounding of *Queen Anne's Revenge* is based on the archaeological record. Wilde-Ramsing and Carnes-McNaughton, *Blackbeard's Sunken Prize*, 36–37, 63; Butler, "North Carolina 1718," 125–26.

3. Rediker, "Under the Banner," 205–8; Rediker, *Between the Devil and the Deep Blue Sea*, 205–50.

4. C. Johnson, *General History*, 4. Originally published in 1724, this popular narrative has been the most influential source on the history of piracy. A complete edition is that of Manuel Schonhorn (1972). The theory that Johnson may have been Daniel Defoe was refuted in 1988. See Cordingly, *Under the Black Flag*, xix–xx, and Cordingly's introduction in C. Johnson, *General History*, xi–xiii. More recently Nathaniel Mist, a Jacobite journalist and publisher, has been identified as Johnson. Bialuschewski, "Daniel Defoe, Nathaniel Mist," 25–26; Woodard, *Republic of Pirates*, 325–26; Brooks, "'Born in *Jamaica*,'" 236. David Moore is not convinced that Mist is the author and notes that some speculate that Defoe or others may have collaborated. Mist had the copyright for the book. D. D. Moore, "Captain Edward Thatch," 150–51, 150n; Brooks, "'Born in *Jamaica*,'" 243.

5. Bridenbaugh and Bridenbaugh, *No Peace*, 3.

6. Peterson, *Funnel of Gold*, 31–119.

7. Esquemeling, *Buccaneers*, 45, 55–60; Rediker, "Under the Banner," 209–11.

8. Leslie, *New History*, 72–73, 77–104; Pope, *Buccaneer King*, 100–353; Talty, *Empire*, 32–305.

9. Louis XIV ascended the throne at the age of five in 1643 and reigned until 1715. The main adversaries of the allied coalitions were France in King William's War (War of the League of Augsburg), France and Spain in Queen Anne's War (War of Spanish Succession), and Spain in the War of the Quadruple Alliance. The treaties of Ryswick (1697) and Utrecht (1713) settled little and provided only temporary breathers.

10. Quoted in Rankin, *Golden Age of Piracy*, 18.

11. C. Johnson, *General History*, 3; Rediker, *Between the Devil and the Deep Blue Sea*, 258.

12. C. Johnson, *General History*, 39.

13. Butler, *Pirates*, 12–13; Cordingly, *Under the Black Flag*, xvii–xviii.

14. Rediker, *Between the Devil and the Deep Blue Sea*, 156, 256, 258–59, 260–61, 264–65; Rediker, *Villains*, 9, 29–30, 53–56. The estimate of 2,000 pirates in the era of Blackbeard and Bonnet (1717–18) is closer to contemporary observations. Rediker doubles this figure for the whole decade of 1716–26. By 1725–26 fewer than 200 were active.

15. C. Johnson, *General History*, 342.

16. Rediker, *Between the Devil and the Deep Blue Sea*, 247, 261.

17. C. Johnson, *General History*, 194–95.

18. *CRNC*, 1:225, 477; Craton, *History*, 64; Craton and Saunders, *Islanders*, 93. The two original proprietors not involved were the Earl of Clarendon, who was in exile, and Sir William Berkeley, who was no longer active. Powell, *Proprietors of Carolina*, 58, 65–66.

19. Craton, *History*, 64–65, 67; Craton and Saunders, *Islanders*, 79, 93–94. Commissioned the first governor, Hugh Wentworth died before taking office and was succeeded by his brother.

20. Craton, *History*, 71–72, 75; Craton and Saunders, *Islanders*, 80, 82, 86–87.

21. Craton, *History*, 79.

22. *CRNC*, 1:466; Rankin, *Golden Age of Piracy*, 19.

23. *CRNC*, 1:225, 466, 477; Craton, *History*, 64, 74, 90.

24. C. Johnson, *General History*, 35–39.

25. C. Johnson, *General History*, 35–36; Peterson, *Funnel of Gold*, 362, 364–75; Woodard, *Republic of Pirates*, 103–12 .

26. C. Johnson, *General History*, 41; Rediker, *Between the Devil and the Deep Blue Sea*, 267–68; Rediker, *Villains*, 29–30, 52–53.

27. C. Johnson, *General History*, 35–38; Cordingly, *Under the Black Flag*, 147, 149–50; Peterson, *Funnel of Gold*, 388–89, 391.

28. A. Moore, "Marooned," 266–67; Craton, *History*, 94, 95; *DNCB*, 2:262.

29. C. Johnson, *General History*, 42; Cordingly, *Under the Black Flag*, 152–53; Woodard, *Republic of Pirates*, 235–36, 268. See Brooks, *Quest*, 643–45, for Pearse's list. The Act of Grace is in C. Johnson, *General History*, 40–41.

30. *CRNC*, 1:347, 467, 674.

31. Coker, *Charleston's Maritime Heritage*, 8–9; *SCE*, 733–34.

32. *CRNC*, 1:467, 475, 527; Hanna, "Protecting the Rights of Englishmen," 300–303.

33. Coker, *Charleston's Maritime Heritage*, 8–9, 13–16.

34. Leslie, *New History*, 202; Butler, *Pirates*, 29–30, 233n. In Jamaican records the family uses "Thache" and "Theach." Brooks, "'Born in *Jamaica*,'" 252–53, 255. Usually written as "Thatch" in North Carolina, the name was likely pronounced with a silent *h*: "Tatch."

35. Brooks, "'Born in *Jamaica*,'" 252–62; D. D. Moore, "Captain Edward Thatch," 154–55; Woodard, *Republic of Pirates*, 38–39. Edward conveyed the estate to his stepmother and half-siblings.

36. C. Johnson, *General History*, 71; D. D. Moore, "Captain Edward Thatch," 155–56; Rediker, *Between the Devil and the Deep Blue Sea*, 267–68; Woodard, *Republic of Pirates*, 160–61.

37. C. Johnson, *General History*, 95–96; Butler, *Pirates*, 52–55.

38. *Boston News-Letter*, 28 October–4 November 1717; D. D. Moore, "Captain Edward Thatch," 156, 160; Woodard, *Republic of Pirates*, 205–9; Butler, *Pirates*, 56–57.

39. D. D. Moore, "Captain Edward Thatch," 157, 159, 162, 164–65; Moore and Daniel, "Blackbeard's Capture," 15, 24–25; Woodard, *Republic of Pirates*, 209–14; Butler, "Blackbeard's Terror," 30–31.

40. C. Johnson, *General History*, 71, 82; Butler, *Pirates*, 29–33, 49; Rediker, *Between the Devil and the Deep Blue Sea*, 267–68.

41. Butler, *Pirates*, 30–31; D. D. Moore, "Captain Edward Thatch," 151–52.

42. C. Johnson, *General History*, 96; *Boston News-Letter*, 16–23 June 1718; Butler, *Pirates*, 57, 59.

43. *Tryals*, 37, 44–45; C. Johnson, *General History*, 96–97; D. D. Moore, "Captain Edward Thatch," 168–71.

44. C. Johnson, *General History*, 74–75, 87–91; *Tryals*, iii–iv, 45; D. D. Moore, "Captain Edward Thatch," 172–73; Woodard, *Republic of Pirates*, 249–53; Butler, *Pirates*, 37–38.

45. *Tryals*, 11, 40, 45–46; C. Johnson, *General History*, 75–97; D. D. Moore, "Captain Edward Thatch," 175; Butler, *Pirates*, 38–40, 60; Konstam, *Blackbeard*, 181–86; Brooks, *Quest*, 374, 530. An extension of the cutoff for crimes from 5 January to 18 August 1718 arrived too late to save Thatch or Bonnet.

46. *Tryals*, 11–14, 46–47, 49–50; C. Johnson, *General History*, 97–99; Butler, *Pirates*, 61–63.

47. *CRNC2*, 7:84–85; D. D. Moore, "Captain Edward Thatch," 178–79; Butler, *Pirates*, 42; Woodard, "Last Days," 40–41.

48. Konstam, *Blackbeard*, 196, 203–4; Woodard, *Republic of Pirates*, 287.

49. *CRNC2*, 7:85–91; Butler, *Pirates*, 42; Woodard, *Republic of Pirates*, 279–80. Bell was a precinct justice who resided on Bell's Island on Coinjock Bay. *CRNC2*, 5:114, 155; Hofmann, *Province of North Carolina*, abstract #3209.

50. *Tryals*, v, 14, 19–22, 30–31, 48, 50; C. Johnson, *General History*, 99–103; Butler, *Pirates*, 63–67; Konstam, *Blackbeard*, 191–96; Hanna, "Protecting the Rights of Englishmen," 309. The intensity of this naval action was unmatched in North Carolina waters until the Civil War.

51. Duffus, *Last Days*, 171–72, 177.

52. D. D. Moore, "Captain Edward Thatch," 182–83; Butler, *Pirates*, 43–44.

53. C. Johnson, *General History*, 78–80, 82–83, 92–94; Butler, *Pirates*, 43–48; Brock, *Official Letters of Alexander Spotswood*, 2:273–74, 275, 316–17; Konstam, *Blackbeard*, 239–64.

54. C. Johnson, *General History*, 77–83; D. D. Moore, "Captain Edward Thatch," 180–81; Butler, *Pirates*, 43–47.

55. *Tryals*, v–vi, 1, 3, 5, 8, 12, 14, 23, 28–30; C. Johnson, *General History*, 105–6; Butler, *Pirates*, 67–69; *SCE*, 733–34.

56. *Tryals*, 37–38, 40, 42–43; C. Johnson, *General History*, 111–13; Butler, *Pirates*, 69–73; Hanna, "Protecting the Rights of Englishmen," 309–10.

57. C. Johnson, *General History*, 92; Butler, *Pirates*, 48–49.

58. C. Johnson, *General History*, 93.

59. *CRNC2*, 7:83–91.

60. *CRNC2*, 5:198–201, 205–9; *DNCB*, 4:109, 303–4, 332–33.

61. *CRNC2*, 7:96.

62. Butler, *Pirates*, 39.

63. Butler, *Proprietary North Carolina*, 32–33.

64. Bailey, Norris, and Oden, "Legends."

65. Watson, *Bath*, 82–83, 92–93.

66. *CRNC2*, 5:431, 6:137–38, 163–64; Duffus, *Last Days*, 171–72, 227.

67. Duffus, *Last Days*, 172–74, 227; Brooks, *Quest*, 372–73.

68. *CRNC2*, 10:255–56.

69. Tinling, *Correspondence*, 1:326, 363–64.

70. *CRNC2*, 10:272–73.

71. Newell, "Man of 'Desperate Fortune,'" 7, 13.

72. Newell, "Man of 'Desperate Fortune,'" 8–9. Ocracoke Inlet faces southeast, and wind from that direction would make it very difficult to put out to sea.

73. Newell, "Man of 'Desperate Fortune,'" 9–11.

74. Newell, "Man of 'Desperate Fortune,'" 12; *CRNC2*, 6:447.

75. Newell, "Man of 'Desperate Fortune,'" 12. Vidal's tale is briefly covered in Rankin, *Golden Age of Piracy*, 155–56; and Shomette, *Pirates on the Chesapeake*, 240–42.

Chapter Fifteen

1. *CRNC*, 3:77–78.

2. Edgar, *South Carolina*, 82–111; *SCE*, 643, 671, 786–87; Weir, *Colonial South Carolina*, 101–3; Clowse, *Measuring Charleston's Overseas Commerce*, 191–94; Scheerer, "Proprietors Can't Undertake,'" 273–74; Sirmans, *Colonial South Carolina*, 126–32.

3. *CRNC*, 3:575; *CRNC2*, 6:174, 7:115; *SRNC*, 23:100–102, 25:212–13; E. L. Lee, *Lower Cape Fear*, 107, 109–10.

4. Brickell, *Natural History*, 8–9.

5. Clowse, *Measuring Charleston's Overseas Commerce*, 30.

6. *CRNC*, 23:40–41, 73–79, 102; *CRNC2*, 483–84.

7. *CRNC*, 2:236–38; *SRNC*, 23:7, 73–74, 101–2; *CRNC2*, 5:291, 6:271, 447, 10:189–90, 354n; Watson, *Bath*, 30, 33, 52, 82–83, 94.

8. Dill, "Eighteenth Century New Bern [Part IV]," 461–63.

9. *CRNC2*, 7:50; Watson, *History of New Bern*, 40–42.

10. *SRNC*, 25:204–5.

11. Berkeley and Berkeley, "'Manner of Living,'" 242; *CRNC*, 3:193.

12. *SRNC*, 23:102, 25:206–9; *CRNC*, 2:454; M. M. Wilson, *Beaufort*, 52–53.

13. Paul, "Beaufort, North Carolina," 373–74, 376–77; Paul, "Colonial Beaufort," 141, 143–46, 151; M. M. Wilson, *Beaufort*, 68, 70.

14. *CRNC*, 3:191.

15. *CRNC2*, 3:368, 402, 420–21; *CRNC*, 1:550; H. R. Paschal, "Proprietary North Carolina," 599–600, 602–3.

16. *SRNC*, 23:95, 25:168, 193; *NCHGR*, 1:120–21, 263; H. R. Paschal, "Proprietary North Carolina," 603–4.

17. *CRNC2*, 5:104, 7:76–77, 144; *SRNC*, 23:97; *NCHGR*, 2:100–101, 147, 191–92; H. R. Paschal, "Proprietary North Carolina," 605–7; Brodsky, *Courthouse*, 14–17; Butchko, *Edenton*, 3–4.

18. *CRNC2*, 7:107–8. Threatened by erosion, the graves of Eden, his wife, Thomas Pollock, and Henderson Walker were removed to St. Paul's church cemetery in 1888.

19. *SRNC*, 25:176–78; *CRNC2*, 10:304.

20. Berland, *Dividing Line Histories*, 107–8.

21. *CRNC2*, 7:61; Edwards, *Celebration of Faith*, 14–18, 22–23, 25–26, 32–33, 40. Preceded by Saint Thomas in Bath (1734), Saint Paul's is regarded as the second-oldest extant church building in North Carolina, although it was not used for worship until 1760. *ENC*, 998.

22. *Boston News-Letter*, 5 September 1715; Meredith, *Account*, 27–28; E. L. Lee, *Lower Cape Fear*, 78–81.

23. *CRNC2*, 6:87, 108; E. L. . Lee, *Lower Cape Fear*, 89–90. "Pedro" would be a typical variation of "Perdreau." Orton Creek was formerly "Perdreaus Creek."

24. *DNCB*, 4:303–4; E. L. Lee, *Lower Cape Fear*, 91. Elizabeth Moore was the widow of Samuel Swann Sr.

25. E. L. Lee, *Lower Cape Fear*, 100.

26. Stone, *Old Town Plantation*, 3–6, 26.

27. E. L. Lee, *Lower Cape Fear*, 94; Bishir and Southern, *Guide*, 268.

28. *DNCB*, 1:53–54; Bishir and Southern, *Guide*, 231.

29. Edmund Moseley, Map of North Carolina, 1733; Jackson, *Big Book*, 112, 117–19, 123–24, 132. Burrington's tract on Walden Creek had been acquired from John Porter.

30. *CRNC2*, 10:324; Wood, *This Remote Part of the World*, 4, 6.

31. *CRNC*, 3:338.

32. *DNCB*, 1:20, 53, 4:65–66, 304, 308, 332, 5:127, 486–89, 6:82.

33. *CRNC2*, 10:324, 500.

34. *CRNC2*, 6:378; Meredith, *Account*, 14–15; E. L. Lee, *Lower Cape Fear*, 101–2, 117–18; South, *Archaeology at Colonial Brunswick*. Since South Carolina claimed eastward to the Cape Fear River, New Hanover west of the river was in dispute until 1735, when the border was anchored west of the Cape Fear at Little River Inlet on a northwest line parallel to the river to latitude 35° north and then west. The western line is significantly south of the thirty-fifth parallel.

35. *CRNC*, 3:259.

36. *CRNC*, 3:469, 470, 471; E. L. Lee, *Lower Cape Fear*, 152. Moseley received a grant of 3,100 acres.

37. Brickell, *Natural History*, 265–67; Catesby, *Natural History*, 2:xxii–xxiii.

38. *CRNC2*, 7:283–85. Blaning became justice of the peace in New Hanover County and later in Bladen County; he represented Bladen County in the assembly. *CRNC*, 3:418, 425, 4:46, 115.

39. Feduccia, *Catesby's Birds*, 3–5, 126, 137–38; Meyers and Pritchard, *Empire's Nature*, 2–7.

40. Catesby, *Natural History*, 1:viii, 2:iv, xxvii; Feduccia, *Catesby's Birds*, 137, 142, 152.

41. Meyers and Pritchard, *Empire's Nature*, 12–13, 20–25; Feduccia, *Catesby's Birds*, 5, 8–10. Having spent his resources on the *Natural History*, on his death Catesby left his family only copies of the book and the engraved plates.

42. *CRNC2*, 7:59, 61, 64–65.

43. *DNCB*, 2:261–62.

44. Grimes, *North Carolina Wills*, 176, 291, 303; *DNCB*, 2:134, 262–63, 4:101, 236–37. Penelope Lovick was married twice more, to George Phenney, former governor of the Bahamas, and Gabriel Johnston, royal governor of North Carolina. Her daughter, Penelope Johnston, became the wealthiest heiress in the colony and also inherited Eden House. Grimes, *North Carolina Wills*, 269, 331, 501; *DNCB*, 2:134, 3:300–301, 5:85.

45. *CRNC2*, 5:256, 7:108; *DNCB*, 2:262.

46. *DNCB*, 5:187; *CRNC2*, 7:74, 193, 10:190, 288.

47. *CRNC2*, 7:142–44; Paden, "'Several & Many Grievances,'" 287–88.

48. *CRNC2*, 6:16–17, 26–27, 141. Burrington's outlay for the passage of Castleton and his daughter was £27.5 sterling, or £109 in North Carolina currency.

49. *CRNC2*, 7:152.

50. *CRNC2*, 7:151, 153, 155, 156.

51. *DNCB*, 4:332. Moseley is listed as president under Burrington in Cheney, *North Carolina Government*, 17.

52. *CRNC*, 2:560, 3:122; *CRNC2*, 7:133–34, 136; Paden, "'Several & Many Grievances,'" 289.

53. *CRNC*, 2:559–62; *CRNC2*, 6:52–53, 116; *DNCB*, 1:284, 2:262–63, 312; Paden, "'Several & Many Grievances,'" 290.

54. *CRNC2*, 7:145–46; *CRNC*, 3:122; *DNCB*, 2:263.

55. *CRNC*, 2:559–62. The proprietors reimbursed Gale £150 for travel to report on the "disorderly State" of the province. *CRNC2*, 7:550.

56. *CRNC2*, 7:147–50; *DNCB*, 1:284. The petition was from legatee Margaret Pugh and her parents Roderick and Anne Eden Lloyd, the governor's sister.

57. *DNCB*, 1:284.

58. *DNCB*, 2:171–72; Haywood, *Sir Richard Everard*, 1, 6–7. Remaining in America, both sons succeeded in turn to the baronetcy but left no heirs. Richard, an attorney in North Carolina, served in the colonial assembly. Hugh lived in Georgia for a time. Anne returned to England and married George Lathbury. Susannah married David Meade of Nansemond, Virginia, and founded a prominent dynasty. Her last years as a widow were spent in Halifax, North Carolina.

59. *CRNC2*, 6:xvn, 7:542–43, 544–49; *DNCB*, 2:171. Sir John Yeamans, baronet, had been governor of Clarendon County.

60. *CRNC2*, 7:155–58, 160, 167–70; *DNCB*, 6:162–63; Paden, "'Several & Many Grievances,'" 291.

61. *CRNC*, 3:526–27; *DNCB*, 5:125; Paden, "'Several & Many Grievances,'" 293.

62. *CRNC*, 2:576–77.

63. *CRNC2*, 6:225–26. Sancho Panza was Don Quixote's squire, a source of comic relief and earthy wisdom.

64. *CRNC2*, 6:226–28.

65. *CRNC2*, 6:220, 228, 271, 447; Watson, *Bath*, 82–83; Paden, "'Several & Many Grievances,'" 295. Kenyon kept the suit active until it was withdrawn in 1729.

66. *CRNC2*, 6:224, 228–29, 231.

67. *CRNC*, 2:608–9, 613–21.

68. *CRNC*, 2:761–63.

69. *CRNC*, 3:142, 333; *DNCB*, 2:171–72; E. L. Lee, *Lower Cape Fear*, 102, 105. Everard's daughters inherited his Hawfields tract.

70. *CRNC*, 3:17–19.

71. *CRNC*, 3:49, 338; *DNCB*, 2:172.

72. *CRNC2*, 10:304.

73. *CRNC2*, 10:304, 317, 321, 462–65.

74. *CRNC2*, 6:280, 304, 327–28, 462; *DNCB*, 1:167–68. The informer was entitled to half the fine, but Blacknall was not punished.

75. *CRNC2*, 10:301–10, 318, 497.

76. *CRNC2*, 6:243.

77. *CRNC2*, 7:569–72.

78. *CRNC2*, 6:229–30, 323, 424–25, 458–59, 468–69, 502, 507–8, 561–63, 645.

79. *CRNC2*, 6:504–5, 507–8, 536, 568–69.

80. *CRNC*, 3:32–47; Lefler, *History of North Carolina*, 1:167–68; Ekirch, *"Poor Carolina,"* 127–28. Following the 1665 charter, Carolina extended from Virginia into northern Florida.

81. *CRNC*, 2:149–50, 393–94; Crittenden, "Surrender," 383–84, 389–93, 398–99; M. G. Hall, *Edward Randolph*, 204–7; *SRNC*, 25:149–50.

82. Berland, *Dividing Line Histories*, 349.

83. Berland, *Dividing Line Histories*, 349, 359, 361; *DNCB*, 2:260–64, 4:73, 101, 332–33, 5:489.

84. Berland, *Dividing Line Histories*, 350, 353–54, 357, 359.

85. Berland, *Dividing Line Histories*, 360–61.

86. Berland, *Dividing Line Histories*, 86.

87. Berland, *Dividing Line Histories*, 87–88, 363.

88. Berland, *Dividing Line Histories*, 89, 265n.

89. Berland, *Dividing Line Histories*, 97.

90. Berland, *Dividing Line Histories*, 98.

91. Berland, *Dividing Line Histories*, 105–6. Byrd was surely familiar with the 1685 ballad "An Invitation to Lubberland."

92. Berland, *Dividing Line Histories*, 114–15.

93. Berland, *Dividing Line Histories*, 122–23, 390.

94. Berland, *Dividing Line Histories*, 124, 199–200. Although there are few contemporary references to buffalo, more telling are the nearly two dozen "Buffalo" place-names throughout the state, mostly in the piedmont and mountain regions, where the prairie and savanna habitats were more common.

95. Berland, *Dividing Line Histories*, 130, 393, 455n. Bainton held land in Nansemond in Virginia and Chowan Precinct, where he had a ferry.

96. Berland, *Dividing Line Histories*, 136, 396–99.

97. Berland, *Dividing Line Histories*, 144, 154–56, 162–63, 405–6.

98. Berland, *Dividing Line Histories*, 166, 168, 415. The Sauratown Mountains are in Stokes and Surry Counties—Pilot, Hanging Rock, and Moore's Knob.

99. Berland, *Dividing Line Histories*, 152, 417, 426, 433.

100. *CRNC*, 3:194; Tinling, *Correspondence*, 2:445, 449. For Byrd's 1733 survey of his 20,000 acres, see "A Journey to the Land of Eden" in Wright, *Prose Works of William Byrd*, 379–415. Byrd subsequently added 6,000 acres on the southern border. Tinling, *Correspondence*, 2:450.

101. *CRNC*, 3:142.

102. *CRNC2*, 7:570–71.

103. *CRNC2*, 7:570–74.

104. In retirement Burrington lived another twenty-five years. Never one to go quietly, on 2 February 1759 he was murdered in St. James's Park while resisting a robbery by an unknown assailant. *CRNC*, 3:142; *DNCB*, 1:284, 5:125.

Epilogue

1. *CRNC*, 3:433.

BIBLIOGRAPHY

Adams, Lars C. "'Sundry Murders and Depredations': A Closer Look at the Chowan River War, 1676–1677." *North Carolina Historical Review* 90 (2013): 149–72.

Adamson, Jack H., and Harold F. Folland. *The Shepherd of the Ocean: Sir Walter Raleigh and His Times.* Boston: Gambit, 1969.

Alexander, Forsyth, ed. *Henrietta Johnston: "Who Greatly Helped . . . by Drawing Pictures."* Winston-Salem: Old Salem, 1991.

Alexander, John, and James Lazell. *Ribbon of Sand: The Amazing Convergence of the Ocean and the Outer Banks.* Chapel Hill: Algonquin Books, 1992.

Alleyne, Warren, and Henry Fraser. *The Barbados-Carolina Connection.* London: Macmillan, 1988.

Allred, Fred J., and Alonzo T. Dill. "The Founding of New Bern: A Footnote." *North Carolina Historical Review* 40 (July 1963): 361–74.

Alvord, Clarence W., and Lee Bridgood. *The First Explorations of the Trans-Alleghany Region by the Virginians 1650–1674.* Cleveland: Arthur H. Clark, 1912.

Andrews, Charles M. "Captain Henry Wilkinson." *South Atlantic Quarterly* 15 (1916): 216–22.

———. *The Colonial Period of American History.* 4 vols. 1936. Reprint, New Haven, Conn.: Yale University Press, 1964.

———. *Narratives of the Insurrections 1675–1690. Original Narratives of Early American History.* 1915. Reprint, New York: Barnes & Noble, 1959.

Andrews, Kenneth R. *Elizabethan Privateering: English Privateering during the Spanish War 1585–1603.* Cambridge: Cambridge University Press, 1964.

———. "Elizabethan Privateering." In *Raleigh in Exeter 1985: Privateering and Colonisation in the Reign of Elizabeth I.* Exeter Studies in History, No. 10, edited by Joyce Youings, 1–20. Exeter: University of Exeter, 1985.

———. *Trade, Plunder and Settlement: Maritime Enterprise and the Genesis of the British Empire, 1480–1630.* Cambridge: Cambridge University Press, 1984.

"Archaeology at Warren Wilson College: The Berry Site and Upper Catawba Valley Archaeology." www.warren.wilson.edu/~arch/berryhistory. Accessed 6 March 2008.

Arnade, Charles W. *The Siege of St. Augustine in 1702.* Gainesville: University of Florida Press, 1959.

Ashe, Samuel A'Court, ed. *A Biographical History of North Carolina from Colonial Times to the Present.* 8 vols. Greensboro: Charles L. Van Noppen, 1905.

Ashley, Maurice. *England in the Seventeenth Century.* 1952. 3rd ed., Baltimore: Penguin Books, 1961.

———. *General Monck.* London: Jonathan Cape, 1977.

———. *The Glorious Revolution of 1688.* New York: Charles Scribner's Sons, 1966.

Ausband, Stephen C. *Byrd's Line: A Natural History.* Charlottesville: University of Virginia Press, 2002.

Bailey, Jane S., Allen H. Novis, and John Oden III. "Legends of Blackbeard and His Ties to Bath Town: A Study of Historical Events Using Genealogical Methodology." *North Carolina Genealogical Society Journal* 28 (2002): 247–306.

Bailyn, Bernard. *Atlantic History: Concept and Contours*. Cambridge, Mass.: Harvard University Press, 2005.

———. *The New England Merchants in the Seventeenth Century*. 1955. Reprint, New York: Harper & Row, 1964.

———. "Politics and Social Structure in Virginia." In *Seventeenth-Century America: Essays in Colonial History*, edited by James M. Smith, 90–115. Chapel Hill: University of North Carolina Press, 1959.

Baldwin, Agnes L. *First Settlers of South Carolina, 1670–1680*. Columbia: South Carolina Tricentennial, 1969.

Barck, Oscar T., Jr., and Hugh T. Lefler. *Colonial America*. 2nd ed. New York: Macmillan, 1968.

Barnwell, John. "Journal of John Barnwell." Parts 1 and 2. *Virginia Magazine of History and Biography* 5 (April 1898): 391–402; 6 (July 1898): 42–55.

Barnwell, Joseph W. "The Second Tuscarora Expedition." *South Carolina Historical and Genealogical Magazine* 10 (1909): 33–48.

Barrow, Thomas G. *Trade and Empire: The British Customs Service in Colonial America, 1660–1775*. Cambridge, Mass.: Harvard University Press, 1967.

Barth, Jonathan E. "'The Sinke of America': Society in the Albemarle Borderlands of North Carolina, 1663–1729." *North Carolina Historical Review* 87 (2010): 1–27.

Bassett, John S. *The Constitutional Beginnings of North Carolina, 1663–1729*. Baltimore: Johns Hopkins Press, 1894.

Becker, Carl. *The History of Political Parties in the Province of New York, 1760–1776*. Madison: University of Wisconsin Press, 1909.

Beckles, Hilary McD. *A History of Barbados from Amerindian Settlement to Nation-State*. Cambridge: Cambridge University Press, 1990.

———. *White Servitude and Black Slavery in Barbados, 1625–1715*. Knoxville: University of Tennessee Press, 1989.

Berkeley, Edmund, and Dorothy S. Berkeley, eds. "'The Manner of Living of the North Carolinians,' by Francis Veale, December 19, 1730." *North Carolina Historical Review* 41 (1964): 240–45.

Berland, Kevin J., ed. *The Dividing Line Histories of William Byrd II of Westover*. Chapel Hill: University of North Carolina Press, 2013.

Beverley, Robert. *The History and Present State of Virginia*. 1705. Reprint edited by Louis B. Wright. Chapel Hill: University of North Carolina Press, 1947.

Bialuschewski, Arne. "Daniel Defoe, Nathaniel Mist, and the General History of the Pyrates." *Papers of the Bibliographical Society of America* 98 (2004): 21–38.

Biggs, Timothy. "A Narrative of the Transactions Past in Ye County of Albemarle in Carolina." Arents Collection. New York: New York Public Library, n.d.

Billings, Warren M., ed. *The Papers of Sir William Berkeley 1605–1677*. Richmond: Library of Virginia, 2007.

———. "Sir William Berkeley and the Carolina Proprietary." *North Carolina Historical Review* 72 (1995): 329–42.

———. *Sir William Berkeley and the Forging of Colonial Virginia*. Baton Rouge: Louisiana State University Press, 2004.

———. "The Transfer of English Law to Virginia, 1606–1650." In *The Westward Enterprise: English Activities in Ireland, the Atlantic, and America 1480–1650*, edited by Kenneth R. Andrews, Nicholas P. Canny, and P. E. H. Hair, 226–42. Liverpool: Liverpool University Press, 1978.

———. *Virginia's Viceroy Their Majesties' Governor General: Francis Howard, Baron Howard of Effingham*. Fairfax, Va.: George Mason University Press, 1991.

Bishir, Catherine W., Charlotte V. Brown, Carl R. Lounsbury, and Ernest W. Wood III. *Architects and Builders in North Carolina: A History of the Practice of Building*. Chapel Hill: University of North Carolina Press, 1990.

Bishir, Catherine W., and Michael T. Southern. *A Guide to the Historic Architecture of Eastern North Carolina*. Chapel Hill: University of North Carolina Press, 1996.

Bjorkman, Gwen B. "Hannah (Baskel) Phelps Phelps Hill: A Quaker Woman and Her Offspring." *Southern Friend* 11 (1989): 10–30.

Black, Jeannette D., ed. *The Blathwayt Atlas: A Collection of Forty-Eight Manuscript and Printed Maps of the Seventeenth Century. . . .* 2 vols. Providence, R.I.: Brown University Press, 1970–75.

Blackburn, Marion P. "Spain's Appalachian Outpost: Failed Ambitions for a North American Empire." *Archaeology* 62 (2009): 38–43.

Boddie, John B. *Seventeenth Century Isle of Wight County, Virginia . . ., Including Abstracts of the County Records*. 1938. Reprint, Baltimore: Genealogical Publishing, 1973.

Bolster, W. Jeffrey. *Black Jacks: African American Seamen in the Age of Sail*. Cambridge, Mass.: Harvard University Press, 1997.

Boyd, William K., ed. *William Byrd's Histories of the Dividing Line betwixt Virginia and North Carolina*. Raleigh: North Carolina Historical Commission, 1929.

Braddick, Michael. *God's Fury, England's Fire: A New History of the English Civil Wars*. London: Penguin Books, 2009.

Bradley, Peter T. *British Maritime Enterprise in the New World: From the Fifteenth to the Mid-Eighteenth Century*. Lewiston, N.Y.: Edwin Mellen, 1999.

Brandow, James C. *Omitted Chapters from Hotten's Original Lists of Persons of Quality and others who went from Great Britain to the American Plantations, 1600–1700: Census Returns, Parish Registers, and Militia Rolls from the Barbados Census of 1679/80*. Reprint, Baltimore: Genealogical Publishing, 1982.

Briceland, Alan V. *Westward from Virginia: The Exploration of the Virginia-Carolina Frontier 1650–1710*. Charlottesville: University Press of Virginia, 1987.

Brickell, John. *The Natural History of North-Carolina*. 1737. Reprint, Murfreesboro: Johnson, 1968.

Bridenbaugh, Carl. *Vexed and Troubled Englishmen 1590–1642*. New York: Oxford University Press, 1968.

Bridenbaugh, Carl, and Roberta Bridenbaugh. *No Peace beyond the Line: The English in the Caribbean, 1624–1690*. New York: Oxford University Press, 1972.

Brinn, Susan H. "Blacks in Colonial North Carolina 1660–1723." MA thesis, University of North Carolina at Chapel Hill, 1978.

Brock, R. A., ed. *The Official Letters of Alexander Spotswood, Lieutenant Governor of the Colony of Virginia, 1710–1722*. 2 vols. Richmond: Virginia Historical Society, 1882.

Brodsky, Marc D. *The Courthouse at Edenton: A History of the Chowan County Courthouse of 1767*. Edenton, N.C.: Chowan County, 1989.

Brooks, Baylus C. "'Born in *Jamaica*, of Very Creditable Parents' or 'A *Bristol* Man Born': Excavating the Real Edward Thache, 'Blackbeard the Pirate.'" *North Carolina Historical Review* 92 (2015): 235–77.

———. *Quest for Blackbeard: The True Story of Edward Thache and His World*. Lake City, Fla.: baylusbrooks.com, 2016.

Brown, Kathleen M. *Good Wives, Nasty Wenches, and Anxious Patriarchs: Gender, Race, and Power in Colonial Virginia*. Chapel Hill: University of North Carolina Press, 1996.

Bruce, Philip. *Economic History of Virginia in the Seventeenth Century*. 2 vols. 1896. Reprint, New York: Peter Smith, 1935.

———. *Social Life in Old Virginia*. 1910. Reprint, New York: Capricorn Books, 1965.

Bryant, Sir Arthur, ed. *The Letters Speeches and Declarations of King Charles II*. 1935. Reprint, London: Cassell & Company, 1968.

Butchko, Thomas R. *Edenton, an Architectural Portrait: The Historic Architecture of Edenton, North Carolina*. Edenton: Edenton Woman's Club, 1992.

Butler, Lindley S. "Blackbeard's Terror." *American Heritage* 61 (2011): 29–37.

———. "The Cape Fear Voyages, 1662–1667, and Their Impact on Southeastern Cartography." *Tributaries* 4 (1994): 21–29.

———. "Culpeper's Rebellion: Testing the Proprietors." In *The North Carolina Experience: A Documentary and Interpretive History*, edited by Lindley S. Butler and Alan D. Watson, 53–78. Chapel Hill: University of North Carolina Press, 1984.

———. "The Early Settlement of Carolina: Virginia's Southern Frontier." *Virginia Magazine of History and Biography* 39 (1971): 20–28.

———. "The Governors of Albemarle County, 1663–1689." *North Carolina Historical Review* 44 (1969): 281–99.

———. "North Carolina 1718: The Year of the Pirates." *North Carolina Historical Review* 95 (2018): 125–46.

———. *North Carolina Genesis: Seventeenth-Century Albemarle County*. Hertford, N.C.: Perquimans County Restoration Association, 1989.

———. *Pirates, Privateers, and Rebel Raiders of the Carolina Coast*. Chapel Hill: University of North Carolina Press, 2000.

———. *Proprietary North Carolina: Politics, Shipping, and Pirates*. Queen Anne's Revenge Shipwreck Project Research Report and Bulletin Series. Raleigh: N.C. Department of Cultural Resources, Office of State Archaeology, Underwater Archaeology Branch, 2007.

Cain, Robert J. "Early Albemarle: Robert Holden's Account of 1679." *North Carolina Historical Review* 91 (2014): 127–43.

Campbell, Mildred. "Social Origins of Some Early Americans." In *Seventeenth-Century America: Essays in Colonial History*, edited by James M. Smith, 63–89. Chapel Hill: University of North Carolina Press, 1959.

Campbell, Peter F. *Some Early Barbados History*. Wildey, Barbados: Caribbean Graphics and Letchworth, 1993.

Canny, Nicholas P. *The Elizabethan Conquest of Ireland: A Pattern Established, 1565–76*. New York: Barnes & Noble Books, 1976.

Carroll, Kenneth. "John Archdale's Quakerism." *Southern Friend* 19 (1997): 51–65.

Carson, Cary, and Carl R. Lounsbury, eds. *The Chesapeake Houses: Architectural Investigation by Colonial Williamsburg*. Chapel Hill: University of North Carolina Press, 2013.

Carson, James T. "Histories of the 'Tuscarora War.'" In LeMaster and Wood, *Creating and Contesting Carolina*, 186–210.

Catesby, Mark. *Natural History of Carolina, Florida, and the Bahama Islands: Containing the Figures of Birds, Beasts, Fishes, Serpents, Insects, and Plants. . . .* 2 vols. London, 1731.

Cecelski, David S. *The Waterman's Song: Slavery and Freedom in Maritime North Carolina.* Chapel Hill: University of North Carolina Press, 2001.

Chafee, Zechariah, Jr. "Colonial Courts and the Common Law." In *Essays in the History of Early American Law*, edited by David H. Flaherty, 53–82. Chapel Hill: University of North Carolina Press, 1969.

Cheney, John L., Jr., ed. *North Carolina Government, 1585–1979: A Narrative and Statistical History.* Raleigh: N.C. Department of the Secretary of State, 1981.

Cheves, Langdon, ed. *The Shaftesbury Papers and Other Records Relating to Carolina and the First Settlement . . .* 1897. Reprint, Charleston: Tempus, 2000.

Clayton, Lawrence A., Vernon J. Knight Jr., and Edward C. Moore, eds. *The De Soto Chronicles: The Expedition of Hernando De Soto to North America in 1539–1543.* 2 vols. Tuscaloosa: University of Alabama Press, 1993.

Clonts, F. W. "Travel and Transportation in Colonial North Carolina." *North Carolina Historical Review* 3 (1926): 16–35.

Clowse, Converse. *Measuring Charleston's Overseas Commerce, 1717–1767, Statistics from the Port's Naval Lists.* Washington, D.C.: University Press of America, 1981.

Coe, Joffre L. *Town Creek Indian Mound: A Native American Legacy.* Chapel Hill: University of North Carolina Press, 1995.

Coker, P. C., III. *Charleston's Maritime Heritage, 1670–1865.* Charleston: Cokercraft Press, 1987.

Connor, Robert D. W. *History of North Carolina: The Colonial and Revolutionary Periods, 1584–1783.* Chicago: Lewis, 1919.

———. *North Carolina: Rebuilding an Ancient Commonwealth, 1584–1924.* 4 vols. Chicago: American Historical Society, 1929.

Copland, Patrick. *Virginia's God Be Thanked or a Sermon of Thanksgiving for the Happie Successe of the Affayres in Virginia Last Yeare.* London, 1622.

Cordingly, David. *Under the Black Flag: The Romance and Reality of Life among the Pirates.* New York: Random House, 1995.

Coxe, Daniel. *A Description of the English Province of Carolana, by the Spaniards Call'd Florida and by the French La Louisiana.* 1722. Reprint, Gainesville: University Presses of Florida, 1976.

Crane, Verner W. *The Southern Frontier, 1670–1732.* Ann Arbor: University of Michigan Press, 1929.

Cranston, Maurice. *John Locke: A Biography.* New York: Macmillan, 1957.

Craton, Michael. *A History of the Bahamas.* 3rd ed. Waterloo, Canada: San Salvador Press, 1986.

Craton, Michael, and Gail Saunders. *Islanders in the Stream: A History of the Bahamian People.* Vol. 1, *From Aboriginal Times to the End of Slavery.* Athens: University of Georgia Press, 1992.

Craven, Wesley F. *The Colonies in Transition, 1660–1713.* New York: Harper and Row, 1968.

———. *The Southern Colonies in the Seventeenth Century.* Baton Rouge: Louisiana State University Press, 1949.

———. *White, Red, and Black: The Seventeenth-Century Virginian.* 1971. Reprint, New York: W. W. Norton, 1977.

Crittenden, Charles Christopher. "The Surrender of the Charter of Carolina." *North Carolina Historical Review* 1 (1924): 383–402.

Crump, Nancy C. "Foodways of the Albemarle Region: 'Indulgent Nature Makes Up for Every Want.'" *Journal of Early Southern Decorative Arts* 19 (1993): 1–35.

Cumming, William P., ed. *The Discoveries of John Lederer with Unpublished Letters . . . and an Essay on the Indians. . . .* Charlottesville: University of Virginia Press, 1958.

———. "The Earliest Permanent Settlement in Carolina, Nathaniel Batts and the Comberford Map." *American Historical Review* 45 (1939): 82–89.

———. *Mapping the North Carolina Coast: Sixteenth Century Cartography and the Roanoke Voyages.* Raleigh: Division of Archives and History, 1988.

———. "Naming Carolina." *North Carolina Historical Review* 22 (1945): 34–42.

———. *The Southeast in Early Maps.* 1958. 3rd ed., rev. and enlarged by Louis DeVorsey Jr., Chapel Hill: University of North Carolina Press, 1998.

———. "The Turbulent Life of Captain James Wimble." *North Carolina Historical Review* 46 (1969): 1–18.

———. "Wimble's Maps and the Colonial Cartography of the North Carolina Coast." *North Carolina Historical Review* 46 (1969): 157–70.

Dahlman, Michael K., and Michael K. Dahlman Jr. *Daniel Island.* Charleston: Arcadia, 2006.

Davies, Godfrey. *The Restoration of Charles II 1658–1660.* London: Oxford University Press, 1955.

Dawdy, Shannon L. "The Meherrin's Secret History of the Dividing Line." *North Carolina Historical Review* 72 (1995): 387–415.

De Beer, Garrin. *Sir Hans Sloane and the British Museum.* London: Oxford University Press, 1953.

Deetz, James. *Flowerdew Hundred: The Archaeology of a Virginia Plantation, 1619–1864.* Charlottesville: University Press of Virginia, 1993.

De Pratter, Chester B. "The Chiefdom of Cofitachequi." In *The Forgotten Centuries: Indians and Europeans in the American South, 1521–1704,* edited by Charles Hudson and Carmen C. Tesser, 197–226. Athens: University of Georgia Press, 1994.

Devine, Christine Styrna (see also Christine Ann Styrna). "Forging Alliances: The Impact of the Tuscarora War on North Carolina's Political Leadership." In LeMaster and Wood, *Creating and Contesting Carolina,* 321–42.

Dill, Alonzo T., Jr. "Eighteenth Century New Bern: A History of the Town and Craven County, 1700–1800." Parts 1–4. *North Carolina Historical Review* 22 (January 1945): 1–21; 22 (April 1945): 152–75; 22 (July 1945): 293–319; 22 (October 1945): 460–89.

———. *Governor Tryon and His Palace.* Chapel Hill: University of North Carolina Press, 1953.

Dowless, Donald V. "Quakers of Colonial North Carolina, 1672–1789." PhD diss., Baylor University, 1989.

Duffus, Kevin P. *The Last Days of Blackbeard the Pirate: Within Every Legend Lies a Grain of Truth.* Raleigh: Looking Glass Productions, 2008.

Dunn, Richard S. "The English Sugar Islands and the Founding of South Carolina." *South Carolina Historical Magazine* 72 (1971): 81–93.

———. *Sugar and Slaves: The Rise of the Planter Class in the English West Indies, 1624–1713.* Chapel Hill: University of North Carolina Press, 1972.

Edgar, Wallace. *South Carolina: A History.* Columbia: University of South Carolina Press, 1998.

Edmundson, William. *Journal of the Life, Travels, Sufferings, and Labour of Love in the Work of the Ministry of That Worthy Elder and faithful Servant of Jesus Christ, William Edmundson.* 1715. 2nd ed., London: Mary Hinde, 1774.

Edwards, Anne R. *A Celebration of Faith 300 Years in the Life of St Paul's: A Brief History of St Paul's Parish, Edenton, North Carolina.* Columbia, N.C.: Sweet Bay Tree Books, 2003.

Ekirch, A. Roger. *"Poor Carolina": Politics and Society in Colonial North Carolina, 1729–1776.* Chapel Hill: University of North Carolina Press, 1981.

Emery, Theo. "Map's Hidden Marks Illuminate and Deepen Mystery of Lost Colony." *New York Times,* 4 May 2012. www.nytimes.com/2012/05/04/us/map-markings-offer-clues-to-lost-colony.html?_r=0.

Esquemeling, John. *The Buccaneers of America.* 1684. Reprint, edited by William S. Stallybrass. Glorieta, N.M.: Rio Grande Press, 1992.

Ethridge, Robbie. *From Chicaza to Chickasaw: The European Invasion and the Transformation of the Mississippian World, 1540–1715.* Chapel Hill: University of North Carolina Press, 2010.

Ewen, Charles R. "John Lawson's Bath: A Subterranean Perspective." *North Carolina Historical Review* 88 (2011): 265–79.

Fagg, Daniel W., Jr. "Carolina, 1663–1683: The Founding of a Proprietary." PhD diss., Emory University, 1970.

———. "Sleeping Not with the King's Grant: A Rereading of Some Proprietary Documents, 1663–1667." *North Carolina Historical Review* 48 (1971): 171–85.

Feduccia, Alan, ed. *Catesby's Birds of Colonial America.* Chapel Hill: University of North Carolina Press, 1985.

Feeley, Stephen. "'Before Long to Be Good Friends': Diplomatic Perspectives of the Tuscarora War." In LeMaster and Wood, *Creating and Contesting Carolina,* 140–63.

First Colony Foundation. "Hidden Images Revealed on Elizabethan Map of America." 3 May 2012. www.firstcolonyfoundation.org/news.

———. "Testing Continues at Site X." 10 August 2015. www.firstcolonyfoundation.org/news.

Fischer, David H. *Albion's Seed: Four British Folkways in America.* New York: Oxford University Press, 1989.

Fischer, Kirsten. *Suspect Relations: Sex, Race, and Resistance in Colonial North Carolina.* Ithaca, N.Y.: Cornell University Press, 2002.

Ford, Worthington C. "Early Maps of Carolina." *Geographical Review* 16 (1926): 264–73.

Franklin, John Hope. *The Free Negro in North Carolina 1790–1860.* Chapel Hill: University of North Carolina Press, 1943.

Frick, George F., and Raymond P. Stearns. *Mark Catesby: The Colonial Audubon.* Urbana: University of Illinois Press, 1961.

Gallay, Alan. *The Indian Slave Trade: The Rise of the English Empire in the American South,
    1670–1717.* New Haven, Conn.: Yale University Press, 2002.
Gallman, James M. "Determinants of Age at Marriage in Colonial Perquimans County,
    North Carolina." *William and Mary Quarterly,* 3rd ser., 39 (1982): 176–91.
———. "Mortality among White Males." *Social Science Quarterly* 4 (1980): 295–316.
Gallman, Robert E. "Changes in the Level of Literacy in a New Community of Early
    America." *Journal of Economic History* 48 (1988): 567–82.
———. "Influences on the Distribution of Landholdings in Early Colonial North Caro-
    lina." *Journal of Economic History* 42 (1982): 549–75.
Goldenberg, Joseph A. *Shipbuilding in Colonial America.* Charlottesville: University of
    Virginia Press, 1976.
Grant, William L., and James Munro, eds. *Acts of the Privy Council, Colonial Series,
    1613–1783.* 6 vols. London: His Majesty's Stationery Office, 1908–12.
Greene, Jack P. "Courts and Society in Proprietary North Carolina: A Review Essay."
    North Carolina Historical Review 60 (1983): 100–104.
Grimes, J. Bryan, comp. *Abstract of North Carolina Wills from Original and Recorded Wills
    in the Office of the Secretary of State.* Raleigh: E. M. Uzzell and Company, 1910.
———. *North Carolina Wills and Inventories.* Raleigh: Edwards & Broughton, 1912.
Hairr, John. "John Lawson's Observations on the Animals of Carolina." *North Carolina
    Historical Review* 88 (2011): 312–32.
Haley, Dru G., and Raymond A. Winslow Jr. *The Historic Architecture of Perquimans
    County, North Carolina.* Hertford: Town of Hertford, 1982.
Haley, K. H. D. *The First Earl of Shaftesbury.* Oxford: Clarendon, 1968.
Hall, Louise. "New Englanders at Sea: Cape Fear before the Royal Charter of 24 March
    1662/3." *New England Historical and Genealogical Register* 74 (1970): 88–108.
Hall, Michael G. *Edward Randolph and the American Colonies, 1676–1703.* Chapel Hill:
    University of North Carolina Press, 1960.
Hampton, Jeff. "Rental Property Dated as Oldest House in N.C." *Norfolk Virginian-Pilot,*
    16 January 2013. www.PilotOnline.com.
Handler, Jerome S., and Frederick W. Lange. *Plantation Slavery in Barbados: An Archaeo-
    logical and Historical Investigation.* Cambridge, Mass.: Harvard University Press, 1978.
Hanna, Mark G. "Protecting the Rights of Englishmen: The Rise and Fall of Carolina's
    Piratical State." In LeMaster and Wood, *Creating and Contesting Carolina,* 295–320.
Hariot, Thomas. *A Brief and True Report of the New Foundland of Virginia.* 1590. Reprinted
    with an introduction by Paul Hulton. New York: Dover, 1972.
Harlow, Vincent T. *A History of Barbados, 1625–1685.* Oxford: Clarendon, 1926.
Harper, Lawrence A. *The English Navigation Laws: A Seventeenth Century Experiment in
    Social Engineering.* New York: Columbia University Press, 1939.
Harris, Tim. *Revolution: The Great Crisis of the British Monarchy, 1685–1720.* London:
    Penguin Books, 2007.
Hassam, John T. *Genealogies: The Hassam Family, the Hilton Family, the Cheever Family.*
    N.p.: Private, 1896.
Haun, Weynette P. *Old Albemarle County North Carolina Book of Land Warrants and Sur-
    veys, 1681–1706.* Durham, N.C.: Private, 1984.
———. *Old Albemarle County North Carolina Miscellaneous Records, 1678–ca. 1737.* Dur-
    ham, N.C.: Private, 1982.

————. *Old Albemarle County North Carolina, Perquimans Precinct, Births, Marriages, Deaths & Flesh Marks, 1659–1820.* Durham, N.C.: Private, 1980.

————. *Old Albemarle County North Carolina Perquimans Precinct Court Minutes, 1688–1738.* Durham, N.C.: Private, 1980.

————, comp. *Perquimans County North Carolina Deed Abstracts 1681–1729, Book 1.* Durham, N.C.: Private, 1983.

Hawks, Francis L. *History of North Carolina.* 2 vols. Fayetteville: E. J. Hale and Son, 1857–58.

Haywood, Marshall DeLancey. *Sir Richard Everard, Baronet, Governor of the Colony of North Carolina, 1725–1731, and His Descendants in Virginia.* N.p.: Southern History Association, 1897.

Hening, William W., ed. *The Statutes at Large; Being a Collection of All the Laws of Virginia, from the First Session of the Legislature, in the Year 1619.* 13 vols. New York: R. W. and G. Barton, 1819–23.

Hill, Christopher. *The World Turned Upside Down: Radical Ideas during the English Revolution.* New York: Viking, 1972.

Hill, Michael, ed. *The Governors of North Carolina.* Raleigh: Office of Archives and History, 2007.

Hilton, William. *A Relation of a Discovery lately made on the Coast of Florida.* London, 1664.

Hinshaw, Seth B. *The Carolina Quaker Experience: An Interpretation.* Greensboro: North Carolina Yearly Meeting and North Carolina Friends Historical Society, 1984.

Hinshaw, Seth Beeson. "Two Epistles from Friends in North Carolina to London Yearly Meeting." *Southern Friend* 19 (1997): 69–72.

Hinshaw, William W., ed. *Encyclopedia of American Quaker Genealogy.* 6 vols. Ann Arbor: Edwards Brothers, 1936–50.

Hobbs, Matthew W. "Complex Networks in Colonial Northeastern North Carolina." MA thesis, University of Delaware, 1999.

Hoffman, Paul E. *A New Andalucia and a Way to the Orient: The American Southeast during the Sixteenth Century.* 1990. Reprinted with a new introduction. Baton Rouge: Louisiana State University Press, 2004.

Hofmann, Margaret M., ed. *Province of North Carolina, 1664–1729, Abstracts of Land Patents.* Weldon, N.C.: Roanoke News Co., 1979.

Hood, Henry G., Jr. *The Public Career of John Archdale, 1642–1717.* Greensboro: North Carolina Friends Historical Society, 1976.

Horne, Robert. *A Brief Description of the Province of Carolina on the Coasts of Floreda.* 1666. Facsimile ed., with introduction by John T. Lanning. Charlottesville: University of Virginia Library, 1944.

Horning, Audrey. *Ireland in the Virginian Sea: Colonialism in the British Atlantic.* Chapel Hill: University of North Carolina Press, 2013.

Hotten, John C. *The Original Lists of Persons of Quality . . . and others who went from Great Britain to the American Plantations, 1600–1700. . . . 1874.* Reprint, Baltimore: Genealogical Publishing, 1962.

Hudson, Charles. "The Hernando de Soto Expeditions, 1539–1543." In *The Forgotten Centuries: Indians and Europeans in the American South, 1521–1705,* edited by Charles Hudson and Carmen C. Tesser, 74–103. Athens: University of Georgia Press, 1994.

———. *Juan Pardo Expeditions: Exploration of the Carolinas and Tennessee, 1566–1568.* 1990. Rev. ed., Tuscaloosa: University of Alabama Press, 2005.

———. *Knight of Spain, Warriors of the Sun: Hernando de Soto and the South's Ancient Chiefdom.* Athens: University of Georgia Press, 1997.

Huggins, Maloy A. *A History of North Carolina Baptists, 1727–1932.* Raleigh: Baptist State Convention, 1967.

Hughson, Shirley Carter. *The Carolina Pirates and Colonial Commerce, 1640–1740.* Baltimore: Johns Hopkins University Press, 1894.

Hulton, Paul. *America 1585: The Complete Drawings of John White.* Chapel Hill: University of North Carolina Press, 1984.

———. "Images of the New World: Jacques La Moyne de Morgues and John White." In *The Westward Enterprise: English Activities in Ireland, the Atlantic, and America 1480–1650,* edited by Kenneth R. Andrews, Nicholas P. Canny, and P. E. H. Hair, 195–214. Liverpool: Liverpool University Press, 1978.

Humber, John L. *Backgrounds and Preparations for the Roanoke Voyages, 1584–1590.* Raleigh: North Carolina Department of Cultural Resources, 1986.

Hume, Ivor Noël. *Martin's Hundred.* New York: Alfred A. Knopf, 1982.

———. *The Virginia Adventure: Roanoke to James Towne: An Archaeological and Historical Odyssey.* New York: Alfred A. Knopf, 1994.

Hutt, Maurice B. *Exploring Historic Barbados.* Bedford, Canada: Lyne, 1981.

"The Indians of Southern Virginia, 1650–1711: Depositions in the Virginia and North Carolina Boundary Case." *Virginia Magazine of History and Biography* 7 (1900): 337–52.

Isil, Olivia A. "Simon Fernandez, Master Mariner and Roanoke Assistant: A New Look at an Old Villain." In *Searching for the Roanoke Colonies: An Interdisciplinary Collection,* edited by E. Thomson Shields and Charles R. Ewen. Raleigh: Office of Archives and History, 2003.

Jackson, Claude V., III. *The Big Book of the Cape Fear River.* 2nd ed., edited by Jack E. Fryar. Wilmington, N.C.: Dram Tree Books, 2008.

Jarvis, Michael J. *In the Eye of All Trade: Bermuda, Bermudians, and the Maritime Atlantic World, 1680–1783.* Chapel Hill: University of North Carolina Press, 2010.

Johnson, Captain Charles. *A General History of the Robberies and Murders of the Most Notorious Pyrates . . . 1724.* Reprint, edited by Manuel Schonhorn, 1972. Mineola, N.Y.: Dover, 1999.

Johnson, William P., and Russell E. Bidlack, eds. "North Carolina Land Grants, 1663–1704." *North Carolinian* 1 (June 1955): 43–48; (September 1955): 77–78.

Jones, H. G. *North Carolina Illustrated, 1524–1984.* Chapel Hill: University of North Carolina Press, 1983.

Jones, Rufus. *The Quakers in the American Colonies.* 1911. New York: Russell and Russell, 1962.

Jordan, Winthrop D. *White over Black: American Attitudes towards the Negro, 1550–1812.* Chapel Hill: University of North Carolina Press, 1968.

Kelly, Kevin P. "'In Dispers'd Country Plantations': Settlement Patterns in Seventeenth-Century Surry County, Virginia." In *The Chesapeake in the Seventeenth Century: Essays on Anglo-American Society,* edited by Thad W. Tate and David L. Ammerman, 183–205. Chapel Hill: University of North Carolina Press, 1979.

Kishlansky, Mark. *A Monarchy Transformed: Britain 1603–1714.* Bristol, U.K.: Allen Lane, 1996.

Konstam, Angus. *Blackbeard: America's Most Notorious Pirate.* Hoboken, N.J.: John Wiley & Sons, 2006.

Kopperman, Paul E. "Profile of Failure: The Carolana Project, 1629–1640." *North Carolina Historical Review* 59 (1982): 1–23.

———. *Sir Robert Heath 1575–1649: Window on an Age.* Woodbridge, U.K.: Royal Historical Society / Wolfeboro, N.H.: Boydell Press, 1989.

Land Warrant Record Book, 1663–1720. Secretary of State, Raleigh, N.C.

Lapsley, Gaillard T. *The County Palatine of Durham: A Study in Constitutional History.* New York: Longmans, Green and Co., 1900.

Latham, Eva C., and Patricia M. Samford. "Naturalist, Explorer, and Town Father—John Lawson and Bath." *North Carolina Historical Review* 88 (2011): 250–64.

Lautzenheiser, Loretta E., principal investigator; Patricia Samford, Jaquelin Drane Nash, Mary Ann Holm, and Thomas Hargrove. *"I Was Moved of the Lord to Go to Carolina . . .": Data Recovery at Eden House 31BR52 Bertie County, North Carolina.* Vol. 1, *The Technical Report.* Tarboro, N.C.: Coastal Carolina Research, 1998.

La Vere, David. "Of Fortifications and Fire: The Tuscarora Response to the Barnwell and Moore Expeditions during North Carolina's Tuscarora War, 1712 and 1713." *North Carolina Historical Review* 94 (2017): 363–90.

———. *The Tuscarora War: Indians, Settlers, and the Fight for the Carolina Colonies.* Chapel Hill: University of North Carolina Press, 2013.

Lawson, John. *A New Voyage to Carolina.* 1709. Reprint, edited by Hugh T. Lefler. Chapel Hill: University of North Carolina Press, 1967.

Lee, E. Lawrence. *Indian Wars in North Carolina, 1663–1763.* Raleigh: Carolina Tercentenary Commission, 1963.

———. *The Lower Cape Fear in Colonial Days.* Chapel Hill: University of North Carolina Press, 1965.

Lee, Robert E. *Blackbeard the Pirate: A Reappraisal of His Life and Times.* Winston-Salem: John F. Blair, 1974.

Lefler, Hugh T. "The Anglican Church in North Carolina: The Proprietary Period." In *The Episcopal Church in North Carolina, 1701–1959,* edited by Lawrence F. London and Sarah M. Lemmon, 1–19. Raleigh: Episcopal Diocese of North Carolina, 1987.

———, ed. "A Description of 'Carolana' by a 'Well-Willer,' 1649." *North Carolina Historical Review* 32 (1955): 102–5.

———. *History of North Carolina.* 2 vols. New York: Lewis Historical Publishing, 1956.

———. "North Carolina History—a Summary of What Has Been Done and What Needs to Be Done." *North Carolina Historical Review* 38 (1961): 216–27.

———, ed. *North Carolina History Told by Contemporaries.* Chapel Hill: University of North Carolina Press, 1934.

———. "Promotional Literature of the Southern Colonies." *Journal of Southern History* 33 (1967): 3–25.

Lefler, Hugh T., and William S. Powell. *Colonial North Carolina: A History.* New York: Charles Scribner's Sons, 1973.

LeMaster, Michelle. "In the 'Scolding Houses': Indians and the Law in Eastern North Carolina, 1684–1760." *North Carolina Historical Review* 83 (2006): 193–232.

————. "War, Masculinity, and Alliances on the Carolina Frontier." In LeMaster and Wood, *Creating and Contesting Carolina*, 164–85.

LeMaster, Michelle, and Bradford J. Wood, eds. *Creating and Contesting Carolina: Proprietary Era Histories*. Columbia: University of South Carolina Press, 2013.

Lemmon, Sarah M. "The Genesis of the Protestant Episcopal Diocese of North Carolina, 1701–1823." *North Carolina Historical Review* 28 (1951): 426–62.

LeShana, James D. "Heavenly Plantations: Quakers in Colonial North Carolina." PhD diss., University of California, Riverside, 1998.

Leslie, Charles. *A New History of Jamaica. In Thirteen Letters from a Gentleman to his Friend*. Dublin: Oli. Nelson, 1741. Reprint, Gale ECCO Print Editions, 2015.

Ligon, Richard. *A True and Exact History of the Island of Barbados*. London, 1657.

Lockyer, Roger. *Tudor and Stuart Britain 1471–1714*. New York: St. Martin's, 1964.

Loftfield, Thomas C. "Lost Charles Towne: Local Manifestation of World Events." *North Carolina Archaeology* 54 (2005): 34–48.

Lorant, Stefan. *The New World: The First Pictures of America*. New York: Duell, Sloan and Pearce, 1946.

Lounsbury, Carl. "The Development of Domestic Architecture in the Albemarle Region." *North Carolina Historical Review* 54 (1977): 17–48.

Lowry, Charles B. "Class, Politics, Rebellion and Regional Development in Proprietary North Carolina." PhD diss., University of Florida, 1979.

Ludwell, Philip. "A Journall of the Proceedings of Philip Ludwell and Nathaniel Harrison Commissioners Appointed for seteling the Limits betwixt Virginia & Carolina Begun July ye 18th 1710 by P. L." *Virginia Magazine of History and Biography* 5 (1897): 1–21.

Lyon, Eugene. *The Enterprise of Florida: Pedro Menéndez de Avilés and the Conquest of Florida, 1565–1568*. Gainesville: University Presses of Florida, 1976.

MacDonald, William, ed. *Select Charters and Other Documents Illustrative of American History, 1606–1775*. New York: Macmillan, 1910.

Mancall, Peter C. *Hakluyt's Promise: An Elizabethan Obsession for English America*. New Haven, Conn.: Yale University Press, 2007.

Mann, Charles C. *1493: Uncovering the New World Columbus Created*. New York: Alfred A. Knopf, 2011.

Margolin, Samuel G. "'Contrary to All Law and Justice': The Unauthorized Salvage of Stranded and Sunken Vessels in the Greater Chesapeake, 1698–1750." *North Carolina Historical Review* 72 (1995): 1–29.

Marley, Branson. "Minutes of the General Court of Albemarle, 1684." *North Carolina Historical Review* 19 (1942): 48–58.

"Maryland Toleration Act, September 21, 1649." Yale Law Library, Avalon Project: Documents in Law, History, Diplomacy. avalon.law.yale.edu/18th_century/Maryland_toleration.asp. Accessed 31 July 2018.

McCain, Paul M. *The County Court in North Carolina before 1750*. Historical Papers of Trinity College Historical Society, Series 31. Durham, N.C.: Duke University Press, 1954.

McCusker, John J., and Russell R. Menard. *The Economy of British America, 1607–1789*. Chapel Hill: University of North Carolina Press, 1985.

McIlvenna, Noeleen. *Early American Rebels: Pursuing Democracy from Maryland to Carolina, 1640–1700*. Chapel Hill: University of North Carolina Press, 2020.

———. *A Very Mutinous People: The Struggle for North Carolina, 1660–1713*. Chapel Hill: University of North Carolina Press, 2009.

McIlwaine, Henry R., ed. *Executive Journals of the Council of Colonial Virginia*. Vol. 2, *August 3, 1669–April 27, 1705*. Richmond: Virginia State Library, 1927.

———. *Executive Journals of the Council of Colonial Virginia*. Vol. 3, *May 1, 1705–October 23, 1721*. Richmond: Virginia State Library, 1928.

———. *Minutes of the Council and General Court of Colonial Virginia*. Richmond: Virginia State Library, 1924.

McPherson, Elizabeth G., ed. "Nathaniel Batts, Landholder on Pasquotank River, 1660." *North Carolina Historical Review* 43 (1966): 66–81.

Meinig, D. W. *The Shaping of America: A Geographical Perspective on 500 Years of History. Atlantic America 1492–1800*. New Haven, Conn.: Yale University Press, 1986.

Meredith, Hugh. *An Account of the Cape Fear Country, 1731*. Edited by Earl G. Swem. Perth Amboy, N.J.: Charles F. Heartman, 1912.

Meyers, Amy R. W., and Margaret Beck Pritchard. *Empire's Nature: Mark Catesby's New World Vision*. Chapel Hill: University of North Carolina Press, 1998.

Middleton, Arthur P. *Tobacco Coast: A Maritime History of the Chesapeake Bay in the Colonial Era*. 1953. Reprint, Baltimore: Johns Hopkins University Press, 1984.

Miller, Helen H. *Captains from Devon: The Great Elizabethan Seafarers Who Won the Oceans for England*. Chapel Hill: Algonquin Books, 1985.

———. *Colonel Parke of Virginia: "The Greatest Hector in the Town."* Chapel Hill: Algonquin Books, 1989.

Miller v. Risco Papers, Suffolk County, Massachusetts, October 22, 1673. North Carolina Archives, Raleigh, PC70.

Milling, Chapman J. *Red Carolinians*. 2nd ed. Columbia: University of South Carolina Press, 1969.

Minchinton, Walter E. "The Seaborne Slave Trade of North Carolina." *North Carolina Historical Review* 71 (1994): 1–61.

Monroe, Haskell. "Religious Toleration and Politics in Early North Carolina." *North Carolina Historical Review* 39 (1962): 267–83.

Moody, Robert E., ed. "Massachusetts Trade with Carolina, 1686–1709." *North Carolina Historical Review* 20 (1943): 43–53.

Moore, Alexander. "Marooned: Politics and Revolution in the Bahamas Islands and Carolina." In LeMaster and Wood, *Creating and Contesting Carolina*, 256–72.

Moore, David D. "Captain Edward Thatch: A Brief Analysis of the Primary Source Documents Concerning the Notorious Blackbeard." *North Carolina Historical Review* 95 (2018): 147–85.

Moore, David G., Robin A. Beck Jr., and Christopher B. Rodning. "Joara and Fort San Juan: Culture Contact at the Edge of the World." *Antiquity* 78 (2004). http://antiquity.ac.uk/ProjGall/Moore/. Accessed 6 March 2008.

———. "Warren Wilson Archaeological Field School 2004." www.warren-wilson.edu/~arch/fs2004/background. Accessed 6 March 2008.

Moore, David D., and Mike Daniel. "Blackbeard's Capture of the Nantaise Slave Ship *La Concorde*: A Brief Analysis of the Documentary Evidence." *Tributaries* 11 (2001): 15–31.

Moore, Rosemary A. *The Light in Their Consciences: Early Quakers in Britain, 1646–1666*. University Park: Pennsylvania State University Press, 2000.

Morgan, Edmund S. *American Slavery, American Freedom: The Ordeal of Colonial Virginia*
    New York: W. W. Norton, 1975.
Morison, Samuel E. *The European Discovery of America: The Northern Voyages A.D. 500–
    1600*. New York: Oxford University Press, 1971.
———. *The European Discovery of America: The Southern Voyages A.D. 1492–1616*. New
    York: Oxford University Press, 1974.
Morton, Richard L. *Colonial Virginia*. Chapel Hill: University of North Carolina Press,
    1960.
Newell, Sam. "A Man of 'Desperate Fortune': The Career and Trial of John Vidal, North
    Carolinas Last Pirate." *Tributaries* 12 (2004): 7–17.
Nickalls, John L., ed. *The Journal of George Fox*. 1684. Rev. ed., Philadelphia: Religious
    Society of Friends, 1997.
Notestein, Wallace. *The English People on the Eve of Colonization, 1603–1630*. New York:
    Harper Brothers, 1954.
Nugent, Nell M. *Cavaliers and Pioneers: Abstracts of Virginia Land Patents and Grants,
    1623–1800*. 5 vols. Richmond: Dietz, 1934.
Oberg, Michael L. *Dominion and Civility: English Imperialism and Native America,
    1585–1685*. Ithaca, N.Y.: Cornell University Press, 1999.
———. *The Head in Edward Nugent's Hand: Roanoke's Forgotten Indian*. Philadelphia:
    University of Pennsylvania Press, 2008.
———. "Manteo and Wanchese in Two Worlds." In *Searching for the Roanoke Colonies: An
    Interdisciplinary Collection*, edited by E. Thomson Shields and Charles R. Ewen, 82–91.
    Raleigh: Office of Archives and History, 2003.
Osgood, Herbert L. *The American Colonies in the Seventeenth Century*. 3 vols. 1904. Reprint,
    Gloucester, Mass.: Peter Smith, 1957.
Paden, John. "'Several & Many Grievances of Very Great Consequences': North Carolina's
    Political Factionalism in the 1720s." *North Carolina Historical Review* 71 (1994): 284–305.
Parker, Mattie Erma E. "Legal Aspects of Culpeper's Rebellion." *North Carolina Historical
    Review* 45 (1968): 111–27.
Parramore, Thomas C. "The 'Country Distemper' in Colonial North Carolina." *North
    Carolina Historical Review* 48 (1971): 44–52.
———. "Tuscarora Ascendancy." *North Carolina Historical Review* 59 (1982): 307–26.
———. "With Tuscarora Jack on the Back Path to Bath." *North Carolina Historical Review*
    64 (1987): 115–38.
Parramore, Thomas C., Peter C. Stewart, and Tommy L. Bogger. *Norfolk: The First Four
    Centuries*. Charlottesville: University Press of Virginia, 1994.
Parrish, Susan S. *American Curiosity: Cultures of Natural History in the Colonial British
    Atlantic World*. Chapel Hill: University of North Carolina Press, 2006.
Paschal, George W. *History of North Carolina Baptists*. 2 vols. Raleigh: Baptist State Con-
    vention, 1930.
———. "Morgan Edwards' Materials toward a History of Baptists in the Province of
    North Carolina." *North Carolina Historical Review* 7 (1930): 365–99.
Paschal, Herbert R., Jr. *A History of Colonial Bath*. Raleigh: Edwards and Broughton, 1955.
———. "Proprietary North Carolina: A Study in Colonial Government." PhD diss., Uni-
    versity of North Carolina, Chapel Hill, 1961.

———. "A State in Search of a Birthday." *The Rebel* 3 (1961): 11–14.

———. "The Tragedy of the North Carolina Indians." In *The North Carolina Experience: A Documentary and Interpretive History*, edited by Lindley S. Butler and Alan D. Watson, 3–27. Chapel Hill: University of North Carolina Press, 1984.

———. "Tuscarora Indians in North Carolina." MA thesis. University of North Carolina, 1953.

Pauketat, Timothy R. *Cahokia: Ancient America's Great City on the Mississippi*. New York: Penguin Group, 2010.

Paul, Charles L. "Beaufort, North Carolina: Its Development as a Colonial Town." *North Carolina Historical Review* 47 (1970): 370–87.

———. "Colonial Beaufort." *North Carolina Historical Review* 42 (1965): 139–52.

———. "Factors in the Economy of Colonial Beaufort." *North Carolina Historical Review* 44 (1967): 111–34.

Penn, William. *A Brief Account of the Rise and Progress of the People Called Quakers*. 1694. Reprint, Richmond: Friends United Press, 1980.

Penney, Norman, ed. *The Journal of George Fox*. 2 vols. 1694. Reprint, Cambridge: Cambridge University Press, 1911.

Perquimans Monthly Meeting Minutes, 1680–. Friends Historical Collection. Guilford College Library, Greensboro, N.C.

Peterson, Mendel. *The Funnel of Gold*. Boston: Little, Brown, 1975.

Pettigrew, William A. *Freedom's Debt: The Royal African Company and the Politics of the Atlantic Slave Trade, 1672–1752*. Chapel Hill, University of North Carolina Press, 2016.

Pope, Dudley. *The Buccaneer King: The Biography of Sir Henry Morgan, 1635–1688*. New York: Dodd, Mead & Company, 1978.

Port Roanoke Book of Registers, 1725–1751. Research Branch, Office of Archives and History, Raleigh.

Port Roanoke Customs House Papers, Volume One (1682–1720). Research Branch, Office of Archives and History, Raleigh.

Powell, William S. "Carolana and the Incomparable Roanoke: Explorations and Attempted Settlements, 1620–1663." *North Carolina Historical Review* 51 (1974): 1–21.

———. *The Carolina Charter of 1663: How It Came to North Carolina and Its Place in History, with Biographical Sketches of the Proprietors*. Raleigh: N.C. Department of Archives and History, 1954.

———. "Carolina in the Seventeenth Century: An Annotated Bibliography of Contemporary Publications." *North Carolina Historical Review* 41 (1964): 74–104.

———. *John Pory 1572–1636: The Life and Letters of a Man of Many Parts*. Chapel Hill: University of North Carolina Press, 1977.

———. *North Carolina: A History*. 1977. Reprint, Chapel Hill: University of North Carolina Press, 1988.

———, comp. *The North Carolina Gazetteer*. Chapel Hill: University of North Carolina Press, 1968.

———. *North Carolina through Four Centuries*. Chapel Hill: University of North Carolina Press, 1989.

———. *The Proprietors of Carolina*. Raleigh: Carolina Charter Tercentenary Commission, 1963.

————, ed. *Ye Countie of Albemarle in Carolina: A Collection of Documents, 1664–1675.* Raleigh: N.C. Department of Archives and History, 1958.

Pringle, Patrick. *Jolly Roger: The Story of the Great Age of Piracy.* New York: W. W. Norton, 1953.

Proceedings: Massachusetts Historical Society. 1st ser., 20 (1883): 402.

Quattlebaum, Paul. *The Land Called Chicora: The Carolinas under Spanish Rule with French Intrusions, 1520–1670.* Gainesville: University of Florida Press, 1956.

Quinn, David B. *The Lost Colonists: Their Fortune and Probable Fate.* Raleigh: N.C. Department of Cultural Resources, 1984.

————. *North America from Earliest Discovery to First Settlements: The Norse Voyages to 1612.* New York: Harper and Row, 1977.

———— . *Raleigh and the British Empire.* Rev. ed. New York: Collier Books, 1962.

————, ed. *The Roanoke Voyages, 1584–1590: Documents to Illustrate the English Voyages to North America under the Patent Granted to Walter Raleigh in 1584.* 2 vols. London: Hakluyt Society, 1955.

————. *Set Fair for Roanoke: Voyages and Colonists, 1584–1606.* Chapel Hill: University of North Carolina Press, 1985.

Quinn, David B., and Alison M. Quinn. *The First Colonists: Documents on the Planting of the First English Settlements in North America, 1584–1590.* Raleigh: Division of Archives and History, 1982.

Rankin, Hugh F. *The Golden Age of Piracy.* Williamsburg: Colonial Williamsburg, 1969.

————. *Upheaval in Albemarle: The Story of Culpeper's Rebellion, 1675–1689.* Raleigh: Carolina Charter Tercentenary Commission, 1962.

Rediker, Marcus. *Between the Devil and the Deep Blue Sea: Merchant Seamen, Pirates, and the Anglo-American Maritime World, 1700–1750.* Cambridge: Cambridge University Press, 1987.

————. "Under the Banner of King Death: The Social World of Anglo-American Pirates, 1716 to 1726." *William and Mary Quarterly* 38 (1981): 203–27.

————. *Villains of All Nations: Atlantic Pirates in the Golden Age.* Boston: Beacon, 2004.

Riddell, William R. "A Half Told Story of Real White Slavery in the Seventeenth Century." *Journal of the American Institute of Criminal Law and Criminology* 21 (1930): 247–53.

Rights, Douglas L. *The American Indian in North Carolina.* 1947. Reprint, Winston-Salem: John F. Blair, 1957.

Roberts, Justin, and Ian Beamish. "Venturing Out: The Barbadian Diaspora and the Carolina Colony, 1650–1685." In LeMaster and Wood, *Creating and Contesting Carolina,* 49–72.

Robinson, Conway, comp. "Notes from the Council and General Court Records, 1641–1664." *Virginia Magazine of History and Biography* 8 (1900): 162–70.

Ronald, Susan. *The Pirate Queen: Queen Elizabeth I, Her Pirate Adventurers and the Dawn of Empire.* New York: HarperCollins, 2007.

Roper, Louis H. *Conceiving Carolina: Proprietors, Planters, and Plots, 1662–1729.* New York: Palgrave Macmillan, 2004.

Rutz-Robbins, Kristi A. "Colonial Commerce: Race, Class and Gender in a Local Economy, Albemarle, North Carolina, 1663–1729." PhD diss., Michigan State University, 2003.

Sainsbury, William Noel, et al., eds., *The Calendar of State Papers, Colonial America and West Indies*. 46 vols. to date. London: Her Majesty's Stationery Office, 1860–.

Salley, Alexander S., Jr., ed. *Journal of the Grand Council of South Carolina, 1671–1680, 1691–1692*. 2 vols. Columbia: South Carolina Historical Commission, 1907.

———. *Narratives of Early Carolina 1650–1708. Original Narratives of Early American History*. 1911. Reprint, New York: Barnes & Noble, 1959.

———. *Records of the Secretary of the Province and the Register of the Province of South Carolina, 1671–1675*. Columbia: Historical Commission of South Carolina, 1944.

Sayers, Daniel O. *A Desolate Place for a Defiant People: The Archaeology of Maroons, Indigenous Americans, and Enslaved Laborers in the Great Dismal Swamp*. Gainesville: University Press of Florida, 2014.

Scheerer, Hanno T. "'The Proprietors Can't Undertake for What They Will Do': A Political Interpretation of the South Carolina Revolution of 1719." In LeMaster and Wood, *Creating and Contesting Carolina*, 273–94.

Schütz, Geza. "Additions to the History of the Swiss Colonization Projects in Carolina." *North Carolina Historical Review* 10 (1933): 133–41.

Secretary of State Deeds, Wills, and Inventories, 1695–1712. State Archives of North Carolina, Raleigh.

Secretary of State Wills, 1712–1722. State Archives of North Carolina, Raleigh.

Shaw, William A., ed. *The Calendar of Treasury Books Preserved in the Public Record Office*. 27 vols. to date. London: His Majesty's Stationery Office, 1904–.

Shea, William L. *The Virginia Militia in the Seventeenth Century*. Baton Rouge: Louisiana State University Press, 1983.

Sherman, Richard P. *Robert Johnson: Proprietary and Royal Governor of South Carolina*. Columbia: University of South Carolina Press, 1966.

Shields, E. Thomson, Jr. *"A New Voyage to Carolina*: Publication History of a Classic of North Caroliniana." *North Carolina Historical Review* 88 (2011): 298–311.

Shirley, John W. *Sir Walter Ralegh and the New World*. Raleigh: Division of Archives and History, 1985.

Shomette, Donald G. *Pirates on the Chesapeake: Being a True History of Pirates, Picaroons, and Raiders on Chesapeake Bay 1610–1807*. Centreville, Md.: Tidewater, 1985.

Simpson, Marcus B., Jr., and Sallie W. Simpson. "John Lawson's *A New Voyage to Carolina*: Notes on the Publication History of the London (1709) Edition." *Archives of Natural History* 35 (2008): 223–42.

———. "The Pursuit of Leviathan: A History of Whaling on the North Carolina Coast." *North Carolina Historical Review* 65 (1988): 1–51.

Sirmans, M. Eugene. *Colonial South Carolina: A Political History 1663–1763*. Chapel Hill: University of North Carolina Press, 1966.

Sloan, Kim. *A New World: England's First View of America*. Chapel Hill: University of North Carolina Press, 2007.

Smith, Henry A. M. "The Colleton Family in South Carolina." *South Carolina Historical and Genealogical Magazine* 1 (October 1900): 323–41.

Smith, H. F. Russell. *Harrington and His Oceana: A Study of a 17th Century Utopia and Its Influence on America*. Cambridge: Cambridge University Press, 1914.

Smith, Margaret, and Emily Wilson. *North Carolina Women: Making History*. Chapel Hill: University of North Carolina Press, 1999.

Smith, William S. "Culpeper's Rebellion: New Data and Old Problems." MA thesis, North Carolina State University, 1990.

Sosin, J. M. *English America and Imperial Inconstancy: The Rise of Provincial Autonomy, 1696–1715.* Lincoln: University of Nebraska Press, 1985.

———. *English America and the Restoration Monarchy of Charles II: Transatlantic Politics, Commerce, and Kinship.* Lincoln: University of Nebraska Press, 1980.

———. *English America and the Revolution of 1688: Royal Administration and the Structure of Provincial Government.* Lincoln: University of Nebraska Press, 1982.

South, Stanley. *Archaeology at Colonial Brunswick.* Raleigh: Office of Archives and History, North Carolina Department of Cultural Resources, 2010.

———. *Archaeology at Santa Elena: Doorway to the Past.* Columbia: S.C. Institute of Archaeology and Anthropology, 1991.

Spindel, Donna J. *Crime and Society in North Carolina, 1663–1776.* Baton Rouge: Louisiana State University Press, 1989.

Spruill, Julia C. *Women's Life and Work in the Southern Colonies.* 1938. Reprint, New York: W. W. Norton, 1972.

Stick, David. *The Outer Banks of North Carolina 1584–1958.* Chapel Hill: University of North Carolina Press, 1958.

———. *Roanoke Island: The Beginnings of English America.* Chapel Hill: University of North Carolina Press, 1983.

Stone, Garry S. *Old Town Plantation, Brunswick County, North Carolina, BW3: The Mansion House Site circa 1725–1755.* Raleigh: N.C. Department of Archives and History, 1970.

Story, Thomas. *A Journal of the Life of Thomas Story: Containing, an account of his remarkable convincement of, and embracing the principles of truth, as held by the people called Quakers. . . .* Newcastle upon Tyne: Isaac Thompson, 1747.

Styrna, Christine Ann (see also Christine Styrna Devine). "The Winds of War and Change: The Impact of the Tuscarora War on Proprietary North Carolina, 1690–1729." PhD diss., College of William and Mary, 1990.

Sunderland, Stella H. *Historical Statistics of the United States, Colonial Times to 1957.* Washington, D.C.: Government Printing Office, 1961.

Suttlemyre, Charles G., Jr. "Proprietary Policy and Development of North Carolina 1663–1729." PhD diss., Oxford University, 1991.

Swanton, John R. *The Indians of the Southeastern United States.* 1946. Reprint, Washington, D.C.: Smithsonian Institution Press, 1979.

Symons Creek Monthly Meeting Minutes. Men, 1699–1785. Women, 1715–1768. Friends Historical Collection. Guilford College Library, Greensboro, N.C.

Talty, Stephen. *Empire of Blue Water.* New York: Crown, 2007.

Terrell, Thomas E., Jr. "The Origins of Religious and Literary Life in North Carolina: Henry White of Albemarle." *Southern Friend* 6 (1984): 5–14.

———. "'Some Holsom Exhortations': Henry White's Seventeenth-Century Southern Religious Narrative in Verse." *Southern Friend* 6 (1984): 3–16.

Thomas, Cornelius M. D. *James Forte.* Wilmington, N.C.: Charles Towne Preservation Trust, 1959.

Thomas, Hugh. *Rivers of Gold: The Rise of the Spanish Empire.* London: Weidenfeld and Nicolson, 2003.

Tinling, Marion, ed. *The Correspondence of the Three William Byrds of Westover, Virginia, 1684–1776.* 2 vols. Charlottesville: University Press of Virginia, 1977.

Tise, Larry E., and Jeffrey I. Crow. *New Voyages to Carolina: Reinterpreting North Carolina History.* Chapel Hill: University of North Carolina Press, 2017.

Todd, Vincent H., and Julius Goebel, eds. *Christoph von Graffenried's Account of the Founding of New Bern.* Raleigh: North Carolina Historical Commission, 1920.

Tolles, Frederick B. *Quakers and the Atlantic Culture.* New York: Macmillan, 1960.

The Tryals of Major Stede Bonnet and Other Pirates. London: Benjamin Cowse, 1719.

Tyler, Lyon G., ed. *Narratives of Early Virginia, 1606–1625. Original Narratives of Early American History.* 1907. Reprint, New York: Barnes & Noble, 1959.

Ver Steeg, Clarence L. *Origins of a Southern Mosaic.* Athens: University of Georgia Press, 1975.

Vigneras, Louis-André. "A Spanish Discovery of North Carolina in 1566." *North Carolina Historical Review* 46 (1969): 398–414.

"Virginia in 1638–1639." *Virginia Magazine of History and Biography* 11 (1903): 46–57.

Ward, H. Trawick, and R. P. Stephen Davis Jr. *Time before History: The Archaeology of North Carolina.* Chapel Hill: University of North Carolina Press, 1999.

Watson, Alan D. *Bath: The First Town in North Carolina.* Raleigh: Office of Archives and History, 2005.

———. "A Consideration of European Indentured Servitude in Colonial North Carolina." *North Carolina Historical Review* 91(2014): 381–406.

———. "The Ferry in Colonial North Carolina: A Vital Link in Transportation." *North Carolina Historical Review* 51 (1974): 247–60.

———. *A History of New Bern and Craven County.* New Bern: Tryon Palace Commission, 1987.

———. "Ordinaries in Colonial Eastern North Carolina." *North Carolina Historical Review* 45 (1968): 67–83.

———. *Society in Colonial North Carolina.* Raleigh: Division of Archives and History, 1996.

———. "Women in Colonial North Carolina: Overlooked and Underestimated." *North Carolina Historical Review* 58 (1981): 1–22.

Webb, Stephen S. *The Governors-General: The English Army and the Definition of the Empire, 1569–1681.* Chapel Hill: University of North Carolina Press, 1979.

———. *Lord Churchill's Coup: The Anglo-American Empire and the Glorious Revolution Reconsidered.* New York: Alfred A. Knopf, 1995.

———. *1676: The End of American Independence.* New York: Alfred A. Knopf, 1984.

———. "The Strange Career of Francis Nicholson." *William and Mary Quarterly*, 3rd ser., 23 (1966): 513–48.

Weeks, Stephen B. *The Religious Development in the Province of North Carolina.* 1892. Reprint, New York: Johnson Reprint Corporation, 1973.

———. *Southern Quakers and Slavery: A Study in Institutional History.* Baltimore: Johns Hopkins Press, 1896.

Weir, Robert M. *Colonial South Carolina: A History.* 1983. Reprint, Columbia: University of South Carolina Press, 1997.

Wertenbaker, Thomas J., and Marvin W. Schlegel. *Norfolk: Historic Southern Port.* 1931. 2nd ed., Durham, N.C.: Duke University Press, 1962.

Wheatley, Henry B., ed. *The Diary of Samuel Pepys*. 2 vols. 1893. Reprint, New York: Heritage Press, 1942.

Wheeler, E. Milton. "Development and Organization of the North Carolina Militia." *North Carolina Historical Review* 41 (1964): 307–23.

White, Stephen J. "From the Vestry Act to Cary's Rebellion: North Carolina Quakers and Colonial Politics." *Southern Friend* 8 (1986): 3–26.

Whitley, Caroline B., and Susan M. Trimble, comps., *North Carolina Headrights: A List of Names, 1663–1744*. Raleigh: Division of Archives and History, 2001.

Wilde-Ramsing, Mark U., and Linda F. Carnes-McNaughton. *Blackbeard's Sunken Prize: The 300-Year Voyage of Queen Anne's Revenge*. Chapel Hill: University of North Carolina Press, 2018.

Williams, Eric. *Capitalism and Slavery*. 1944. Reprint, Chapel Hill: University of North Carolina Press, 1994.

———. *From Columbus to Castro: The History of the Caribbean 1492–1969*. New York: Harper and Row, 1970.

Wilson, Mamré M. *Beaufort North Carolina*. Charleston: Arcadia, 2002.

Wilson, Thomas D. *The Ashley Cooper Plan: The Founding of Carolina and the Origins of Southern Political Culture*. Chapel Hill: University of North Carolina Press, 2016.

Winkler, Wayne. *Walking toward the Sunset: The Melungeons of Appalachia*. Macon, Ga.: Mercer University Press, 2004.

Withington, Lothrop. "Virginia Gleanings in England." *Virginia Magazine of History and Biography* 15 (1908): 298–99.

Wolf, Jacquelyn H. "Patents and Tithables in Proprietary North Carolina, 1663–1729." *North Carolina Historical Review* 56 (1979): 263–77.

Wood, Bradford J. "Struggling to Find Proprietary North Carolina." *Reviews in American History* 38 (2010): 601–6.

———. *This Remote Part of the World: Regional Formation in Lower Cape Fear, North Carolina, 1725–1775*. Columbia: University of South Carolina Press, 2004.

———. "Thomas Pollock and the Making of an Albemarle Plantation World." In LeMaster and Wood, *Creating and Contesting Carolina*, 211–33.

Woodard, Colin. "The Last Days of Blackbeard." *Smithsonian* 44 (February 2014): 32–41.

———. *The Republic of Pirates: Being the True and Surprising Story of the Caribbean Pirates and the Man Who Brought Them Down*. Orlando: Harcourt, 2007.

Wootton, David, ed. *John Locke Political Writings*. 1993. Reprint, Indianapolis: Hackett, 2003.

Wright, Louis B., ed. *The Prose Works of William Byrd of Westover: Narratives of a Colonial Virginian*. Cambridge, Mass.: Harvard University Press, 1966.

Wroth, Lawrence C. *The Voyages of Giovanni de Verrazzano, 1524–1528*. New Haven, Conn.: Yale University Press, 1970.

INDEX

Page numbers in italics refer to illustrations.

CPSIA information can be obtained
at www.ICGtesting.com
Printed in the USA
LVHW102300280422
717483LV00009B/1450